Glimpse

Systematic Theology from a
Metaphysical Christian Perspective

2nd Edition

Thomas W. Shepherd, D.Min.

Theosis House
Kansas City, MO

Thomas W. Shepherd

Glimpses of Truth: Systematic Theology from a Metaphysical
Christian Perspective, 2nd Edition

ISBN-13: 978-0615969923

For

Rev. Rachel

Open my eyes, that I may see
Glimpses of Truth Thou hast for me;
Place in my hands the wonderful key
That shall unclasp and set me free.
Silently now I wait for thee,
Ready my God, thy will to see;
Open my eyes, illumine me,
Spirit divine![1]

Clara H. Scott
(1841-1897)

CONTENTS

Preface to 2nd Edition

Although originally written in 1986 as a project for Unity Books, *Glimpses of Truth* went unpublished until the summer of 2000, when UFBL Press launched the first edition. Browsing my original text in preparation for the current update, it became painfully clear the world has changed dramatically since the turn of a new millennium. The world and the author.

Two decades ago I was much more optimistic about the flow of history toward higher, greater good. The prophetic vision elucidated by Pierre Teilhard de Chardin of humanity's unstoppable, evolutionary rise toward the Omega Point seemed patently obvious in the days after the Cold War ended. We had not reached the Promised Land, but the lull at the close of a stormy twentieth century anticipated calmer seas ahead in the twenty-first. Unfortunately, the period of relative calm only marked the passing eye of the storm, which began with the euphoric fall of the Berlin Wall and ended in the horrific collapse of the World Trade Towers.

It all seemed so...*unfair.* My Baby-Boomer generation grew up under the looming threat of nuclear war with the Soviet Union. I remember the Cuban Missile Crisis. We went to bed literally not knowing if the world would still be there in the morning. Suddenly the fearsome old words of the night time prayer my grandmother had taught me took on new meaning: *"If I should die before I wake, I pray the Lord my soul to take."*

East-West tensions lingered through my youth and adulthood. While serving in West Germany as a US Army Chaplain, I took an orientation tour along hem of the Iron Curtain. We stood on a hill while a plain-clothes official on the other side of the wire snapped our photographs under the watchful eyes of well-armed East German guards. Soldiers from two worlds, staring at each other across no-man's land. Nobody thought any other arrangement was possible in our lifetimes. Boomers looked at the Doomsday Clock and wondered if humanity would survive into the next century.

And then it was over. Economic and cultural factors overcame political ideology. The Soviets renounced their costly empire. Germany re-united. Communism got outsourced to better, more productive markets. Even the Chinese—once the ultimate zealots for Marxist collectivism—went over to the Dark Side and began selling warm up suits to joggers in New England. What is the new political philosophy which today guides the largest communist dictatorship on earth? According to a quip attributed to a former Chinese official: *"We'll do whatever we want and call it socialism."*[2] Whether the quote is straightforward news or political satire, the point is well taken. The opportunistic socialist-capitalism of Mao's successors would have given the rotund Chairman a brain-freeze.

Just when we began to relax—just when optimism about an end to widespread conflict began to rise—worldwide terrorism rushed forward to pierce the peace bubble. Islamic extremists brought a whole new dynamic to the global scene: suicide-murder in the Name of God, with the goal of jamming a sectarian wedge between civilizations. The conflict between militant Islam and the West was not new; it had roots in the middle ages and branches on both sides of the historic battle lines. One cannot read the account of Christian Crusaders as they describe the joys of massacring Muslim infidels without hearing the same kind of hateful language used by Osama Bin Laden and Islamic terrorists of the current age. Suddenly, we were back to peering across no-man's land between two alien, hostile worlds.

The East-West nuclear standoff is effectively gone, but religious violence in the guise of anti-Western terrorism has the potential to linger until humanity realizes it cannot settle old disputes with new brutality. That may take a while. Thousands of Iraqi and Afghan men, women, and children who died in the aftermath of the US invasions had nothing to do with 9-11, just as the innocent victims in the USA who died as a result of those criminal attacks had no part in the grievances which drove eighteen educated young men to commit suicide by flying hijacked airplanes to destruction in a misbegotten attempt to please God. Gandhi's remark about the fallacies of an *eye for an eye* is painfully appropriate.

> The shreds of individuality cannot be sewed together with a bayonet; nor can democracy be restored according to the Biblical injunction of an "eye for an eye" which, in the end, would make everybody blind.[3]

While frankly acknowledging the potential for choosing evil which free will allows, the Mahatma advocated hope that good will triumph over ignorance.

> You must not lose faith in humanity. Humanity is an ocean; if a few drops of the ocean are dirty, the ocean does not become dirty.[4]

Some events are watersheds, e.g., the First World War snuffed out the sunny optimism of 19th century idealism. A similar wake-up call pealed in the cultural thunder of 9-11, which affected human consciousness in ways most people have not yet realized. Given the recurring patterns of dysfunction in the human family, confidence in the onward-and-upward progress of our species toward spiritual transcendence no longer seems incontestable.

Today, I am less inclined to re-read-f Teilhard than to re-examine Reinhold Niebuhr and the neo-orthodox theologians. These crucial issues cannot be side-stepped or swept under an imaginary rug labeled "the Absolute," which conveniently allows people to ignore any potential design flaws or signs of incompleteness in human nature as humanity stumbles forward in this "relative" existence.

Another way to look at human shortcomings might be to consider the shadow side of humanity, identified by Carl Jung. How does the whole picture of what it means to be human come into focus without embracing self-delusion or species denigration? Shall we evolve into an affirming community, which extends outward to embrace the whole human family, or are we genetically bred for tribal conflict, from the sports teams we cheer about to the military forces we send into the field? Given an evolutionary model of life, what evidence do we have that humanity's niche in the ecosystem is not a network of competitive predators but a non-combative, cooperative flock? Lion or lamb—the jury is still out.

This is where theology empowers us to clear away the emotional clutter and boldly explore the hard questions we should be asking ourselves but have hesitated because it felt like lack of faith. No belief, however sacrosanct, gets a pass. Theology invites us to turn every idea upside down to see if there is an expiration date stamped on the bottom. There are important issues any modern faith must address if it is to speak meaningfully to a confused, divided, lion-and-lamb world. To be heard beyond its village of like-minded congregations, Metaphysical Christianity must speak the language of theology.

Obviously, the volume you are reading does not attempt to raise all the questions humans face today, let alone supply all the answers. Its goals are to equip feeling-thinking people with spiritual technology (i.e., theological tools and the knowledge of how to use them), in order to analyze life critically, shape a personal religious faith, and integrate the results into the specific thought-world in which we live.

This revised Second Edition of *Glimpses* owes a mounting debt to a long list of people who abetted me during dark nights of the long re-writing process. Many people offered passing comments, others offered lines of thought, and still others took time to read the text, make editorial suggestions, and locate typos undetectable to the word processing program. Some of my present and former students who read and commented on the work-in-progress include: John Beerman, Deborah Hill-Davis, Beth Hitesman, Mona Krane, Judith Marshall, Christine McFarland, Jim Mullis, David Old, Jennifer Sacks and Mark Fuss. Countless others have contributed ideas and corrections over the intervening years since the first edition appeared from UFBL Press in the summer of 2000. You know who you are, even though my faulty memory does you the disservice of anonymity.

I could not have produced this *minimum opus* without the ongoing encouragement of my patient and supportive life-mate, Carol-Jean. She continues to be my primary source of sanity in this world (at least on days when we're not driving each other crazy).

To readers who are discovering *Glimpses of Truth* for the first time, welcome to the joys and angst of living an examined life in a cosmos where surprises are sometimes called miracles and, despite appearances to the contrary, selfless love remains the mightiest force of all. Theology is a set of tools. Use them well, and your world will make better sense through glimpsing the truth that all knowledge is connected. And God, however conceived, will be with you every step of the way.

Thomas W. Shepherd
Lee's Summit, Missouri
Spring, 2014

I am born into the great, the universal mind. I, the imperfect, adore my own Perfect. I am somehow receptive of the great soul, and thereby I do overlook the sun and the stars and feel them to be the fair accidents and effects which change and pass. More and more the surges of everlasting nature enter into me, and I become public and human in my regards and actions. So come I to live in thoughts and act with energies which are immortal.[5]

Ralph Waldo Emerson

Foreword

"God doesn't give a fig about theology." That was what I thought when I began my path to ministry. Theological inquiry sounded dull and even a little frightening. Who was I to question the deeply held historical beliefs and teachings in my circle of faith?

My spiritual community at home had focused on experiencing God rather than trying to understand God. We had proudly chosen "heart over head" and dismissed theological inquiry as heady and pretentious. An experience of God, we reasoned, was available to everyone, while an understanding of God was reserved for the scholarly.

But then—Rev. Dr. Thomas Shepherd entered my life.

I had first become aware of "Dr. Tom", as he is affectionately known at Unity Institute & Seminary, through his popular Q&A column, "Good Questions" in *Unity Magazine*. He answered his readers' often difficult questions with insightful, provocative, well-reasoned replies, and a light touch that included humor and warm wit. Dr. Tom never claimed to have all the answers, but was willing to question and reconsider everything. I hungrily read his column each month without stopping to think why. Now I can see it was through his column that Dr. Tom first began making theological inquiry accessible and applicable to my everyday life.

I became a seminary student of Dr. Tom's in the summer of 2006. As professor of systematic and metaphysical theology at Unity Institute and Seminary, Dr. Tom gleefully turned my belief system upside down and inside out for the next three years. Through his deft use of theological inquiry, he led me to dig up my deeply embedded beliefs to re-examine, redefine, reshape, and in some cases, release or replant. He taught me how to exercise my "sacred intellect."

Glimpses of Truth has been a central part of my spiritual journey. It provided a gateway to understanding that led to deep personal healing and professional readiness. Now I see theology not as heady and academic, but as mind and heart expanding. I see how my *understanding* of God informs my *experience* of God. The two are intertwined.

Theology is not just for ministers, teachers, and academics. The search for and articulation of an inspiring, motivating, uniting theology serves each of us as individuals, and all of us as the future of humanity. Through theological inquiry, we come to understand those who came before us and the ideas and decisions that have shaped our history. We also broaden our view to include multicultural and multi-faith perspectives, and begin holding ourselves accountable for accepting and honoring our differences. Imagine the impact of open and honest theological inquiry in our congregations and among spiritual seekers everywhere!

Glimpses is a comprehensive, thoughtful, provocative examination of theology from a Metaphysical Christian perspective. It provides the tools and methodology for "doing theology," including thought-provoking discussion questions at the end of each chapter.

If we are to reshape historical patterns and beliefs—to be contemporary influences—we must seek understanding through theological inquiry. We must be willing to ask the hard questions. As Dr. Tom says, "Theology invites people to turn every idea upside down to see if there is an expiration date stamped on the bottom."[6]

Theological inquiry is not to be feared, but embraced. *Glimpses of Truth* provides the tools and the roadmap to do just that. Who am I to question the deeply held beliefs and teachings of my circle of faith? I am a theologian. And so, my friend, are you.

Read on, fellow theologian, read on.

Rev. Mark A. Fuss
Director of Admissions
Unity Institute and Seminary

THEOLOGY AND LIFE

Christmas Faith in an Easter World

The Reverend Dietrich Bonhoeffer—pastor, chaplain, theologian, and committed pacifist—conspired with fellow countrymen to kill Adolf Hitler. Although he never fired a gun or planted a bomb, the historical evidence clearly implicates Bonhoeffer in the German resistance movement, which eventually led to an abortive attempt on Hitler's life by military officers on July 20, 1944. Hollywood fictionalized this real-life assassination drama in the motion picture *Valkyrie* (2008) starring Tom Cruise.[1] Bonhoeffer did not appear in the storyline, but as early as 1940 he had told friends:

"If we claim to be Christians, there is no room for expediency. Hitler is the anti-Christ. Therefore we must go on with our work and eliminate him..."[2]

In his willingness to act without regard for "expediency," Dietrich Bonhoeffer was a lonely figure. Speaking as a German-American clergyman, I am deeply saddened by the fact that most European German clergy of the Nazi era either enthusiastically supported the Fuhrer, whom they hailed as the opponent of godless Communism, or implicitly condoned Hitler's policies by a conspiracy of silence. In his book *A History of Christianity,* Paul Johnson says the German church was poorly prepared to resist a powerful leader who went astray. European Christianity has long a history of allegiance to the government. To this day, German churches receive billions of Euros each year from taxes levied by the government, which effectively makes the clergy a category of civil servants. In a political system gone awry under the Nazis, the tradition of Church-State collusion proved fatal for the faith of Jesus.

Some self-described Christians greeted Hitler with wild enthusiasm. On April 3, 1933, the first National Conference of the Faith Movement passed the following resolution: "For a German, the church is the community of believers who are under obligation to fight for a Christian Germany...Adolf Hitler's state appeals to the church: the church must obey the appeal."[3] One pastor told a gathering of church leaders: "Christ has come to us through Adolf Hitler...the Savior has come... We have only one task, be German, not be Christian." [4]

Personally, Hitler despised Christianity, even though he required his high officials to pretend otherwise. Hitler said on one occasion that the conspiracy of silence would prevail:

> "Do you really believe the masses will ever be Christian again? Nonsense. The tale is finished...but we can hasten matters. The parsons will be made to dig their own graves. They will betray their God to us. They will betray anything for the sake of their miserable little jobs and incomes."[5]

Nazi State Church: Hymns to Hitler

The Nazi's spurned the Faith, even while German Christianity was wooing the fascists like an unrequited lover. In fact, Hitler planned to replace the church of Christ with a Nazi State Church. There were Nazi creeds, baptism ceremonies, burial and wedding services. Sometimes propaganda became religious absurdity. Bizarre lyrics were written to make old hymns fit Nazi theology:

> Silent night, holy night,
> All is calm, all is bright,
> Only the Chancellor steadfast in fight,
> Watches o'er Germany by day and night,
> Always caring for us.[6]

The motto of the nationalistic German Christian organization was, "The Swastika on our breasts, the Cross in our hearts." At church council meetings, "the pastors dressed in Nazi uniforms, and Nazi hymns were sung."[7]

Nor were the Germans the only nation to award unmerited trust in Hitler. Surprisingly, the British government at first refused to believe Hitler had any plans beyond securing his borders and recovering from World War I. The British Empire was exhausted from fighting the "Great War," (1914-1919); His Majesty's Forces worldwide had suffered 3,190,235 casualties with over 900,000 killed. War fatigue was so profound in England that in 1933 the Oxford Student Union at that most British of institutions passed a resolution which read "This House (Oxford University) will in no circumstances fight for its King and country."

Their Gandhi-esque outbreak of pacifism came less from an aversion to taking up arms than a lingering fatigue after the cataclysm of the Great War, which brought widespread destruction and devastated the world economy.[8] Small wonder why the thought of another war on the European continent turned most Britons into isolationists even while maintaining the most far-flung Empire on Earth.[9] Only Winston Churchill sounded the anti-Nazi alarm, but his persistent cries for action against Hitler kept him a back bencher in Parliament, at the periphery of English politics.

Hitler shared none of England's distaste for battle; he wanted revenge for the humiliating defeat at the hands of the Allies. Germany attacked Poland in 1939, dragging the weary, unprepared British government into a Second World War. This time it was *blitzkrieg*, lightning war, and France fell quickly before the Nazi onslaught. Then British cities took ceaseless punishment from Luftwaffe air strikes that frequently set the city on fire. As the lone voice against Nazi terror for almost a decade, Churchill rose to Prime Minister.

Back in Germany Dietrich Bonhoeffer's patience had expired. He secretly flew to Sweden in 1942 and conferred with his friend, British churchman George Bell. Bonhoeffer revealed to Bell the details of the plot against Hitler, asking him to relay to his government the hopes of many Germans for a speedy end to the war and the Nazi terror. When the Allies refused, pushing for unconditional surrender, the fledgling German resistance movement tried to assassinate their Caligula. The conspirators arranged to have a bomb slipped under the table in a bunker briefing room, which detonated without seriously harming

Hitler. In the aftermath of the botched assassination, Hitler went on a rampage of revenge. Hundreds of people died, including General Erwin Rommel. The Desert Fox wanted rid of Hitler, too.

Modern Martyr

Dietrich Bonhoeffer was not immediately implicated because he was already in prison when the bomb exploded, but his part in the conspiracy was impossible to conceal. T.A. Kantonen describes what finally happened to him:

> ...in February, 1945, he disappeared from the Berlin prison and his family did not learn his fate until the war was over...from Berlin he was taken to Buchenwald and then to Flossenberg. On Sunday April 8 he conducted a worship service for his fellow prisoners. He had hardly finished his closing prayer when two men came in and said, "Come with us." After a court martial that night he was hanged at dawn on Monday, April 9, 1945.[10]

German Christianity was about to lose a hero. Dr. H. Fischer-Huellstrung paints a painfully vivid portrait of Bonhoeffer's execution:

> On the morning of that day between five and six o'clock the prisoners...were taken from their cells...through the half open door in one room of the huts I saw Pastor Bonhoeffer, before taking off his prison garb, kneeling on the floor praying fervently to his God. I was most deeply moved by the way this lovable man prayed, so devout and so certain that God heard his prayer. At the place of execution, he again said a short prayer and then climbed the steps to the gallows, brave and composed. His death ensued after a few seconds. In the almost fifty years that I worked as a doctor, I have hardly ever seen a man die so entirely submissive to the will of God.[11]

It was not a quick death. They hanged Bonhoeffer from a meat hook by a noose of piano wire. Five days later, Flossenberg was liberated by the Allies. Bonhoeffer had been executed by special order of Heinrich Himmler as World War II was ending. He was 41.

Bonhoeffer as Theologian

If that were his only contribution—heroic involvement in the fight for freedom and a martyr's death—he would have made a worthy contribution to humankind. However, Dietrich Bonhoeffer was not just a pastor, but a theologian. He acted from deeply held Christian beliefs which he sketched in a scant few books, poems and letters smuggled from his prison cell during the madness of war. The day after Hitler escaped assassination, Bonhoeffer wrote:

> Faint not nor fear,
> but go out to the storm and the action,
> trusting in God
> whose commandment you faithfully follow;
> freedom, exultant, will welcome your spirit with joy.[12]

Not everyone will agree with all the points of his doctrine, but something in the tragic heroism of Dietrich Bonhoeffer evokes appreciation from Christians of diverse theological persuasions. Bonhoeffer suffered the dilemma of the philosopher-king; called to live by high principles, he nevertheless had to practice in a world which he perceived to be ruled by brute force. He had to decide whether to dwell in a land of academic exercises, a safe, happy place where truth and goodness always rule, or descend to the muddy battlefield where the children of God were hacking each other to pieces. It was a nasty choice.

Few of Bonhoeffer's contemporaries in the German clergy had the courage to abandon their ivory towers for a perilous journey down the valley of the shadow of death. Most found it easier to preach theoretical sermons about the eventual triumph of God's goodness than to speak out against a tyrannical regime that was plunging the world into a holocaust. Dietrich Bonhoeffer—safe in New York City, teaching at an American seminary, knowing full well the peril he would face—caught the last ship home to Germany on the eve of World War II. It was the cost of his discipleship, and he paid in full.

Religionless Christianity

Bonhoeffer took a look at the churches of his day and called for a "religionless Christianity" cut free of rigidity to historic doctrines, able to declare universal truths to modern humanity. "I should like to speak of God," he wrote, "not on the boarders of life but at its center."[13]

For Bonhoeffer, religionless Christianity meant a belief system liberated from both the irrelevant other-worldliness of traditional Christianity and the brooding cynicism of modern secular thinking. However, Bonhoeffer invoked the R-word in a much narrower sense than found in this study. Glimpses uses the term *religion* to indicate a community of faith which is distinguished by a generally held system of beliefs and practices and advocated by a recognizable body of believers. Bonhoeffer's distinction was between dead ceremonialism and living faith. He called for a commitment to Jesus Christ which included a willingness to change, grow and die to oneself and live for God and neighbor.

> This is not achieved by dint of efforts to 'become like Jesus,' which is the way we usually interpret it. It is achieved only when the form of Jesus Christ itself works upon us in such a manner that it molds our form in its own likeness.[14]

At first glimpse, this seems diametrically opposed to one of the central ideas of Metaphysical Christianity, i.e., everyone is capable of outpicturing the Christ-within as demonstrated by Jesus of Nazareth. However, closer scrutiny of Bonhoeffer's words suggests his analysis is not necessarily antithetical to Christian metaphysics. A person can never "become like Jesus" because Jesus Christ was absolutely unique, just as everyone is absolutely unique. For Bonhoeffer, Jesus Christ is not a hero with exploits to mimic but a life-transforming Lord whose power reshapes anyone choosing to plug into the Christ-source.

Certainly, when "the form of Jesus Christ itself works upon us in such a manner that it molds our form in its own likeness," we shall become Christ-like. But *Christ-like* does not require everyone to become *Jesus-like*. The process outpictures differently in every life.

Bonhoeffer never lived to follow this idea to its logical conclusion: when people let God mold them, they become the Christ in still another form, an idea which brings a whole new meaning to words attributed to Paul, "Christ in you, the hope of glory." (Colossians 1:27, NRSV).

Cheap Grace

Bonhoeffer believed change comes by commitment to God. He called all attempts to become religious without changing the inner person "cheap grace." It is one of his most powerful and important terms. Against this superficial religiosity he set "costly grace," which is total commitment to Christ.

> Cheap grace is grace without discipleship, grace without the Cross, grace without Jesus Christ, living and incarnate... costly grace is the gospel which must be sought again and again, the gift which must be asked for, the door at which a man must knock. Such grace is costly because it calls a man to follow Jesus Christ. It is costly because it costs a man his life, and it is grace because it gives a man the only true life.[15]

Dietrich Bonhoeffer knew following Jesus Christ takes moral courage. Yet, only by accepting the cost of discipleship can people become what God intends them to be. In his lifetime Bonhoeffer watched men and women trade principles for temporary security. Anyone can understand how this happened. Everyone wants stability and safety in their lives, and some moral choices expose them to danger. It is not an easy decision. Courage reads better than it plays in real life. It is far easier to stand aside. "Why should I be the one to act?" the fear-motivated person asks. "I don't want to get involved." Who has not heard reports from news media about victims who bleed to death while people hurry by? Yet, focusing on the failure of human courage is to miss the point of Dietrich Bonhoeffer's life. He was one of us, too. He remained faithful unto death.

Even while admiring Bonhoeffer's moral courage, it is possible to disagree with his moral conclusions. Events during his short lifetime drove Bonhoeffer from pacifism to tyrannicide. One might legitimately ask how his resort to violence differs from the jihadist who kills for God. Perhaps the answers lies in the target chosen by Bonhoeffer, Adolf Hitler, as opposed to the random violence of a suicide bomber. Others will side with Gandhi and insist that under no circumstances is violence justified.

The ethical discussion, which engages mind and heart, is not simply about right and wrong; theological ethics operates in the vast gray center of life where many answers are possible. Theology offers tools of critical inquiry to assist people slog through the ethically murky regions of life.

Some may not admire his decision to conspire in an act of violence, but when put to the supreme test Bonhoeffer returned to the forgiving, loving faith of Jesus even while imprisoned by a world gone mad. Hitler was wrong. Bonhoeffer did not betray everything for the sake of worldly security, nor did many others, most of whose names are lost to history but known to God. If he could do it, anyone else can.

Theology's Failure

The brave Germanic theologians who stood up for the Jesus faith had little impact upon their world. As both a theologian and German-America, I find it paradoxical that, while the flames of war spread across Europe, Germanic theology was experiencing an intellectual renaissance. German-speaking giants like Karl Barth, Rudolf Bultmann, Emil Brunner and Paul Tillich developed their theological systems from safe enclaves in Switzerland or behind the ocean barrier in North America. Yet, for all their brilliance, academic theology was powerless to halt the stampede to World War II. Although those mentioned above actively opposed Fascism—some fled for their lives when Hitler came to power—Christianity had ceased to influence European socio-political life before the Nazi era. After World War I, Christian thought had become an intellectual game played by professional theologians, generally ignored by everyone else. Where abided the faith to move mountains? Not in the church.

Free Market Religion

What happened? How did the Church, which had once dethroned kings, become so impotent that no one listened to her anymore? Except for the vociferous insertion of the Religious Right in American politics—which is generally dismissed by intellectuals and ignored by people outside the circles of zealotry—today the socio-intellectual trend is to consider the Church peripheral to daily life. Questions of social and political ethics and are seldom addressed theologically, unless an official "religious position" is sought by the news media. Quaint relics of a bygone era, churches give people someplace to go on Christmas and Easter, sanctified spaces in which to be christened, married and buried.

Even so the institutional church of today, totally oblivious to her inability to sway the multitudes, keeps churning out position papers and passing resolutions at conferences which the faithful keep ignoring. People seem to have decided they can make decisions of great importance without benefit of clergy. Strangely, surveys indicate many people still self-identify as members of various faith groups, but they tend to ignore the teachings of their church. One example is the deepening chasm between American Roman Catholicism and the Vatican party line. The following quote from a 1986 article in *U.S. News and World Report* suggests Catholic dissent is not exactly breaking news:

> Today, the polling data show, the average Catholic believes that it is possible to disagree with the church's teaching on moral issues and still remain a good Catholic. Despite Rome's prohibition on birth control, for instance, a majority of (American) Catholic women say they practice it. [16]

One might argue that the unique conditions of American church life contribute to this perfidy by the laity. In several European countries, Catholic and Protestant churches, still receive the bulk of their income from tax revenues and not offerings.

> In Belgium, Greece and Norway, churches are financed by the state. Churches in Austria, Switzerland and Sweden all use the state to collect taxes from members, but the contributions are either

predetermined amounts or, compared with Germany, a more modest 1 to 2 percent of the annual assessed income tax. Spain and Italy allow congregants to decide whether they would like a percentage of their income to flow to religious organizations or be earmarked for civic projects.[17]

Historically, this government financing of Churches has made European Christianity less dependent upon the good will of its parishioners than highly competitive, North American Christianity. Since church-goers can literally overturn religious institutions by voting with their dollars, American churches must pay attention to the needs and beliefs of their congregations. Both systems have their defenders and critics.

European church leaders might reasonably argue that a clergy independent of the pressure to conform to the whims of parishioners can provide a more effective witness against the excesses of secular culture. However, the very fact that churches must meet the needs of secular men and women suggests the major strength of American churches. If Christianity does not exist to meet actual human needs, why does it exist at all? It is no coincidence that cathedrals in Europe remain virtually empty on Sundays, while big churches in the USA either pack in the crowds or close their doors.

A sample of the articles and books published by American Catholic scholars shows that the Catholic laity, although powerless to affect the doctrinal anachronisms proclaimed by Rome, have nevertheless influenced the tone of theology preached by the American Catholic clergy. But more importantly, Christianity in North America operates in a free market consciousness. Many Catholics and Protestants, not to mention non-observant Jews, apparently have decided to retain basic religious identities while ignoring the doctrinal specifics of their ancestral faiths.

Contrary to their European counterparts, large numbers of Americans ignore church troublesome teachings while continuing to attend church regularly! How can a person stay a member of a religious faith that espouses ideas contrary to what he/she actually believes? Very easily, given the individualism of North Americans. It's rather like having an eccentric old aunt who rails against this or that newfangled idea. Dissenters just smile and say, "You can't take her seriously. She lives in the past, you know."

An interesting dynamic in Roman Catholic scholarship has developed in recent years, which underscores this disconnect between official doctrine and existential practice. Speaking extemporaneously during the Q&A segment of her paper to Unity Institute's Lyceum 2011 conference, Catholic scholar Aimée Upjohn-Light said the official policy barring women and gays from service in the Church hierarchy has driven them to scholarly professions as the highest avenue of upward mobility within the Church. The result, Upjohn-Light explained, is a Roman Catholic academia which has become progressively more liberal and resistant to official Church doctrine. Since academic freedom is the hallmark of higher education in the USA, Catholic scholars have frequently been able to resist attempts by the hierarchy to impose Church doctrine on courses of study at Catholic colleges and universities.

Clearly, schools with stronger ties to Roman Catholicism, i.e., those with faculties heavy in clergy and other religious professionals, will likely be more receptive to guidance from bishops and other official sources, but the tension within the Catholic Church between magisterial authority and academic freedom in more diverse educational communities continues to build.[18] The 2013 election of progressive new Pope Francis, the first Roman Pontiff from Latin America, might bring much-needed reforms to the Church. At this writing, it is too soon to tell whether he can rejuvenate the largest denomination in the world. Even with a farsighted captain ordering course corrections, a ship that large will take some time answering to its helm.

This is not meant to single out Catholicism as the only church experiencing membership dissent. Stepping back for a wider view of religious America, the Pew Forum on Religion and Public Life found in recent interviews with more than 35,000 American adults that a large percentage of the religiously mixed American population describes itself "spiritual, not religious," (18%). [19]

All told, about two-thirds of U.S. adults (65%)

describe themselves as religious (either in addition to be being spiritual or not). Nearly one-in-five say they are spiritual but not religious (18%), and about one-in-six say they are neither religious nor spiritual (15%). Among all those with a religious affiliation, about three-quarters (75%) consider themselves religious, one-in-six (15%) consider themselves to be spiritual but not religious, and fewer than one-in-ten (8%) say they are neither.[20]

The paradox of contemporary religious life is that, while more and more people are self-describing as "spiritual, not religious," a significant plurality of American Protestants continue to call themselves evangelicals or born-again Christians, or embrace the culturally pejorative label *fundamentalists*. The largest growth in Protestantism has been among "non-denominational" churches, which usually preach some form of anti-modernist, biblical literalism.

Another group that shows a net gain is nondenominational Protestants, whose share of the population has more than tripled as a result of changes in affiliation; 1.5% of the population was raised within nondenominational Protestantism, compared with 4.5% who currently report such an affiliation.[21]

A word of clarification is needed here. The term *nondenominational* may be misleading to some readers, since it's used by a few liberal religious organizations—for example, historically New Thought churches—to distinguish themselves as *inclusive* rather than *exclusive* among spiritual fellowships. In that context, the word indicates an acceptance of varying points of view. However, most churches which self-designate as "nondenominational" actually mean "anti-denominational," and are signaling their doctrinal purity. "Nondenominational" usually indicates a staunchly conservative, "turn-or-burn" theology that is wholly incompatible with the universalism of churches descending from New Thought Christianity.

Why Conservative Churches are Growing

Despite the signals some disaffected people are sending about traditional religion, the fact remains that conservative Protestants outnumber the mainline/liberals in North America by significant numbers. In a recent study, one third of all Americans indicated they believed the Bible was literally true, and another third said the Bible was God's word but not necessarily true in all aspects. Slightly more than one fourth held the generally accepted position among biblical scholars, i.e., that people wrote the Bible.[22] Even more disturbingly for American civilization in science-based world, forty-six percent of the people surveyed agreed with the statement, "God created human beings pretty much in their present form at one time within the last 10,000 years or so." The disappointing results strongly correlated with a population composed of so many people clinging to conservative religious affiliations. [23]

Given the vitality and persistence of anti-scientific, anti-intellectual, socially conservative churches, a fair question to ask is, "What needs are being met?" A generation ago, Dean M. Kelley contrasted the religious groups that were popping up like dandelions with religious groups withering on the vine. Presenting an impressive battery of charts and statistics based on studies done in the 1970s, Kelley decided American churches were dividing into two basic groups, which he described as follows.

1) Liberals: reasonable, rational, ecumenical, tolerant, easy-going, non-dogmatic, nonsectarian churches

2) Conservatives: unreasonable, irrational, exclusivist, intolerant, demanding, dogmatic, sectarian churches

A visitor from another planet who saw the above might assume the tolerant, progressive churches would be attracting members and the intolerant, sectarian churches would be turning people off. Kelley's data indicated the opposite:

...precisely the sectarian and theologically conservative religious groups have made amazing gains in recent years. Amid the current neglect and hostility toward organized religion in general, the conservative churches, holding to seemingly outmoded theology and making strict demands on their members, have equaled or surpassed in growth the yearly percentage of the nation's population.[24]

Instead of attending to church to find better ways to live in the world, Kelley's data suggested that many people came to church to escape the complexities of a world hurling change at them at an accelerating pace, a world both too large and too shrunken, too hidebound and too innovative, too banal and too ghastly for the human mind to entertain, encompass, endure. Rather than seek new answers to age-old questions, these rapidly growing churches offered sanctuary and a full-scale retreat from modern life. It was a conclusion which Kelley, a member of the "liberal" United Methodist Church, did not find at all satisfying. [25]

If the most "successful" churches in North America have been encouraging people to retreat from bewildering contemporary reality since the end of the Vietnam era, Kelley's research suggests that passionate religionists are not looking to the church for ways to interface with modern life, but to deny its inconvenient trajectory on issues like climate change, marriage equality, universal health care, abortion rights, immigration and gun control. Kelley insisted that churches exist to provide religious answers to the great questions of life and to weave what Peter Berger called a *Sacred Canopy*. Here is Kelley's rather poetic analysis:

> If a man can see his sufferings--the bad things that befall him and those he loves--as part of a cosmic purpose or a long range good, he can often overcome them, or at least regain some of his zest and resilience and possibly go on to significant achievements. Meaning...has historically and repeatedly proven to be the remedy for severe disorganization of persons and groups. It has been the antidote for anomy, the rehabilitation of criminals, the rescuer of alcoholics, the deliverer of drug addicts, the preventer of suicide, the cure for psychosomatic disabilities, and the sure

solution for many cases of poverty, failure, and despair. [26]

Applauding Evangelical Joy

Metaphysical Christianity might quibble over Kelley's word choice—preferring not to dwell on "sufferings" or "bad things that befall" the individual—but his point about the power of meaning to heal mind, body and relationships rings true. Could the answer to Kelley's questions be a strongly spiritual view of the world, providing a framework of meaning by which men and women can understand life religiously in the twenty-first century, while still affirming the unity of scientific and religious truth? If a greater vision of life captures the mind, empowering people to live more effectively, does this not provide the strongest of all religious systems, i.e., a comprehensive worldview integrating heart and head?

Authentic Christian theology always responds to human needs with healthy interpretations of the ancient faith grounded in the real world, not by nourishing the fears of its clientele. Promising heaven does nothing to correct ineffective living in this world. Fear-based fantasies may have been popular in bygone eras—Jonathan Edwards and his sermon "Sinners in the Hand of An Angry God"[27] comes to mind—but today fear-based Christianity is a dinosaur in search of a tar pit, large and loud but totally incapable of adapting to survive the social and intellectual climatic changes that will surely come in the twenty-first century. It should be noted that, while this study is frequently critical of the theology of conservative Christianity, to their credit many evangelical churches have moved from fear to faith, emphasizing prayer and praise rather than turn-or-burn. People attending those large, nondenominational "cathedrals in a cornfield"[28] usually get a strong, spiritual high from uplifting music, inspiration preaching, and fervent prayer. Although their theology is distant from the Metaphysical Christianity which informs this study, I cannot resist applauding the bushels of blessings in transformed lives, spirits lifted, spiritually empowered communities, and unbridled bliss of celebrating the Presence and Power of God, which evangelical Christianity brings to so many people. Hooray for joyful faith. May your tribe increase while your vision of the world's complexities expands.

First Paradox: Asceticism vs. Activism

Bonhoeffer saw the danger for Christianity from two extremes: either flight from this world to the Ivory Palaces of heaven on one hand, or a cynical "God helps those who help themselves" attitude on the other. Both represent real religious needs, the need to find divine order in an apparently mad world, balanced by the equally important need to make this world a better place because of our commitment to God and neighbor. Continuing the overview of theology and life, this is the first paradox which confronts religionists who want to live their faith: Asceticism vs. Activism—withdraw or engage?

The New Testament clearly shows that Jesus took time to pray and center Himself, then marched back to the marketplace to engage contemporary people with his words and healing touch. His spirituality flowed directly to action. Sometimes, the followers of Jesus become, in the old preacher's cliché, *So heavenly minded they ain't no earthly good.* Spiritual pursuits are delightful, but acute other-worldliness can lure people so far from the marketplace they cannot, or will not, hear the cries of the poor in spirit.

During my seminary days, I heard about a professor at another school who staged a dramatic lesson for his students. On the day he was lecturing on the parable of the Good Samaritan, he stationed an actor beside a bush outside the classroom. The pretender looked dreadful —broken, bloody and moaning, smelling like a homeless drunk who had fallen among bad company. All the students rushed by, eager to get to their lecture on the Good Samaritan! Apparently the idea of actually touching a ragged, bloody man occurred to them. Why study religion, if it makes no contact with everyday life? Yet, doesn't religion offer comfort precisely because it offers sanctuary from a world which can be so unpleasant at times? Religious leaders struggle to keep their work relevant to the real world. However, some have become so hot for social and political justice they've grown cold to their calling as spiritual leaders. Late in the twentieth century, two forms of this activism arose, one conservative and the other liberal.

In the 1980's and 90's, evangelical Christians, spurred by electronic evangelists like Jerry Falwell and Pat Robertson, rallied around conservative political leaders to battle for a multitude of socio-political causes. Anti-abortion, anti-feminism, anti-gay activism became the litmus test for Christian faithfulness; cutting the size of government became a mission field. On the far left, Liberation Theology attempted to crossbreed Marxism with Catholicism, sometimes promoting armed revolution on behalf of the landless, oppressed peoples of the Third World. Liberal Christians created shibboleths of their own: feminists insisted on gender-neutral translations of scripture and pro-choice politics; theologians from minority communities pushed for affirmative action and condemned cuts in government programs to aid the poor. Gun control, the death penalty, immigration policies—most social and political issues took on religious overtones, and the rightness or wrongness of any particular contest usually depended on which set of cultural lenses a person wore to the arena. Too often, religion and politics are played like team sports. You don't cheer the other guys.

Although avowed enemies, the goals of the Religious Right and Liberation Theology are essentially the same, i.e., to bring their vision of the ideal Christian community and the just society into existence by taking direct action in the world. Making the world a better place is an admirable goal (which will be considered at length in Chapter 15), but socio-political activism can submerge spiritual teachings and drown people in a sea of bitterness. Too frequently, campaigns are waged against institutions, against groups, against opposing viewpoints. Theologies which advocate socio-political activism run the risk of becoming intolerant, self-righteous, and prone to anger. They seem to say, "If we don't act now, God's kingdom won't come." Yet, as Dietrich Bonhoeffer discovered, the church must address the problems of the world or risk descending into trivia. He prayed hard, but saw no alternative to Hitler's overthrow. Grappling with the paradox leads directly to a sea of misty possibilities.

Anchoring the Asceticism-Activism paradox requires answers to questions about appropriate involvement. When does theology need to concentrate on spiritual matters (hunger for God so rampant in our world), and when does theology need to turn its attention to socio-political issues (human rights, racism, gender discrimination, homophobia, poverty, drugs/crime, teen pregnancy, economic justice)? This study will steer a middle course between otherworldly asceticism and socio-political activism, holding the two poles in tension. Missouri mystic Charles Fillmore suggested a solution to the paradox might be to acknowledge troubles in the world and help the cause of justice when possible.

> The church of Christ covers every department of man's existence and enters into every fiber of his being. "He carries it with him day and night, seven days of the week. He lives in it as a fish lives in water and is transformed into a new creature. [29]

Second Paradox: Pessimism vs. Idealism

Historically, Christian orthodoxy has resolved the Asceticism-Activism problem either by withdrawing from society to form cloisters of the Elect (as did the Jewish Essenes of the Qumran community and Christian monastics of the high Middle Ages), or by attempting to control all aspects of life (as did Rabbinical Judaism and the Medieval Church). The problem is exactly the same for Ascetics and Activists: How shall we live in an imperfect world full of imperfect people?

Belief systems in recent years have reflected this age old question about the worth of humanity. Glancing at history, we can understand how sensitive souls might ask whether human society were incontrovertibly evil. This is going to be a point of contention between metaphysical Christianity and virtually every other Christian perspective. Generally speaking, modern theologies are grounded in extreme pessimism about the perfectibility of human beings. Metaphysical churches appeared during the Victorian era when a different set of values and a more optimistic intellectual climate dominated Christendom.

The closing years of the nineteenth century were exciting times. Science had come of age; empirical research was beginning to enrich human life. First telegraph then telephone shrank distances for the first time, bringing instant communications possible from the other side of the world. Edison lit the night, then gave us recorded music and moving pictures. Henry Ford perfected an automobile almost everyone could afford, mass produced on an assembly line. New advances in health brought vaccines against smallpox, the Pasteurization process, and the long-overdue comprehension of the part microorganisms play in disease. Charles Darwin capped the progress of that brilliant century by quietly observing birds and animals for years and publishing his world-shattering *Origin of Species*, laying the foundation for modern biology by showing how life evolved from simpler to more complex organisms. Humanity was poised to transform smoothly into a world of peace and harmony, governed by reason and law.

In the intellectual realm at the turn of the twentieth century, Absolute Idealism dominated the philosophical and theological landscape. Absolute Idealism was metaphysical; spiritual categories were identified with Ultimate Reality. It was monistic, believing in One Power/One Presence without a distinct line between Creator and creatures. It spoke about things as universal rather than particular; it looked at the incarnation of Jesus Christ as typical (universal) rather than unique. Absolute Idealism was also unapologetically optimistic. British theologian John Macquarrie wrote:

> At the present day there will be no ready response to the optimism of idealist like Sir Henry Jones, who concluded his Gifford Lectures by assuring his audience of "the friendliness and helpfulness of man's environment'; or like Josiah Royce, who asserted that 'the world, as a whole, is and must be absolutely good."[30]

The "friendliness and helpfulness" of the world. One Presence/ One Power. Reality itself is "absolutely good." Science and education are the magic keys to social progress and spiritual evolution. These were the dominant themes of the late nineteenth century. It seemed things would continue to get better until God's Kingdom was established, or at least a human utopia.

And then the system began to unravel. Nation-states squared off in two world wars. Humanity compelled its scientists to design more efficient ways to kill people. First, poison gas and machine guns; then dive bombers, gas chambers, and atomic bombs. But two World Wars didn't slake the human appetite for carnage. Korea, Vietnam, the Kennedy and King assassinations, drive-by homicides, and drug related crime—small wonder a cynical pessimism has settled over the world, replacing the sunny optimism of the previous century.

Newer, gloomier philosophies appeared, like Existentialism, which promised nothing but full awareness of squalid human life. Existentialism became the worldview of Western intelligentsia. And since professional clergy are educated by the intellectual community, religious thinking quickly followed suit. Mid-twentieth century theologians, like Reinhold Niebuhr, were soon proclaiming that humanity is unqualified to follow the model of Jesus because we are fatally flawed. Salvation must break into human existence by God's action; we are part of the problem and cannot be part of the solution. [31]

Science and education as the answer? The Nazi's flourished in Germany, among some of the most highly educated, scientifically advanced people on earth. We learned that when you educate a bigot you often get a better educated bigot. Still worse, we learned that education could be a weapon of tyranny as totalitarian states indoctrinated millions in their school systems.

Given the events of the twentieth century, it's not hard to see how disbelief in the perfectibility of humankind has become the only acceptable viewpoint, not just in theology but across society. Anyone who expects the best is seen as hopelessly naive. Next time you watch the evening news, listen carefully. The only people predicting good results today are politicians claiming success and their spin doctors trolling for votes. "Sure things are getting better, because our policies are working!" Anyone else "reached for comment" looks at the future as guarded at best.

Negativism is so pervasive that media reporters, when announcing an encouraging statistic, feel compelled to drain the optimism from their coverage in the name of balanced reporting. Does the government report a nationwide lower-than-expected unemployment rate? Watch the media scour the nation until they find someone standing in an unemployment line in Boise, Idaho, to show that not everyone has benefited from the upward trend. The twenty-first century has become the age of urbane pessimism.

Founded in an era of bright hopes, metaphysical Christianity now finds itself in sole possession of the optimistic highlands once crowded by theologians from virtually every major denomination. Yet, we would be living in cloud castles if we did not admit that the pessimists have a point. Humans have done terrible things to each other, often in the Name of God. But is their conduct normal or aberrant? Was the Nazi movement an isolated phenomenon or a typical episode in human history? As we ask ourselves whether pessimism or optimism is the appropriate attitude for Christian thought, we are really asking questions about our views on metaphysical anthropology. What is the nature of humanity--devil or angel, evil or good?

Third Paradox: Human vs. Divine

How can anyone believe that humanity, with its many flaws, is somehow related to the Divine? Is Homo sapiens a lowly being, dust of the earth, given permission to glimpse toward heaven only by Divine mercy? In the words of the Episcopal prayer book:

> We have erred, and strayed from thy ways like lost sheep.
> We have followed too much the devices and desires of our
> own hearts. We have offended against thy holy laws. We
> have left undone those things which we ought to have
> done; And we have done those things which we ought not
> to have done; and there is no health in us. [32]

Are we lost sheep, or powerful sons and daughters of God, unaware of our birthright because we have not yet learned how to claim it? Can we blithely affirm, with Sir Henry Jones, "the friendliness and helpfulness of man's environment", or with Josiah Royce, that "the world, as a whole, is and must be absolutely good"? Miserable sinners, or divine offspring?

Emerging from the Shadows

As the surviving remnant of nineteenth century idealism, Metaphysical Christianity offers a compromise to the tension of the Human-Divine Paradox. Those who stand in the idealist tradition believe in the perfectibility of men and women, but not through blinding themselves to the atrocities humans have visited upon their brothers and sisters. They just recognize God isn't finished with humanity yet.

Walk into a second grade classroom. Ask a bright seven-year-old this question: "Jessica, how do you find the area of a rectangle?" You'll draw a blank stare, frown, or nervous giggle. Seven-year-olds aren't ready for math problems that complicated. But that doesn't mean they're flawed, evil or corrupt, with "no health" in them. It means they are at another level of development, the proper stage for them, now. Ask the same question of a Ph.D. candidate in computer science and you'll draw the same frown or nervous frown, but this time it's because she'll be wondering if you're serious or if you're merely insulting her intelligence. A graduate student isn't better than a second grader, she's just further along the path of knowledge.

So with humanity. Certainly, the journey is not over. People are still capable of extreme cruelty. Nevertheless, all but the bitterest cynics must admit Homo sapiens has leaped forward in modern times. Slavery has been abolished except in small, illegal pockets far from civilization. Colonialism is almost gone, racism is socially unacceptable, and the East-West Cold War has melted away. People of all sorts of lifestyles and orientations are slowly becoming part of the social and political mainstream. Even more encouragingly, although we may not agree with the choices newly liberated countries make, it is clear that democracy is winning the worldwide battle against totalitarianism.

Ironically, the conflicts which threaten human stability in this post-911 world are rooted in religious strife. Will humanity overcome its longstanding tendency to self-destruct in the Name of God? The jury of history is still out, but there are positive signs. For example, Pope Francis has affirmed every good person can go to heaven, even atheists. Francis also declared, "To say that you can kill in the name of God is blasphemy."[33] Perhaps the current madness of religion-excused violence is a last gasp of medievalism, and the good, cooperative side of humanity will emerge from the shadows at last, making world peace no longer a wild dream.

Instead of adopting the wide-eyed optimism of the nineteenth century or the cold cynicism of the mid-twentieth, a balanced theology might solve the Human-Divine Paradox by acknowledging the problems of humanity while boldly affirming our indwelling Divine spirit. Isn't that the model of Jesus Christ? Instead of forcing a choice between humanity and divinity for the starting point of a renewed theology, the Jesus Christ model provides both: God-with-us and God-in-us. Humanity has a long way to go, but many forward-looking people are eager to get on with the journey. For those in the Christian tradition, Jesus Christ is guide, destination and map; appreciation for diversity draws a stiff breeze into the sails of humanity. Metaphysical Christianity raises a lighthouse over the turbulent seas of life.

Calm Weather, Eye of the Storm?

As stated in the *Caveat*, our perspective begins with the central premise of Metaphysical Christianity--there is One Presence and One Power in our lives and in the cosmos, God the Good, Omnipotent. The three paradoxes (Asceticism vs. Activism, Pessimism vs. Idealism, Human vs. Divine) will emerge again and again as we survey the vast domain of Christian theology. Since the emphasis in current Christian thought remains pessimistic, the positive insights of Practical Christianity offer hope. John Macquarrie, writing his critical evaluation of Idealism in the early 1960's, first brushed optimism aside, then asked a prophetic question:

> Idealist theologians (like idealist philosophers) are likewise in eclipse, and the doctrine of divine immanence has been replaced by a stress on transcendence. Of course, it is a question whether, if the Western world should come through its present turmoils—political, social, and intellectual—to a settled and stable period once more, something like absolute idealism may not reappear. For the present, however, it is out of favor, and is not even seriously discussed, much less defended.[34]

Macquarrie wrote this passage before 9-11, and today it is obvious the winds of change blowing across the "political, social and intellectual" seas have not yet carried us to "a settled and stable period once more." However, despite the ongoing terrorist threats to stability, a developing worldwide marketplace and burgeoning internet might yet succeed in uniting the planet where armies of conquest have failed. Perhaps the global village will soon be ready once more to discuss seriously the possibility that all human beings are worthy children of a benign cosmos. This sets up next question: What biblical event serves as the best model to understand God's relationship to humanity?

Easter or Christmas?

In recent years there has been an increasing pressure from clergy in traditional churches to de-emphasize Christmas in favor of Easter. Though ordinary believers (non-believers as well) seem to identify with the Nativity, the most important event in Church history for clergy has long been the Crucifixion-Resurrection. This has been especially true for theologians. Browse the index of any book on Systematic Theology; you will find plenty of Easter images but almost nothing about Christmas. Lots of crosses, very few mangers.

Contrast this theological emphasis with the popular/secular celebrations of each holiday. The Christmas euphoria begins in November and lingers until January. For a month and a half, a vast portion of the human family dreams about *peace on earth* and sends gifts and greetings to folks they ignore the rest of the year. Christmas gathers a huge cloud of humanity into a quasi-religious community, which lingers until well after the New Year's Day clean up.

Easter gets a half-day. Even then, the Christian church has to share its most sacred observance with a big white bunny pushing chocolate figurines and pastel painted, hard-boiled eggs; an ersatz Halloween with Roger Rabbit as master of ceremonies. Certainly, Santa Claus has eclipsed the baby Jesus in some celebrations of Christmas, but at least he's a saint, theoretically based on a real person, who represents the virtues of love, kindness, and generosity. The popular aspects of Easter—fuzzy rabbits and colored eggs, new clothing and excessive carbohydrates—often represent a secularized holiday silenced of every whisper of religiosity, perhaps because the image of an innocent man suffering capital punishment is too unpleasant for a celebration of new life amid spring blossoms. Consider the widespread embrace of Christmas, which is celebrated even in Japan, where Christianity is a distinct minority. Does this hunger for Yuletide reflect deeper religious yearnings than the Crucifixion-Resurrection emphasis of Easter? What makes Christmas so special?

Ask children why they love Christmas, you'll get a

straightforward answer: *"The presents!"* And so it is. Christmas gift-giving is love-giving, pure and simple. It's too easy to chalk holiday presents up to crass commercialism. Nothing sells unless people buy it; advertising cannot guarantee a market. Ask Hollywood.

Although we harry ourselves by all the holiday activities squeezed into busy lives, Christmas rings the love bell, even if while we're grousing about it. Not by accident, people have discovered Christmas is the holiday of hope, the day when people dare to believe that it's really possible to hear the angels sing, and know that God comes to us in every newborn child. Although this will sound like rank heresy to most orthodox clergy and theologians, it is possible to contend that the main event of the Christian Faith occurred not at Calvary but Bethlehem.

The Birth of the Christ—God-within-us—is at the very least equal to the crucifixion- Resurrection event. Easter shows us God's triumph in the face of suffering and despair; Christmas reveals God's brightest hopes for every human child. Who says which message is more important?

Theologically, the cross has been central in Christian thought because our religious frame of reference has been built upon what historical theologian Matthew Fox calls a Fall-Redemption centered theology. Fox sees this as a mutant off-shoot, not representing the main branch of Jewish and Christian biblical tradition. [35]

My book *Friends in High Places* described the fifth century controversy between St. Augustine and the Celtic monk Pelagius. Augustine pushed for a non-biblical, Fall-and-Redemption Christianity based on his dualistic, pessimistic, Manichean background. Fall-Redemption centered religion holds that humans "fell" from some kind of pristine goodness to a state of brokenness. Humanity wallows in its fallen state, sinful and lost, until a divine agent cleanses and restores us to wholeness and harmony with God. [36]

In its Christian expression Fall-Redemption theology interprets the Garden of Eden story as both an historic and a metaphysical event which led to original sin that stains every human soul. We inherit sinfulness from our parents, a spiritual disease transmitted *in utero*. The biblical worldview is quite different from the alien, non-Christian, pagan viewpoint which sneaked into the church through the writings of

25

frustrated celibates like St. Jerome and St. Augustine. A fresh look at the Bible shows a few passages which mutter about the dark side of humanity and a lot of verses, chapters and whole books proclaiming creation's wholeness before God.

Matthew Fox replaces Fall-Redemption with a model based on Creation Spirituality; he believes humanity lives under *original blessing*, not original sin.[37] In the Middle Ages, Meister Eckhart reminded Christians that after God created the world *good*, it remained *good*. It's a short hop from Eckhart's mysticism to a faith based not just on the lessons of the Cross but also the grand vision of *Incarnation*. Christmas is the world's birthday, because every cradle is the Manger and every child is the Christ. The hunger for something to believe in bursts forth each December, when even stolid cynics must allow themselves a moment of "maybe".

> Maybe it could be true.
> Maybe there could be peace on earth.
> Maybe God comes to us this way, clothed in flesh.
> Cradled in ordinary straw.

A world of challenges still awaits us as we walk back from candlelight services each Christmas Eve, but for one shining moment, heaven has touched earth. If we could bottle that feeling and carry it with us all year around, we might be able to handle any circumstance with courage and faith. In a Creation Centered theology, Christmas gives us the light to walk by, for God dwells within us, empowering our every step on the upward path. The world is still a dangerous place; "bad" things can still happen to us. But the Nativity reveals God's Presence and Power reaching the weakest link in the human chain; even a newborn baby has the Divine Spirit within. Despite appearances to the contrary, God has everything under control. Life is trustworthy and good, even when it leads to Calvary.

Although scholars are rightly skeptical whenever any group declares they alone are teaching the authentic, pristine faith of Jesus Christ, Metaphysical Christianity might arguably recover a central goal from primitive Christianity implied in the stories of the Nativity and the Crucifixion: To be the Christmas faith in an Easter world.

CHECK YOUR KNOWLEDGE

1. "Bonhoeffer suffered the dilemma of the philosopher-king." What does this mean, and what choice did he make?

2. What does recent data indicate about people who find the teachings of their religious faith difficult to follow? Are they leaving to join other groups?

3. Three paradoxes are discussed. Name and explain each.

4. Explain "Creation-Centered" Theology. How is it helpful to Metaphysical Christians?

5. Is most Christian theology today pessimistic or optimistic? How did theology achieve its current position?

6. Why does the author suggest Metaphysical Christianity might see itself as the "Christmas faith in an Easter world"?

QUESTIONS FOR DISCUSSION

1. Should we make life better or concentrate on spiritual pursuits?

2. Would you have joined Bonhoeffer in fighting the Nazis?

3. Is violence justified in war? What about trying to kill Hitler? Would Jesus Christ approve of tyrannicide?

4. How can Metaphysical Christianity maintain its sunny optimism about human perfectibility after the Holocaust? Has 9-11 affected the way you look at the world?

5. In what ways is Jesus Christ calling you today? What is "The Cost of Discipleship" for you?

6. The author also says some positive things to say about evangelical churches, especially their emphasis on joy and praise. What do you think?

- 2 -

TOOLS OF THEOLOGY

Describe before You Prescribe

In the introduction to *The History of Christian Thought*, Paul Tillich admitted his task was impossibly large:

> Actually, nobody would dare to present a complete history of what every theologian in the Christian Church has thought. That would be an ocean of contradictory ideas. The purpose of this (work) is quite different, namely, to show those thoughts which have become accepted expressions of the life of the church. [1]

Tillich went beyond describing ideas which "have become accepted expressions" of religious thinkers. His writings teem with analysis, critique, and synthesis. How could it be otherwise, since he frankly admitted that theology is a process of sifting through "an ocean of contradictory ideas"?

Describing Theology

The general rule we shall follow in this study is *describe before you prescribe*. As a teacher of theology, I have noted that many students come bouncing into class the first day of graduate theological education with all the answers worked out, and this before learning what the questions are. Theology requires hard work; it is not shuffling opinions back and forth among people who have no clue what the great minds of the human race have been saying on these critical tropics for thousands of years. Theology is to religious and spiritual thought as math is to chemistry and physics. It provides the tools to critically reflect on the most important questions the human mind has ever conceived. And you have a personal stake in this study.

Have you ever stood under the night sky and gazed at the stars, suddenly seized by the majesty and vastness of the cosmos, and asked yourself, "What is life all about?" Congratulations, you've doing theology. Since you were not the first member of species Homo sapiens to ask that question, you might be interested in some of the more intriguing answers cooked up by your ancestors. You will not agree with all of them; your task here is not so much to find the truth, but to find what others have *said* is the truth. Theology will give you the analytic tools to dissect and describe great thoughts about God, life, eternity, love, justice, salvation (hold your fire—Hindus use that term, too), the Trinity, the Bible, church, ministry, prayer, and many other subjects which lend themselves to theologically inquiry. But first, aspiring theologians need to learn how theological inquiry is done.

Theology, as the root words suggest (*theo-logos*, words about God), is the study of God. The word *God* itself requires several chapters to unpack in this volume, so let's temporarily roll past that roadblock with the annotation "however defined" tacked to the warning alarms going off in your head. As already stated, the all-purpose rule to follow in this study is *describe before you prescribe*. Here's my attempt at a comprehensive, inclusive description of the subject field to be investigated in this text.

> **THEOLOGY:** Organized, rational reflection on ideas and practices pertaining to the Divine, God and Ultimate Concerns, evaluated from within the boundaries of a chosen circle of faith.

This definition brings along a trunkful of ideas, so let's begin unpacking it. Saying theological inquiry is "organized, rational reflection" separates it from devotional, inspirational or strictly personal studies about divine actions or ideas. Theology is *organized* because it proceeds from point to point in a logical sequence, and it is *rational* because the whole picture should fit together without blatant contradictions in its *reflections*.

Theology concerns itself with *ideas and practices*. Not just concepts but the deeds done in the name of God are fair game for theological analysis. One theologian might examine a concept like the Trinity, while another studies the Lord's Supper as celebrated by different communions. Both are doing theology.

Subject matter for theological reflection must be *pertaining to the Divine, God and ultimate concerns.* Anything which concerns humanity in an ultimate way (What happens after death? How shall we treat neighbors? What is the purpose of life?) can be studied as a theological subject. Religious ethics, human relationships, healing, prosperity anchored in a Jesus Christ consciousness--any subject which opens itself to the influx of Divine power is a theological topic. Since these questions of Ultimate Concerns move beyond data available to the physical sciences, they are inherently metaphysical.

Lastly, the definition locates theological efforts *within the boundaries of a chosen circle of faith.* This is how theology differs from the philosophy of religion. Theoretically, philosophy begins without commitment to any particular worldview. For example, philosophers of religion might examine ideas attributed to the Prophet Muhammad or Jesus of Nazareth without claiming either Islam or Christianity as home base. Theologians, however, begin with certain ineluctable assumptions.

If a Jewish theologian decides the Qur'an is true and Mohammed is the prophet of God, she can no longer call herself a *Jewish* theologian. If a Muslim theologian studies Buddhism and decides to embrace the Noble Eightfold Path, he is no longer a *Muslim* theologian. Jews do theological analysis of the Qur'an, of course, and Muslims study Buddhism, but they study these books from "within the boundaries of a chosen circle of faith." The yardstick for the Jew is Torah and Talmud. For Muslims it's the Qur'an. The yardstick for the Christian is...? Answer that question, and you're doing Christian theology.

Embedded Cultural Influences

At first blush, the way of the philosopher of religion seems closer to the self-image of many open-minded Christians. For example, Metaphysical Christianity takes pride in affirming that truth (sometimes a capital T) can be found in all the religions. Aren't labels just arbitrary barriers fencing people in or out? Let's call ourselves *Interfaith* and embrace all religions as one.

Interfaith religion sounds nice, but it's not an accurate picture of the rich, cultural diversity which everyone brings to the spiritual quest.

Although great insights and inspirational guidance reside in all religions, everyone comes to the table of interfaith discussion with a cultural history and embedded theology. My book *The Many Faces of Prayer* (Unity Books, 2013), recounts the following urban legend:

> During the Protestant-Catholic disturbances in Northern Ireland of the mid-twentieth century, a young man approaches a barricaded checkpoint and is halted by the guard.
>
> "Catholic or Protestant?" the sentry demands.
>
> "Atheist," the stranger replies cockily.
>
> The guard is not impressed. "Would that be Catholic atheist or Protestant atheist?"[2]

Pre-set categories of thought shape the world and influence people even when they categorically deny being influenced. By nature, humans grope in the dark to find answers, yet often the *questions* elude them. Those who forsake Christianity seldom abandon Jesus' ethical mandate to love your neighbor as yourself, return not evil with evil, treat neighbors and strangers with equal respect, show kindness to the poor and afflicted and gentleness toward children, and work for justice and equality for all people. Yet, not every human culture has subscribed to all those values. Plains Indians hardly treated neighbors and strangers with equal respect. A more accurate presumption was that members of other tribes had the right to kill or enslave you whenever the opportunity arose.

For a contemporary example of embedded theologies, take the concept of *revenge,* which has no official sanction in Western civilization. New Testament passages clearly forbid extracting personal vengeance, even when perfectly justified. In Matthew and Luke, Jesus orders his disciples to go beyond shunning revenge and to do good to evil-doers.

> But I say to you that listen, Love your enemies, do good to those who hate you, bless those who curse you, pray for those who abuse you. If anyone strikes you on the cheek, offer the other also; and from anyone who takes away your coat do not withhold even your shirt.[3]

The idea that vengeance belongs, at most, to God runs deep in cultures impacted by the New Testament. Although some Christian ethicists look at vengeance as a perfectly acceptable motive for capital punishment or lengthy imprisonment of wrongdoers, the state, not the individual, administers justice in retributive systems of moral theology. Other theologians say any form of punishment centered on vengeance is contrary to the teachings of Jesus. Crime-and-punishment theories based on models other than vengeance will often endorse penalties, like incarceration, to isolate criminals for public safety, or provide inmate education to correct recidivism, or go even further and attempt to rehabilitate the offender into a productive member of society. None of these allows vengeance by individuals. Citizens can't legally do that in Western societies. However, not all cultures are part of Western society, and not all cultures view criminal or personal offenses equally. Islamic law allows much wider latitude in response to wrongdoing.

> (In Islam) one is entitled to exact revenge from an offender, but only provided one remains within the limits so that wrongs are commensurate. The Koran warns that one may lapse into evil when one attempts to requite evil with evil. The path of forgiveness is preferable to that of revenge, though taking revenge, and even feuding, are permitted if one does not carry things too far.[4]

Islam prefers forgiveness but allows selective acts of vengeance; Christianity officially does not. Individual Christians certainly have violated this cultural taboo and taken revenge, but they risk incurring social disapproval to the point of criminalizing their behavior. There is no clause for feuding, and dueling was outlawed centuries ago. This example was not selected to suggest the superiority of Christian unconditional forgiveness over Islam's ethical vengeance. Indeed, I cheered loudly when Ralphie finally beat the stuffing out of the bully Scut Farkus in *A Christmas Story*. Culturally embedded values—e.g., *bullies should get what's coming to them*—can influence religiously observant and non-observant people alike.[5]

Culturally Christian, Spiritually Unlimited

The historical evidence clearly shows a Metaphysical Christian stream flowing from nineteenth century progressive Protestant thought, especially the powerful renaissance unleashed by New England Transcendentalists Ralph Waldo Emerson and Henry David Thoreau. Emerson is a common link in the evolution of New Thought and historic Unitarian-Universalism, although the metaphysical churches and the congregations which constitute today's Unitarian-Universalist Association parted company around the turn of the twentieth century and have no connection at the present. Add to these intellectual movements the spiritual healing breakthroughs of the *Christian sciences*—originated by Phineas Parkhurst Quimby, Christianized by Mary Baker Eddy, and expanded by great teachers like Emma Curtis Hopkins, and Charles and Myrtle Fillmore—and the evolutionary picture snaps into focus. All these sources acknowledged their practical and intellectual debt to Christian tradition while reserving the right to reject or reinterpret parts which no longer worked for them.

Metaphysical Christianity is not some remote island but an archipelago just off the Christian mainland. Even while honoring the luminous insights of a teacher like the Buddha, people of Western culture experience the light of Gautama Siddhartha through a window irrevocably shaped like Jesus Christ. Recognizing this cultural influence does not in any way denigrate the unique, powerful message of Buddhism, nor does it imply Christianity offers a superior point of view. Acquiring an embedded worldview is value-neutral, not a form of original sin, just as learning a mother tongue from parents and other caregivers suggests no linguistic superiority.

The Judeo-Christian worldview shapes the dialogue. For theists or atheists,[6] the God-concept, accepted or rejected, is not so much a *God* concept as it is a *Jesus* concept. What are the attributes of God? Selfless love, healing mercy, infinite kindness, overwhelming forgiveness, endless warmth, non-judgmental intelligence, life-empowering confidence, vast oceans of grace. Where do we get these ideas? From centuries of reflection on the life and teachings of Jesus the Christ. For a cogent, inclusive definition of *Christian*, look at the following from Catholic theologian Hans Kueng:

> A Christian is not just any human being with genuine
> conviction, sincere faith and good will. No one can fail
> to see that genuine conviction, sincere faith and good
> will also exist outside Christianity. But all those can be
> called Christian for whom in life and death Jesus Christ
> is ultimately decisive.[7]

Kueng's prescription extends the widest umbrella; it is a maximum definition, including virtually everyone who claims to follow Jesus. Theologians often erect elaborate screening devices to filter out the heretics, yet here we have a Catholic thinker proposing an almost fenceless Christian pasture for all the Lord's sheep to range far and graze freely. The first edition version of this chapter, written in the mid-1980s, referred to Kueng as "delightfully heretical" for proposing such an inclusive definition of Christianity. Times are a-changing so rapidly that now, in the second decade of the twenty-first century, Kueng's wide umbrella may have found an ally in Pope Francis, who has already declared every good person moves onward to God, not just Catholics.

Although Kueng's definition is broad, it sets boundaries. Limitations are not inherently bad. Every choice necessarily eliminates other options. Marrying one person ordinarily shuts down certain kinds of intimate contact with others. A decision to buy *this* car instead of *that* car, limits the choice of conveyances when driving to work. Structure is not always equal to bondage, especially if the structure is freely chosen and provides space within it to operate in some measure of freedom. The rules in a football game provide necessary structure without which no game could be played. Rules become a problem only when they are imposed, arbitrary and oppressive.

Metaphysical Christianity straddles a paradox. It acknowledges cultural influences shape religious thought, yet it has acknowledged the rich heritage of the dominant religion of that culture, the Judeo-Christian faith. And people who live in this quandary are not alone. According to the conservative online news magazine *Christian Post,* recent studies have shown that while seventy percent of the American population self-identifies as Christian, increasingly more of us (37%) are exhibiting "post-Christian" behavior, including an aversion to formal prayer, Bible reading, and church attendance.[8] Not everyone is clear about what they disbelieve.

> For example, many self-described atheists also claim to pray to a deity. Long-time churchgoers often lack basic orthodox beliefs. People who effortlessly self-describe as "Christian" may live like practical atheists in most other parts of their lives.[9]

Although most Americans self-identify as Christians, not everyone who fits under Hans Kueng's rainbow definition likes that word. Some zealous devotees of today's Jesus cults have so poisoned the well with anti-intellectual, flagrantly ethnocentric theologies that some progressives shy away from the Christian label. (Heard recently: *"If that's Christianity, I'm damn sure not a Christian!")* Especially among young people, it's becoming fashionable to reject any link to the word *Christian.* Others grimace at traditional terms like *church*, preferring the neutralized word *center* for progressive houses of worship. This is a live debate in Metaphysical Churches today.

Even though some of his intolerant friends do their best to drive people away, something in the birth, life, teachings, death/resurrection and ongoing presence of Jesus Christ keeps people coming back for comfort and spiritual strength, including people of all theological perspectives. There is something about Jesus that broadcasts unity in diversity, even if his friends haven't always gotten the message. Jesus is the common ground which all Christians share, although they may disagree about the particulars.

And there are other guides to the Divine available in the world. Doubtless the prophets and sages of other world faiths are effective shepherds and teachers for who travel with them. Likewise, despite the best efforts of a vocal minority to claim him as their exclusive property, Jesus the Christ is an all-purpose Wayshower by whom divergent communities of the Christian family of religions have found their path to the One Presence/One Power God standing beneath all our traditions.

Jesus shows the way to be human and divine and points beyond to a spiritual reality in which all things live, move, and have their being. As previously noted, the specific variation of the Jesus Faith which generally frames the theological discussion in this volume is called

Metaphysical Christianity. Some have identified this expression of the historic faith as *post-Christian*, meaning a new religion emerging from Christianity as the Jesus Faith originated within Judaism.

Another possibility is *trans-Christian*, which describes Metaphysical Christianity as the branch of the church which transcends and includes its heritage.   My favorite descriptive phrase is *Culturally Christian, Spiritually Unlimited.*[10]

Six Functions of Theology

After locating Metaphysical Christianity's place in the family Christian thought, let's consider what theology should be doing to pay its way as an intellectual activity within any spiritual tradition. I call these *Six Functions of Theology*. They are not the only tasks of religious inquiry, but they will serve as a handy framework to introduce theological thinking for now.

1. Ongoing Re-interpretations of the Faith.

When theology is doing its job, it challenges the clichés and outmoded ideas of previous generations, translating the Christian faith into the language of today. The first function of theology, then, is to provide an ongoing re-interpretation of truth for each new generation. Scientific research methods have taught us a valuable lesson: truth must be faced and accepted even if it kicks the pillars out from under our most cherished hypotheses.

Charles Darwin expounded his theory of evolution with no intention to endanger God's truth. A lifelong Anglican, Darwin is buried in Westminster Abbey. He did, however, shoot holes through existing concepts about how life arose on this planet and shook up the established paradigm of instantaneous Creation. Since Darwin's day scientists have learned to be more open to new ideas. Although "orthodoxy" exists in the scientific community, science is much more willing to accept radically new concepts than almost any other field of knowledge.

A case in point is what happened as the Voyager I space probe passed near Saturn in late fall-winter 1980-81. The camera-carrying spacecraft sojourned briefly, sending pictures back to Earth before resuming its trajectory, which eventually took Voyager out of the solar system. (At this writing, Voyager I has reached 18.8 billion kilometers from Earth and officially exited the solar system.)[11] When the first computer-enhanced photographs flowed back across millions of miles of space from the ringed gas giant, researchers were enthralled at the beauty of Saturn's ring system. Then their rapture turned to astonishment as Voyager focused on the inner rings of the sixth planet.

To their utter amazement they found the clear images of the F-rings showed an intertwined pattern. How could orbiting particles of frozen gas twist themselves into an elongated braid around the girth of Saturn's atmosphere? One scientist moaned that this new discovery meant they might have to throw out everything they knew about orbital physics. "Braiding defies the laws of orbital mechanics for several reasons," he said. "But obviously these rings are doing the right thing."[12]

In an earlier age, people consulted ancient authorities if they wanted to know what was true. If Aristotle or St. Augustine said it was true, then it was true forever. No one considered examining nature to learn what is true, because learned men had already passed judgment. "Who are we to contradict the great ones?" medieval scholars demanded. The problem, of course is that ancient authorities, perhaps wise in spiritual matters, have often missed the mark when straying into the scientific arena.

If scientists were still functioning from the authority model they would have looked at those crisp, color photographs of the braided rings of Saturn and said, "Well, that can't be right. The camera must be broken. Our books on astronomy say those F-rings can't be braided, so the pictures must be wrong." Saturn, having never read the textbooks, didn't know it wasn't allowed to braid its rings. The objective of science is not to prove theories but to find out what is true. Scientists studying the Voyager data had to get right with Saturn, because the ringed planet wasn't about to change its physical properties to suit their theories.

A more rational approach to religious studies might also be to accept the probability of change and to welcome it. What is important, after all, is not one particular religious theory, comfortable though it may be, but finding a continuously upgradable, working model of truth as it is currently understood. A faith to live by in the ages to come must be absolutely fearless when facing the accelerating pace of new knowledge streaming into human consciousness. Rather than deciding what God has done and requiring all new data to comply with our self-made religious systems, religious thinkers will need to modify their cherished beliefs as we learn what actually exists, what is actually true, what God has actually wrought. Anything less is an insult to the Creator and Source of all life, love, and intelligence.

New knowledge is no threat to God. Scientific advances and historical discoveries only threaten those who have shuttered their windows against the light of divine possibilities. An ongoing re-Interpretation of faith allows people to correct their blind spots.[13] This transitions nicely to the second function of theology.

2. Provide Critical Analysis of Religious Ideas.

When theologians are doing their jobs, theology becomes the science of religious analysis, a gadfly pestering people to re-think assumptions and re-design paradigms. In short, effective theology is critical. This may be a new concept in Metaphysical Christianity, deserving special attention. The word "criticism" has fallen on hard times. Originally it meant to evaluate and analyze, but these days criticism is almost always equated with negative comments. In today's language, "Don't criticize me!" actually means, "Don't pick on me!"

Some exceptions reflect the original sense of the word: art critics, movie critics, and drama critics evaluate works from their specialty fields and pass the information along to non-specialists. Since everyone is an amateur in someone else's field, people often rely on the critical opinions of experts before plunking down cash for a Broadway show, a new car, or a house in the suburbs. This is the sense in which the term is used in theology.

Practical Christianity has usually emphasized points of agreement and tried to play down conflicting ideas. In a world frequently torn by religious strife, some have concluded that to follow Jesus Christ means, in the words of a well-known ditty, it's important to

> Accentuate the positive,
> Eliminate the negative,
> Hold fast to the affirmative
> an' don't mess with Mr. In-between.[14]

Positive thinkers can be analytical as well. Sometimes they must choose among alternatives based on our best analysis of the situation.

Some folks are comfortable within Roman Catholicism; others find their Jewish or Muslim or Hindu heritage works best; still others find some form of Protestantism meet their religious needs. But every selection implies non-selections. To choose one church is to reject the others. Critical evaluation doesn't mean to dislike, disapprove of, or even disagree with the other spiritual paths. It means to sort through the possibilities and pick what works best for the individual.

Theological analysis is that sort of work. Many are the ways to look at the great issues, as Paul Tillich indicated. When someone examines the concepts, practices and lifestyles offered in the religious marketplace, then selects one for our personal faith—that is critical analysis. Practical Christianity has always encouraged people to think for themselves, i.e., be independently minded and prove truth ideas in their lives. One of the goals of this book is to open dialogue on the subject of theological analysis and to offer help for people as they now self-consciously do what they have intuitively been doing all along. Hopefully, any critical analysis of theological topics will retain the more positive tones of Christian tradition while still remaining faithful to the principles of religious scholarship.

However, a note about the limitations of theology is in order before proceeding. Some religious questions will remain open, forever. A healthy religious faith rejoices when it doesn't have all the answers. As Eric Gill said in a moment of outrage, *"Good Lord! The thing was a mystery and we measured it!"*[15] Thankfully, some things are immeasurably deep. In a remarkable passage from *Dynamics for Living*, a "best of Fillmore" compilation, Charles Fillmore laid the foundation for new systematic theologies:

> To think in an independent, untrammeled way about anything is foreign to the habit of the races of the Occident. Our lines of thought and act are based upon precedent and arbitrary authority. We boast much of our freedom and independence, but the facts are that we defer from custom and tradition. Our whole civilization is based on manmade opinions. We have never thought for ourselves in religion, consequently we do not know

how to think accurately and consecutively upon any proposition. We have not been trained to draw conclusions each for himself from a Universal Pivotal Truth. Consequently, we are not competent to pass judgment upon any statement so predicated. Our manner of deciding whether or not certain statements are true or false is to apply the mental bias with which heredity, religion, or social custom has environed us, or else fly to some manmade record as authority. In the study of practical Christianity all such temporary proofs of Truth are swept aside as chaff. We entertain nothing in our statements of Truth that does not stand the most searching analysis, nothing that cannot be practically demonstrated.[16]

When theology does its job, it offers *Glimpses of Truth* from a new vantage. Its method will be analytical rather than devotional/inspirational, since theology seeks "to think in an independent, untrammeled way" about central concepts of theology from "a universal pivotal truth" turning upon solid, foundations. Fillmore also insisted that religious truth must "be practically demonstrated." This brings us to the third function of theology.

3. Integration of Religious Ideas with Everyday Life.

When I was a boy, I attended a Sunday school at a mainline Protestant church. Like most kids, I enjoyed the Bible stories. However, moving into my teens I began to notice that we were always reading stories about men who wore robes and sandals and had no electricity. Jesus met the woman at the well because she frequented the village square to draw water. Even in the 1950s, my family had indoor plumbing, walked under street lights, and benefitted from public sewage systems.

Why was everything religious so doggone ancient? Sunday school teachers applied the stories, of course. Help people like the Good Samaritan; forgive people like the father of the prodigal son. Morally educated children are important to any society. But what was the specifically *Christian* content of those everyday applications? Didn't *all* good people in *every* culture help innocent victims and forgive the repentant family member?

When problems crashed through our Ozzie-and-Harriet world, bringing health challenges and relationship problems never shown on black-and-white television, how could ancient Christianity help? When visiting patients in the hospital, can pastors offer anything but bedside comfort and Rogerian counseling—*Could you say more about that?* Indeed, compassion for people facing health challenges is part of the job description of the pastor, who is not there to cure but to *care*. However, do clergy today believe there is actually a chance that spiritual efforts— prayer, for example—might affect healing?

Later I found that ministerial training at traditional theological seminaries helped a little. Prospective ministers were taught to let the people express their feelings and to be a caring person, an important skill for a pastor. However, pastoral education rarely progressed beyond the psychological treatment phase of ministry. During my years of graduate theological education, I cannot recall hearing a seminary professor express the belief that Divine power could heal people of disease, let alone that we should encourage people to have faith in their God-given power to overcome any obstacle. Thumbing through the index of books on Christian theology, "healing" is often conspicuous in its absence, seldom listed as a topic worthy of discussion. When healing is mentioned, it more likely refers to overcoming emotional scars rather than curing disease or other physically challenging conditions.

The same is true for relationships. We were trained as communications facilitators, treating relationship problems by applying the principles of non-directive counseling. And, of course, there was no mention of prosperity consciousness, even though we learned in the first year at seminary that the number one problem couples fight about is money. Essentially, we were taught the clergy's job is to help people suffer with dignity while remaining faithful to the Church.

The Bible is full of healing miracles, so where is God-power today? Did God only act back in the days of camels and sandals? When theology is doing its job, it helps people apply religious insights to everyday life. Shouldn't clergy talk about prosperity when people are hungry, healing when people are sick, and wholeness in relationships when love falters? One could argue that if there is a fundamental heresy in modern Christian thought it is this: Too many pastors and theologians no longer believe God is capable of doing anything in the real world.

Because the Metaphysical churches grew up as lay movements within Protestantism, they were free of ecclesiastical strings and they could, like Pinocchio, dance freely wherever they wanted to go. This hard-won freedom gave neo-Luthers of the nineteenth century an unfettered opportunity to pursue ideas and lay the foundation for the movement some have called *New Thought Christianity*. In 1897, Charles Fillmore assured readers of his magazine he taught nothing he had not proved for himself. [17]

Like Pinocchio and the Prodigal Son, some Metaphysical Christians have wandered homeless for a long while. The very freedom they enjoyed has given a sense of independence which isolated the movement from its Christian heritage. I wrote *Friends in High Places* to re-introduce long-lost relatives in church history. The continuing popularity of that book suggests some people are as eager to see themselves as "real Christians" as Pinocchio wanted to be a "real boy" and the Prodigal wanted to return home.

Practical Christianity has much to contribute to the greater community of faith; it also has much to gain, it we would share resources and study metaphysical theology with scholars and laypeople from other traditions. This introduces the fourth function of theology.
4. Establish Dialogue within the Theological Circle.

Scientific research begins with known facts and proceeds to learn about the unknown. Religious inquiry is different. We have certain "pivotal truths" from which we begin and to which we must return. For example, belief in God is fundamental to Christian theology, however differently we may understand what "belief" and "God" mean. A theologian who refuses to acknowledge God in his work can scarcely call himself a Christian theologian. Tillich named this space, in which religious thinkers must operate, the "Theological Circle".[18]

There are certain givens within which every theoretician must function if he/she is doing theology. Real theological dialogue is not a hostile harangue but a marketplace/meeting place for exchange of ideas. Lively, lovely disagreements have regularly brightened dry, theological discussion, as with the famous exchanges between Karl Barth and Emil

Brunner. The Barth-Brunner "paper debates" lasted for years and were characterized by mutual respect and a sincere desire of both for new insights. Sadly, the history of Christian thought has seen a lot of scathing denunciations and too few instances of real dialogue. Theological dialogue widens the circle of faith when it include discussions with other Christian traditions.   We have much to learn from each other. Good theology is tolerant and promotes openness. God-inspired theology is a bridge of light.

5. Interpretation of Symbolism.

Everything humans say about God is symbolic, because human language never quite captures the Divine. Even when people share their mystical experiences, those encounters must be translated into word symbols which limit readers' experience to linear, descriptive sentences on a page. All religious writings are symbolic, some more than others. Theology interprets those symbols and explains their meanings to each new generation.

Our grandchildren will rediscover the excitement we felt when we grasped the basic principle of Metaphysical Christianity: God's one presence and power. How will language and symbols change in the next hundred years? In the next thousand? We have no way to know. New, young theologians will arise whose task it will be to re-state the ancient truths for the children of the twenty-first and twenty-second Centuries and beyond. This realization triggers the final category.

6. Raise New Issues and Suggest Answers.

Could anyone envision the moral/political crisis which shook the United States during the second half of the twentieth century? Suddenly, we became aware our institutions were promoting racism, war and sexism. Could anyone dream big enough to see the Berlin Wall toppling and the winds of democracy blowing through the gap to melt the Cold War? Free elections in Eastern Europe; the dissolution of the last great empire state, the Soviet Union? And now, in the post-9-11 world, ancient rivalries and the clash of civilizations threaten to tangle the emerging global community in cords of conflict which stretch back thousands of years. Attitudes have changed, and theology must address those changes.

In fact, some of the changes were first brought to our attention by "radical" theological opinions, notably in the areas of world peace, and civil rights.

Dr. Martin Luther King, Jr. was more than a political leader: King was a brilliant thinker with a Ph.D. in Systematic Theology from Boston University. His activism grew from a deep spirituality; his theological interpretation of Jesus and Gandhi in terms of nonviolent struggle gave him strength and courage. Like Bonhoeffer, he remained faithful to his vision until death.

What will be the new issues that motivate the "radicals" of the future to re-interpret the ancient message and find new answers? We cannot guess. But theology must never let itself become the private chaplain to the status quo, smiling approvingly as powerful people try to keep their power at the expense of needed change. Theology carries a divine mandate to seek, understand, and speak the Word of God to each new generation.

The Unity Quadrilateral

The purpose of this book is to offer a broad overview of theology which can inform the skeptics and mystics within twenty-first century Christianity. A second aim is to interface those two thought-worlds so we can dialogue across that "bridge of light" linking islands of modern truth churches with the liberal Protestant mainland from which they floated free a hundred years ago. It is a task fraught with peril. John Naisbitt, author of the 1980s bestseller *Megatrends*, summed up the plight of the systematic thinker when he noted that his work was

> ...synthesis in an age of analysis. Its purpose is to provide an overview. To do that, it is necessary to generalize...Yet, I think it is worth the risk. In a world where events and ideas are analyzed to the point of lifelessness, where complexity grows by quantum leaps, where the information din is do high we must shriek to be heard above it, we are hungry for structure. With a simple framework we can begin to make sense of the world. And we can change that framework as the world itself changes.[19]

To erect a "simple framework" upon which to discuss modern Christian theology, this study will borrow a schema from the *United Methodist Book of Discipline*. Originally known as the *Wesleyan Quadrilateral,* I have modified the system for doing theology from a Metaphysical Christian perspective and re-baptized the technique as the *Unity Quadrilateral*, with apologies to and appreciation for John Wesley, founder of Methodism. To prepare the workbench for the task ahead, let's take a brief look at this impressive set of tools.

To think theologically means to examine existing beliefs as well as striking out in new directions. While many people frequently question religious beliefs and practices, few have paused to consider the sources of those convictions. And the more successfully embedded a viewpoint is, the less likely someone will question its source or validity. For example, most people believe *God is good*, but where does that widely held concept originate? (See Fig 2-1.)

Scripture

One possible answer is Scripture. The Bible is often called the textbook of Christianity; its students and teachers are legion. People study the Bible to gain new insights and hear what God is saying today through the voice of prophets, teachers and apostles. Chapter 5 will dig deeper into Biblical interpretation, but for now let's just say the Bible alone can never serve as the basis for faith. All branches of Christianity have access to the Bible, yet look how differently a Catholic charismatic or a Russian Orthodox priest, a Mormon or a Presbyterian reads this same Bible. Each person brings to the Bible his/her own peculiar brand of Christian Tradition.

Tradition

Narrowly defined, tradition is that which one's personal branch of the Christian family has believed. A wider definition might include the whole of the Christian history, even at the risk of sailing onto that ocean of contradictions. The whole body of Christian history belongs to all of us, although we certainly won't want to affirm every absurdity which has ever been declared in the name of Jesus. Tradition tells us who we are and what we accept as true.

For example, Metaphysical Christians usually affirm some variation of the following affirmation from Myrtle Fillmore's *Healing Letters*: "There is but one Presence and One Power, God the good."[20] This is the cornerstone belief, the "Universal Pivotal Truth" on which Practical Christianity turns. Metaphysical Christians are certain that One Presence/One Power (my shorthand: OP^2) is a fundamental principle of the Universe. I posted a small note on my wall which reads: "One Presence/One Power—Everything else is commentary." Regardless how much I resonate with the mystical vision of God as OP^2, as a theologian I'm duty bound to ask a hard question: *Who says?*

> ➤ It isn't biblical.
> ➤ It isn't advocated by most Christian churches.
> ➤ It isn't discussed beyond the metaphysical community.
> ➤ In fact, OP^2 isn't even *attacked* by theologians, suggesting its irrelevance to contemporary theology. [21]

Where, then, do metaphysical churches get the idea that God is the only Presence/Power in the cosmos? It is a part of mystical tradition going back to Meister Eckhart, the medieval preacher, and other thinkers who both predated and followed him. Certainly, someone can find OP^2 in the Bible when looking for it, but nowhere is this doctrine (teaching) elucidated as a plain statement of fact in the pages of Scripture. Alluded to? Yes. Required by the life and teachings of Jesus? Very possibly. But given as an outright teaching? *Not in the Bible.* Don't worry. Quite a few orthodox beliefs are non-biblical, too. For example:

> ➤ Original sin
> ➤ The Trinity
> ➤ Sundays as the Sabbath day
> ➤ Existence of an immortal soul (biblical model is *resurrection of the body*)
> ➤ Eternal hell (at least it's not found in Paul)

All of the above are traditional ideas developed externally and read back into Scripture. In fact, how did *scripture* become Scripture? What makes the bizarre *Letter of Jude* a New Testament book, while the fascinating early Christian treatise known as the *Didache*, or *Teaching of the Apostles*, didn't get in? You guessed it.

Unity Quadrilateral*

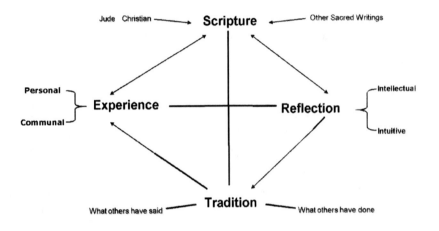

*Theological toolkit developed for Unity by Thomas Shepherd, with appreciation for John Wesley, founder of Methodism, whose original version provided the basis for this adaptation.

Fig. 2-1

Take the familiar Christmas story. Ask someone to describe the events, and they might come up with this:

> Joseph and Mary (his wife) come to Bethlehem in late December because of a census ordered by the Roman Emperor Augustus. They are given a stable to stay in by a kindly innkeeper, where Jesus is cradled in straw. Earlier that night, angels sing while flying above shepherds, who are dazzled by the star hanging over Bethlehem. At the stable, the shepherds meet three Kings—Balthazar (who is black), Melchior and Caspar. Shepherds, magi and the animals kneel in worship of the Christ child. The scene in our Christmas crèche is complete. *Gloria in excelsis Deo.*

It's a beloved scene, deeply meaningful to Christians around the world. Except for one small glitch: except for the Roman census, which did not happen historically, *none of the above is in the Bible.*

First, we must separate the two birth narratives of Luke and Matthew. Luke has the shepherds, the angels (who never sing, fly or hover) the census (by Caesar Augustus, who never ordered it). Luke provides the manger but never mentions straw or even a stable. And the kindly innkeeper and adoring animals are totally absent from Luke's Nativity. So are the star, the wise men, and the kneeling worshippers. And—with apologies to those who thought this was a G-rated narrative—Luke's Mary isn't Joseph's wife; *she's his pregnant girlfriend.* (Technically, "betrothed wife," which meant a fiancée who had vowed fidelity.) Prudish Matthew has them married but chaste.

That isn't Matthew's only problem with Luke. Matthew stages the whole affair in a *house*, mentioning nothing about a manger or a crowded city. He assumes Joseph lives in Bethlehem so the author does not need to invent a census to get his holy family in town by Christmas. There are wise men, but the text neither names them, nor describes their ethnic origins, nor indicates how many dignitaries joined the caravan. We surmise three visitors because he does list three gifts: *gold, frankincense, and myrrh.* The word *kings* is nowhere found in Matthew, nor are there *shepherds* and the *angel* bands which Luke hired for the gala occasion.

Most profoundly, Luke's Jesus is announced as "good news of great joy for all the people: to you is born this day in the city of David a Savior (or *Healer*), who is the Messiah (Greek, *Christos*), the Lord." That fits Luke's universalism very well. Matthew was a Jewish Christian and not at all interested in a savior for the whole world. He wanted the Messiah. Listen to how the "wise men from the East" inquired after the baby at the palace of Herod the king: "Where is the child who has been born king of the Jews? For we observed his star at its rising, and have come to pay him homage."[22]

Finally, Christmas borrows from December holidays in New Testament times. *Saturnalia,* the Roman holiday of serious partying, drinking, gambling, and exchanging places with servants, began December 17. Heads of households prepared meals for the slaves, and everyone wore hats which were ordinarily reserved for free citizens.

Gifts were exchanged among a wide network of friends and business associates. Later the holiday of *Sol Invictus*, the Unconquerable Sun, joined the celebrations. Since this winter solstice festival fell on December 25th, early Christians borrowed the date as the birth of the Son of God, cleverly converting the pagan festival of winter solstice to Christ's Mass.

The popular model for the first noel is really a collage of interwoven traditions. And why not? Holidays are usually a combination of memories and adaptations that stick to the calendar. If an idea or practice works for a community of faith, the action will bind with thought patterns and lifestyles as part of that church's traditions. No one is immune from this tendency. Even avowed non-traditional groups have traditional ways of doing things. Tradition only terrorizes when it withers into traditional-*ism*. In describing the Wesleyan Quadrilateral, the United Methodist *Book of Discipline* cautiously recognizes this danger:

> An uncritical acceptance of tradition amounts to traditionalism, deliverance from which requires an adequate understanding of history as well as a resource for acquiring new wisdom. Traditions are the residue of corporate experience of earlier Christian communities. A critical appreciation of them can enlarge our vision and enrich faith in God's provident love.[23]

Some people are uncomfortable with traditional-ism. Does that mean, when setting up the Christmas crèche and singing about angel choirs and stars leading three kings of orient to the stable, we need to prune the crèche, segregate Luke's shepherds from Matthew's wise men, and take away the stable and farm animals? The stories have merged, not because they happened as historical events, but because together they tell a more complete truth than possible as separate narratives. They are the genesis myths of Christian faith, testimonial tales, proclaiming something special happened when Yeshua ben Joseph was born in Roman Judea two thousand years ago.

Some might argue that the Bible is whatever God wanted it to be, and apparently God wanted the birth of Jesus to be a good story. Tradition enriches life.

Experience

Experience seems to divide naturally into two categories, *communal* and *personal*. Sometimes individuals are swept along when their whole culture undergoes a sea change, like the abolition of slavery, recognition of women as unrestricted and equal members of society, or the movement toward marriage equality. The tidal surge toward recognition of marriage equality demonstrates how values shift with the momentum of *communal* change.

Studies done by the Pew Research Center in 2001 and 2013 showed marked differences. In 2001, Americans opposed same-sex marriage by a 57% to 35% margin. By 2013, the cultural tide had turned; polls showed 50% of Americans in favor and 43% opposed. The same study showed almost one fourth of all white evangelical Protestants favored marriage equality; over half of the mainline Protestants and Catholics agreed.[24]

Humans are more than just products of cultural events. There is a *personal* dimension to experience. Everyone has been shaped by life to believe certain things and doubt others. Beyond the obvious accidents of geography (most Algerians are Muslim, most Italians are Catholic) other factors which shape religious thinking can be traumatic life experiences (such as the death of a parent) ecstatic life experiences (a powerful love relationship) or dramatic life experiences (near death encounters, serving in war, surviving a divorce, discovering a new spiritual dimension to life). Also important to belief systems are encounters with parents, peers, and professors who shape the way people think. Everyone comes to the study of Christianity with a basketful of beliefs already in full bloom.

However, experience is not irresistible. A bright kid growing up in the ghetto has different role models than a bright kid growing up in suburbia. The center city child sees the effects of street crime, drug use, and violence. The suburban child sees neatly manicured lawns, white collar workers driving their BMW's, and old people out for a stroll in the evening wearing designer jogging suits. How will these vastly different environments slant the development of the two? The suburban child might go to an Ivy League university and become a stock market tycoon who turns into a notorious Ponzi scheme operator and defrauds many people; while the ghetto youth might go to night school, study law, begin as a public defender and one day become a widely respected federal judge. Communal and personal experiences may influence, but choices still matter.

Reflection

The final source to consider is *Reflection*. During this study of systematic theology, Reflection is the source employed more than any of the others. I presented a series of ideas; you reflected on what I wrote. Reflection has two components, *intellectual* and *intuitive*. The *intellectual* side takes precedence when people use their capacity to reason, analyze, compare/contrast. *Intuitive* energies come into play when moved by love, compassion, joy, sadness, or grief. Metaphysical Christianity has long understood these two modes of Reflection. In *Twelve Powers,* Charles Fillmore includes descriptions of divine-human faculties which function primarily in the intellectual realm— *understanding* and *judgment*—while others are mostly intuitive, such as *imagination* and *zeal.*[25]

Sometimes the two functions are associated with the two hemispheres of the brain, but most research seems to suggest that both hemispheres contain intellectual and intuitive processes. There is a recorded case of a forty-seven-year old man whose entire left hemisphere had to be removed due to cancer. Remarkably, his other hemisphere was able to adjust and take up the bodily and logical/intuitive functions normally found in the missing hemisphere. In the case of the *Twelve Powers*, every faculty seems to possess both intellectual and intuitive components. Left brain/right brain chitchat is popular and trendy but perhaps not as conclusive as some would like to believe.[26]

The intellectual and intuitive aspects of reflection shape everyone's theology. In fact, all four sources of the Unity Quadrilateral guide everyone's religious and spiritual thinking, whether or not they acknowledge multiple sources. Groups which vehemently claim to depend on nothing but the Bible must use their powers of Refection to interpret *Scripture*. No one exists without a distinct cultural background, their *tradition*. Everyone brings personal history and a lifetime of *experience* to the religious quest. Because the Unity Quadrilateral is so important for thinking theologically, this study will continually refer to the four categories in our ongoing study. Scripture, Tradition, Experience and Reflection provide, but measuring those new ideas to determine what works best is the process to which this study now turns.

CHECK YOUR KNOWLEDGE

1. How does this chapter define *theology*? Explain the definition.

2. What is the difference between *philosophy of religion* and *theology*?

3. Describe each of the *Six Functions of Theology* introduced in this work.

4. What do theologians mean when they speak of *biblical criticism*?

5. What is the *Unity Quadrilateral*? Whose thought inspired this adaptation?

6. Evaluate the pros and cons of *Tradition*.

QUESTIONS FOR DISCUSSION

1. The author says theology always operates within a *circle of faith*. Do you agree?

2. Do you see yourself more like a philosopher of religion or theologian? What are the starting points and limitations of each?

3. Which of the *Six Functions of Theology* do you recognize in your religious community?

4. Is the Bible "true"? What kind of biblical criticism is practiced at your church?

5. Do you think churches should be more or less "churchy"? Ideally, what balance should Metaphysical Christianity seek?

6. How might you use the Unity Quadrilateral in personal studies? Are the four sources equal for you?

- 3 -

EPISTEMOLOGY

How Do I Know What's True?

They went to Capernaum; and when the Sabbath came, he entered the synagogue and taught. They were astounded at his teaching, for he taught them as one having authority, and not as the scribes.

Mark 1:21-22

Pilate asked him, "So you are a king?" Jesus answered, "You say that I am a king. For this I was born, and for this I came into the world, to testify to the truth. Everyone who belongs to the truth listens to my voice." Pilate asked him, "What is truth?"

John 18:37-38

Bumpy Path to Ministry

Seminary students from various denominations often come to graduate study for the professional ministry with wide-eyed innocence. It's all so simple that first semester: The Bible is God's Word, Jesus' clear teachings can be found in the Gospels, and all we have to do is love the people and they'll grow under our wise pastoral guidance. Although each of these illusions shelters a germ of truth, the new seminary student at most mainline Protestant schools of theology often approaches studies for the professional ministry with a benign ignorance as to the problems

54

he/she is about to encounter.

Students learn that modern biblical scholarship starts with the premise that humans wrote the Bible; scripture reflects a struggle for better understanding rather than transcripts of Divine dictation. Rather than declaring the Bible *is* the Word of God, the common assumption which dominates biblical scholarship today is that the Bible is a set of human documents which, at best, *contains* the Word of God. The difference between those two concepts may sound slight, but in fact it is quite profound. Scholars are more likely to see the words of Jesus in the Gospels as interpretive statements of the first century Church rather than news bulletins quoting Jesus verbatim.

And that's just Bible study. In classes on Pastoral Care and management of a church, most seminary professors frankly admit that we Christians are not always teachable. When I studied for the ministry a generation ago, we studied books like James Glasse's *Putting It Together in the Parish* and *Profession: Minister*, and Oliver Read Whitley's *The Church: Mirror or Window?*, which dispelled myths about a carefree life among God's Elect. Being a pastor is tough work. We learned that even the most faithful Christians will resist your leadership from time to time. Another popular book among religious professionals was *Church Fights* by Speed Leas. There would have been no market for the book if squabbles in the family of God were not rampant.

It quickly became apparent to me that religious leadership is a strange job, and I began to reflect on the audacity required to do ministry. Oddly, both humility and a healthy ego seem like required equipment. After all, what gives someone the right to stand in front of a group of people and teach them about God Almighty? Everyone who has ever spoken at a gathering of believers has probably asked themselves the question Martin Luther struggled with while formulating his theology during the Reformation: *"Are you alone right?"* By what authority do you stand here and tell other people how to live their lives? Ministers continually call people to a standard which they themselves have not yet achieved. Isn't that the very definition of hypocrisy? Yet, the job requires setting the bar high and the goals lofty. If clergy had to limit what they taught from the pulpit to things they have already mastered, Sunday talks would seldom show people the high possibilities toward which Jesus called his followers.

If this is true of those preparing for the professional ministry, it also applies to those of us who are simply trying to live the best lives possible as Children of God. Luther believed in the priesthood of all believers, which is a way of saying everyone who follows Jesus Christ is called upon to "minister" unto others in the selfless, affirming way of the man from Nazareth. This is one reason so many teachers and writers have insisted on the importance of comprehensive, critically grounded religious education for anyone who claims the Christian heritage. "To be a Christian at all is to be a theologian. There are no exceptions."[1]

Epistemology: Teachings *of* or *about* Jesus?

The bedrock question which underlies every effort to understand things of God is to ask, *"How do I know this is so?"* Some people shuffle the question into a "hold" box in their brains, but theologians won't let us get away with that for very long. Theologians throughout history have challenged us to think through our assumptions and re-think our prejudices. Like new seminarians, this may cause us some pain at first, but the growth which results from pruning dead ideas from our trees of knowledge makes the pangs of progress worthwhile.

Theology is not the gift of prophecy. Prophets seldom explain themselves. They teach "as one having authority, and not as the scribes." Prophets seldom disagree with one another. Theologians always do. But without the creative re-interpretations of theologians, prodded by skeptics and free-thinkers, the dynamic quality of the prophet's message chills to cold stone as we carve idols of the prophet who walked in our midst. In a provocative passage from his book *Discover the Power Within You*, Eric Butterworth observed:

> What did Jesus really teach? The answer is not easy to formulate, simply because we have been so conditioned by the religion about Jesus. For the religion *of* Jesus, we can only turn to the four Gospels of the New Testament and read the words as they have been recorded.[2]

James Dillet Freeman adds:

> We like to say that we are not so much the religion *about* Jesus as the religion *of* Jesus. We believe that He is the

Son of God; we believe that everyone is a son of God, yes, even the least of us. We believe that this is true, whatever your faith, Christian or other, and we respect your faith...a new approach to Christianity ...interprets Jesus Christ's teachings in a slightly different way than some of the religions that have been around for a longer time.[3]

To consider the difference between religion *of* Jesus and the religion *about* Jesus requires skill in epistemology. *How do we "know" what we know?* What gives anyone the right to interpret things differently? Freeman is right when he says that the metaphysical churches have a distinctive flavor not found elsewhere in Christianity; he could have strengthened his argument by recalling that, although the wrapper may be only a century old, the goods inside are as ancient as anything taught by the Christian faith. That's why metaphysical some thinkers have claimed to be teaching the religion *of* Jesus instead of the religion *about* Jesus. Of course, *every* group wearing the Christian label believes the same thing about their fundamental doctrines. The danger in affirming one's unique take on truth can sound elitist, exclusivist, and dismissive of other ways to understand the faith of Jesus.

Let's be honest. No modern religion actually practices the faith *of* Jesus, which was Temple centered Judaism of the pharisaic model, tinged with the radical reformism of John the Baptist. Jesus seemed to believe the world was ending in the immediate future, after which there would be a Judgment of the righteous and unrighteous and the establishment of the Kingdom of God. He was wrong, historically speaking. But Rabbi Jesus' message of faithfulness to God and inclusive embrace of all others as "neighbors" has persisted to this day, even though layered with massive cultural adjustments heaped upon his work by successive generations.

Review of Classical Epistemologies

Metaphysical Christianity is more than a rediscovery of ancient principles which we believe Jesus taught; it is built upon work done throughout the history of the Christian Faith by those pesky mystics and theologians. Wherever Christianity has blossomed, good teachers have asked the hard questions and found solutions appropriate to their time and locale. Many of these thinkers operated from the assumption that they possessed, within themselves, the ability to know truth when they encountered it. The idea is so widely accepted today that we may wonder why it needs to be discussed. Yet, there are schools of thought which remain dubious to the ability of sinful humanity to achieve truth. We cannot summarily dismiss these doubts as error-belief without hearing what they have to say, any more than new students of Christian metaphysics can continue in old consciousness just because a new idea scratches them where they don't itch.

Metaphysical Christianity has much to say on questions people are still asking today. Therefore, before plunging into a study of topics like Biblical Theology (Ch.5), Christology (Ch.8), or Ecclesiology (Ch.13) it is important to examine the standards by which people judge from un-truth. First let's briefly review epistemology's classic answers to the problem of how to know truth, followed in each case by a critique of the various solutions, and concluding with an attempt to create an epistemology which incorporates the insights of the mystical path and yet is faithful to the faith of Jesus Christ as presented in the gospels.

Authority

Aristotle insisted that two objects of different weights, like a coin and a ship's anchor, would fall to the earth at different speeds, the heavier faster. Since Aristotle was a major authority for western civilization, nearly two thousand years passed before anyone challenged this idea. Then Galileo climbed to the top of the leaning tower of Pisa and dropped two objects of varying weight. They plopped to the ground simultaneously, overturning centuries of erroneous thinking.

This, of course, is the problem with Authority as a source of truth. Even though people like to think of themselves as self-sufficient, in reality everybody trust authorities every day. Very few of us can fly a jumbo jet, inspect the cables of an elevator, or cut away an infected appendix. When wandering beyond their individual specialties, all people must rely upon other specialists to make the highways go where the maps point and to keep food inside those wrapped packages fit to eat. Modern life makes humans unavoidably dependent on the expertise of others, but dependence need not be blind faith. We must be educated consumers, requiring our authorities to toe the line and provide the services we need.

When thinking theologically, someone can listen to what other thinkers have said and gain insights from their wisdom. People unconsciously do this whenever they quote the Bible, which is seen as somehow authoritative by most Christians. Why reinvent the wheel every generation? Isn't it better to defer to greater minds who have struggled with these problems and let them guide us? Although authorities in any field are important, there have been too many instances when religious authority has turned *authoritarian*. Today's practical solution becomes tomorrow's dogma which must be followed even though life situations change.

Because Jesus spoke with his own authority instead of arguing from external authorities, people said he taught "not as the scribes." He did not hesitate to cite those religious thinkers of previous generations; Jesus quoted scripture freely throughout his ministry. He also reserved the right to reinterpret truth by looking at the circumstances even if some venerated person in Hebrew history had said otherwise. Jesus felt comfortable both invoking and breaking with Tradition.

Tradition

Non-industrialized societies are often steeped in *Tradition*, and for good reasons. At its most basic level, tradition passes information down through the generations about how to survive in a world without social safety nets or community food banks.

> Of all sources of truth, tradition is one of the most reassuring. Here is the accumulated wisdom of the ages, and he who disregards it may expect denunciation as a scoundrel or a fool. If a pattern has "worked" in the past, why not keep on using it?[4]

This is a highfalutin variation of the old truism: *If it ain't broke, don't fix it.* Let's take a concrete example. For as long as anyone can recall, slash-and-burn agriculture has fed the rural peoples of the Philippines. Find a level place in the jungle; cut down everything and burn the vegetable matter to ash; plant a crop in the charred plot after it cools; and in a short while you will harvest yams or whatever you have planted.

It works. Rural Filipinos have farmed this way for generations. Bring in new methods fertilizers, crop rotation, new machinery, exotic crops--and the people face a serious problem: Shall try the new ways and risk starvation when the old ways have fed our families for so long? Tradition, for simpler societies, is more than just a system of beliefs; it's a father-to-son, mother-to- daughter technical manual about what to do in the most common situations.

This is the healthy function of tradition. However, as noted in Chapter Two, tradition can be so overbearing that it deteriorates into traditional-*ism*, preventing new ideas from improving the system just because they are new. Sometimes, new ideas are eagerly accepted but twisted by an incomplete understanding so that, instead of an improvement, the new idea becomes part of a reconstructed network of superstition. There have been some recent examples of this latter phenomenon which have been studied by social scientists.

Cargo Cults

One of the most fascinating instances of new ideas upsetting an established culture is the bizarre phenomenon of Cargo Cults. These religious revitalization movements have flourished spasmodically for almost a century among the Melanesian islands of the South Pacific.

Western missionaries came to teach the native populations the Christian faith, but what the natives learned was more than the spoken word. They saw affluent people with bright new gadgets like rifles and steamships. They saw great bags of foodstuffs. They listened to Christian promises about the return of Christ and a day of judgment when good would be rewarded and the dead shall rise. Then they promptly translated this into Melanesian thought, deciding:

1) The End is Near.
2) Our dead ancestors will rise, and
3) they will load up steamships with rifles, rice and flour,
4) bringing the cargo here to us.

The earliest account of Cargo Cult activity comes in 1893 at Milne

Bay in New Guinea where a "prophet" arose to foretell volcanic eruptions and tidal waves which would herald the arrival of the ancestors' ship and the cargo. All available food had to be consumed before the ship would dock, so they slaughtered all their pigs and went on an eating frenzy. After the tidal wave failed to appear, the prophet was jailed by colonial officials to prevent further disturbances.[5]

Other experiences were not so benign. Prophets began to point accusing fingers at European settlers and colonial officials when the cargo did not arrive as predicted. On the island of Espiritu Santo in the New Hebrides in 1923, a plantation owner was murdered by cultists when the prophet Ronovuro predicted the Europeans would prevent the cargo ships from landing. Officials suppressed the movement for a while but it reappeared in 1939.[6]

The following analysis of Cargo Cult phenomena by anthropologist Marvin Harris (1927-2001) borders on theological inquiry and points to the power tradition holds over people, especially when that tradition is the worldview itself:

> The confusion of the Melanesian revitalization prophets is a confusion about the workings of sociocultural systems. They do not understand how the productive and distributive functions of modern industrial society are organized, nor do they comprehend how law and order are maintained among state level peoples. To them, the material abundance of the industrial peoples and the penury of others constitutes an irrational flaw, a massive contradiction in the structure of the world. Their attempt to resolve this contradiction strikes us as a pathetic or even ludicrous aberration. It should be pointed out, however, that almost all of the cargo cults have occurred among people who have been exposed to intensive conversion efforts by Christian overseas missions...they have been provided with a view of the world that is fundamentally supportive of the logic and standards of that revitalization process...After all, strong justification for the logic of the cargo prophets is to be found in the New Testament. Here, too, there are prophecies, visions,

ghosts, and reunion with ancestors. While Christ did not
offer cargo he did offer an even greater gift, "the gift of
eternal life." [7]

Tradition, as a source of truth, is limited by its inability to adjust to
new circumstances. Sometimes, as in the case of the Cargo Cults, when it
does adjust to new circumstances that adjustment is irrational,
superstitious. Tradition can be a valuable source of ideas and customs
which give us a link with our heritage. But traditional-ism can hold us
back from growth necessary to thrive, while radical, irrational changes in
tradition can put us even further out of touch with effective living in the
real world. Tradition alone is insufficient in modern epistemologies.

Intuition

Transcendentalists of the nineteenth century supposed that *Intuition*
was the key to knowledge. Real insights come not by step-by-step
procedures of logic but by flashes of creative inspiration. Where did
those flashes of truth come from, if not from within?

The problems with this method are twofold. First, intuition is not a
reliable process because it relies upon chance insights. What do we do if
inspired flashes don't come and we must decide anyway? As a
supplement to other ways of understanding, intuition is fine, but we
cannot rely on intuition alone. That is why Metaphysical Christians read
the Bible, pray, and discuss ideas with other Christians. Second, these
supplementary methods are needed because intuition is really a source of
truth, not a way to determine what is true.

Intuition is one half of the formative factor of Reason, discussed in
the previous chapter. We can get an idea by intellectual, step-by-step
procedures or by a burst of insight, but is the idea true or false? Intuition
works subjectively, like a baker sampling fresh bread to see if it tastes
good. Whether we cook our ideas by intuitive insights or rational
processes, we must find an objective way to taste them to see if they are
wholesome fare for a spiritual life. [8]

Revelation

The same applies to *Revelation*, which is intuition supposedly received from a higher Source outside the individual consciousness, presumably God or an agent speaking for the Divine. Some Christian epistemologies have been developed that identify revelation as the only source and criterion of truth. Those who take the message of Jesus Christ as recorded in the Bible as the sole source of truth can further use that message as a standard of what is true and judge everything else that claims to be true by the yardstick of scripture.

Obvious problems arise as soon as we identify any fixed source of truth like a set of sacred writings which are considered special revelations from God. Even granting that God speaks to us through the pages of scripture, how shall we understand what those pages mean? How shall we interpret the revelation? Whatever criteria we use, they are the real basis for our epistemology. Since so many people read the same message in scripture and arrive at such diverse conclusions, how can anyone assert that the Bible is a clear, apparent yardstick by which we can measure all truth?

Chapter 5 will delve into biblical theology more thoroughly, but for now let's say Scripture also constitutes a *source* of ideas, but cannot test its own concepts because the value of revelation must be assumed by faith. Revelation fails to provide a working basis for an epistemology because it is susceptible to all the problems we encountered when considering *intuition*. The brief look at Cargo Cults shows what can happen when special revelations crowd other factors from the worldview.

Are we foiled in the search? Is there no way to verify ideas and insights that is available to anyone and repeatable under similar conditions?

Scientific Method

When Galileo dropped those weights off the tower at Pisa, he was employing the scientific method. Science tests ideas by experimentation under controlled conditions in a way that is repeatable by anyone and will produce similar results. If you want to test Aristotle's hypothesis, take two weights and drop them from a tower. You should get the same results as Galileo did, provided some other factor doesn't intervene (like high winds, or one weight striking the side of the tower) Controlled experiments allow researchers to vary one factor and see how this change will affect the outcome.

Let's take an example, drawn from the author's household. When he was in high school my son, Bill, needed to come up with a science fair project. He took three plants and exposed the greenery to different types of music for one hour each evening. Two little pepper plants listened to either classical or hard rock music while the third got an hour of silence. His hypothesis, not surprisingly for a teenager, was that rock music is better for living things than stale, old junk like his Dad listens to.

All three plants were about the same size when the experiment began; all three received the same, measured amount of moisture and sat in the same window the rest of the time. Which grew tallest?   With blissfully reinforced prejudices, I can report the triumph of classical tunes over the tone-deaf mayhem of rock music. Nature herself validates the great masters. But my victory lap was tempered by design flaws in Bill's research technique.

1) Sample was too small. How do we know if the "classical" plant was genetically superior, so that it would have grown much taller had it NOT listened to Mozart, Bach and Handel, which stifled its growth?

2) Exposure was too brief. Every day the plants had one hour of music and twenty-three hours of something else. How do we know if other sounds or environmental exposure influenced their grown?

3) Too many other variables. He carried the plants to different rooms to hear their music. Humidity, temperature, and outside noises varied.

4) Bill cheated. He talked to the rock music plant, telling it he was hoping it would win. Encouraging a species which has no auditory system probably had little effect, but who knows?

Because rock music failed to win hardly means an outside factor had no influence on the outcome, which is why conventional scientific research is generally useless for spiritual endeavors. The sampling we are dealing with is always too small. Emily wants to know what's true, so she tests idea A and concept B. Concept B works for her; idea A leaves her cold. Lindsey runs the same "test" and finds neither A nor B will work for her. She opts for C, producing immediate results. Why? There are too many variables, because humans often react differently to exactly the same stimulus. As the old maxim goes, *one person's meat is another's poison.*

Good research occurs in highly controlled environments with masses of subjects to study. Sociologists Horton and Hunt frankly admit religious topics are not within the charter of scientific study:

> Since science is based on verifiable evidence, science can only deal with questions about which verifiable evidence can be found. Questions like, "Is there a God?" "What is the purpose and destiny of man?" or "What makes a thing beautiful?" are not scientific questions because they cannot be treated factually. Such questions are terribly important, but the scientific method has no tools for handling them. [9]

Scientific methods work quite well when dealing with quantifiable, measurable results, even given the fact that there will be erratic events within the framework of the best research techniques. However, science stops where religious inquiry begins. Horton and Hunt rightly note that science does not—cannot—answer questions about Ultimate Concerns.

So Far, So Bad

So far that the classical solutions to epistemological questions all have good and bad points.

Authority can be helpful, since everyone is a layperson when they stray beyond their fields of expertise. However, authority too easily becomes authoritarianism, demanding concurrence without bothering to show evidence.

Tradition is a kind of community authority, a collection of do's and don'ts which tell members of a society what the ancestors did and how they did it. Tradition can be helpful, in that it relates people to their heritage and provides tried and true methods for doing things which have worked before. Tradition can also prove harmful when it deteriorates to traditional-ism, where new ideas never receive a fair hearing, the group suffers because it cannot learn and grow.

Intuition seems, at first, a likely candidate for an epistemological model, since mystics have usually held that each person has the Divine Spirit within which can guide and direct him/her. However, a belief system built strictly on intuition no readily available, really dependable method for dealing with everyday situations. Intuition is actually a method for *obtaining* insights, not for checking their validity. When epistemology asks, "How do we know it's true?" intuition falls short in regard to consistency. Jack is considering whether some new idea is true or false, so he intuitively decides, "It's true because I feel it is true." Jill, his partner may intuitively contradict him, "No, it's false because I feel it is false." What negotiation is possible if intuition alone is the standard? Reasonable discussions about rightness or wrongness, better or worse, healthy or unhealthy are meaningless and impossible. Intuition can't answer questions with repeatable, consistent results.

Revelation fails the same application test. Information claiming to originate in a divine source outside of the individual is beyond criticism. Yet so groups which claim to have received divine revelation seldom agree with other factions. Is God really that inconsistent, or does this disclose a basic flaw in any revelation-based epistemology?

The Scientific Method of experimentation is more helpful, especially when dealing with questions about the physical Universe. However, science deals in facts and theories, not wisdom and truth. Science has nothing to say about theological ethics, socio-political rights, or the nature of love. Science is value neutral, unable to ask the question, "Does God exist?" Anything which goes beyond study of observable phenomena goes beyond science, too.

This has been a hurried look at classical ideas about how we know truth; it has not been a comprehensive survey of epistemology. I could have mentioned common sense, majority rule, or instinct. None of these meet the need for a flexible yet consistent tool to measure ideas. Is any epistemological method possible since religion sails upon Tillich's "ocean of contradictory ideas." Isn't all religious opinion just that-- *opinion* about religion?

Pragmatic Idealism

Without suggesting that we can solve all the problems of epistemology for time immemorial, let's take a look at a system of truth-testing suggested by Charles Fillmore and other great mystical Christian thinkers. For lack of another term, let's call the process *Pragmatic Idealism*. We have already looked briefly at Absolute Idealism as an antecedent of Metaphysical Christianity. Without going into deep historical details, Idealism was the belief that everything in the manifest world has its origins in spirit. The idea goes back to Plato.

> Plato believed that there are two worlds. The first is the spiritual or mental world, which is eternal, permanent, orderly, regular, and universal. There is also the world of appearance, the world experienced through sight, touch, smell, taste, and sound, that is changing, imperfect, and disorderly. This division is often referred to as the duality of mind and body.[10]

Idealists generally believe the good, perfect, and beautiful exists in an unseen realm of ideas, sometimes referred to as the Absolute. The world which we perceive is a temporal outpicturing of the patterns which exist in an eternal realm. Because the good, perfect and beautiful have no possibility of being overcome by anything in the manifest world, idealists are supremely optimistic about the nature of reality and the ultimate triumph of good over evil. If you have ever heard any person or notion dismissed as "idealistic" it is probably because idealism sounds *Pollyannaish when confronted with the existential suffering of people in a concrete world where good does not always triumph.*

Pragmatism is a philosophical school which essentially says things that work are true. It leans on the work of Plato's disciple, Aristotle, who reversed his master's thesis and said abstract models (ideals) only exist because we create them to explain things we have observed in the concrete world. Pragmatism went further and said the nature of reality isn't abstract, perfect forms but change and growth. "The Universe is dynamic and evolving, a 'becoming' view of the world. There is no absolute and unchanging truth, but rather, truth is what works."[11]

William James (1842-1910), the philosopher/ psychologist and perhaps the best known Pragmatist, wrote: "True ideas are those that we can assimilate, validate, corroborate and verify. False ideas are those that we can not..." [12]

In other words, truth works. If it doesn't work, it isn't truth. But isn't this just the scientific method again? How can anyone verify religious questions? James would never push his system this far, but here is my proposal: *True ideas are those which demonstrate good results in the real world.* In February 1897, Charles Fillmore placed an announcement in *Unity Magazine* describing a new class which he would begin teaching March 15 of that year. The little note reads, in part:

> These lessons are in a large measure the outgrowth of my experience in the regeneration through which I have been passing for several years, and are therefore very practical. I do not follow any teaching, but give the Truth as I have gotten it from spiritual experiences, which I find corroborated in a wonderful way in the Hebrew Scriptures.[13]

Fillmore discovered ideas which he could "assimilate, validate, corroborate and verify" in his own life. He spoke of "going to headquarters," by which he meant spending time in contemplative prayer. The insights he received were then tested in the laboratory of daily living and referred to other Christians for discussions, testing, and application. His method was *pragmatic*; truth was truth because it worked for him.

That methodology characterized Practical Christianity. More than just working, it was repeatable. Other people tried the techniques suggested by Charles and Myrtle Fillmore and the same principles brought healing, prosperity, and wholeness to their lives as well. It was also Bible-based, because the gospels are fully staffed with people who received healings, enlightenment and prosperity by applying the Jesus Christ principles to their daily lives. Multiple Fillmorean publications carried this declaration:

> Our objective is to discern the Truth and prove it. The
> Truth we teach is   not new, neither do we claim
> special discovery of new religious principles. Our
> purpose is to help and teach mankind to use and prove
> the eternal Truth taught by the Master.[14]

This is the basic definition of Pragmatic Idealism, as we are coining the term: True religious ideas are those which demonstrate good results in the real world. Religious ideas which are demonstrated true by existential reality have inner-personal validity. You prove them true when they work for you.

How else does one "prove" religious ideas if not by living them and enjoying their fruits? We noted Paul Tillich describes the "theological circle," as the place a theologian begins to work. Philosophers, in theory, proceed empirically toward who-knows-where as they develop their systems. Theologians begin within a community of faith and interpret existential reality (i.e., life's experiences) for that community. As a religious movement, Metaphysical Christianity begins within the circle of the faith of Jesus. Our epistemology starts with a pragmatic question: What Christian interpretation of everyday life works for me?

The result of such an inquiry will not be scientifically valid because God cannot be measured or quantified. A person-centered epistemology provides personally valid theology, which is the only kind worth having, anyway. Beliefs which make textbook sense but fail to outpicture in the lives of people are more examples of those theological computer games.

Jesus said to the people of his day, "You have heard it said...but I say unto you..." People were attracted to his teaching. It changed lives; it brought peace that passes understanding. The validity of any theology is closely bound up to its value as a faith to live by. Spiritual principles may or may not repeat always in the lives of others because there are too many variables, but because they work for many people they constitute an aggregate of "proof" of their basic validity.

Four Tests of Pragmatic Idealism

An epistemology which could inform Metaphysical Christian theology would build on the resources of the Unity Quadrilateral— Scripture, Tradition, Experience, and both intellectual and intuitive

Reason. Because the method stresses action, we can test religious ideas four ways:

1) *Existentially* (everyday life) - "Does this idea work?"

2) *Comparatively* (dialogue with other believers) - Does it make sense intellectually and intuitively? (Does it think/feel right?)

3) *Holistically* (cultivating spirituality) - Does it promote wholeness/growth?"

4) *Christologically* (measuring by Jesus) - Does it meet the toughest standard of all—is it consistent with the life and teaching of Jesus Christ?

But Is It *Science?*

Some will claim the above system, the elements of which certainly did not originate with this author, is an example of scientific Christianity. The word "scientific" has been popular in Metaphysical Christian circles since the turn of the twentieth century, when a lot of New Thought groups were trumpeting the "scientific basis" of their beliefs. Indeed, they were not alone. Even secular philosophers of the era were defining their enterprises as "the scientific treatment of the general questions relating to the Universe and human life."[15]

That might be an appropriate description of the goals of astronomy, evolutionary biology or physical anthropology, but it hardly describes the scope of theology, whose very subject matter—Ultimate Concerns—by definition lies beyond the scientist's domain. To be intellectually honest, this is not truly a scientific method, because different persons will receive differing results from the same treatment. There is no such thing as scientific Christianity, but admitting this does not doom religious thought to congenital absurdity. Our methodology must be as rigorously objective as theology can be, given the metaphysical (beyond-the-physical) nature of epistemological questions.

Truth is a dynamic, growing process. All theological ideas must be brought into contact with reality by application and dialogue or suffer the fate of a Cargo Cult. Jesus "taught with authority" but demonstrated what he said was true by his willingness to be faithful to Divine Principles even unto death.

Religious teachers cannot speak with authority until they are willing to leave the blackboard for the marketplace, testing their beliefs in the only arena that counts, everyday life. Jesus Christ calls us to go and do likewise, to put feet on our prayers and test the ideas we cherish, and then to speak with the authority such experience will bring.

The first three chapters of this work have discussed applications of the Christian faith as it meets the needs for spiritual understanding, both inside the believer and outside in human community as followers of Jesus interact with the world. This inward/outward movement will continue during the whole course of study because it is imperative for theology to deal with inner and social needs. It is not enough for one person to reach enlightenment in isolation. Jesus came back from the desert to practice love among the people, and he is the model for a Metaphysical Christian.

Today the world shrinks with every new technology. Communications make us one world, even though political and social harmony are far from being achieved. No Christian theology can ignore the stark reality that followers of Jesus are a minority faith of humanity at large, that most human beings are not and never shall be Christian. Therefore we turn next in our study to a discussion of the relationship of the Christian faith and the other religions of our world.

CHECK YOUR KNOWLEDGE

1. What is *Epistemology*?

2. Give the advantages/disadvantages to the following as standards of truth: Authority, Tradition, Intuition, and the Scientific Method.

3. Why can't everyone read the Bible to get the same truth? What's wrong with Revelation?

4. How did Melanesian tradition, modified by contact with Christian missionaries, emerge as the superstitions of the Cargo Cult phenomena? What danger does this disclose about leaning too heavily on tradition?

5. Define *Pragmatic Idealism*, and tell how it works.

6. Describe the author's four tests of Pragmatic Idealism.

QUESTIONS FOR DISCUSSION

1. What kind of traditions are helpful? Harmful? Where is the line?

2. Do Metaphysical Christians really have the religion "of Jesus"? Isn't that arrogant? What gives us the right to interpret the faith our special way and then insist this is what Jesus taught?

3. The writings of Metaphysical teachers—like Charles Fillmore, Ernest Holmes or Mary Baker Eddy—are studied and treated as important documents in some churches. What kind of implicit "authority" do great teachers have, and how do you think they would view their status as authority figures?

4. If truth cannot be "proved" but can be "demonstrated", what happens when a given technique works for you but not for me?

5. Is Metaphysical Christianity *scientific*? Defend your answer with the tools of theology.

6. Discuss *Pragmatic Idealism*.

– 4 –

CHRISTIANITY AND CULTURE

No Tiger Gods without Tigers

Before considering specific problems of Christian thought we must complete our study of the basics. So far, we have examined *theology* and discovered why thinking about the Divine in an organized way is important. We have also noted a dynamic epistemology is possible if we are willing to test ideas by action and dialogue. Next, it is vital look at more social science tools to understand how faith is shaped by the culture in which it developed.

Our methodology is theological, i.e., we organize our reflections on the meaning of life according to religious presuppositions. No one needs to prove God exists for a Christian because God's existence is part of the structure of reality for us. Another way of saying this is to use the yardstick analogy. When measuring three feet of cloth we take the fabric to the yardstick; we don't figure the length of the yardstick from the cloth. God's existence and other basic beliefs (i.e., God's Absolute Goodness) are the standard against which we measure other ideas. They are neither provable nor disprovable; they are accepted on faith.

Note carefully: We are not speaking of *blind* faith. All presuppositions have demonstrated their validity in the crucible of life. Accepting ideas on faith is no excuse for embracing any absurdity that comes along. Theological ideas must stand before the judgment seat of Scripture-Tradition- Experience-Reflection, and submit themselves to the ultimate standard for Christians, the life and teachings of Jesus Christ. Finally, theology demands that all elements of faith must undergo continuous review and critical analysis. Even the teachings of Jesus are themselves subject to theological enquiry, and a glance at the history of biblical interpretation shows how radically the portraits of Jesus have shifted throughout the centuries since he walked among us.

Having passed those tests, an idea must work in the real world and demonstrate truth by application. Since new ideas in religious thought are always being put forth, tough epistemological standards driven by a healthy skepticism is the best insurance policy for a healthy theology. Everything beyond the basic premises of a religious system must continually come under review and correction. And even the basics need a check-up from time to time. As Harry Emerson Fosdick said so appropriately:

> The fact that astronomies change while the stars abide is a true analogy of every realm of human life and thought, religion not least of all. No existent theology can be a final formulation of spiritual truth. [1]

Before proceeding to explore the relationship of Christianity to other world faiths, we needed to review and understand the very tentative nature of religious ideas. Yet there are some definite things we can say about theology that makes it similar to other forms of knowledge.

It has *content*, meaning specific beliefs and systems of belief. It is *organized* into a system that can be analyzed to detect any contradictions or blatant factual errors. Finally, theology must interact with other ways of knowing and not separate itself into a special category wherein the rules of knowledge do not apply; it must be *compatible* with other established truths. The job of the systematic theologian is to make sure all of the above happens.

Looking at religious systems and how they interact, some might suggest that a better way to go would be via sociology or anthropology or a history of religions approach. There is much theologians can learn from the humanities and social sciences, especially since those studies represent an empirical methodology and theoretically have no points to prove, no axes to grind.

Of course, social scientists and historians have religious viewpoints and their work will be shaped, even slightly, according to those assumptions. We would do well to remember that science is no longer the god-replacement it seemed to be earlier in this century. Scientific methods, although admirable, are certainly not foolproof. As one of my junior high school teachers said, in a conversation just inside the edge of ancient memory, *"Foolproof? Give a fool enough time and he'll prove anything!"* Theology needs no apologies for its methods or results. But it does need to continue dialogue with its sister studies in the social sciences and humanities. Religion without science degenerates into superstition and dogmatism; science without religion becomes amoral and inhumane.

Let's take a quick look at some social science ideas which can point our theological inquiry in the right direction. We'll begin with a model for understanding how religious beliefs develop drawn from renowned anthropologist Marvin Harris, whose book *Culture, Man and Nature* provided the fascinating data about Cargo Cults in Chapter 3. Then we'll move on to a discussion of *ethnocentrism* and *cultural relativism*, which are pretty much standard fare in introductory courses in sociology. All this sounds a lot more complicated than it really is, so hang in there. If we do it right, there will be some exciting new ideas presented during this digression into the social sciences, which may forever change the way you look at your religious system.

Social-Systems Model of Marvin Harris

Human beings everywhere have arranged themselves into social systems displaying remarkable differences. Despite the diversity social scientists can identify common patterns. Looking at the universal need to establish working human communities, Marvin Harris drew some startling conclusions. His work is based on social theory going back to Frederick Engels, but Harris organized the ideas into a highly original and controversial model. The Harris system consists of environmental-cultural elements which interact in sequence.[2] (Figure 4-1.)

1) ENVIRONMENT interacts with TECHNOLOGY. No culture exists in empty space. Geography, weather, terrain, and food availability will influence group behaviors. Yet, environment alone does not determine culture. There is also technology, which social scientists define as tools plus the knowledge of how to use them. Give a Stone Age hunter a

tractor, and his cultural level still has not leaped forward to the modern age. Why? Because he lacks knowledge of how to operate complicated machinery. By the same principle, a farm family stranded on the proverbial desert island does not have a tractor technology either, because they lack to tools necessary to implement their knowledge--no tractor.

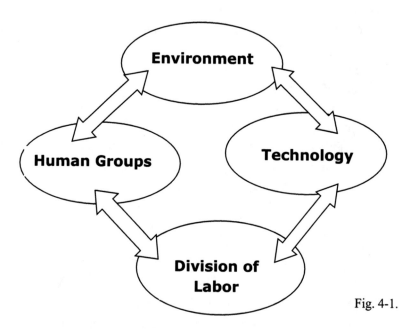

Fig. 4-1.

Illustration: Seacoast to Deep Woods

Tools/knowledge must realistically apply to the environment or the group will not survive. Let's suppose a tribe of seacoast dwellers are chased away from their fishing nets and driven inland to the forest by another, stronger tribe. They face an immediate problem: Life in the deep woods requires a different technology than life along the seacoast. If a deep-woods tribe insisted on fish as their main source of protein they would likely starve until someone was able to convince the pacesetters of the group that modifying their technology--"Let's hunt deer and gather nuts"--could feed their families. Then the tribe would need to learn how to track and kills wild animals, identify edible plants and cook what they bagged.

Life in a "simpler" society was far from simple, as Ruth Beebe Hill has shown in her historical novel *Hanta Yo*. Hill writes enchantingly about the Lakota Sioux during the first years of their contact with European society. Training for Lakota youth was extensive, complicated and demanding. No young person was allowed to wander out on the prairie until they reached full adulthood, and even grownups seldom felt they knew enough to survive alone.

2) TECHNOLOGY interacts with the DIVISION OF LABOR. Once a group establishes its technology in a given environment, they will then divide up the work to be done. Continuing with our illustration of a seacoast tribe driven into the deep woods, if hunger forces them to change their technology from fishing to hunting and gathering, they must next decide who will do the hunting and who will do the gathering. Perhaps everyone will do both, or the women will hunt and the men gather, or young people of both sexes will hunt and old people gather. Many combinations are possible.

Techno-environmental factors will play a key role, too. If the supply of animals to be hunted is great, both sexes may hunt locally. If animals are scarce, requiring long trips to bring back large game, most probably young men will go off and leave women of child-bearing age to perform that most vital of all functions. Please note: we are not passing judgment on the ethical values of this kind of arrangement. What works well in a culture of hunters-gatherers will hardly work in a post-industrial, computer-driven society like ours.

3) TECHNO-ENVIRONMENTAL factors and the DIVISION OF LABOR interact to influence the next category, HUMAN GROUPS. In our tribe of uprooted sea coasters, their technology and the forest environment will give them an opportunity to divide the work among themselves various ways. When they choose who will do what, this will influence the way their family structure and other social groupings take shape.

For example, if the men leave the community circle for long periods of time there will most likely be some kind of extended family arrangement. Several generations will share one large dwelling or a complex of dwellings; children will be raised communally by the extended family; and the senior woman of each sub-group will usually organize domestic chores.

Arrangements like this often lend themselves to *polygyny*, one husband married to more than one wife. But not necessarily so. Single-family dwellings are more likely had the tribe lingered by the sea, where the men would not be gone for long periods of time, thus promoting— but not requiring—monogamous marriage. An interesting variation on family systems is *polyandry*, one wife married to more than one husband.

> Julius Caesar wrote that the ancient Britons were a polygamous society in which sometimes men could have multiple wives and sometimes women could have multiple husbands. The Irigwe people of Nigeria practiced a woman having co-husbands, until their council voted to outlaw it in 1968. Until then, women moved from house to house, taking on multiple spouses, and the children's paternity was assigned to the husband whose house the woman lived in at the time. Women in the ancient Amazon had multiple husbands, as well as men having multiple wives.[3]

Some cultural conditions have occurred under which a pair of living brothers will share a wife or a group of wives. This has happened, but quite rarely in human societies. The point here is that no single system of marriage and family has been baptized from On High as the "correct" one. Anthropological studies support a broader view of possibilities. In fact, any combination seems to work if people believe in the practice and if it meets the needs of society to regulate child-raising, sexual access, and other economic/ educational functions which must take place in the family. The definition of marriage and family worldwide is quite varied, despite what traditionalists in the USA might believe. If the model of "one man, one woman" were applied to biblical figures, all the Hebrew patriarchs and kings of Israel would be disqualified.

The single most important factor in every culture is human ingenuity. We might call it craftiness or adaptability or, to use a metaphysical term, wisdom. Many possible combinations can work under the same conditions, but humans are so creative that they work out solutions to their techno-environmental and social problems that are astoundingly varied and diverse.

4) THE RELIGIOUS FACTOR applies when all these problems have been resolved. Social scientists and historians have observed that belief systems change to accommodate changes in the status quo. More than accepting change, the religious/ethical thinking of the tribe displays a marked *preference* for the new way of life. That's what happen to the former sea coasters, now comfortable as woods people. (See Figure 4-2.)

Before, the tribe worshipped sea gods and prayed to the moon goddess for favorable tides. Now they worship spirits of the deep woods, praying to the goddess of the hunt to insure that deer and elk are plentiful. Along the coast they could not imagine anyone living away from the magnificent, roaring waves and they celebrated their rites of passage under a tent of stars that stretched to the rim of the world. Now they feel safe under the shelter of the Eternal Wooded Canopy, celebrating their rites of passage in meadows where only a glimpse of the sky is allowed because they are unprotected from its glare. Soon, they will not be able to imagine why anyone would want to live along the seacoast, away from their home in the deep woods.

Religion develops to tell them that what they are doing is right, proper and good. It is manly to hunt deer and gather nuts. Who would want to catch squiggling fishes with a net? Why get wet and risk exposure to the dangerous sky when a man can be safe under the eternal canopy of Father Forest?

Does Behavior Cause Ideologies?

At this stage the model becomes controversial. Most people believe that *ideologies cause behavior*. People believe something, which prompts them to action. Harris reversed the conventional model and suggested *behavior causes ideologies*. People act, which prompts them to develop new beliefs. We act in a certain way and then develop religio-political systems of thought that ratify our existing practices, giving what we do the sanction of church and society. Harris wrote:

> Ideology also embraces all thoughts and patterned
> expressions of thought that describe, explain, and justify
> the parts of social structure; that give meaning and

purpose to domestic and political economy and to the maintenance of law and order in domestic and political relations; that describe, justify, and plan the delegation of authority, the division of labor, the exchange of products, the sharing or non-sharing of resources. [4]

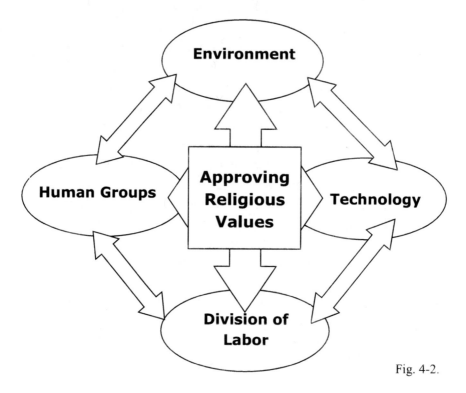

Fig. 4-2.

Historians of religion tend to support Harris. Whenever any of the four primary factors (Environment, Technology, Division of Labor, or Human Groups) has changed, human religious faith has adapted to the new circumstances by insisting this is the way things were always meant to be.

A case in point is the destruction of the Temple by the Babylonians in the sixth century B.C.E. The Promised Land of the Hebrews had the environmental misfortune to straddle the major north-south land route between the formidable empires of Mesopotamia and Egypt. Although Israel faced the sea on its western flank, it was a landed kingdom, adapted to semi-arid terrain, but possessing no natural barriers to thwart invading armies.

When the Assyrians carried off the Northern Kingdom in eighth century B.C. (the so-called "lost tribes" of Israel), Jerusalem rejoiced that she was spared. Judean theology comforted the people by declaring Jerusalem the very throne of God, and that the House of David would be established forever, despite its powerful neighbors. Was this not vindication of her special status as the Chosen People? Unfortunately, the jubilation would not last. Nebuchadnezzar, King of Babylon, marched against Judah early in the sixth century B.C. and pillaged the city of Jerusalem. He denuded the Temple of its sacred relics and treasure and burned the "House of God" to the ground.

The Ark of the Covenant disappeared from history, ostensibly until Indiana Jones temporarily recovered it in *Raiders of the Lost Ark*. Now, it is probably tucked away at *Warehouse 13* or Area 51. Good thing Hollywood completed the biblical record, or the Ark might be somewhere in Ethiopia by now.[5] How did Hebrew religion deal with this crushing blow to its self-esteem? At first, quite bitterly. Psalm 137 records the reaction of temple musicians en route to captivity in Babylon. Read carefully to the end. It will shock you.

> By the rivers of Babylon—there we sat down and there we wept when we remembered Zion.
>
> On the willows there we hung up our harps.
>
> For there our captors asked us for songs, and our tormentors asked for mirth, saying, "Sing us one of the songs of Zion!"
>
> How could we sing the Lord's song in a foreign land?
>
> If I forget you, O Jerusalem, let my right hand wither!
>
> Let my tongue cling to the roof of my mouth, if I do not remember you, if I do not set Jerusalem above my highest joy.

Remember, O LORD, against the Edomites the day of Jerusalem's fall, how they said, "Tear it down! Tear it down! Down to its foundations!"

O daughter Babylon, you devastator! Happy shall they be who pay you back what you have done to us!

Happy shall they be who take your little ones and dash them against the rock![6]

Other voices began to rise. This was not a failure; it was the Hand of God, punishing the Chosen People for their faithlessness. Instead of a defeat, the exile in Babylon was purgative, preparing a small number of next-generation Jews for their triumphant return to rebuild the Temple. With the approval of the new conqueror, Cyrus the Persian Emperor, of course. Hebrew Prophets reinterpreted these events and insisted that the God of Israel engineered it all. Metaphysical Christians today might call it faith in Divine Order, but there is evidence the prophetic messengers spoke after the exile as interpreters of history rather than oracles predicting its future course. Prophetic voices may have been raised to overcome the cognitive dissonance created when the one Temple of the one God was sacked by pagan Babylon.[7]

The Hebrews behaved exactly like other defeated peoples. In fact, religion has often come along after the fact to reinterpret what has happened as Divine Justice, regardless how painful the circumstances. Anthropologists like Marvin Harris may eventually force theology to acknowledge the link between religious thought and socio-cultural practice recognized by secular scholarship. On my desk as I write is an issue of "Christianity and Crisis", a journal of ethical-political issues from a liberal religious viewpoint.

The following is from an article by the Right Reverend Dr. John S. Spong, former Episcopal Bishop of Newark, New Jersey:

The relativity of truth is as established today in theology as it is in the world of physics. A study of its history reveals that Christian theology emerges out of debate and compromise within the church as Christian thinkers interact with their understanding of truth as well as with the culture and the times in which they live. Only later, long after the smoke of battle has cleared, do these debates get codified into doctrines and dogmas that are called infallible. Then those who have no sense of history proclaim that they were received by revelation.[8]

The idea that religious thinking often comes after behavior poses no threat to the principles of Metaphysical Christian churches. Recall, we said truth must be proved in everyday experience and good theology is dialogue, often touching base with Scripture-Tradition-Experience-Reflection. If life compels us to draw other conclusions than what is taught our religion, we are better off with the changes which emerge from those new circumstances. Just like good science, good theology is willing to overturn its most cherished beliefs in the pursuit of truth.

Only those religions which seek to carve the ideas of today on the milestones of tomorrow will be threatened by a frank acknowledgment of religion's debt to cultural influences. We must admit that even those cornerstone concepts, by which we define ourselves as people of faith, are subject to review and reconsideration. Only those beliefs which serve as yardsticks which we shall cling to with tenacity, because without yardsticks there can be no measurement of truth.

Of course, the possibility exists that someone will invent a better yardstick (meter stick?) and our whole religious orientation will change sometime in the future. Certainly, it happened to a small number of first century Jews, who left established religious practices to embrace the revitalization of Judaism brought by Jesus of Nazareth. Even more amazingly, vast numbers of polytheistic gentiles across the Hellenistic world climbed aboard the Jesus boat and sailed into Christianity without ever making port in traditional Judaism. Yet, even that was not a complete break with yardsticks of the past. Jewish Christianity and gentile Christianity joined forces to find in the life and teachings of Jesus a fulfillment of all the promises God had made to his people, Israel, and a way of life which non-Jews could wholeheartedly embrace. It was nothing short of a religio-cultural miracle.

Arguably, believers of all faiths should cheer new discoveries in physical and social sciences as gifts wrapped by the hands of God. The

Prophets were right after all. God did not cause the terrors of the Babylonian exile, but stood with the Children of Israel as they struggled to "sing the Lord's song in a foreign land."

Norms, Folkways, Mores

What we have been discussing is the cultural element in religious thought. To better comprehend how pervasive culture can be in theology, we need a few more terms from sociology. This will not be a crash course in that discipline but a quick brush-up for those who have studied the social sciences and a running summary of a few basic ideas for those who have not previously looked at human groups and their practices.

The source for this material is the popular college textbook *Sociology* by Paul B. Horton and Chester D. Hunt, whose work we quoted in the previous chapter. We shall look at *norms* (which will take in *taboo, folkways*, and *mores*), then *institutions, cultural integration* and *ethnocentrism*. From this light-speed survey we'll move on to consider the key concept addressed by this chapter, *cultural relativism*, and see how it applies interaction between communities of faith in the twenty-first century.

All cultures develop norms, which are ordinary ways of doing things that become standardized. In Western societies we shake hands with the right hand, but we may use either hand to scratch our heads. If certain parts of our bodies itch, we may not use either hand in public to scratch those private parts. Our culture has a right-hand norm for hand-shaking, no norm for head scratching, and a prohibition or *taboo* on scratching genitals and other areas publicly. Norms divide into two basic types.

Folkways. These behaviors "... are simply the customary, normal, habitual ways a group does things...eating with knives and forks, wearing neckties on some occasions and sports shirts on others...and eating toast for breakfast are a few of our many American folkways."[9]

Mores. Some norms are more important than others. Choosing the wrong fork for a salad is embarrassing; choosing public nudity will land you in jail. Horton and Hunt describe two kinds of norms:

> "Those which SHOULD be followed as a matter of good manners and polite behavior" and "those which

MUST be followed because they are believed essential
to group welfare." [10]

These must-do behaviors are called *mores*. To understand religious behavior it is vital we realize how powerfully our sense of right and wrong are shaped by the unspoken assumptions we are taught to make. Cultures like the Aztec made it a religious act to tear the heart from a living person and burn it to their bloodthirsty gods. Today, such religious ceremonies would be considered mass murder.

> Our mores define the killer as either a villain or a hero according to the circumstances. Medieval mores made it right for the church to tolerate prostitution and even share in its income. Most of the Reformation churchmen, both Protestant and Catholic, who ordered the torture and burning of heretics were not cruel or evil, but were decent and often kindly men who did what the mores of the time and place required them to do. Mores of our recent past have approved child labor, slavery, and persecution of minorities, and have condemned pacifism, women's suffrage, and sex education. And at all times and places, good people feel pure and righteous when following the mores, whatever they may be. [11]

Nothing could speak more eloquently for the constant review of religious beliefs and the need for dialogue. Unchecked and unexamined standards of conduct, heavily sanctioned by church and society, can retard social progress and hamper personal freedom. When a culture stones its prophets for raising unpopular issues, later generations come along, shaking their heads and sighing, "How could they have been so blind?"

Groups of folkways and mores organized into a complex pattern which centers on a major human activity are called an *institutions*. Industrial societies have five basic institutions which are the *family* (in its many forms), *religion*, the *government, education,* and *economic activities.* [12] These may be identifiable as separate institutions, but they are not islands unto themselves.

Cultural Integration: Buffalo and Temple

"Just as a pile of bricks is not a home," write Horton and Hunt, "a list of traits is not a culture." [13] Cultures are integrated into a system that works smoothly. Cultures which do not provide *cultural integration* can suffer the spasms of disunity, normlessness and lack of self-identity. Modern Western society, many would contend, fits the description of a culture lacking integration. A culture can even be intentionally denuded of its identity, as were the Native Americans.

> The culture of the Plains Indians centered upon buffalo. From its carcass they drew most of their material culture, as they used its flesh, hides, tendons, bones, sacs, membranes, and many other parts for one purpose or another. Their religion was mainly directed at ensuring the success of the buffalo hunt. Their status system measured success largely according to a man's hunting skill. Their nomadic way of life was attuned to the buffalo migrations. In other words, the different parts of the culture all fitted together in an interrelated system of practices and values. When the white man killed off the buffalo, he did so in a deliberate and successful effort to demoralize the Indian by destroying the focal point of his culture. [14]

Exactly this kind of crisis faced the ancient Israelites when the center of their religion, the Temple, was destroyed first by the Babylonians and again by the Romans. When an integrated culture suffers such a traumatic injury to its self-image, seldom does it survive without radical change. Judaism developed the synagogue worship system to replace its Temple ritual, making the written Word the new focal point of Jewish faith.

Native American culture is still recovering from the shock of its amputation from its heritage. Some members of that culture have been absorbed totally by the white-European social order that replaced its ancient ways. Others have tried to recover the tribal practices of pre-

European America with some success. It is too soon to tell whether Native American culture will survive as coherently as Judaism has.

Cultural integration means the building blocks of a functioning society must fit together. "It is no accident," sociologists Horton and Hunt say, "that hunting peoples worship hunting gods, fishing people worship sea gods, and agricultural peoples worship sun and rain gods." [15]

The sobering realization which must follow is that we are greatly shaped by our culture. As the old axiom says: *There are no tiger gods where there are no tigers.* Inherited religious faith shapes the way people look at the world, but the world also shapes the way individuals look at religious faith.

Ethnocentrism

Ethnocentrism is the tendency of each group to assume the superiority of its beliefs and practices. [16] All cultures are ethnocentric to some degree. Everyone assumes their way the proper, correct, natural way for humans to live. It may shock Americans, but not everyone wants to be like us. Wade Davis has brilliantly observed:

> The world in which you were born is just one model of reality. Other cultures are not failed attempts at being you; they are unique manifestations of the human spirit. [17]

Members of so-called simpler societies often admire the material goods of industrial nations while feeling quite superior in other ways. For example, in the eyes of the indigenous peoples of New Guinea:

> The Europeans were not regarded as all-powerful, but rather pathetic, ignorant people who could be easily cheated or stolen from. Their ignorance of sorcery was lamentable. [18]

Some degree of ethnocentrism is necessary for group cohesion and self-respect. It is healthy and helpful for a black American to feel proud of his African heritage, to enjoy soul music and soul food. Hispanics, Asians, Indians and other identifiable groups justifiably revel in their uniqueness. How could anyone grow up anywhere in the world, speak the native language, belong to a religious tradition, participate in an ethnic community, observe its taboos and lesser mores, and *not* see that cultural neighborhood as normative? Even people who renounce their cultural milieu are unconsciously paying homage to the rejected standards, which shape the rebellion by their absence. American atheists seldom write scathing denials of the Hindu goddess Lakshmi, or Zoroastrianism's supreme deity, Ahura Mazda. Ethnocentrism is localized, inconspicuous and agreeably self-congratulatory.

Ethnocentrism only becomes a problem for a group when it draws an unflattering conclusion: If our way is good, your way is un-good. The damage becomes obvious when groups segregate themselves from inferior or unsaved members of alien cultures or other religions. Love of country becomes nationalism that spills over into fanaticism and provokes wars of conquest. People whom Western society brands as terrorists are called "heroes" and "freedom-fighters" in other religio-political settings.

What fate might have awaited George Washington and the other "heroes" of the American Revolution if the rebellion had failed? Would our textbooks speak of them today as our "Founding Fathers," or as the traitors who almost caused us to break away from our rightful King? In the Broadway musical *1776*, Benjamin Franklin dryly reminds John Adams of the subjective nature of politics:

> A rebellion is always legal in the first person, such as "our rebellion." It is only in the third person—"their rebellion"—that it becomes illegal.[19]

Ethnocentrism is everyone's enemy when it justifies acts of brutality. Any government that sponsors *freedom fighters* in selected regional conflicts and opposes *terrorists* closer to home is either lying to its people or has sunk so deeply into ethnocentrism it does not recognize the contradiction in its foreign policy. Virtually every government with significant military power has been guilty of excessive use of force at one time or another in its history. This tendency does not make it morally wrong to maintain reasonable defensive forces. Peace at any cost is a price that free people cannot afford to pay. Nazi Germany is the supreme example of what happens when power and hate coincide. While pushing forward to the goal of a peaceful a world community, the conflicts of the twentieth century remind us that compassionate men and women of every society must be on guard against the dangers of ethnocentric nationalism at home and abroad.

If modern cross-cultural studies chip away at intolerance and outright rejection of other religious views, over-eagerness to embrace alien belief systems presents a danger in the other extreme. Speaking with members of Metaphysical Christian churches, one encounters a significant number of persons who have rejected the "One Way" mentality of their backgrounds and have moved in healthier directions.

To overcome narrowness is no small task, and those who have embarked on the long pilgrimage from *turn-or-burn* religions to Christian universalism have come a long way. Legions of believers have yet to realize how outrageous, how sub-Christian, the concept of hellfire-and-damnation truly is.

However, there is always the possibility that the pendulum might swing too far in the opposite direction. In their eagerness to leave ethnocentrism behind, some religious liberals have moved so far from narrowness that they have become wishy-washy about their own Christian heritage. Dangerous as ethnocentrism may be, lack of commitment is no answer to the problem, either. And while open-mindedness is absolutely essential to real spiritual growth, ambivalence about religious faith is not open-mindedness. Religious progressives must ask hard questions when contemplating the relationship between Christianity and other world faiths:

1) At what point does tolerance become lack of commitment?

2) If your faith is as true as mine, why follow any?

3) How do I dialogue with another faith while remaining faithful to mine?

To answer the first question, we need only look at the most successful tolerant religious system the world has ever known, that complex of mini-faiths practiced in the Indian Subcontinent in some form for at least five thousand years, Hinduism (which is a useful misnomer). Hindu religion assumes there is truth everywhere but still retains its distinctive flavor. Seeing God incarnate in many ways, the sophisticated Hindu is not threatened when others find God elsewhere. He/she does not feel the need to worship every way possible, but recognizes many possible ways.

This model is not universal; there have been Hindu fanatics, one of whom murdered Mohandas Gandhi in 1948. But the age-old spirit of Hinduism breathes open-mindedness and tolerance without the signature lack of commitment so prevalent in liberal circles today. The difference? A tolerant faith is not a tolerant skepticism. Hindu emphasis is on *belief*, not unbelief. Western liberals snicker about the blind faith of fundamentalists, but is the blind faithlessness of religious liberals any better? No wonder that some critics of liberal theology have seen in its doctrines a *thanatos*, or death-wish, which forbids progressive religionists from enjoying life because of their gloomy views about the future. (I entitled the first sermon I ever preached, delivered in 1974 to a Unitarian-Universalist congregation, "Is It Ethical to be Happy?")

Refugees, Emigrants, & Home-Growns

I sometimes tell New Thought congregations, tongue-in-cheek, that they are not really Metaphysical Christians, they're ex-Baptists, ex-Catholics, and ex-Methodists. I used to stop there, assuming Metaphysical Christianity is a refugee movement. But in recent years it has occurred to me that there are really three major demographics attending Sunday services in many denominations: *Refugees, emigrants,* and *home-grown natives.*

Refugees left their religious homelands because they found conditions there too intolerable to remain. They are true refugees, effectively driven out of their childhood faiths by some combination of oppression, spiritual neglect or lack of opportunity.

Emigrants, like me, were never threatened, abused, nor otherwise treated badly in their religious upbringing. They just felt the call for higher possibilities, not unlike leaving a good home to seek their fortune.

Home-grown natives are people with the karmic luck to be born in a religious community which understands the benefits of an affirming, positive spiritual education.

There are probably other subgroups you could identify. Increasingly more people are growing up without formal religious affiliation in households headed by "no preference" parents. And what about those who continue attending a church because they like the rhythm of regular Sunday worship yet their spiritual needs are far from being met?

I am not suggesting people in other churches are unhappy or misplaced; millions find peace and joy through religious traditions which the great diversity in human spiritual practices. The above is just a thumbnail sketch of what I have observed about some people who find their way into an inclusive, progressive Christian community. Nor am I rejecting other religions. The world is a marketplace of possibilities, and history shows that people will seek ways to meet their spiritual needs either privately or in communities of faith.

Fortunately, a kindly spirit dominates many churches today. Diversity is affirmed; love is shared. Progressive Christian communities are usually places where everyone feels welcome. Credit women and men in ministry for attracting open-minded people with positive faith. Every generation faces the challenge to continue in the spirit of tolerance without withering our commitment to Jesus Christ. Healthy self-examination and dialogue with other Christians guards against the dangers of religious ethnocentrism.

Superficially, the second question ("Why mine instead of yours?) sounds easier to answer: Obviously, I embrace my faith because it works for me. If it did not work for me, I would migrate to another religious tradition which better suits my needs. However, there is an undetected briar patch ahead for ministers or laypersons who fail to understand why people sharing a common religious heritage often grapple over what works best. Members of a local congregation, while sharing a common theological foundation, will go to war over micro-issues and trivia. Battles break out involving the order of worship, church policies, finances, and plans for the future.

After experimenting with changes to the order of service in several churches, I became convinced one of my seminary professors had been right when he said that there should be a sign over the front door of every congregation in North America which reads: *"But we've always done it that way!"* And another one over the back, *"But we've never done it that way!"*

Life experiences created different needs in people, and the lenses they wear make any other point of view look like an unnatural distortion. When people see through a glass differently, their tendency is to shout, "No reasonable person wants that!" Awareness of incompatible views without judging the people who express them marks the first step in negotiating a nonaggressive solution to problems of church conflict. Lacking time to investigate this phenomenon completely, it might still be helpful to explore the functions of diversity awareness in a specific circumstance, for example, differences about Sunday worship needs.

Four Reasons to Attend Church

As an instructor of religious studies who is also an ordained clergyperson, I try to remember an important factor when invited to preach at a Sunday worship service: *Not everybody is here for the theology.* The late Dr. James Glasse, former President of Lancaster Theological Seminary of the United Church of Christ, said during a class I attended in the 1970s, there are at least three reasons why people attend church. Glasse divided churchgoers into categories that he called, small "c" catholics, small "r" reformed, and small "e" evangelicals. Each type, he said, represents a different spiritual need. Here is the gist of Dr. Glasse's description, as well as memory can reconstruct the lecture four decades later. It has proven invaluable as a tool to help me understand why people with divergent worship needs often cannot understand each other.

Small "c" catholics are not the same as *Roman Catholics*. Many Catholics fit the description, but so do a large number of Baptists. These folks come to church for a multi-sensual *encounter with the holy*. They need visual and auditory signs and wonders—things like stained glass windows and vaulted ceilings; candles, crosses, and ceremony; majestic organ music with choral refrains; vestments, scripture readings, holy sacraments and soaring prayer—anything which connects the worshippers with the ancient, sacred traditions of the Church. Some of these people could sit in an empty cathedral and feel they had "been to Church" in its fullest sense.

Small "r" reformed people come to church for *ideas*. They want to hear stories from the Bible explained in a new, thought-provoking way.

Sermons which appeal to the small "r" reformed churchgoer provide insights about spiritual principles and current events, theological ethics, the nature of God, the meaning of life, and how everything works together for the good. The classic paradigm for the small "r" reformed people is an old Unitarian joke about two road signs which appear to a soul who has just departed this life.

> A Unitarian Universalist dies, and on the way to the afterlife encounters a fork in the road with two options: The left path has a sign "to heaven;" while the right has a sign "to a discussion of heaven." Without pausing, the UU turns right, to the discussion of heaven.[20]

As a Unity minister who also holds ordination in the Unitarian-Universalist Association, I've always enjoyed the self-effacing humor of my fellow UUs.[21] Some people discover Ultimate Concerns—God, Truth, Peace, Justice, or Love—through the Sacred Intellect. They require something which contacts them intellectually to feel they have been to an authentic church experience. This need is not inferior to those who want deep meditative experiences or sacred music which uplifts the soul, it is simply represents a *different* primary worship need.

Small "e" evangelicals come to church to find a better way of living their lives. *Practical spirituality* could be their battle cry. They want to learn techniques to deepen themselves spiritually, get along better with their significant other, and become a better parent, sibling, friend, and neighbor. When they hear about problems in the world, they want to know what they can do to fix or ameliorate them. They might be social conservatives who want to know how to avoid sin, or progressive activists who want economic justice to make the world a better place. They hunger for action, either strictly within their own consciousness or outwardly as a member of the global community.

Surely, there are other possibilities. Reflecting on the above paradigm in the decades since my seminary years, I added a fourth category.

Small "k" koinonia people come to church for the hugs. They attend primarily because of the loving fellowship and support they receive from a community which accepts them, as Mr. Rogers used to say, just the way they are. The biblical term for that kind of beloved community is *koinonia* (Greek, κοινωνία). Sometimes scholars translate the word as *fellowship* (I Cor. 1:9), other times *communion*, as in the "communion of the Holy Spirit" (2 Cor. 13:14). My personal preference is to think of koinonia as the beloved community, where all are welcome. The sense of the language indicates a special harmony among those who gather in the name of Jesus. In every church I have served, the small "k" koinonia people appeared. They were not there for a mystical sense of the holy, or great teaching/preaching, or lessons to carry with them into the week ahead. They wanted the warmth of *koinonia*, the beloved community.

Summary: The disconnect occurs in a local congregation when people, who are not aware of these and other specialized needs, look at a multi-spectrum church program through their unique set of lenses without realizing they are only seeing part of the color scheme. If members of the congregation who are small "c" catholics hear great insights about the Bible or new ideas about how to get along with houseguests, but the service contains no sense of the holy, they will not feel like they've been to church. Similarly, if small "r" reformed members hear magnificent music and an energetic talk entitled "Ten ways To Love Your Neighbor," but no fresh insights or new ideas to challenge their thinking, they will not feel like they've been to church. And if the liturgy is majestic and the sanctuary feels like a pep rally outside heaven's gates, complete with a good talk on new theories about the Book of Revelation, but there is nothing they can do about it during the upcoming week, they will not feel like they've been to church. And if small "k" koinonia seekers cannot find unconditional love, none of the above will matter to them.

Ministers do well to remember: *Every Sunday all four types will be sitting side-by-side in your sanctuary.* The best kind of worship experience—for me, at least—offers something of each category. A sense of the holy and ongoing continuity with the ancient Church; good ideas which challenge the Sacred Intellect for those who find God with their minds (yes, we're out there); and something which calls forth a response in action on the part of the community, which author Connie Fillmore believes is a requirement for effective living:

Knowing and understanding the laws of life, also called
Truth, are not enough. A person must also live the truth
that he or she knows.[22]

Any religious faith works best when it addresses the six functions of
theology:

1) Provides ongoing re-interpretation of the faith that makes sense
   to sensible people.
2) Critically analyzes ideas and practices.
3) Helps to integrate religious concepts into actions in everyday
   life.
4) Gives people a place to dialogue with others, expanding the
   theological circle.
5) Interprets symbolism of the faith and makes it intelligible to
   everyone.

6) Raises new questions and provides new answers to problems of
   the present and future.

There are other reasons why Metaphysical Christianity works for
many people, to include providing a flexible environment in which all
three worship-types identified by James Glasse can flourish.
Healing/Prosperity/Relationship issues are integration of religious ideas
with everyday life. Coherent interpretation of the Bible requires
unpacking its symbolism, and the chance to exchange ideas without fear
of criticism or threats of excommunication will establish dialogue within
the theological circle. The place of worship can be churchy or plain,
indoors or out, private or communal. Mindfulness, the lovely Buddhist
term for self-conscious awareness, is the key to loving others and
knowing peace within.

Cultural Relativism

Finally, we asked, "How do I dialogue with followers of another
religious faith while remaining faithful to my own?" This is potentially a
difficult question. If we approach the "gentile" as a nonbeliever who
must be converted, tolerance is in jeopardy. If we come to the other

acknowledging the truth in his faith, our own commitment is suspect and he might see us as a poor representative.

To avoid both intolerance and unbelief, we have said, a positive, tolerant religious faith must be nurtured. *Cultural relativism* is a social science concept which may be extremely helpful when seeking a link between tolerance and commitment. Anthropologist Melville J. Herskovits (1895-1963) forcefully advocated this position. According to Herskovits, we must view each culture as having *intrinsic value*. He saw the norms and institutions of any culture to be of self-validating, since they held their respective societies together. All social systems are worthy of respect because they evolved to meet some kind of need.[23]

> A trait is neither good nor bad in itself. It is only good or bad with reference to the culture in which it is to function. Fur clothing is good in the arctic, but not in the tropics. Premarital pregnancy is bad in our society, where the mores condemn it and where there are no comfortable arrangements for the care of illegitimate children; premarital pregnancy is good a society such as that of the Bontocs of the Philippines, who consider a woman more marriageable when her fertility has been established, and who have a set of customs and values which make a secure place for the children. Adolescent girls in the United States are advised that they will improve their marital bargaining power if they remain chaste until marriage. Adolescent girls in New Guinea are given the opposite advice, and in each setting the advice is probably correct...any cultural trait is socially "good" if it operates harmoniously within its cultural setting to attain the goals which the people are seeking.[24]

Does this mean that anything goes? As long as society says it is acceptable, can we cut loose and do it? Not quite. Read on:

> The concept of cultural relativism does not mean that all customs are valuable nor does it imply that no customs

are harmful. Some patterns of behavior may be injurious in any milieu...The central point in cultural relativism is that in a particular setting, certain traits are right because they work well in that setting, while other traits are wrong because they would clash painfully with parts of that culture. This is another way of saying that a culture is integrated, and that its various elements must harmonize passably if the culture is to function efficiently in serving human purposes.[25]

This sounds a lot like St. Paul's advice to the Corinthians:

"All things are lawful for me," but not all things are beneficial. "All things are lawful for me," but I will not be dominated by anything.[26]

Adaptive or Maladaptive?

One way to organize critical thinking about the wild proliferation of choices humans make in daily life is to consider the effect on any action on individuals and their society. All behavior can be classified as *adaptive* or *maladaptive*. *Adaptive* behavior contributes to the health, well-being and competitive success of a group. *Maladaptive* practices are harmful to group health and prosperity.

...the existence of adaptive culturally transmitted human behavioral strategies (i.e. behavior that actually aids us in our survival and reproduction) is due to processes that are in some ways similar to natural selection – they are adaptive processes that reliably fix or generate behavior that aids the survival and reproduction of human beings.[27]

Some theorists believe maladaptive traits cannot long endure, because either the group will cease doing business the maladaptive way or the social system will cease to exist in its present form. Unfortunately, maladaptive traits often take a long time to extinguish and the price in human suffering can be quite high.

Quick Review: Putting It Together

We now have a vantage point from which to look at religion, provided by social scientists. Religious behavior consists of *norms*, which are made up of common ways of doing things (*folkways*) and strict rules (*mores*) which require some kinds of behavior while prohibiting other actions (*taboos*). Theologies are built on *organized reflection upon the beliefs and practices within the theologian's institution (circle of faith)*. A society which functions harmoniously (with a minimum of *maladaptive* behavior) displays *cultural integration*, which is another way of saying that its practices are *adaptive* to the circumstances and provide for the health, well-being and competitive success of the larger group. Attitudes which say that our folkways/mores are the "natural" way and other behaviors are "unnatural" or wrong are called ethnocentrism. Finally, *cultural relativism* suggests that all cultures/beliefs have value as long as they are not harmful to the group which is practicing the behavior.

Of course, nobody has to approve customs which seem foreign and unnatural in order to accept cultural relativism as a working hypothesis. People merely have to accept that others see the world quite differently than they do. Are there standards which apply everywhere? Probably, but how does anyone know for certain? What measures the measuring stick? What perch can the individual find to look down upon the world untainted by previous values and assumptions? Modern Christian theology has tried to find such a lofty pinnacle and failed miserably. Neo-orthodoxy claimed it was the revealed Word of God, but biblical criticism shows that the Bible is a different book in each person's hands.

Traditionalists in various churches claim this or that authority, but the day of unquestioned religious authority is over. Theology came of age during the twentieth century when some thinkers began to admit that no transcendent vantage point exists: we all do our ethical/religious thinking within a circle of faith.

A worldview comes with the baby shower. All people are to some degree ethnocentric. This really isn't so bad as long as we keep an open mind and are aware of our ethnocentrism. If we assume that God does speak through all the religions of humankind, then God must speak through our religion, too.

For a member of Western society, this means exploring the Judeo-

Christian heritage *to find the voice of God* through prophets, apostles and teachers, not blindly following whatever a prophet, apostle or teacher might have declared. It means finding the truth that works for you while allowing neighbors to go and do likewise. To be grasped by a religious faith requires *faith*. To accept God may speak differently to someone of another worldview calls for the rest of St. Paul's equation, *hope and love*.

CHECK YOUR KNOWLEDGE

1. How is theology similar/dissimilar to other forms of knowledge?

2. Draw and explain Marvin Harris' controversial social system model.

3. Episcopal Bishop John S. Spong said that after the "smoke of battle has cleared," doctrines which were open to debate are declared infallible, then proclaimed infallible, and finally "those who have no sense of history proclaim that they were received by revelation." What does this mean for Christian thought?

4. Explain the following: *norms, taboos, folkways, mores, institutions, cultural integration, adaptive/maladaptive.*

5. How does *cultural relativism* overcome *ethnocentrism*?

6. Explain the adage "There are no tiger gods where there are no tigers"

QUESTIONS FOR DISCUSSION

1. If God speaks through all the religions of humanity, why follow Christianity instead of the Hinduism, Judaism, or Islam?

2. Make a list of religio-cultural DO's and DON'Ts. What kind of adaptive significance can you find for each?

3. Is *cultural relativism* possible when looking at atrocities like massive human sacrifice offered by the Aztec? Where does tolerance draw the line?

4. Are you a *refugee, emigrant,* or *home-grown native*?

5. Did you identify primarily with the small "c" catholic, small "r" reformed, small "e" evangelical, or small "k" koinonia?

6. What ideas do you take for granted as "normal" that are not necessarily accepted by every culture on the planet?

BIBLICAL THEOLOGY

What were the authors saying to their generation?

Biblical theology mingles historical research with theological analysis. Biblical theologians ask: "What were the authors saying to their generation?" This is a vastly different question from, "What does it mean for us today?"

Biblical theology tries to arrive at just that--the theology expressed in the Bible. A person studying the actual message contained in a section of the biblical library might ask these questions: What God-concept shapes the book of Genesis, as opposed to the gospel of John? Did Paul believe in hell? How is Matthew's Jesus different from the Jesus found in Luke-Acts?

Mining the text for the author's message is called exegesis (reclaiming the original meaning of the text by in-depth study.) To do exegesis properly we must acquaint ourselves with the hermeneutical principles (techniques of interpretation) used by virtually all modern biblical scholars.

Today's biblical theologians begin by assuming that the Bible is the recorded memories of our spiritual ancestors, written to express to their generation what they believed God was doing in their lives and in the life of the greater community of faith. The Bible speaks of issues, concepts, and expectations which make sense only when we understand the time in which each piece was written, which is the task of the biblical theologian.

This is known as the historical-critical (or historical-analytical) method of interpretation. Historical-critical studies treat the Bible as literature produced by a partisan community of faith, not as a divinely dictated source of infallible guidance. In the words of a seminary professor under whom author studied, "The Bible wasn't lowered from heaven in a basket." Here are a few guide points.

Most Important Question: *When?*

Knowing the date when the piece was written is more important than knowing the era it discusses. A work of art or literature better represents the time in which it was produced than the period it portrays. Walk through the Louvre and study the magnificent Renaissance paintings of biblical scenes. You will be mildly amused to see the Virgin Mary wearing fifteenth century velvet dresses, sitting inside a gothic arch, with steep-roof houses in the background. There may even be a gondola floating by, medieval castles towering on the horizon. Hardly ancient Judea. Renaissance art opens a window to the only world the artists knew. They reproduced the fashions, architecture, and topography of their era when painting biblical times. Historians study the paintings, not to learn about ancient Israel, but to peek into the daily life of fifteenth century Europe.

White Hats

Another clue to understanding the Bible is found in the history of American cinema. If you are old enough to recall the 1950's movies, or have seen vintage re-runs, you know the scenario. Good Guy wears white hat, Bad Guy wears black hat. Good Guy goes to the saloon and orders--remember?--milk! Or, at the most, sarsaparilla. They fight, and Good Guy never loses his hat. He needs it to keep his head warm, since he wore his hair short. Good Guy is always good; Bad Guy is always bad. Villains had no disturbed childhoods or psycho-social problems-- they were just bad guys.

If you have read or studied the American west during the late 1800's you know that his model is plainly ridiculous. Photographs of that era show ragged, bearded, long-haired men in dark hats. It is impossible to tell the good guys from the bad guys without footnotes on each picture page. Milk would have spoiled in the heat rather promptly, if a saloon even bothered to carry such a drink. Saloons, were usually gambling dens and houses of ill repute as well as watering troughs for whiskey-and-beer drinkers. Gun fights weren't the *High Noon*, quick-draw affairs of Hollywood, either. Hand guns weren't accurate enough for long-range, one-shot combat. The combatants drew slowly and blasted away, trying to hit the other *shootist* (not gunslinger) before taking lead themselves. Although fanciful, the old westerns provide a look at the morality, dress-codes, lifestyles and attitudes of another era--the 1950's. Good was good, bad was bad, hair was short, and heroes always played fair. Or so we believed, back in the *Happy Days*.

If future historians watch some of these old westerns two thousand years from now, they will face the same problem encountered by twenty-first century people exploring the Bible. To unscramble the context, historians assume works of art or literature better represent the period in which they were produced than the period of the subject portrayed. The black-and-white 1950s movies and TV shows about the 1870s in the American West cast none but clean-cut, young men and prim females; all characters were played as white, straight, and honest to a fault. That world never existed, not even during the Eisenhower era.

Recognizing the importance of when a work is produced becomes an especially important precondition for biblical studies, since almost every passage was written well after the events it describes by generations of believers whose issues, insights, and interests were not the same as those of the earlier time. When people approach the Bible looking for texts to support an agenda of socio-political and theological biases, the problem multiplies.

The Author, Not the Characters, is Speaking

Biblical theology tries to understand what the authors were probably saying to say to their audiences. To determine the content of the original message requires an understanding of its context, so postmodern readers must find out when the passage of scripture was written and what was happening when the author wrote the passage. Reading the Sermon on the Mount, biblical theologians are likely to ask, "What is *Matthew* saying to his readers?" rather than, "What is *Jesus* teaching here?"

This is only a disturbing thought if readers are operating out of a model of biblical literalism. Biblical theology seeks the intent of the author, not the intent of the characters portrayed within the narrative.

Troublesome though it may be to some people, the overwhelming historical evidence suggests the gospels are not impartial biographies of Jesus. They are shared memories of the Christian community, less like evening news reports, more like pamphlets displayed in a church lobby.

Today's New Testament scholarship generally holds that no apostle wrote a gospel, a fact apparently confirmed by Luke in the first four verses of his gospel. The closest reference to a possible author of Luke was made by in Colossians 4:14 and II Timothy 4:11, (both passages from books scholars doubt were written by the Apostle Paul). Mark may have been the John Mark mentioned frequently in Acts and in various New Testament epistles, but we have no direct evidence for this assumption. John Mark was not an apostle anyway but a traveling companion and assistant to Paul.

Aramaic or Greek Originals?

Matthew was long thought to be the tax collector called by Jesus (Matthew 9:9), but scholarship has established fairly well that whoever wrote that gospel used Mark's gospel as a source document and that both were written in Greek. George Lamsa's theories about an Aramaic New Testament are not shared by the vast majority of scholars. Insights about Semitic idiom can come from studying Lamsa's works, but the bulk of New Testament scholarship stands firmly behind an all-Greek original edition.

Certain concepts, such as the logos of John 1:1, are difficult to express in Aramaic, a Semitic tongue related to biblical Hebrew. Aramaic shares the richness of Hebraic pictorial imagery but struggles to express abstract ideas as the logos. Koine Greek, on the other hand, is highly abstract. The difference comes across vividly, even in English translation. Read Genesis 1:1-5 then skip to John 1:1-5 for two Creation accounts, the first translated from Hebrew and the latter from Greek. Notice the action-oriented imagery in the Semitic idiom and the intellectual abstractions offered by the Greek.

However, students of the New Testament can learn about the thought-world of the Aramaic-speaking community from Lamsa's studies. Aramaic teachings of Jesus probably stand behind the New Testament's Koine Greek as part of an oral tradition, even though any Aramaic texts from the first generation church are long since lost.

Identify Viewpoint and Target Audience

These books which today we call the gospels of Matthew, Mark, Luke and John originated late in the first century, not the first generation. Interpreters need to identify Matthew's underlying theology and to realize what special interest keeps cropping up in Luke. Why does the rough simplicity of Mark's Jesus contrast with what John's invocation of the *logos* of Greek philosophy to explain the Christ-event?

Do these radically different pictures of Jesus he is unavailable in scripture? Of course not. It means struggling, growing human beings, like us, recorded their ideas for their communities of faith. When we read the Bible, we are looking over their shoulders at the best sketch of the Nazarene they could draw in their concrete historical circumstances. In the words of the Prophet Isaiah:

> Go, now, write it before them on a tablet,
>   and inscribe it in a book,
> that it may be for the time to come
>   as a witness for ever.[1]

Nevertheless, it is important to remember, when reading the words of Jesus in Scripture, the biblical word-images have passed through a series of filters, beginning with the mind of the author/editor and ending with the particular screening process of the reader. Looking behind the filters and find the historical Jesus is always an "iffy" task, as Albert Schweitzer discovered. The great medical missionary was also a first-rate theologian. In his book *The Quest of the Historical Jesus*, Schweitzer declared it was impossible to peel off the layers of tradition and arrive at the authentic, undoubted Jesus of history. Our best efforts yield only memories. Perhaps he was right; there are limits to historical scholarship. Yet, Schweitzer believed he had found in the teachings and life-stories about Jesus a spiritual force which he called the "religion of love."[2]

Jesus of history is the energy-force that stirred the New Testament authors to tell their tales. There can be no doubt that Jesus existed and that he stands behind the gospel traditions as their driving, motivating Force. As such, he is present in personalized accounts of the Christ-event, an event played out in the generation immediately before theirs.

Readers today still find his footprints in the gospels, only the faintest hint that a flesh-and-blood Human-Divine paradox walked the earth. Some stories test credulity, tales which smack of mythology-- virgin birth, walking on water, magically transforming water into wine. Other times the historical person shines through the editorial haze of gospel authors in his parables, his treatment of women and children, his ringing words of faith in the Sermon on the Mount, his triumph over doubt and fear at Gethsemane.

Even these encounters with the Great Teacher are subject to the filtration process of history and colored by the stained-glass windows of human imagination, including the reader's. However, the task of biblical theology is not completely impeded by these problems, because its goal is to determine what the author meant to say to his target audience, regardless of how historically valid his sources were. This is both the advantage of biblical theology and its greatest limitation.

If God speaks through Scripture, as most Christians believe, the question becomes how can someone hear the divine voice through the clatter of countervailing opinions, ancient worldviews and mythological language of the biblical authors? Biblical theology provides a starting point, but today's interpreters must push beyond antiquarianism, which is mere fascination with the past, and find new ways to release the spiritual power which the biblical authors experienced. As a starting point for Christians, the gospel narratives offer the only reputable information about the life and teachings of Jesus, even though the four gospels were written half a century after the crucifixion. Even an arms-length encounter is welcome. The Bible is the raw material of the Christian faith. If the historical Jesus isn't here, He's unavailable to us.

In my book *Jesus 2.1*, I called for people to let the Bible be what it is, ancient spiritual literature written by human beings. Biblical theology is an attempt to clarify the message of scripture in its ancient context. When modern readers rediscover the original context, or as much of it as they can discern from historical and archeological studies, many enigmatic passages speak with new clarity.

Medieval Paradigms

The Bible has always been important in the Church, even though it did not achieve preeminence until the Reformation era when Protestants proclaimed Holy Writ as the sole authority for Christian faith and morals. The great cry of the Reformers was Sola Scriptura—only the Scripture. Yet the library of biblical documents has been a constant companion of clergy and educated laypeople since the earliest Christian centuries. Theologians searched for passages to buttress their arguments. Monks chanted its passages in daily "offices" of the Church. Priests drew homilies from the standard Latin text, which eventually required unofficial, paraphrased explanations of the chosen passages in the languages of the people. With so much public exposure, even in a world of widespread illiteracy, it soon became apparent that certain texts required clarification. By the Middle Ages biblical interpreters frequently adopted the four-fold method proposed by St. John Cassian (360-435 C.E.), who was in turn indebted to Origen of Alexandria (185-254 C.E.). Cassian suggested a passage might be taken any of four ways:

> Historical - literally
> Tropological - morally
> Allegorical- prefiguring later events
> Anagogical- alluding to spiritual mysteries

When Cassian spoke of allegory he was referring to prefiguring future events, which is a limited, oracular understanding of the word. A better definition of allegory is "a story in which the characters and events are symbols that stand for truths about human life."[3] Not all medieval interpreters understood the four-fold model the same way. For example, it was explained in a ditty from Nicholas of Lyra in the fourteenth century, which has become known as the *Quadriga:*

> Littera gesta docet, quid credas allegoria,
> Moralis quid agas, quo tendas anagogia.[4]

This Latin jingle translates: The letter teaches what happened, the allegorical what you are to believe, the moral what you are to do, the anagogical where you are going. A frequently cited example is the word *Jerusalem,* which can be interpreted four ways through the Quadriga.

> The same Jerusalem can be taken in four senses:
> historically as the city of the Jews; allegorically as
> Church of Christ, anagogically as the heavenly city of
> God "which is the mother of us all," tropologically, as
> the soul of man, which is frequently subject to praise or
> blame from the Lord under this title.[5]

For Nicholas of Lyra, *Allegory* was both prophetic and
morally binding: the city of Jerusalem means the Church, which
if obeyed will bring spiritual blessings to all. Yet by the modern
definition, *allegory* is the use of symbolism to interpret human
life, which means all four elements in the *Quadriga* are forms of
allegorical clarification. Even the literal events, taken as history,
inform people about the nature of God.

Christological Interpretation

Some interpreters use allegory to read the Scriptures
Christologically, finding prophecies and veiled references to Jesus Christ
scattered throughout its sixty-six volumes. A few Old Testament
passages have taken on such powerful Christological significance it is
difficult for Christians to hear them without reading Jesus into the text.
Rabbinic scholars understandably reject such conclusions. Advent
readings often include the following passages from the Prophet Isaiah.

> The people who walked in darkness
> have seen a great light;
> those who lived in a land of deep darkness—
> on them light has shined.

> For a child has been born for us, a son given to us;
>   authority rests upon his shoulders;
> and he is named Wonderful Counselor,
>   Mighty God, Everlasting Father, Prince of Peace.[6]

Judaism has never been impressed with the Christological

paradigm. A Jewish website spins this perennial Advent passage quite differently:

> Isaiah 9:5-6 is not a messianic prophecy according to the Jewish perspective. The correct context of this passage is that it describes events that had already taken place in Jewish history, namely, the birth and naming of this particular child (believed to be Hezekiah... According to one interpretation, this passage speaks of the wonders performed by God for Hezekiah as King of Judah, and in it, the Prophet expresses his praise of God for sparing Hezekiah and his kingdom from demise...[7]

Implicit in all of these methods of interpretation is the creative identification of symbolism and its explication through allegory. As early as the Second Century AD, Alexandrian Christianity was busily painting a grandly inclusive picture of the faith under the bold brush strokes of Clement, Origen, and host of lesser figures. They believed that Christian truth was the same as philosophical truth. Armed with Plato's worldview, those early allegorists found images, illustrations, and insights tucked between the lines of scripture. The method is creative and elastic to the point of shapelessness.

By its very flexibility, allegory bends to any master. Allegorical interpretation justified racism, sexism and homophobia. In fact, allegory is so plastic it was the weapon of choice when theologians battled over difficult texts in earlier times. If one side in a dispute quoted scripture that seemed to support its position, the other side would offer an allegorical interpretation that "proved" otherwise. Today, however, theologians proceed differently. They seldom quote scripture as the authority for their ideas; proof-texting is considered an exercise in futility because of the above. Since there are so many scripture passages that could be called upon to contradict other texts, any discussion which resorts to proof-texting has deteriorated from legitimate theology to legalistic nit-picking.

Theology today tends to refer to biblical concepts and ideas rather than citing Isaiah to prove some abstract idea first enunciated by Luther or Calvin. However, religious conservatives continue to proof-text, blithely ignoring the reality of modern biblical analysis. The best known example of this approach was Billy Graham, whose "Crusades" featured biblical preaching as a jaunt through theologies of yesteryear. Lutheran theologian T.A. Kantonen wrote:

> It (fundamentalism) is the theology undergirding mass evangelism such as that of Billy Graham. With complete disregard for the original connotations and situations as elucidated by biblical scholarship, the evangelist proves his point with a simple indiscriminate "the Bible says..."[8]

Question of Authority

Biblical authority is the issue. If we see the Bible as the only source of truth—*sola scriptura*, the cry of the Reformation—then we must make sure it agrees with what we are doing. One way to achieve harmony with Scripture is to change our practices to bring them in line with biblical mandates. This is important if one believes, in the words of Luther's Small Catechism: "Every word of the Bible is God's word, and therefore the Bible is without error."[9]

A common way to reach accord between Bible and practice is to apply creative methods of interpretation to places where contradictions or difficulties appear. Luther claimed the right to critique the canon of Scripture, calling the Letter of James an "Epistle of straw" because it contradicts the basic premise of salvation only through faith and not through works. The author of James challenges people to show him their faith by their deeds, not just in pretty words.

> What good is it, my brothers and sisters, if you say you have faith but do not have works? Can faith save you? If a brother or sister is naked and lacks daily food, and one of you says to them, "Go in peace; keep warm and eat your fill," and yet you do not supply their bodily needs, what is the good of that? So faith by itself, if it has no works, is dead.[10]

Even a cursory reading of the biblical library shows it contains an amazing array of ideas. One would have to be a titan of interpretation to harmonize the brutality of Nahum with the self-giving love of Jesus. Even if the Bible were inerrant—which it is *not*—the denominational smorgasbord available on Sunday morning in North America makes it difficult to comprehend how an error-free text still manages to confuse most of Christendom.

More importantly, the religious thinker must frankly admit that he/she is not an unbiased observer. No one comes to the Bible without opinions about God, Jesus Christ, heaven and hell. We see scripture through the stained-glass windows of our beliefs. Granted, some degree of objectivity in Bible study is possible, but only we continually examine our uncritical assumptions when reading Scripture. For example, does the book of Revelation really forecast a future time of the end, or is it better understood as underground literature of the first century Christian community with symbolism related to people, places and events of that era? Most biblical scholars today would argue the latter.

Metaphysical Interpretation: A Brief Critique

This book has set as a goal the critical discussion of deeply held beliefs and practices. So, before introducing a new approach to the method, let's take a moment to summarize a few reasonable critiques which could be leveled at metaphysical interpretation. To continue the full disclosure mode begun earlier in this work, I must confess my doubts about the future of biblical studies grounded solely in allegorical interpretation. Although crafting a metaphysical interpretation can be enjoyable and edifying, quite frankly I wrestled with a strong inclination to drop this technique from the Second Edition for several reasons.

Allegory marginalizes. Any method of interpretation grounded in allegory further marginalizes Metaphysical Christianity from the wider community of historic Christian faiths. Biblical allegories built on word studies are seen as an archaic, eccentric methodology, practiced by a decreasingly smaller number of churches and seldom found beyond the New Thought habitat.

Eisegesis distorts. As with all methods based on allegory, metaphysical interpretation often makes the scripture say whatever an interpreter wants to hear. Scholars call this importation of bias into reading a text *eisegesis,* the polar opposite of what biblical theologians are attempting, i.e., *exegesis,* to discover what the text was actually saying to its target audience and to ask how that message applies today.

Easily discounted. Finally, metaphysical interpretation provides an easy, quirky substitute for the harder task of understanding the Bible in a context of historical-archaeological discoveries, new manuscript evidence, principles of literary analysis and data from the social sciences. If the New Thought churches exclusively promote an allegory-based methodology to mine the rich deposits of spiritual insight in Scripture, we have no one to blame if our efforts to speak to a wider world are discounted as unschooled happy-babble.[11]

Historical-Metaphysical Interpretation

Notwithstanding all the difficulties and potential for capricious application, creative use of religious literature for personal insights is an age-old practice.[12] Is there a role for personal interaction with biblical texts which allows the creative chemistry of human consciousness to experiment with meanings without dismissing modern scholarship?

Three decades ago, while attending a conference on biblical studies in Colorado, I asked eminent biblical scholar Krister Stendahl a question during his Q&A session. After making the admiring noises of a theological groupie who had read Stendahl's works in seminary, I raised an issue which everyone at the conference probably thought had been settled centuries ago. "Is allegorical interpretation still valid today?"

Every head in the room turned sharply to the questioner. The audience was packed with professional scholars; I was not an academic but served as a U.S. Army Chaplain. Nevertheless, I knew allegory was in great disfavor because of its erratic tendencies toward religious fantasy. His response startled the learned assembly but delighted the questioner: "Yes, it is a wonderful way of playing in God's garden." Dr. Stendahl went on to warn that it could become a way to rationalize ideas that were unhealthy unless we check our interpretations out with the broader community of faith. Stendahl further acknowledged that allegory is widely mistrusted today, but actually has deep roots in New Testament mysticism.

Stendahl's caveat informs the presentation in the remainder of this chapter, which will present a method which blends the foundational achievements of two methodologies: historical biblical studies and the word studies found in supportive literature, such as the *Metaphysical Bible Dictionary*. There are several methods of doing metaphysical interpretation, but all of these generally begin by examining the root meanings of words in a biblical passage to discover possible alternative ways to read the passage. The guiding star of metaphysical interpretation points to all places, people, things and events in the text as *symbolic statements about the growth of the individual soul*. If we add brief historical analysis to the process, the result is often quite illuminating, albeit creatively achieved.

To interpret the Bible symbolically while keeping the historical context of the original passage, we need the right tools. A competent biblical commentary, like the *Interpreter's One-Volume Commentary* (Abingdon) is absolutely essential. To do linguistic research we'll need a Bible dictionary which delves into the root meanings of the Greek and Hebrew words. Unity's *Metaphysical Bible Dictionary* is still the best, but other fine biblical reference works will give you root meanings. Best of all would be to study Greek and Hebrew, but few of us have the time to study that deeply. A good translation of the Bible is also essential, like the *New Revised Standard Version*. Once we have the proper tools--a good historical-critical commentary and an MBD or another root-word source book--we can get to work.

The process is actually quite simple. We are trying to set the biblical passage in its historical context and discover what the author was trying to say to his readership, then find a concept-bridge in the root meanings which can enable us to see deeper meanings in the text   through metaphysical analysis. It's actually kind of fun, too. We'll take it step-by-step.

Before we begin, let's remind ourselves that we are *not* unlocking some deep secret meaning the author really meant for us to find. We are taking the pieces handed to us by Matthew, Mark or Luke and rearranging them in other patterns, quite possibly in ways that would scandalize the editor-writers of the Bible. Our license to create new images draws its authority from two sources:

1. The Historical Context. We must begin with the best insight into what the author really did mean to say to his target audience. When the unknown author of Ephesians went off on a jag about slaves obeying their masters, we need to know he believed the end of the world was fast approaching; one's social status was not important in an apocalyptical context. A symbolic understanding of the context means we don't have to discard the text, because the divine can speak to us through all sorts of media, even historically outdated moral values. Now we're ready for the second reference point.

2. One Presence/One Power. God the good is the only power that exists. Not two forces, light and dark—there is only light and shadow (non-light).

These provide a starting point. Of course, as with all religious ideas, we submit the insights of allegorical interpretation to the Scripture-Tradition-Experience-Reason test, ask that they meet our epistemological criteria for Pragmatic Idealism (chapter 3), and hold them up against the yardstick of Jesus Christ. Disciplined by a guiding principle and aware of the method's limitations, we can venture into the exciting world of biblical allegory.

Fair enough. Open your Bibles—any number can play! With apologies for the lame acronym, this interpretative technique can be called the B-I-B-L-E method.

B--> Background of the Book. Read the introduction to the book from your commentary, studying when it was written and for what purposes. Who were the bad guys? Did the author try to make us believe he was somebody else? Scholarship has shown this was often the case. What was happening in the world and in the target community when this passage was written? Remember, some books (Psalms, Isaiah, Genesis, and others) were written by more than one author over a period of time longer than one lifetime. Focus down to your specific scripture passage by using the commentary. This brings us to the next step.

I-->Interpreter's Insights. Go to the textual commentary and see what the interpreter has to say about your passage of scripture. Try to set the verses in their context. What does the interpreter suggest that the biblical author wanted to say or accomplish with this passage? When you feel you understand what the ancient author probably meant to convey to his readers, you are now ready to move into symbolic interpretation.

B-->Breakdown to Basics. Find the names, objects, and places mentioned in the text. Personal names such as Aaron, Moses, Jesus, Zedekiah, or Jezebel. Objects like animals, plants, or mountains. Structures like temples, inns, shrines, tents, houses. Places like Jericho, Egypt, Syria, or the Red Sea. Make a list of all the persons, places and things mentioned in your text--animal, vegetable, or mineral. And don't forget abstract nouns: love, hate, war, peace, faith, hope. Next, take your *Metaphysical Bible Dictionary* in hand and move to step four.

L-->Look up List. Find the key concept-words from your passage in the *MBD*, looking for root meanings and variant readings. See if patterns emerge.

E-->Exchange and Editorialize. Using the new insights based on the root meanings of the text and recalling the historical context, try to find an allegorical or symbolic teaching in the passage. Listen to the new meanings you've uncovered and see if the mists rise over your verses. This is the fun part, because you get to play with the meanings until some new ideas snap into focus.

Application of Technique

Let's try a quick example. Remember, biblical authors often use self-conscious symbolism when they choosing place-names, character names or physical objects. However, not every verse in the Bible can be interpreted "metaphysically". Lots of passages are hymns of praise or wisdom stories requiring no symbolic interpretation, for example, Paul's "Hymn to Love" in I Corinthians 13. Pick a passage with strong images and action. For example, here's how one might do a historical-metaphysical workup on Mark 10:32.

And they were on the road, going up to Jerusalem, and

Jesus was walking ahead of them; and they were amazed, and those who followed were afraid.

Journey with me on a stream- of-consciousness study of this passage and we'll walk through the B-I-B-L-E method.

B--> Background of the Book

First, investigate the background of the book. Open the *Interpreter's One-Volume Commentary* to the section on Mark.

We want to discover when the book was written and for what purpose. Writing in the *IOVC*, biblical scholar Lindsey P. Pherigo, says the book was probably written after the death of the Apostle Peter (ca. 64 A.D.) by a missionary companion of Peter and Paul. It was written far from the local traditions about Jesus, perhaps at Rome, by someone who did not participate in the events himself.

I-->Interpreter's Insights

Pherigo says this is a "Gentile Christian" gospel, as opposed to the "Jewish Christian" message of Matthew. Hmmm. That means Mark was an advocate of Paul's concepts about the message of Jesus being for everyone and not just for the lost sheep of Israel, as Matthew's gospel suggests. The commentator notes that the disciples did not understand what was happening; that's typically Marcan. He often minimizes the importance of the Apostles because he's trying to establish a world-wide Christian message that need not be linked strictly with the leadership in Jerusalem. Also, Pherigo says to notice way they were walking, strictly in order of seniority with Jesus leading. He says that was a formal procedure in first century Palestine. This suggests we have a piece of authentic history here. If Mark was not one of the original circle but his storyline reflects a local custom he could not have known otherwise, it probably happened. Jesus leads the way, followed by his disciples...and the disciples are scared and amazed that he is going to Jerusalem, the commentator notes. Time for step three.

L-->Look up List

The text presents the following characters and places:

1 - Jesus

2 - Disciples (not specified in this passage; implied as "them")
3 - Jerusalem
4 - Road to Jerusalem

Other significant relationships to note:

> They were going *up* to Jerusalem.
> The first group *behind* Jesus was amazed.
> The *second group* was *afraid* ("those who followed").

Moving to the *Metaphysical Bible Dictionary*, with help from *The Revealing Word*, we have alternative images to consider based on the Greek words of the text.

> Jesus - the *MBD* lists these meanings for the name: "...whose help Jehovah is; deliverance; safety; salvation; Savior; Deliverer; helper; prosperer; deliverance through Jehovah." Also describes Jesus as God's idea of humanity in expression.

> Jerusalem - habitation of peace; dwelling place of peace; possession of peace; foundation of peace; constitution of harmony; vision of peace; abode of prosperity.

> Disciples - *MBD*: the twelve "faculties" (Divine-human powers natural to everyone); *RW*: (cross-ref to Apostles) those who are sent forth; messengers; ambassadors; active spiritual thoughts.

> Road to Jerusalem - not mentioned in *MBD* or *RW*.

E-->Exchange and Editorialize

Armed with these informative bits, let's move to the interpretation stage. Jesus represents *deliverance*. He leads the way and the *active spiritual thoughts* we have follow him. But on the upward path toward the *abode of prosperity/peace/harmony*, our thoughts become confused, falling into two camps. First we have those spiritual thoughts which are simply amazed. Can all this be true? Amazement is not necessarily bad, but if we are paralyzed by the wonder of our unfolding spiritual growth—if we feel this can't be happening—confidence will erode into doubt.

The second group represents fearful thoughts and attitudes. They are behind and therefore lower than the amazement-thoughts, since we are moving upward after Jesus. These thoughts could stop altogether, but if we continue on the upward path we shall break through fear into amazement, which is directly beyond fear. The important thing is to keep pressing on, traveling upward after Jesus, who is safety and deliverance from all lesser states of consciousness. Just as the first century Church broke through their fears about the unknown (gentile world), so must we move beyond our fears that lack or apparent dis-harmony will prevail. Jesus leads us onward toward a habitation of peace; our deliverance is secure because God is within us.

This was a rough-cut example of how to link historical critical insights with allegorical interpretation. Wherever names, places or objects are present, a symbolic interpretation is possible. However, we must face a tough question before moving on to our next topic: Is Metaphysical Biblical Interpretation an authentic method of study, or is this merely a Bible word-game invoked by Metaphysical Christian churches to "prove" points of doctrine that are not otherwise biblical?

How Biblical Is Metaphysical Interpretation?

Just how *biblical* is this method? What right do we have to turn the meaning of scriptural words inside-out and make them say what we want them to say? Can anyone honestly believe that Mark (whomever he was) meant for us to interpret the text the way we did in the above example from his gospel? Or shall we fall back on that old Gnostic drivel about hidden, secret meanings in the text which only specially initiated persons--members of our elite group--can comprehend?

The most serious challenge to metaphysical interpretation is that an allegorical reading does not faithfully represent the ideas penned by the author so long ago. Facing the issues squarely, readers must acknowledge that metaphysical interpretation does not reach a truer, deeper meaning, which God intended for a select few. To pretend the writer intended anything but the plain, literal meaning when he said Jesus was "on the road, going up to Jerusalem," is to fool oneself; it does no justice to the profound insights of metaphysical interpretation.

The great danger facing any interpreter of the Bible is the tendency to prove this-or-that religious idea by twisting the text to a biased conclusion. Given the proclivity of Metaphysical Christianity to slide into Gnosticism, one cannot say this strongly enough: *There is no secret key which unlocks the true, hidden meaning of the Bible.* Except for a few instances of self-conscious symbolism, such as the books of Genesis and Revelation, no significant "secret" meanings exist. What, therefore, gives us the right to do metaphysical interpretation? Let me suggest three possible justifications for playing this creative mind game with the text of Sacred Scripture.

First, substitutionary allegory is practiced in the Bible. Interpreting texts symbolically is one of the methods used by biblical authors themselves. New Testament authors often see references to Jesus Christ throughout the pages of the Hebrew Scriptures. Remember, there was no New Testament when Paul and the apostles went barn-storming around the Mediterranean with their evangelical message. Paul didn't hand out pocket New Testaments, but he did quote the Hebrew Bible—the only Testament at the time. Fortunately, the Jewish Scriptures had been translated into Greek long before the time of Jesus, so the Greek-speaking world knew about the sacred writings of the Jews.

Paul and his fellow evangelists quoted the Old Testament freely, using this Greek translation (called the Septuagint or LXX). They also freely reinterpreted the symbolism of Psalm, Prophet and Torah to find references to Jesus Christ everywhere.

Jesus Himself re-interpreted and spiritualized the scriptures. What gave his the authority to change the meanings? The author of John 10:34 shows Jesus invoking Psalm 82:6 out of context to authenticate the early church's claim that Jesus is certainly divine, since we are all divine. As much as modern readers might want to believe those words were spoken by Jesus, the likelihood is that we are listening to one side of the doctrinal battle about the nature of Jesus that waged for centuries after his crucifixion. Nevertheless, even the most radical interpretation of the passage falls short of a literal reading, i.e., that we are actually gods and goddesses after the ancient model of a polytheistic cosmos. It must be read symbolically.

But what about *metaphysical interpretation*? There are several examples, the most obvious is where Paul explains the meaning of Abraham's two wives. Significantly, he begins: "Now this is an allegory: these two women are covenants..." (Gal. 4:24) How can allegorical interpretation be "unbiblical", when New Testament authors use it themselves?

Dangerous, yes. We have already addressed the fact that, like an online computer with no operational anti-virus program, allegorical interpretation can expose people to all sorts of weird tangents which become religio-cultural extremes. That does not invalidate the method; it just makes us aware of our responsibility to ground our mystical interpretation in principles which meet the criteria of a sound Christian theology. The teachings of Jesus Christ, mediated through the principles of systematic theology presented in this work, can prevent maladaptive ideas from infiltrating any through study of the Bible to gain spiritual insights. However, if we are faithful to the basic principles of modern biblical interpretation and guided by a Metaphysical Christian perspective, good results will be forthcoming.

Secondly, allegorical interpretation is at least as old as literalism. Two schools of biblical interpretation developed in the first Christian centuries. One, which was centered in Antioch, stressed literal interpretations of both the established Jewish Bible and the Christian documents vying for a place in a New Testament. The other school of thought sprang from the rich intellectual/spiritual soil of Alexandria on the Egyptian coast. This second center of Christian interpretation followed the lead of Greek stoicism and the great Jewish philosopher Philo, who lived during the missionary period of the Apostle Paul.

Philo learned allegorical interpretation from the stoics, who were uncomfortable with a literal interpretation of Greek mythology. As a Jew who was schooled in both Torah and philosophy, Philo sought to synthesize those two thought worlds by interpreting the Jewish scriptures allegorically. When Christianity came to town, its learned adherents-- notably Clement and Origen--adopted the same method of interpretation. Allegorical interpretation was widely popular among educated Christians for the first few centuries after Christ. Eventually, Antiochian-style literalism became the dominant method of biblical interpretation, and then only after the light of Greek scholarship had been snuffed out by anti- intellectual zealots who ushered in the Dark Ages.

Finally, art *requires* interaction. Appreciation is a creative act. As compelling as these arguments from scripture and history may be, there is a still stronger reason for doing metaphysical interpretation. Any work of art or literature will evoke a response in us that goes deeper than words. Poets write of the Mona Lisa with little thought of what Da Vinci had in mind when painting. In fact, one researcher has concluded that Da Vinci's greatest work is a secret self-portrait: the eyes, mouth and other facial features provided a perfect computer-enhanced match. Will that affect the way our grandchildren see her? Probably not.

Millions hear the William Tell Overture and associate it with the *Lone Ranger*, a connection which scarcely occurred to the composer, Gioachino Antonio Rossini (1792-1868). Christians read prophecies in the Hebrew Bible and point to these as proofs of Jesus' messiahship, yet Jews read that same Bible and have decided these proofs do not apply to the man of Nazareth. Who's right? Is it possible both are? Is it possible a work of art or literature can deliver a powerful, symbolic message, whether or not the artist-author intended to say exactly that?

One of Robert Frost's best beloved poems is "Stopping by Woods on a Snowy Evening." Listen to the haunting simplicity of the closing verse:

> These woods are lovely, dark and deep.
> But I have promises to keep,
> And miles to go before I sleep,
> And miles to go before I sleep.[13]

Countless English teachers have swooned over Frost's picture of life's journey which will end in rest one day. This noble soul has paused along the path of life, anticipating the sleep of death, but knowing there are hard times ahead and feeling the need to press onward faithful to that calling.

Then someone asked Mr. Frost what he meant by the poem, and the poet shrugged and said it was a straightforward narrative about a person who stops to see the snowfall on his way home. Frost said the poem means, "...it's all very nice but I must be getting along, getting home."[14] Some English teachers will probably never forgive him.

When so many people see the symbolism of life and death in a poem, who's to say, "That's *not* what Robert Frost meant to say. You may not hear life's end in this poem." The same applies to words of Scripture. Sometimes a biblical passage expresses ideas which its authors never intended to convey.

Repeating the cautionary note: This method is only valid if practiced self-consciously, with full knowledge it requires reshaping the author's message into the images of Christian metaphysics. As noted above, mental integrity proscribes fooling ourselves into thinking we have discovered what the author *really* meant to say and are merely unlocking his coded message. What we are actually doing is breaking down the message and re-coding it into symbolism more congenial today. Allegorical interpretation gets people into trouble only when they refuse to acknowledge what they are actually doing: creating something new from the energy source of the original. It is more art than science.

Lectio Divina

There are other ways to encounter the Bible. My grandmother breezed through verses from the scripture every night at bedtime and found great comfort in texts she had heard since childhood. Some people find the Bible speaking directly to them, even though prophet, psalmist or Evangelist is long dead. Devotional reading requires no special context. Along this line, an old style of visiting the Bible has recently become popular again, the technique called *Lectio Divina*. The goal here is not about learning or even understanding a passage, it is about *experiencing* the text the way you might experience a walk in the forest. There are usually four steps in the process:

> Lectio—Read aloud until encountering a key passage.
> Meditatio—Reflect on the text; imagine freely.
> Oratio—Respond by prayer; talk to Divine Spirit.
> Contemplatio—Rest in silence with the passage; be open to God

Lectio Divina is a rich practice which is fairly easy to master. There is plenty of literature available about it, including a chapter in my book *The Many Faces of Prayer: How the Human Family Meets Its Spiritual Needs.*[15]

No Easy Job

Even for scholars, exploring the Bible can be a difficult, complex task. Yet, as we have seen, there are many beneficial ways to read Scripture, and the question is not really, *"Which method is right?"* Surely, God speaks with many voices, influenced by cultural comprehension and personal needs. The Bible is a different book in everyone's hands, as it must be. It is a treasure chest from which we can receive deep insights and high standards, good stories and fine poetry, inspiration to reach for goals beyond our grasp, and power to make our dreams come true.

No single method of biblical interpretation will meet the needs of everyone. We have merely suggested a method which seems to blend the best elements of historical-critical study with metaphysical-allegorical interpretation. Any insights gleaned from adventuresome reading in the allegorical hinterlands must be compared with the ideas current in the Christian community through dialogue and discussion in an atmosphere of mutual respect.

A rabbi once told the author, "You cannot be a Jew alone. It takes a community—it is a lifestyle as much as a religious faith." Hillary Clinton famously said that it takes a village to raise a child. We know from our study of cultural influences that every one of us has been powerfully influenced by the norms of our communities, and that this influence is not inherently bad but provides a necessary context for living an effective, rich and meaningful life. Good biblical interpretation is therefore both intensely personal and irrevocably public, because it links our private communion with God's Word to the beliefs, practices and thoughts of people in our religious tradition, and through that window we should be able to see the world.

CHECK YOUR KNOWLEDGE

1. What is biblical theology; how does it differ from a metaphysical interpretation of the Bible?

2. List and explain the three rules for historical-critical interpretation.

3. Why does the author think George Lamsa's translation of the New Testament from the Aramaic is not as accurate as Lamsa claims?

4. How is allegory at once an exciting yet dangerous tool?

5. What are the five steps in the historical-metaphysical method introduced in this chapter?

6. Describe *Lectio Divina*.

QUESTIONS FOR DISCUSSION

1. How do you feel about the Bible? What experiences brought you here?

2. Which new ideas in this chapter do you find helpful? Which ideas were problematic?

3. If modern biblical scholars are right when they say the people in the Bible are literary characters, what does it mean for your faith to realize the "words of Jesus" are really the "words of Matthew"? Is Jesus Christ really present in the New Testament? How?

4. Why is metaphysical interpretation both exciting and dangerous?

5. In your opinion, what are some advantages and disadvantages to Historical-Metaphysical interpretation?

6. How important should the Bible be in our churches today?

- 6 -

HOLY SPIRIT

God as Dynamic Expression

The Holy Spirit is continually inspiring me. My thoughts
are fresh, and new, and clear, and powerful with the might
of Omnipotence. My prayers are the handiwork of the
Holy Ghost--powerful as the eagle and gentle as the dove.

Emmett Fox[1]

Traditionally, studies of the Trinity begin with God the Father and
sooner or later get around to the Holy Spirit, as though this aspect of
God's activity were an afterthought. This study reverses the tendency
and begins with Spirit, because arguably the mystical Christian point of
reference is *spirituality* as opposed to the creative/ruling facility of
Divinity. Neglect of the Spirit's importance is not limited to modern
theologians. The author of Luke-Acts says Paul found the same sort of
benign ignorance in his missionary encounters with new Christians:

> Paul passed through the upper country and came to
> Ephesus. There he found some disciples. And he said to
> them, "Did you receive the Holy Spirit when you
> believed?" And they said, "No, we have never even
> heard that there is a Holy Spirit." [2]

Apparently, whoever taught the first Christians at Ephesus didn't
consider the Holy Spirit important enough to include in the basic course
on being a Christian! This tendency lingers in theology, partly because
the idea of spirit is so vague when juxtaposed against such readily

comprehensible symbols as Father and Son. Most people have known fathers and sons; few have held conversations with a spirit.

Spirit is an ephemeral concept, and its vagueness can lead to confusion. Mainstream Christianity has shied away from emphasis on Spirit, partly because of its identification with exotic practices of the past. Several radical sects have financed their assault on orthodoxy by claiming special revelations from the Holy Spirit. Western theology's reluctance to acknowledge the importance of Spirit also flows from the historic problem of charismatic experiences, especially the phenomenon of Glossolalia or speaking in tongues. In several mainline Protestant denominations this phenomenon has driven away long-standing members, split some churches and yet revived sagging spirituality in others.

This chapter examines some of these problem/objections by looking at God through the first window, Spirit, in the three-sided cathedral of faith known as the Trinity. First, however, it is important to step back and take a broad look at the whole category of Spirit and things spiritual, followed by an analysis of the concept of Holiness, which forms the combination term *Holy Spirit*. From a discussion of the Holy Spirit in biblical and theological perspectives, the study moves on to Gifts of the Spirit/Fruit of the Spirit to see how these special gifts and ubiquitous fruit helps some believers understand what God is like.

One could argue that knowledge of God comes through knowing the divine-human nature of people, because the summit of God's ultimate nature remains forever shrouded in mystery. Any God humans fully comprehend could hardly be God. Although God, by any reasonable definition, must be immeasurably vast, perhaps infinite, seekers can follow a trail of clues to a clearer vantage point. Those clues come from observing God at work in the lives of other people—made in the image and likeness of the Eternal—and from organized reflection on the basic categories of belief, the task of systematic theology. To improve any Christian model of what God is like requires a look at *spirit*.

The Trinity—Spirit First?

Before considering a metaphysical Christian view of *God the Father* or *God the Son*, an understanding of God as Spirit seems necessary, because spirit is the underlying reality behind all matter, energy, thought, and creativity. "God is Spirit," says Jesus to the Samaritan woman at the well, "and those who worship him must worship him in spirit and in truth." (John 4:24)

One need not delve too deeply into philosophical studies before encountering a serious problem with theologies based on the existence of Spirit. First, as Immanuel Kant (1724-1804) showed, all knowledge comes to us through the senses, and things of the Spirit are not sensory phenomena. John Macquarrie explains:

> Kant, as everyone knows, showed in his Critique of Pure Reason that human understanding is limited to the phenomena of sensory experience. When we try to go beyond these and ask questions about transcendent objects—God, freedom, immortality—we land ourselves in contradictions. The ultimate reality is unknowable, and rational metaphysics is impossible. [3]

Humanity is like a feral child groping for its humanity. People learn through the senses. We encounter stimuli in the physical world, hear ideas, see events unfold, and make religious/ethical decisions based on sensory data. We never experience the essence of "things-in-themselves" (Kant's term) but must process in the brain the input received from bodily senses. Looking at a chair cannot bring the observer into contact with the chair's true nature; observation presents the chair as an image in the brain. Senses of smell, sight, hearing, taste, and touch file their electronic reports with brain central, where the sensible smelling, seeing, hearing, tasting and touching moves into consciousness. If this is true for an object as simple as a chair, how much more is it true that sensory input delivers all knowledge about God?

But where do people get the sensory input—stories and readings, visual images, great songs of faith, ceremonies of food and sacred scents— that teach them about God? From other people, who have already decided to believe. Kant held that nothing can be *proved* about religion, because all evidence comes through the senses and the transcendent realm of God lies far beyond sensory experience.

Leap of Faith

To believe in God requires what Danish philosopher Soren Kierkegaard called a "leap of faith" from the limitations of sensory input to a place of certainty which philosophy cannot provide. Things of God are beyond the physical world (meta-physical). They cannot be comprehended by the senses, therefore cannot be called authentic knowledge in a scientific sense. For this reason, Kant insisted, a rationalistic metaphysic is impossible. Divine Ideas must be understood through a combination of faith and intuition.

To understand what the Kantians were saying clarifies why some of the founders of modern metaphysical Christianity got downright snarky when they wrote about sensory knowledge and those who claimed it was the only source of information. Charles Fillmore, among others, believed "pure reason" was capable of achieving perfect knowledge of God, although he never replied directly to Kant's powerful critique.

Again, space for a full reply to the Kantian position is not available in a work this broad, but a few remarks seem appropriate since we have already cast our lot with Spirit as the underlying Reality upon which all matter and energy and consciousness is built.

First, we must frankly admit that Kant was right when he asserted that all knowledge comes to us through the senses, if we define "knowledge" as learning about things external and detached from ourselves. But if there is an inner dimension to human consciousness, then we can look within ourselves to find direct information which does not come through the senses. If God is within us, as metaphysical Christianity believes, then we should be able to make contact with God internally. We should be able to "go to headquarters" directly, as Fillmore claimed.

Secondly, we have more than sensory input; we have our own response to that input. Why do humans feel love if there is not some kind of power moving through us? Why do we respond with anger sometimes and with astonishment other times? What is consciousness itself, if not evidence of Spirit?

Most importantly, we have Jesus Christ to hold before us. If all things about God are necessarily symbolic, as we said in the previous chapter, then sensory input is just another form of symbolism. Jesus Christ, the ultimate symbol for things divine, comes to us through senses, through emotions, through meditation and prayer, through intuition and through insight. Our knowledge about the Jesus of history may come strictly from our senses, but our knowledge of the Christ-within comes from that data as it is processed by the faith faculty. Kant would agree that belief is more than a hopeful guess. It is input plus faith plus a willingness to let some questions hang unanswered in space.

Spirit: The Final Frontier

Paul Tillich said God is not *a* Being but *being-itself*; God does not exist but is existence itself or the very power to be. Imagine a lamp hooked into a power source, spreading warm light across a room. Electricity flows through the cord and the lamp squeezes light from the raw energy, thanks to Thomas Edison. Now, leap from science to science fiction for a moment. Suppose there were a power source that not only produced light but generated the lamp as well. Flip a switch and the power-package causes a lighted lamp to appear.[4] Turn off the switch and the physical lamp, as well as the light, disappears. Energy and matter are the same thing in different form according to current scientific theory, so the idea of an energy- generated lamp is not entirely beyond possibility. We are not talking about the image of a lamp, like a holographic model, but an actual, touchable, solid object which comes into existence because energy is transmuted into matter. Got it?

Now think about the Universe. God is the very *power-to-be.* Everything exists because God is the Energy Source which causes everything to exist. "In him we live and move and have our being," Paul said the Apostle, paraphrasing Epimenides the Cretan poet (Acts 17:28). Spirit is the true underlying Reality that causes everything to be.

Of course, as Kant showed, this cannot be proved. It also cannot be disproved, Kant admits. But the reality of Spirit can be demonstrated by the inward life of each person and the out-picturing of Spirit through application of spiritual principles in the world. The previous study of Epistemology (Ch. 3), suggested that spiritual matters must be practically demonstrated, not proved after the manner of empirical science or deductive reason. Kant supports this argument, because he readily agrees that things of the Spirit are the province of faith and cannot be apprehended by human intellect. In fact, he goes as far as to say that the way people look at the world shapes the world itself:

> In metaphysical speculations it has always been assumed that all our knowledge must conform to objects; but every attempt from this point of view to extend our knowledge of objects...has ended in failure. The time has now come to ask, whether better progress may not be made by supposing that objects must conform to our knowledge[5].

Our perception of reality, far from originating in the outer world, begins within us. We all have that stained-glass window of personal beliefs and imagination through which we filter all the helter-skelter sensory and intellectual data flying at us. Take snow for an example. When most people see snow they see a white mass; but a Native Alaskan looks at snow and sees many types, textures, and weather indications. The languages of the circumpolar peoples are rich in snow words, most of which are not translatable without complex descriptive phrases.

Green Jumble or Precision Parts?

Another example comes from a personal experience. I was bivouacked with the troops as an Army Basic Training chaplain back in the 1970s. Fort Leonard Wood, Missouri, is affectionately known as "Fort Lost-in-the-Woods" to soldiers. One afternoon during a break in training, a young officer and I went for a walk in the rural Missouri forest. My companion was a trained wildlife ecologist, not an ignorant city-boy like me. It soon became apparent that we were not seeing the same forest or even sharing the same world. Instead of a jumble of green and brown, he saw order and organization, a magnificent ecosystem of interdependent animals and plants. He strolled down the forest paths through a world he knew well. I walked joyfully among the pretty trees—which is a good spiritual exercise—and so did my friend, who saw the woods from a much broader perspective.

We shape the world perceptually, but our ability to influence the reality in which we live extends beyond perception alone. We shall look at this provocative concept later. For now, let's just say Spirit, as the Reality undergirding all that exists, operates through and with us, because *It is us, and we are It.* Our discussion of the Trinity begins with

Spirit because Metaphysical Christianity considers Spirit as the fundamental building block of existence..

Spirit in Pre-Christian Thought

In earliest form, the idea of spirit probably found expression through *animatism* a term coined by anthropologist Robert R. Marett. Animatism is the belief that spirit exists separate from individual supernatural beings, and it can manifest itself anywhere. Rocks, cooking utensils, storms, mountains, or any other person, place or thing may have special divine power. It is the life-force in both animate and inanimate objects. This is *not* to say there is one presence and one power, God omnipotent. Rather, there are outcroppings of universal spirit power in special places and things.

> Animatism is the belief in an impersonal supernatural power which can be controlled to some extent. It's not physical but can be seen by its (physical) effects on the world. It is often referred to as *Mana*. This supernatural power is not a part of supernatural beings (whether spirits or deities), instead being more of universal 'magical' power which is everywhere.[6]

Animatism differs from the more common anthropological term *animism* because the former does not require a soul-force behind it. Some anthropologists believe primitive people looked at the majestic peaks and felt the mountains had spiritual power without personifying the mountain as a spirit or a god. To the animatist, nature does not have a spirit; nature is spirit.

Later, humans began to worship the power of spirit wherever it broke through: sunrise, flood, rainstorm, thunder, and seasons. These and other powerful occurrences took their place beside mountaintops and forests, stars and meteors, to become separate spirits which eventually acquired names and personalities as gods and goddesses.

If we take Hinduism as a typical model of religious evolution, the gods and goddesses continue grow in stature until they all become omnipotent and omnipresent. How could there be hundreds of deities, each omnipotent? The only logical answer is that they are all expressions of the One Presence and One Power. Thus we come full circle, back to undifferentiated spirit-power which is everywhere present. The circle is really a spiral which brings us back to an entirely different level.

Modern Hinduism is not really animatistic (i.e., believing in ambiguous spirit-force behind nature) but Pantheistic or Monistic, seeing a conscious Intelligence at work and present in all things. Dr. John B. Noss wrote in his widely read textbook *Man's Religions*:

> Ultimately, (in Hindu thought) all things are bound together, not only by likeness of activity but in actuality, that is to say, in Being. Man comes to see not his separateness from the gods and his fellows but his and their identity with an eternal, all-inclusive Being or Reality, and begins to seek his deliverance (moksha) from separateness by mystical union with it.[7]

Since Hindu monistic belief arose from polytheistic religion, one cannot help but play with a fascinating question: What might have happened to Greco-Roman paganism if the Christian takeover had not radically altered the religio-cultural direction Hellenistic society? Would the gods and goddesses of Rome have merged into a form of cosmic monism? Already in the first century there were large numbers of "God-fearing Gentiles" (i.e., monotheists) who attended public meetings at Jewish synagogues and openly professed disbelief in the existence of so many mini-gods. A few centuries before Jesus, Socrates was executed for teaching, among other things, that there was only one God. These proto-monotheistic tendencies are interesting, but will ever remain speculative. Greco-Roman religion was ill equipped to deal with a vital, new faith that proclaimed one God and maintained connections with antiquity through the history of a well- known ethnic group, the Jews. Spirit, as understood by this new faith, would take Hellenistic religion to a very different place than the spirit-concepts found among the mini-religions of the Indian subcontinent, which Westerners describe by the collective misnomer of *Hinduism*.

Spirit in Biblical Context

Interestingly, the Old and New Testaments chose similar words for the concept of spirit. The Hebrew *ruach* is roughly equivalent to the Greek *pneuma*; both mean "wind, breath, and, by extension, a life-giving element." [8]

It is likely some ancients quite literally believed that the wind stirring in the treetops was the very breath of God, the Divine Spirit passing overhead. However, most biblical descriptions of God's spirit as breath or breeze must have been poetic license not unlike these words from a well-known hymn:

> This is my Father's world: He shines in all that's fair;
> In the rustling grass I hear him pass,
> He speaks to me everywhere. [9]

Three Modes: Creative, Inspirational, Communal

Hebrew scripture describes three modes as movements of the Spirit. First, there is the *creative* aspect. God's presence and power can be awesome, as in Genesis 1:2 and Ezekiel 37:1-10. Spirit also manifests as *inspiration* in Old Testament passages. This mode breaks through as prophetic utterances, wisdom literature, and courageous acts by heroes-- Joshua, Gideon, and David--empowered by divine prompting. Finally, there is a *communal* presence of Spirit among the people of Israel. Some biblical authors described a unique destiny Israel had among nations and a singular status as the platform from which the Messiah would address the world. God's spirit (read: inspiration) may depart from individuals like King Saul or Eli the Priest because of their disobedience, but God can never renounce his pledge to love Israel. [10]

Of course, "Israel" is not just a religio-cultural group but the whole body of humanity. Thus later prophets would cry that Israel must become "a light to the gentiles," a prophecy which, Christians believe, came true in the life and teaching of Jesus Christ. It must be noted before we go further that Old Testament writers, although virtually unanimous in describing God as spirit, were not at all convinced that humans shared this spiritual nature.

The idea of a disembodied spirit is totally foreign to Hebrew thinking; most of the OT passages which are translated with the English word *soul*, for example, could just as easily read *life force*. This difference surfaces abruptly in the Hebrew view of life after death.

For most of the OT period, few Israelites believed in life after death. When Hellenistic Jewish thinkers, under pressure from Greek-dominated culture, began to tinker with the idea of personal survival, the model they built bore no resemblance to the Platonic idea of life after death as a disembodied spirit. Hebrew thought has usually held that life and bodily existence go hand-in-hand. Liberal-thinking Pharisees in the days of Jesus believed in life after death, but they taught a doctrine of bodily resurrection to eternal life, not immortality as a soul or spirit. It was the only option ancient Judaism allowed.

New Name for God

New Testament authors carry over most of the Hebrew ideas about God's Spirit. Christian innovation on Jewish thought begins when NT writers start describing "Holy Spirit" as the activity of both the Father and the Son. We find this in Paul's letter to Galatia:

> And because you are sons, God has sent the Spirit of his Son into our hearts, crying, 'Abba! Father!' So through God you are no longer a slave but a son, and if a son then an heir.[11]

Paul uses the word pneuma (spirit) several ways, but he usually speaks of Spirit as a power which is available to everyone (Romans 8:6, 8:13; I Corinthians 2:10, 3:16; etc.). If Luke's account of the Sermon at Mars Hill is accurate (Acts 17:22-31), Paul quotes two Hellenistic philosophers to show that we "live and move and have our being" in God's Spirit, "For we are his offspring." Quite an advanced concept for first century Christianity. These two quotes taken in context seem to move toward understanding Spirit as the Reality undergirding all existence. Is this a hint of Platonism?

Probably not. Or if it is, then it probably isn't Paul but Luke speaking. Paul leaned more toward the Stoic metaphysic than the Platonist, although he was not above flavoring his messages to suit the tastes of his target audience. True Christian Platonism will come two centuries later, funneled through people like Clement and Origen.

However, Paul is unhesitant about the benefits we can receive from Spirit. More about that later.

Looking at the four canonical gospels—admittedly written after Paul, probably by his supporters and opponents—Jesus sometimes regards Spirit as equal to God the Father. This is especially apparent in the episode of his baptism (Mark 1:10). Other times the gospels refer to Spirit as the life-force within each person (Mark 14:38, Luke 23:26), and still other verses show Spirit as the empowering divine presence within the believers (John 3:6, 6:63, 7:39, 14:17). This clip-and-paste selection suggests that the New Testament authors were neither certain what Spirit meant nor in agreement on what part this concept should play in the emerging Christian faith. Very early they began calling an aspect of God's activity the work of Holy Spirit, which quickly became the Holy Spirit and acquired distinct characteristics.

Hebrew Scripture refers to God's holy spirit twice (Ps. 51:11, Isa. 63:10), but both are descriptive phrases much like "God's justice and great mercy" or "God's steadfast love." In the Hebrew Bible "holy spirit" is adjectival, never a noun. For the OT authors, God *has* a holy spirit; in the NT, God *sends* the Holy Spirit.

The difference is crucial for theology. OT texts lend almost no support to the doctrine of the Trinity, but NT authors use Holy Spirit as a proper noun. This new name for God gives Christianity a whole new way of looking at the Divine and prepares us for refinements which will come later, when the Church begins to see that God is the Holy Spirit.

Holiness Is Wholeness

To understand what "Holy Spirit" means requires a brief review of *holiness* in Jewish and Christian scripture. Fortunately, like spirit, the idea of holiness is virtually identical in both Testaments. In *Harper's Bible Dictionary:*

> HOLINESS, a term in Hebrew probably meaning separate from the ordinary or profane. Also in Hebrew and Greek "holy" implies connection with God or the divine. Thus God is holy and people, things, and actions may be holy by association with God. Holiness may also include the ideas of consecration to God and purity

from what is evil and improper.[12]

The Revealing Word emphasizes the connection with God:

> Holiness is wholeness in Spirit, mind, and body. In this
> state of consciousness man is aware of the all-pervading
> glory of God.[13]

Since mysticism is the identification of self with and movement toward the Divine, Charles Fillmore identified holiness with awareness of "the all-pervading glory of God." Awareness is all that is required by this definition to achieve holiness. Getting that kind of awareness is the obvious difficulty. However, the two definitions require a follow-up question about dualism. In many religious systems—for example, Orthodox Judaism, traditional Christianity, Islam and Baha'i—*holiness* means the association with something divine, a *Holy* Other that is *wholly* Other. This also usually means avoiding contact with people or things which are considered ritually unclean or ethically improper by the standards of the particular religion.

For the mystical Fillmore, *holiness is consciousness;* God is not *wholly* Other, existing beyond space-and-time as a separate, Supreme Being but dwells within everything and everyone as a singular, all-pervasive Presence and Power. If God is the very structure of reality, as Paul Tillich proposed, goodness and holiness must lie at the heart of all things. Individuals may distort that goodness by using their divine power of free will, nevertheless all mortals "live and move and have our being" in God's Spirit, "For we are his offspring."

Some might be skeptical about finding holiness through avoiding evil. Such a negative concept says nothing about what holiness is, unless the definition of holiness means simply to refrain from sin. Mystical Christianity has usually emphasized holiness as wholeness, completeness. Human beings are more than flesh-and-blood creatures with a body and mind: we are also spiritual. There is something within every person that tells of our kinship to God. As we flow with the divine will, we experience wholeness. When moving against our higher nature, brokenness and estrangement results.

This is an element in the classical definition of *sin.* Paul Tillich, himself no mystic, frequently identified *sin as separation* from neighbor, loved ones, and God. But one could argue that separation occurs in mind, not in reality. How can anyone really be separated from an Omnipotent/Omnipresent God? For the Metaphysical Christian, holiness means identification of the person with God's intentions for us. This comes close to the definition of holiness as "connection with God" or "consecration to God," but lacks the negative implications of "avoiding evil."

Purity: More than Avoiding Evil

Harpers Bible Dictionary also mentioned *purity*, a concept closely related to holiness. Again, this term is frequently defined in the negative—*"Here's what to avoid..."* rather than *"Here's what you should strive for..."* when seeking purity. This odd tendency to see goodness as a double negative (lack of evil-doing) is not limited to the Judeo-Christian mythos. Listen to an abridged version of the seemingly endless "Negative Confession" found on the walls of the tomb of Nu, a high official in Eighteenth Dynasty (1570-1305 B.C.) Egypt:

Homage to thee, O Great God (Osiris) Lord of Double Maati, I have come to thee, O my Lord, I have brought myself hither that I may behold thy beauties.
I have expelled wickedness for thee.
I have not done evil to mankind.
I have not oppressed the members of my family.
I have not wrought evil in the place of right and truth.
I have no knowledge of worthless men.
I have not brought forward my name for exultation.
I have not ill-treated servants.
I have not belittled a god.
I have not defrauded the oppressed one of his property.
I have not given the order for murder to be done for me.
I have not inflicted pain upon mankind.
I have not committed fornication.
I have not encroached upon the fields of others.
I have not carried away the milk from the mouths of children.
I am pure! I am pure! I am pure![14]

I cannot help wondering whom Nu was trying to convince—the gods or his wife? His attitude is not confined to the ancient world. How many people do we know who define holiness and purity as non-action, not breaking certain behavioral taboos?

Pastor James Dyson was minister of the Community Church of Moscow, Idaho in the early 1970's when I was attending the University of Idaho. He liked to tell the story about the man who came up to him and said: "Preacher, I'm trying to live a pure, holy life. I don't smoke; I don't drink; I don't cuss; I don't play cards and I don't dance." Rev. Dyson replied: "Congratulations. You've got a lot in common with a *rock.* Now, tell me—what do you do?"

Purity is more than avoiding wrong, or humanity would all be better off comatose. Language gets in the way here, because sciences speaks of "impurities" in a formula, and people think of freshly fallen snow as "pure." And there is a programmed, almost Pavlovian response to people of my generation when we see a bar of Ivory Soap: *ninety-nine and forty-four one hundredth percent pure...*[15]

Sacrifices to Achieve Holiness / Purity

Perhaps the ancients are still with us in many ways. Biblical Hebrews believed in a ritual purity which included washings, cleansing, and proper handling of food. These customs survive today in observant Jewish homes. In biblical times, women were required to perform special acts of purification after menstruating and after childbirth.

There was an intricate system of Hebrew taboos which rendered a person "unclean" (impure) which then required other actions to reinstate the alienated one to purity. To enter the house of a gentile, to touch the dead, or contact swine or a leper—any number of events in the daily life of a first century Jew could render him impure and require ritual acts of cleansing. Sacrifice was about more than recovering lost purity. Cross-culturally, systems of animal sacrifice attempted to maintain, recover, or establish the balance between heaven and earth, the gods and humankind, the individual worshipper and some form of super-natural power, often divinely indifferent to human plight. Our ancestors believed offering sacrifice of grain or blood kept the seasons on track, held enemies at bay, augured a long and healthy life, and granted that most precious of divine gifts, increased fertility of field, flock, and family.

The Hebrews had specialized their sacrificial system to depend on taboo. Without sacrifice there was no forgiveness of offense against the divine, which they called *sin*. But, in Hebraic thought, without sin (violation of taboo) who needed sacrifice? If a person broke a taboo or committed some kind of offense, the Israelites believed there was a blood-curse upon him. Something literally had to die, shedding blood to lift the curse. It was an objective transaction, and they saw it functioning as immutable law. If the offender did not provide a sacrificial animal to die, he would pay the price himself.

During sacrificial worship the priest, as representative of the god, often placed one hand on the head of the sinner and the other hand on the sacrificial animal thus transferring the guilt from offender to his blood offering. The priest or his assistant then ritually killed the animal and, depending on what type of an offering it was, burned its blood along with other inedible parts of the carcass. Since in most cases the priests kept at least some of the meat offered on the altar, taboo was good business for the clergy. Small wonder there were so many possible offenses!

This type of ceremony can be found in the history of peoples around the world and is still practiced in remote locations where angry spirits must be placated. Early Christians, searching for euphemisms to describe the great sacrificial offering of Jesus upon the cross, succumbed to the metaphor of animal sacrifice, so that by the end of the first century the author of John's gospel could proclaim: "Behold, the Lamb of God, who takes away the sin of the world!"[16] How literally the early church took this prescription is a matter for scholarly debate. But the imagery worked cross-culturally, since virtually everyone offered blood sacrifices to this or that god. One can almost hear a polytheistic Greek or Roman saying, "So, you're saying Jesus died as a sacrificial offering for everybody? That's a little weird, but I get it." The majority of Christian communions eventually accepted blood atonement as a doctrinal position, although they continue to differ on what his sacrifice meant and how Jesus took sin away.[17]

To the metaphysical Christian, *holiness* is not something poured into the believer from outside but an ever-increasing awareness of the Christ within. Several NT authors provide theological support for this viewpoint. Paul wrote to the church at Corinth:

> Or do you not know that your body is a temple of the
> Holy Spirit within you, which you have from God, and
> that you are not your own.[18]

However, the meaning of this passage is ambiguous. Is it about gratitude for God's Holy Spirit, which has been poured into the believer, or a divine spirit welling up from within? NT passages often describe the Holy Spirit "descending" from on high, taking up residence in bodily temples only after the believer has accepted Jesus Christ. Paul becomes vague on this point, as the above quote shows. The difference is not sophistry but a fundamental variance in the way people look at the work of the Holy Spirit. Do all human beings—perhaps all sentient beings— have God's spirit within them? Or must God send his Spirit in a special way to those who achieve some sort of select status by virtue of their correct beliefs and practices? Is the goal of spiritual growth to open ourselves to the inflow of the Holy Spirit, or to discover the Spirit within us and let it shine forth? I call this the *Let It In / Let It Out Controversy*, and the implications of this dispute require a little unscrambling before pressing on to a fuller understanding of the Holy Spirit. [19]

"Let It In / Let It Out" Controversy

Traditional thinking has pictured the Holy Spirit as an alien power which benignly takes possession of human nature and either causes us to do good things or opens us to divine blessings. How else could the dichotomy between human sinfulness and an in-dwelling Spirit of God be overcome? The problem is anthropological. If humanity is inherently bad, any hope for improvement must come from God. Some theologies insist God must prepare the soul to accept his blessings by giving the gift of faith. The term for this is *Prevenient Grace.*

> GRACE, PREVENIENT, is, according to Roman
> Catholic teaching, the supernatural power that quickens
> and assists the will to have faith. In Protestantism, it is
> often used more generally to refer to the grace preceding
> man's decision but is not always identified with a
> specific quickening power.[20]

Such a view makes it impossible to conclude humanity possesses any indwelling divinity to let out; only "Let It In" works here. If God must make us willing to accept faith before we have faith, all talk about the divine within becomes sheer nonsense. Since much of traditional Protestantism rests on this idea of Prevenient grace, built squarely on a foundation of Calvinist notions about the total depravity of humanity, the mystical vision of union with God has seemed far-fetched indeed. When Hindus and New Thought Christians speak of the indwelling divinity of all people, the idea sometimes sounds blasphemous to listeners brought up in Western Christianity. Historically, most churches have seemed to enjoy stressing the sinfulness of human nature and our total inability to do anything to improve ourselves without massive infusions of divine power from beyond.

However, taking a cue from Jesus Christ, some progressive Christians find the whole idea of human depravity to be slightly depraved. What kind of person can look into the eyes of a toddler and say with conviction: "You are born a miserable sinner and have no power to grow closer to God without his pulling you toward his against your own perverted will"? Most people have known individuals who epitomize malevolence and others who radiate saintly vibes, but the majority of species Homo sapiens fall somewhere between the extremes. Whenever life experience crashes a theological system, it has identified a theology in need of repair.

Jesus-the-Christ reveals a flesh and blood man who plausibly knew his Oneness with God yet called humanity his brothers and sisters. If Jesus had the Divine Spirit and humanity is his kinfolk, people can reasonably assume the same Spirit dwells in everyone. Why else did Jesus continue to exhort his followers to do what he had done? If men and women are incapable of self-directed goodness, his admonition in the Sermon on the Mount ("Be perfect, even as your Father in heaven is perfect...") amounts to nothing but divine teasing.

Besides scriptural and existential evidence, Christian history abounds with individuals who looked within and discovered the radiance of God's Holy Spirit. Spiritual seekers like George Fox, one of the founders of the Society of Friends (Quakers), believed that each of us has an "inner light" which guides us. Mystics like Meister Eckhart, who saw God and humanity as essentially one, so godliness depends on willingness to receive what we already have. Eckhart wrote:

> The authorities in the schools ask often how it is possible
> for the soul to know God. It is not from God's strictness
> that he requires so much of man, but rather from his
> kindness that he expects the soul to progress to that point
> where it may receive much, as he gives so much to it. No
> one ought to think that it is hard to attain this, however
> hard it sounds and however hard it may be at first... God
> is always ready but we are not ready. God is near to us
> but we are far from him. God is within; we are without.[21]

One resolution to the "Let It In / Let It Out" controversy might be to find a middle path. Certainly, any conceivable God must to be "out there" in the Universe as well as "in here" within the individual. Most religions show the Divine as working, whispering, motivating, comforting, commanding or nudging all Creation toward a set of exalted ideals. But God must also dwell within every sentient being, or the gap between finite human consciousness and Infinite Goodness becomes impossibly vast.

Some theologians do hold this latter position, insisting that only an infinite sacrifice by God in Jesus Christ could bridge the infinite gap. Even if that were the case, the problem remains: How does finite humanity avail itself of an infinite sacrifice unless we are somehow part of the program, somehow related to Divinity itself? Programming Jesus into the Godhead doesn't solve the equation; it merely puts more distance between people and Jesus. However, since Jesus claimed kinship both to humanity and God, one could assert that he offered a handy link to divinity precisely because he is *not* special. Jesus was a normal human being, which means every one of us has a divine nature. In such a viewpoint, Jesus was an example of humanity's true nature. (More about Christology in Chapter 7.)

The middle path would also accept both God-out-there and God-within. Sometimes I become aware of the presence and power of God in the world—watching the sun set over the great, blue sea; gawking into the Grand Canyon; ambling through a mountain forest and catching glimpses of snowy peaks from wildflower meadows. Other times I go within and hear that still, small voice. Why must theology opt for an either/or? Why not "let God in" when I experience the Divine beyond myself, and "let God out" when I contact the Inner Light? A theology which strongly emphasizes God as One Presence/One Power can offer a formula for prayer to God beyond oneself. (Personally, I have no problem with my part of God talking to the Spirit filling the cosmos.)

A survey of systematic theology allows insufficient space in to discuss such problems at length. However, raising questions is often as important as providing answers, especially if the question is vital and neglected. As metaphysical Christianity continues to grow and expand its agenda to include greater emphasis on legitimate theology, other thinkers doubtless will find themselves pressed to untangle complex controversies like "Let It In / Let It Out."[22] One of the more satisfying aspects of identifying knotty new problems is the ability to step professorially aside and allow the resultant cognitive dissonance to bedevil generations to come. It is also a sneaky way of confessing an inability to answers all the questions and to invite more participants to share the joyful headaches of systematic theology.

So far this study has looked at the concepts of spirit, holiness and purity, i.e., does God dwell within, or stand aloof? Along the way it has touched on themes such as sacrificial worship, theological anthropology, and the attitude of biblical and traditional mystics toward in-dwelling Spirit. Now the discussion turns to the main event. What is the *Holy Spirit*? What does the Holy Spirit do, and why is it essential to understand Spirit before discussing the Father and the son in a study of the Trinity? A brief look at the Gifts of the Spirit and the Fruit of the Spirit as taught by the Apostle Paul will complete the survey, hopefully showing how all this fits together in metaphysical theology.

What Does *Holy Spirit* Mean?

Harper's Bible Dictionary defines the Holy Spirit as "the mysterious power or presence of God in nature or with individuals and communities, inspiring them with qualities they would not otherwise possess."[23] Note the traditional position—if the Holy Spirit did not inspire individuals, they would not otherwise possess positive qualities of the Spirit. This definition walks a fence line separating the two sides of the "Let It In / Let It Out" controversy. Nowhere does the *HBD* say whether the Holy Spirit comes from outside or from within. A foreign element in our natures, to be sure. But does it well up from inside us or crash over us like a divine avalanche?

Charles Fillmore is more helpful, but he, too, very carefully avoids pontifications about Spirit always coming from within or without. Fillmore was no fence straddle, in fact he frequently leaped at the chance to take sides in a debate. Listen to Fillmore's delicate handling of the controversy:

> SPIRIT, HOLY. The source of all manifestation is in mind...The Holy Ghost, or Holy Spirit, is the law of God in action; and in that action it appears as having individuality. From this the Hebrews got their concept of the personal, tribal God... The Holy Spirit may also be defined as the whole Spirit of God, and can be known by man only through his spiritual nature. The prayer of the soul alone in its upper room (state of high spiritual aspiration) brings down the Holy Ghost. (Parenthesis original) [24]

Comparing the above to Fillmore's mini-treatise in the *Revealing Word*, we find the fence-walking continues:

> HOLY SPIRIT—The activity of God in a universal sense. The moving force in the Universe as a whole. The Spirit is the infinite "breath" of God, the life essence of Being... To be "filled with the Holy Spirit" is to realize the activities of Spirit in individual consciousness. The quickening of a man by the Holy Spirit is peculiar to each individual and must be experienced to be understood. [25]

Did Fillmore recognize the Holy Spirit as active both outside and inside the individual? God in the world contacts God in the consciousness to become "God with us." *Harper's Bible Dictionary* and Fillmore's *Metaphysical Dictionary of the Bible* identify the Holy Spirit as a power of God which cannot be understood separate from divinity. There is a going-forth and a calling-forth aspect to the work of the Spirit, each roughly paralleling one side of the controversy. God goes forth into the world and actively seeks humanity. When people discover God, it is like finding a long-lost relative Who calls forth something from within their deepest selves. Metaphysical Christianity defines this activity as the Holy Spirit. In a very real way, the Holy Spirit is kinetic divinity—God in action in the world and within ourselves. This is a working definition and certainly not an all-encompassing one. But at least it allows us to proceed to the second question.

What Does the Holy Spirit Do?

Scattered bits of this question have already been considered. God sends *the* Holy Spirit, or God comes to humanity *as* Sprit in holiness, encountered at whatever level of spiritual/emotional growth required. Most Christian traditions say the HS also nurtures, comforts, and encourages. It is that still, small voice of calm, but also God in action, displayed preeminently in the life of Jesus Christ. This flexible understanding allows a new resolution to an old argument in the Church, about whether the Holy Spirit "proceeds" from both the Father and the Son.

A Metaphysical Christian interpretation of the Trinity must begin with the premise that all reality exists within God, a fundamental union of everything, One Presence/One Power (OP²), which is the expression of eternal, omnipotent Spirit.[26] The Son (i.e., the Christ, the Buddha consciousness, or whatever the Indwelling Divinity may be called) provides a perfect example of the Creative Divine (Father-Mother God), by which the Son-within-us (or daughter-within-us) is able to recognize kinship to divinity, and know the oneness of Spirit. Without this divinity in expression—the Holy Spirit—the activities of God remain inscrutable. Holy Spirit is the cosmos outpicturing, the knowledge of how everything works, and the love glue which holds ontological reality together.

Those who haven't known love experientially, or suffered the heartbreak of a dysfunctional relationship, may be skeptical about trustworthy love when it finally appears. The same could be said about the gifts of God. Christians have generally found in Jesus Christ a Wayshower to divine love; looking at that one solitary life provides the believer with something profoundly metaphysical, a glimpse into what God is like. It is much easier to recognize universal in-dwelling divinity when it outpictures in the specific life and teachings of Jesus.

Can God do anything in the real world, or does Spirit just deliver uplifting guidance? Any divine power incapable of action in the concrete world is little better than no god at all. Others might say that to deliver "uplifting guidance" *is doing something*. Spirit's primary job is to quicken awareness, which releases power of the divine-human nature within every person. That alone is enough.

Many religionists worldwide have long believed God's activity exceeds moral example and encouragement; God is not a great Cheerleader in the sky. However, this does not necessarily mean God operates through supernatural activity. There are natural ways for God to act: pointing humans to discover that which empowers the greater good; sending people to assist those in need; making connections that somehow work things out for the best; and standing beside the individual to offer the strength of prayer when disaster happens, as it most certainly does, even to the most spiritual person alive. The words of the Shepherd's Psalm have offer countless generations the assurance of that kind of divine presence.

> The Lord is my shepherd, I shall not want.
> He makes me lie down in green pastures;
> he leads me beside still waters;
> he restores my soul.
> He leads me in right paths
> for his name's sake.
> Even though I walk through the darkest valley,
> I fear no evil;
> for you are with me.[27]

Note the active verbs. God *makes me lie down, leads, restores.* Christian faith points to this kind of nonviolent leadership. "In the presence of my enemies," God acts with a different kind of power than the world normally understands. People want their heroes to destroy the bad guys and emerge rich and famous. But the Judeo-Christian Scripture shows a paradoxical model of triumph through suffering and death. The nation or Israel suffered terribly at the hands of its enemies. Hebrew Bible tells how the bad guys sacked the Temple of the Jews in the sixth century BCE. Even Jesus failed miserably by modern standards. When Jesus was executed as a criminal, his friends scattered while the executioners gambled for his clothing. Jesus died penniless, friendless, and defeated.

As an aside, it's worth noting that for centuries Christians mistakenly blamed the Jews for the death of Jesus. In 2011, although way overdue and somewhat condescending, Pope Benedict absolved the Jewish community of responsibility in Jesus' death. Benedict's belated *mea culpa* brought the Catholic Church into line with the biblical narrative. The gospels clearly show Jesus wasn't killed by the Jews. It was the Italians. [28]

Even though the chapter ended badly, the story continued for both Jesus and Israel. The survival of Judaism through thousands of years of oppression shows God did not abandon the "Chosen" people. For Christians, who were at first a sect of Jewish reformers, Christmas showed hope for people of all nations; Good Friday seemed to dash that hope at the foot of a blood-soaked cross. But Easter broke the hold of death and proved that inclusive love is the only power which endures. Conventional models of power—armies, physical prowess, wealth, political clout—are shadows passing in the night. Nonresistance to the flow of God's goodness is the only real power, the only lasting power.

The Holy Spirit prompts people to look for the footsteps of Divinity in the disasters of human existence. The power of God protects, not from pain and suffering, but from the most terrible fate of all—futility. Some Eastern religions, like Buddhism and Hinduism, believe if someone gains the whole world but fails to learn life's lessons well, the soul shall be reborn to repeat the process again and again until the lesson is learned. Spirit is the Great Educator, the Counselor promised by Isaiah, the Guide Who continuously points toward the best, most expeditious path up the mountain to Christ consciousness. God is able to do this so subtly that it has been going on for eons and yet many people still wonder if there is a divine power at all.

Miracles?

Does God intervene in time-and-space to perform miracles?

Miracles, as understood in the pre-scientific worldview of the biblical authors, require interventions in time and space; the Divine Power violates the laws of science to bring about it Will. Yet, wouldn't a little prior planning make the *zap-crash-boom* of miraculous intervention unnecessarily crude? Surely, God doesn't need to break carefully made rules by which the Universe operates. Some might argue that events which seem miraculous to humans merely show God works in a natural way not yet comprehended by science. Sorcery and science are indistinguishable to the prescientific mind. Science fiction writer Arthur Clarke said in his oft-quoted Third Law, *"Any sufficiently advanced technology is indistinguishable from magic."*[29]

The Metaphysical Christian movement has believed from its inception that God's activities are orderly if properly understood. However, life experience brings many people to a contradictory realization, i.e., though illogical and unscientific, miracles happen anyway. Or, at the very least, there are things in the cosmos more wonderful than anyone could imagine. (Think Saturn's rings and Voyager.) Whether a powerful healing demonstration which confounds the experts or a simple coincidence that brings a special blessing, anyone who has experienced a miracle knows the mystery of life cannot be contained in any theological or scientific system. A popular poster in the 1970s, drawn by Sister Mary Corita Kent, quoted the Italian author Ugo Betti:

> *To believe in God is to know that all the rules are fair and that there will be wonderful surprises.* [30]

The Holy Spirit is also called the *Comforter*, the One Who nudges people toward wholeness/holiness. The future lies with God. Whenever people grasp that concept in deeper, more meaningful ways, the Holy Spirit has been at work in their lives. It is interesting that this is the manifestation of the Spirit which Jesus explicitly promises to send--the Comforter, God's Presence and Power, to walk with humanity regardless of the circumstance.

Spiritual Benefits: *Fruit & Gifts*

The Apostle Paul listed two kinds of spiritual benefits given by God. The first category appears Galatians 5, usually designated *Fruit of the Spirit.* Paul liked to draw up lists of good and bad qualities to illustrate his teaching points. Perhaps his best-known litany of positives and negatives appears in the "Hymn to Love" in I Corinthians 13.

> Love is patient; love is kind; love is not envious or boastful or arrogant or rude. It does not insist on its own way; it is not irritable or resentful; it does not rejoice in wrongdoing, but rejoices in the truth. It bears all things, believes all things, hopes all things, endures all things. Love never ends.[31]

The Apostle's zeal often crescendos when listing the no-no's. In the Galatians passage, Paul can only think of nine spiritual fruits to contrast with a shopping list of fifteen "works of the flesh," which he ends with the Greek equivalent of *"and lots more!"* Paul relished the salacious side of human nature, which he could gleefully castigate.

Fortunately, he did not dwell exclusively on the negatives but moved to accentuate the positive. Here's the complete list of bad and good qualities in Galatians 5:

> Now the works of the flesh are obvious: fornication, impurity, licentiousness, idolatry, sorcery, enmities, strife, jealousy, anger, quarrels, dissensions, factions, envy, drunkenness, carousing, and things like these. I am warning you, as I warned you before: those who do such things will not inherit the kingdom of God. By contrast, the fruit of the Spirit is love, joy, peace, patience, kindness, generosity, faithfulness, gentleness, and self-control. There is no law against such things.[32]

The second list, Fruit of the Spirit, are worth plucking from the pile to review separately: Love, Joy, Peace, Patience, Kindness, Generosity, Faithfulness, Gentleness, Self-Control. Within these words—hastily ticked off by a ticked-off Paul in the midst of a battle with opponents in the Galatian church—there lurks the ingredients for a comprehensive moral theology. Conceivably, Christians might change their lives and make the world a better place by centering themselves in thoughts guided by Paul's basket of spiritual fruit.

Fruit of the Spirit differ from *Gifts of the Spirit* in that every Christian is expected to harvest spiritual fruit, but the gifts are special talents awarded to various persons in varying degrees. Paul was not as certain about how many gifts there were; he listed four different groups of special talents. Some scholars suggest that since the lists are not identical they are not intended to exhaust the possibilities for other gifts.[33]

Speaking in Unknown Tongues

A word must be said about the well-know and sometimes divisive phenomenon of glossolalia, or *speaking in unknown tongues* as it is popularly called. People who experience glossolalia describe themselves as possessed by the Holy Spirit. They utter strange sounds which must be interpreted for others to understand. Charismatic utterances are not strictly a Christian phenomenon. There is scriptural evidence that praying or chanting in unknown sounds was practiced as early as the time of the Judges (I Samuel 10:9-13).

Cross-cultural studies show that various kinds of ecstatic awakening are practiced in nearly every human society. These may include chanting, dancing, and possession by good or bad spirits, vision quests, or ritual of sympathetic magic. Doubtless those within Christian Pentecostal circles would be outraged by listing the "gift of tongues" with these other practices, but anthropologists of religion rightly study human behavior and categorize religious acts according to functional similarities. Since it is not within the charter of the social sciences to pass judgment on the appropriateness of a particular religious practice, just to study the behavior as a phenomenon. For the anthropologist, ecstatic experiences of charismatic Christians and tribal rituals of pre-industrial societies fall under the same scrutiny.

Occasionally, speaking in tongues has resulted in a kind of charismatic elitism within the church, when those who have the gift express doubts about the salvation of those who do not. If one reads chapters twelve through fourteen of Paul's First Letter to the Corinthians in sequence, it is almost impossible to draw any other conclusion than the Apostle Paul wrote his sequence—including the Hymn to Love—to deal with divisive elitism caused by glossolalia in the first generation of the Church. His solution identified different gifts, given to each as a "manifestation of the Spirit for the common good." And therefore, "If I speak with the tongues of men and of angels, but have not love, I am a noisy gong or a clanging cymbal."

Middle Ground: Active Meditation

Does the gift of tongues actually represent people possessed by the Holy Spirit, enabling them to "speak with the tongues of men and of angels"? Some Christians say glossolalia was a gift of the Apostolic Church only; others declare it active today. Studies are inconclusive, and much subjectivity is involved. The phenomenon cuts across socio-cultural lines and appears in churches from the predominantly black Church of God in Christ, to the predominantly white Assemblies of God. The largest Christian denomination in the world, the multi-cultural Roman Catholic Church, has a significant plurality of charismatic Catholics within ranks of laity and clergy alike.

> While the Roman Catholic presence has always been strong in much of South and Central America, the current trend in all of the majority world (or 2/3's world, what used to be known as the "third world" but now holds around 2/3's of the world's population) is that there is an unprecedented growth among the charismatic and pentecostal movements.[34]

People *experience* the gift of tongues, they don't simply read about it. Because speaking in tongues is a subjective event, no definitive study can establish the validity or the frivolity of glossolalia. For someone who has uttered unknown sounds in private prayer or public worship, the outpouring is self-validating. Consequently, in any critical consideration of the gift of tongues, theology merges metaphysical and psychological speculation. This is risky but unavoidable. As a religio-cultural phenomenon, the charismatic movement is too important to ignore.

A possible answer to glossolalia as a religious phenomenon is to see it as a form of *nonverbally articulated prayer* in which the cognitive processes detaches from vocalization during the act of praise. In this explanation, speaking in tongues is more like active meditation, like chanting a mantra, rather than possession of the worshipper by a benign supernatural agency.

The advantages of this view are many. First, it complies with the evidence of scientific studies, which seem to show glossolalia as a series of unconnected sounds rather than an organized language. Second, it does not belittle the gift, since spiritual benefits from such active, non-intellectual prayer have been well documented in studies of Eastern meditation forms. Also, this view offers a middle ground between those who insist that tongues is a gift from God and others who flatly reject the notion that it is a language of men and/or angels. This offers a middle view which says glossolalia can be a gift of the Spirit without being an angelic tongue. Finally, the idea that tongues is a form of active meditation removes the gift from the fringes of the occult, so people who fear loss of control or some other negative impact on their spiritual life are more likely to try nonverbal prayer.

Ancient traditions of chanting or singing to prevent the intellect from interfering with our feeling faculties show there is nothing to fear. Long ago King Saul "prophesied" with the explicit blessing of God's spokesperson, Samuel. Ecstatic utterance is firmly rooted in the Judeo-Christian heritage.

Glossolalia as meditation does not completely solve the old problems of elitism and loss of control, but this approach can offer a compromise that points in a spiritually healthy direction. Metaphysical Christians have traditionally believed many avenues of spiritual growth await the seeker. Marcus Bach, described his "Holy Spirit baptism" in the book *Questions on the Quest*: "It was, as I recall, a pure exclamation of adoration, and I am willing to let it go at that."[35]

Amen, Brother Bach. Amen.

Mystery & Worship

The Holy Spirit is an exciting concept with vast possibilities for theological inquiry and metaphysical speculation. The sacred intellect within each person allows access to profound insights about the workings of God and the mystery of life. However, great religious thinkers have always insisted the deepest insights into the Spirit come from a life lived in prayerful communion with the *God-within* and the *God-in-the-world*. In a sense the animatists correctly identify spirit as divine power pulsating through the cosmos.

Those who want to open themselves to this spiritual power (the "let it in" party) rightly yearn for God's grace to come upon them and raise them to new life in Christ-consciousness. But those who have discovered God in the world could scarcely have done so if God had not first stood within them to point the way, and in this respect those who teach "prevenient grace" also have a piece of the truth. The mystery of life and intelligence originates from Holy Spirit both within/without, pointing to the underlying unity of all things and hinting of God the Good, omnipotent. Ruth Furbee caught the sense of this eternal mystery in a poem simply named but majestically spoken.

Worship

God made my cathedral
Under the stars;
He gave my cathedral
Trees for spires;
He hewed me an altar
In the depth of a hill;
He gave me a hymnal
A rock-bedded rill;
He voiced me a sermon
Of heavenly light
In the beauty around me--
The calmness of night;
And I felt as I knelt
On the velvet-like sod
I had supped of the Spirit
In the Temple of God.[36]

CHECK YOUR KNOWLEDGE

1. Explain the following: *glossolalia, holiness, animatism, pantheism, monism, and pneuma.*

2. How do the *Fruit of the Spirit* differ from *Gifts of the Spirit* in St. Paul's writings?

3. If someone broke a serious taboo in ancient Israel, what had to happen in order for the "blood-curse" to be lifted? How does this memory affect New Testament authors' imagery when they wrote about Jesus Christ?

4. What is the "Let It In / Let It Out" controversy?

5. Why is it essential to understand Spirit first when studying the Trinity?

6. The author suggests *glossolalia* is a form of *active meditation.* What does this mean, and how is it a middle way between two extremes?

QUESTIONS FOR DISCUSSION

1. The author suggests that Greco-Roman polytheism might have grown into a Hindu-like faith. How did Christianity prevent that? What would Western culture look like today if Jesus Christ had not come?

2. Do you believe speaking in tongues is a real gift of the Holy Spirit today?

3. On which side of the *"Let It In / Let It Out"* controversy do you find yourself?

4. What is *purity* and how can it be achieved in a secular age? Should you strive for purity?

5. Does the *"Holy Spirit"* remain a meaningful term, or have you abandoned it?

6. What evidences of the Holy Spirit have appeared in your life?

- 7 -

DIVINE MIND

God as Father-Mother-Creator

Ineffable is the union of man and God in every act of the soul. The simplest person who in his integrity worships God, becomes God; yet for ever and ever the influx of this better and universal self is new and unsearchable. It inspires awe and astonishment. How dear, how soothing to man, arises the idea of God, peopling the lonely place, effacing the scars of our mistakes and disappointments. When we have broken our god of tradition and ceased from our god of rhetoric, then may God fire the heart with his presence.

Ralph Waldo Emerson[1]

Trinity is a compound noun, consisting of three interlocking concepts. Christians across multiple faith traditions tend to believe that each "person" of the Triune God must be understood in reference to the other two. Even a mystic like Charles Fillmore deferred to this ancient formula when elucidating his metaphysical system, although he reserved the right to reinterpret each *persona* of the classic Trinity in highly creative—some might say wildly speculative—ways. The current analysis of the Trinity presented by this book reserves the same right to rethink the faith critically. Beginning with the Holy Spirit, because *Spirit* is the basic category to understand all things divine, the descriptive-prescriptive process now turns to the first person of the Trinity, God as Father-Mother-Creator.

It hardly seems necessary to mention, but let's be very clear: God is not three persons sitting on a cloud in some heavenly dimension. As Catholic feminist scholar and theologian Sister Sandra Schneiders said, "God is more than two men and a bird."[2] The Trinity is a chosen

155

viewpoint, not necessarily identical with absolute reality. Theologian Paul Tillich argued that every word about God must be symbolic, because no language comprehensibly measures the ground of our being. The Trinity is an effective way to represent symbolically that which is impossible to fathom in depth. Other ways of appraising may be equally valid, but for Christians the time-proven symbol for the Omnipotent, Omnipresent God is *Father, Son* and *Holy Spirit*.

The Christian worldview has provided a useful paradigm, but obviously no template works forever, and even long-lasting patterns need continual maintenance or they slip into pious superstitions that no longer speak contemporary language. Reinterpreting the persons of the Trinity marks one way to re-shape a faithful prototype for today.

God: The Central Concept

No attempt will be made to prove God exists, which cannot be done conclusively. This is nothing to lament. God's existence cannot be disproved, either. In fact, a wide assortment of cherished truths cannot be proved or disproved:

> Love is superior to hate.
> Peace is better than war.
> All human lives are of equal worth.

Enlightened people today universally accept these principles, yet no matter how self-evident these sentiments may be, not one of these deeply held beliefs can actually be *proved*. Only scientifically measurable events can be proved or disproved. Someone might demonstrate the overwhelming good sense of love over hate, but that conclusion remains an opinion, not a computable fact. Even science requires a substantial body of supporting evidence, replicated many times, before a fact is established. I can measure the distance from my lips to your ears, but I lack quantifiable tools to determine scientifically whether I should speak words of kindness or anger. Science and the realm of facts must be guided by a moral compass, which operates from wisdom rather than technologically verifiable understanding. Fact-based science shows how to split the atom, but only opinion-based wisdom guides this discovery to peaceful applications. Buddha, Jesus, and Muhammad were not scientists; they were teachers of spiritual truths without which all the technical data in the cosmos becomes helpless to guide humanity.

Great attempts have been made in the past to prove the existence of God, the most famous of these by medieval scholastic Thomas Aquinas. Some people have been convinced, others have not. Napoleon Bonaparte asked one of his top scientists, Pièrre Simon Laplace, where God fit into his cosmological system. Laplace replied: "Sire, I have no need for that hypothesis."[3] Other scholars have found room for faith. The Pew Research Forum discovered that 51% of scientists either believe in God or in some kind of universal Spirit.[4]

This work will not duplicate the effort to prove or disprove God's existence. A spiritual dimension to life, whether it includes a personal God or not—is one of those grand ideas which grasps human consciousness and provides a helpful way of looking daily existence. Besides, if people have no use for God-talk, words will not change their minds. Although expressed in many iterations and cultural variations, *God* is alive and well for billions of people. They believe in the Divine— however understood—because "that hypothesis" works for them. Therefore the goal of this study is to examine various ideas about what God is like, not to validate God's existence. Besides, considering our finite starting point, any human adjudication on God's legitimacy rather quickly begins to sound a little arrogant. We'll begin by stipulating what theologian Charles Hartshorne called *The Divine Relativity*[5] and move on to explore the God-concept with a preliminary definition.

> God, Spirit, is the only presence in the Universe, and is
> the only power. He is in, though, and around all creation
> as its life and s sustaining power.[6]

Considering life from a cosmic perspective might be a fool's errand. Humans know so very little about the Universe; how can anyone speak with certainty about God, which is greater than the cosmos? Chapter 2 looked at a way to organize thinking about life. Everyone has some concept about how the Universe hangs together, even people who seldom think in such grand terms. The question is not "Faith or no faith?" but, "What kind of faith shall we have?" Human beings are irrevocably religious. Even the agnostic trusts the routine of daily life and the healing power of the human body. Faith allows people to deal with the great questions and find answers which permit them to live in a stable mental/emotional worldview.

No Presence / No Power: Atheism

At this writing, to deny the existence of God is still an offense punishable by death in some places.

> In 13 countries around the world, all of them Muslim, people who openly espouse atheism or reject the official state religion of Islam face execution under the law, according to a detailed study issued on Tuesday. And beyond the Islamic nations, even some of the West's apparently most democratic governments at best discriminate against citizens who have no belief in a god and at worst can jail them for offenses dubbed blasphemy, it said. [7]

However, today's resurgence of atheism in the West has transformed this feisty, anti-traditionalist perspective far more socially acceptable on a global scale. Talented authors like Richard Dawkins, Sam Harris and the late Christopher Hitchens—sometimes called "The Unholy Trinity" in the media—have popularized the atheist attack on organized religion. They argue cogently and make a plausible case for skepticism. I frequently assign readings by Sam Harris to students preparing for the ministry, telling the clergy-in-training, "You don't have to agree with their conclusions to benefit from their thinking." Subsequent classroom discussion is usually lively.

Reflect for a moment on the meaning of the word. A-theist, *without god*. Christians were accused of atheism by Romans and Greeks, and with good cause. Followers of Jesus denied the existence of the pagan gods. In fact, everybody is an atheist about something. Few people today believe the Roman deities have any metaphysical reality; Jupiter, Venus, and Neptune are planets, not gods. Most people reading this book would likely agree the "angry god" of Jonathan Edwards does not exist. Jews and Muslims believe in a solitary God; Hindus worship a medley of gods and goddesses.

All people are all selective atheists--believing in some religious ideas and dismissing others. And if humans are willing to be painfully honest, everyone must admit the possibility looms that no god exists anywhere; that is why belief in a Divine Power is called *faith* as opposed to knowledge. The Atheist is in exactly the same position as believers. Disbelief is, at best, an argument from silence. Atheism is faith that no god exists.

Two Presences, Two Powers (Or More): Dualism

Dualism is the belief that two spheres of influence exist simultaneously. In some dualistic systems, one force is the good, the other evil. Usually, activities of the mind and spirit are good while experiences of the senses and material world are evil, or at least inferior to the mind-spirit activity. Plato fell into this trench warfare between material/spiritual realms, and since his thinking influenced early Christian theology, much of orthodoxy dove into the same ditch.

Dualism, more accurately defined, means the existence of more than one power or condition. When polytheists worship the sun god, rain god, and moon goddess, they affirm divine power is comprised of multiple pieces, operating from distinctly separate sources. This provokes some difficulties theologically: If there are various powers rather than a unified God-power, where did those powers originate? Further, how can each of multiple gods be said to be "All-powerful"? And lacking omnipotence— or even supremacy among peers—how can a pantheon of deities be the source of all reality?

Dualism often assumes some power is good and other power is evil. Dualistic religion personifies that power into evil, supernatural beings: Satan, the Devil, Loki, Lucifer, Ahriman, Eblis, Apollyon, Satyr, Mephistopheles, Beelzebub, or filmmaker George Lucas's dark side of the Force. Mildly dualistic religions emphasize the good power while barely acknowledging the presence of the other option. Mainline Protestantism and American Catholicism are examples of minimally dualistic religious faiths today. The important point is that dualism proceeds from a premise which says that there is more than one power behind the Universe, whereas atheism began with the proposition that is no spiritual power at all. Only one more option is possible.

One Presence / One Power: Monism

Monism says that there is only one power and one presence. Any power which exists outside of the divine means God is not omnipotent. Theologian Charles Hartshorne suggests God can do everything needed to be done. Hartshorne would substitute *adequacy* for omnipotence, putting forth a model of God that is omni-competent, able to do all things necessary but incapable of overcoming paradox or acting against the divine nature of love.[8]

Harsthorne's clever sophistry fails to solve the problem for dualistic theologies. If there is any other power, God cannot be said to be the Omnipotent Good we have worshipped. World religions scholar John Noss remarked that monism, which says no power exists but God-power, is the only true *mono*-theism.[9] Although quite ancient monism has become popular in the West since the 19th century, chiefly through nineteenth century Transcendentalists. Ralph Waldo Emerson, a formative figure in that movement, declared:

> Once men thought Spirit divine, and matter diabolic; one Ormuzd, the other Ahriman. Now science and philosophy recognize the parallelism, the approximation, the unity of the two: how each reflects the other as face answers to face in a glass: nay, how the laws of both are one, or how one is the realization. [10]

Today's science and philosophy no longer encourage speculative metaphysics, so Emerson's cheery confidence died young. The closing years of the nineteenth century—about the time New Thought was born—philosophy was already moving away from metaphysical studies. By the middle of the twentieth century, existentialism, with its emphasis on here-and-now, demonstrable and empirical evidence, had carried the day. And since God is neither empirical nor demonstrable, in the manner that scientists can control laboratory experiments, God-talk fell to death-of-God talk. Atheism, since it seeks to prove nothing metaphysical, became the respectable religious philosophy for philosophers. Theology retreated to regroup behind walls of special revelation, biblical exceptionalism and dualism, thinly disguised as Christian existentialism.

Parenthood of God?

Christians often declare that one of the more revolutionary concepts brought by Jesus declared the God of Israel—YHWH, the self-proclaimed jealous tribal deity who smote the firstborn of Egypt—could be better understood as the forgiving Father of the Prodigal Son.[11] Certainly, the idea of God as a loving parent was not new; the metaphor dominates the biblical text, usually presented as the steadfast love of Yahweh for the fickle Hebrews. God's parenthood of the children of Israel repeats throughout the First Testament. The concept is implied or stated outright in places as diverse as Exodus 4:22; Deuteronomy 14:1, 32:6; Hosea 11:1; Jeremiah 3:4, 19, and 31:9; and Psalm 103:13. It is important to note the theology of community implicit in these passages: God was the Father of Israel as a people, not of individual Israelites.[12]

In the Second Testament, Jesus individualized the profound intimacy of the divine-human relationship. The carpenter boy from Nazareth spoke as if the Creator of the Universe were Joseph and Mary; he was God's son. More importantly, Jesus taught his disciples to claim the same relationship as he enjoyed. His greatest prayer does not begin *"My Father"* but draws a great circle, including all humanity: *"Our Father, who art in heaven..."* Universal intimacy with God outpictures in the portraits of Jesus drawn by gospel authors, even though at least one of them (Matthew) was no universalist. This suggests the Jesus of history—veiled by curtains of written and oral tradition, lost in the mists of time—stands firmly behind the New Testament church's confession of universal childhood under God.[13]

Problems with Ethical Monotheism

Such intimacy with the Deity is unique in monotheistic religions. Islam regards God as an awesome, completely transcendent Being. Jewish mysticism and charismatic movements like Hassidism speak of God as an all-consuming flame, a love that drenches the soul and whirls it to ecstasy. Yet, to this day Judaism will not utter the biblical Name of G_d aloud.[14] No prophet-founder of a world religion has alleged personal kinship with God, save the Man of Nazareth. Jesus is a scandal in the family of faiths, a bastard Who claims to be King of Kings.

We noted in the previous chapter that simpler concepts of animatism (spirit-force) may have yielded to animism (worship of distinct spirits or powers of nature) which in turn gave rise to polytheism (personification of those powers into gods and goddesses). Monotheism (belief in One God) has its problems, too.

One difficulty is that any *Ethical Monotheism,* in which the Divine cares about right and wrong, rewarding right and punishing wrong, will be inherently intolerant. After all, if there is only one God, Who cares enough about what people do/think/believe to reward the good folk and punish the nonsubscribers, everyone must follow the same religion, the faith of the One True God. If you disagree with the doctrine or moral teachings of the church--which are, really, the religious/ethical opinions of the church's leadership--you are wrong. In fact, since there is only one truth and God will punish those who do not affirm it, those who disbelieve are not merely wrong, *they are evil.*

While every major faith group has generated its share of fanatics, Ethical Monotheism has a far worse record of abuses than polytheism, which tends to be tolerant toward those who worship another deity. Our study of world religions quoted sociologists Horton and Hunt who said church officials during the Spanish Inquisition—who tortured nonbelievers to accept their faith and then killed them to save their souls—probably operated from a perverse sense of moral duty. Only an Ethical Monotheist could consistently argue in favor of suppressing dissent so violently because only believers in a single supernatural being who punishes wrong and rewards right have the One-Way premise explicit in their theologies.

Though some may be surprised, Ethical Monotheism is not the only Christian option. At various times during Church history ideas like Deism, Naturalistic Theism, and Pantheism have had their heydays. The best we can get from any god-concept is a clean shadow of the Unknowable. But sometimes we learn things from the odd-looking shapes of other god-images which are denied to us because of the very familiarity of our own theological shadow-pictures. We do not need to review the complete history of God-concepts at this time (see "Evolution of the God Concept," Appendix III.), but the three images mentioned above are significant enough for our study to demand at least brief consideration.

God as Slum-Lord: Deism

Deism reached its zenith during the late l eighth century as the dominant God-model for radical thinkers of the Enlightenment. The most common image for deism's God is a clockmaker, a supreme engineer who has fashioned the mechanism of the Universe, wound it up like a clock, and stepped back to let it run without further intervention. Quite a few founding fathers of the United States of America—George Washington included—embraced intellectual deism. Since God created the Universe and set it in motion but does not interfere with its daily operations, deism's best feature is its ability to deal with the problem of evil. If not involved with the mechanics of everyday life, God can hardly be held accountable for suffering, disease and war.

However, the God of deism is as remote as an absentee landlord ruling over struggling tenants from the safety of the spiritual suburbs. Such a God, while intellectually satisfying, might be accused of apathy, ambivalence, and impotence. The God of deism is next to no God at all.

Nature is God: Naturalistic Theism

Essentially, the adherents of Naturalistic Theism push beyond deism and arrive at no-god. Nature is god for them, and there is no need to postulate any kind of intelligence behind the operations of scientific principles. Albert Einstein and Carl Sagan are two of the best modern examples. There is a reverence for life in some of the writings of naturalistic theists, a sense of awe at the mystery of the cosmos, but no Divine Mind at work. We are star-stuff, Sagan said, but nothing more.

This kind of secular thinking found theological expression during the "God is Dead" debate of the 1960's, especially in the writings of Thomas J. Altizer and William Hamilton. Altizer and Hamilton insisted God must be denied for humanity to be liberated. For Altizer, God has incarnated himself in the world and given up his distinct otherness, freeing us from dependence upon a power outside ourselves. While "Death of God" theology may have died a swift, natural death, secular forms of atheism are alive and well in the opening decades of the twenty-first century, as mentioned previously. The discussion will briefly revisit this topic in chapter 14, when looking at providence.[15]

An obvious advantage to Naturalistic Theism is its sense of harmony with the Universe. Humanity is not some alien entity plopped down within time-and-space for three-score-and-ten years, later transplanted to heaven or hell for all eternity. Like Max Whemann said in his "Desiderata," *we have a right to be here*.[16] This provides a much more reverent way of looking at ecology, human misery and the responsibility of science to make the world a better place than classical theism with its dualistic destinations and transient status for humanity.

An obvious disadvantage to Naturalistic Theism is that it speaks of mystery without allowing things to be genuinely mysterious. For life and consciousness to evolve from dead matter and energy makes no more sense than postulating a Divine Mind pushing the whole process along.

Atheistic and yet still optimistic, Naturalistic Theism has no basis for hope other than a blind euphoria about the ability of science to overcome all our difficulties. Listening to the fascinating yarns of Carl Sagan during his epic *Cosmos* series on PBS, one could almost begin to believe that all we need to achieve the Kingdom of Heaven is better research.

Human history discloses otherwise. Unless there is some kind of spiritual growth, smarter folks just make smarter weapons. And if there is "spiritual growth," what standard does the Naturalistic Theist hold up as a model for humanity to emulate? Usually, it is an unconsciously religious model, a mixture of pop-psychology and the parables of Jesus. In any other enterprise, that would be called plagiarism. In theology, it's acute myopia compounded by intellectual elitism. Naturalistic Theism will never work as a Christian system because it is essentially unnatural and nontheistic.

God is the World: Pantheism

If Naturalistic Theism sails off the map by reading God out of the cosmos, pantheism does the same in the opposite extreme. For the pantheist, God is the cosmos. Everything is God. This means every act, thought, being and thing in the Universe can be added up and the grand total equals God. The pantheistic God is coextensive with the cosmos, therefore could not have created it or we land in the contradictory conclusion of a self-created Creator. Both God and the Universe must be eternal, since God is that Universe.

Pantheism finds expression in the philosophies of Spinoza, Hegel and Royce and in the theologies of great Christian mystics like Dionysius the Aeropagite, John Scotus Erigena, and Meister Eckhart. Eastern religions are almost unanimously pantheistic, but Ethical Monotheists within Judaism, Christianity and Islam have energetically suppressed God-is-All as a doctrine smelling of universalism. Certainly, a consistent pantheism does not allow any dichotomy between the saved and the damned. If God-is-All, then heaven and hell are at worst adjoining chambers in God's consciousness.

Pantheism's one major advantage is its grasp of the all-pervasive Presence of God. The Divine is not remote but totally immanent. God works in everything, not just a few spectacular moments of Divine intervention. God is impersonal, because the energy of the cosmos is not geared to redeem the individual soul but rather to express the Divine in many forms.

One theological problem of pantheism is that it cannot explain why there are imperfections in the world, therefore it tends to deny that suffering, pain and discord exist. This puts the pantheist in the very unenviable position of denying that his neighbor really hurts. A simpler way of stating the problem comes to us from William and Mabel Sahakian's *Ideas of the Great Philosophers*:

> Since every person is part of God, it follows that if a child (also part of God) believes erroneously that 2+2=5, while at the same time his teacher (part of God as well) knows that 2+2=4 and that the child is mistaken, the entire situation is one in which God must be assumed to be simultaneously aware and not aware that he is in error. Thus, Pantheism injects contradiction in the mind of God, an inconceivable impossibility.[17]

Despite its tendency for detachment, or maybe because of it, some pantheists are among the most pacifistic people on earth. Many pantheists refuse to eat animal products and others watch where they step for fear of causing the death of insects underfoot.

What's Left?

So far we have looked at these God-concepts: Ethical Monotheism, Deism, Naturalistic Theism, and Pantheism. This does not exhaust all the possibilities; there are many options yet unexplored. To name a few: the Deistic Supernaturalism of Soren Kierkegaard, John Dewey's Religious Humanism , British and American forms of Impersonal Idealism, and the conglomerate of god-models in the theologies of Neo-Paganism. Although each view offers insights which may provide still another piece to the infinite puzzle, overall they are unsatisfying to people looking for a new understanding of God grounded in historic Christianity.

Progressive Christianity demands a God-concept which holds in dynamic tension the disruptive experiences of everyday life and the faithful assurance that *God*—however that word is understood—has everything under control. Practical Christianity requires a way of looking at the Infinite God as Infinite Good without undermining God's role in the real world or human freedom. Compassionate Christianity insists on a God-model which reconciles the personal, caring nature of God with the suffering of real life; a method of understanding how God can be in-and-through everyone while we are still capable of atrocious error-beliefs and flagrant attempts to rip ourselves free from the good that God wants to give us. A tall order, but it can be done. Several excellent thinkers have pointed the way.

Creation Implies Risk: Panentheism

Panentheism is not pan-theism, although the former borrows some of pantheism's best elements. Pantheism (all *is* God) says God is the Universe, but Panentheists find that concept too limiting. Pan-*en*-theism (all *in* God) says the Universe exists *within God*. Divine power interpenetrates the cosmos but transcends it.

> God possess self-identity and is independent of the particular objects of nature, though immanent in them. Panentheism differs from Deism which posits only a transcendent God; it also differs from Pantheism which identifies God with nature. That is to say, it agrees with Pantheism that the being of God includes nature, but adds the belief that God surpasses and embraces more than nature.[18]

Although the term *panentheism* was coined by K.F.C. Krause

(1781-1832) early in the nineteenth century, people like Albert Schweitzer, Alfred North Whitehead and Charles Hartshorne are among its subscribers. Panentheism says God is *in* the world, inhabiting the very atoms of the physical Universe, but *beyond* the world as well. Historical theologians have traced the concept from the writings of medieval mystics like Meister Eckhart. God incarnates in and through the world but, contrary to the Death of God theologians, God is not exhausted by going forth in creation.[19]

A key point in panentheism is that God perceives the world through creating sentient creatures and therefore is gaining new experiences as we live and grow. In that case, we are adding to the sum of God's being by our choices. Neither God nor the Universe can ever be complete, i.e., *finished* like a perfectly sculpted statue, because there is always more to learn and do. And the process surprises God, because the Divine Spirit does not have our choices as actual events until after we choose. Much like a parent who knows a child will go off to school, suffer scraped knees and get in fights until the child learns how to live with others, God "knows" generally what people shall experience but does not know exactly which possibility they will choose. Otherwise, there would be no real choice. If billions of eons ago God knew what choices we would make today and created every sentient being knowing those distant choices already, no real freedom could exist. By giving the gift of freedom, God relinquished foreknowledge about specific events. As people make selections God "grows" with them. According to Hartshorne, God needs people as much as people need God, because the divine nature is creative expression itself, and sentient beings are the fulfillment of that nature. Hartshorne wrote:

> A new era in religion may be predicted as soon as men grasp the idea that it is just as true that God is the supreme beneficiary or recipient of achievement, as he is the supreme benefactor or Source of achievement.[20]

John Macquarrie said, "Creation implies risk."[21] To send forth creative expressions, God must free those expressions to act in ways contrary to the divine will. Sentient beings must be able to choose dastardly, cruel behavior in order to freely choose to walk the paths of peace and love. Freedom cuts both ways or not at all. Believing that God the Good empowers everything does not guarantee happy outcomes in all instances, because God's greatest gift is freedom, and freedom means risk. William G.T. Shedd (1820-1894) delivered a great one-line sermon, which preachers, designers of inspirational calendars and poster makers have enthusiastically pirated: "A ship in a harbor is safe, but that is not what ships are built for."[22] Macquarrie adds:

> It is by no means obvious that "in everything God works for good," but then this was not obvious to St. Paul who wrote these words. It has to be insisted again that this doctrine begins as an act of faith and hope, an attitude to life; it does not begin as a speculation about the world, and certainly not a speculation that can be thought up in the study away from the actual conflicts and decisions of life.[23]

Panentheism avoids the contradiction of pantheism's self-creating God by asserting that God is not exhausted by the act of creation. Plenty of divine substance remains after all the matter-and-energy cosmos springs forth from that primordial act of creation/organization. This is metaphysical speculation of the highest order. But if Sagan can step back fourteen billion years to the explosion which gave rise to the physical Universe and call it science, we can certainly tiptoe into the primeval dark before the Big Bang to peek at what was happening in the name of theology. Science cites the expanding Universe as evidence for the Big Bang; theology cites the existing Universe as evidence for God-substance. The two theories are wholly compatible when properly understood. When we look at Eschatology (Ch. 10) we shall discuss Creation and cosmology in greater depth.

One Presence / One Power: Monistic Panentheism

Monistic panentheism expands the concept of panentheism to include the transcendent and imminent; all the principles and laws of existence as well as physical matter, energy, and any spiritual realms which may exist. More than fish and ocean, God embraces the all the principles of chemistry and physics by which the ocean exists and operates. Applying the term to Fillmorean theology: *God is mind, idea, expression.*

The wellsprings of Metaphysical Christianity flow from this cardinal principle. It is neither explicitly biblical nor traditional but results from experience and reason. In that respect OP^2 falls under the same heading as other non-biblical doctrines (like the Trinity) and represents a minority view in the history of Christian thought (like universalism). It is worth noting that, although the Trinity and Christian universalism are non-biblical and non-traditional respectively, both positions are staunchly defended by churchmen as orthodox as Macquarrie—who was Lady Margaret Professor of Divinity at Oxford University—and a host of other high-visibility theologians of both Catholic and Protestant persuasions.

Christian mysticism has hinted the OP^2 concept for centuries, but so far there have been few attempts to state theologically what this idea means and to show how it relates to the totality of Christian thought. A possible linking concept is *process theology.*[24]

Process Theology

As previously noted, some thinkers have insisted God can be better understood as the principle of existence. Paul Tillich said God is not a solitary Supreme Being but Being-Itself. God does not exist, in the way creatures, planets and stars exist; God is the power of existence itself. The Book of Acts has Paul quoting Epimenides the Cretan, sixth century B.C. Greek philosopher: "In him we live and move and have our being."[25] Note the philosopher does not speak of God as *becoming*, but *being*, suggesting a static perfection from which all mortals descended and continue to exist.

But is God best understood as *being* or *becoming*? In previous generations, it was blasphemous to suggest that God—whether Supreme Being or Divine Principle—could ever change. How could the all-mighty, all-potent, all-knowing Deity transform into something else? The thought is a little scary. Yet there are responsible Christian theologians who contend that God does change, even grows. The school of thought which holds this view is called *process theology*; its chief advocates are the intellectual heirs to the work of Alfred North Whitehead (1861–1947). Whitehead was a rather ponderous yet profound thinker who began as a philosopher of mathematics then moved on to religion.

Life is a Process

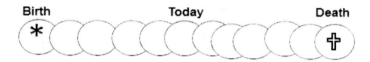

Which one are you?

Fig. 7-1 Process view of life.

Whitehead believed God is not a static entity but an evolving process. In fact, Whitehead said consciousness is a *process*. You were once an infant, then a child, adolescent and young adult. Which of these stages is you? Obviously, all of them, as well as all the stages of life you have yet to experience. You change and grow, yet every stage of your existence is an authentic out-picturing of your real self. Whitehead held that God is so integrated into the fabric of reality that God experiences this progression of thoughts, feelings and day-by-day activities in all sentient beings.

But how does God change? Process theologians would say that by participating in the events of your life and the existence of all sentient beings, God gains more experiences. By receiving and giving love, God absorbs those exchanges and "realizes" the increased love. T. A. Kantonen describes the God of process theology:

> Far from being enthroned in remote, solitary splendor, he [God] is a responsive and responsible give-and-take relation to the world. He receives, treasures, and remembers everything that happens and uses it to further his purpose of cosmic advance from the potential to the actual. In Whitehead's own words, he is "the fellow-

sufferer who understands," and in him our perishing experiences "live forevermore."[26]

The idea that God is a process is highly controversial in Christian theology. At first glance, it also seems out of step with metaphysical Christianity, which has always held that God is "Absolute Good." But the word absolute doesn't have to mean "changeless." It can mean "total" or "endless" as well. As a Metaphysical Christian, one need not agree with everything process theologians say, but I suspect that most people would like to think their interactions with the Divine can in some way add to the total good of the cosmos. Process theology contends God is not constrained by time and space; God is the whole process of life, evolution, time and space.

Study your life experiences for a localized illustration. (Figure 7-1.) You have pictures of yourself as an infant, toddler, grade-schooler, adolescent teen, young adult and so on. If your life pattern continues normally, you'll have photos of yourself as an octogenarian someday. Lay them out chronologically—which one would you say is *you*? The answer is, of course, all of them. You are not a slice in time; *you are a process*.

Process theology says, so is God. A Metaphysical Christian way to put it would be to see Divine Mind as the *panentheistic process* in which every subordinate process exists. As the process of existence unfolds, God grows. As the cosmos expresses itself in creative diversity, God experiences new events. God changes by experiencing that which creative freedom of the cosmos co-creates with its empowering share of the divine energy. In a Platonic sense, the principles which guide the divine creative process are the true God-behind-God, and these never change. But God-power continually expresses in new creative, combinations, which by definition means change.

Theodicy: How Good is God?

OP[2] forms the cornerstone of the God-concept in Metaphysical Christianity. However, the idea that no power can exist outside of God requires making one of two choices about the nature of suffering. Either physical-emotional pain is an illusion which must be denied, or suffering comes from our state as incomplete manifestations of God's Presence and Power. In other words, either bad things really don't happen (which life experience shows to be absurd) or God is somehow involved in the pains and failures which invariably visit every human life. This lands us in the old problem of *theodicy*, which is theology's attempt to square the idea of a loving, all-powerful God with the suffering of the world.

In the words of ancient Greek philosopher Epicurus:

> Is God willing to prevent evil, but not able? Then he is not omnipotent.
>
> Is he able, but not willing? Then he is malevolent.
>
> Is he both able and willing? Then whence cometh evil?
>
> Is he neither able nor willing? Then why call him God?[27]

If a quick answer occurs to you, re-read the problem; you aren't thinking deeply enough. Theodicy is the primordial question which has given theologians sleepless nights for untold centuries. It calls every religious system to task.

How does Metaphysical Christianity answer its challenge? Let's review: God is the only Power and Presence in the Universe, Good Omnipotent. The problem of evil and suffering evaporates in the paradigm of Incarnational Monism. If each sentient being is an incarnation of God, theodicy morphs into growth-experiences. God incarnates in every sentient being. The Divine Father-Mother sends the "children" off to learn, grow and create, knowing they will potentially experience pain and suffering as the price of freedom in an unpredictable world. This sending forth is not an act of Deism's absentee God or Ethical Theism's Supreme Judge. God goes forth as you and me to love, learn, grow, design and savor life's experiences. Knowing creation implies risk, God is willing to gamble with disaster because jeopardy opens doors to infinite possibilities. Meister Eckhart said the Word becomes flesh because, until God expresses as the children of the Universe, God the Creator is not yet Father-Mother Creator.

> The word "Father" implies a Son and the phrase "Father of Lights" implies an immaculate birth and a universal principle. The Father begets the Son in the eternal mind

and also begets the Son in the soul as if in his own nature...Thus we are all in the Son and are the Son.[28]

God does not cause earthquakes, wars or diseases. God is Omnipotent Good, wanting nothing but the best for all creation. God-power operates through a free cosmos where earthquakes, wars and disasters can occur. God "begets" such a Universe for the sake of creative growth, creative expression, loving-giving. Spirit has provided ways to learn and grow in the most adverse situations, and has organized Reality itself to be supportive and health-giving. Because there is a loving-giving Father-Mother God empowering the cosmos to exist, this is a basically friendly Universe. Offspring of God can affirm One Presence / One Power, even in the face of apparent evidence to the contrary, because the transpersonal Father-Mother Spirit binds the Universe together through the attractive power of love. Fillmore wrote: "In Divine Mind, love is the Power that joins and binds in divine harmony the Universe and everything in it; the great harmonizing principle known to man."[29]

Onward to Christology

Christian theology cannot address the question of God without taking as its starting point the best example of God-with-us. Jesus Christ, we have said, was absolutely unique because he gives us a window through which God's light can shine and by which we can see what we are truly meant to be. In Jesus Christ we have a summary of all the good that God wants for his children. As the Apostle Paul wrote in his second letter to the Church at Corinth:

> For in him every one of God's promises is a "Yes." For
> this reason it is through him that we say the "Amen," to
> the glory of God.[30]

We turn now to the unqualified *yes* of those Divine promises, Jesus Christ, as we look at the final person of the Trinity, God the Son-Daughter.

CHECK YOUR KNOWLEDGE

1. Define the following: *monotheism, atheism, deism, naturalistic theism, pantheism, dualism, and monism.*

2. Describe the author's critique of the ideas held by Pierre Teilhard de Chardin.

3. Describe how Ethical monotheism can quickly become judgmental.

4. What is *panentheism*?

5. Explain the basic concepts of Process Theology.

6. What is theodicy? Describe the author suggestion that panentheism can solve theodicy's deep conundrums.

QUESTIONS FOR DISCUSSION

1. Discuss the comment by Sister Sandra Schneiders: "God is more than two men and a bird." What does she mean?

2. If everybody is an atheist about something, what are you an atheist about?

3. Which of the models presented in this chapter appeal to you? (More than one answer is acceptable, perhaps desirable.)

4. If God is All-Good, why do innocent people suffer?

5. Discuss the ideas of Process Theology. Is God a process? Does God change?

6. What kind of God-concept works best for you?

- 8 -

GOD THE SON-DAUGHTER

Perfect Example of the Divine-Human Paradox

Once I was asked what the Father is doing in heaven. I replied that he begets his Son and that this activity is so pleasant to him and suits him so well that he never does anything else and that from the two there blossoms forth the Holy Spirit. When the Father begets his Son in me, I am that Son and no other. "If we are sons, then we are true heirs." He who knows the truth knows very well that the word "Father" implies the immaculate birth and the having of sons. Thus we are all in the Son and are the Son.[1]

Meister Eckhart (1260-1327)

Metaphysical Christianity is Trinitarian, but just barely. The classical doctrine of the triune God—one substance, three "persons" or modes of expression, proceeding from each other and uniquely Divine— is too anthropocentric and mythological to accept literally. Classical Trinitarianism provokes more questions than it answers: If only the persons of the Trinity are Divine, what about the rest of us? Is there more than one kind of consciousness, some Divine and some not-divine? If God is not our true "Abba!" the way Jesus taught, what commerce could finite beings have with a holy, pure and distant Supreme Being? If Jesus alone is the Second Person (Son) of the trinity, ordinary mortals are at best admiring followers who wonder how He did it. And how can God be three, and yet one, without tri-theism or other contradictions?

Who's Hiding in Your Pantheon?

Most Trinitarians have a much larger concept of spiritual realities than orthodox theology allows, albeit unconsciously. Mono-theism, we have said, insists there is only one God. This concept is interpreted in so many ways that some interesting variations occur within orthodoxy.

Insisting on only one God, most Christians nonetheless believe in a host of other super- natural entities which coexist in the divine realm. Anthropologist Anthony F.C. Wallace observed that Roman Catholicism's official system of supernatural beings—saints, demons, angels, etc.—pales into minimalism when compared with the multifarious entities actually recognized by people in his own hometown.

Even the so-called "monotheistic" religions invariably include an elaborate pantheon. Thus in the small Christian community in which I grew up, "the religion" (in the summative sense) included at least the following categories of supernatural beings in its pantheon:

1. God (the high god)
2. Jesus
3. The Virgin Mary
4. The saints
5. The Devil
6. Ghosts (souls of the dead on earth found in old houses and around cemeteries)
7. Souls in heaven, hell, or purgatory
8. The souls of normal living human being
9. Witches, who could take on the form of animals and harm people
10. Santa Claus (believed in only by children)
11. The Easter rabbit (also believed in only by children)
12. Souls of animals
13. Fairies (who bring quarters when teeth fall out, and live in closets or in woodsy places)
14. Superstition: beliefs concerning good or bad luck.[2]

Wallace noted that not everyone believed in the whole list and there was always pressure to reduce the numbers. Who hasn't heard a sermon on Easter or Christmas bemoaning the "secularization" or "commercialization" of those high holy days? Most people are not accustomed to thinking of religion in such broad terms. As a cultural anthropologist studying the phenomena of religion, Wallace has no qualms about listing all the supernatural beings people acknowledged in his hometown. Stepping back to look at the larger picture, quite visibly the belief systems which pass as monotheistic are really thinly veiled polytheism (belief in more than one god) or, at best, henotheism (belief in one overwhelmingly powerful god among many supernatural beings and gods).

Rudolf Bultmann: De-Mythologizing

This paints a rather disturbing picture of mythologies intertwined with theologies, a fact pointed out by theologian and New Testament scholar Rudolf Bultmann in his shattering essay, "The New Testament and Mythology." Published in 1941, the work should be read by every serious biblical student. Bultmann wanted to *de-mythologize* the New Testament, strip away its pre-scientific worldview, while preserving the *kerygma* (kernel of truth) wrapped within archaic thought-forms:

> If the truth (kerygma) of the New Testament proclamation is to be preserved, the only way is to demythologize it...The real purpose of myth is not to present an objective picture of the world as it is, but to express man's understanding of himself in the world in which he lives.[3]

People look out at a world they did not create and attempt to arrange life into a coherent whole, so that they can go grocery shopping without worrying about evil powers cursing their homes while away or supernatural beings striking them dead on the freeway. Religious systems which picture a plethora of gods and demi-gods vying for custody of the human soul will invariably give rise to a complex mythology and a ritual system designed to insure safe passage down the corridor of life and eternal reward at some final destination.

Simpler systems do not necessarily mean simpler mythologies, as anthropologists like Anthony Wallace have shown. Every worldview will contain some mythological elements because human consciousness cannot fully comprehend the cosmos. Today's secret mythologies hide behind more appropriate socio-cultural fashions: Salvation through romantic love leading to marriage; science will solve all our problems; life evolved from the primordial soup to sentient human beings by accident of nature; the better educated a person is the less problems he/she will have in life.

Myths: Not Untruths

It is important to be very careful the word *myth*—which properly describes a *story told in a legendary, non-historical genre*—does not degenerate into a synonym for *falsehood*. The above list of modern myths is essentially a negative one because we can more readily see the mythical elements in ideas based on half-truths. There are other myths to explain life that are not so easily recognized: Democracy is better than dictatorship; chastity until marriage is the best way; all people are created equal. None of these are provable, yet millions of people--the author included--will organize their lives according to "myths" which explain how the world operates and how good people behave.

The parables of Jesus may not reflect historical incidents. There may not have been a "good Samaritan" or a "prodigal son." Nevertheless, those stories teach some profound insights about effective living. They are, in the larger sense of the word, myths. Bultmann and other biblical scholars call people to recognize the prescientific elements in New Testament literature while preserving the kernel of truth contained within its mythological husk. As this study delves deeper into Christian thought, a by-product of the process will be to encourage students to construct new mythologies, an exciting enterprise more-or-less required for renewal of all religious thought, but especially in building a new Christology.

Renewed Christology

Is it possible to believe in Jesus Christ as the Second Person of the Trinity while remaining faithful to One Power/One Presence and to the biblical witness? The answer is a qualified, "Yes." Seeing Jesus as the Second Person of the Trinity only works if we see his as representative of the divinity-in-everyone. When we move Jesus of Nazareth to the right hand of God and make him uniquely divine, he loses all value to mortals. If Jesus was the only God-man, he cannot represent achievable goals, for mere humans have no access to that level of divinity. In 1910, Harvard Professor of Church history Ephraim Emerton took issue with those who wanted to make the historical Jesus the only God-man:

> No, it is belief in the perfect humanity of Jesus that alone
> commends him to us as an attainable example. Without
> that he remains a mere abstraction, a shadowy image of
> humanity, a divine apparition clothed with the
> semblance, but lacking in the reality, of a man.[4]

Fortunately, Metaphysical Christianity solves the problem by seeing Jesus Christ as *typical* rather than unique. He is the Second Person of the Trinity, because all sentient beings are that Second Person, the "Son" of Divinity. Jesus is typical because he displayed the qualities which everyone has in potential. In Metaphysical Christian thought, every sentient being harbors the Christ incarnate. More than *harbors*. Every form of higher consciousness actually *is* an incarnation of God. The Hindu idea of abundant gods did not go far enough. In the words of a popular hymn in Metaphysical Christian circles:

> I behold the Christ in you,
> Here the life of God I see;
> I can see a great peace, too
> I can see you whole and free.[5]

Mystical thinker Charles Fillmore described his speculative vision of the process behind those poetic words.

> God, the Father, Divine Mind, had an idea of man, and
> this idea is his Son, the perfect-man idea, the off- spring
> of God-Mind. This Son is the Christ, the only begotten
> of the Father...Manifest man should be as the ideal. He
> will be when the individual identifies himself with the
> Christ. When he is identified with anything less than
> perfection he manifests some degree of imperfection.[6]

Jesus Christ as a paradigm for the Christ-within interfaces nicely with One Presence/One Power, yet stresses the importance of Jesus. A favorite motif for Jesus-models is the *Wayshower*.

Jesus is the Way-Shower. He came that we might have life more abundantly. He came to awaken man to the possibilities   of his own nature. He came to bear witness to Truth. He used the one true way to the realization of eternal life and universal consciousness, therefore His influence on the (human) race cannot be measured. It is infinite and eternal.[7]

Rather than a sacrificial victim proffering his bloody body to appease an angry god, Jesus as Wayshower unfolds a map for the road through life. A story told to me by a Catholic priest illustrates the mapmaking process. A Catholic layperson was lunching with his best friend, a Jewish Rabbi, when he excitedly told the Rabbi his son was entering seminary to study for the priesthood.

"So?" The Rabbi stirred his coffee.

"But don't you understand?" said the Catholic. "He could become a bishop!"

"So?"

"Don't you realize he could become a Cardinal, or even the first American Pope?"

The Rabbi yawned. "So?"

At that point the future priest's father lost it. "For God's sake! What do you want him to be—Jesus Christ?"

The Rabbi smiled. "Well, one of our boys made it."[8]

All humor aside, the Rabbi inadvertently made the point under consideration in this chapter; the humanity of Jesus reveals the divinity in everyone. *One of our boys made it.* An ordinary human being achieved such unity with God that the Gospel of John has him saying aloud with complete conviction, "I and the Father are one." (John 10:30). To declare Jesus was human in no way diminishes his divinity. The greatest creeds of the Christian heritage have affirmed consistently Jesus Christ was fully divine and fully human. Two examples follow, drawn from the folio of unimpeachable orthodoxy.

The Nicene Creed:

> We believe in one Lord, Jesus Christ, the only Son of God, eternally begotten of the Father, God from God, Light from Light, true God from true God, begotten, not made, one Being with the Father. Through him all things were made. For us men and for our salvation he came down from heaven: by the power of the Holy Spirit he was born of the Virgin Mary, and became man.[9]

Luther's Small Catechism:

> 125. Who is Jesus Christ?
> Jesus Christ is true God, begotten of the Father from eternity, and also true man, born of the Virgin Mary.

> 128. What two natures, then, are united in Christ?
> The divine and the human natures are united in Christ, both natures together forming one undivided and indivisible person (personal union).[10]

Metaphysical Christianity can affirm the above historic doctrines about the nature of Jesus Christ without reservation. Unquestionably, Jesus was fully human and fully divine. The difference is that traditional Christianity wants to make the Jesus-event unique, while Metaphysical Christianity sees Jesus as *normative*. Otherwise, Metaphysical Christology is highly orthodox, but it is an "otherwise" that makes all the difference in the cosmos. Studying Christology requires studying anthropology. Investigating of the nature of Jesus Christ is really peeking into the potential of all sentient beings. This makes an understanding of Jesus' divine-human nature tantamount to knowing the inner workings of human consciousness.

Christological Groundwork

Early in Christian history, the Church fathers steered a middle course between the two extremes of *Adoptionism* and *docetism*. These two tendencies—both considered heretical in historic Christian thought—must be understood before proceeding because they linger today.

Adoptionists said that Jesus was only human, that he had been *adopted* into a special supernatural status when God the Father chose him as the Son. Nineteenth Century Unitarianism was almost wholly Adoptionist, indicated by the passage quoted from Ephraim Emerton's book, *Unitarian Thought*. Although rejected by most Christians, Adoptionism is actually more popular today than it was when progressive thinkers of the early-modern era were struggling with their Christologies.

Docetism, on the other hand, has always been popular with the masses. docetism is the general term used to describe any Christology which says that Jesus was exclusively Divine, bearing no relationship to humanity other than physical resemblance. When infiltrating Christian theologies, *Gnosticism* often took this position. Some docetists insisted that Jesus, being God Omnipotent, could not really have been born, grown up, gotten hungry, suffered and died. And he certainly could not have felt angry, sexually aroused or in need of bodily elimination. Jesus was pure spirit, no crass matter or human material tainted his nature, or so Gnostic docetism declared.

Docetism is more alluring than Adoptionism. While studying at a liberal Protestant seminary, the author was told by a professor that the Divinity of Jesus always preaches better than his humanity. A flagrantly heretical, docetic sermon could be preached from almost any orthodox Christian pulpit without raising an eyebrow, but a sermon stressing the humanity of Jesus Christ will provoke midnight sessions of the governing board. People want a Savior, not a fellow-servant with issues.

Despite the popular appeal of *Jesus is God* language, traditional Christian theology—both Catholic and Protestant—has attempted to steer the hard, middle course between the rocky shore of Adoptionism and the whirlpool of docetism. The Nicene Creed insisted Jesus "came down from heaven...and became man..." Luther called him "true God...and also true man." On this point Metaphysical Christianity stands firmly with the historic creeds and wizened scholars of the ancient church: Jesus was fully divine and fully human. Where Metaphysical Christians differ is on the point of his *unique* divinity, about which most are skeptical. To believe God is One Power/One Presence, Metaphysical Christian theology must infer that Jesus represents *normative* humanity. If there truly is only One Power and Presence in the cosmos, God-power, the consciousness of Jesus as Christ must be identical to God-consciousness. Any putative difference must be purely quantitative, not qualitative.

Reasoning from this model, i.e., Jesus as an expression of the divine idea of consciousness, one could argue that Jesus achieved and understood more than other humans only because he reflected more of the Divine light than they presently do. Jesus as normative supports the idea that every self-aware entity enjoys the same *imago Dei*. The incarnation of the divine-within includes *all sentient beings*—human, dolphin, or alien on a distant world. The question arising from this conclusion is based on everyday observation: Reasoning from this brazen assumption—i.e., I am putatively an example of the Divine-within—why is the *imago Dei* so cleverly disguised when I look at God's face in the mirror every morning? If the gospel accounts are correct, the same impediment to greeting the divinity in Jesus occurred to his friends and neighbors.

> Is not this the carpenter's son? Is not his mother called Mary? And are not his brothers James and Joseph and Simon and Judas? And are not all his sisters with us? Where then did this man get all this?" And they took offense at him. But Jesus said to them, "Prophets are not without honor except in their own country and in their own house."[11]

Good question. For a possible answer, follow me out the door of orthodoxy into a replanted garden of ancient, delicious heresies.

Kenosis: Emptying of Divinity

We have already identified the key concept, *Incarnational Monism*. The root idea goes back to Paul's Letter to the Philippians:

> Let the same mind be in you that was in Christ Jesus, who, though he was in the form of God, did not regard equality with God as something to be exploited, but emptied himself, taking the form of a slave, being born in human likeness. And being found in human form, he

humbled himself and became obedient to the point of death— even death on a cross. Therefore God also highly exalted him and gave him the name that is above every name, so that at the name of Jesus every knee should bend, in heaven and on earth and under the earth, and every tongue should confess that Jesus Christ is Lord, to the glory of God the Father.[12]

Kenosis is the Greek word Paul used to describe the origin of Jesus Christ. He said Jesus "emptied himself" of preexistent "equality with God" when he was born into this world. But while Paul probably believed this act of kenosis was the unique prerogative of Jesus as the only Son of God, mystical Christian thought has often seen divinity as the essential ingredient in all consciousness. Medieval churchman Meister Eckhart:

I have read many writings of both Pagan masters and the Prophets of the old and new Covenant (Testament), and have investigated seriously and with great zeal which would be the best and highest virtue by which Man could resemble again the archetype such as he was in God when there was no difference between him and God until God made the creatures. [13]

Eckhart goes on to suggest the gift of kenosis, which allows humans to express in this world as separate entities, necessarily separates people from original oneness with God. Eckhart's solution calls for "seclusion" to renew the primordial relationship with God lost in the kenotic descent to flesh required to incarnate in the world. This call for communion with God, both beyond and within, echoes down the corridors of time. Eckhart's appeal for solitude rings like a temple bell in the work of pastoral theologian Henri Nouwen, who wants urban culture to find an inner, desert place to commune with God in the hustle of workaday life.[14] Both these ideas resonate in the spiritual pilgrimage of Charles Fillmore, who wrote constantly about the need to find time for meditative quiet, solitude with God.

When one goes into the silence he enters the "secret place of the Most High," the closet of prayer within. He closes the door and in the stillness of that meeting place he prays to God, he communes with God, and he meditates on Truth. Then he listens to what God has to say to him.[15]

Meister Eckhart had asserted as far back as the thirteenth century that such dogged determination, when couple with love, will flush God from towering state transcendence and draw the Divine down to humanity. The circulation of God-essence continues until people unite with God and resume some degree of oneness with the Creator. Eckhart was absolutely convinced that God must come "down" to our level:

But it is much more important that I force God down to me than that I force myself up to God. For my eternal bliss rests upon my being united with God. For God is more able to penetrate into me and become united with me, than I with Him.[16]

To the untrained ear, that sounds blasphemous. People seldom think of prayer as a way to "force God down" to them. The passage makes better sense when noting that Eckhart believed God could not resist a heart turned toward its Source in sincere prayer. God's nature is loving-giving, an inseparable whole expressed by another New Testament Greek word, *agape*. As hearts reach for God, a loving Father-Mother can no more refuse to express that loving-giving nature than the sun could refuse to shine once the rainclouds are swept aside after a storm. "God cannot help abandoning Himself to a secluded heart," Eckhart wrote.[17] As the First Letter of John had said: *"God is love (agape)."* The One Presence/One Power is selfless love itself.

Kenosis as Normative

Here's where the paradigm gets personal. If *kenosis*, God's self-emptying, is a onetime phenomenon manifested exclusively in Jesus of Nazareth, there can be no actual relationship with God like the oneness glimpsed by Eckhart and Fillmore. God's Fatherhood of the human race is a mere figure of speech, much like all Americans having the same "Uncle Sam." However, *if kenosis is the norm for all sentient beings*—if we are all bits of divinity flung to the far corners of the cosmos, where we are to express creativity and love as we become increasingly aware of our Oneness with God—then the best of panentheism and incarnational theology merges in the concept of God as One Presence/One Power. Even the traditional problems of Ethical Monotheism are mitigated by kenosis. Certainly, God "cares" about right and wrong, but if God is acting in and through everything, it makes no sense for one part of God to interfere with the operation of another part. If you are God expressing as you and I am God expressing as me, each "emptied" of full divinity by the primordial act of creation/expression, we must learn to see the divinity in each other without some outside force compelling us to act in a responsible, God-conscious manner.

If we are all incarnations of God, the notion of reward-and-punishment becomes ludicrous. Would God send a bit of Divinity to hell? Would any parent condemn his/her child for all eternity? There might be built-in rewards for choosing the best path, and less satisfactory responses from life if we choose otherwise, but no permanent damage would be experienced unless the model includes a God who enjoys self-inflicted wounds.

Kenosis also answers the objection about contradictions in the mind of God. If both pupil (thinking 2+2=5) and teacher (knowing 2+2=4) are kenotic incarnations of God (i.e., shards of divinity in a finite locus, emptied of full divine awareness), the apparent contradiction resolves. As those grow spiritually, finding harmony with their true nature by choosing the path of loving-giving walked by Jesus the Christ, they become more Christ-like until they become so convinced of their identity in God they can say with complete confidence, "I and the Father are one." (John 10:30)

Incarnational Monism is a useful term to describe this unity-in-diversity brought about through kenosis and summarized for all time in the life and person of Jesus Christ. Incarnational Monism, if true, would explain the origins of intelligence, consciousness and evolution. If the part of God that is Jesus Christ was "emptied" of its full divinity when he took "the form of a servant, being born in the likeness of men," and if Jesus regarded humanity as his brothers/sisters, calling us to recognize our Abba-Father "in Heaven," then each sentient being can be regarded as an incarnation of God with the same potential demonstrated in Jesus Christ.

There are several effective ways idea of kenosis as normative can be critiqued. First, it can be attacked at its panentheistic foundation. Everyday experience seems to contradict panentheism. How can everything be "in" God with so much ungodliness rampant in the world? Humans hardly behave like divine beings, unless there is an unknown god of bank robbers, drug pushers, or terrorists. But God in His/Her/Its fullness is not what panentheists are talking about, which is where kenotic theology begins to make sense. God "emptied" the fullness of divine perfection and came to earth in Jesus Christ. The spark of divinity was there, but not the All-powerful, All-knowing, All-present Creator/Ruler of the cosmos. Jesus, mortal child born at Bethlehem, reveals an immortal God in microcosm. So powerful is Jesus Christ in Western culture one could argue we have a Jesus-model for God, not a God-model for Jesus. Jesus the Christ is not God-like; God is Jesus-like. Jesus is the window through which the Light of God shines, and the window determines the shape of that light. If Jesus was fully human as well as fully divine, which most orthodox theologies agree, kinship to Jesus as children of God implies all the qualities expressed in the Nazarene are available to everyone. Humanity awaits its awakening as kenotic incarnations of God, the One Presence/One Power.

Cornerstone for the House of Tomorrow?

Incarnational Monism gives us a way to understand how God can be born in a stable, grow up an apprentice carpenter, and bleed to death on a Roman cross. Like panentheism, Incarnational Monism shows a God Who is in and through all and yet beyond all. It is a flexible, biblical model to understand God as the OP2 behind all that is, while still affirming the reality of suffering and human freedom without implicating God in the snares of theodicy.

As Metaphysical Christianity begins to develop theologians who will provide leadership for the twenty-first century, Christian Incarnational Monism could become the rallying-point for the Church of the future. It might provide another bridge of light for Metaphysical

Christians to rediscover and reconnect with our heritage as part of the mainline/liberal Protestant movement in the Western world. Incarnational Monism may be an idea whose day has not yet come, a cornerstone laid in waiting for the house of tomorrow.

This discussion clears the field to consider one final question: Does an incarnational, monistic Christology work from a biblical perspective? One can reasonably argue that monistic Christology is completely faithful to the biblical record. In the end, Jesus reflected so much light the world could not hold him. The New Testament authors were not certain how it happened, but the crucified man Jesus became the risen Lord. At first, the faith was little more than   proclamation of the resurrection of Jesus. Studying the preaching of the first century church, as preserved in the letters of Paul, the synoptic gospels and the book of Acts, we see the main thrust of their mission was to tell the world the Jesus has risen from death.

How seriously can anyone take such claims today? Some biblical scholars take a radical position, arguing Jesus had little self-consciousness of any role as Messiah, let alone as the Divine Son of God. Others flatly reject the resurrection as a historical event; it is a good myth which gives insights into the nature of life but cannot actually have occurred. These are not rabble-rousers from the fringes of academic cultism; these opinions are held by some of the top biblical scholars of our time. Of course, being a world-class scholar—which I am not—offers no guarantee of historical accuracy. There are just as many first-rate professors of biblical studies who believe some kind of resurrection event happened in history. What we can say for certain is this: Whether the disciples could explain it or not, the early Christian community believed in the fact of Jesus' resurrection so completely they were willing to die for the new faith.

Saved by Faith?

This chapter discussed Jesus as kin to all humanity, referring to the concept by its biblical name, *kenosis*, based on the description of the Christ-event found in Philippians 2:5-13. Paul declares that Jesus the Christ left his creative union with God--a union in diversity--to empty Himself (Greek, kenosis) of that Oneness and take on the form of a "servant." Kenotic theology is in general disrepute today because it causes severe problems for any theology built upon the Gospel of John. In the fourth gospel Jesus is painted as a God-man possessing supernatural powers and knowledge not available to a mortal. Presumably, that precludes an "emptying" of the kind described by Paul.[18]

However, the Johannine materials are generally believed to be the latest and least historical of the gospel narratives. Written after 90 A.D., John's Gospel comes at least thirty years after Paul wrote his letter to the church at Philippi. That means the kenotic idea pre-dated John's Christology by several decades and represents one of the earliest Christological formulations in the Bible. As noted earlier, modern biblical scholarship sees the Jesus pictured in each New Testament source as a literary character through whom the author is trying to market his personal theology. This distinction is so important, and so seldom recognized by casual students of the Bible, that it almost cannot be over-emphasized: When people read the words of Jesus in Matthew, Mark, Luke and John they are not necessarily reading the words of Jesus. They are reading the words of a *literary character* by whom Matthew, Mark, Luke and John tout their religious views.

Think of Abraham Lincoln, a verifiably historical figure who lived in nineteenth century America. Evidence for Lincoln's existence is irrefutable: countless photographs, documents in his hand, and newspaper articles which mention the 16th president by name. But even this indisputably historical figure appears as a *literary character* in books written about him. Reading the speeches of Lincoln gives a glimpse of the historic figure in his words. All other forms give us Lincoln through someone else's eyes—reporters, historians, novelists, even film makers. (Did you know he was a vampire hunter?)[19] The same problem occurs when looking at the life and teachings of any figure from the past.

John's gospel is the easiest to identify as blatantly re-worked theology. At several places the author departs on long, intricate theological discourses which are thinly disguised as sermons, admonitions and even prayers by his Jesus. Johannine literature knows nothing of the fear shown by the Jesus-character drawn by Mark. John's Jesus is a being of light who has access to supernatural knowledge and whose theology reflects late first century thinking influenced by Greek ideas such as the Logos.

Don't be too hard on the author of John, whoever he was. If you sat down to pen a gospel based on stories you heard from others, Jesus would speak with your colloquialisms, too. First century Christians had no precedent other than the Hebrew Bible and no information other than oral tradition and a few second-hand written accounts. Sometimes the authors declare their indebtedness to earlier sources. Here's the introduction to Luke's gospel, apparently dedicated to an unknown Roman official named Theophilus.

> Since many have undertaken to set down an orderly account of the events that have been fulfilled among us, just as they were handed on to us by those who from the beginning were eyewitnesses and servants of the word, I too decided, after investigating everything carefully from the very first, to write an orderly account for you, most excellent Theophilus, so that you may know the truth concerning the things about which you have been instructed.[20]

Sifting the limited data available, gospel writers told us a story. Their efforts gave us priceless information about Jesus and valuable insights into what the various schools of thought within the first century church were saying about him. We owe to the gospel writers our deepest appreciation and respect; it is through them alone we learn about the life and ministry of Jesus. In an age before electronic news media, they can perhaps be forgiven if the image they present to us is colored by the passion of their faith. But although they are our sole authentic source for stories about Jesus's life, there is a still better source to learn about Jesus' faith.

Pauline Christology to the Rescue

Paul wrote all his letters at least ten years before the first gospel, presumably Mark, was written. That makes Paul's Christology older and closer to the events than any other extant source. In fact, readers get better information about the apostolic church from Paul's letters than from books specifically about that first generation, such as the gospels and Acts. Since the post-Paul books were written forty to sixty years after the ministry of Jesus, teachings, stories and tales in the New

Testament actually reflect issues and ideas of the second generation church, not the problems faced by the founding apostles. This   is obscured by the general misconception about who wrote the gospels. They were not written by the first generation apostles, as Luke clearly testifies in the preamble to his gospel, but by second or third-hand authors who conceived to write "an orderly account" of the events "just as they were delivered to us by those who from the beginning were eyewitnesses and ministers of the word." Reading Paul's authentic letters, however, is not reading *about* the first generation church; it is peeking over Timothy's shoulder as he takes down the rambling, feisty dictation pouring from the mind of the first theological giant of the Christian church, Paul of Tarsus. Paul's Christology is, perhaps surprisingly, quite amiable to Metaphysical interpretation.

Keying on Paul, whose Christ-figure is a pre-existent entity subservient to the Divine, it is possible to construct a paradigm that yields a high mysticism from Paul's mythological construction: If Jesus descended from union with God, emptying Himself of Divine Mind, and if humans are his brothers and sisters, then we did, too. As previously identified, the cornerstone of Metaphysical Christology rests on God as One Presence/One Power. This deep conviction implies Jesus is the representation of that which everyone can be; he is the Wayshower. If he were uniquely Divine, his deeds and words would be utterly useless to mortals. How can sinful, alienated humanity emulate the Divine? Only as a sacrificial lamb to be slaughtered in our place to rescue us from an angry God would Jesus Christ have value. Frankly, that kind of God would be no bargain.

Eric Butterworth said, "Fundamentalists believe Jesus was God becoming man. I believe that Jesus was man becoming God."[21] This is such a radical concept that to many Christians it may sound offensive. If Jesus the Christ was truly human, everything said about him can be said about humanity. You and I are the Christ. To understand how the divinity of Jesus as normative for humanity requires a whole new orientation toward the historic Jesus, consider the Divine vs. human paradox discussed in Chapter 1. Instead of a peerless spiritual being, Jesus is the guy who worked the carpenter shop down the street, and by that ordinary life provided the blueprint for divine-human union. Instead of a heavenly demi-god who visited Earth because of his compassion for hominid ineptitude, Jesus *emerges from our ranks*, as Butterworth suggests, and this simple carpenter shows everyone where to find Jacob's ladder in human consciousness. Instead of showing how far beneath the Divine we humans are, Jesus shows us how high we can go. In the words of a popular song, the Jesus event "lifts us up where we belong."[22]

For Butterworth, Jesus-the-Christ was a bridge-concept linking human nature with an incarnation of God. Like Jesus, all humans emptied themselves of intimate contact with divinity and took on the form of a servant. The process is more open to us now that we have seen his example. One of our number has demonstrated the God in everyone; a hometown boy has made the big time. If we believe he did it, and that he is our older brother, we must believe in our own potential as well. Belief in the possibility of unity with God empowers us to make greater strides in spiritual growth. By faith people are saved from futility, anxiety, and meaninglessness.

Ticket into the Thicket: Soteriology Ahead

Chapters 6-8 looked at the Trinity. The study began with Spirit, because the mystic believes spirit undergirds everything, supplying the very cosmos with the Power to be. Father is the term used by Christians to describe their relationship with that Presence/Power; many Metaphysical Christians prefer Father-Mother God, or Spirit, or just God. Neither raw energy nor uncaring mechanics stand beneath Reality, spinning galaxies on their mindless journey to oblivion. At the heart of the cosmos something like the voice of Jesus cries, *"Abba! Father!"* Life itself cares, because God-power is love. Jesus, as Wayshower pointing to the Son, is both unique and normative. He is unique because, in the words of Ralph Waldo Emerson:

> Alone in history he estimated the greatness of man. One
> man was true to what is in you and in me. He saw that
> God incarnates himself in man, and evermore goes forth
> anew to take possession of his World.[23]

Jesus as normative demonstrates the pattern all sentient beings must eventually achieve. As Dietrich Bonhoeffer pointed out, no one will "become like Jesus;" because that was the Nazarene's distinct identity.

Everyone will become the Christ, fully attuned to his/her Divine spirit. This kind of Trinitarian theology is both orthodox and radical, biblical and experiential. It is orthodox because these views are based on the middle ground walked by Church thinkers between the two extremes of Adoptionism (which said Jesus was strictly human, chosen by God for a special task) and docetism (which held Jesus was pure Divinity with no humanity whatsoever); it is radical because such a Christology makes Jesus a universal example of the divine-human paradox instead of the one and only God-man of dualistic theologies. It is biblical because it uses concepts like *kenosis* (emptying of divine nature to become fully human) and yet existential because, after de-mythologizing the message of its pre-scientific worldview, it allows people to find God in their own consciousness and in the community of believers as well as a lonely, faithful Jew hanging from a cross.

This study has also noted that Christology becomes anthropology because Jesus Christ is true man, the image of God written in large print for even the spiritually nearsighted to see. But theology cannot stop here, for Jesus was more than a good example. His incarnation, life, teaching, crucifixion and resurrection accomplished something for the sake of the human race. Biblically, this has often been likened to a sacrificial lamb offered for the sins of others. The ancient metaphor of blood sacrifice to calm an offended god lingers in Christian thought, although as we shall see in the following chapter on soteriology, *appeasement* is only one of many competing ways to interpret the death and resurrection of Jesus Christ.

Tough questions still remain in the struggle to make sense of the Jesus Christ-event in the light of mystical awareness of the God-within. How does a rational, spiritual person understand the work of Jesus Christ? How could one man's obscure life and senseless death fling open the prison doors and set free the spirit of humanity? In what way did he overcome sin and death, making eternal life readily available to all? Can anyone speak meaningfully of sin, guilt, atonement, and redemption without sacrificing the high insights of Incarnational Monism? The discussion has prepared us to dive into the great thicket of countervailing theories which describe the "work" of Jesus, *soteriology*.

CHECK YOUR KNOWLEDGE

1. Explain the following: *tritheism, henotheism, kerygma, demythologizing, Wayshower, Adoptionism, docetism, unitarianism, logos.*

2. Which concept is more "popular" among the rank-and-file of mainline Christianity, *docetism* or *Adoptionism*? Why? Describe the difference.

3. According to the text, does Metaphysical Christianity agree or disagree with orthodoxy on the full humanity/full divinity of Jesus? What is the difference?

4. What is the Pauline concept of *kenosis*? How does this chapter suggest kenosis applies to Metaphysical Christianity?

5. How does Pauline Christology help mystical/metaphysical theology? Is he in agreement with the Johannine materials?

6. How are people like Jesus? How is Jesus absolutely unique?

QUESTIONS FOR DISCUSSION

1. Why isn't it blasphemous to suggest we are sons and daughters of God? What gives you the right to make such an audacious claim?

2. List and discuss the supernatural beings in your childhood pantheon. In what ways are you still dualistic?

3. How does myth differ from falsehood? Can myth be truer than an historical event? How?

4. In what respect is Jesus the Wayshower for Christians? Is his role as Wayshower closer to a docetic or Adoptionist Christology?

5. What do you believe about the divinity of Jesus, and why? Is it biblical, traditional, experiential or rational?

6. The Apostle Paul thought Jesus "emptied himself" of full divinity when he became a man. What do you think this says about every human?

- 9 -

SOTERIOLOGY

Sin, Atonement and the "Work" of Jesus Christ

So if anyone is in Christ, there is a new creation:
everything old has passed away; see, everything has
become new! All this is from God, who reconciled us to
himself through Christ, and has given us the ministry of
reconciliation; that is, in Christ God was reconciling the
world to himself, not counting their trespasses against
them, and entrusting the message of reconciliation to us.

II Corinthians 5:17-19

Trapping Euthyphro

In the fourth century B.C.E. the philosopher Plato composed a series
of running debates between his mentor, Socrates, and a few citizens of
Athens otherwise unknown to history. Fortunately, most of the
"discussions" have survived in whole segments generally called the
Dialogues of Plato. Socrates is the star of Plato's *Dialogues,* just as Jesus
of Nazareth holds center stage in the gospels. Both sets of documents
confront modern readers with *literary characters* whose words come
from sympathetic biographers rather than the spoken or written words of
the actual historical figures. We read Socrates through the lens of Plato
and Jesus through the complex filtration system of New Testament
authors and the divergent, developing communities each represents.

It is highly unlikely young Plato lingered behind a pillar of the
temple, quill in hand, copying the words of the master philosopher in
Greek shorthand, however the only person today who worries about

whether Plato put the words into Socrates's mouth in the *Dialogues* is the occasional Ph.D. candidate wrestling with a dissertation in classical studies. It is also highly unlikely that eye-witnesses transcribed the Galilean master's Sermon on the Mount or its parallel version in Luke's Sermon on the Plain (6:17-49). Yet when biblical scholars identify secondary sources and conflicting testimony within New Testament documents, some people find their faith threatened. Nothing like that happens when professors of classical literature look at mere philosophers. The life and teachings of Jesus still speak with authority to devout believers. When authentic scholarship rightly questions what Jesus actually said or did, the four corners of the Universe tremble for those who, as Bishop Spong has said, "have no sense of history."

It may seem peculiar to begin a discussion of the traditional Christian doctrines about sin and atonement with a foray into the Platonic dialogues, but listen to a few key exchanges between Socrates and the Athenian youth, Euthyphro. The young man is on his way to testify against his own father for impiety. Socrates will be forced to drink hemlock for the same offense, which probably explains why Plato raises this central issue in the Dialogue.

In typical style, Socrates feigns ignorance and asks Euthyphro to define the nature of piety, in other words, to tell him what makes something *good* or *bad*.

> EUTHYPHRO: Yes, I should say that what all the gods love is pious and holy, and the opposite which they all hate, impious.

> SOCRATES: Ought we to enquire to the truth of this, Euthyphro, or simply to accept the mere statement on our own authority and that of others? What do you say?

> EUTHYPHRO: We should enquire; and I believe that the statement will stand the test of enquiry.

> SOCRATES: We shall know better, my good friend, in a little while. The point which I should first wish to understand is whether the pious or holy is beloved of the

gods because it is holy, or holy because it is beloved of the gods.

EUTHYPHRO: I do not understand your meaning, Socrates.[1]

This is actually the first question Socrates asks at the beginning of the passage quoted above. How much *authority* should we give to *Authority*? Shall we accept all traditional ideas, because questioning key beliefs sends us groping in the dark? The more profound our respect for the authority, the greater our terror if it should prove unstable. Most folks like to live in a world where the rules stay constant; questioning minds like Socrates would challenge us to examine our deepest assumptions.

Euthyphro doesn't realize what he's admitted when Socrates lures him into the trap. Speaking with a renowned philosopher, the lad has to agree that inquiry is better than authority. Ideas must be tested, both by critical analysis and practical application. Once Euthyphro accepts that premise, all external authorities have fallen, *even the gods*. He is defeated already.

But Socrates is only beginning. After wringing this concession from the unsuspecting Euthyphro, Socrates (or is it Plato?) next asks the most profound theological question found in classical Greek philosophy. Properly understood, the answer to this question divides people into two camps and creates a nearly irreconcilable rift between those opposing forces. One view or the other must be true. Everything in theology depends on how we answer.

Socrates asks Euthyphro "whether the pious or holy is (1) beloved of the gods because it is holy, or (2) holy because it is beloved of the gods?"

Euthyphro frankly confesses Socrates has lost him there. He needn't feel alone. Most people need to read the formula several times to grasp its importance. The distinction is not trivial, but absolutely definitive in religious thought. Socrates' question is not mere sophistry. Its implication for theology are staggering. Before any religion can speak of *sin,* it must clarify what makes an act good or evil. Appeal to authority won't do. People must look at the question and decide what constitutes the holy and the unholy. To crank up the gravity of this question for later

Christian theology, Socrates shows that, viewed from a theocentric perspective, there are only two possible answers.

1) **An act or belief is good/holy because the gods approve of it.**

At first glance this viewpoint looks admirable stressing loyalty in God. However profound difficulties occur with a theology which says goodness is determined by the Divine Will. (See Fig. 9-

---

ACTION / BELIEF + GODS' WILL = GOOD

Fig. 9-1 "Good" depends on whether or not the gods approve.

There is no *good* except those acts, beliefs, events, practices which God has blessed with an endorsement. If an action is good because the gods approves of it, the gods can operate by complete whimsy. While we might be inclined to allow a moral God, like the One proclaimed by Jesus, to act whimsically, religious zealots have used this argument to justify all manner of heinous misdeeds. If we are convinced God approves, any act of greed or violence can be justified as morally acceptable. People can feel justified in their racism, sexism and religious prejudices as long as they can find a proof-text from their favorite source of authority (the Bible, Qur'an, Chairman Mao's *Little Red Book*, etc.) Shakespeare saw the danger. In *The Merchant of Venice,* Bassanio grumbles:

> In religion,
> What damned error, but some sober brow
> Will bless it, and approve it with a text?[2]

With option #1, there is no standard of good or bad, right or wrong, except divine decree. God could declare black is white and night is day; both would be correct if our theology is predicated on God's authority and not some sort of eternal principle undergirding all Reality. This brings us to the other option.

2) An act or belief is beloved by the gods because it is good.

Reversing the equation (Fig. 9-2), we see that divine approval comes because an act or belief is inherently good. This model suggests there is a standard of good which so sublime even the gods must conform to it.

ACTION / BELIEF + GOOD = GODS' WILL

Fig. 9-2 The gods' approval depends on whether or not the ACTION / BELIEF is GOOD.

Plato's position is that goodness is self-validating, because it is a Standard (Principle) to which even the gods must conform. Of course, this means the true Divinity is that Standard. Nothing can be higher than God, so if there is a principle of goodness to which God must conform, that *Principle* must be God. This, of course, describes Platonic idealism, the godfather of all idealistic philosophies and theologies built on faith in the Absolute Goodness of God. No doubt Plato wanted his students— including you and me— to choose this latter definition of the Divine Nature. In Platonic thought the Beautiful and the Good are eternal categories having inherent value. God cannot be less than the Beautiful and the Good, nor can God change the Beautiful and the Good by an arbitrary decree.

There are profound socio-political implications to Plato's metaphysics. If the gods cannot make un-good into good by personal authority, how can mere mortals? Kings cannot violate the eternal truths by which the cosmos operates, and many of those principles have moral and ethical implications. The divine right of monarchs does not extend to making their unjust deeds morally justifiable. The king's word is law, but he cannot hold back the tide or make evil into a good. Good is good because it possesses inherent goodness, not because gods—or kings or any government—validate its goodness with their approval.

No wonder they poisoned him, even in democratic Athens.

Metaphysical Christianity has been practicing a modified Platonism for over a century. *God is Principle,* the standard of goodness. Plato forces a choice between God who stands above goodness, validating it with divine fiat, and God as the Goodness-principle Itself. The biblical record speaks inconsistently on this subject, with the OT generally in favor of whimsy (e.g., Joshua, I & II Kings) the NT usually supporting God-as-Goodness (e.g., synoptic gospels, John's gospel, I John, James, most of Paul). Church tradition is also divided on the question, although Christian mysticism has generally refused to see God apart from goodness, often insisting (as with Meister Eckhart) that God's nature compels the OP[2] to be loving, good, kind, and responsive to the receptive soul. This brief background enables consideration of the nature of sin and its consequences.

Unless we agree what constitutes *good,* we cannot hope to construct a meaningful theology of sin and atonement. If sin is the absence of good, we need to know what we're missing. So we must focus our discussion on good and its lack, which we call *sin.*

Taking Sin Seriously

Metaphysical Christianity is frequently criticized for Pollyannaish responses to the frequent suffering and occasional horror of life. "Sin" is a dirty word for a lot people, some of whom come from religious traditions which battered them with the dangers of sinfulness since childhood. Not everyone shares this history of fear-based religion. I grew up in a healthy, positive-thinking Protestant church. All the standard Calvinist doctrines were technically still on the books, but, like Catholics who practice birth control, my church dealt with Calvinism by ignoring all that totally depravity and predestination lingo. The Sunday school teachers at Zion's Reformed Church were more interested in developing young people with compassion who loved God and Jesus.

Whether suffering from Sunday school PTSD or harboring fond memories of singing "Jesus Loves Me" while munching animal crackers, growing numbers of self-identified Christians today describe themselves as "spiritual, not religious" and share a common lack of interest in critical reflection about the implications of sin and guilt. However, humans continue to make grievous choices and violate their own standards with disquieting frequency. The Apostle Paul announced his frustration about the problem almost two thousand years ago.

> I do not understand my own actions. For I do not do what I want, but I do the very thing I hate. Now if I do what I do not want, I agree that the law is good. But in fact it is no longer I that do it, but sin that dwells within me. For I know that nothing good dwells within me, that is, in my flesh. I can will what is right, but I cannot do it. For I do not do the good I want, but the evil I do not want is what I do. Now if I do what I do not want, it is no longer I that do it, but sin that dwells within me. So I find it to be a law that when I want to do what is good, evil lies close at hand.[3]

Paul wants to do what is right, yet too often he finds himself drifting into choices conscience cannot abide. He infers some kind of power within him wars with his desire to do "the good I want." Paul is attempting to blame something other than himself because he plainly does not want to do evil. Does that sound familiar? Addictive personalities understand completely what Paul is describing here. People in the grip of alcoholism or drug abuse frequently know they are killing themselves but believe they lack the power to stop. Doing something you know is wrong fits almost anyone's definition of *sin*, and it does not require outside or inside forces to work destructive consequences. In fact, blaming behavior on external or internal demonic powers or metaphysical forces is one of the constituent elements for sin itself. We shall explore these concepts and others more deeply.

Understanding Sin

Religious conservatives tend to think of sin as *individual acts of immorality* like murder, theft, criminal dishonesty, or acts of violence against the innocent. Religious progressives often view sin as *harmful group activities* such as racism, sexism, homophobia, economic injustice, ecological irresponsibility, or waging aggressive war. My unscholarly definition is *bad stuff chosen by people who ought to know better*.

Any decision that works against the health and well-being of individuals and groups might be called *sin*. No reference to spiritual blights transmitted from mythological first parents is required to see how *everyone*—even the great saints among us—struggles with choosing healthy, adaptive behavior over unhealthy, maladaptive activities. An understanding of *sin* might offer a glimpse into the problems of the divine-human power of *Will*, because any imaginable definition sin requires an act of volition. A study of will is needed to unpack the symbolism of sin and make it intelligible to modern minds.

Obviously, sin should not be trivialized as merely "missing the mark" without taking into consideration the target that was actually hit. No one can talk to a big city police officer or study the bloody history of genocidal atrocities without realizing monstrous evil is real and hurts real people. Yet, to balk at calling everything *good-good-good* in no wise acknowledges a *power* of evil. Humans need no Mephistopheles, hot from hades, to behave fiendishly toward each other or demonically abuse the Earth. The angels and demons dwell within us, and the blessing of free will curses all sentient beings to spend eternity sorting the tares and wheat, choosing the right over the wrong. The Jesus of scripture totally gets this; he takes evil seriously while refusing to acknowledge any power but God. In Luke's gospel, Jesus actually instructs his Satan-vision: "Do not put the Lord your God to the test."[4]

Who would argue that *sin* is a tepid subject? It has kept preachers fired up for two thousand years. As noted in the discussion of Gifts/Fruit or the Spirit (Ch. 6), the Apostle Paul particularly relished cooking up long lists of no-no's. The popularity of daytime soap-operas and prime-time dramas show the seamy side of human nature, suggesting Paul knew how to stir up an audience. Gossip, the soap-opera of everyday life, continues to be a favorite pastime among church people and brings new recipes to serve up sin.

A complete discussion of sin moves into the realm of *theological ethics*, also known as *moral theology,* a topic to be discussed later. While the intent this chapter is to focus on remedies and not the disease, we must briefly discuss the nature of sin in order to speak meaningfully about ways to overcome sinfulness. As we said earlier, this means we must decide what constitutes good, because sin is the absence of that goodness. Since that which is ultimately good is synonymous with God, the discussion must begin with God's nature itself.

Hebrew Consciousness

The biblical library is no place to look for harmony, but on this point there is a surprising degree of agreement. God is goodness itself, and divine goodness is described in the First Testament as 1) steadfast love (Hebrew: *hesed*), 2) justice tempered by 3) mercy or kindness. Although the formula is expressed frequently throughout the First Testament, perhaps the finest statement of God's character comes from the prophet Micah:

> "With what shall I come before the Lord, and bow myself before God on high? Shall I come before him with burnt offerings,
>
> with calves a year old? Will the Lord be pleased with thousands of rams, with ten thousands of rivers of oil? Shall I give my first-born for my transgression, the fruit of my body for the sin of my soul?"
>
> He has told you. O mortal, what is good; and what does the Lord require of you but to do justice, and to love kindness, and to walk humbly with your God?[5]

The quality of justice is an interesting concept which alone could be the subject of a whole volume; it has inspired quite a few works on theological ethics. From a metaphysical point of view, Justice can be seen as combination of the four divine-human powers studies thus far: Understanding, Wisdom and Power as enacted into being by the Will. Some theologians, notably the earlier writings of Reinhold Niebuhr, have said that steadfast love is not likely to break out in society at large, but justice is possible.

Steadfast love (Hebrew, *hesed*) means loyalty, the kind of devotion a good king could reasonably expect from his subjects. Implied in the term is a contract between two parties, called the *covenant* or *testament* in biblical terms. The ruler treats his subjects with justice and they respond with steadfast love, i.e., dutiful service and faithfulness. Of course, this exactly describes the Hebrew idea of a covenantal relationship between Yahweh, the God of Israel, and his chosen people.

But even divine justice must be mitigated by an even greater divine *mercy,* often translated *kindness.* Jewish thought has usually held, contrary to widespread belief in Christian circles, that people are capable of keeping the Law, all of the Law. However, Jewish pragmatism surfaced when ancient writers stressed the merciful kindness of Yahweh. Knowing that humans could keep the Law was no guarantee they would readily do it. God was merciful with humanity, because few could stand before the King and Judge in a state of righteousness under the Law. In fact, the entire body of the Law and the sacrificial system for forgiveness of sin was another example of God's merciful kindness. He could have easily abandoned Homo sapiens to drift aimlessly in lawlessness and sin, which are synonymous in Judaism.

The OT concept of divine goodness describes loyal love, supreme justice and even greater mercy. Life, too, must reflect that steadfast love, justice and mercy, or the whole system is a contradiction. Therefore, to the Hebrew, the world was a system which operated according to divine principles. To the ancient Hebrew, sin was any attempt to negate that orderly flow by stepping outside the protective constraints of Torah. Lawlessness, in its many forms, was sin. The greatest sin for the ancient Hebrew was idolatry, i.e., to worship anything other than Yahweh. If God is One, any attempt to move beyond Oneness to worship god in the plural was a threat to the whole system of divine Law and Order. There could be no other gods beside Yahweh. The hope of fallible humans for reconciliation with their neighbors, with the orderly flow of life itself, rested on his steadfast love, justice, and merciful kindness.

First Testament writers generally gave Yahweh credit for personal authority above any abstract standard of good, but none would be so rash to suggest that he ever acted in any manner contrary to his holy nature. The God of Abraham, Isaac and Jacob simply could not be unloving, unjust, unkind or merciless, but people could demonstrate all of the above. It was the communal experience of human fallibility that generated the cry of the prophets to national repentance. All the Children of Israel required forgiveness. Sin was an attempt to negate the Law, which was summarized so aptly by Micah: "Do justice, love kindness, and walk humbly with your God."

Second Testament Consciousness

Heeding the words of Jesus, Christian writers saw their task as fulfilling the Law rather than setting it aside. Even so, post-crucifixion Christian thinkers began re-thinking the ancient faith almost immediately. No one knows what actually happened, but after Jesus made his transition from earthly ministry, his followers began reporting continued contact with their Master. Whether through visions, dreams, meditation experiences, memories, or tangible encounters with a resuscitated corpse, the community believed they were still being led by Jesus, who now had become Risen Lord. Like a sea change in Jewish thought, which would rise like a mountain from the deep to become the largest family of religions on the planet, Christianity began slowly, developing its theology as in expanded its base. New ideas emerged in the light of that world-changing phenomenon.

No longer was justice enough, even when softened by merciful kindness. No longer did people owe *dutiful love* to God and neighbor; Jesus introduced the radical new concept of *selfless love* (*agape*), and ordered Christians to squander love recklessly on even the most unlovable. God's nature was now understood in reference to the life, teachings and character of Jesus Christ. Not a benign despot who doles out mercy, God was a loving Father who longs for his children to return unto him even when they are in full rebellion and have raced off to attempt to overturn every divine law.

In the New Testament we meet a different God concept, a God Who comes to us in worldly weakness and Whose power is set free through utter defeat: Not Caesar on a throne but Jesus on a cross. In Dietrich Bonhoeffer's *Letters and Papers from Prison*, printed posthumously, he wrote the following poignant, cryptic words:

> Here is the decisive difference between Christianity and all religions. Man's religiosity makes him look in his distress to the power of God in the world: God is the *deus ex machina*. The Bible directs man to God's powerlessness and suffering; only the suffering God can help.[6]

In Greek theater the playwrights often solved the problems of their heroes by bringing a god (*deus*) out of a box (*ex machina*) to perform some miracle and save the day. Bonhoeffer, who had seen his country ravaged by war brought on by a madman in power, thought the New Testament knew nothing of this sort of god. According to Bonhoeffer, the role God portrayed in Jesus Christ was a powerless son of man, involved with his people through sharing in their suffering. Bonhoeffer believed only a God so intimately involved with the world can help, because that God alone can speak the authentic word of faith the language of everyday life. Although Jesus the Christ appears powerless before Pontius Pilate, through powerlessness his truth is set free to transform lives and move humanity forward to Christ-consciousness. Miracles are not necessary if the system contains self-correcting, self-healing tendencies. In the paradox of this central Christian image—Jesus Christ crucified—rests the key to the absolute goodness of God. The self-giving love which breaks the power of even the most terrible circumstances sets everyone free to experience the good of life, to express creativity, appreciate the beauty of the Universe, and share in the mystery of love.

The crucifixion has always been a problem for Christians. Even though some branches of the faith have chosen to emphasize the suffering of Jesus almost to the point of morbidity, the early Church agreed with Paul that the cross was a "scandal" and a "stumbling-block" (my irreverent paraphrase: banana peel). The cross was not used a symbol for the faith of Jesus until several centuries had passed, partly because it was still the Roman government's treatment of choice for criminal conduct, and partly because the Church had to answer a lot of questions within its ranks about what sense it made for Jesus to die such an ignoble death. Christians began to see the paradox of the Cross as a powerful symbol which speaks to something deep inside everyone: It is the very absurdity of Calvary which makes the crucifixion of Jesus Christ so real.

Could Jesus have avoided this nasty fate? Certainly. He had several escape routes open, including simply leaving Jerusalem before they arrested him. Instead, like Bonhoeffer two thousand years later, Jesus chose to fide out the storm, even though it meant embracing the cross. His choice demonstrated that even in the midst of scandalous defeat and apparently utter failure, God's One Power/One Presence is at work. The symbol of defeat becomes the central image of Christian triumph. Good Friday gives way to Easter morning. All bets are off. People need not fear disaster anymore, because God empowers humanity to higher love, even if utterly ruined by worldly standards. Look to the cross as a mystical symbol of the One Power/One Presence, God the Good, regardless of appearances to the contrary. (More about the symbolism of the cross later in this study.)

Understanding Sin: Rabel's Recipe

To talk about Sin and Atonement, we first need to define sin. That is a tough task. Modern life suggests that one person's sin is another person's freedom. Yet, life is full of heroism and horror, and we could not live in a world which provided no clues to decide between good and un-good. For our working definition we'll turn to Ed Rabel, an original thinker and teacher at the Unity School of Christianity. Rabel blended biblical concepts with modern Christian mystical thought by this simple recipe: *Sin is any attempt to negate Divine Ideas.*

OT consciousness held that sin is an attempt to negate the Divine Ideas of loyal love, justice and merciful kindness (Micah 6:8). NT writers viewed sin as an attempt to negate the Divine Ideas of love, life, prosperity, health, and forgiveness. Rabel's recipe is both comprehensive and easy to apply; it bridges OT and NT views of sin.

Rabel's classification works for theology, too. Virtually everything today's theologians might call *sin* are anti-human deeds and unhealthy attitudes: murder, racism, sexism, homophobia, and drug abuse, irresponsible use of resources, stealing, and inflicting emotional or physical pain. All these can be understood as attempts to negate Divine Ideas. Murder is an attempt to negate the Divine Idea of *Life*. Theft is an attempt to overturn the orderly flow of *Prosperity*. Racism, sexism and nationalism are attempts to violate the Divine Idea of *agape*, selfless love. Rabel would probably agree with Paul Tillich's dictum that *sin is separation*. By choosing sin instead of love, people separate themselves from the image of God within them.

This brings the conversation back to Plato. Good is good because of its inherent goodness, not because a supernatural power wills it, which dovetails nicely with the model of Metaphysical Christianity presented in this study. Divine ideas are Spiritual Law under which God's Holy Spirit functions. Rather than a set of rules governing divine action, divine ideas are kinetic law, God-in-expression. God the Father is the same as God the active Spirit, both are the same as God the Son, or Christ-consciousness. As discussed previously, in recent years it has become fashionable for theologians to speak of God as a *process*. Metaphysical Christianity works comfortably with the option of seeing God-as-Process, God-as-Totality, God-as-Unity. God is the goodness-principle in action, the process of goodness unfolding in the real world. Any attempt to negate divine ideas—to work against the good which God is always trying to manifest in our lives—is bound to have an unhealthy effect on the individual. Theology, borrowing a term from anthropology, might call such behavior *maladaptive*.

Radical Freedom Requires Option for Error (Sin)

Implicit in the human condition is freedom. Not all Christian thinkers have agreed, notably Reformation theorizer John Calvin, but progressive theology is fairly unanimous in affirming that we humans are free to behave as outrageously as we can imagine. To wander as far from the optimum path as error beliefs can carry us. People have a divine right to be wrong. This also means humans have the power to choose. Without the ability to choose *un-good* (evil), there is no freedom to choose *good*. Radical freedom gives the tools to follow the rules. Without the power of Will operating in a totally free person, no growth is possible.

Wrong choices are part of learning. Children cannot master solid geometry before stumbling around in simple arithmetic, floundering before the dragons of multiplication, subtraction, addition, division. Every step of the way, errors mark the road is by staking out its edges, showing where the road is not. In snow country, tall sticks dot the outside edges of vanished highways for snowplows to clear the path. Errors provides information, steering a clear path by showing the drifts of snow or tangle of weeds along life's highway.

However, it would be a mistake to romanticize misdeeds; some errors are more painful and less innocuous than a slip in math or wandering off a snow drifted highway. There is a vast difference between arriving at an incorrect quotient in long division and arriving at a supermarket to commit armed robbery. Thankfully, for most behaviors as blatantly harmful as armed robbery have been fenced off life's highways by moral standards (mores) built by good experiences. If someone seriously argued in favor of armed robbery as a morally correct action, people might question his sincerity or sanity.

Humans live very closely with other humans, so we must have codes of behavior which facilitate cooperation and harmony while allowing for healthy competition. Codes will vary quite profoundly from culture to culture, but the key element in each is that the approved behavior will contribute to the health and well-being of the society at large, hence will be Adaptive. To rob a grocery store is an act which is harmful to the good of the greater society, hence stealing in that context is an error, a sin. It is also an attempt to negate the divine idea of Prosperity and therefore qualifies metaphysically as Sin.

However, stealing horses from another tribe was an act of bravery for the Lakota Sioux. Young men proved their courage and enhanced the tribe's wealth/prestige by raiding other tribes, which by the definition this study has been applying would make such behavior *adaptive* and therefore not sinful. Steal a horse from a rival tribe and you're a hero. Steal the same horse from a brother Lakota in the next lodge was just plain horse-theft and an act of disloyalty totally repugnant to their value system, a cardinal sin. Why? Because the greater good of the larger society was not served by intra-tribal theft.

If you cannot lie down at night without worrying that your cousin in the next lodge might cut the ropes and make off with your prize ponies, who would band together? Mutual defense, corporate food gathering and cross-family marriage would be impossible.

Does horse theft by Lakota youth meet the metaphysical definition for sin? Was it an attempt to negate a divine idea? Right the contrary. Raiding enemies for horses, which was seldom a violent act in the days before the white man, opened Plains Indians to increased prosperity by redistributing wealth through the vehicle of the raid. No encampment could hoard horses, because at some point the herd became too large to defend from stealthy raiders.

In a way, raiding for horses was a kind of primitive reverse-income tax, the poorer groups receiving compensation from their richer neighbors and thus leveling wealth in Native American culture. Riding also provided a rite of passage for young braves to leave childhood and become full adults, an important function in any social system.

Today, parents hand young people the keys to the car; eventually, they earn diplomas and perhaps higher degrees. In the society of the Plains Indians, becoming an adult male required acquiring your own transportation by raiding another tribe for a horse. The only diploma was the right to dance the deed by the fire once the young man returned from his exploits. To be consistent with what we have said so far about human behavior and religious teaching, horse theft among the Lakota was no more sinful than taking student loans to pay for college today.

Anthropology comes to the rescue of theology at this point. Murder, in-group theft, adultery and incest are outlawed because they are maladaptive. These prevent group cohesion, growth, happiness and well-being. Societies which have allowed murder, unrestricted theft, open adultery and incest may have existed in human history, but these behaviors are so destructive that any social order which mistakenly calls them "good" will not last long. There is an objective quality to sinful behavior which outpictures in the life of the individual and in society at large.

Although no known society has openly advocated such maladaptive behaviors as murder or adultery, every group of humans has had its murderers and adulterers. Sin defines the road, but there are those who stray so far afield they have difficulty finding the path again. Human nature seems to work against us just when we need clear thinking the most. Studies show that people tend either to rationalize their errors by blaming them on people or circumstances, or assume responsibility for events over which they had no control. Psychologists call these two tendencies *under-responsible* and *over-responsible* behavior.

Under-Responsible Behavior: "It's *not* my fault!"

An under-responsible person refuses to admit she could ever be wrong; it is always the other person's mistake, or events forced them to act that way. The slogan for under-responsible people is, *"But I didn't do nothin'!"*

Al Capone earns the prize as history's most under-responsible gangster. When he was finally brought to justice, did the great mobster express remorse for his misdeeds? Hardly. Al Capone—murderer, extortionist, leader of a vast crime syndicate—actually said:

I have spent the best years of my life giving people the lighter pleasures, helping them have a good time, and all I get is abuse, the existence of a hunted man."[7]

Over-Responsible Behavior: "It's *all* my fault!"

If under-responsible folks refuse to admit their errors, over-responsible blame themselves for everything. If you have a flat while driving him to the hospital for an emergency appendectomy, the over-responsible person will apologize for causing your mishap. These folks mistakenly believe they have the power to work havoc on a wide-scale just by coming in contact with people, places and things. "If I had not asked Uncle Chester to eat Christmas dinner with us, he would never have slipped on the ice in front of his house late that night and broken his hip," they moan. They feel guilty if someone else mistreats them; returning a badly burned steak at a restaurant is impossible. They even feel guilty if the weather is bad on a day they planned a trip, because if they had not planned to go the bad weather might not have arrived to punish them and spoil the day for everyone.

Objective Guilt

This study has suggested sentient beings could be understood as a divine-human paradox, a complex of spiritual and physical energy brought into existence through Divinity's emptying Itself of fullness so that a bit of itself can know creativity and growth. When people do things which run afoul of that process—trying to invalidate the divine idea stamped in each person's spiritual nature—the individual strays into sin. There is little doubt that people suffer real, actual disadvantages by acting on those error-beliefs, much like a person butting his head against a stone wall. God, however, does not need to punish sin any more than society needs to jail people who butt into stone walls.

If we hurt anything by sin it is ourselves. *Objective guilt* is another way of describing *such self-chosen spiritual self-harm*; some people have described S-I-N as "Self Inflicted Nonsense." Under-responsible people. i.e., those who will not face their culpability for maladaptive behavior, nevertheless suffer from sinful choices, just as the person beating his head against the wall will experience pain whether or not he acknowledges its source.

Sometimes objective guilt results from things people do, but other times the harm comes by choosing not to act. Refusing to help someone in genuine need, the sin of the priest and the Levite in the Good Samaritan parable, misses an opportunity for growth. Laziness in devotional life keeps spiritual batteries discharged and less able to meet those daily mini-crises with Divine Ideas. Falling into a rut in marriage allows even the brightest love to fade. Those failures have traditionally been called *sins of omission*, and there is no good reason for abandoning the term. Conversely, actions which willfully attempt to negate a divine idea are *sins of commission*. Both generate objective guilt because both stunt the perpetrator's spiritual growth.

Subjective Guilt

If under-responsible people harm themselves objectively, over-responsible behavior results in *subjective guilt*, which is *the anxiety suffered when doing something that should have been avoided or avoiding something that should have been done.* Subjective guilt can be extremely self-critical, as with an over-responsible person, but it can also be right on target. When caught in a self-protecting lie, the moral person rightly feels guilty.

This kind of guilt, held in balance by a healthy ego, generates the energy needed to take corrective actions in our attitudes and behavior. If getting caught in a lie were not painful for most people, human society would be a network of falsehoods. It could be argued that a little more consciousness of subjective guilt- is occasionally necessary to tone up sagging truth muscles, especially for political leaders. Here again is an example of the middle path, which this time occurs from the dichotomy of under-responsible/over-responsible behaviors. Too little responsibility for maladaptive actions and people suffer objective guilt with scant opportunity to correct the problem because they experience no anxiety to energize the quest for improvement. Too much responsibility for actions, taking the blame when only a bystander, and personal self-confidence is so paralyzed by anxiety so that no growth is possible.

Obviously, this can happen whether or not people consciously realize the misery they are creating for themselves and others. An under-responsible person will blame everyone else but suffer nonetheless. Misery knows no distinction between objective and subjective guilt:

whether a person feels guilty or not, error belief (sin) works its mischief by de-humanizing the sinners, robbing them of opportunities to grow in Christ-consciousness. Racism, sexism and religious prejudices can be unspoken assumptions—sins of omission, never acted upon—but will nevertheless keep the bigot from understanding the universality of God's spirit in all sentient beings.

Some of life's most miserable circumstances can masquerade as success and happiness, so we can never judge by external appearances how spiritually advanced a person might be. Too many outwardly happy marriages show the first signs of distress only after they file for divorce. Too many seemingly successful men and women end their lives by suicide. The price paid for objective and subjective sins of omission or commission is collected in poor quality of life. Billionaire Howard Hughes lived in fear of disease and became a virtual prisoner of his own wealth. Who would call him *prosperous*? Athletes who pump their bodies full of performance enhancing drugs cannot be called *healthy*.

Misery is the outpicturing of bad choices and error-beliefs. The Apostle Paul had the best commentary on where unchecked sin finally leads: "For the wages of sin is death, but the free gift of God is eternal life in Christ Jesus our Lord."[8] Death need not mean the immediate end of life. Both Luke and Matthew reported that Jesus told his disciples, "Let the dead bury their own dead." Luke's Jesus added, "But as for you, go and proclaim the kingdom of God."[9]

Find Bedrock or Collapse

Our study has been diagnostic thus far. We have discussed sin and its effects on the person, charting those effects in a downward fall from the path which God wants us to find and walk. But how shall we regain the road once we are lost in the tangle? Will better information do the trick? Hardly. Merely listing the requirements for God-consciousness is like telling a drowning man how to swim. New Testament writers were adamant that mere knowledge is not enough. It takes action to bring wandering humanity back on course again. This mandate of Jesus to take action has influenced everything from pastoral ministry during the Black Plague to the Christian Social Gospel movement of the twentieth century. Mentioned previously, Connie Fillmore's "Five Principles" concludes with the requirement to take spiritual insights into the world:

> Knowing and understanding the laws of life, also called
> Truth, are not enough. A person must also live the truth
> that he or she knows.[10]

To follow the Christ-within, many have decided to turn their lives over to the Omnipotent Presence and Power, and begin "to walk humbly" with our God. This is the basis for countless decisions of faith throughout the millennia. More recently, in Metaphysical Christian history, the "decision for Christ" undergirds the Covenant written by Charles and Myrtle Fillmore when they began their prayer and publishing ministry that would eventually become the Unity movement:

> We, Charles Fillmore and Myrtle Fillmore, husband and
> wife, hereby dedicate ourselves, our time, our money, all
> we have and all we expect to have, to the Spirit of Truth,
> and through it, to the Society of Silent Unity.
>
> It being understood and agreed that the said Spirit of
> Truth shall render unto us an equivalent for this
> dedication, in peace of mind, health of body, wisdom,
> understanding, love, life and an abundant supply of all
> things necessary to meet every want without our making
> any of these things the object of our existence.
>
> In the presence of the Conscious Mind of Christ Jesus,
> this 7th day of December A.D. 1892.
>
> Charles Fillmore
> Myrtle Fillmore[11]

Their act of sheer trust would be unthinkable without a role model in the historic person of Jesus, to whom the Fillmores to dedicate their life's work, "In the presence of the Conscious Mind of Christ Jesus..."[12] To discuss this idea we must grapple with concepts which are wholly alien to Metaphysical Christianity, although they form the mainstay of traditional Christian theology. This brings us to the critical point in bridge building, the moment at which we drive into the mucky bottom and search for bedrock to support the final span linking our Metaphysical Christian island with the church of Jesus Christ on the mainland. There is no avoiding this messy task. Either we find our foundation here or the bridge comes tumbling down.

Atonement: Christ Died For Your Sins

The New Testament is unequivocal on this point: Jesus Christ came to save humanity from bondage to the law of sin and death. This idea can be found in all four gospels, the Pauline and deutero-Pauline letters, Acts, and the general epistles. It is implicit everywhere else. NT thought builds upon a foundational belief that Jesus of Nazareth somehow gave humanity access to eternity, ways to throw off the burden of sin, and power for effective living. Paul said it boldly, simply, and no allegorical gamesmanship can siphon the power away.

> While we were still weak, at the right time Christ died for the ungodly. Why, one will hardly die for a righteous man-- though perhaps for a good man one will dare even to die. But God shows his love for us in that while we were yet sinners Christ died for us.[13]

Students of Christian Scriptures are sometimes surprised to learn there is no clear NT explanation about how the death of Jesus saves the "ungodly." Looking back through centuries of interpretation, it is difficult for us to factor out the shades of meaning which Christian theology has given to the work of Jesus Christ. We are so familiar with orthodox interpretations of the Jesus-event that something must be said about these various Atonement theories before moving on to consider a restatement of Jesus' mission in metaphysical Christian language. The primary source for this brief foray into the history of Christian doctrine is *Understanding the Christian Faith* by theologian and biblical scholar Georgia Harkness.

There are, of course, many possible ways to contemplate the work of Jesus Christ. Some explanations contain elements which most modern theologians reject outright, but looking at these solutions to the Easter problem provides better insight into the whole spectrum of historic Christian thought offers a springboard for leaping beyond those limited concepts to a higher, more worthy interpretation of Atonement.

Before beginning, it is worth to note it was the crucifixion, not the resurrection, which caused problems for early Christians. Jewish followers of the Nazarene expected a resurrection at the end of time. What they did not expect was their messiah to be publicly crucified. Almost immediately after the Easter appearances, Christians began trying to interpret the crucifixion in the light of their historic faith and their firm belief that Jesus had risen from the dead. Soon, they fell back upon Temple imagery. By the end of the first century, John's gospel was proclaiming that Jesus was the "lamb of God, who takes away the sin of the world."[14]

Rather than an act of violence ending the career of their messiah, the crucifixion morphed into an integral part of the plan for the salvation of the world. Even so, biblical authors never quite got around to explaining how the death of Jesus "takes away the sin of the world." That effort, which began in writings of the early Church, goes on today in the volume you are reading. Here, then, are some of the more well-known theories of Atonement.

Appeasement Theory

Dr. Harkness prefers the word propitiation, from the King James translation of I John 2:2—"...he is the propitiation for our sins; and not for ours only, but for the whole world." A better translation comes from the *New Revised Standard* version: "He is the atoning sacrifice for our sins, and not for ours only but also for the sins of the whole world."

Appeasement theory, however, follows the older, King James wording. God is an All-Holy, All-Righteous Supreme Being who cannot stand the sight of sin. Life in this world implicates human beings in free choices which result in errors, therefore people invariably break God's rules and sin. This makes God angry, because he doesn't like sin and cannot seem to separate his dislike for sin from his reputed love for the sinner. God's righteous anger demands punishment for sinful humanity.

Enter Jesus Christ. Appeasement theory says the only way to placate God is for Jesus to die as a sacrificial offering, just like blood sacrifices offered by pre-Christian religions to mollify angry gods. God accepts the blood of Jesus and his wrath is soothed by this eternal sacrifice. Besides the comic figure of a God whose own temper gets the best of him, there are some serious theological problems with Appeasement Theory. John Macquarrie pointed to the most serious defect:

> It is necessary indeed that some particular historical event should bring to light in a signal way the "mystery hidden for ages and generations," but no historical event changes God's attitude, or makes him from a wrathful God into a gracious God, or allows his reconciling work to get started--such thoughts are utterly to be rejected.[15]

Harkness added:

> When this (propitiation) is taken to mean, as it too often has been, that an angry God has to be appeased, the modern Christian rightly rebels. It sounds like primitive religion, and clearly is not the kind of God that Jesus worshipped and served! Jesus' God of fatherly love for all men, even sinners, needs no sin offering to propitiate his wrath.[16]

Some passages in Paul support Appeasement/Propitiation theory, but Macquarrie said these verses can be read differently depending on the context. Further, he insists the idea is so abhorrent that it fails other tests such as reason and experience.

> Even if it could claim support from the Bible or the history of theology, (Appeasement theory) would have to be rejected because of the affront which it offers to reason and conscience.[17]

Ransom Theory: Sucker-Punching the Devil

This may be the oldest official doctrine of the Atonement, dating back to the early centuries of Church history. According to Ransom

Theory, humanity is enslaved to evil powers, especially the Devil, and must be purchased from Satanic influence like a slave bought at the auction block. There are a number of Pauline passages which lend proof-text support to this clearly incredible notion, most notably these remarks in Paul's First Letter to the Corinthians:

> Or do you not know that your body is a temple of the Holy Spirit within you, which you have from God, and that you are not your own? For you were bought with a price; therefore glorify God in your body.[18]

Besides the inability of proof-texting to "prove" any doctrine in the eyes of modern theologians, these passages could be interpreted as merely emphasizing the costliness of Jesus' self-sacrifice, much the way we might say that we bought a much-wanted item but it cost us "a King's ransom." No sensible person would ask, "Who's the king you paid a ransom to get this?" We understand figures of speech for what they are and never take them literally in everyday conversation. Has anyone ever "dropped you at the corner"? Did it hurt?

Adding the gospel references (Mk 10:45 and Mt 20:2) to Paul's comments in I Corinthians and the mention of "the man Christ Jesus, who gave himself as a ransom for all" in the pseudo-Pauline First Letter to Timothy (I Tim 2:6), still falls far short of a biblical theory of the Atonement as a payoff to the forces of evil.

Some scholars have said Ransom theory is helpful because it points to the high cost of the Atonement, but it presupposes evil powers who hold title to the world and the souls of humanity. Such metaphysical dualism marks Ransom theory as more akin to the Gnostic rejection of the good of this world than the world-affirming theologies generally found in mainline Christian thought today.

Ironically, one of the ancient "friends" of Metaphysical Christianity, Origen of Alexandria, firmly believed God paid Satan with the death of Jesus for the souls of humanity which the Devil held in captivity. Satan was duped when he failed to hold a mere Jewish Carpenter in bondage as he held other mortals. In effect, Jesus the Christ had sucker-punched Old Scratch. According to Origen, when Jesus rose from the grave he threw off the shackles of satanic control and led humanity out of bondage like

Moses departing from Pharaoh with Israel and the booty of Egyptian households.

Even adding the impressive name of Origen to its pedigree, the Ransom theory doesn't work for metaphysical Christianity, which builds its theology on the unshakable rock of One Presence One Power. Recently a more sophisticated version of the Ransom theory has resurfaced, chiefly through the views presented by Swedish theologian Gustaf Aulen in his book *Christus Victor*. Aulen is no crude literalist and numbers people like John Macquarrie in his camp of admirers, but his conclusions still require a theology of Gnostic dualism which Metaphysical Christian thinking rejects as totally inconsistent with God's nature. To his credit, Aulen frankly admits the problem:

> ...the classic idea of the Atonement is dualistic and dramatic: it depicts the drama of the Atonement against a dualistic background. If Dualism is eliminated, it is impossible to go on thinking of the existence of powers hostile to God, and the basis of the classic view has been dissolved away.[19]

Here is a scholar at war with his own theology. For his solution to work requires an unseen, evil force lurking in the shadows causing frail humanity to slip. He tries to clean up his metaphysics with footnotes. Aulen's notes explain he is not speaking of "metaphysical dualism between the Infinite and the finite" or "absolute Dualism between Good and Evil typical of Zoroastrian and Manichaean teaching..." His variant of dualism means "the opposition between God and that which in his own created world resists his will; between the Divine Love and the rebellion of created wills against Him."[20]

But his very punctuation gives Aulen away. Good and Evil, Dualism, Infinite--all receive capitalization, suggesting they have ultimate meaning for him, or at least A.G. Herbert, his translator, believed so. It makes no sense philosophically or theologically to dispense with "metaphysical Dualism" and then insist that dualism really exists in some other form, i.e., as the opposition to God's Will by our created, finite wills. Either there is One Presence and Power in the Universe or there is not. If not, then what we have is not classical dualism but multifarious powers and presences, returning us to the age of polytheisms.

The possibility of free will operating within a unitary system—i.e., sentient beings existing as expressions of God with complete freedom, to include the ability to attempt to negate divine ideas—does not occur to him, or if it did he must have dismissed it without comment. Like most metaphysical dualists, Aulen also rejects two equal and opposite dualistic powers—God and Satan—at war for eternity. No one, not even the Zoroastrians, has been hardy enough to claim that kind of split-apple Universe, because two equal and opposite powers cannot be said to possess Omnipotence, unless held in some kind of unity such as seeing them as two ends of the same process, which would make nonsense of the whole concept of goodness.

Macquarrie faults Aulen for failing to demythologize the biblical sources of his soteriology, but a greater problem lies at the heart of any theology built on dualism, i.e., locating the source of those "principalities and powers" which hold humanity prisoner. If everything comes from God, there can be no "power" of evil. If everything does not come from God, he is no god. In eternity as in the created cosmos, the only available resource is God-power. Incarnational Monism is a logically consistent answer to the dilemma, tempered by an understanding of kenotic emptying as normative for all sentient beings. This necessarily precludes any evil power gripping at human souls. Shadows have no talons.[21]

Penal Substitution Theory

Also called Vicarious Atonement, this is possibly the best-known theory. Interestingly, Penal Substitution theory is not an ancient doctrine of the Church, like Ransom theory, but a relatively new development. The idea originates in the Middle Ages from the work of St. Anselm of Canterbury.

> As Anselm propounded it, man's sin before God is a
> debt so great that no mere man, but only the God-man,
> could pay it; and he could make atonement, not by any
> act of duty that was required of him, but only by
> something not required--the giving of his life.[22]

Looking at Christianity through the lens of the legal system had antecedents as far back as Tertullian (second century C.E.) who was well versed in Roman law. Not surprisingly, one of the names used to describe vicarious atonement is Penal Substitution. Here's how it works: God is the Judge. You stand before the bar, guilty as charged, awaiting your sentence of eternal damnation, demanded by God's justice and righteousness.

But, wait! Here comes Jesus Christ, offering to take the penalty for your sins by suffering on the cross in your place. God accepts Jesus as substitute. (How much you are involved in the deal gets theologians hopelessly entangled in arguments about "subjective" and "objective" views of vicarious atonement; we shall avoid that jungle.) A guilty sinner is set free from the curse of the sin and death by Jesus' willingness to suffer in your place.

Unquestionably, there are some highly appealing elements to this story. The idea of Jesus loving individuals enough to die for them has brought genuine tears of gratitude to countless people. The emotional and spiritual release believers have felt through the centuries due to this narrative of divine self-sacrifice cannot be underestimated. Until individuals learn to recognize their self-worth and realize they are not standing as condemned criminals before the bar of divine justice, the conviction that God accepts and releases them because of the atoning love of Jesus can heal many wounded hearts.

Beyond its philosophical difficulties, three main objections to Penal Substitution leap out at modern Christians. First, the whole idea is morally untenable. Who could ethically allow another to be punished in his place? Suggesting that Jesus willingly went to Calvary still fails to remove the act of cowardice on the part of humans who are not willing to face the consequences of their actions. If another person goes to prison for a crime committed by someone else, how do we feel about the person who allows his substitute to suffer in his place? To accept this kind of replacement would be an act of selfish cruelty, which is one of the definitions of sin, which means vicarious atonement works only if *sin* saves people from the curse of sin.

Secondly, Penal Substitution negates grace. As usually defined, Grace is God's goodness which floods people's lives whether they deserve it or not. It seems reasonable that God wants everyone to enjoy the good, if people will accept divine blessings—but that is the very problem with vicarious atonement. If God wants good for humanity, eternal punishment is not just unnecessary, it is absurd. Casting God as some kind of Cosmic Judge who enforces the moral code is contrary to the vision of grace, which offers unearned mercy.

The Penal Substitution theory turns the Divine drama into a comedy. Why should God be encumbered with a legal system, which God ostensibly created, in which God must circumvent by bribing God?

Finally, the result of Penal Substitution is an unchanged sinner set loose on heaven. No growth is required, no spiritual development. Just forgiveness slopped out to creatures who have no need to reach for the stars because heaven has been lowered to their level, handed to them gratis. Charles Manson goes to Disney World. In fact, those who advocate vicarious atonement most strenuously insist that any effort on the part of sinful humanity to improve itself amounts to a denial of God's free gift of salvation. "Works righteousness" or "salvation by works" earns the label of heresy for these people because it suggests we can do something for ourselves beyond humbly accepting the slot in heaven reserved for us by the death of Jesus on the cross. Small wonder Dietrich Bonhoeffer pronounced such an easy-to-afford, no-money-down ticket to heaven "cheap grace."

The valuable element in vicarious atonement theory is, of course, its emphasis on the free flow of good to humanity from a gracious God. Penal Substitutionists make a good point when they say no one can earn salvation, because God's approval comes through grace and not deeds. However, if *salvation* means avoiding hell and achieving heaven, no gracious act of self-sacrifice can compensate for the infinite atrocity of establishing a place like perdition. Beyond the logical inconsistency of a loving God Who created and sustains a place of fiery, eternal torment for people who do not agree with Church doctrine during their brief stay on Earth, it is abundantly clear no such place could have ever existed. (The utility bill alone would be cost-prohibitive.)

God's forgiveness need not be earned because, as Eric Butterworth liked to say with his penchant for turning truisms inside out, God cannot forgive us, having never been angry with us in the first place.

How does God forgive? Our answer may seem startling,

possibly even sacrilegious. God doesn't really forgive sin...God is love. God hasn't held any unforgiveness. There is nothing to forgive in his sight...[23]

Fosdick and the Prodigal

In the parable of the Prodigal Son (Luke 15:11-32) the father never lets his spendthrift child provoke him to anger. Harry Emerson Fosdick was senior pastor of New York's Riverside Baptist Church, author of a stack of books, a popular radio ministers and one of the great preachers of the twentieth century when he wrote the following analysis of vicarious atonement as contrasted with the teaching explicit in the parable of the forgiving father:

> The Prodigal has sinned against his father, and the father—not a feudal lord but an honest-to-goodness father—sees the returning son, penitent and ashamed, coming home from the far country. According to Anselm and his kind, can the father run and fall on the prodigal's neck and kiss him? Oh, no! A legal reparation must first of all be made. There must be an elder brother, of another sort altogether from the one described in Jesus' parable, who will volunteer to let himself be flogged to death, crucified, or what you will, after seeing which the father, his legal honor satisfied, can welcome the returning son. Can you imagine Jesus thinking in such terms as that? These legalistic theories of the atonement are in my judgment a theological disgrace.[24]

Any God who demanded a blood-guilt sacrifice would be unworthy of worship. Fortunately for the whole of creation, there is no need for Substitutionary Atonement to justify sinners. In the courtroom language of that legalistic theory, we need not be acquitted because no charges have been filed.

Moral Influence Theory

This idea, popular in some liberal churches today, sees Jesus Christ as the One whose life and death point to the perfect pattern for humanity to emulate. Georgia Harkness found much in this model to commend itself. It has the advantage of linking Jesus' death to his life and teachings, which gives us reason to study his words and try to follow him. It also counters the tendency to see the cross as somehow magically changing God's mind about humanity.

Harkness raised some objections to any theology of Atonement built strictly on the Moral Influence Theory, and we must admit her points are well taken. If Jesus died as a martyr to his own teachings, how does his death differ from the death of any other human—Socrates, Lincoln, Dietrich Bonhoeffer—who was faithful to high principles to the end? Furthermore, other theologians have noted that the high standards set by Jesus often lead to frustration rather than inspiration. If Jesus is uniquely divine, as orthodoxy claims, any standard he sets will be necessarily unattainable, hence useless. Moral Influence works better than other theory yet discussed but falls short of a complete explanation of the Atonement which Metaphysical Christian students can affirm.

Reconciliation Theory

As mentioned earlier, the key to Easter may be Christmas. Metaphysical Christianity cannot say God is present in some ultimate way in the incarnation of Jesus Christ—since all sentient beings are incarnations of the Divine Presence and Power—but because God's radiance floods through that one solitary life, Jesus Christ becomes the window into every sentient being. "If one wishes to speak about God," T.A. Kantonen wrote in his analysis of Karl Barth, "he must say Jesus Christ over and over again."[25]

Barth saw Jesus as ultimately unique; Metaphysical Christianity sees the opposite. The man of Nazareth shows us God-within because Jesus is ultimately typical. Christmas is the entry-point where Jesus Christ breaks through walls of darkness and ignorance to let the light of Divine goodness shine through. Jesus so perfectly reflected that Divinity that our whole God-concept in the Western world is really a Jesus-concept. Metaphysical Christians can fully agree with Karl Barth: Whoever would see God can look to Jesus for an example of the Christ. Easter confirms that decision.

Process Theology Strikes Again

Jesus has changed through the centuries as human consciousness has evolved. Here we encounter another thorny problem. Generations of Christians looked at Jesus and still found no problem in owning human slaves, beating their wives, waging wars of territorial conquest, and approving child labor. As numerous modern authors have shown, Jesus has been characterized by each successive generation in the terms of their own consciousness. To put another way, we have made Jesus in our image and will probably continue to do so. This is the central theme of my book *Jesus 2.1: An Upgrade for the twenty-first Century* (Unity Books, 2010).[26]

There simply is no transcendent vantage point where observers can shuck their ethnocentrisms and see Jesus with the eye of complete objectivity. We are part of the process, and human interaction with Jesus throughout history has shown a constant struggle to reinterpret, re-evaluate, re-make, and re-work both the Christ-concept and whatever soteriology would be based on the current model. Taking this as a given—that Jesus-models are all in transition—it is possible to see positive strengths flowing from a dynamic, ever-changing Christology and its resultant soteriology.

First, a process theory of Atonement offers another form of dialogue about spiritual growth. As the Jesus-model/ salvation-model interacts with life-experience, both are changed. If God works through Jesus Christ to affect human "salvation," the process of dialogue-change-growth-dialogue is the actual means for grace to flow to humanity. Rather than bemoaning the fact that people have altered the Jesus model through history, those changes might be the clearest evidence that God is at work in Jesus. A static Christology hangs a series of millstones around the necks of future generations, tempting reformation and schism. However, seeing new things in the Jesus-model throughout history demonstrates God will continue to prompt humanity to look deeper as future circumstances warrant.

God really does come to us in Jesus, not as a once-and-for-all-time revelation but through a process of continuous discovery by which we find the Good who seeks us.

Reconciliation: A Working Model

When Paul wrote, "In Christ God was reconciling the world to himself,"[27] he gave us a clue to understand Atonement as an unfolding, continuous process. This is exactly what happens when people look at the life-death-resurrection of Jesus. The model interacts with whomever encounters and personalizes the pattern, seeing God at work reconciling the world to the perfect (i.e., best) template for them through the prototype of Jesus Chris; he outpictures the potential in everyone. Charles Fillmore thought Jesus was the window to see God.-

> Christ is the perfect idea of God for man. Jesus is the perfect expression of the divine idea Man. Jesus Christ is a union of the two, the idea and the expression, or in other words, He is the perfect man demonstrated.[28]

Most forms of Christianity refer to God in language of fatherhood. Today a better term might be *parenthood*, removing the gender bias which has plagued the Judeo-Christian heritage. Parents require children—"For we are indeed his offspring," Luke's Paul reminds the Athenians (Acts 17:28). Taken seriously, this means all people are God's children; God is the forgiving father of the Prodigal Son story (also found uniquely in Luke). The runaway child is "reconciled" to God by returning to the love of a parent who does not need to forgive anything.

To reconcile the world unto God the Father-Mother means to assist all sentient beings on their journey to spiritual union with God, a union which does not blur individualities but recognizes everyone as fully unique, irreplaceable expressions of God's Omnipotent Presence.

God's reconciling acts could not be realized if not for two factors: Christ-indwelling each sentient being, and some method to show the way. Not as a moral influence, although that is important, but as a Wayshower to stake out the road up ahead. People are not usually aware of their indwelling divinity, because human freedom includes the right to be wrong. In the long history of humanity, very few people have achieved any kind of high-order spirituality which would suggest indwelling divinity

Enter Jesus of Nazareth, fully human, yet pointing like an arrow at the Divine-within. If he did it, we can do it, too. By freely embracing the cross, Jesus chose to be a road sign for the rest of humanity. But more than a road sign, he is somehow the map, path, and destination. All the pieces of a paradigm outpicture in the life of Jesus the Christ.

People look to Christmas and say, "He was born, like anybody else." They listen to his stories and study his life and say, "He struggled against the same kind of negative-thinking everybody faces in this world." They look at the cross and say, "That's probably the worst that could happen to anyone. To die shamefully, alone, innocent and undeserving of punishment." Finally, they look at the empty tomb and say, "This event cancels the worst possible fate, because it confirms God's power over death and the presence of grace even in the face of apparent disaster."

Putting the four revelatory events together—Christmas, life/teachings, Good Friday and Easter—a clearly Metaphysical Christian interpretation of soteriology emerges: Life brings hope of growth toward Christ-consciousness. All sentient beings are incarnations of God, struggling to know as Jesus knew their Oneness with the Divine-within. Life brings challenges and suffering because people are truly free. But even in the face of the worst that could happen, God is working through it all to bring perfect, long-term results. There really is only One Presence/Power, and the birth, life, teachings, death & resurrection of Jesus show that God's goodness will triumph.

Preserving the Best

The Reconciliation model for the Atonement gathers up in itself the positive elements of all the others discussed in this chapter. The costliness of Jesus' sacrifice cannot be underestimated, as the Ransom Theory holds. He had to endure, for love of humanity, a cruel and wholly undeserved fate. As the Substitution Theory insists, people cannot earn God's approval, but Reconciliation differs by insisting that God's approval has never been withdrawn from humanity therefore need not be won back. God certainly does not want people to harm themselves by self-destructive choices, but God never lapses in relentless love for even the nastiest, most negative person. A house divided cannot stand.

It is possible to find some agreement with the Appeasement Theory, because Sin (error-beliefs which outpicture in the life of an individual as attempts to negate Divine Ideas) must be taken seriously. Sin may be Self-Inflicted Nonsense, but people feel the sting of it nonetheless. Reconciliation theory does not rest on the merits of the Savior, because people are called to become aware of *their* Christ within, and represent Christhood in diverse forms. Individuals are reconciled to God when the whole process culminates in Christ-consciousness; until then, reconciliation is an ongoing process of regeneration and growth.

Because it is only through faith (i.e., consciousness) that people are "saved" from whatever error-beliefs may be bogging them down, individuals can appropriate the solution to the human predicament only through a free act of Will; they must let the model of Jesus Christ work in and through their lives. This can break the power of sin and release humanity to its full divine potential.

Symbolism of the Cross

Arguably, the best symbol for God's One Power/One Presence in the face of existential evil and human suffering is the cross. The horizontal bar represents the Omnipresent love of God in everyday life, regardless of appearances to the contrary; the vertical bar shows the down pouring Power of God into the world, God's willingness to shower goodness on everyone who is open and receptive and turn toward the Divine Source. Placing a circle around the junction of those two bars forms a Celtic cross, which is a great symbol for Metaphysical Christianity. The circle stands for eternity and oneness, which, when added to OP², describe the cornerstone affirmation the Metaphysical Christian in visual form: One Presence/One Power, God the Good, Omnipotent. In the cross God truly was "reconciling the world unto Himself." The process goes on today; the Christ within is Alpha and Omega, first and the last. From God-consciousness everything came, and in God we live, move and have our being. Life may not always look like the Kingdom of God, but Jesus told his followers the Divine Presence and Power it represents is within you.

With this thought in mind, let's turn next to Eschatology, last things.

CHECK YOUR KNOWLEDGE

1. Identify the following: *steadfast love (hesed), merciful kindness, agape, divine ideas, over-responsible /under-responsible behavior, radical freedom, propitiation dualism, moral influence theory, reconciliation.*

2. What, according to the text, is *sin*? Give your critique of the author's definition/evaluation.

3. Would stealing a horse from another tribe be the same as stealing a horse from a kinsman for the Plains Indians? Which was "sin" and why?

4. Describe the difference between the *appeasement* and *penal substitution* theories of atonement.

5. What part does Satan play in the Ransom theory of atonement?

6. What is the difference between the Moral Influence and Reconciliation theories?

QUESTIONS FOR DISCUSSION

1. What does *sin* mean to you?

2. How do you deal with both subjective and objective guilt in your life? Should we even be discussing "Sin" and "guilt"?

3. Compare and contrast the OT concept of *hesed* with the NT's *agape*. Do any differences resolve themselves in Reconciliation Theory? How?

4. Do you tend to be an *over-responsible* or *under-responsible* person? Which is healthier? What alternatives are there to both?

5. How do you interpret these words from Paul?--"But God shows his love for us in that while we were yet sinners Christ died for us." How did the death of Jesus Christ save us? Or did it?

6. In what respect is Jesus the "Wayshower" in your life?

ESCHATOLOGY

Where Do We Go from Here?

> ESCHATOLOGY - that area of theology which is directly concerned with the "study of the last thing(s)"...death, particular judgment, heaven, hell, purgatory, Second Coming of Christ, resurrection of the body, general judgment, consummation of all things in the perfection of the Kingdom of God.[1]

On the bathroom wall of the student center at the seminary I attended, some wag had scribbled two lines of theological graffiti:

> Repent, ye accursed, for the End is near!
> (If you've already repented, please disregard this notice.)

As much as religionists would like to know, they really don't. No one knows what destiny awaits the individual soul after death. People have been born and died for countless generations, still no one knows for certain where human consciousness comes from and whether it continues beyond mortal existence or evaporates with the last brain waves at death. Throughout history some people have claimed firsthand knowledge of an afterlife, which has encouraged the faithful. Religious literature frequently reports instances of contact between the living and the dead.

For a biblical example, take the strange incident of King Saul ordering a spirit medium to summon the life-force of the dead prophet, Samuel. The medium at first refuses, because King Saul ordered the death of anyone who displays paranormal abilities or practices occult arts. When the King solemnly pledges her safety in the name of the Lord, she brings up a vision of the departed prophet Samuel, which the medium alone can see. Samuel complains about being disturbed from eternal rest, then devastatingly predicts the downfall of Saul on the morrow. [2]

Even if this incident occurred historically, which is questionable, it represents a second-hand report at best. Not even Saul witnessed the apparition but had to take the medium's word for its presence and accept her transcript of what the dead prophet said. Today, hearsay accounts of supernatural events provoke grim skepticism. Modern science knows about the power of the brain to generate illusions which appear concrete, so even if a genuine apparition materialized before people today, there is no guarantee spectators would believe in the specter. The problem of credibility goes back to the prescientific days of Jesus, as Luke's gospel recounts in the parable of the rich man and poor Lazarus:

> The poor man died and was carried away by the angels to be with Abraham. The rich man also died and was buried. In Hades, where he was being tormented, he looked up and saw Abraham far away with Lazarus by his side... He called out, "Father Abraham... I beg you to send him to my father's house—for I have five brothers—that he may warn them, so that they will not also come into this place of torment." Abraham replied, "They have Moses and the prophets; they should listen to them." He said, "No, father Abraham; but if someone goes to them from the dead, they will repent." He said to him, "If they do not listen to Moses and the prophets, neither will they be convinced even if someone rises from the dead."[3]

The Lord had a point. Subjective factors in reported sightings of spiritual life-forms cannot be overlooked. Hindu's seldom encounter departed Muslim saints; Jews are rarely visited by the Virgin Mary. Ethnocentric expectations color what we see when these visions occur. When Native Americans living on the Great Plains went on vision-quests, they received their goal only after sensory deprivation, starvation and sleeplessness. What they saw took its shape from the symbolism of the religion of the Plains tribes. They did not see Jesus on the Mount of Transfiguration or Mohammed arriving triumphant at Mecca. As noted earlier, *there are no tiger-gods where there are no tigers.*

While personal experiences cannot be convincingly cited as proof of life after death, they cannot be discounted purely on intellectual grounds by those who have not experienced such dramatic encounters. The very subjective nature of these "contacts" can empower belief in those who experience them, and the power of an unexpected rendezvous with something beyond rational thought and resulting in a raw discharge of emotional energy can profoundly affect the worldview of an individual. Perhaps that is one reason why quite a few religions, the Judeo-Christian among them, have absolutely forbidden any activity involving contact with the dead or the use of spirit-mediums. However, even granting the validity of some paranormal encounters, theology is an intellectual discipline which cannot summon phantoms to divulge a comprehensive explanation of last things, so supernatural encounters offer little help to a critical study of eschatology. Indeed, many religions introduce complex visions about life after death, but cultural reveries may not properly be called *knowledge*. Organized beliefs comprising an eschatology must come from creative reflection on the whole corpus of ideas about the nature and destiny of life rather than relying on personal or communal experiences.

Validity of Faith

Of course, there is nothing wrong with beliefs based on faith rather than verifiable evidence. Earlier in this book we said that religious insights are subject to personal validity, not scientific validity. Those beliefs must be tested in the larger arena of theological dialogue—either formally, in the case of academic discourses between theologians, or informally over a cup of coffee after the Sunday sermon. Love is probably the most important human attribute, yet it is more closely related to faith, hope and charity than pure logic. What would you say if asked why you love your spouse? You might reply with a litany of his/her good qualities: kindness, generosity, sense of humor, sexual attractiveness, sensitivity, altruism, etc. But those are just attributes, not facts proving love. Most of us know any number of kind, generous, humorous, sexy, sensitive, altruistic people. Yet we love only one person with the kind of lasting intensity and depth that brings two people together as mates for life. Marriage is based on faith, not fact, but good marriages begin with faith which has its eyes open, has done its homework and has made a loving, careful decision. Most religious systems propose faith is a choice, but spiritual preferences need not be synonymous with the kind of ignorance caricatured by Mark Twain: "Faith is believing something you know ain't true." [4]

More Speculative

Because of the nature of Eschatology, this chapter will deal in thought-forms which are much more speculative and metaphysical than almost any other section of the book. It is unavoidable. Eschatology is inherently speculative, which is one of the reasons that talk about "the end of the world" has remained so popular throughout the ages.

A word must be said about those "popular eschatologies" before plunging into the topic from the perspective of legitimate theology. If we rule out the brief flash of hippie-Eastern apocalypticism—which during the Vietnam War era sent droves of long-haired, blue-jeaned college dropouts scurrying to form communes in remote areas before the End— most other pop-eschatological movements in Western society have been based on woeful misunderstandings of the book of Revelation. To read the Apocalypse of St. John as a program for the end of the world is to overlook several important points about that feisty, First Century treatise.

Initially, it is important to note *every generation* since the ink first dried on the original autograph of Revelation has believed they were living at the time of the End. New Testament authors generally considered themselves the last generation. So passionate was this belief that II Peter (circa 150 C.E.) deals with growing restlessness in the Christian community because Armageddon has not commenced. Listen to the author, obviously not the Apostle Peter, as he deals with serious objections to the dwindling Christian hope of a rapid *Parousia*, or Second Coming of Jesus Christ and resultant Final Judgment of the living and the dead:

> First of all you must understand this, that in the last days
> scoffers will come, scoffing and indulging their own

lusts and saying, "Where is the promise of his coming? For ever since our ancestors died, all things continue as they were from the beginning of creation!"[5]

New Testament authors scribbled at white-hot speed, certain the *Parousia* would occur before the writer could finish his manuscript. Sometimes their apocalyptic hope has disappeared in the reading and re-reading of familiar texts. For example, Matthew's Jesus says, "Let the little children come to me, and do not stop them; for it is to such as these that the kingdom of heaven belongs." Is Jesus expressing sentimental thoughts about the openness of childhood, or is Matthew citing this memory in the belief that those children (Matthew's late first century generation) will actually live to see the kingdom arrive? Millennialists through the ages have shared Matthew's hope. Western culture alone has spawned over two hundred widely believed predictions of doomsday since New Testament times. End-of-the-world forecasts will continue far into the future, partly because John's Apocalypse is bizarre enough to find signs and indications in every age.

Another key point is the book of Revelation was written as underground literature. The volume speaks to an oppressed community, encouraging Christians to remain faithful under persecution. Its promises of the End are more cheerleading than prophecy. The central message of the Revelation seems to be prophetic exhortation: *Don't worship the Beast*. Don't abandon your faith in the face of private or public harassment. The *Beast* was most likely the Roman emperor, whose loyalty oath included offering wine and incense to an image of the reigning Caesar, an affront to both Christian and Jew.

Today the Beast can be anything that prevents people from following the Christ-within. Christian conservatives continue to insist the Beast of John's Revelation has a real identity and will show himself soon. Like predecessors in earlier generations, some believe they have decoded the symbolism of John's Revelation. To them fall of the Soviet empire, the rising tide of Chinese economic power and Islamic fundamentalism are clearly harbingers of the Apocalypse. Earlier candidates for anti-Christ and the Beast included Napoleon, Kaiser Wilhelm, Hitler, and Stalin, but these are tactfully omitted in the mountains of brightly jacketed drivel which ultra-conservative presses keep churning out for an eager readership. Eschatology is good business for publishers, provided they are willing to ignore the towering historical evidence generated by the never-ending stream of frivolous end-time proclamations.

We have probably spent enough time on pop-eschatology. If further study is desired, many good sources are readily available. An excellent introduction to the book of Revelation is the chapter on that subject in William E. Cameron's *Great Dramas of the Bible* (Unity Books, 1998). Cameron presents selected stories from the Bible with clarity and wry wisdom. His chapter on the Revelation to John does a remarkable job of demythologizing that complex jumble, recovering the freshness of its ideas for scientifically based people today. Although Cameron is not formally trained as a biblical scholar, the book is a solid work built on good scholarship. Highly recommended for people who want to reclaim their Christian heritage from the mind-numbing train-wreck that American evangelical conservatism has wrought upon the deeply mystical faith of Jesus the Christ.

Also, the *New Interpreter's Bible One-Volume Commentary* (Abingdon, 2010) has an excellent monograph on biblical-era apocalypses by Carol A. Newsom of Emory University and an introduction to the Revelation to John by Judith L. Kovacs of the University of Virginia. The real message of Revelation is timeless and will continue to inspire generations to come as they struggle with the "beasts" which threaten their faith. Hopefully, more intelligent biblical study will replace printed diagrams ticking off the countdown to Armageddon.

Ends & Beginnings

Eschatology comes from the Greek word *eschaton*, meaning literally "the end." Eschatology, therefore, is a study of endings, of last things. Since an ending presupposes a beginning, Eschatology is an idea wholly alien to several schools of Greek philosophy, notably the Eleatics, who held that Ultimate Reality is changeless Being. If there was no creation, there can be no end. Some philosophers reasoned that life is cyclical, so preternatural talk about the end of the world devolves into meaninglessness. Of course, not all Greek philosophers agreed, but it is fair to say Hellenistic philosophy generally favored a cyclical view of time that allowed little room for a doctrine of last things.

Conversely, Hebrew thought has generally been linear, not circular. Genesis leaves no doubt about the march of time starting with God's primordial act: "In the beginning God created the heavens and the earth." (Gen. 1:1) Both the Hebrew Bible and the New Testament end with prophetic notes about the future, suggesting the founding fathers of the Judeo-Christian faith never lost sight of the linear dimension to life and the moral responsibility which an onward-and-upward flow brings to mortal existence.

Is there some way to combine the forward-motion of history with the cyclical nature of life itself? Later this chapter will explore whether the linear and cyclical models can be true simultaneously.

Looking at "Last Things"

Eschatology is usually divided into two general categories, individual and corporate human destinies. A further subdivision might be made between the destiny of a given group, such as Israel or the Church, and the destiny of humanity at large. Or we could opt to explore the grandest question of all and ask, "What shall happen to the cosmos at the end of time?" Although our space is limited, we shall attempt to address the wide range of related subjects by focusing on three categories:

1) Individual destinies—where, if anywhere, do we go after death?
2) The human race—what is our ultimate fate?
3) The Universe—will it end?

Such a controversial subject is bound to stir up disagreement, but a topic as important as individual and corporate destinies of humanity and the cosmos cannot be skipped simply because controversy makes some folks uncomfortable. Controversy is not injurious to rational thought. Some of religion's finest insights have come only after the clash of countervailing ideas. Let's attack the problems of Eschatology hopeful anticipation of healthy disagreement, remembering these are not the last words on the last things.

Individual Destinies

What happens when we die? Few questions evoke greater interest. In fact, life after death comprises perhaps the largest sub-category in the world's religious scriptures. Christianity owes its existence to a particular life-after-death experience recorded in history. The New Testament can be thought of as a discussion from both sides of the Easter event, before and after, since the post-resurrection appearances of the Risen Lord powerfully shaped everything the primitive Christian community thought, taught and wrote.

Discourses about life-after-death are by no means limited to Christian tradition. Islam holds before its followers the vision of paradise for the faithful and perdition for the infidel; Hinduism teaches various forms of reincarnation leading to absorption into the One. Great religions of antiquity devoted vast energies to projects that would insure eternity for believers--albeit only high-ranking ones like the king or the nobility. Priest-craft has included funerary rites, magic and necromancy in order that the soul of the believer may pass into the spirit world. The *Tibetan Book of the Dead* provided guidelines for the dying as they departed this life. Similar practices survive in other religions, such as Extreme Unction, sometimes called the last rites of the Catholic Church.

Of the major religious teachers of humanity, only Buddha remained silent on the question of individual survival after death, preferring to let his disciples dwell on right living and following the Eightfold Path. Buddha believed a well-ordered life prepares individuals for whatever awaits beyond life's boundaries. Of course, some of his followers through the ages could not allow such a burning question to go unanswered. Pure Land Buddhism, for example, developed a complex theology of last things.

Is Hope Universal?

According to evangelical theologian John Marks Hicks, "The New Testament is a thoroughly eschatological, if not apocalyptic, message. The practices of the early church, consequently, are likewise thoroughly eschatological.[6] Liberal churchman John Macquarrie calls the belief that life will somehow make sense in the end "the universal presence of hope in mankind."[7] But eternal life has also been called a wishful projection (Feuerbach), a consolation for the oppressed (Marx), a denial of the eternal return of the same (Nietzsche), and an unrealistic regression of the psychologically immature (Freud).[8]

Hans Kueng counters with a statement of faith: "If I believe in eternal life, then it is always possible to endow my life and that of others with meaning."[9] Without the possibility of eternity, life falls into meaninglessness, the cosmos becomes empty space punctuated with energy-sources burning themselves out; and sentient beings are chemistry accidents. Eschatology, therefore, either validates or voids the whole theological enterprise.

Even a brief survey of the literature of theology uncovers a wide variety of ideas about individual destinies across the Christian theological spectrum. Afterlife options differ quite profoundly in the thinking of laypeople, something I learned when conducting multi-denominational religious retreats. Frequently I would ask people to write down what they believe awaits after death, I recorded their responses on a big sheet of white paper with a thick, felt-tip pen so that everyone could see the growing list. Here are some of the notes from one session, which was from a mixed group of Protestants and Catholics (no avowed Metaphysical Christians).

WHAT HAPPENS AFTER DEATH?

➢ Heaven or Hell immediately.
➢ Heaven or Hell or Purgatory.
➢ Sleep until judgment, then Heaven or Hell.
➢ Eternal life in paradise for Jehovah's little flock; eternal death for unbelievers.
➢ Oneness with God if ready, otherwise reincarnation.
➢ Nothing happens--when you're dead, you're dead.
➢ Heaven for everybody.
➢ Heaven for good people; everybody else goes to Enid, Oklahoma.
➢ I don't know. I don't like to think about death.

Some of the responses are admittedly facetious, but there are a few painfully honest replies in this short list. One person professed belief in reincarnation; another said death ends consciousness. Remember, this exercise took place on a religious retreat and the replies came from active church members, not unchurched agnostics. Maybe the most honest response of all was, "I don't know." Doubts about personal survival after death can easily honeycomb the bedrock of anyone's belief system. It could scarcely be otherwise. Living requires us to take this life seriously, and if we were absolutely certain that a better life awaits us in the hereafter who wouldn't elect a quick death?

Doubt keeps us on the job, working at the spiritual growth we need to achieve in this world. Shakespeare's Hamlet struggled with this question and arrived at a similar solution. It is that "unseen country" in the shadows beyond life which both beckons and frightens. If humans could see it more clearly, we might be tempted to abandon spaceship earth or, if the afterlife vision were not a happy one, despair could crush any ability to live the best possible life in the here-and-now. Some doubts are healthier than certain knowledge.

Life after death must remain in the realm of possible-but-uncertain because lack of absolute knowledge instance is probably good for us. However, religious thinkers continue to speculate about personal survival because it is such an important question. Remembering that all eschatologies are educated guesswork, we shall take a look at some of the commonly held beliefs about life after death in Western traditions.

Extinction

Belief that death ends consciousness is the oldest personal eschatology in the Judeo-Christian heritage. This may surprise some, but there is ample evidence in the Old Testament that extinctionist eschatologies predated any form of survivalism in ancient Hebrew thought. Some examples of extinctionism in the Old Testament are Jeremiah 51:39, 57; II Samuel 14:14; Job 7:21; Psalm 39:13. By the time of Ecclesiastes the Hebrew community was pondering this issue, reflected in the brooding, Hamlet-like soliloquy by its unknown author:

> For the fate of humans and the fate of animals is the same; as one dies, so dies the other. They all have the same breath, and humans have no advantage over the animals; for all is vanity. All go to one place; all are from the dust, and all turn to dust again. Who knows

whether the human spirit goes upwards and the spirit of
animals goes downwards to the earth?[10])

By the time of Jesus, Jewish theology was divided on the question
of personal survival after death. Newer ideas about life after death were
needed if the scales of the cosmos were to balance in favor of Divine
justice. Too many times people of God had suffered defeat at the hands
of pagan conquerors. Although the prophets kept calling Israelites to
repent, promising divine retribution if they did not, most people simply
did not believe they were bad enough to suffer that kind of brutality from
the hand of Yahweh. When the Maccabean revolt produced martyrs who
died after offering sacrifice, i.e., in a state of ritual purity after receiving
forgiveness of sin, many Jewish thinkers decided that God's moral
integrity demands life after death and a final judgment at which justice
prevails. The old idea that suffering comes from sin no longer met their
actual life experiences, since the martyrs were technically sinless when
they died. Jewish theology had to evolve to accommodate this historic
event. God's goodness and righteousness were unimpeachable, so the
account must be settled at a last Judgment preceding eternal life.

It was not entirely a new idea, but it was new enough for
intertestamental Judaism. Grappling with theodicy produced a rift in
Jewish thought which prevailed into New Testament times. Theologians
took sides, depending on whether they were pro or con about the
continued existence of human consciousness after death. Liberals, who
believed in life after death and those were known as the *Pharisees*. The
old guard conservatives and members of the priestly aristocracy, who
clung to the ancient teaching of *extinction*, became the *Sadducees*. (See
Mark 12:18-27 and Acts 23:6-10 for some interesting biblical anecdotes
about the rift.) Modern extinctionist eschatologies of the Western world
fall into three broad categories: Absolute, Conditional, and
Redemptionist.

Absolute extinctionists agree with the person who said, "Nothing
happens--when you're dead, you're dead." Death ends consciousness
permanently for all sentient beings. Religious humanism leans in this
direction; extinctionism is the eschatology of all true atheists.

Conditional extinctionists believe some people will cease to exist, usually wicked ones, or those who fail to affirm some particular beliefs, Jehovah's Witnesses believe everyone who fails to worship Jehovah will cease to exist after the resurrection to come. The "condition" required for extinction of consciousness is lack of faith. The Apostle Paul can arguably be called a conditional extinctionist.

> For it is indeed just of God to repay with affliction those who afflict you, and to give relief to the afflicted as well as to us, when the Lord Jesus is revealed from heaven with his mighty angels in flaming fire, inflicting vengeance on those who do not know God and on those who do not obey the gospel of our Lord Jesus. These will suffer the punishment of eternal destruction, separated from the presence of the Lord and from the glory of his might.[11]

Even though scholars question the Pauline authorship of Second Thessalonians, extinctionist sentiments dot the undisputed letters of Pau. For example Romans 9:22 reads: "What if God, desiring to show his wrath and to make known his power, has endured with much patience the objects of wrath that are made for destruction...?"[12] Also, conspicuous in its absence is any Pauline theology of eternal punishment, other than destruction. The word *hell* is not found in his writings.

Redemptionist eschatologies of extinction try hard not to be extinctionist, but fail at last because they hold that human consciousness ends at death. Although death terminates individualized awareness (extinctionism), some theologians believe God still "remembers" us and therefore, somehow, we are preserved in the Mind of God. We are redeemed, although we'll never know it.

This should not be confused with the mystical union with God, through which the individual overcomes the *I-Thou* dichotomy and merges with the Divine. Redemptionist eschatologies of extinction insist that consciousness actually ends--we die and live no more. Yet, because God "remembers" us, our essence is somehow preserved.

Critique: Extinctionism

All forms of extinctionism fail to address the central question which provokes men and women to look beyond life to a continued existence: If death ends consciousness, what is the purpose of achieving consciousness at all? Is the high intellectual/spiritual awareness represented by the human mind simply a tool to gather more food, to defend the human creature in a hostile world, to outwit enemies? If death ends it all, life itself is the ultimate absurdity in a scandalously wasteful, bitterly cruel Universe. This, of course, is the old Jewish dilemma written anew. Does God's nature require self-aware beings to continue? Consciousness, once given, cannot be rescinded without creating an absurdity in the constitution of the Universe. Feeling this frustration to the bone, our ancestors made gods in their own image and argued with them about the persistence of life.

Heaven or Hell

Traditional eschatologies have usually offered two fates for the soul: heaven or hell, a place of unlimited happiness or endless misery. Medieval artists pictured wailing souls in fiery agony and blissed-out semi-angelic beings reclining on billowing clouds. In *Letters to the Earth*, Mark Twain satirized the classical paradise. We pick up the action as Twain's Satan—correctly identified as a member of the heavenly court exiled to Earth[13]—reports on the human concept of heaven:

> Now then, in the earth these people cannot stand much church--an hour and a quarter is the limit, and they draw the line at once a week. That is to say, Sunday. One day in seven; and even then they do not look forward to it with longing. And so--consider what their heaven provides for them: "church" that lasts forever, and a Sabbath that has no end![14]

Satan is dumbfounded by the human portrait of heaven:

> Meanwhile, every person is playing on a harp--those millions and millions!—whereas not more than twenty in the thousand play an instrument in the earth, or ever

wanted to. Consider the deafening hurricane of sound-- millions and millions of voices screaming at once and millions and millions of harps gritting their teeth at the same time! I ask you: is it hideous, is it odious, is it horrible?[15]

Admittedly dated satire, but still relevant today. Twain forces people to ponder the silly images still widely associated with heaven: Would anyone really want to live there?

Apparently so. A recent New York Times bestseller, *Heaven is for Real,* tells the story a near death experience by four-year-old Colton Burpo, son of Nebraska evangelical minister, Rev Todd Burpo. Colton's father recruited bestselling author Lynn Vincent to co-author the book. The verifiable facts: Colton is suffering from a severe illness, and "…during emergency surgery slips from consciousness and enters heaven. He survives and begins talking about being able to look down and see the doctor operating and his dad praying in the waiting room."[16] The four-year-old vividly recounts what heaven is like, which coincidentally resembles the puffy clouds and winged creatures pictured in Sunday school literature. Colton embellishes the standard vision of heaven with things a child might relish. "He describes the horse that only Jesus could ride, about how 'reaaally big' God and his chair are, and how the Holy Spirit 'shoots down power' from heaven to help us." Super-powered angels and heroic Christians from heaven later fight the forces of evil with power-swords.[17]

Although that kind of gamers' heaven sounds more appealing than Twain's endless church meeting, it's clear both originate in popular mythologies. Less obvious are the subtler expectations of reunion with loved ones, sunny pathways lined with flowers leading to spacious homes; fun and fellowship forever in an eternal, gated retirement community. All that's missing is golf and an early bird special.

There is also a model of heaven which resembles a spiritual retreat center. Fellowship, joy, and personal development. But a look at the world suggests not many people find monastic existence appealing, even if it brings time for quiet reflection and prayer. Most humans crave a little commotion in life, either personally through physical activity or outings with friends, or vicariously through video games, television shows, or sporting events.

Eternal existence which does not occasionally challenge, perplex, or confound the individual would be supernaturally boring, more like lapsing into never-ending coma than reaching the highest good. For heaven to be a worthwhile existence, the *highest good* should always recede from approach. As Robert Browning said, "Ah, but a man's reach should exceed his grasp, or what's a heaven for?"[18]

Hell, No?

Hell is another image that artists have enjoyed painting, but their motives have not always been religious. Some painters and sculptors liked to portray souls en route eternal damnation because an artist could hardly get away with representing the naked human form in an age when women's ankles had to be covered. For example, art critic Laura Gibbs says, "the story of the Harrowing of Hell provided Renaissance artists a rare opportunity to paint female nudes in a work of religious art."[19] Tintoretto, Bronzino, even Michelangelo showed nudes in their visions of the Last Judgment and hell. Arguably the greatest sculpture of all time, Michelangelo's *David*, represents the muscular young shepherd *au naturel*. A cynic might wonder if the masters occasionally injected a little nudity to spike their popularity among the masses. More likely, the stiff moralism of European culture forced artists to find virtuous, defendable venues to explore the human form. Heaven and hell are biblical categories. Yet, the Bible's *descriptions* of heaven and hell are not the source of popular imagery. The true source is probably medieval mythology which had its culmination in the greatest eschatological farce ever written, Dante's Inferno.

Reading New Testament accounts of hell it is clear, for example, Satan is not the overlord of hellfire, the divinely appointed jailer of damned humanity found in Renaissance art. That image thoroughly un-biblical comes from Dante. In the minds of first century Christians, Satan represented the ultimate evil of the Roman Empire. He is cast into a fiery lake in John's Apocalypse, not put in charge of the place. Evil, like death, is done.

Beyond the biblical problems churned up by eternal hellfire presided over by Satan, even greater difficulties appear for modern people who believe in any kind of an eternal punishment, especially when considering such a horrendous concept from an ethical/moral perspective. No less a distinguished Churchman than theologian John Macquarrie ripped into the dragon skin of "the barbarous doctrine of an eternal hell." Macquarrie wrote:

> Needless to say, we utterly reject the idea of a hell where God everlastingly punishes the wicked, without hope of deliverance. Even earthly penologists are more enlightened nowadays. Rather we must believe that God will never cease from his quest for universal reconciliation, and we can firmly hope for his victory in this quest, through recognizing that this victory can only come when at last there is the free cooperation of every responsible creature.[20]

Lutheran theologian T.A. Kantonen agreed:

> Every sincere Christian shudders at the idea of eternal perdition as the fate of anyone, and if we err in trusting that God's infinite resources will provide a happy ending for all, we may hope to be forgiven.[21]

Belief in an eternal, burning hell, although popular with some rank-and-file churchgoers, is simply not the concept taught to students preparing to enter the Christian ministry at mainline Protestant theological seminaries. I have attended three Protestant schools of theology—two United Methodist, the other United Church of Christ—and cannot recall anyone on the faculties speaking in favor of a literal, burning hell. Also, very few members of the student body reflected this outdated, sub-Christian notion in their personal belief systems. Certainly, religious conservatives warn their flocks about eternal damnation while holding up a vision of bliss in paradise, but hell-preaching churches give signs of full retreat from the complexities of modern, pluralistic society. Rejecting evolution, global climate change, marriage equality, religious pluralism, gender equality, even the geological age of the Earth, conservative Christianity haunts dark, empty thought-castles, which history has condemned as uninhabitable, in a real world intellectual culture that broadly rejects their outdated theologies of hellfire and damnation. The dragons of yesteryear belong in fantasy, not twenty-first century public policy or social ethics, and are destined to go the way of other maladaptive religious beliefs of the past.

People who still cling to some kind of hell—and they are legion— most likely have never reflected on the ghastly character of damnation doctrine. Punishment of any kind is only justified when the end result is improved character or prevention of future offenses. Today any parents who beat their children because the little ones had erred would rightly be considered child-abusers. Enlightened parenting sets the example and lovingly corrects the child's natural mistakes rather than dishing out merciless punishment. Even criminals are imprisoned in the hope of rehabilitating them or, at the very least, preventing them from committing other crimes.

Yet, why do the tortured masses suffer in hell? To learn some lesson? Hardly. To prevent further sin? Not at all. Hell exists to inflict pain and immortal anguish upon those unlucky souls who failed to get their spiritual act together during a brief lifespan on Earth. Could any concept be more monstrous? If some want to argue that Jesus taught an eternal hell, therefore the concept must be good, listen to Kantonen:

> It is inconsistent with all we know about God to suppose that he is more vindictive towards his children than we are toward our own worst enemies. This position (nonexistence of eternal punishment) has been supported by appealing to various passages in the teaching of Jesus and the apostles. 'I,' says Jesus, 'when I am lifted up from the earth, will draw all men to myself' (John 12:32). He pictures the shepherd-love of God as persistently seeking the lost one 'until he finds it' (Luke 15:4)...Many of Paul's sayings seem to point to the same conclusion. (E.g., Phil. 2:10-11, Rom. 11:32, I Cor. 15:28.)[22]

Perhaps gospel authors or editors inserted the language of punishment and despair into the message of Jesus. Perhaps Jesus invoked existing imagery about hell from the Greco-Roman worldview when he taught..

Or perhaps Jesus of Nazareth actually believed in eternal punishment, which would reflect some of the cultural norms of his day. He also seemed to accept slavery and the subjugation of women, even while treating all people as equals. As a human, Jesus lived in a culture which gave him certain values and lenses through which he saw the world. Had he been born in India, he likely would have spoken about gods and goddesses. Perhaps Jesus used the cultural images of Roman Judea as metaphors to drive home other points. It was not the rich man's suffering in agony that was the moral of the story in the parable of Dives and Lazarus, rather the selfishness of one particular rich man prevents Dives from experiencing the presence of God and makes him less than he should be

Whether the biblical texts about hell came from his lips or the imagination of his successors, the undisputed example of Jesus Christ was a seminar in forgiveness. He recognized nothing less than universal membership in the Kingdom of God. In his lifestyle and personal faith, Jesus went far beyond such limited concepts. He spoke about hell, but he acted like a universalist. Heaven is the other extreme, but it too has met with criticism in the modern world. What kind of existence would provide no challenge to grow, no new learning, no creative work to be accomplished? If the classical heaven and hell are the only two possible choices, eternity offers bleak prospects, indeed.

Reincarnation. Contrary to general belief among the metaphysical churches, reincarnation never was widely popular in Christian theology. Belief in the return of human consciousness in another human body has always smacked of Far Eastern religious thought, something imported from India by way of sea trade routes and overland caravans. Let's start with a broad definition:

> **reincarnation,** also called transmigration or metempsychosis, in religion and philosophy, rebirth of the aspect of an individual that persists after bodily death—whether it be consciousness, mind, the soul, or some other entity—in one or more successive existences. Depending upon the tradition, these existences may be

human, animal, spiritual, or, in some instances, vegetable.[23]

Metempsychosis (μετεμψύχωσις), as the early Church fathers called reincarnation, occupied only peripheral importance in their speculations. We are fairly confident that reincarnation was not a widely held belief in early Christianity because an idea as explosive and, in the classical definition of the word, as heretical as metempsychosis would have been refuted at great length by the highly combative apologists for orthodoxy. The fact that no such body of refutations exists suggests very few people knew about the concept of reincarnation or, more likely, it was seen as so foreign that no responsible Church Father gave it any serious credibility. There are some points, however, where familiar biblical passages could be reinterpreted to support reincarnation. When Jesus asked his disciples a profound question, their answer could easily mean the apostles believed in reincarnation:

> And Jesus went on with his disciples, to the villages of Caesarea Philippi; and on the way he asked his disciples, "Who do people say that I am?" And they answered him, "John the Baptist; and others say, Elijah; and still others one of the prophets."[24]

Jesus seldom hesitates to correct his disciples when they commit major thought-blunders, yet according to all three synoptic gospel writers (Matthew, Mark and Luke) he steps right over an opportunity to express disapproval of a reply which seems to favor reincarnation. Some commentators have concluded Jesus tacitly approves of reincarnation since the apostles have suggested he might be a reborn prophet and he has not bothered to rebuke their mistake. It is an argument from silence, but there is another problem as well.

Are the Disciples really suggesting reincarnation? Elijah, the only prophet mentioned by name, flew to heaven in the sky aboard a fiery chariot while he was still quite alive.[25] Other prophets might have done likewise, so Jesus could be the original Elijah, or another long-gone prophet, without being a reincarnated seer. The fact that his contemporaries wondered if Jesus were "John the Baptist" suggests some people, living in an age before electronic media, had either not heard or refused to believe the prophet of the Jordan was dead. Jesus could scarcely be John unless he was John's ghost, or John resurrected, neither of which would have been impossible for ancient minds to conceive. None of these conclusions pointed to metempsychosis.

An interesting prospect for reincarnationist eschatologies arises in the fourth gospel, where Jesus famously chides Nicodemus: *"You must be born again."*[26] Traditionally, this passage has been spiritually interpreted as the purifying renewal which occurs after someone accepts the lordship of Jesus Christ. The New Revised Standard abets that interpretation by rendering the passage: *"Very truly, I tell you, no one can see the kingdom of God without being born from above."*[27] There is nothing in either version, or the Greek text, which specifically prohibits a reincarnationist interpretation.

Although nothing in the gospels precludes reincarnation, a passage from Hebrews seems to more directly contradict the concept of rebirth: *"It is appointed for mortals to die once, and after that the judgment."*[28] However, looking at the whole passage shifts the emphasis away from single-life doctrine to a statement about the sacrifice offered by Jesus.

> For Christ did not enter a sanctuary made by human hands, a mere copy of the true one, but he entered into heaven itself, now to appear in the presence of God on our behalf. Nor was it to offer himself again and again, as the high priest enters the Holy Place year after year with blood that is not his own; for then he would have had to suffer again and again since the foundation of the world. But as it is, he has appeared once for all at the end of the age to remove sin by the sacrifice of himself. And just as it is appointed for mortals to die once, and after that the judgment, so Christ, having been offered once to bear the sins of many, will appear a second time, not to deal with sin, but to save those who are eagerly waiting for him.[29]

Note the text specifies that without the complete nature of his sacrifice, Jesus might have had to be re-born *"to suffer again and again since the foundation of the world.*" Separating the two key factors in this passage, one need not embrace an appeasement theology of the atonement to notice the author of Hebrews believed Jesus *could* have physically been born again and again. If Jesus could reincarnate, why not others? We have already noted that, before the divinity of Jesus was commonly held, some people believed Jesus was "one of the prophets" returned to Earth.[30]

Characteristically, biblical authors fail to deliver conclusive, consistent testimony for or against the doctrine of reincarnation. However, multiple re-birth has remained relatively alien to Western thought. The idea that reincarnation was a widespread belief which the Catholic Church somehow suppressed has no basis in history. The best argument against the anti-reincarnation conspiracy theory comes from surviving documents by Christian authors. Theologians exerted vast energy writing massive tomes to refute ideas which they found unorthodox and to defend their versions of the Faith.

Throughout its first five hundred years, the developing Church waged civil wars over minute points of doctrine. Today most of these arguments seem trivial, but to the Church Fathers (alas, all men) the ideas they debated were the building blocks of Christian thought. Surprisingly to modern readers, not only professional theologians engaged in this debate. According to Gregory of Nyssa, ordinary people at Constantinople followed complexities of the Christological argument like today's sports fans track statistics about their favorite players.

> If in this city you ask a shopkeeper for change, he will argue with you about whether the Son is begotten or unbegotten. If you inquire about the quality of bread, the baker will answer, "The Father is greater, the Son is less." And if you ask the bath attendant to draw your bath, he will tell you that the Son was created ex nihilo [out of nothing]." [31]

Foundational principles could not be knocked over without collapsing the temple of faith. Early Christians debated the precise nature of Jesus Christ to the point of absurdity. They argued about the Trinity, atonement, baptism, forgiveness of sin for backsliders, and countless doctrines which were so technical that studying them requires a separate course in the history of Christian thought.

Pick your favorite heresy—*Marcionism, docetism, Gnosticism, Donatism, Apollinarism, Monophysitism, Arianism, Sabellianism*, to name a few. Refuting the ideas of this or that school of Christian thought received lengthy treatment. However, the literature is relatively silent on reincarnation. Considering the mountains of invective early Christians heaped upon each other, if any significant Christian groups or teachers who had proclaimed an idea as incendiary as reincarnation the early church blogosphere would have exploded with rebuttals. There is an occasional outburst against the early writings of Origen, who held that human souls existed prior to birth, but very little about birth and rebirth for the purposes of spiritual growth or overcoming karmic debt.

One figure sometimes mentioned is Valentinius, second century Gnostic Christian who was a contender for Bishop of Rome, an office today known as the papacy. Contemporary theologians excoriated Valentinius for his incontestably bizarre teachings, which included thirty gods and the creation of the world by an inferior semi-divine being. However, it is unclear whether his complex, arcane system actually included multiple rebirths for every human. General reincarnation is hard to imagine in Valentinian Gnosticism, especially since he believed only the Elect had a spark of divinity within them. Nineteenth century Transcendentalist Christians—like Theodore Parker, Henry David Thoreau, and Ralph Waldo Emerson—dabbled in Eastern thought and toyed with the idea of reincarnation. Metaphysical Christianity is heavily indebted to Transcendentalism. In the twentieth century the Beatles helped to popularized Hindu ideas for the West.

Critique: Reincarnation as Eschatology

Reincarnation as eschatology raises some serious questions. First, why return at all? To redress grievances, conclude unfinished business, connect loose ends, perhaps to enjoy missed opportunities? Or do souls reincarnate to as mentors, like *Jonathan Livingston Seagull* returning to help other birds learn to fly? Reincarnation can be a penalty for errors.

Buddhists believe karma lasts more than one lifetime. Reincarnation is like walking the wheel of life, but being born over doesn't have to be in the same state. You can be reborn in different situations. Buddhists believe when you are reborn in different situations you can be born a god, titans (anti-god), human, animal, hungry ghost, or a demon. Materialized karma will keep accumulating and coming to your next life but once it is set free your new karma will be calmed and you can enter the stream leading to Nirvana where making good karma is not a goal anymore.[32]

Bad karma.

The doctrine that rebirth is chosen for some needed soul growth can have serious moral side-effects. The idea that children born with physical disabilities have chosen their lot can relieve cognitive dissonance among those who believe in a loving, just God, but it can also excuse us from taking corrective action. After all, the individual chose it, so all is well. Kama-heavy theologies have been critiqued for the tendency to drift into fatalism, a charge vigorously denied by some religionists from faiths which espouse reincarnation.

> Karma is not fatalism...quite the opposite in fact! The teaching about Karma revolves around the concept of self-created destiny. The Law of Karma is the law of cause and effect, the law of action and reaction, the law of sequence and consequence. It says that for every cause we set in motion – and we are always continually setting causes in motion, through our actions and deeds as well as our words and thoughts – there will be a corresponding effect which will come back to us, since we were the originators of the cause.[33]

Actual fatalism is more common to starkly monotheistic systems like Islam or Calvinist Christianity. However, any religious system where misdeeds accrue harmful consequences, which must be annulled by future virtue, gives power to negatives. Karmic debt is only a half-step away from an appeasement theory of atonement. Bad karma effectively creates a power of evil, something to which Metaphysical

Christianity has traditionally given no power.

Returning for learning.
The idea that we can return for remedial lessons is much more appealing than paying off karmic debts. A missed learning experience can be made up but need not be ameliorated. And while we're discussing new learning, let me share something I discovered during this study which changed my mind about the potential frequency of rebirths in human form. For many years I've objected to reincarnation as a widespread phenomenon, assuming there were not enough lives in human history to accommodate everyone currently alive with multiple past visitations. Working on this 2nd Edition I re-did the math and discovered my error. According to the World Population Clock of the US Census Department, there are 7,098,383,401 people in the world at the moment I write these words. Rounding the figure to 7 billion, that means only 6% of the people who have ever lived—approximately 108 billion—are alive now.

Even assuming people cannot have lived as their parents and will not likely return as their own children, the number of potential past lives is still more than ten. That's enough for a lot of past-life options. So, I recant my earlier critique of reincarnation based on population. There *are* enough lives in human history for everyone alive today to have lived at least ten times. Even a theologian can live and learn. And maybe repeat the process.[34]

Universalism. The belief in universal salvation is ancient within Christianity. As previously mentioned, there are clear indications of emergent universalism dot in the writings of Paul and gospel parables and sayings attributed to Jesus. Perhaps these passages allow some of the Master's Universalist theology to slip past later editors, who by the time of the great persecutions at the end of the first century had a vested interest in seeing the wicked punished. In the second and third centuries, great churchmen like Origen were openly proclaiming that God would not allow anyone to be lost. Some kind of eternal life awaited everyone; eternal punishment loomed over none.

Universalism, however, is not without its problems. If everyone goes to the same place (i.e., heaven), what is the purpose of life on earth and why did Jesus Christ come? If the mass-murderer is rewarded alongside his victims, how can we speak at all about God's justice? What happens to those who refused to learn and grow? Does St. Peter order everyone to don angel wings at heaven's gate, one size fits all?

Fresh Look at Purgatory

Some theologians, like John Macquarrie, believe growth must continue after physical death; dying accomplishes nothing other than changing the locale of human education. Macquarrie actually wants to resurrect the old High Church idea of *Purgatory*, which may send a chill down the spine of Metaphysical Christians who checked out of high church traditions to find happier lodgings.

An Anglican churchman and progressive thinker, Macquarrie suggests Purgatory fills the gap between incomplete spiritual growth and diversity-in-union with God:

> Heaven, purgatory, and hell are not sharply separated, but form a kind of continuum through which the soul may move, perhaps from the near- annihilation of sin to the closest union with God. Indeed, the concept of purgatory served the valuable purpose of introducing the dynamic, moving element into the traditional scheme, where heaven and hell could easily be mistaken for fixed immutable states.[35]

Note that Macquarrie's purgatory fits our category of universalist eschatologies because he flatly rejects any eternal punishment and believes everyone will eventually find "union in God." However, his use of a word which has such a medieval sound to the modern ear does little to reach those who want the Church to address itself to the present and future. A less provocative term like *sanctification* or its modern equivalent, *spiritual growth*, might convey the sense of what Macquarrie is addressing without unnecessarily arousing unpleasant memories of remedial suffering before proceeding to paradise. In any event, those of us who claim the Metaphysical Christian tradition have little quarrel with

Macquarrie's basic idea of growth continuing after life. One could argue that Eternal life ought to be attained through stages of growth, rather than crossing some salvific boundary line to avoid the transitory hothouse of purgatory or flaming eternity in hellfire.

Collective Eschatologies: What's Up for the Cosmos?

Individual destinies are only part of the problem, albeit the most essential share for every individual. Two other metaphysical questions asked by eschatology are equally important, "What will be the fate of the human race?" and "Will the Universe come to an end?" Although people are not as intimately caught up in these questions as in contemplating personal survival after death, nevertheless humanity has an investment in this Universe. It is natural for people to be curious about how the currents of time will treat our heirs upon the only world we have ever known. Of all speculations so far in this study, this will doubtless be the most speculative, but science does offer some possible answers which can help theology. We move now from personal to collective eschatologies.

Ultimate Fate of the Human Race

If history is any indicator, humanity is a wandering species. From our African genesis we drifted northward and learned how to survive in the snows of Eurasia; still farther and we adapted to warm waters of the Indian Ocean, learned to build rafts that carried our seed to tiny specks of rock in a vast, uncharted sea. It is no accident some of our greatest works of literature tell of travel to strange, new lands. There is something in the human consciousness that beckons us onward, away from the security of old ways and into the open sea where all things are possible to those who believe.

Earlier this study quoted the popular proverb attributed to William G.T. Shedd, "A ship in a harbor is safe, but that is not what ships are built for." Humanity is a shipbuilding race, a species of adventurers and explorers. And the greatest years of human exploration arguably loom ahead of us as people begin to dip their toes into the ocean of galaxies that comprises our cosmos. If science can find a way to circumvent the light barrier—which at this writing is still believed to be the absolute speed limit of the Universe—our descendants shall surely take their needlecraft, Bibles and candy bars aboard starships to other worlds. Perhaps the destiny of the human race lies beyond earth. Perhaps not. But if God empowers a cosmos in which starlight is possible in a reasonable amount of time, doubtless our descendants will discover the secret and take the treasures of the human heritage with them as they embark on the greatest adventure of all time.

Even Macquarrie agrees that this is no longer the stuff of fantasy but must be seriously addressed by responsible theologians. He quotes Alice Meynell's futurist poem in a visionary passage from his book *Principles of Christian Theology*:

> The overwhelming probability is that countless billions of "histories" have been enacted in the cosmos, and a space-age cosmology calls for a vastly enlarged understanding of divine grace and revelation. Now that man is reaching out into space, Alice Meynell's prediction is not so improbable:
>
> > *Doubtless we shall compare together, hear*
> > *A million alien gospels, in what guise*
> > *He trod the Pleiades, the Lyre, the Bear.*[36]

If humanity abandons Earth before the sun explodes in the distant future, its descendants might endure in some form to the very end of the cosmos—if there is to be such an end.

The Universe—Final Season?

There are only two possible answers to this question and both of them are scientifically based. Either humanity lives in a continuously re-creating Universe, or the cosmos is a one-time phenomenon headed for burn-out and oblivion. Biblical images of the end seem to represent only one possibility. Divesting the mythological trappings from NT accounts of end times, what remains is a totally re-created heaven and earth. No hint of an all-encompassing death appears in the wildly optimistic words of John's Apocalypse:

Then I saw a new heaven and a new earth; for the first heaven and the first earth had passed away, and the sea was no more. And I saw the holy city, the new Jerusalem, coming down out of heaven from God, prepared as a bride adorned for her husband. And I heard a loud voice from the throne saying, "See, the home of God is among mortals. He will dwell with them; they will be his peoples, and God himself will be with them; he will wipe every tear from their eyes."[37]

Although written in a prescientific age, the New Testament's complete trust in divine order transcends the limitations of a flat-earth cosmology, providing insights which apply to the space age and beyond. Notice there is no guarantee this cosmos will survive eternally. A "new heaven and a new earth" are promised *after* the old one passes away.

Scientists are divided about the fate of the Universe. While most agree that the present cosmos began after a Big Bang some fifteen-plus billion years ago, some believe that the Universe will continue to expand outward from that explosion until the last star burns out, and others believe an implosion will occur which will eventually result another Big Bang. The latter group, in effect, sees the Universe as a kind of cosmic accordion which exploded outward and collapsed inward any number of times—perhaps infinitely, without beginning or end.

Still another possibility comes from Einstein. If space is curved—and that's a big IF—theoretically one could continue in a straight line and end up at the point of origin without turning from the original course. If that is true, some scientists say that all matter could have exploded outward fourteen billion years ago only to reconvene at some moment in the far future. This counterintuitive scenario sees the Big Bang in warped space operating like a burst from the North Pole on a globe, which will reconvene at the South Pole without ever changing trajectory.

These are scientific ideas about the future of the cosmos. Although the question does have profound theological implications, it remains a scientific question and not a metaphysical one. Science and religion have a working partnership as long as science continues to look for new information about the physical Universe and religion offers its insights about ways to live more effectively in whatever cosmos actually exists.

When science starts making pronouncements about spiritual truth or religion begins to publish decrees about the origin or fate of the Universe, both are out of their areas of expertise. Progressive religionists accept the discoveries of science as gifts from the God Who created/organized the cosmos; spiritually minded scientists turn to progressive religion for lessons in cooperative living on a dangerous, weapon-ridden planet.

Second Coming, Revisited

Unfortunately, some religious groups continue to make noise about an end of the world by a supernatural intervention of God in time and space. With all due respect to brothers and sisters in churches which specialize in end-time predictions, that is simply not how God operates, nor is it faithful to the message of the New Testament when freed from its mythological packaging.

Jesus Christ taught a kingdom that was "not of this world," but he proceeded to give men and women teachings that would enable them to live at peace in a world without end. Most of all he showed people a natural way of life, a practical faith. There were no magical, superhuman powers in his healing miracles—he told his disciples they could do these things, too.[38] He called himself as the Son of Man, i.e., an ordinary human, and told men and women they had power to work wonders. His answer to the criticism from the religious leaders who accused him of making himself God was to quote Psalm 82:6, "I said, you are gods."

This admittedly represents late first century thinking, since it comes from John's gospel and represents a misreading of Psalm 82. [39] But even the Synoptics (Matthew, Mark, and Luke) show Jesus marveled when others marveled at his works. Johannine theology might represent a few decades of mulling this over in the minds of First Century Christians, but it might also represent strains of tradition originating with Jesus Himself. It is unlikely a person who believed other humans could attain the same degree of spirituality as Jesus would also believe only supernatural intervention by God in time and space at the Last Judgment will right the wrongs of this world and usher in the Kingdom of Heaven for an elect few.

How better to see the "Second Coming" as a continuous process whereby Jesus the Christ "comes" to men and women of succeeding generations with a freshness that speaks to each new situation in words of Christian hope? For Jesus, the Kingdom of Heaven is always in our midst, always within us. If that is true, the natural order shall roll on and God's kingdom shall find ways to manifest itself in and through the cosmos as we know it. Supernaturalism is not required in a well-planned Universe.

Any discussion of eschatology can only be an exercise in shortcomings, but Christian Theology in all its diversity is our topic and we shall pursue the broad course of studies as we continue our survey. People have wondered about what lies after death, what stands at the far end of time, from the earliest days of human life. Archeologists find that even prehistoric peoples like the Neanderthal buried their dead with tools and artifacts as though they wanted to send their loved one into the next world with the proper equipment to live well.

Books by pop-religious authors will continue to warn people that The End Is Near, and Armageddon approaches. Intelligent, well-educated people will spend vast sums of money on psychics, fortunetellers, and various self-designated seers because they want to know what lies ahead. But, if truth be told, we *don't* know, because we *can't* know. And that's why they call it "faith."

Personal View

A few years ago the author was pondering Life, Death and Eternity over a chef's salad when a sudden realization became clearer than ever before. Like many of the great riddles of life, we cannot know for certain what fate awaits the cosmos in general and ourselves in particular. It was not a terribly original thought, but the realization which followed sounded new to me: I can't know for sure, and that's OK. It makes for a better life of service to *believe* rather than to *know*. Taking a pen and notebook, these words flowed easily. They are not the last words on last things, but they say what one theologian sees when he stands looking into the face of sprawling, lovely, incomprehensible mystery.

A WORTHY SACRIFICE

If I offer my whole life as a sacrifice
  on the altar of Thy service,
If I provoke people to ask spiritual questions
  and love them into greener pastures of mind and soul,
If I expend my life-energies in ceaseless striving
  for World Unity and individual Christ-consciousness,
If I give my talents and strength
  so long as I have breath and awareness
To help others walk the path of peace
  in the footsteps of our Lord Jesus Christ,
Then whatever awaits after the life-force
  has flowed from my body—
  eternal progress, eternal bliss, or eternal oblivion—
Will do just fine,
And my life will have been worthily lived.[40]

CHECK YOUR KNOWLEDGE

1. Identify/explain the following: *eschatology, Parousia, eschaton, apocalypse, extinctionism, universalism, purgatory, metempsychosis.*

2. What was the main difference between Hebrew and Greek conceptions of time? How did this affect the theology of each?

3. Explain the three kinds of *extinctionist eschatologies.*

4. What was John Macquarrie's position on hell?

5. What is *bad karma*; why does the author say this may be a problem for Metaphysical Christianity?

6. What three possible fates await the physical Universe?

QUESTIONS FOR DISCUSSION

1. Could "purgatory" be a useful concept today? How would you interpret it?

2. What happens to consciousness after physical death? How do you know?

3. Do you believe in reincarnation? Elaborate on your answer based on the tools of Scripture, Tradition, Experience and Reflection

4. Metaphysical Christians tend to be universalists. If so, what kind of eternal destiny awaits people like Adolf Hitler?

5. Do you agree with the author's contention that humans will explore the stars? What might happen to Christian theology if Alice Meynell's poetic vision comes true?

6. What does the "Second Coming of Christ" mean in your belief system?

SACRAMENTAL THEOLOGY
A New Look

> For I received from the Lord what I also handed on to
> you, that the Lord Jesus on the night when he was
> betrayed took a loaf of bread, and when he had given
> thanks, he broke it and said, "This is my body that is for
> you. Do this in remembrance of me." In the same way he
> took the cup also, after supper, saying, "This cup is the
> new covenant in my blood. Do this, as often as you drink
> it, in remembrance of me." For as often as you eat this
> bread and drink the cup, you proclaim the Lord's death
> until he comes.[1]

Martin Luther and Ulrich Zwingli had a lot in common. Both were
German-speaking leaders of the Protestant Reformation: Zwingli (1484-
1531) helped the Germanic Swiss provinces break with Roman
Catholicism, while the anti-establishment escapades of Luther (1483-
1546) made him undisputed leader of the religio-political rebellion in
Germany proper. Luther and Zwingli decided to meet at Marburg,
Germany, in the Fall of 1529 to discuss unity in the struggle to establish a
reformed church in Europe.

Possibly, the two great revolutionists could close ranks and join
forces against a central church in Rome, which they saw as unbending,
obdurate and arrogant. A United Protestant Church was visible on the
horizon as the reformers met that long-ago Autumn. Roland H. Bainton
comments on that meeting in his book The Reformation of the Sixteenth
Century:

> A truly surprising measure of agreement was attained.
> Only one point was accord impossible, and that was the

Supper of the Lord. The great rite of Christian love had become the ground of contention.[2]

They agreed on all major points, save one. The historic Church recognized seven sacraments; chief among these was the Lord's Supper, sometimes called the Eucharist, Holy Communion or the Table of the Lord. Upon this rock of the faith Zwingli and Luther failed to build their church. And, like the testimony of an American President five centuries later, it all hinged on the meaning of a tiny word. The gospels report at the Last Supper Jesus said: "This is my body." To understand the significance of that two-letter word, is, requires a little background work in classical theologies of the Lord's Supper.

Crash Course in Eucharistic Thought

Catholic theology says the elements of bread and wine, after consecration by an ordained priest, are miraculously transformed into the "substance" of the body and blood of Jesus Christ. In Catholic thought the bread and wine remain physically the same, but their essence is now changed so that they are literally Jesus Christ himself.

For Catholics, celebration of the Mass replays the events of Calvary; every time a priest raises his hands with the tray containing bread, Jesus' body is sacrificed anew upon the altar. Since Jesus Christ is seen as uniquely God, those who hold such a "high" theology of the Eucharist often venerate the bread and wine as a physical manifestation of God. Once the act of priestly celebration transubstantiates the bread and wine into the body and blood of the Savior, the elements become God, not figuratively but actually. The next time you visit of a church with such a "high" sacramental theology, look for a small flickering flame at the front of the sanctuary. This indicates a portion of the sacrament has been held "in reserve" and is present for adoration. Catholic Eucharistic theology holds bit of consecrated bread is literally a chunk of God Almighty.[3]

And the Reformers said...

The founding fathers of Protestantism brought two different interpretations of the Eucharist to their Marburg Colloquy. Zwingli thought Jesus really meant, "This signifies my body," or, "Let this bread represent my body when you do this in remembrance of me." The Swiss position was a radical break with ancient tradition. For Zwingli, the Eucharist (Greek, "to give thanks") is merely a commemorative meal. In his Seventy-Seven Articles, the Swiss reformer wrote:

> Christ, having sacrificed Himself once, is to eternity a certain and valid sacrifice for the sins of all faithful, wherefrom it follows that the mass is not a sacrifice, but is a remembrance of the sacrifice and assurance of the salvation which God has given us...Christ is the only mediator between God and us.[4]

No two positions could be further apart than the Zwinglian idea of symbolic remembrance and the Catholic doctrine of transubstantiation. Luther, however, disagreed with both. In Zwingli we find rationalism, a faith that appeals directly to the mind. In Martin Luther there is a strain of mysticism which gave him the tendency to look deeper into things of the Spirit. Luther developed a remarkable theology of the Lord's Supper which held the Christ is present everywhere. Paul Tillich summarized Luther's thought:

> Christ is present in everything, in stone and fire and tree, but for us he is present only when he speaks to us. But he can speak to us through everything...In a Lutheran service during the Sundays in spring, you always find a tremendous amount of flowers and things of nature brought into the church, because of this symbol of the participation of the body of Christ in the world.[5]

"Christ is...in stone and fire and tree." The Christ is in the light of the farthest galaxy; the Christ is in the lily pad, the cactus and the dung heap. But at some places the presence of the Christ (i.e., God's presence) is more discernible than others. There are events in time-and-space where God's presence becomes elevated, and limited human thought become aware of Spirit which pervades everything. Bona fide encounters with the numinous are infrequent and mysterious, yet widespread enough to qualify as a recognizable phenomenon. Rare moments of mystical encounter offer vantage points where people can glimpse the true nature of the divine-human paradox.

Where does humanity find God in the world? How can finite human minds contact the infinite God? Upon what common ground does Homo sapiens stand when communing with the Creator? Or, as some might ask, how do people reach upward, to take part in the life that God can offer us, when all they can build is a Tower of Babel? These questions must be addressed prior to any meaningful discussion on regular encounters with the Divine through the Sacraments.

How Is God Known?

Until now, this ongoing study has assumed God can be known by finite human beings. Yet, the discussion has not yet offered theological reflection on how such contact is possible, or whether the Divine or human side initiates the encounter, or what form this contact might take. The differences for Christian thought are profound, depending on the options selected.

Assuming such divine-human interaction does happen, we are left with the question, "Who does what?" Usually two solutions are considered to the problem of human traffic with the Divine. Either God comes to humanity, revealing unto us that which we never would have otherwise known, or we search for God until we find divine footprints, then piece together the story and discover God's truth. The question represents another variation of the "Let It In / Let It Out" Controversy (Chapter 6). If someone says, "God can be known through prayer," does that mean humanity approaches God, or God approaches humanity? In the mythological language of the biblical three-story Universe, do humans finally succeed in build a babble-free Tower to the heavens, or does God descend like a dove? Raising human consciousness through acts of revelation, or soul ascend to God by discovering its power within? The difference is not frivolous. Let's look at both options.

Revelation: God Comes to Humanity

One of the best recent descriptions of revelation came from John Macquarrie, whose work we continue to consult while wandering the intricate maze of Christian thought:

...essential to the idea of revelation is that what we come to know through revelation has a gift-like character. If, in general terms, we say that what is disclosed in revelation is the dimension of the holy, then, in the revelatory experience, it is as if the holy "breaks in" and the movement is from beyond man toward man.[6]

"Revelation" means the movement is downward from God to woman/man. Macquarrie said religious communities are built around a primordial revelation given to the Founder by the Divine. But communication between God and human does not stop with the initial downpour of information, after which everyone is reduced to shuffling through accounts of that initial experience like Supreme Court Justices arguing the precedents of Constitutional law. There must be continuous contact with the Divine, or the founding revelation will deteriorate into antiquated meaninglessness. Macquarrie's comments set a careful tone when dealing with extracurricular, personal instruction allegedly received directly from God by individual believers. He wrote:

> We do not normally dignify our day-to-day experiences of the holy by the name of "revelation," and no theology properly called so could be founded on private revelations, for, as has been stressed already, theology expresses the faith of a community. Yet on the other hand we would never have believed that anyone had been the recipient of a revelation unless we ourselves had some experience of the holy. Indeed, the very notion of revelation would be completely unintelligible to us unless we knew first hand some experience that bears some analogy to revelation.[7]

There is the problem in a nutshell. How does one decide if an idea represents authentic "revelation" or just someone's fantasy? In many ways, this is the problem raised during the discussion on epistemology (Ch. 3). However, this chapter focuses on testing a single source of religious information, i.e., revelation, rather than scanning the various ways to know truth. If God is known by revelation, it is important to apply the tests of epistemology to any message which claims to speak with a divine voice. The first task is determine whether such God-to-humanity communications even exist. Macquarrie thinks so, but he says the community of faith provides the best testing ground for religious ideas, especially new ideas from alleged divine revelations.

> It is present experience within a community of faith that gives rise to theology and that enables us to recognize the primordial revelation as revelation; but if theology is to be saved from the dangers of subjectivism, the varieties of experience within the community must be submitted to the relatively objective content of the classic revelation on which the community is founded.[8]

Chapter 9 (epistemology) suggested a dialectical model of knowledge. Seek and be fearless, but bring all to the yardstick of Jesus Christ as present to us in Scripture, mediated through Tradition, and examined by Reason. Only this give-and-take keeps the ancient teachings from becoming fossilized, which Macquarrie agreed would provide us no revelation at all. Dialogue and critical analysis permit us to evaluate new ideas and practices encountered in everyday life-experience.9

Natural Theology vs. Revelation

If we find God in such a community experience or through the primordial revelation, we still face the same question: Did God come to us or did we discover him? Macquarrie is far gentler with humanity that some recent theologians like Karl Barth (pronounced Bart.) In the 1930s, Barth was invited to present the Gifford Lectures. According to the testament left by the late Lord Gifford, guest speakers were supposed to lecture on Natural Theology. Today an archaic term, Natural Theology meant Barth was to discuss religion based on reason rather than divine revelation. Barth accepted the commission, presumably took their money, but totally disregarded its stipulations:

> I certainly see--with astonishment--that such a science as Lord Gifford had in mind does exist...I am convinced that so far as it has existed and still exists, it owes its existence to a radical error.[10]

Kantonen says that in Barth's theology:

> Man's ultimate need is God but his attempt to think or to find God is futile. God is not the object of man's rational apprehension, moral striving, or religious feeling. The God who is set up as the object of human religiosity is only a man-made idol. The true God is always subject, not object, one who stands over against man, one who takes the initiative, one who speaks to man by his own sovereign word, one who in Christ reveals himself and acts to restore man into personal fellowship with himself.[11]

Neo-orthodox thinkers like Barth, Brunner and Bultmann insisted the impetus must come from God, not humanity. Barth said if there were no divine revelation, humans would know nothing about God. In a gracious act of self-disclosure, God comes to us as Jesus Christ. We do not come to God. That would be as impossible as the Tower of Babel. We cannot reach God because we are part of the problem, the giants of neo-orthodoxy said; humanity's spiritual science is flawed.

Discovery: Math & Mysticism

A radically different opinion holds that all knowledge is discovered. Even if God lowers instructions from heaven in a basket, someone will have to find the basket and interpret the instructions. Discovery is the basic procedure for all information, spiritual subjects included. When beginning his spiritual quest in the 1880s, Fillmore wrote:

> I noticed, however, that all the teachers and writers talked a great deal about the omnipresent, omniscient God, who is Spirit and accessible to everyone. I said to myself, "In this babel I will go to headquarters. If I am Spirit and this God they talk so much about is Spirit, we can somehow communicate, or the whole thing is a fraud."[12]

Charles Hartshorne, Unitarian-Universalist layperson and professor emeritus, leaned in the direction of discovery in his weighty little book The Divine Relativity. Hartshorne believed certain religious ideas (i.e., God's existence) can be logically demonstrated, and he had no patience with those who say God is just too mysterious to understand:

> The very people who choose the soft words, paradox and mystery, for what, so far as they have shown, are simply contradictions in their own thinking, resort to the harsher terms, absurdity or contradiction, do they not, when they meet with difficulties not essentially different in systems which they oppose?...an illogical position is hardly strengthened by the apparent logic with which it furnishes reasons for its own illogicality.[13]

Hartshorne's point is well taken. One need not embrace absurdity in order to pledge loyalty to Jesus Christ. However, faith is more than logic. A possible critique of Hartshorne is that he relies too heavily on pure logic, since the rational mind represents only half the process of reflection, i.e., intellectual reflection. The other half, intuitive reflection, is just as important, but does not submit easily to the constraints of formal logic. Add to this experience, mediated by dialogue with a larger community of believers, which can be measured against the standards of Tradition and compared with the record of the "primordial revelation" (Scripture). This four-fold interaction—previous called the Unity Quadrilateral—provides tools to deepen and extend the dynamic Metaphysical Christian Faith.

Yet, Christian theology is really not a group effort but an individual encounter between the believer and the Lord, however understood. The individual does the work, experiences faith, dialogues with other Christian and members of other faith groups, and compares the result with the Jesus Christ yardstick as known both in the life of the community and through the primordial, scriptural revelation. Arguably, because everyone's spiritual growth is an individual learning plan, God does not make faith-decisions for anyone. Jesus Christ acted as though he believed every person he encountered had the divine power to choose a best path. Jesus presented alternatives from which his listeners had to choose. After telling the story of the Good Samaritan, he asked his questioner, "Which of these three, do you think, was a neighbor to the man who fell into the hands of the robbers?"14 He told an assortment of stories to reach a variety of learning styles.

In the two models of spiritual growth discussed so far, *discovery* says *we find God*, but *revelation* disagrees, insisting *God finds us*. The choice between these polar opposites is powerfully affected by the attitude of the theologian toward human capabilities. If humans have the inherent capacity to recognize divine truth, *discovery* seems most logical. However, if we are fatally flawed—more charitably, limited by the existential predicament and shaped by culture—our only hope for knowledge of God must come from God's initiative, *revelation*. Yet, there may be a third alternative.

Seek and Ye Shall be Found

Anglican novelist Madeleine L'Engle said, "We seek God until He finds us."15 Perhaps the quest is two-sided. In the parable of the Prodigal Son, the Father sees his wayward progeny approaching from a great distance and rushes out to meet him. If this parable represents the model of Divine-human interaction favored by Jesus, as many scholars believe, then we can see initiative is required on both sides. To preserve human freedom, God cannot force goodness and truth upon us. God must patiently wait until we move in a Godward direction. That is Discovery. However, as soon as people come to their senses and head homeward to the divine Father-Mother, God comes rushing to greet them with blessings unanticipated. Catholic Theologian Hans Kueng is confident everyone will be found.

> ...every man is intended to find his salvation within his own historical condition...within the religion imposed on him by society... A man is to be saved within the religion that is made available to him in his historical situation. Hence it is his right and duty to seek God within that religion in which the hidden God has already found him.16

Other parables of Jesus suggest God does not loaf around in heaven while the children are wandering in the wilderness. The Good Shepherd goes after the lost sheep; the woman lights her lamp and sweeps her house until she finds that misplaced coin. In Jesus Christ we find Discovery and Revelation perfectly integrated. To paraphrase Eric Butterworth, Jesus was a human like us who discovered the power within him, and by that great discovery he reveals something of our indwelling Divine Spirit. With this two-fold, dialectical understanding, we can now turn to the study of those places in life where Gods presence is revealed/discovered for us.

Sacramentum: Two Early Mistakes

Luther believed the points of contact were the Sacraments of the Christian church. Before we can reconsider sacramental theology we must first look at some traditional views of these time-and-space happenings which are celebrated in some form by every congregation that calls itself Christian. First, a word-study of the term seems to be in order. The English word sacrament comes into the language by way of dual misunderstandings, one linguistic and the other theological.

The Latin word *sacramentum* was a common term in pre-Christian times to describe a bonding procedure of the Roman judicial system. When two adversaries went to court, each was required to deposit a sum of bond money, called a sacramentum, which the loser would forfeit to religious charity after the case was adjudicated. Sacramentum also referred to the oath of allegiance a new recruit took when entering the army. Consequently, the term gradually became a synonym for an oath or covenant.

By the second century the church father Tertullian equated conversion to the Christian faith with this oath of allegiance, calling the process sacramentum. Pliny the Younger (ca. 112 A.D.), when reported suspicious activities of this new religion, told Emperor Trajan that Christians bound themselves by an oath. Pliny wasn't certain what kind of crimes Christians were committing, but anyone so completely dedicated to a secret society must be up to no good and should be punished. As a pagan, he could scarcely understand the significance of the Christian sacramentum, even though he rightly saw that joining the faith required a commitment on the part of the convert. Adding his confusion to Tertullian's misnomer was the theological misunderstanding.

We can forgive Pliny for his ignorance; few people understood Christian theology in its early days. Some would say the situation changed little through the ages. Go beyond the ranks of the professional religious thinkers and you encounter an amazing variety of ignorance as to what the Church has really taught. Perhaps this is the way it must be. Theology is like any other profession: specialized vocabulary, technology (tools + knowledge), and procedures. Laypeople seldom care about the ideas which excite us theologians, but that is probably a blessing masquerading as a deficiency.[17]

On the other hand, the linguistic mistake (*sacramentum*) comes to us by way of a professional theologian, the greatest linguist of the early church. In the fourth century Pope Damascus commissioned St. Jerome to translate the Bible into the common language of their day, Latin Vulgate. To accomplish this Herculean feat, Jerome moved his desk to Jerusalem where he studied, conversed and debated with the preeminent rabbis who still lived in the land which gave birth to both testaments. The result was a superb translation, based on ancient texts, which could be studied by anyone who read Latin vernacular.

A secondary purpose, but one which was even more important for the still-young Church, was that Roman Catholic priests reading the Sunday text during worship in the Western church were reading in the language of the common people. Peasants, tradesmen, wives, young children--all heard the gospel in their language. Jerome's Bible did for the fourth century Latin-speaking churchgoers what the modern translations of scripture have done for twentieth century Christians.

However, Jerome's translation was not without flaws. When he rendered the passage *"Repent, for the kingdom of Heaven is at hand,"* into Latin, it came out, *"Do penance, for the kingdom of Heaven is at hand."* Jerome also translated the New Testament Greek word *mysterion*, which biblical authors used to describe church practices such as baptism and the Lord's Supper, into Latin as *sacramentum*. You don't have to be a linguist to grasp the difference in the root words. Instead encounters with God's mysterious Presence and Power, they would be would be seen by the Western Church as oaths of allegiance, sealing the recipient to the faith.[18]

St. Augustine (A.D. 354-430) defined a Sacrament as a "visible sign of an invisible reality," which is often described in modern churches as a visible sign of invisible "grace."[19] To investigate properly what that short phrase means we would have to discuss "grace," "signs," and the distinction between the "visible" and "invisible" activity of God. Instead of wallowing into that thicket, let's invoke artistic license and paraphrase Augustine's definition with help from Luther.

Defining Sacrament: Encounter with God

The operational definition for this study will be as follows: Sacraments are occasions in life where God's Presence becomes discernible.

People who grew up in traditional churches might be surprised at a sacramental theology which begins with such a broad brush stroke. Since the Council of Trent in 1545, Catholic thought has tended to limit the sacraments to seven: baptism, confirmation, the Eucharist, penance, extreme unction (last rites), ordination, and matrimony.

Protestant reformers took issue with this list and defined a sacrament even more narrowly. Not only did the act have to be a way for God's grace (goodness in action) to manifest itself, a genuine sacrament must have been inaugurated by Jesus and explicitly commanded by him. According to the earliest account of the Last Supper (I Corinthians 11:23-25), Jesus did this only in regard to the Eucharist. Only baptism, ordained by the risen Lord in Matthew 28:19, also qualifies as a legitimate sacrament for most Protestants. In general, Protestants also differ from Catholics by insisting, in John Calvin's words, that the sacraments "communicate no grace from themselves, but announce and show, and, as earnests and pledges, ratify, the things which are given to us by the goodness of God."[20]

Protestant sacraments are not a "medicine of immortality," as Ignatius of Antioch called them in the second century. They do not give the recipient something which he/she did not have before the sacramental act. Baptism and the Lord's Supper play a part in Protestant theology roughly equivalent to the Bible: they are places where the believer can receive inspiration but are not funnels through which God pours Himself out to people regardless of their receptivity.[21]

The ancient church defined the mysterion/sacramentum much more broadly than either Protestant or Roman Catholic doctrines presently allow. Writing in Harper's Dictionary of the Bible, George Wesley Buchanan says early Christians accepted almost any evidence of God's activity as a sacramental event:

> Although baptism and the Eucharist were considered the primary sacraments, the term "sacrament" was used in the early church to describe many kinds of religious ceremonies and practices. By the twelfth century Hugo of St. Victor listed some thirty sacraments. This was probably the result of Augustine's definition of sacraments as signs pertaining to things divine, or visible forms of invisible grace. Since there is no limit to the number of ways God's grace can be expressed, the number of sacraments increased with Christian sensitivity and imagination. Therefore the Council of Trent (A.D. 1545) decreed that not all signs of sacred things had sacramental value. Visible signs become sacraments only if they represent an invisible grace and become its channels.[22]

Hugo's list of sacraments included making the forehead of Christians with ashes at the beginning of Lent, but he also recognized sacraments under the "old law," Jewish practices to include offering tithes and animal sacrifices.[23]

Access to the Sacraments

Sacramental theology has always intrigued mystics, mainly because it revealed God dealing with people One-to-one. Yet, some theologians have been suspicious of church-administered, liturgical sacraments. Access to those "visible signs" has been controlled by professional clergy. If you can't get to heaven without the sacraments, and if the clergy is empowered to withhold those rites from communicant believers—guess who's really in charge of heaven? In medieval times the church had the power to bludgeon kings and lesser rulers into submission. When a secular ruler defied Church decrees, the Pope's arsenal of spiritual weaponry included the Interdict. When it was imposed, every church in the region affected closed its doors. Serious business in those days. No weddings, funerals, baptisms, or Eucharist. No forgiveness of sins.

When the whole Western world worshipped as one universal Catholic Church, the interdict was the equivalent of a spiritual nuclear bomb. Interdicts were effectively laid upon France in 998, Germany in 1102, the city of Rome in 1155, and England in 1208. The events surrounding an interdict were so overwhelming to the medieval mind that people behaved as though the culprits named by the church were carriers of the plague. Will Durant describes an episode in his massive, multi-volume Story of Civilization:

> When King Robert of France was excommunicated (which led to the interdict of 998 against the whole country) for marrying his cousin he was abandoned by all his courtiers and nearly all his servants; two domestics who remained threw into the fire the victuals left by him at his meals, lest they be contaminated by them.[24]

Later, the interdict would be ignored or laughed off by rulers and large segments of the Christian world, especially after the Reformation. Today, even personal excommunication seems like a medieval anachronism, and the idea of putting a whole nation on a spiritual starvation diet is, hopefully, an idea whose time has passed.[25]

Thankfully, denying the sacraments has lost its power to control people through fear. Furthermore, the new definition for what constitutes a sacrament, described in this chapter, redirects human consciousness toward the mysterion of God's Presence and Power, which we shall explore in the following chapter. Some will be experiences of corporate worship in a very traditional sense, such as the Lord's Supper. Other sacraments will be private, personal moments when God is able to catch an individual's attention. Who has not stood under the mysterion/sacramentum of the night sky and breathed the awe-inspiring Presence? What is more evocative of the Divine than deep meditation, heights of prayer, or episodes of love?

It may be helpful to discuss some of these life-events as sacramental encounters, especially if we are serious about constructing a systematic theology that is thoroughly mystical and touches base with the great themes of Christian thought. Looking at sacramental theology from this wide, inclusive viewpoint it is important to remember Metaphysical Christians are members of the Church Universal, heirs to all that has gone before, not curious spectators watching a religious procession. We may even differ with some of our ancestors in the central premises of the Ancient Faith, but we do so as participants in the body of Christ. The sacraments, perhaps more than anything else, can have the potential build a bridge linking Metaphysical Christianity to the mainland of Christian faith.

Twelve Powers / Twelve Sacraments

The operating definition of a sacrament introduced in this study is any occasion in life where God's Presence becomes discernible. This means sacraments are an existential events in the course of daily life. Under this definition a sacrament is less like a novel and more like a stage play, a drama in which people are players, not mere spectators. You experience a sacrament; you don't watch it like a television show. Any number of space-time occurrences could be sacraments, but for the sake of economy let's consider a limited number of events at which God's presence becomes discernible to the receptive person. Hugo of St. Victor's thirty sacraments is too many to treat in a single chapter. Limiting the sacraments at two, as Protestant Reformers insisted, seems grudgingly restrictive, almost punitive.

Since Christians discover God consistently in their spiritual lives, one could call any number arbitrary depending on who's scoring the list. For our purposes, we shall limit the discussion to twelve points. There is an unconcealed artificial structure in this system, but all attempts to describe mystical points of contact will necessarily involve some kind of flimsy framework at best. Jesus Christ spoke in parables, not systems, perhaps because systematic thinking limits the subject matter to the shape of the pigeonholes provided by the system-builder.[26]

To provide cohesion and structure, each sacramental event will be linked to one of Charles Fillmore's Twelve Powers, so a few brief comments on that work is required before venturing further. There are many other possibilities, many ways to approach sacramental theology depending on the angle of attack desired. We could have chosen a classical religious theme, like the fruits of the Spirit listed by the Apostle

Paul (Galatians 5:22), or the Beatitudes of Matthew's Gospel. Social psychology could have given us a working framework, like Abraham Maslow's pyramidal Hierarchy of Needs, Don Beck's Spiral Dynamics, or the behaviorism of B.F. Skinner.

However, since this work represents an attempt to do systematic theology from a Metaphysical Christian perspective, Charles Fillmore's Twelve Powers provides a flexible yet comprehensive way to achieve that starting point while standing fully within the wider circle of modern Christian thought. Fillmore struggled with the problem of how to organize his thinking about the divine-human paradox. What ingredients do human beings have within them that come from the original recipe cooked up by the Creator? Borrowing from contemporary New Thought writers like Emma Curtis Hopkins, Fillmore linked twelve Divine-human traits with twelve New Testament characters. Just as the church created patron saints to represent various professions or activities, Fillmore matched the disciples with the Twelve Powers.

There is a certain artificiality to any theological system. Fillmore's twelve categories suffer if we push the model too far. Still, there is something intriguing about the way these twelve interact and interface. Although some of his ideas are controversial—few moderns will agree with Fillmore's views on human sexuality in the chapter on Life in Twelve Powers—any reasonable reader could concede that every human being needs traces of each "power" to be a whole person before God and in community with other people. Fillmore's system is neither psychology nor yet theology but a wise man's overview of the human condition as it could be under Divine guidance. His twelve categories will provide a framework for investigating the sacraments from a wider, more inclusive perspective.

Whither Cometh Sacramentum / Mysterion?

Sometimes the door to mystical awareness will open during a highly liturgical event, such as the Eucharist; other times it may be a lonely encounter or even an experience not usually considered religious in a traditional sense. The key turns when any event presents people with a heightened awareness of the Divine Presence. Christian faith is not a game of peek-a-boo with discorporate spirits, nor an attempt to manipulate magically the cosmos to squeeze blessings from an impersonal, uncaring supernatural realm. Christianity is a relationship to God through Jesus Christ. All the sacramental experiences to be described are ultimately valid for the Christian only if approached as paths leading to the God revealed in Jesus the Christ With that caveat in mind, move on to discuss twelve points at which God's presence can be known to modern mystical Christians, the Twelve Sacraments of Life.

CHECK YOUR KNOWLEDGE

1. Explain/identify the following: Eucharist, Transubstantiate, Revelation, Discovery, Primordial Revelation, Mysterion / Sacramentum, Latin Vulgate, St. Jerome, Interdict.

2. Why were Zwingli and Luther unable to agree?

3. What was Karl Barth's objection to "Natural Theology"?

4. What did Madeleine L'Engle say about finding God?

5. What is the definition of a "Sacrament" given by the text?

6. What "linguistic mistake" did St. Jerome make and how has it affected the way the Church views the sacraments?

QUESTIONS FOR DISCUSSION

1. In what way, if any, is Christ present in the Holy Communion in your view?

2. How do we know about God, revelation or discovery?

3. How does the "primordial revelation" of the Christian faith keep from becoming "fossilized"?

4. Are there places when/where God's presence becomes more discernible to you? Are those your "sacraments"?

5. What do you think life would be like in a medieval town under the Interdict?

6. Do you like a church service rich in symbolism and ritual, or do you prefer the low-church "hymn sandwich" liturgy with a bare minimum of ceremony? How could different worship needs be met by the same church?

- 12 -

TWELVE SACRAMENTS OF LIFE

A Dozen Places Where People Have Encountered God

Finally I am coming to the conclusion that my highest ambition is to be what I already am. That I will never fulfill my obligation to surpass myself unless I first accept myself, and if I accept myself fully in the right way, I will already have surpassed myself.

Thomas Merton[1]

Having discussed the concept of a sacrament from a traditional perspective and offered an alternative definition, i.e., occasions in life where God's Presence becomes discernible, it is now possible propose a revised list of sacraments for Metaphysical Christianity. Any catalogue of spiritual subjects brings an element of organizational subjectivity, but offering a structure to consider moments of sacramental encounter might be helpful. Fillmore's *Twelve Powers* will provide a framework for identification of old and new sacraments in this chapter, the *basic seven* and *bonus five*.

The *basic seven* categories roughly correspond to classical sacraments of the ancient church:

1. Faith – creating sacred space by worship, Eucharist, Lord's Supper, music

2. Life – experiences of parental Love, infant baptism/christening

3. Zeal – dedication, adult baptism, ordination

4. Love - experience of selfless love, marriage, adoption ceremony

5. Power - inspired teaching/preaching, Confirmation

6. Renunciation - assurance, forgiveness, rededication

7. Strength - healing prayer, memorial service, Extreme Unction (Last Rites)

The first two sacraments are agreed upon by nearly all Christian churches—Lord's Supper and Baptism. Note that "agreed upon" does not mean all Christians agree about what these practices mean or who should officiate or participate. Right the contrary! More than one Protestant denomination has splintered specifically because the breakaway people failed to agree on sacramental theology. In place of *infant baptism*, some churches substitute *adult baptism* (sometimes called *believer's baptism*). This system differentiates between these two practices by associating the term *adult baptism* with the Sacrament of Zeal. Conservative Protestant churches often have a problem with infant "baptism," but no difficulty in "Christening" new babies in a ceremony that closely resembles a waterless baptism. (Sometimes, water is used!) We shall explore the differences between infant and adult baptism when looking at the two sacraments, *Life* and *Zeal*.

Five new sacraments are introduced in this chapter. The "bonus five" sacraments expand consciousness by recognizing ways people experience the mystical in everyday life, Omnipresent God in mundane theophany, described in the Eighth Psalm:

> When I look at your heavens, the work of your fingers, the moon and the stars that you have established; what are human beings that you are mindful of them, mortals that you care for them? Yet you have made them a little lower than God, and crowned them with glory and honor.[2]

With those lofty thoughts in mind, behold the *bonus five*:

8.. Order - "Starry Night" experience, nature-communion

9.. Understanding - the "ah-ha!" experience; grasping spiritual insights

10. .Wisdom – meditation; moments of intuitive insight; the Silence

11. .Imagination - creative outpouring; "The Muse"

12. .Will - confident prayer; "knowing the truth" despite appearances

Each category represents a Divine-human encounter which, under the definition established in this work, qualifies as sacramental. Frankly, to do justice to this complex, important topic requires an entire volume devoted to nothing but the study of sacramental theology from a Metaphysical Christian perspective. But it may be helpful to begin the work by staking a footpath for others to follow into this rich but neglected country of mystical studies.

With apologies for its scanty nature, let's turn to a brief jaunt through the Twelve Sacraments of Life. The trail begins with a fresh look at the traditional "basic seven" sacraments, reinterpreted through the lens of Metaphysical Christianity.

1. THE SACRAMENT OF FAITH

EVENT: High moments of worship when a person "feels" God's presence through prayer, music, spoken words, or other elements in a worship experience.

SPIRITUAL ACTIVITY: Corporate worship or mystical communion, such as inspirational music; especially the Eucharist (Lord's Supper).[3]

Following Luther's lead, the "body" of Jesus Christ (i.e., Divine presence) could theoretically be discerned in everything and every place, but divinity is best experienced in those high moments of worship that elevate the God-within to the range of human perception. Luther wanted this to apply only to the Eucharist, but once he had opened the door to mystical awareness there was no stopping those who would come after him from finding God in other places. Indeed, the whole sacramental theology presented in this work builds on Luther's assertion that the Christ is everywhere if we only would discern the divine substance which outpictures as the Universe. God's Presence is always present.

There is some biblical support for this as the viewpoint of the ancient church. In last chapter of the Gospel of Luke we find recorded a remarkable story, known popularly as the *Walk to Emmaus*. Two of Jesus' followers—one called Cleopas, the other unnamed by Luke—are walking toward Emmaus late in the afternoon on the original Easter day. They are discussing the events of Holy Week when Jesus appears to them. Significantly, at first they fail to recognize their Master as He walks with them and explains the Hebrew prophecies about how the Messiah must suffer, die and rise again on the third day--today! Only when they stop for the night do these intimate followers of Jesus realize who he is, then only in conjunction with an action he performs. The gospel of Luke reports:

> When he was at the table with them, he took bread, blessed and broke it, and gave it to them. Then their eyes were opened, and they recognized him; and he vanished from their sight... The two explained to them (other disciples) what had happened on the road, and how they had recognized the Lord when he broke the bread.[4]

This describes Luther's theology of the Eucharist. The presence of the living Christ becomes discernible in the communion meal. The stranger was Jesus all the way along the road to Emmaus, but it was only after "he took bread, blessed and broke it, and gave it to them" that "...their eyes were opened and they recognized him."

A sacramental encounter marks the point where God's Omnipresence elevates into view. Like a card labeled *"Look here!"* pops up from a file box, sacraments occur when something Divine gets human attention. Behold the Christ, and realize he was strolling beside you all the way to Emmaus. All this makes perfect sense metaphysically. One can affirm, with the higher Christologies and ancient traditions, the Real Presence of the Christ is found in the bread and wine of the Lord's Supper. After all, if the Christ-spirit is in the stone, the fire, the air we breathe, it certainly must be in the bread and wine of Holy Communion.

What does this mean for innovative worship? What examples of new ways to celebrate the Eucharistic meal have been attempted by Christian churches? Not surprisingly, quite a few varieties exist and have met with success. Quakers sometimes describe their traditional silent meeting as a communion sacrament.

> This sacramental language may seem strong from a group that discarded rituals. But Quakers only abandoned rituals in favor of what they considered inner sacraments full of spiritual power. They found that they came to God and God came to them in holy silence. They feasted on Jesus in their hearts. Then they found power to live lives of faithful practice.[5]

A number of churches offer "spiritual communion," where the minister leads the congregation in a guided meditation which seeks to honor the command to "remember" Jesus. William L. Fischer advocates this practice in his slim book, *Alternatives*:

> Let's consider the sacraments, in a deep sense. Wine represents blood, and blood represents life. Therefore, wine is symbolic of the Life of God coursing through our bodies. Bread represents the body of Christ, and this in turn is representative of divine substance. If the flesh profits nothing and the words are the important thing, why not observe communion by using our words in prayer?[6]

Indeed, why not? A sacrament is any place where the real presence of God/Christ can be discerned, so wouldn't a commemorative meditation in remembrance of him qualify as a Eucharist of Spirit? Yet, here it is important to keep in mind James Glasse's three worship needs. People who value physically celebrating the Lord's Supper and actually eating bread/drinking wine, probably the small "c" catholics, may find Fischer's meditative alternative or Quaker silent prayer too abstract to meet their spiritual needs. Since contemplative communion ingests no physical elements, the process might probably work best in churches with strongly non-traditional leanings.

Many groups celebrate the Lord's Supper by substituting grape juice for wine. The sacrament offered by the Latter-Day Saints distances the communicant even further from alcohol. At the Marriage at Canaan Jesus reportedly turned water into wine. The LDS celebration reverses the process:

> Our primary family worship service is called sacrament meeting. This meeting is held in our chapels on Sunday and lasts approximately 70 minutes. Visitors are welcome to attend...The sacrament consists of prepared bread and water, which is blessed and passed by priesthood holders to those in attendance who wish to do so.[7]

It's also possible to go the opposite direction on the wine question. During my career as military chaplain, I spent three years ministering to soldiers and their families in the forty-ninth state. Traveling with the troops in the vast, pristine wilderness was often exhilarating. Alaska has warm, sunny summers when it literally never gets dark. But I paid a karmic debt for all that sunshine when the seasons shift. Temperatures between December and March sometimes plummet to *sixty below zero*. The super-cold winters challenged my priestcraft skills. When attempting to do field worship services at subzero temperatures, I quickly discovered the regular communion wine had a tendency to freeze solid. So, I took the liberty of changing the wine into fire-water by carrying freeze-resistant brandy in my communion kit. Not surprisingly, when the word spread throughout the battalion attendance at field services skyrocketed.

More frequently, I have offered civilians and military churchgoers communion with two cups—one containing wine, the other grape juice—so people could chose whichever met their needs. I've also done a "First Century" dinner at which Mediterranean foods were served, followed by the Eucharist at the dining table.

As a frequent visitor at a variety of churches, I have seen cookie and milk communion for children, and flower communions in the Spring. The flowery Eucharist invites people to bring garden blossoms to the church and exchange their gift for the flowers grown by another. The Lord's Supper can be offered at a home prayer circle, choir practice, or youth worship service Many hospital chaplains carry portable communion sets for bedridden people who want the comfort of the sacrament. The Lord's Supper is sometimes offered in Protestant marriage ceremonies, but more commonly in Catholic nuptial rites. Since Catholics define the *Mass* by the absence or presence of the Eucharist, Catholic Rites of Wedding come in two forms: wedding with Mass (with Holy Communion), or without the Mass (no Eucharist).

All these variations have been successful in the right context. Sensitivity and common sense are the key to any worship experience. A flower communion might work better in a less traditional church setting than in a heavily liturgical program. But who knows? Experimentation has permeated all sectors of the church. Even more liturgical congregations are finding they have freedom to try innovative approaches to sacramental ministry, especially if the event is in a non-traditional location, away from the main worship service.

Some will argue it trivializes the Eucharist to consider it just another theophany in a Universe teeming with divinity. If God's presence were conspicuous—i.e., easily recognizable to everyone, everywhere—this critique would be irrefutable. But the numbing routine of modern living mitigates against universal awareness of the Divine Presence. It should not be necessary to *find* God in a world made of God-stuff, but it is. And thankfully, there are places where God's presence breaks through. Like a supernova announces what previously was an ordinary star, God appears when sentient beings allow themselves to perceive the Divine.

Other high moments of corporate or private worship fall into this category. Whenever people recognize God in the burning-bush moments of their lives, the commonplace becomes holy ground.

Music: A Form of Worship?

A special word must be said about music as worship and its power to bring a person to awareness of God's reality. Music is often employed by worship leaders as background sounds for movement--offertories to move the offerings, processionals/recessionals to move the worship leaders or the choir into position and back again at the close of the service. However, properly understood, music is a form of worship and not an interlude. To sing unto the Lord is to *pray*. It is no accident of preservation that gave us musical directions "To the Choirmaster" between the verses of many psalms. Music can sometimes lift heart and mind when words fall like tin raindrops on shuttered ears. Some of the finest spiritual experiences occur during corporate worship through music. People often report their highest worship experiences occur when listening to classics like Handel's *Messiah* or chanting prayer songs individually or in congregation. Music can be a sacramental experience.

2. THE SACRAMENT OF LIFE

EVENT: Experience of parental love.

SPIRITUAL ACTIVITY: Christening, infant baptism.

What parent has not felt a wondrous Presence when gazing into the eyes of a child? The Christian community recognizes parental love by a rite of passage, infant baptism. When life comes to us renewed in the face of a child, the result can be a genuine sacramental encounter. Although the mystical words of Karen Drucker's song, "You Are the Face of God," apply to everyone, it is almost impossible not to see the Divine in a newborn child.

> You are the face of God.
> I hold you in my heart.
> You are a part of me.
> You are the face of God.[8]

Love for children—that sense of continuity with the Creator—is the Sacrament of Life. Bringing forth new life from old, establishing a new generation to serve God and humanity, is what people celebrate when they gather to welcome a new child as a member of the covenant community. The awe-inspiring power of life renewed, moments of silent communion between parent and child, constitute genuine sacramental encounters.

3. THE SACRAMENT OF ZEAL

EVENT: The "God is with me" feeling when acting in his service.

SPIRITUAL ACTIVITY: Dedication, adult Baptism, Ordination, Consecration of person or place; also the "conversion experience," when a person accepts Jesus the Christ as Wayshower and Lord.

Biblical authors frequently take time to narrate in great detail the dedication of some great shrine, like the Temple at Jerusalem, or consecration of a new leaders like Samuel, David, or Jesus. Something special happens when people decide on a new spiritual venture; walking with God is always easiest the first few paces. At those high moments when we make a conscious decision to follow God's guidance, often we can feel the Divine Presence in a unique way. Under the expanded definition this study has offered, experiences of new beginnings, when we feel that God is with us, are sacraments in the truest sense. Adult Baptism, certainly, would fall under this category. So would ordination to the clergy, installation of a pastor or dedication of a church officer, or consecration of a new religious facility such as a worship center or Sunday school building.

Another sacramental encounter which falls under this category is the "conversion-experience." Do people who make a conscious decision to follow Jesus Christ experience God in a unique way? Evangelical Christians are often encouraged to make a "Decision for Christ," meaning to accept Jesus as guide and Lord and to regard his sacrificial death as an atonement for their personal sins. No matter what theological lenses people wear when examining of the "born-again" phenomenon, there is no doubt the believer has experienced God-presence in a new and powerful way. If I love realism in painting, I do not have to share a love for expressionism or abstraction to accept that other people are passionate about those very different artistic styles. Finding God is the art of living spiritually, and there are many forms.

Looking at "decision" theology, obviously the same volume of omnipresent God-power permeated the cosmos *before* the person decided to recognize God-in-Christ. But *after* the decision to follow Jesus, more God-presence became discernible. A conversion-experience fits the new description of a sacramental encounter.

Baptism: Kids or Grown-Ups?
Something should be said about baptism of adults in this context. A

raging controversy has split church after church on this subject, even though some Metaphysical Christians find it difficult to understand what all the shouting is about. Before the sixteenth century there was no real controversy about baptism. The Church baptized babies and adult converts. With the Reformation, Protestants began to question to validity of infant baptism. If baptism means joining the church, how can an infant choose to follow Jesus Christ? If the sacrament of baptism gives the believer a full measure of God's grace, how could anyone but a consenting adult receive it?

Furthermore, did the example of Jesus include infant baptism? He waited until thirty years old to accept baptism. The New Testament knows nothing of babes in arms receiving the blessings of clergy by a fount of holy water. Some Protestants considered this such an important point that they broke with mainline thinkers like Luther, Zwingli and Calvin to form newer, more radical sects that practiced only believer's baptism. Since these groups insisted all adults must be baptized, even though many had received infant baptism, they were known as Anabaptists. Nearly all modern Baptist churches descended from the rebels of the radical Reformation.

Middle Way

A more moderate position is an inclusive, both/and theology rather than the either/or positions of earlier times. Certainly, adults who feel they have had a significant renewal of belief or have professed their Christian faith for the first time should be invited to celebrate this encounter by receiving baptism as part of a corporate worship experience. Baptism, like the Eucharist, is not a private affair but is a welcoming of the Christ-spirit by the whole community. It should ideally be part of a regular worship service at which the candidate for baptism and the congregation of faith both covenant together to help the new member grow spiritually.

However, infant baptism is also perfectly logical and biblically defensible when related to the circumcision rituals of ancient Israel. A Jewish male child was circumcised on the eighth day as a sign of the covenant community of Israel. In place of the painful experience of circumcision, Christians substituted infant baptism, a rite practiced widely in the ancient world and neither specifically Jewish nor exclusively Christian. Taking their cue from John the Baptist, who seems to have begun the practice for Christians, and Paul, who argued against being circumcised of the flesh because it frightened too many gentiles away from the new Faith, early Christians baptized both babies and adults as they joined the ranks of the Church. By the Middle Ages, when Christianity had become the universal religion of the Western world, babies provided most new members and adult baptism was seldom required.

Arguments from *Scripture, Tradition* and *Reflection* support for both adult and infant baptism. The deciding factor for most Christians today will doubtless be the fourth source of religious values, *Experience*. For those who grew up in churches which applied water to babies during baptism, infant baptism seems natural and acceptable. If only believer's baptism was allowed, dunking adults will seem normative. Theologically, the "best" form of baptism is the one which works within your comfort zone. From a Metaphysical Christian perspective, any tasteful practice will do. It is worth noting that several major denominations—among them the United Methodist Church—allow for virtually any form of baptism: Adult or infant, immersion, pouring or sprinkling. And there are, again, other options available to those in the more experimental communions under our expanded definition of Sacramental Theology.

Other Options

One alternative is to substitute some other medium for water of baptism. Some churches "christen" their babies with a name-giving ceremony that ends with the minister sprinkling rose petals on the head of the infant. This delightful variety preserves the form of baptism but incorporates a new element through the colored petals in lieu of water.

Another alternative is to *christen* infants and *welcome* new adult members, usually during a worship service. This is quite popular among churches founded since the nineteenth century, especially some New Thought groups. However, where water drips equally on the baptized and the unbaptized, there is little difference between a name-giving ceremony of christening and the tradition of infant baptism. Why not revert to the older practice, reinterpreted for a modern age? Metaphysical Christian groups have much to gain from participating in the historic sacraments, not only in personal growth but in wider fellowship within the "Body of Christ".

Credibility Issue: Bottom-Line Sacraments

Baptism and the Lord's Supper, in some form, seem to be the bottom line for most Christians. Any church which discards these two entirely does so at great peril to its historic connection to the Church Universal. Those movements which specialize in seeing themselves as non-Christian "churches" may not be troubled by cutting themselves off from their heritage, but a Christian movement can step only so far beyond the Circle of Faith before it ceases belonging to the family of Christ Jesus.

Great Metaphysical Christian teachers—from pioneers like Ernest Holmes, Charles Fillmore, and Nona Brooks to James Dillet Freeman, Eric Butterworth, and Johnnie Colemon—have always steered the Metaphysical Christian movement away from more radical expressions of occult/esoteric studies or paranormal experiences to supplant the leadership of Jesus Christ. All religious thought, for the Christian, must ultimately be measured against the *God-with-us* in Jesus Christ, however interpreted.[9] Christian churches, to be worthy of their heritage, must come to terms at least with the two sacraments practiced by the Church Universal, the Lord's Supper and Baptism. Many variations are possible; some variation is necessary unless a congregation wants to leave the Christian family in pursuit of other circles of faith.

4. THE SACRAMENT OF LOVE.

EVENT: An experience of agape, selfless love; "true love," when a person realizes he/she has found the one with whom he/she wants to spend forever; love on many levels of such as deep friendship that brings one to selflessness and joy, love of a group or a nation, love of humanity as a whole; supremely, love of God.

SPIRITUAL ACTIVITY: Marriage

Obviously, love is not limited to marriage, but no other institution better demonstrates the potential for joy and disaster that love represents. This generation has witnessed the historic movement toward equal marriage for all people, including members of the gay and lesbian community. At this writing (October 2013), same-sex marriage is recognized in fourteen states, plus the District of Columbia, and among five Native American tribes. Despite the hysteria among conservative groups, marriage equality has not threatened the end of male-female relationships. There has not been a flood of heterosexual couples rushing to the divorce courts to bail out of their relationships because opposite-sex union is no longer the exclusive form of marriage legally recognized by the state. (And the sun keeps rising.) The idea of marriage as a union between "one man and one woman" has not been outlawed, just expanded to include two men or two women. Also at this writing, several major religious denominations still cling to ancient taboos limiting marriage to opposite sex couples. The beauty of a free society is that people who don't believe in same-sex marriages are not required to participate in one, just as members of the LGBT community will not be forced into what is, for them, the unnatural state of heterosexual union. God bless America. Let's move on. Love beckons.

In modern times a swelling chorus of poets, philosophers and theologians have observed that popular culture places too much emphasis on the romantic/passionate aspect of love and not enough on camaraderie, cooperation and friendship. When I was pastor of a local church, I often cautioned newlyweds that the wild, giddy amusement park of new romance usually lasts six to twenty-four months, after which they will begin to discover what they really have in common and whether they like each other enough to stay married.

Make no mistake, passion is terribly important. Most happy marriages begin with the throbbing, over-powering urge to make love. But the sexual intensity couples initially feel marks the entry-level of relationships. Honeymoon level physical intimacy does not—*cannot*—last a lifetime. Like the tide, passion will come and go in the months and years ahead. What partners have left after the tide goes out will determine whether or not they enjoy low tide enough to wait for the flood.

Marriages based only on passion are like tent-cities set up at a gold rush. When the ore is gone, nothing is left to hold the people to the location and they pack up and leave for newer claims. The problem with this pack-and-move lifestyle is that it is operating out of a mythology. There is no eternal vein of gold that will never run dry. Hollywood lied to us, because we wanted them to. It's time to clear the campground and lay the cornerstone for long-lasting intimacy by acknowledging there is no eternal, passionate relationship that will never cool down. Human beings aren't made like that.

Three Greek Words

If relationships are based solely (or even primarily) on *Eros*, i.e., the passionate nature, they are doomed from the start. If they are based on *Philia*, friendship, they have a much better chance to survive. However, if they are based on *Agape*, selfless love that puts the other person first, then the moments of Eros and Philia will reinforce an already solid foundation of caring and commitment.[10]

In fact, one could argue that all relationships would fare better if they were grounded in agape. Friendships often break down when one party says or does something reprehensible to the other. Jesus knew this would happen, so he told a bushel of parables about forgiveness. But his greatest teaching about friendship—the parable of the Good Samaritan—explores the nature of agape and stands as a radical statement about our responsibilities to help other people regardless of how different, alien or foreign they may seem to us.

Those times when we reach the fringes of our potential, those infrequent moments when we feel/sense love as it could be if we truly lived agape, are the experiences we have grouped under this heading as The Sacrament of Love.

5. THE SACRAMENT OF POWER.

EVENT: Inspiration from the words of scripture or a teacher; ministry of the Word that touches mind and heart to bring awareness of God's presence.

SPIRITUAL ACTIVITY: Confirmation, scripture reading, sermon, teaching, any form of exhortation or instruction in a spiritual context.

Most people belong to the Christian family because Jesus came to them through others. Someone spoke words of truth. A typical evangelical Christian upon hearing those words will find herself confronted, convinced, converted and confirmed in the faith. Perhaps she knows the date when she felt grasped by God's power for the first time. For others, the Sacrament of Power came slowly; they could not look back in a datebook and find a notation which read:

> October 21. Accepted Jesus Christ as Lord & Savior.
> Tuna fish sandwich for lunch.

Both experiences—dramatic decision and gradual growth—have been reported for nearly two thousand years by faithful Christians. A common difficulty faced by anyone trying to convey ideas about the gospel occurs in all religions, i.e., profound spiritual insights can be either too complex and too lofty to capture with words. Long ago several schools of Eastern thought abandoned the attempt to explain the path to enlightenment with verbiage. For example, Zen masters crafted a linguistic technique to overcome human inability to express the inexpressible with language. "In Zen Buddhism, koans are small presentations of the nature of ultimate reality, usually in the form of a paradox."[11]

Western religion plods along, refusing to forsake the search for better words to describe ultimate experience. Although probably a Quixotic quest, the search for God through the Sacred Intellect and by forging words of power is deeply woven into the cultural DNA of Western thought. Sometime around twenty years after the crucifixion/resurrection of Jesus Christ, a teacher took time to dictate a letter that began like this:

> Paul, Silvanus, and Timothy,
>
> To the church of the Thessalonians in God the Father
> and the Lord Jesus Christ:
>
> Grace to you and peace. We always give thanks to God
> for all of you and mention you in our prayers, constantly
> remembering before our God and Father your work of

faith and labor of love and steadfastness of hope in our
Lord Jesus Christ.[12]

After writing Q&A columns in *Unity Magazine* for more than
twenty years, I can sympathize with Paul as he took a few moments to
respond to issues and problems originating with the Christian community
at Thessalonica. He was schooled as a Pharisee, a lifelong, passionate
lover of the Jewish Testament (Covenant) as Scripture testifying to the
mighty acts of God. Doubtless Paul would have been appalled at the idea
he was writing the first lines of a *new* Testament. First Thessalonians is
widely considered the oldest writing in the Christian canon. The epistle
represents an attempt to instruct people in the faith by the written word,
an effort which would be repeated by countless writers throughout
Christian history. But efforts to instruct people in the faith are doomed to
fail unless backed by a living *community* of faith where people witness
truth in action. Emerson's archaic words jingle with nineteenth century
male-centeredness but, when mentally corrected for gender inclusion,
manage to convey something grand about all human beings:

> The spirit only can teach. Not any profane man, not any
> liar, not any slave can teach, but only he can give, who
> has; he only can create, who is. The man on whom the
> soul descends, through whom the soul speaks, alone can
> teach. Courage, piety, love, wisdom, can teach; and every
> man can open his door to these angels, and they shall
> bring him the gift of tongues.[13]

Another paradox emerges here. People cannot learn the
indispensable qualities of *reconciliation, love, wisdom, peace* from mere
words. Yet, without words individuals cannot communicate their efforts
to experience God. Words are, as Paul Tillich said, symbols pointing to a
reality far transcending their limitations. Without symbols, handles by
which people grasp the utterly ungraspable, humanity could not share its
insights with others. Jesus could not have taught us so much about truth;
the Bible could not have been written; the light brought by prophets,
teachers and mystics would hide under a bushel.

Most great spiritual truth is opinion rather than verifiable fact. Facts are decided based on empirical measurement. Facts can be tested, and the results will repeat themselves regardless of who does the testing. Opinions—even opinions so compelling that no sane person would dispute them—nevertheless cannot be tested scientifically. Good opinion, like *caring for the poor is better than self-centeredness*. Irrefutable opinion, like *love is better than hate*. But opinion no less.

Religionists have often misunderstood the difference, and confused strongly held opinions with verifiable fact. Perhaps that is why the inspiration which comes from words must be checked at least two ways, by *application* to everyday life and *critical discussion* within the covenant community. The first effort, application, is what Charles Fillmore called Practical Christianity; the second is thinking theologically.

When the "voice" of God breaks through via the spoken/written word, people experience the Sacrament of Power. It can be a life-changing, empowering event. Some ways we can experience God through the spoken/written word include: Listening to or reading Scripture; hearing a gifted teacher, especially a powerful preacher; group study of spiritual topics; hearing the words of a spoken prayer or guided meditation; watching a dramatic presentation on stage, TV or at the movies (this can be the most powerful teaching tool of all); hearing spiritual themes in music. This is only a partial list; you can doubtless add experiences from your life.

A continuously popular method of spiritual instruction for young people is the ancient practice of giving special classes to young candidates for church membership which leads to a worship service celebrating their joining the Christian fellowship. This has traditionally been known as the sacrament of Confirmation. Generally, the more ceremonial the regular church service is on Sunday morning, the more likely it will offer a formal Confirmation program for young people. Churches as diverse as the very liberal United Church of Christ and the solidly conservative Wisconsin Synod of the Lutheran Church both practice Confirmation.

James Glasse told a story about the different ways to look at the function of Confirmation. Rev. Glasse, raised in the North, spent several years as a young Presbyterian pastor in the Deep South. When he offered Confirmation classes to the young people in his church, a traditional

Presbyterian practice elsewhere, the new pastor was greeted by polite refusals. Mystified, Glasse kept trying to no avail. He finally cornered a likely candidate for Confirmation and invited her to join a new class. She said, "No, thank you."

When the young Rev. Glasse asked his younger parishioner why she didn't want to join the church, she told him he had it all wrong. Of course she wanted to join the church! In fact, she was going to Christian Camp next summer and would "get saved" there. So, she didn't need to attend Confirmation class to become a church member.

A wiser-and-older Dr. Jim Glasse later explained us seminary students that he now realized "getting saved" was often the equivalent to Confirmation classes for young people in the rural South. The experience of Christian Camp provided the same opportunity to hear teaching, study scripture, and respond with a commitment to Jesus Christ as classes taught by the minister back home. Whatever the process, the end result was achieved: a young person responded to the Sacrament of Power, an epiphany of God through the medium of the spoken/written word.

6. THE SACRAMENT OF RENUNCIATION.

EVENT: Experiencing the release of forgiveness; letting go and letting God; releasing any hindrance to spiritual growth or any belief/practice that is keeping someone from spiritual renewal/growth.

SPIRITUAL ACTIVITY: Traditionally, the acts involved in the rite of *penance*, i.e., confession of one's shortcomings and assurance of pardon; alternatively, any technique which brings one to awareness of the forgiveness/acceptance that God continually showers upon humanity.

Guilt and guilty feelings are not a popular topic in liberal religious circles in general and Metaphysical Christian churches in particular. They are the people who left all the guilt-trips behind and discovered a progressive vision of Christianity. But even the most affable, unapologetically positive theology of divine approval cannot prevent feelings subjective guilt, which this study has defined as *the anxiety suffered when doing something that should have been avoided or avoiding something that should have been done.* Subjective guilt is not only unavoidable, a little remorse can be healthy when it marks an ethical boundary line. If I lie to my boss to stay out of trouble, if I cheat a friend for personal gain, if I tell a racist or sexist or homophobic joke— and if I am mentally healthy—I *should* feel subjective guilt.

Subjective guilt is only worthwhile when it energizes people to make positive changes. When the American public was confronted with TV images of police dogs and fire hoses unleashed on peaceful Civil Rights protestors, the flagrant racism shamed the whole nation and brought many otherwise reluctant whites to a new recognition of the need for equality. Guilt dissolves when flooded by positive action.

Some forms of personal subjective guilt are so intense they require spiritual-psychological repairs, and a tiny infraction can cause extraordinary emotion pain, like stubbing a toe in the darkness. Finding relief in those circumstances requires action and reflection, sometimes including help from competent professional counselors. More often people seek remedies from personalized rites of absolution. Historically, Jews and Christians have brought their sins to the altar for reconciliation with God, which carries the believer to self-forgiveness as a side effect.

Roman Catholics and Eastern Orthodox Christians have practiced the Sacrament of Penance continuously since the early days of the church. Penance in the Catholic Church empowers the priest-confessor to grant absolution for sin. In the act of Confession as practiced in Eastern Orthodox churches the priest performs many of the same functions, but his job is theoretically advisory since the confession is made directly to God in the presence of the priest. Formal acts of confession usually involve naming the offense, claiming responsibility for actions in the past, and pledging to repent, i.e., change destructive behavior into Godly conduct.

> The Greek term for repentance, *metanoia* (μετάνοια), denotes a change of mind, a reorientation, a fundamental transformation of outlook, of man's vision of the world and of himself, and a new way of loving others and God.[14]

While this has led to some abuses—the most notorious involved selling "indulgences" as exit-visas from purgatory during pre-Reformation days—the actual, day-by-day effect of this process is of great psychological and spiritual benefit if practiced in genuine faith. Protestant theologian John Macquarrie testified to the effectiveness of soul-cleansing:

> Perhaps we should not pay too much attention to pragmatic considerations, but we can hardly ignore the fact, attested by Jung and other psychoanalysts, that Protestants are much more likely to end up on the psychiatrist's couch than Catholics who practice the sacrament of penance.[15]

The idea of "confessing" to a professional religious leader is not likely to catch on in Protestant churches because of our strongly individualistic streak. Although we feel, as children of the Reformation, that confession is a private matter between the believer and God, we shall be spiritual wastrels if we omit this step in our prayer life because of some vague notion that we "shouldn't feel guilty."

Confession of one's shortcomings to another human being is so vital to a mental/spiritual healing process that it is an imprint step in the Alcoholics' Anonymous program. A.A. and all its offshoot groups (Gamblers, Parents, Overeaters, Narcotics, and others-Anonymous) insist to one's life back under control a person must confess to God *and to another person* those things which are burdensome from the old way of doing business. People who have gone through 12-step recovery programs describe this milepost as the hardest and most meaningful to reach along their recovery program. Charles Fillmore spoke of the process in his chapter on Renunciation in *The Twelve Powers*:

> All Christians who have had experiences variously described as "change of heart," "salvation," "conversion," and "sanctification" will admit that, before they experienced the great change of consciousness represented by these names, they had been "convicted of sin" or had determined to give up the ways of the world and do the will of God...If the system has been burdened with congestion of any kind, a higher life energy will set it into universal freedom. But there must be a

renunciation or letting go of old thoughts before the new
can find place in the consciousness.[16]

Before people can fill up with God-stuff, they must off-load the
junk. Of course, God-stuff permeates everything, even the junk of life.
But the polar star of the new Sacramental Theology introduced by this
work has been the idea that a true mysterion/ sacramentum occurs only
when individuals recognize the omnipresence of God in a specific
moment in time. Although humans are not guilty before God for petty
failures, or even great sins, behavior must change in order to avoid the
disastrous consequences of self-inflicted wounds and offenses against
others. Jesus the Christ reveals the forgiving love of an *Abba-
Father/Mother* who, like the parent of the Prodigal Son, wipes away
tears and greets all confessions with an unconditional embrace.

But sometimes people *need* forgiveness for emotional and spiritual
reasons, even though it is unnecessary in the sight of God. Such
forgiveness can only come with bleeding the poisons of self-hate from
the soul. This is the true purpose of Renunciation: To open the door of
the hear so to accept unconditional forgiveness. The Sacrament of
Renunciation is the first step the Prodigal took when he came to his
senses and decided to go back to the place he belonged.
Renunciation is the front porch of the greatest Christian concept of all,
Reconciliation. Renunciation means to let go of that which is harmful,
renounce un-good, embrace only good. Reconciliation means to bless
and release self-hatred, putting faith in the Christ-within.

If Reconciliation begins with Renunciation, Renunciation begins
with emptying. When praying about things that have generated guilty
feelings, people draining the foreign matter from their spiritual engines
before filling up with pure God-fuel. The point where someone feels the
release of forgiveness marks an encounter with a genuine Sacrament.

7. THE SACRAMENT OF STRENGTH

EVENT: Life-experience that demonstrates God's presence, e.g., a
prosperity demonstration, healing, or "coincidence" that speaks to us;

also, when becoming aware of finitude and death such as the transition of a loved one.

SPIRITUAL ACTIVITY: Healing prayer, memorial service; traditionally, Extreme Unction (Last Rites) and the anointing of the sick.

Alfred North Whitehead (1861-1947),[17] began his professional life as a mathematician. Turning to philosophy of religion, Whitehead offered some interesting calculations about the way life in the cosmos adds up:

> God is in the world, or nowhere, creating continually in us and around us. This creative principle is everywhere, in animate, and so-called inanimate matter, in the ether, water, earth, human hearts. But this creation is a continuing process, and 'the process is itself the actuality,' since no sooner do you arrive than you start on a fresh journey.[18]

The excerpt begins with Whitehead's well-known quote: *"God is in the world or nowhere."*[19] It is a statement which indicts progressive religionists for their lack of faith in divine activity today. During a prayer breakfast at Fort Wainwright, Alaska, in the early 1980s, I heard Chaplain (Major General) Kermit Johnson, who was then U.S. Army Chief of Chaplains, declare that the dominant heresy of modern life was the inability to believe God can do anything in the real world.[20]

Yet, Sagan has described a modern world which is necessarily secular, humanistic. We emerged from a cloud of superstition and magic, for such was the world of our ancestors. Romanticize the golden ages gone by as we may, the reality is that until the last few decades the vast majority of humanity believed their lives were threatened by evil spirits and controlled by dark forces from realms beyond the physical Universe. Sociologists Paul B. Horton and Chester L. Hunt describe an existing culture, the Dobuans of Melanesia, in their widely-acclaimed college textbook *Sociology*:

The Dobuan child soon learns that he lives in a world ruled by magic. Nothing happens from natural causes; all phenomena are controlled by witchcraft and sorcery. Illness, accident, and death are evidence that witchcraft has been used against one and call for vengeance from one's kinsmen. Nightmares are interpreted as witchcraft episodes in which the spirit of the sleeper has narrow escapes from hostile spirits. All legendary heroes and villains are still alive as active supernaturals, capable of aid or injury. Crops grow only if one's long hours of magical chants are successful in enticing the yams away from another's garden. Even sexual desire does not arise except in response to another's love magic.[21]

The New Testament presents an ancient cosmology, clumsily manipulated by supernatural powers, lacking any concept of natural laws. In fact, more people have lived in this kind of superstitious world than have lived in the modern, scientific age. Today the pendulum has swung to the opposite extreme. Twenty-first century humans no longer look supernatural causes. When the Challenger space shuttle exploded killing seven astronauts, no one seriously proposed that witchcraft was involved. Dobuan investigators would have insisted someone had destroyed the spaceship by brewing black magic. Thankfully, we have come a long way from fears about evil spirits and witchcraft. Yet, the danger facing modern humanity is not attributing all events to the Divine, but cultural amnesia about Divine activity in the everyday world. When God breaks through the no-God program of modern life and gets our attention, people experience the Sacrament of Strength.

Fillmore refers to this power by three names: *Strength, Stability*, and *Steadfastness*. This sacramental encounter promotes renewed strength, not brute force but a rejuvenated equilibrium, a balance of harmony at the center of life. The activity need not be overwhelming, and it is likely to be impossible to explain to others. For example, moments when God speaks through coincidences that do not translate into anyone's understanding but your own. They are highly personalized, somewhat spooky events, like hearing the same old tune several times from different media before realizing the words of the song are speaking to some problem happening in life, right now. When you have such a moment—an old friend pops into your life and says something that gives exactly what you needed to hear—you might feel God is speaking through this mundane circumstance, yet there is no possible way to explain such a subjective encounter so that someone else can feel their faith renewed as well.

These encounters are solitary, tailor-made for the person receiving them and non-transferable. As you read the words on this page, I am certain that some heads are nodding "Yes!" and others shaking a hearty, "No way." If you have experienced a faith-strengthening, mini-theophany, you know what it is, but stand helpless as anyone else in describing the event logically for another person. It is a *mysterion / sacramentum* that knows your name but vanishes like morning mist when you try to imprison it in a cage of rational thought.

Personal Example: ἀγαθός

Here is a personal testimonial. Do not expect Mount Sinai or some other dramatic event. I find spiritual insights often come through reflection upon coincidences. One day I performed a funeral of a church member, a difficult task for any minister. Standing by the grave I pondered how to talk of *good* in a world where there is so much suffering and death. As I contemplated the meaning of life in the face of death, my eyes drifted to an old tombstone next to the fresh grave. It was carved with a single name: *Good.* Later that afternoon while driving home and thinking about this coincidence, I happened to notice the New Testament Greek flashcard ring hanging from my mirror—a way of keeping up with my Greek vocabulary by flipping to a new "Word of the Day" each morning. The word hanging there in front of my eyes was ἀγαθός (*agathos*), which means—you guessed it—*good.*

Did this mean God was gently reminding me that good is all around, even in the midst of tragedy? I took it that way. It was an ephemeral encounter, yet it gave me renewed strength. Driving along the front range of the Colorado Rocky Mountains, that Greek flashcard dangling in the red sunset, I experienced the mysterion/sacramentum of Strength. (Told you it doesn't explain well, but I can live with a little life-spicing incongruity.)

Traditional religious practices to celebrate the Sacrament of

Strength are found in the ceremony of Last Rites (Extreme Unction, i.e., anointing with oil and commending into God's hands for healing or transition to the next phase of existence); healing prayer of many kinds; and the funeral/memorial service. Unfortunately, people have looked to Last Rites as death preparation, like the readings for a soul about to pass which can be found in the Tibetan or Egyptian *Book of the Dead*. The fact that so many cultures have transitional preparation for the dying suggests weakness requiring fortification, but the Sacrament of Strength is about recognizing the Presence and Power of God despite appearances of frailty.

Properly administered, unchanging ritual can provide a meeting place for believers to encounter God. More frequently, the Divine-human congruence occurs in quiet moments and solitude. Early in the history of the church, souls in search of solitude went off to the desert where they could be alone with God. Well-known Catholic spiritual writer and pastoral theologian Henri Nouwen believed solitude was terribly important in this rush-rush world. Nouwen thought we have far too little time for spiritual pursuits. Writing in his book *The Way of the Heart: Desert Spirituality and Contemporary Ministry*, Nouwen sounded a warning for busy clergy that is equally applicable to overcommitted laypeople:

> Precisely because our secular milieu offers us so few spiritual disciplines, we have to develop our own. We have, indeed, to fashion our own desert where we can withdraw every day, shake off our compulsions, and dwell in the gentle healing presence of our Lord. Without such a desert we will lose our own soul while preaching the gospel to others. But with such a spiritual abode, we will become increasingly conformed to him in whose Name we minister.[22]

This study has presented from a new perspective the seven sacramental encounters recognized by the traditional church. But the discussion does not end here. Next, let's move beyond historical categories to five places where God's mysterious Presence becomes discernible.

Five New Thoughts

All experiences discussed so far have been at least peripherally related to the seven traditional sacraments. Now we go beyond, to explore five additional points of contact between the individual and the Divine. Some of these require very little elaboration; they are common experiences for every human being. Others will need more explanation. Nevertheless, each new sacrament steps out into no-man's land between established theological ideas (like the Lord's Supper) and practices not normally regarded as religious in a Christian sense (like *satori*). We turn to these new ideas about what constitutes a sacrament with the measuring-stick of Scripture/Tradition/ Experience/Reflection in hand, mindful that in all things spiritual the definitional authority is the Christ within everyone.

8. THE SACRAMENT OF ORDER.

EVENT: The starry night experience; awareness of Divine omnipresence and majesty; captured by the awesome immensity of the cosmos.

SPIRITUAL ACTIVITY: Nature communion; prayer-walk; *satori*.

Volumes have been written on this topic; doubtless they will continue to be. For our purposes we shall allow a brief space to discuss the Sacrament of Order because it is such a common human experience that few words are necessary to introduce it. Who has not walked under the starry night sky and sensed the Presence of God? The psalmist wrote long ago:

> The heavens are telling the glory of God; and the firmament proclaims his handiwork. Day to day pours forth speech, and night to night declares knowledge. There is no speech, nor are there words; their voice is not heard; yet their voice goes out through all the earth, and their words to the end of the world.[23]

When the starry night sense of wonder merges with an awareness of God's presence in all things, the believer catches a glimpse of Divine

Oneness. That is the *Sacrament of Order*. In the East it is called, among other things, *satori*. A full-blown experience of satori can be world-shattering, life-changing. Hindu mystic Paramahansa Yogananda described an evanescent moment of union in the transcendence of God:

> An oceanic joy broke upon calm endless shores of my soul. The Spirit of God, I realized, is exhaustless Bliss; His body is countless tissues of light. A swelling glory within me began to envelop towns, continents, the earth, solar and stellar systems, tenuous nebulae, and floating Universes. The entire Cosmos, gently luminous, like a city seen afar at night, glimmered within the infinitude of my being...[24]

It could not last, of course. Even Yogananda had to come down to earth eventually. He continued:

> Suddenly the breath returned to my lungs. With a disappointment almost unbearable, I realized that my infinite immensity was lost. Once more I was limited to the humiliating cage of a body, not easily accommodative to the Spirit.[25]

What was the reaction of Yogananda's teacher to this momentous experience? He brought the young mystic back to earth where he belonged:

> My guru was standing motionless before me...He held me upright and said quietly: "You must not get overdrunk with ecstasy. Much work yet remains for you in the world. Come, let us sweep the balcony floor; then we shall walk by the Ganges."[26]

Most people in western society find this kind of spiritual experience, frankly, difficult to accept. If a satori-like encounter of omnipotent/omnipresence described by Yogananda is too much to believe, let it describe the upper limits of the Sacrament of Order, and let those quiet moments when we can feel God's presence in nature provide the more attainable lower end of the spectrum. Any contemplative exercise which takes aspiring mystics to higher realms must bring that same person back to earth again.

There is a delight old story, perhaps apocryphal, about a young Catholic monk who reported joyfully to his spiritual adviser, "Father, I have been so successful in prayer in my cell that for the last few nights I have beheld an apparition of the Virgin at the foot of my bed!"

The wizened elder monk replied, "That is very good, my son. Now, if you persist in prayer, it will go away."

The objective of a spiritually disciplined life is not visions and ecstasy; it's to sweep the balcony and know God is with you while the dust clouds engulf your feet. The visions will go away, but the Presence of Power of God will walk with you along the Ganges.

9. THE SACRAMENT OF UNDERSTANDING.

EVENT: The "Ah-ha!" experience when intellectually grasping a spiritual truth.

SPIRITUAL ACTIVITY: Studying, reflecting or discussing spiritual ideas.

Even more common to everyday life is the moment when something clicks and a new spiritual understanding drops into place. At that moment, people have grasped something new—or perhaps are grasped by something very old—which imparts new insight. Clarity of thought reveals God working in and through a specific experience, *now*. It is a genuine sacramental encounter.

Something must be said here about one of the most neglected subjects in Metaphysical Christian studies, the Sacred Intellect. Historically, it has been fashionable to denigrate the intellect in favor of the emotional/feeling nature of humanity.

Intellect and its plane of activity are not pure mind as the realm of matter is not Spirit. The same essences of being enter into both, but wisdom is sadly lacking in the intellectual realm. Intellect has formulated its conclusions from the sense side of existence instead of from the spiritual side, and these two sides are divergent.[27]

Ironically, Fillmore used the intellect as his main tool when presenting his metaphysical system. In fact, as a young man he exchanged letters about critical thought with Myrtle Page, who as Myrtle Fillmore would become known as the Mother of Unity. Here is Myrtle writing to Charles before they were married:

You question my orthodoxy? Well, if I were called upon to write out my creed it would be rather a strange mixture. I am decidedly eclectic in my theology—is it not my right to be? Over all is a grand idea of God, but full of love and mercy.[28]

This study proceed from the assumption that human consciousness operates by thinking and feeling, and neither is superior. Some people find God primarily through the feeling nature through meditation, worship experiences, prayer, and intuitive insight. Others find God largely through exercise of the Sacred Intellect. Certainly, no one can fathom all of God's Omnipotent-Omnipresence, but that limitation applies equally to the thinking and feeling natures.

Exercise of the Sacred Intellect is a spiritual path as surely as meditation in the Silence, Sufi dancing, or immersion in joyful spiritual music. Jesus said it was necessary to "love God with all your heart, and with all your soul, and *with all your mind*, and with all your strength."[29] Within the words of the "Greatest Commandment" Jesus gave the Sacred Intellect his seal of approval.

10. THE SACRAMENT OF WISDOM.

EVENT: Moments of Divine Guidance.

SPIRITUAL ACTIVITY: Meditation; entering the Silence

Prayer is talking to God; meditation is listening. When people "hear" an answer, they have experienced the *Sacrament of Wisdom*. This encounter differs from the Sacrament of Understanding, which is an intellectual, "Ah-ha!" insight that seems to drop in from higher consciousness. Wisdom is more than knowledge or intellectual comprehension; wisdom encompasses all levels of thought and feeling. Wisdom is more than knowing how, it's knowing when, where, and why. Wisdom is closely related to faith and love; it flows like a whole-person experience. Instances of divine guidance—especially encounters of the Divine in meditation—may be classified under this Sacrament.

For example: A young woman faces a choice of whether to accept a proposal of marriage from a certain young man or postpone marriage until she completes her college education. Intellectually, she knows all the facts. She can answer the how questions easily. When she applies herself to prayer and meditation about this question, she will be seeking Wisdom to make the right choice. For this reason, Charles Fillmore also called this Divine-human attribute the *Power of Judgment*. "Wisdom, justice, judgment, are grouped under one head in spiritual consciousness."[30]

Cora Dedrick Fillmore, second wife to Charles after Myrtle's death in 1931, pushed the idea further in her book, *Christ Enthroned in Man*:

> Every soul has free access to the source of wisdom within. As we approach the divine source of wisdom and begin to realize our oneness with it, we find that we are evolving a higher intelligence than that of the intellect and that we are learning the greatest of all sciences, the science of mind...Divine wisdom, divine judgment, has in it the essence of goodness.[31]

When people feel overtaken by Divine guidance, they are experiencing the Sacrament of Wisdom.

11. THE SACRAMENT OF IMAGINATION.

EVENT: Moments of creative insight when "the muse" works for us.

SPIRITUAL ACTIVITY: Any of the creative arts—dance, writing, painting, etc.

This sacrament is better known to creative artists—writers, poets, painters, and people who work with their hands and minds to create something that did not exist before. When Divine Guidance breaks through mental blocks and walls of unwillingness, the *Sacrament of Imagination* has occurred.

Although "artistic" people will recognize this encounter most readily, it outpictures when anyone experiences the power of creative imagination in life. Streams of creativity flow through every conscious mind. Perhaps it's just looking for a new way to walk home or discovering a new recipe, but part of the job-description for Homo sapiens is to be a creative thinker. Adaptability made human beings the dominant life form on this planet. Our hunger for tools grew hand-in-hand with a thirst for objects of beauty to revere. The evidence for the antiquity of this sacrament is indisputable. Archeologists find in prehistoric graves not only cooking utensils and digging stones but images shaped like buffalo, deer and other people. Creativity is as natural to humans as walking upright. Only modern humanity, with its pre-packaged lifestyle, has restricted creative expression to an elite handful of professional artists. The rest of us get *some-assembly-required* and coloring books.

When people open themselves to the Sacrament of Imagination, a rainbow of creative energy will pour from them. Maybe not the next Rembrandt, but each human soul has the power to create original beauty. Everyone can experience the God-given flow of Imagination.

12. THE SACRAMENT OF WILL.

EVENT: Moments of Prayer when we "know the truth."

SPIRITUAL ACTIVITY: Affirmations and Denials, Centering Prayer.

Our last Sacrament to consider is, in many ways, the key to them all. Charles Fillmore thought goal of spirituality was to merge with God so fully that the Divine-human encounter became a union of wills.

> It is possible, however, for man so to identify his consciousness with Divine Mind that he is moved in every thought and act by that Mind. Jesus attained this unity; when He realized that He was willing not in the personal but in the divine, He said: "Not my will, but thine, be done."[32]

One way people experience God by establishing a prayer-relationship with the Divine through an act of Will. This exactly describes Fillmore's well-known "go to Headquarters" experience. After he decided he had read enough and thought enough, but still had no personal experience of the Divine, he set time aside to commune directly with God. Through what was surely an act of will, Fillmore kept his nightly appointment for months, until he received his guidance through dreams and personal insights. He saw no visions, heard no voice, but this act of will proved to his satisfaction that God was real. The same technique might do nothing for you or me, because people must find the path leading to God from their starting point. Stepping off boldly requires an act of will, not unlike Kierkegaard's leap of faith.

One good pattern for prayer is the widely practiced method of Affirmation and Denial. We shall discuss a Theology of Prayer in Chapter 17, but for now let's look at this prayer-form in action without analyzing it too deeply.

Affirmation/Denial

In conventional prayer, people "talk" to God. Affirmation/denial means talking to yourself by repeating words of truth, which puts people in touch with ideas about God they already believe with their heads but are unable to feel confident about. The well-known Twenty Third Psalm opens with this sequence:

The Lord is my shepherd, (Affirmation)
I shall not want. (Denial)

Affirmation tells us what God is capable of doing; denial reminds us not to worry because everything is in divine hands. Both are acts of Will. When we feel overshadowed by the Presence of God, reassuring us that all is well, we have experienced the Sacrament of Will. Only an act of Will on our part makes the all-pervasive Presence and Power of God available to us. God-within does not compel people to act. Faith begins when we choose to respond to the nudging, whispering, "still small voice" available to every conscious being.

Entering the Silence: An Act of Will

One final point about this Sacrament: The strange paradox is that, when individuals seek God with the mind, Divine Infinity sprawls before them, unfathomable to finite intelligence. By releasing the need to comprehend God, people discover how near the Divine has always been. It requires an act of Will to capitulate to God through non-resistance, to willfully give up willing. The heart which longs for God must have control enough to relinquish control. Discovering God is not unlike falling in love. It is a matter of the heart, which resists all efforts to organize the experience into language intelligible to anyone who does not love as deeply as we do.

Great mystics speak of "The Silence" beyond speech where we know God's presence as certainly as we know who we are. It is not reached through intellectual pursuits, although good thinking can clear away much of the mental underbrush that clogs our path to Christ-consciousness; this is the task of the theologian.

The Silence is not just sitting quietly and cannot be achieve in a minute or two of silence meditation during a church service. (Whenever I hear a minister say, *"We shall now enter the Silence..."* I cannot help mentally muttering, *"No, we won't."*) The Silence is reached only by moving beyond words to adoration, quiet communion, and openness to "hear" the unspoken Presence of God. It takes a while to get there, and awhile to get back. Entering the Silence requires an act of Will which moves beyond willing to a place of utter receptivity. It is losing the self to gain the Christ-self, releasing the world in order to gain a new way of dealing with the world.

312

St. Francis' Summary

Hundreds of years ago one of the greatest mystics who ever lived gave us the finest summary of the life spent in service to God and humanity. It still reads as crisply as if some enlightened pastor just jotted it down as a closing prayer for next Sunday's worship service. Perhaps the best way to understand the Sacraments is to read the famous "Prayer of St. Francis of Assisi" every day of our lives. In this blank-verse hymn, the mystical mixes with the practical, the paradox of giving-to-receive finds one of its highest expression in the Christian faith. The result is a soul which reflects the omnipresent light of God, a life that presents itself like a sacrament for all the world:

Prayer of St. Francis

Lord, make me an instrument of Thy peace;
Where there is hatred, let me sow love;
Where there is injury, pardon;
Where there is doubt, faith;
Where there is despair, hope;
Where there is darkness, light;
And where there is sadness, joy.
O Divine Master,
Grant that I may not so much seek
To be consoled as to console;
To be understood as to understand;
To be loved, as to love;
For it in giving that we receive,
It is in pardoning that we are pardoned,
And it is in dying that we are born to eternal life.[33]

CHECK YOUR KNOWLEDGE

Match the Power/Sacrament with it's the way it outpictures.

POWER/ SACRAMENT	SACRAMENTAL ENCOUNTER
1. FAITH	[ ] PRAYER MOMENTS
2. LIFE	[ ] MARRIAGE/SELFLESS LOVE
3. ZEAL	[ ] ASSURANCE/FORGIVENESS
4. ORDER	[ ] "AH-HA!" EXPERIENCE
5. POWER	[ ] INSPIRED TEACHING/PREACHING
6. RENUNCIATION	[ ] HEALING PRAYER
7. STRENGTH	[ ] DEDICATION/ADULT BAPTISM
8. IMAGINATION	[ ] "STARRY NIGHT" EXPERIENCE
9. UNDERSTANDING	[ ] MEDITATION
10. WISDOM	[ ] HIGH WORSHIP/EUCHARIST
11 LOVE.	[ ] CREATIVE OUTPOURING
12. WILL	[ ] PARENTAL LOVE/INFANT BAPTISM

Thoughts/Notes:

QUESTIONS FOR DISCUSSION

1. The author strongly asserts that at least baptism and the Lord's Supper must be observed in some form or a church severs "its historic connection to the Church Universal." What do you think?

2. How would you change the list of Powers/Sacraments? What would you delete? Add? Modify?

3. Isn't all this sacramental heritage part of the baggage we must discard in order to free ourselves from seeking God in the outer and concentrate on the inner where Christ indwells? Can we do both? Should we?

4. Can symbolism and ritual bring you closer to God? Explain.

5. What is the value of "confessing" to another human being as practiced by Roman Catholicism and various "Anonymous" groups?

6. Describe any personal moments of *Mysterion / Sacramentum* you have experienced

---

Thoughts/Notes:

- 13 -

PROVIDENCE

How Does God Interact with the Universe?

"God did not deprive thee of the operation of his love, but thou didst deprive Him of thy cooperation."[1]

St. Francis de Sales
(1567-1622)

Is there an inescapably dualistic assumption built into the question of providence, i.e., how does God interact with the Universe? Another way to frame the question, and perhaps factor our some of its underlying theism, is to ask how does God outpicture *as* the Universe? But even a sturdy monist looks out her window and realizes she is not the world, not other people, and not God in the fullness of the word. Scooping a cup of seawater from the surf, a beachcomber can accurately say, "I hold the ocean in my hand." But this metaphoric realization can become delusional nonsense unless tempered by realism; while eight ounces of brine contains the chemistry of the open sea, one cannot hold the ocean depths in a ceramic mug. Panentheism, described in Chapter 7, solves this problem by placing the cosmos *within* God. We are *in* God as fish is *in* the ocean. In fact, as a product of organic evolution inside the ocean's chemistry, the fish effectively *is* the ocean in a finite locus. We are *in* God, *as* God; individual consciousness is not an example of divine omnipotence but of divine omni*presence*.

An idea embedded deep within Christian tradition, *aseity,* may be helpful here. Thomas Aquinas, among others, said God is uncaused and self-sufficient, requiring nothing to exist outside of the Divine and nothing to sustain that existence but God's eternal essence. Aseity recognizes God as One Presence/One Power, however from that starting point—God's completeness—it is difficult to understand how a self-contained God can change, as process theology describes (Chapter 7). One solution to the apparent contradiction is to ask if the Divine experiences the Universe as human consciousness encounters daily living.

Process theology, as we have previously seen, says nothing about God's *essence* or self-sustaining power shifting. What changes when we experience life is the result of free choice in a cosmos which allows a vast cafeteria of possibilities. When a finite expression of God outpictures as me and makes choice A instead of choice B, God has encountered a fresh set of variables and the results of that choice. Artists paint and sculpt and dance and beautify the world; poets write, musicians compose, parents love their children in new and creative ways. Why would an infinite Presence/Power create a Universe at all, unless to experience it all, through all expressions of divine energy? Aseity does not say God can have no new experiences, just that the Divine needs no assistance. A model for Metaphysical Christianity, which operates from panentheistic monism, could easily see everything as an outpicturing of God, a connection which allows *aseity* and *process theology* to coexist as logical extensions of each other.

Platonic Dualism

Another dualistic model of the Divine-human relationship comes from Plato. In his dialogue *Timaeus*, the Athenian philosopher shows indebtedness to earlier Greek thought when forming his theory of spiritual growth. Drawing on ideas from the Pythagoreans, plus the life renewal rituals of the goddess Demeter and the Eleusinian mystery cult, Plato describes a pre-existent soul which lived among the stars until plummeting through various intervening planes of existence to crash land upon the earth where it was united with a body. During its fall from grace, the soul took on characteristics of the lower levels while en route to this material world. Like a high-flying bird somehow forced to earth, the task of the soul according to Plato is to learn how to fly and reclaim its rightful place in the realm of spiritual perfection. Gnosticism will later embellish this myth with elitism that 1) designates only certain human souls as immortal, and 2) consigns the vast majority of humankind to eternal darkness after death.[2]

Proto-orthodox Christianity[3] eventually commandeered the Platonic worldview and applied it, out of context, to Adam and Eve. In Hebrew thought, the Garden of Eden fable, with its talking snake and magical trees, was simply a way of explaining how things got the way they are. When Christian thinkers looked back through the Christ-event to reinterpret the Adamic tales, Genesis became the entry point in human history for all sin, and Adam's disobedience became "the Fall" which brought the curse of sin-death-judgment upon all humankind.

In doing so they brought Platonic imagery in synch with Hebrew mythology. The result was a Christianized Platonism centered round the fall of humanity. The part about humanity's exalted status in pre-existent communion with Divine Mind became a subject of controversy among the Ante-Nicene Fathers. Origen said *yes* about pre-existent perfection; others, like Tertullian, voted *no*. Christian Platonism, like all theological schools, had dissent within its ranks, however most Christian Platonists said humankind fell from a higher state to its present condition of spiritual disrepair.

To establish the need for a plan of salvation, Fall-and-Redemption theology required a humanity created in divine perfection but still refractory enough to reject God's sovereignty through an act of defiance in Eden. Although not exactly what the biblical story actually says, it was close enough to make a plausible case for the Fall. The connection was important, because hacking into a respectable philosophical system like Platonism could help the fledgling Christian church to achieve desperately needed intellectual credibility. A small circle of sophisticated thinkers among the early believers knew that without a veneer of respectability, the Church would never reach beyond her natural constituency of lower classes, slaves and women to attract educated members of Hellenistic society.

Plato built no bridge to Hebrew thought; it's doubtful the Athenian sage knew much about the faith of Israel. Finding that connection was a task assumed by the great Jewish thinker Philo (c. 20 BCE – c. 50 CE), and the subsequent Christian Platonists of the Alexandrian School. But mixing the chemistry of Hebrew thought and Greek Platonism was dangerous as brewing moonshine for the early church. Frankly hedonistic cults also borrowed from Plato, and his strict dichotomy between spirit and matter made much of the Jewish Bible meaningless.

Church leaders at Antioch, the other great center of early Christian intellectual life, dismissed symbolic interpretation as too subjective and took a hard line against pagan influences on the Bible. If Alexandrian Christianity was born of gentile-genteel Platonism with roots in the gymnasium (community center), Antiochian Christianity looked homeward to its Hebrew source, the synagogue. The Antiochian school emphasized literal meanings when interpreting the Bible, suspicious of the speculative metaphysics going on down in Alexandria. Soon, Christian thinkers in general would deplore the drift toward Hellenistic ideas. Second century North African church father Tertullian famously cried: *"What has Athens to do with Jerusalem?"*

> What indeed has Athens to do with Jerusalem? What concord is there between the Academy and the Church? what between heretics and Christians? Our instruction comes from "the porch of Solomon," who had himself taught that "the Lord should be sought in simplicity of heart." Away with all attempts to produce a mottled Christianity of Stoic, Platonic, and dialectic composition! We want no curious disputation after possessing Christ Jesus, no inquisition (further study) after enjoying the gospel! With our faith, we desire no further belief.[4]

Theologians re-baptized the myths about the Garden of Eden as historical events. Ironically, the Platonic concept of a *fall*, which has never been a central part of Jewish thought, survived the purge of Christian Platonism. So did the dichotomy between matter and spirit, body and soul, achieving a disconnection which invites a little further examination. Contrary to popular belief, there is nothing approaching the concept of an eternal soul in either the Hebrew or Christian Scriptures. Jewish thought originally held that only God is immortal, and with death all people cease to exist. The Jewish life after death concept was a late bloomer, developing in the intertestamental period, traditionally the 400 years between the last works of the Hebrew Bible and the beginning of the New Testament canon. It never included a doctrine of the soul. For the faction within Judaism which wanted to move beyond extinctionism, eternal life was not immortality as a discorporate soul but a typically concrete Hebraic notion of *bodily resurrection*. In Hebrew thought, you do not *have* a body; you *are* the body.

In developing Christian theology, most Church Fathers rejected Jewish resurrection theory in favor of the Platonist ideal of an immortal soul. However, the idealist construction which eventually prevailed also managed to preserve some of the worst ingredients in the Greek worldview. Proto-orthodoxy abhorred Origen's monism, which worked from a Platonic base but moved far beyond its jarring dualisms to a vision of underlying oneness. But the emergent Church consensus rejected Origen. Instead of unity with God, which was the goal of Alexandrian Christianity, the Western Church adopted an eschatology entangled with human worthlessness and inability to approach the Divine. Instead the Wayshower, the archetype of what people ought to be, Jesus became the pre-existent, only begotten Son, sent to earth to repair the damage by giving tickets to heaven to be earned by affirming the right doctrine.

Any number of ideas might have carried the day. Unfortunately for the Church, some of the less savory worldviews fused to form a far-reaching negativism about humanity and the world. Hebrew thought, with its emphasis on health and wholeness of people before God, was abandoned in favor of a radical other-worldliness that made the Platonists look like speculative amateurs. Eventually, Original Sin became the official doctrine of the Church. Since leading churchmen were usually celibates and ascetics, not surprisingly they soon identified Original Sin with sexuality, a conclusion which baffles Jewish scholars to this day. Apparently the celibates, who wanted to disparage even healthy sexuality, were not dismayed by the Hebrew propensity to see the Creation as good. Zealously negative thinking allowed some Church fathers to find sexual travesty in a story of simple disobedience. Where is the sexual crime in Eden? Of course, not everyone was swept along by the tidal wave of anti-Platonism and anti-intellectualism. My book, *Friends in High Places* (iUniverse Press, 2006), traces in broad terms the undercurrent of mysticism in the history of Christian thought. I won't duplicate that effort here, however incomplete the study of ancestors in the faith remains.

The purpose for reviewing the formative process of traditional theology is to spotlight a series of choices Christian thinking made in its infancy. The Church rejected its life-affirming Hebraic and mystical Platonist options in favor of a negativity about life in the world. Official doctrine saw humanity as disconnected from God, incurably out of harmony with neighbor. Most unfortunately, traditional Christian thought declared Jesus Christ the unique Son of God whose blood-sacrifice paid the price of admission to an undeserved heaven. Other options presented themselves; some were holistic and positive (like Pelagianism), some even more extreme and life-denying (like Gnosticism). Eventually, a sin-and-redemption package emerged as the majority view. For a highly readable study of roads not taken, see Bart Ehrman's *Lost Christianities: The Battles for Scripture and the Faiths We Never Knew* (Oxford University Press, 2005).

In fairness to Eastern Orthodoxy, the Greek-speaking church, plus its historical descendants in various national and ethnic expressions, has continued to emphasize union with God as the goal of salvation, preserving some of the Christian Platonic ideals. In Orthodox thought union with God is not an abstract term for higher spiritual awareness; it is a concrete merging of human life-energy into the Godhead. Eastern Orthodox thinkers have called this process *theosis*. Two millennia after Tertullian's blast from Carthage, Archimandrite George, Abbot of "The Holy Monastery of St. Gregorios," Mount Athos, Greece, replied in gentler language. Study the amazing passage below and you will find Platonic return-to-grace alive and well in the Christian East.

> Our life's purpose is declared in the first chapter of the Holy Bible, when the Holy author tells us that God created man "in His image and likeness." From this we discover the great love the Triune God has for man: He does not wish him simply to be a being with certain gifts, certain qualities, a certain superiority over the rest of creation, He wishes him to be a god by Grace... Since man is "called to be a god" (i.e. was created to become a god), as long as he does not find himself on the path of Theosis he feels an emptiness within himself...[5]

Theosis actually presumes humanity is *not* inherently divine and only has the potential to become one with God because of what God does, not because of what we are. Metaphysical Christianity usually proceeds from a different set of assumptions, which this study has called *monistic panentheism*.

Although legalism had triumphed through the power of the Western Roman Empire, other ways of looking at the Christian faith continued to rise and fall through history. In the twentieth century Karl Barth, Rudolf Bultmann, Reinhold Niebuhr and others developed what is commonly called *neo-orthodoxy*. This new look at traditional Western theology expanded on the pessimistic philosophy of existentialism, but neo-orthodoxy shunned biblical literalism and welcomed scientific discovery enthusiastically. Another sub-school built on existentialism, Leslie Weatherhead and others legitimized thoughtful skepticism in a movement known as *Christian agnosticism*.

Perhaps the most radical thinker in a century filled with innovative theologians was Thomas J. J. Altizer, who scared the bejesus out of everyone from seminary professors to gray haired grannies. Altizer's work on the *Gospel of Christian Atheism* triggered a national debate, thanks in part to the cover of *Time* magazine in April 1966, which asked provocatively, "Is God dead?" and sold more issues than any other edition in the previous twenty years. Four decades later *Emory Magazine* declared in a burst of commemorative zeal, "With one simple proclamation, Thomas J. J. Altizer set religious scholarship on fire and gave Emory a name as a bastion of theological liberalism."[6] It was shameless self-promotion for the school, but completely true.

> It is perhaps the ultimate paradox that Thomas J. J. Altizer, the former Emory professor whose radical 1960s "death of God" theology earned him a glaring media spotlight, international infamy, and dozens of personal death threats, is utterly fixated on God...religion scholar Mark C. Taylor calls Altizer "the last theologian" and "the most God-obsessed person I have ever known."[7]

At this writing, God and Altizer are both alive and well. Many other possibilities, not listed above, could provide models about God's interaction with the cosmos. Any comprehensive look would require a multi-volume series, an impossible task for a survey of the whole theological enterprise. Consequently, this chapter will provide a few options of special interest to Metaphysical Christianity and trust interested students to engage in further scholarly discussion on their own. We shall be exploring ideas about God's providential interaction with the world, linking this old concept with the metaphysical term *divine order*.

Divine Order as Grace

> Ask for wisdom; then affirm divine order. Put yourself in unity with Spirit. Then you will come into the consciousness of a new world of thought and act and find yourself doing many things differently because the orderly Mind that directs the universe is working through you. A harmonious relation will be established in all your ways. Whatever there was in mind, body, or affairs that was out of harmony will easily be adjusted when you open the way in your mind for the manifestation of divine order.[8]

Note how Fillmore defines divine order as action: "...the orderly Mind that directs the universe is working through you." Not surprisingly, the mind and heart of this discussion relies upon the *sine qua non* of Metaphysical Christianity, which this study has referred to as OP[2] (One Presence/ One Power). We shall synch this relatively modern idea with an older, more traditional term for the grand interaction between God and the Universe, a popular word in devotional literature with mystical dimensions which roughly parallel divine order, the concept of *grace*.

It might surprise Metaphysical Christians to know the term *divine order* is used by other traditions with vastly different connotations. Catholic theology refers to divine order as God's natural pattern and encourages believers to yield to the Divine plan. "It is by a well-regulated heart that one is united to the divine action; without this everything is purely natural, and generally, in direct opposition to the divine order. God makes use only of the humble as His instruments."[9] Another variant meaning, this time among evangelical Protestants, is the divinely established structure of society, which includes spiritual priorities in life's relationships: first God, followed by marriage, family, church/ministry, and human governments (social contract).[10]

Metaphysical Christians sometimes invoke divine order in "coincidences" (with air quotes), or hint at God's providential involvement when good things happen unexpectedly. Divine order is not exactly synonymous with *luck*, because people who use the word usually see God's handiwork instead of happy happenstance. An older parallel can be drawn with the mysterious yet oddly satisfying concept known as *grace*. Some definitions include:

> Grace means good will, favor, disposition to show mercy.[11]

> Unmerited divine assistance given humans for their regeneration or sanctification.[12]

> A divinely given talent or blessing.[13]

> Elegance, loveliness, and beauty. *The swan glided over the lake gracefully.*[14]

Support for the idea of divine order as grace can be found in Fillmorean writings. Note in the following passage the "Missouri mystic" links an orderly flow of life's opportunities to human receptivity without requiring any particular struggle to achieve the good.

> If there is a tendency to hurry, let us stop and affirm divine order and rest ourselves in its poise. Geologists tell us that our world has been whirling around the sun for over five hundred million years. So you see there is no need to hurry. Remember that you live in eternity now. This thought of omnipresent eternity will alleviate nervous tension. Put every thought and act under the divine law. Even if you think you are going to miss a car, do not hurry. Another car will be right along, and if

your mind is in divine order, it will be your car.[15]

A nineteenth century man, Fillmore miscalculated the age of the Earth, but even that illustrated his point. When waiting patiently on God's eternal grace (divine order), what's a few billion years, plus or minus? This idea does not require a theistic deity to intervene; God as the ground of all being contains the process of divine order while retaining the possibility of surprises. Secret doors, loopholes, time-space wormholes, and plain old mysterious events too ephemeral to nail down with rational language. An earlier chapter in this study quoted Science fiction writer Arthur Clarke's Third Law, *"Any sufficiently advanced technology is indistinguishable from magic."*[16] Metaphysical Christian movement has long believed divine activities are orderly if properly understood, but let me propose a theological counterpart to Clarke's Third Law: *"Any sufficiently gracious act of the Universe is indistinguishable from miracle."* Ugo Betti's "wonderful surprises" become encounters with divine providence which transcend human understanding.

Divine order as *grace* may be an idea which can speak across the fence between Metaphysical Christianity and more traditional expressions of the Jesus faith, but there is a greater depth to divine order when linked to God as One Presence/One Power. Fillmore wrote:

> Order is the first law of the universe. Indeed, there could be no universe unless its various parts were kept in perfect order. The facts of Spirit are of spiritual character and, when understood in their right relation, they are orderly. Orderliness is law and is the test of true science.[17]

H. Emilie Cady linked the spiritual nature to matter-energy:

> There is but one power in the Universe, and that is God—good. God is good, and God is omnipresent. Apparent evils are not entities or things themselves. They are simply apparent absence of the good, just as darkness is an absence of light. But God, or good, is omnipresent, so the apparent absence of good (evil) is

unreal. It is only an appearance of evil.[18]

At a lecture attended during my seminary years, I heard world religions scholar and textbook author John Noss say something profound about the doctrine of One Presence/One Power. An octogenarian and *Professor Emeritus* when I studied with him in 1976, Dr. Noss declared *monism* was the only genuine *mono*-theism, because if any power exists outside of the Divine, God is not all-powerful.

Yet, everyone has experienced sickness, suffering, and willful acts which any sane person would classify as evil. How can anyone deny evil exists? Monists say usually say, as Cady has done, evil and suffering represent an "apparent absence of the good," because good is the only true reality. But it makes no sense to turn off the lights, sit in a dark room, and declare, "There is no such thing as darkness." Perhaps a better summation is to say, "I have no light by which to see, because I've deprived myself access to illumination." Darkness owns no force to suppress light, but individuals can empower darkness by their dismal choices.

Some authors and teachers have emphasized the positive nature of goodness so completely that Metaphysical Christians frequently refuse to acknowledge adverse circumstances can occur. This can lead to unfortunate side effects, such feeling of spiritual incompetence and guilt when illness or misfortunes occur. No moral failure exists if a healing-oriented person gets sick; no lack of faith is indicated when prosperity fails to demonstrate in every single instance. Well-intended supporters need not rush to the friend who has suffered a terrible loss to assure them there is no such thing as loss for everything is *good, good, good!* That kind of metaphysical malpractice discloses not only turbid thinking but a lack of clarity about the needs of suffering persons.

The greatest mystics throughout the ages have *not* insisted that pain and suffering do not occur; they declared "evil" events have no power over us, because humans are essentially spiritual beings. Spiritual beings cannot get sick or suffer permanent damage. God really does have everything under control, although the present circumstances may argue to the contrary. Bad things *do* happen to people. Some situations are so heart-breaking it appears like there is no good at all, at least none visible to human eyes. Nazi death camps were certainly the classic example of places where the light of God's goodness grew terribly dim.

Jewish psychiatrist Viktor Frankl described what morning was like at the Nazi death camp, Auschwitz:

> The most ghastly moment of the twenty-four hours of camp life was the awakening, when, at a still nocturnal hour, the three shrill blows of a whistle tore us pitilessly from our exhausted sleep and from the longings in our dreams. We then began the tussle with our wet shoes, into which we could scarcely force our feet, which were sore and swollen with edema. And there were the usual moans and groans about petty troubles, such as the snapping of wires which replaced shoelaces. One morning I heard someone, whom I knew to be brave and dignified, cry like a child because he finally had to go to the snowy marching grounds in his bare feet, as his shoes were too shrunken for him to wear.[19]

Even in those horrible places, people were sometimes able to offer each other loving help and reflect the faintest hint of God's goodness. Frankl wrote:

> I remember how one day a foreman secretly gave me a piece of bread which I knew he must have saved from his breakfast ration. It was far more than the small piece of bread which moved me to tears at that time. It was the human "something" which this man also gave me--the word and   look which accompanied the gift.[20]

Viktor Frankl discovered the death camps could strip human beings of every shred of dignity save one. No one could take away the power to choose how he responded. Buddhists long ago recognized the problem is not evil or suffering but how people handle to it. Freedom to shape consciousness is humanity's greatest blessing and challenge. Everything depends on this selection. In both mundane and extreme circumstances, people respond and their choices shape the world.

Providence is sometimes confused with predestination, but they are distinctly different. Predestination says long ago God planned everything; human beings are merely players in a cosmic drama who simply do not know the outcome, even though already decided. Divine order—which might be a Metaphysical Christian synonym for Providence—says freedom rules.

> The day of days, the great day of the feat of life, is that in which the inward eye opens to the Unity in things, to the omnipresence of law:—see that what is must be and ought to be, or is the best. This beatitude dips from on high down on us and we see. It is not in us so much as we are in it. If the air come to our lungs, we breathe and live; if not, we die. If the light come to our eyes, we see; else not. And if truth come to our mind we suddenly expand to its dimensions, as if we grew to worlds. We are as lawgivers; we speak for Nature; we prophesy and divine.[21]

The direction and goal of divine order is often spoken of as reaching Christ-consciousness. Now we must look at the process by which this proceeds. To examine the underlying beliefs of any theology requires critical analysis; to do so in an attitude of respect for those who have given us so much good thinking requires Christian charity.

The definition for theology used in this study begins with "organized reflection on God, the divine and Ultimate Concerns," which obliges the theologian to recognize no taboo when exploring the far corners of any belief system. In the spirit of healthy respect and great indebtedness to our recent ancestors in Metaphysical Christianity, let's consider whether some of the most fundamental premises agreed upon by most of the early-modern metaphysicians are in fact still a valid way to do business. From the careful tone set by this introductory paragraph, you have probably already guessed the answer. First, we must sweep aside classic metaphysical assumptions and ask whether we actually live in a Universe governed by immutable law. Next, we need to re-examine the deepest metaphysical question of them all, i.e., does divine order function as immutable law or probabilities and tendencies?

Immutable Law or Probability/Tendency?

When the New Thought pioneers did their work, the dominant images they drew upon were from the physical sciences. Teachers like H. Emilie Cady, Emma Curtis Hopkins, Mary Baker Eddy, Ernest Holmes, and the Fillmores speak about Law and Science by which things of the Spirit function in an absolute cause-and-effect chain of events.

These ideas flow from a worldview which is essentially mechanical and which originated in the thinking of Sir Isaac Newton. Before Newton (1642-1727), science was an oddity among university studies. Men (not yet women) poured over ancient texts or engaged in lengthy verbal and written duels to find answers to their questions. As we saw in our study of Epistemology (Ch. 3), the experimental method to obtain data, which can be analyzed to determine scientific truth, was foreign to the medieval mind. Look at what happened to one of Newton's predecessors:

> ...when Roger Bacon (c. 1220-1292), the most celebrated European scientist of the Middle Ages, sought "to work out the nature and properties of things"—which included studying light and the rainbow and describing a process for making gunpowder—he was accused of black magic. He failed to persuade Pope Clement IV to admit experimental sciences to the university curriculum, he had to write his scientific treatises in secrecy, and was imprisoned for "suspected novelties."[22]

Like the Zuni and Dobuans, Medieval people explained their world by unseen forces, some benign and some malicious. Rain came through divine action and sickness could be attributed to witchcraft or a broom closet full of other supernatural agencies, including the Supreme Being. God made the sun rise and set; brought frost and thaw; sent drought and flood. It never occurred to the vast majority of human beings that there could be natural laws standing behind the observable phenomena of the world.

Not until Isaac Newton.

Newton popularized the scientific method. He didn't originate the principles of experimental science, but his contribution was so important that one scholar calls him "the first popular hero of modern science."[23] Newton showed how everything which happens in the world has a natural cause which can be expressed mathematically. He completely stripped the physical world of its supernatural premise. God did not turn the earth or crank up the curtain of night; such crude analogies were the product of human imagination. Rather than a comic figure racing about backstage to drop the night sky and roll the sun into place every morning, Newton's God was a Grand Designer Who planned the Universe according to Divine Law. Listen to the biblical cadence of Newton's laws:

- ❖ For every action there is an equal and opposite reaction.
- ❖ Gravity holds planets in their orbits and humans upon the earth.
- ❖ Objects in motion or at rest tend to remain in motion or at rest.
- ❖ Light is composed of colors which break down according to mathematical values.

Newton poured out scientific elixir to cure ignorance, and the real marvel of his system was its methodology. The results of Newtonian physics replicated precisely by experiment, measured and calculated by anyone. The world would never be the same again.

Law Rules

All the great discoveries of the Age of Enlightenment can be summarized in a single phrase: This is a Universe governed by laws. Understand the law, fathom the mechanics of the cosmos, and you can confidently predict the outcome. Just as $2+2=4$, so does Newtonian physics show us a world that is ordered, precise and mechanical.

When the great Metaphysical Christian thinkers of the modern era did their primary work, Newtonian physics still shaped human thought about the cosmos. As Emerson's theories about *God-in-us* began to find practical expression in the healing work of Quimby, Eddy, the Fillmores and others. These practitioners naturally sought to understand why and how their ideas worked. They knew *what* worked, but giving those practices a theoretical base was not easy. Some thinkers—Emilie Cady and even Charles Fillmore—sometimes recommended against too much study when it took the place of practice. Their point was well taken, but usually ignored. People neither read too much nor practiced enough.

Newtonian physics was the unspoken scientific model of the day, just as Hegelian idealism in its American Transcendentalist expression was the dominant philosophical system. Remember, we are talking about worldviews, which are often so pervasive and subtle that we are not aware of their existence.

Metaphysical Christians of the nineteenth and early twentieth Centuries assumed Newton's mechanical Universe was identical to Reality, that everything could be reduced to absolute law and science. And since truth is one, metaphysical truth must be law and science, too. "This is a Universe governed by laws." All we need to do is understand the laws and apply them correctly to demonstrate a given result. Metaphysical absolutism was born a natural birth.

Then the elegant, orderly Universe of Isaac Newton—with its sublime mechanical principles that always apply everywhere, calculable world without end, *Amen!*—began to crack. Physical scientists, peering deep into the sub-atomic levels of matter, discovered that things just ain't what they seem.

In the mid-1970s I had the honor of regularly speaking to the Unitarian-Universalist Fellowship of Rolla, Missouri. One of the board members was Dr. Charles McFarland, then professor of physics at Missouri University of Science & Technology. The professor remarked that students entered his discipline because they loved the precision of Newtonian physics taught in high school. Then students in the physical sciences reach college begin to realize the building blocks of the cosmos are wobbly, stringy, dark and empty.

For openers: There is no such thing as matter and energy. Everything is matter-and-energy. Just as water, ice and steam are the same substance in different form, energy and matter are one and the same, force/object. We can no longer speak of one without the other. But that's not all. A bigger shock was coming. At the heart of the Universe—in the sub-atomic microverse of which everything is composed—there is no such thing as law. There are only probabilities and tendencies. Instead of the absolute certainty of classical Newtonian physics, science now knows that random factors operate at the sub-atomic level.

This does not mean "when the relationships are understood by better theories, we'll be able to explain why certain sub-atomic particles behave a certain, unpredictable way." It means there is unpredictable behavior woven in the fabric of the Universe. The most basic level of the cosmos operates in chaos, not order. Sub-atomic particles are ruled by tendencies, not law .This new approach is called quantum mechanics. There is no need to understand its complicated structures, but a brief passage from *Harper's Dictionary of Modern Thought* will help:

> Whereas in classical physics the state of a system is specified by a precise simultaneous determination of all relevant 'dynamic variables' (position, momentum, energy, etc.), the Uncertainty Principle asserts that this specification cannot be made for small-scale systems. Thus complete determinism is lost, and in quantum mechanics systems are specified by stating the probability of given values...[24]

In the larger world around us, mechanical laws operate with predictable precision. Water boils at 100 degrees centigrade at sea level all over the earth. But even a cup of water contains a staggering number of molecules. If one molecule per second has been removed from that cup of H_2O since the creation of the Universe, the water level would not be visibly different.

When we peer down into the atomic level, certainty becomes probability. We know this vast pool of molecules in a cup of water will boil at a given combination of temperature and air pressure, but we don't know when this pesky water molecule will choose to boil. We can predict with absolute certainty things in the aggregate, but with no certainty whatsoever when taking of the particulars.

Even more astonishingly, the way we look at a given phenomenon can influence its behavior! (Hang on; this is going to get weird.)

For example, light. Is it a wave or a particle? Well, that depends on how we look at it. Looking at it as a wave, certain principles and rules apply. Looking at it as a particle, other rules and conditions take over. Both sets are true, and yet they are mutually exclusive. There is no consolidating theory to bring them together. Light is wave-particle, neither and yet both. Furthermore (I'm not making this up!), the observer who measures the spin of a subatomic particle at one location will force a twin particle miles away to spin in the opposite direction. Quantum physics has revealed a cosmos that unified yet peculiar, in which the observer co-creates the reality which is being measured.

Time is another fun topic for those who crave an orderly cosmos. We now know that as an object's velocity begins to approach the speed of light, the flow of time slows down. It is even theoretically possible to reverse the process, to make time flow backwards. This is the stuff of science fiction, yet it could be playing at a physics laboratory near you in the near future.

Social Science Model for the Cosmos?

Social sciences contribute to our understanding of the probability principles of life, too. Listen to sociologists Horton and Hunt as they discuss the unpredictability of human behavior:

> ...most scientific prediction deals with collectives, not individuals. The agronomist predicts what proportion of seeds will grow, without telling which little seed will die. The chemist predicts the behavior of several billion hydrogen and oxygen atoms, without predicting the behavior of any single atom of hydrogen or oxygen. The sociologist (or any social scientist) can rarely predict what any one person will do, although he may be able to predict what most of the members of a group will do. In other words, the sociologist may predict the probability of an action...[25]

When the Denver Broncos scores a touchdown at the home opener, even an amateur sociologist can predict with 100% accuracy that the crowd will cheer. At this writing, every Broncos opening game has been sold out since 1970. If this book becomes the classic the author envisions it will be, no doubt the Broncos will still be selling out the stadium as

333

you read these words in the twenty-second century, and the home crowd will still be cheering whenever the home team scores a touchdown.

But no sociologist can predict whether Person X, sitting in seat Z-47, will cheer or not. Neither psychologist, psychiatrist, clergyperson nor seer can tell if an individual will respond a certain way with any kind of accuracy. The seat might be empty. There are always a few no-shows for NFL games. Or the person sitting in seat Z-47 might be a visitor from another town, or he might not care about football; maybe he bet on the other team, or his mother died last night.

Human beings are intricate, complex, matter-energy events who possess the same kind of randomness found at the sub-atomic level: They are free agents in the middle of a crowd. That's why medical science is an inexact enterprise. Give Mr. Jones a dose of medicine, and he gets healthier. Administer the same drug to Mr. Smith, and he suffers a violent allergic reaction and almost dies. Medicine is a participatory endeavor, relying as much on the response of the patient as the treatment of the doctor. We know that aspirin tends to suppress pain and inflammation, but will aspirin relieve Mrs. Smith's headache or relieve Mr. Johnson's bursitis?

Spiritual science can help here. Ample evidence suggests that medicine works better when people believe in the treatment. In fact, a lot of people have gotten healthy while taking placebos, sugar pills which were given in place of strong drugs. Those people got well because their minds took over and did the job instead of depending on chemical healing. Now, there is nothing wrong with medicine. I am not suggesting that everyone taking prescription drugs should flush their pills down the toilet and go cold turkey. However, some studies show medical treatment more frequently succeeds if incorporated into a mental and spiritual dimension. Science generally recognizes that people who think healthy thoughts get healthier quicker and tend to stay well longer. Does this suggest that all healing comes from the God-power in the cosmos and within the individual, whether released by mental or medical means?

The "science" of mental healing is the basic discovery which gave rise to all the Metaphysical Christian churches. When that discovery occurred late in the nineteenth century, early experimenters in what was then called the "Christian sciences" looked to the physical sciences for a theoretical model that explained what was happening. Since all the world was Newtonian, classical physics with its mechanical laws provided the framework by which our founding mothers (later, founding fathers) described their new "spiritual science." It was thought to be a true science, because truth teachings demonstrated results again and again.

Myrtle Fillmore was healed of tuberculosis, and then sitting at her kitchen table she taught others who came to her because they learned through the grapevine of Myrtle's healing. Others got healthy, too. These ideas spread like an infection of healing, and the movement which later came to be called "Unity" was off and running. Similar stories are told of Mary Baker Eddy and Nona Brooks, founders of the Christian Science and Divine Science churches, respectively. This was no abstract concept brewed up over tea at a gathering of academic theologians. These ideas brought healing, prosperity and wholeness when applied by almost everyone. And so they were taught as law and science, based on the model of Newtonian physics, for so they were believed to be.

Except for one factor: truth teachings had to be applied by human beings, Homo sapiens, thinking/feeling persons. We are not interchangeable cogs in the wheel of the cosmos. We are matter-energy events with a thinking/feeling nature. Humans are less like Newtonian physics and more like quantum; even if Mrs. Smith affirms health with deep faith and energy and Mr. Johnson does likewise, there is still no absolute guarantee they will be healed. As medicine is a participatory sport, so is spiritual science.

If humanity at large applies metaphysical principles we can predict with reasonable confidence that increasing numbers will experience healing and prosperity demonstrations. But we cannot guarantee that you or I will get healthy or prosperous in a given circumstance because we are free to respond unpredictably. This in no wise negates the power of divine order any more than recognizing the human factor in medicine negates medical science.

But if the foregoing is an accurate description of reality, then Metaphysical Christian churches have some major re-tooling to perform in their theological assumptions. The great bulk of metaphysical writings speak of *law* and *science* when referring to the theologies which would come to be called *New Thought*. Operating in a traditional Christian milieu, early New Thought teachers had to combat the notion that God dotes out favors according to his inscrutable emotional Nature. Like

Santa Claus in the sky, the god of classical theism nods here, frowns there. "Yes, you may have a new car. No, your mother may not recover from her heart attack." Small wonder people have turned aside from a God who could be so arbitrary.

In place of the God of classical theism, which was really a projection of the emperors and despots of the ancient Near East, some metaphysicians turned to a modified Deism. God is the First Cause, who draws plans and never, never varies from precise, predictable operations. Thinkers who took this direction peppered their texts with bromides about Absolute Law, which effectively degraded metaphysical theology to pre-Jobian thinking. A balance mechanism governs the Universe. Right action (thought) produces right results absolutely; wrong action (error-belief) produces unfavorable results in an equally absolute manner.

Again, the problem with such a tally-sheet cosmos is that it doesn't bear the scrutiny of personal experience. (If every wrong thought I've issued since birth has negative consequences with any shelf life whatsoever, I should have died decades ago.) Life is under no obligation to be fair. Good people suffer. Bad guys win big. Right thinking powerfully affects the outcome, but happy endings don't happen 100% of the time, even for super-positive thinkers. People still need to grieve when they lose a friend. Humans must be free to hurt with someone who is walking the valley of the shadow. Although speaking of neither physics nor metaphysics, the Apostle Paul tied a neat package for the church at Rome: "For sin will have no dominion over you, since you are not under law but under grace."

Carried to its logical conclusion, the concept of God as immutable Law means suffering must come through some fault of the person. To avoid disaster and acquire the greatest good, all anyone needs to do is affirm the right truth idea. Healing, prosperity and wholeness must follow. That's not how the cosmos operates. Certainly, there are numerous demonstrations of healing, prosperity and wholeness, and people have generalized those practices which work best into bundles of laws and rules. However, when dealing with the free agency of human response, human freedom, no law or rule applies 100% of the time.

Four Choices for Modern "Job"

What happens to the Job's among us, people who work spiritual "laws" with all their heart and yet experience no healing? There are four possible responses to this dilemma.

1) You didn't do it right. If the Law always works when properly applied, then failure to demonstrate means improper application. This is probably the most common reaction of people when they fail to demonstrate healing or prosperity, and it is usually correct. More times than not, something is missing and the demonstration will be forthcoming as soon as the person gets back on track.

But not always. Who doesn't know someone who has worked prosperity or healing principles with no apparent result? In the Old Testament, Job's friends urged him to repent and confess his sins because God would not send such calamities on a person who was living a righteous life. Job knew better, and his reaction brings us to the second possibility.

2) God is welshing on his contract. Sounds outrageous? Think about it. Job had the temerity to insist that God was cheating. Everyone knew that good was rewarded and evil punished, so why was he suffering? He knew in his heart that he was innocent, a fact which the Lord confirmed by asking Satan (God's prosecuting attorney) a provocative question.

> One day the heavenly beings came to present themselves before the Lord, and Satan also came among them. The Lord said to Satan, "Where have you come from?" Satan answered the Lord, "From going to and fro on the earth, and from walking up and down on it." The Lord said to Satan, "Have you considered my servant Job? There is no one like him on the earth, a blameless and upright man who fears God and turns away from evil." [26]

The Lord had an audience—the heavenly court—and couldn't resist the opportunity to brag a little about his law-abiding human creations in the face of the chief prosecutor. The future Devil took the bait:

> Then Satan answered the Lord, "Does Job fear God for nothing? Have you not put a fence around him and his house and all that he has, on every side? You have blessed the work of his hands, and his possessions have increased in the land. But stretch out your hand now, and touch all that he has, and he will curse you to your face."[27]

When Job realizes he is doing everything according to the Law of God and still suffering miserably, the one possible conclusion is that God has reneged on his promises. Much of the Book of Job contains the hero's complaints about the injustice of God. Not a very patient fellow, Job. At least he didn't succumb to the temptation of metaphysical agnosticism, which is the third and final reaction to unanswered prayer.

3) The "spiritual law" is not true. This is frequently the conclusion of people who have been peripherally involved with the Metaphysical Christian movement, who float into our churches and try a few affirmations, succeeding awhile. But when they meet a real challenge that doesn't go away as soon as it is denied three times, they march out the door in hot pursuit of the next religio-psychological fad. Sometimes it takes tenacity to break through the walls people have erected in their subconscious.

So far, this study has considered three possible responses when people apply spiritual laws and fail to receive successful results. A fourth possibility needs to be considered.

4) Spiritual principles are not immutable laws but probabilities and tendencies. Why? Because *people* are involved. With thoughts of healing, will Mr. Johnson's bursitis go away? Affirming prosperity, will Mrs. Smith definitely attract abundant into her life? Will a lonely person, declaring faith in divine order, find a soul mate? We simply don't know. Teach a billion people to affirm health, prosperity, and joy. What will happen? There will be a lot of healthy, prosperous, joyful people living long and productive lives. But sometimes desired results do not follow. It even happened to the Apostle Paul.

> Therefore, to keep me from being too elated, a thorn was given me in the flesh, a messenger of Satan to torment me, to keep me from being too elated. Three times I appealed to the Lord about this, that it would leave me, but he said to me, "My grace is sufficient for you, for power is made perfect in weakness."[28]

Let's de-mythologize the passage of the supernaturalism endemic to first century consciousness. By the time Paul wrote the letter, Satan no longer worked as attorney general for the heavenly council, as he had in the book of Job, but graduated to consulting work as ruler of Hades. Here is one of the undisputed heroes of the Christian faith suffering with a "thorn in the flesh," which means some kind of painful physical malady, i.e., a health challenge. We have no idea what it was. Like a faithful student of metaphysical studies, he turns to God and affirms belief in divine healing. Three times he prays to God for healing. You figure a guy this well connected should go straight to the head of the line for divine surgery. But God basically says, no doubt in Paul's consciousness, "My grace is sufficient..." That roughly translates, *"Deal with it, dude."* Sometimes power comes through releasing the outcome, as Buddha taught six centuries earlier. Paul got the message, finally.

> So, I will boast all the more gladly of my weaknesses, so that the power of Christ may dwell in me. Therefore I am content with weaknesses, insults, hardships, persecutions, and calamities for the sake of Christ; for whenever I am weak, then I am strong.[29]

To contend that truth is immutable law, an assumption unconsciously based on the now-defunct Newtonian worldview, generates a real problem when specific individuals fail to demonstrate in specific instances. Newtonian-based metaphysics requires one of the first three remedies:

1) You didn't get it right; do it again.

2) God is welshing on the contract; abandon all thoughts of divine justice.

3) Truth is not true; find another religion because yours is false.

There are no other alternatives when our system operates from a Newtonian premise. However, approaching the problem from the insights of quantum physics offers a perfectly logical, scientific explanation:

4) Spiritual principles are not immutable laws but probabilities and tendencies.

Principles, Not Laws

Even while allowing God's grace is changeless and God is always good, rational persons must acknowledge theologically what we have all experienced privately. Sometimes a spiritual technique doesn't get us anywhere, regardless how faithfully we apply it. Sometimes a Metaphysical Christian dies while affirming divine healing. After all, if we are serious about immortality and growth-potential throughout eternity, even though death is a form of healing. Sometimes prosperity does not demonstrate in the immediate circumstance, even while people are diligently "knowing the truth" about their eternal prosperity in God-substance.

This stark fact of life in no way questions the faith or sincerity of the individual. God never reneges on promises or whimsically changes the rules because spiritual principles are true in all instances once we recognize they must operate within the limitations of the Divine-Human paradox as *principles* rather than grind on as inexorable law.

Some spiritual teachings work so well that we tend to think of them as mechanical laws, but that model does no justice to the random factor which God has apparently programmed into the cosmos under the rubric of freedom. If, however, spiritual teachings are principles instead of laws, we have a much more flexible theoretical model to explain why some people have dramatic results and others experience frustrating failure to demonstrate healing, prosperity or wholeness in their lives. Principles are not equations which always apply, like Plato's abstract world of perfection where geometrical forms float in an ethereal soup that could not spill into reality without contamination.

Although the word principle can mean unchanging law, it also can mean "a guiding sense of the requirements and obligations of right conduct: a man of principle."[30]   Charles   Fillmore's   definition   of *principle* in *The Revealing Word* seems to allow for such a loose interpretation, especially if we differentiate between Divine Principle and the application of those principles by faulty human consciousness:

> PRINCIPLE--Fundamental Truth. Divine Principle is fundamental Truth in a universal sense, or as pertaining to God, the Divine. It is the underlying plan by which Spirit (God) moves in expressing itself...God immanent in the Universe is the great underlying cause of all manifestation; the source from which form proceeds. Although Principle is formless, it is that by which all form is produced.[31]

Is God trustworthy or not? It is not an easy question when asked from a world where chaos sometimes reigns supreme, where nice people get cancer and bad guys are not always punished. In this cosmos of billions and billions of sentient beings, natural events and freak accidents, one could argue that God has engineered spiritual principles as a response mechanism to the exigencies of life in a free Universe. But they are principles rather than laws, because the Universe is truly free, even down to the sub-atomic level. Truth does not seem to function as immutable law but rather as high-probability tendencies.

This does not invalidate Metaphysical Christian principles any more than to understand the response of a patient's body invalidates medicine. If one patient receives an anti-biotic and his infection gets worse, medical science doesn't throw away all the antibiotics and let infections run their course. Humans are highly individualized, bio-psychological entities whose response can be predicted only in large numbers. Most people will not go into shock when given a life-saving anti-biotic, but some will. It is no concession to shamanism for the medical establishment to admit they cannot determine how our individual bodies will receive/reject treatment.

When the spiritual dimension is added, the situation becomes even more complex. Sometimes a person will fail to follow Divine Principles properly and, obviously, will fail to demonstrate. Other people seem to demonstrate so easily that they become lazy about learning more. Paul may have been one of those.

Still others follow spiritual principles faithfully but are not healed, receive no prosperity demonstration, gain no better toehold on healthy relationships. In those circumstances, God's words to the Apostle Paul seem to apply: "My grace is sufficient for you, for my power is made perfect in weakness."

One could argue that early-modern New Thought teachers were absolutely correct when they attacked the notion of a whimsical god, but to counter this error-belief they fell back upon the Newtonian model of a mechanical Universe operating precisely within changeless law. What I am suggesting here is that these teachings are better understood by the quantum terminology as tendencies and probabilities rather than immutable law. Principles, rather than equations. Guidelines, not mechanics. More art than science. Less like the principles of mathematics, more like the principles of good writing.

An example from my years as a Little League coach will help here. I taught the boys and girls on all my teams three basic rules for hitting a baseball:

1) Swing level.
2) Keep your eyes on the ball.
3) Try to make contact, not to kill the ball.

These were the principles of hitting. Did they always work? Of course not. But kids who applied these principles consistently hit the ball more often than those who allowed themselves to chop away, lose sight of the ball, and swing like a tornado.

God-power, working in and through the cosmos, cannot be limited just because a particular strategy fails to demonstrate healing or prosperity. When medical treatment sees that a particular drug or therapy is not helping the patient, doctors back off and try a new approach. They don't discard the first treatment, knowing it may work perfectly well on another patient even though failing miserably this time.

Treatments as they are sometimes called, might work more effectively if we followed the same procedure. Some people give up too quickly. When demonstrations do not follow, spiritual veterans know, divine order must be affirmed. There is no better time to remind ourselves that there is a natural flow to life, a divine order behind the organized chaos of the cosmos, which functions even when randomness and accident seem to rule the day. God's power comes to us most powerfully when we recognize that no matter what happens to us, we are his children and shall return unto him.

Job's complaints about God not playing fair were finally answered in the fortieth chapter of that remarkable book. Speaking to Job from the whirlwind, the God asks a question which both undermines and strengthens his faith: "Will you even put me in the wrong? Will you condemn me that you may be justified?" [32]

Job's system was wrong; his worldview put too many restrictions on God. In this life, good is not always rewarded, evil not always punished. Truth teachings apply, but in some instances demonstrations will not happen the way we expect. At those times, we need to remember God's question to Job and his answer to Paul, for they fit together perfectly.

Divine order is the whole system, not a portion of it. God could not have created a Universe with the precious gift of freedom if everything worked like Newton's mechanical cosmos. It is worth noting that Newton labored mightily to stay within the fold of the Anglican church and succeeded; he is buried in Westminster Abbey. Newton wrote over 1.3 million words on biblical and theological topics alone. However, many of his successors found the idea of a self-perpetuating, orderly Universe luring them into deism, which is one hop from nontheistic humanism.

Today, with a scientific worldview that accepts the unitary nature of matter-energy (scientifically, there really is only one kind of power-presence), and quantum theory accepts tendencies and probabilities, God and the spiritual realm don't seem all that improbable anymore.[33] Divine order is the summary term we have chosen to describe this ongoing, tendency-probability process which allows maximum freedom for all participants. Not everyone will cheer each time the home team scores, but by the time the game is over everyone will be on the same team and everyone will be cheering. Divine order in all things means we know where we're going even while momentarily lost.

Yet, we now know that human beings are amazingly complex, matter-energy-beings who respond differently under identical circumstances. So, although Principle is eternally true, results will vary depending on how the person interfaces with God's power. God never overwhelms us, forcing us to accept divine goodness. Spiritual health is always elective surgery. Even so, not everyone who affirms health and follows all known formulae for prosperity will always manifest healing and abundance. Both Principle and person must resonate in harmony. As we have shown the freedom-factor knit into the fabric of the Universe does not allow us to say that such-and-such will always produce this result.

Science, therefore, is an accurate description of God's operations, but only if we understand the post-Newtonian Universe. God is *Law*, if we use the word the way science now does. "Laws of science" are high degree probability-tendencies which show the same results when applied in identical circumstances, in nearly every instance. Good science is forever skeptical, denying itself the luxury of words like "always" and "never" because it has been burned too many times. God is Law, but the Law must interact with free human beings. Perhaps that is why the great mystics have told us to relax and let God work through us regardless of the circumstances, always knowing that divine order is at work despite our inability to get desired results.

If we use these terms carefully, conventional metaphysical language can make sense theologically, biblically and practically. We need always to remind ourselves that God's truth is greater than any system, and a Universe without the possibility of surprises and mystery would be intolerably drab. As Fillmore wrote:

> The Principle of Being is not only all good, but it is all intelligent. It is the fount of your intelligence. When you study it you will find yourself becoming one with the principle of all wisdom. To be one with the principle of All Intelligence is to know. When you know you will

find yourself so broad in judgment and understanding
that you will have charity for all who differ from you in
religion, metaphysics, and even politics.[34]

The problems we have been addressing in the teachings of the
founding mothers/fathers of modern Metaphysical Christian churches are
not of application but of explanation, not practice but theory. Many
students of spiritual principles, the author included, find themselves
totally agreeing with the early-modern New Thought teachers when they
say what works and disagreeing when they try to explain why it works.

Excited by their discoveries, pioneers of Metaphysical Christianity
rushed to explain these concepts in the scientific language of the day.
Thus we have Charles Fillmore describing the non-existent "ethers"
which he believed surround earth and talking about "ganglionic centers"
in the human body where none can be found. Scientific language has the
power to bestow credibility today, just as Greek philosophy brought
respectability to a radical, new belief system taught by that stubborn
band of Christians in the First Century of the faith. Twenty centuries
later, early-modern Metaphysical Christian teachers continued to explain
why those Jesus Christ ideas work. Borrowing the respectable thought-
language of their day, they never realized how dramatically science
world reverse itself. That was their only real error.

Christian thought must never wed itself to a particular worldview or
scientific orientation, or the "God of the gaps" will evaporate when better
science crushes old models in favor of new ones. Even the quantum
theory is not without its critics. Perhaps the next generation of Christian
thinkers will wonder how we could have ever cast God's
healing/prospering power in such limitations as either Newtonian
Mechanical Law or Tendency-Probability of quantum theory. We send
them our prayers across the gateway of time, hoping they will realize we
are children of our own age as surely as were the founders of
Metaphysical Christianity.

Thomas W. Shepherd

CHECK YOUR KNOWLEDGE

1. Explain/identify: *Providence, grace, aseity, process theology, theosis, Christian Platonism, Alexandrian School, Antiochian School, Philo, Origen, Sir Isaac Newton, Immutable Law vs. Probability/Tendency.*

2. Which "school" won the argument, Alexandria or Antioch?

3. What are the three logical possibilities, mentioned in the text, if a person believes the concepts of Metaphysical Christianity functions as immutable law, and yet he/she does not receive a demonstration?

4. Compare/contrast Newtonian and quantum views of reality and show how they impact on mystical/metaphysical thought.

5. Why did early-modern New Thought teachers describe their findings as "law" ? What alternative does the text suggest?

6. What is the difference between Newtonian and Quantum Physics?

QUESTIONS FOR DISCUSSION

1. Did early-modern Metaphysical Christian teachers made a mistake in aligning their discoveries with the Newtonian worldview? What are the arguments on both sides? Are there other options?

2. What does *divine order* mean to you? How is it different/similar to predestination?

3. How will a switch from "Immutable Law" to "Applied Principles" change Metaphysical Christian thought?

4. What would you say to people who tell you they have applied spiritual principles for healing, prosperity, etc., and it didn't work?

5. Discuss divine order and grace.

6. Is this chapter likely to provoke controversy, as the author anticipates?

ECCLESIOLOGY

Church and Ministry

One...(Metaphysical Christian) minister who fascinated me and who had an extraordinary   following used none of the old techniques that ministers in the historic churches commonly subscribe to. He made no parish calls; he had no use for membership drives. He shunned financial campaigns and carried on no special social relationship with the members of his congregation. In fact, there were any number of people on his church roll who scarcely   knew him. To analyze his success was impossible for those who did not understand...They knew nothing of his intuitive power or the fact that he carried his church in his heart.[1]

Marcus Bach

Who Speaks for The Church?

During my years as a military chaplain, two facts became clear about the state of religious education among American Protestants. First, most young men and women in uniform I encountered in the late twentieth century (1976-1988) generally did not know what a *Protestant* was, or which churches fit that broad category. Second, almost everyone's paradigm about what makes someone a *Christian* was a stereotype of biblical literalism and socio-political conservatism.

To judge by the way the media continue to present Christianity today, nothing has changed. Historical and theological deficiencies at this order of magnitude suggest that doctrinaire conservatives have successfully marketed their *Johnny-come-lately* form of biblicism as the historic Christian faith, and their socio-cultural branding has powerfully affected the public realm. Shrill theologies of the Religious Right invaded politics in the 1980s and hijacked the formerly mainstream Republican Party, tossing its centrist-right policies aside in favor of ultraconservative doctrinal purity. When the majority of a national party's candidates for President in the second decade of the twenty-first century continue to reject the hard science of evolution and global climate change; uniformly oppose marriage equality and immigration reform; conspire to suppress minority voter turnout and to deny a woman's right to manage her own reproductive choices; and refuse to address the biblical issues of universal health care and income inequality, supporting instead an agenda of oppressive policies which accelerate concentration of wealth among the super-rich at the expense of a struggling population—who can doubt the theological dinosaurs have escaped their theme park?

It is somewhat maddening when mainstream Christian scholars must convince the public that looking to science for answers about the origins of life on the Earth and supporting responsible efforts to save the global ecosystem is *not* hostile to the faith of Jesus Christ. Why is Jesus opposed to gay rights but a strong supporter of the right to bear arms? Does the man of Nazareth really embrace the death penalty, considering he unjustly suffered capital punishment at the hands of the Romans? And must faithful Christians declare the planet Earth is *seven thousand years old? Seriously?* If so, the biblical town of Jericho, which archeologists date to 9,000 B.C.E., existed four thousand years before the world was created.

To be fair, there are also members of the Democratic Party who represent staunchly conservative districts and waffle on the science and social issues, but that merely defines the problem. Religious and political values emerge from cultural context. As the broader context changes, worldviews adjust or perish. If wild tigers go extinct, someday none of us will have tiger gods or even living memories of the great cats. North American nature worshippers today are hard pressed to find a shrine to the Sabre Tooth, the woolly Mammoth or the Giant Beaver outside natural history museums. But there is hope. Values which upheld chattel slavery as the handwork of a godly society have gone with the wind. Human history repeats, corrects, adapts. Postmodern societies will work this out, but not without the passing of extinct creatures of the mind.

Fundamentalist Christianity, the most reactionary of the larger conservative factions, is far more idiosyncratic than evangelical Protestantism and represents a twentieth century throwback to early American revivalist movements. Writing in the *Trinity Journal*, historian John Fea divided fundamentalism in four phases.

> Protestant fundamentalism in America can be understood best by viewing the movement through four distinct periods, or "phases": 1) an "irenic phase," which runs from approximately 1893–1919 and serves as a harbinger to fundamentalism "proper"; 2) a "militant phase," that runs from 1920–1936 and which encompasses the now famous "fundamentalist-modernist controversies"; 3) a "divisive phase" from 1941–1960, associated with the intramural fragmentation of fundamentalism into "evangelical" and "separatist" factions; and 4) a "separatist phase" from 1960 to the present, in which the term fundamentalism is applied to those Protestants who choose to remove themselves from the mainstream of American culture and religion.[2]

Metaphysical Christian movements, like New Thought and Unity, are actually older than American fundamentalism, which some scholars date to the publication of a series of pamphlets before World War I.

> The term "fundamentalism" was first coined in 1920 by a Baptist periodical, the *Watchman-Examiner*, and has its origins in a series of twelve booklets entitled "The Fundamentals: A Testimony to Truth," underwritten by oil magnates Milton and Lyman Stewart and authored by a variety of 64 Evangelical preachers and scholars. Three million copies were circulated free of charge to U.S. clergymen between 1910-1915...[3]

As an observer of the American religious scene for over half a century, it has been my experience that few Americans can name churches committed to progressive Christian values, and almost no one can describe actual the pluralism of Protestant thought. Some Christian progressives—previously called *liberals*, but the word has astonishingly become toxic—have become frustrated by the ubiquitous identification of the word *Christian* with mindless anti-Darwinism, homophobia, racism, sexism and jingoism, and are nearly ready to abandon the ancient label for the faith of Jesus. This may be the true genesis of the "spiritual, not religious" hullabaloo. What this growing reluctance to proclaim Christian allegiance says above all is that ultra-conservative churches have been much more successful in publicizing their viewpoint than moderate and progressive denominations. Some authors, like retired Episcopal Bishop John Shelby Spong, have written extensively about this religio-cultural battle within Christendom. However, failure of the liberal church at the grass roots level to engage evangelicals and fundamentalists theologically has allowed conservative theology to brand itself as the default definition for what it means to be a Christian in the collective mind of America.[4]

Progressive Christian values, which arguably better represent the character of Jesus as social reformer and champion of the poor, have taken a backseat to the vociferous, hyperbolic persona of fundamentalism. Yet, the strong tendency persists, even within Metaphysical Christian communities, to lump all traditional churches into the same kettle as fundamentalism. To appreciate the contribution of Metaphysical Christianity and recognize its obligation to dialogue with other communions of faith requires pushing beyond simplistic generalizations and grasping the pluralistic nature of Christian thought. Even a casual study shows fundamentalism is not traditional Christian theology, neither in a New Testament nor Protestant Reformation sense of the word. The origin of this anti-modernist species traces back to movements rising in reaction to scientific discoveries and modern biblical scholarship of the nineteenth century. Like theological Luddites, the leaders of this reactionary wave tried to smash the machinery of modern thought before new ideas destroyed their comfortable zone of ignorance. In his book *The Christian Faith Today*, quoted earlier in this study, T.A. Kantonen listed three reasons why Mainline Christianity rejected fundamentalism. After praising their zeal and loyalty to the Bible, Kantonen delivered a withering critique:

First, fundamentalism is incompatible with the Bible's own method of self-authentication. Heaping extravagant praise on the book and claiming miraculous origin for it places the Bible in the same category as the Koran and the Book of Mormon. Mere appeal to the authority of the Bible proves nothing, for every sectarian and fanatic quotes Scripture to prove his own position. The Bible provides its own vindication when we appeal with Luther from the letter of the Bible to Christ, its living center.[5]

Merely claiming to "follow the Bible" suggests a person has no need of Tradition, life Experience or Reflection. This view is both simplistic and untenable. Everyone is biased. Life gives them a language and culture which invariably shape their world. No one goes to the Bible or any sacred text without pre-formulated ideas. Cultural lenses unavoidably bend the light which illuminates the search for truth. The best anyone can hope for is an active dialogue with others to shape a working understanding of what God is trying to do in the lives of all people. While engaging others in conversation, an awareness the Buddhists call *mindfulness* can correct for flaws in the lenses, not by dismissing embedded theologies but by being aware of its influence on the process of dialogue. Fundamentalists of all faiths will deny any of the above applies to them, since they have a special pipeline to ultimate truth. Kantonen continued:

Second, fundamentalism is incompatible with the method of divine revelation in general. God's revelation of himself is marked throughout by a bipolarity of the human and the divine. This is true of Christ, of the church, of the sacraments, and also of the Word. The deification of a book into something divinely inerrant is a form of the docetic heresy, a denial of the human nature of the Word.[6]

The Divine-human paradox is central to an understanding of God's actions in the world. If the Bible represents a clear stream of pure divinity, then it stands alone in all creation, occupying a place of perfection Jesus Christ did not even claim for himself. On the other hand, if the Bible represents God speaking through human minds--with all the typical, healthy misunderstandings and limitations to which human minds are subject--then the message of the scripture can talk to us in our language because its authors have walked our path and caught a glimpse of truth that transcends human limitations. The Bible can be freely interpreted because it was freely given; it is more poetry than science, more love letter than law book. This leads to Kantonen's final point:

> Third, fundamentalism is incompatible with the mission of the Holy Spirit to teach new truth. It freezes revelation to a fixed period in past history and transforms the Bible into a collection of proof-texts for corroborating doctrinal preconceptions. The Bible is the living Word when the Holy Spirit uses it to create faith and provide vital new insights into divine truth.[7]

Acquiescence to fundamentalist ideology is even more remarkable considering poll after poll shows the public at large growing is growing more theologically inclusive all the time. Even among seminary students of the more conservative denominations, studies have shown a marked tendency toward such typically liberal ideas as gender equality, racial justice, and freedom of choice in personal ethics and lifestyle.

What's going on in American Protestantism? Catholics seem to be lunging ahead on social and cultural issues. Pope Francis has declared gay priests are not to be excluded because of their sexual orientation. Speaking at an impromptu press conference on the plane ride back to Rome, Francis candidly charted a new course for the largest Christian denomination in the world:

> For decades, the Vatican has regarded homosexuality as a "disorder," and Pope Francis' predecessor Pope Benedict XVI formally barred men with what the Vatican deemed "deep-seated" homosexuality from entering the priesthood. "Who am I to judge a gay person of goodwill who seeks the Lord?" the (new)

pontiff said, speaking in Italian. "You can't marginalize these people."[8]

Now we have a puzzle before us. Studies show that people tend to identify Protestant Christianity with ultra-right theologies, but other studies indicate that greater numbers of people are becoming more liberal in thought and lifestyle even while becoming more conservative in their "official" religious beliefs. It's almost as though the Protestant movement in the United States has splintered three ways:

1) Vocal, ultra-conservative minority who think they're the only true church,

2) Confused majority of people who claim they're conservative on Sundays but who follow inclusive, progressive lifestyles the rest of the week, and

3) Quiet minority of progressives who have allowed conservatives to define what is and is not American Protestant Christianity.

What a mess! And not only Protestantism. Despite an energizing new Pope, Roman Catholics show an even greater rift between what they do and what they're supposed to do as communicant members of their Church. By the mid-1970s American Catholics had pretty much decided to rely on freedom of conscience rather than Church teaching on birth control, premarital sex, and divorce. Does Pope Francis's receptive attitude toward gays in the priesthood reflect the next phase in this trend toward progressive values, and does this mean the Church has decided to lead instead of allowing herself to be dragged into modernity? Even some Protestant conservatives are calling for responsible discussion of topics previously shunned by the Religious Right. For example, climate change. Laurie Goodstein writing in the *New York Times:*

> Despite opposition from some of their colleagues, 86 evangelical Christian leaders have decided to back a major initiative to fight global warming, saying "millions of people could die in this century because of climate change, most of them our poorest global

neighbors." Among signers of the statement...are the presidents of 39 evangelical colleges, leaders of aid groups and churches, like the Salvation Army, and pastors of megachurches, including Rick Warren, author of the best seller *The Purpose-Driven Life.* "For most of us, until recently this has not been treated as a pressing issue or major priority," the statement said. "Indeed, many of us have required considerable convincing before becoming persuaded that climate change is a real problem and that it ought to matter to us as Christians. But now we have seen and heard enough."[9]

While some religious conservatives are interested both in preserving doctrine and saving the planet, a vast swath of American Christians flatly deny anything that challenges their anti-modernist worldview. Affirming Darwinian evolution, for example, denies Creationism and overrules any claim of biblical infallibility. Accepting the scientific evidence for evolution shuffles the Christian holy book from its unparalleled status as divine revelation into the literary category shared by every world religion, i.e., inspirational writing about the Divine, created by human thought. If any part of the Bible is not literally true, inerrancy's house of cards collapses.

One final word about the label *fundamentalist.* I have heard Metaphysical Christians refer to their more conservative friends and neighbors as *very fundamental.* The tendency to tar everyone beyond the walls of our liberal-progressive compound with the brush of fundamentalism does a disservice to liberal and conservative alike. Christian fundamentalism is a historically dateable development within American Protestantism, and its adherents are quite proud to claim the title. Plenty of conservative churches, while professing highly traditional religious values, have distanced themselves from the label of fundamentalism, preferring to call themselves *evangelicals.* Mainstream Christian theologians flatly reject everything fundamentalists cherish, from the inerrancy of scripture to the reversal of Roe vs. Wade.

Productive dialogue with fundamentalists over these and other issues is practically impossible today. However, there are plenty of moderate and progressive Christians, Jews, and members of other faiths with whom constructive and mutually edifying discussion is possible. It remains my fervent hope that such a conversation over the back fence with neighbors from other religious families will continue to enrich all participants.

It has also been a central thesis of this survey of Christian theology that the faith of Jesus Christ is a diverse family under his lordship, and that within the Christian family there is plenty of room for half-cousins and in-laws. Our critique of fundamentalism, like any critical analysis, is only justified as it helps define who we are and what we are trying to accomplish. Otherwise, it would be a destructive blow to the "Body of Christ," as the church has been called, and to the family of faiths and philosophies celebrated by humanity.

The Church: *Ekklesia* and *Koinonia*

Having reiterated the right and obligation of Metaphysical Christianity to speak for-and-to the Church, let's do a little theology about the community of faith. The starting point for investigating the Church will be the first source in the Unity Quadrilateral, *Scripture*. New Testament authors chose two words to describe their community of faith: *ekklesia* (Greek, ἐκκλησία) and *koinonia* (κοινωνία). The first term (*ekklesia*), generally translated by the modern English word *church*, is root word for the word *ecclesiastic*, which means clergyperson. Ecclesiology is the study of the Church and her ministries.

Ekklesia has an English equivalent word, *ecclesia*. Used by historians to describe the popular assembly of ancient Athens, the word can also mean any sort of assembly. From this archaic meaning we find the idea of the Church as the first century Christians saw it. *Ekklesia*, the assembled congregation; a community gathering of those called to serve, much like a state legislature. Christians believed the Church could be the popular assembly of all humanity, a great town-meeting of all humankind. There is no trace of elitism in the word.

Koinonia is a term which has become widely favored by modern theologians to describe the fellowship of Christians. Van A. Harvey defines it in his *Handbook of Theological Terms*:

Koinonia is a word frequently used in the New

Testament to refer to the peculiar kind of communion Christians have with God and with one another in Christ...The word is frequently used in contemporary theological literature to refer to the kind of community that should characterize the churches instead of the undisciplined occasional gathering of individuals for worship, on the one hand, or a kind of superficial friendliness characteristic of the fraternity or lodge on the other.[10]

Theologically, *koinonia* means the fellowship of believers as it ought to be. The word suggests selfless love, disciplined study, sharing and commitment to truth. It is an excellent word for Metaphysical Christians, because it so clearly reflects the kind of energy and love that usually characterizes a progressive, prayer-centered church.

Beyond defining the words, a student of New Testament Christianity finds the early church saw herself as a movement with a destiny unprecedented in history. Christians were to carry the Good News to the ends of the earth. Because of this mandate to teach truth, every believer was a deputy town crier. Every Christian was expected to tell others about the Good News of Jesus the Christ. Not everyone was a teacher, as Paul pointed out in I Corinthians 12, but everyone was able to live the Christian life and show others how truth works.

Church Becomes Cathedral

Another key point is the Church was not a building. At first believers met in their homes, but even after permanent structures rose and great cathedral towers pointed skyward, the Church was not supposed to be the edifice at which the people met. The Church was the people of God. Sometime in the Middle Ages this sense of people as the Church surrendered to institutionalization. *Ekklesia* became *basilica*; the gathered community became identified with the stone-and-stained-glass gathering place where services were held. The Protestant Reformation temporarily challenged this view, restoring in theory the older concept of church as people. Even with a well-educated clergy reminding Christians of this distinction, people today still tend to think of their church as the building standing at Fourth & Main, not the people who go there.

Why is this tendency to identify religion with building so strong in human consciousness? People across multiple cultures and religions have built large, lovely structures to honor the Divine, exquisite places to experience the holy mystery. The most ancient structures known to archaeology have been religious gathering places beginning in the dim past. Evidence for the antiquity of human urges to erect holy buildings came to light by the recent discovery of the 11,500-year-old ruins of the temple complex at Göbekli Tepe in southeastern Turkey near the Syrian border.[11] Humans seem to raise basilicas from floor plans in their DNA.

Today, most Christians say they *go* to church, when in New Testament times the believers *were* the church. In a biblical sense, this was a grievous error, equivalent to idolatry. However, to build permanent structures for Christians to meet and carry on the work of study, teaching and proclaiming the truth was not really a mistake; organization and institutionalization is both inevitable and desirable. Nor is there anything wrong with beautiful buildings and great works of art, like statuary or stained glass windows.

> The word basilica is derived from a Greek term meaning "royal house." In the Catholic world, a basilica is a church building that has been accorded special privileges by the pope... basilicas are traditionally named because of their antiquity, dignity, historical value, architectural and artistic worth, and/or significance as centers of worship.[12]

The problem would be the same if the people met at St. John's Storefront Church or St. John's Mighty Fortress Church at Fifth and Main. When we begin to confuse the place we meet with the institution which meets there, we have taken a step backward from a biblical understanding of what the Church is.

When "the Church" is located at First and Main, we can come and go, leaving our faith in the vestibule and returning to the "real world" where science and reason rule. Next Sunday, we can return to "the Church" and pick up our religious mindset again. For one hour plus-or-minus we can pay our respects to morality, goodness and decency, then drop our Sunday-go-to-meeting mentality in the vestibule again when we sally forth into the nonreligious world.

But if we are the Church, no such dichotomy is possible.

Biblically, there is no question that the believers in Jesus Christ lived their faith. When Paul wrote his letters to the Churches at Thessalonica, Corinth, Ephesus, Galatia, Colossae, and Rome he was not writing to a building on the corner of Forum Street and Gladiator Square. He was writing to people who knew themselves as the Church.[13]

Church Tradition

As theologies hardened during the infighting which characterized the first few centuries of the faith, the Church at large (i.e., the *catholic* or *universal* church) began to see itself as a world apart from the common experience of humans. Men and women retreated from a plague-ridden, war-torn society to shut themselves behind monastery walls where they could pursue spiritual and intellectual pastimes without interruption from the unhappy outside world. So complete was the withdrawal that some churchmen wondered if anyone could be saved outside a monastery's stern disciplines.

Those who reflected on the Church during the Middle Ages often saw her as an ark bobbing on a troubled sea. Little thought was given to the possibility that the poor peasants scratching the soil to coax forth crops year after year were full members of the body of Christ and were, in fact, the Church itself. It was a time of aristocracy when minor nobles ruled great districts, often with life-and-death power over citizens. Absolute monarchies controlled the nobles, and the Church exerted power over the monarchs from time to time, for example, the Interdict. In the thirteenth century Pope Innocent III placed Norway and England under the Interdict, excommunicating the rulers. The King of England was formerly the real-life Prince John, the villain in the fictional Robin Hood tales. The standoff with the Pope continued until the King John complied, and Norway's King Sverre died. Innocent had less luck with suppressing the Magna Charta, which English nobles forced a hapless John to sign in 1215. The Pope felt bestowing rights upon the English nobility was a slippery slope away from his vision of absolute monarchy presided over by a universal Pontiff (himself).

By now the Church was no longer the people, nor was it yet the stone walls of the cathedral. That would come much later with the development of free denominations after the Protestant Reformation. In Medieval Europe, the Church was the political/ecclesiastical system which supervised Western Christianity, from parish priest to Pope. All over Europe, there was one Church only. If a man were not baptized into it, he was not a member of society.

Anyone excommunicated by the Church lost his political rights as well. At the same time, it was the Church which provided sanctuary for those endangered souls who took refuge within its walls. It was the Church which insisted that the poor did not have to fast as much as the rich, and which forbade servile work on Sunday. It was the Church which provided the poor with social services—free food and free hospitalization. For a long while, the Church was the sole source of education and scholarship. Its hold on people's affairs, no less than their minds, was enormous.[14]

Long Road to Multi-Faith Tolerance

Politically, the Medieval Church organized itself along feudal lines. The basic local unit was called a diocese, which was supervised by a Bishop with his headquarters in the largest town. Deacons assisted him, and in rural communities the duties of visiting the sick and caring for the poor were carried out by the lowest-level clergyman, a Presbyter as he was sometimes called. All these officials were ordained clergy. The latter expression, *presbyter,* is the source of the modern term *priest.* Above them loomed a complex hierarchy of regional bishops, known as Archbishops and Patriarchs or, in the Western Church, Cardinals. Above this whole superstructure sat the Pope, whose power grew through the centuries until reaching its apex in pre-Reformation times.[15] Monastic communities had their own hierarchy, generally related to but separate from the power structure of the locality in which the monastery stood.

A peasant attending Mass in a high-vaulted church would feel as though he were entering another world, the world of the Holy. His thoughts about the Church probably centered on relationship with the local priest and the ceremonies and feasts of the Christian year. If Medieval Europe was more religious than our time, it was a religiosity which kept the worshipper locked into the role of the consumer with the Church as the supplier of salvation. The priestly hierarchy held the keys to heaven. Only through obedience and proper attendance to one's duties as a Christian could a medieval layperson dream of fellowship with God. The rift between the people and their Lord became so complete during this time that the ceremonial portion of the Mass—where the priest raises the elements and *transubstantiates* them into the body and blood of Jesus Christ—was consider too sacred for the profane eyes of the multitudes to behold. Churches screened off the ritual of the Mass from the masses, although the nobility sat in special boxes to the left and right of the altar in the cross-shaped sanctuaries, where they could watch the Mass without sharing the holy event with commoners and serfs.

With the Protestant Reformation of the sixteenth century, screens began to fall. Luther overturned centuries of elitism when he proclaimed the "Priesthood of all believers." He meant quite literally every believer in Jesus has the same obligations and shares the same rights before God. No one stands as an intermediary between the person and God according to Luther. The Church became once more the people. But this new populism would give way to new elitism as the developing Protestant denominations evolved their systems of training, placing and depending upon ordained clergy. Some Protestant ministers grasped at authoritarian heights, which would have been the envy of Medieval Popes like Innocent III, by establishing theocracies ruled jointly by cadre-clergy and laypeople who held the proper beliefs. Experiments in church-states blossomed for a while in Geneva under John Calvin and in New World locations.

Americans often forget that, although the original thirteen colonies eventually adopted policies of religious tolerance, a multi-faith society was not the original intent of settlers from Europe. For example, the Plymouth colony, later known as Massachusetts, fled religious persecution in England and promptly set up its own form of intolerant theocracy in the New World. Quakers and Baptists found themselves imprisoned. In 1659, William Robinson and Marmaduke Stevenson, who came from England to escape religious persecution, were executed under the provisions of "a law passed by the Massachusetts General Court the year before, banning Quakers from the colony under penalty of death."[16] Assorted Protestants banned other Protestant groups; Protestants discriminated against Catholics; and, of course, everyone discriminated against the Jew.

American and Canadian political thought today fiercely defends the rights of religious minorities, but the New World colonials hardly arrived at religious pluralism through open-minded acceptance of the beliefs of others. It is probably accurate to say the faith groups which formed American religious scene came to accept the *necessity* of multi-faith tolerance even though originally opposed to the idea of religious freedom. Government support of religious institutions began when the American colonies were founded. The last vestige of state support lingered until 1833, when Massachusetts abolished its Standing Order for the support of Congregational clergy by local tax revenues—*forty-two years* after the First Amendment to the US Constitution had declared:

> Congress shall make no law respecting an establishment
> of religion, or prohibiting the free exercise thereof; or
> abridging the freedom of speech, or of the press; or the
> right of the people peaceably to assemble, and to petition
> the Government for a redress of grievances.

This is a new paradigm for many readers, who have been raised to believe America was founded to promote religious freedom for all, but historical evidence fails to support that golden age myth. Scholars of American studies have found a pattern of begrudging acceptance which followed a pattern not unlike Marvin Harris's social systems theory: *Behavior causes ideologies.* When forces compelled members of assorted religious communities to share this new land and work together for the greater good, the necessity of religious tolerance eventually became a virtue, dear to the heart of American civil religion. However liberty in religion was not their first choice.[17]

Although there are ethnic enclaves where exposure to heterodoxy is limited, like the Amish or Hassidic Jewish communities, most people growing up in twenty-first century North America today will encounter a cultural mix of Protestant denominations (256 at last count), Roman Catholicism, Eastern Orthodoxies, Judaism, a growing Islamic community, and a smattering of other faiths. How does multiculturalism shape the Christian Church and ministry? To answer this requires examining the theological source of *Experience*.

Experience: Culture and Religious Thought

What constitutes "the Church"? A young girl growing up in the Bible belt of Kentucky, will probably have a highly developed idea of the Church. It will be rural, evangelical and lively. As the Rev. Dr. James Glasse discovered, she will join the Church by "getting saved," which means an emotional/intellectual decision to accept Jesus Christ as Lord and to acknowledge the Bible as the infallible Word of God. Her religious faith will shape the way she looks at the world politically. She will probably be anti-gun control, pro-defense, anti-environmentalist, pro-life, pro-death penalty, and homophobic.

However, for a boy growing up in a Boston Catholic parish, the Church means priests and nuns, midnight Mass and CCD classes, confession and penance. His method of joining the Church will be to make First Communion by the time he is seven years old and Confirmation in his early teens. The Bible will be a holy book, but the clergy is his real source of authority; their view of Scripture will greatly shape his thinking. And the possibility of priesthood moves with him in the background of life, so the young man will have that opportunity for service. This option is denied the girl from Appalachia, whose church has no female clergy...*yet.* The young man's politics might exhibit a wider range than his contemporary from the rural South, but as a devout Catholic he most likely will be pro-gun control, anti-war, pro-environmentalist, pro-life, anti-death penalty, and moving toward a pro-gay position on marriage equality.

Both portraits are caricatures. Some progressives spring from the heart of Dixie; some conservatives come out of the San Francisco Bay Area. The point is that anyone growing up in a culture will be influenced by the culture, if only to rebel against its propensities. *There are no tiger gods where there are no tigers.* And nobody publishes a *fatwa* against the worship of prowling jungle cats where no wild *felids* roam the wilds. Even people railing against their upbringing are paying homage to this background by opposing its cherished values. One cannot be dead set against confessing sins to another person unless somebody else thinks this is the proper way to achieve forgiveness.

Therein lies the irony of opposition. Expending vast energies to battle a system of belief shows as much dependence upon that system as rigidly following its most minute dictates. If a cornerstone of the faith rests upon rejection of any opposing viewpoint, the believer lives in the shadow of someone else's religion. Too many people come to progressive churches in a spirit of rebellion, certain what they don't believe but never taking the time to find out what they do. Metaphysical Christian churches are thick with many fine ex-Catholics, ex-Baptists, and ex-Methodists who continue to define themselves by what they reject rather than what they accept. There is a time and place for legitimate critical analysis, but if attacking and defending defines one's religion, what kind of *faith* is that?

Experience plays a huge role in shaping religious identity. Chapter 12 looked at the Dobuans, a cultural group in Melanesia which trains its children to be suspicious because of the dark forces which they believe stand behind everyday life. As a contrast, take the Zuni Indians of New Mexico whose worldview is the polar opposite of the Dobuans. Zuni supernatural entities are all benign and frequently helpful. Magic is practiced through long, careful ceremonies, but there is no trace of frenzy or orgiastic elements. The Zuni lives in a happy world of moderation where children are welcomed and cooperation is a cardinal virtue. Individual Zuni seek no power or leadership; tribal headmen have their duties forced upon them against their wishes. Horton and Hunt describe the ethical system, which is radically different from the Dobuans:

> The Zuni have no sense of sin. They have no picture of the Universe as a conflict between good and evil, nor any concept of themselves as disgusting or unworthy. Sex is not a series of temptations but part of a happy life. Adultery is mildly disapproved, but is largely a private matter and a probable prelude to a change of husbands. Divorce is simple; the wife simply piles her husband's things outside the pueblo, where he finds them, cries a little, and goes home to his mother. Since the family is matrilineal (descent follows the mother's family line, and family residence is with the mother's family), a divorce and the disappearance of the father does not seriously disrupt the life of the children. Yet divorce is not very common, and serious misconduct is very rare.[18]

Which view of reality is correct? That really depends on whether you are a *Zuni, Dobuan,* or none of the above. As we have seen from this study, life experience shapes religious values so profoundly that people are usually unaware how culturally dependent they are. The conclusions from this contrast are important to systematic theology in a pluralistic world. Any planet which could produce social systems and worldviews as vastly different as the Dobuans and Zuni certainly has room enough for theological diversity among its religions.

Theology of the Church & Ministry

Taking seriously all the problems mentioned above, let's move toward a view of the Church which fits the life-experience of Practical Christianity, draws upon the biblical heritage, and preserves the best elements of traditional Ecclesiology. Many have raised voices in the name of "the Church," quite often in an attempt to silence others who see the Christian faith differently. It is here that Metaphysical Christianity has an important contribution to make, as legitimate heirs to the long history of creative, critical Christian thought. Accepting that culture plays an important role in shaping worldview, progressive religionists can boldly speak truth as they see it while allowing for diversity within the family of faiths.

Unfortunately, the word *church* itself has fallen on hard times in Metaphysical Christianity. For example, the organization which accredits Unity congregations and ordains ministers, formerly called the Association of Unity Churches, has started doing business as Unity Worldwide Ministries because of "branding" concerns about calling itself a church. Local churches in several denominations have drifted away from calling their campus a *church*, converting to language like *center, fellowship, community,* or simply *Unity of (place name)*, dropping the designation noun entirely. Ironically, abandoning the word *church* to describe what is essentially a local congregation is perhaps the most archaic form of all. As noted in this chapter, the *basilica* (physical plant) was never meant to equal *ekklesia* (gathered community).

However, if the reason for abandoning the word *church* comes from a hesitancy to identify with the Christian heritage for fear of offending or excluding non-Christians, this constitutes the exact opposite of the biblical model of church as a people committed to Jesus Christ. While the world in which churches operate is increasingly more pluralistic, denying one's heritage is not required to take healthy steps toward multiculturalism. Many Buddhists affirm the truth can be found in many faiths, but they simply would not understand the need to deny Buddha in order to affirm the contributions of Jesus, Moses, or Muhammad. In my wildest dreams, I would never expect my friend the Venerable Bhante Wimala, a Theravada monk, to re-brand Buddhist structures as *centers* or *communities* because Christians might feel uncomfortable with the designation *temple.*

. Jesus Christ was about inclusive love and multicultural diversity. Perhaps it is time for Metaphysical Christianity to remake his church for the twenty-first century, starting with the three basic ingredients: *ideas, heritage* and *people.* All are equally important; none can exist without the others.

The Church is Ideas.

First and foremost, the Church is the storehouse of great ideas about God, which the ancients discovered in the primordial Judeo-Christian faith and which continues to speak to people today. In recent years a growing army of authors and ministers have retreated from pledging allegiance to traditional creeds. Some have claimed the Christian faith isn't even a *religion* but a living relationship with God through the Lordship of Jesus Christ.

> To set Christianity apart from other religions, some like to use this line when witnessing to others. They will say that Christianity is not a religion in the dictionary sense that involves a system of impersonal rites, rituals and worship to an abstract impersonal deity. But rather, it involves a personal one-one-one relationship with Jesus Christ. And that's what makes it special because you are having a personal relationship with a living being.[19]

Theologians have said this before, yet the paradox is that any rejection of ideas-based religion is itself an idea, a concept, a way to organize thought about life and faith. Protestants gather not simply for ceremonies but for the Word of God, which is not limited to the written words of a book but comes alive when two or more gather in his name. More than a storehouse, the Church is workshop, marketplace and hothouse for growing, shaping and exchanging ideas. No system can capture the truth of God so perfectly that it will stand forever without need of revision. Rethinking the faith in each generation is the continual task of theology and the continuing challenge for every serious religionist. The Church is both the product of that thinking/rethinking and the location where theologizing gets done.

The Church is Heritage.

Beyond the *ideas* which define whom we are as a people, the rich *heritage* of the Christian faith constitutes another ingredient of the Church recipe. Although this study has unashamedly celebrated the Sacred Intellect, the Church is not just head-stuff. Christianity flows from art and music and ceremony, too. The Church is candlelight services on Christmas eve, white lilies on the altar at Easter. Defining the Church without bringing pictures of religious symbols and memories of ceremonial customs is like explaining San Francisco without mentioning cable cars or the Golden Gate Bridge. Metaphysical Christianity has its own special story and its own impressive heritage to add to the Church Universal. From Centering Prayer, discovered in the medieval monasteries, to congregations joining hands to sing "The Peace Song," Metaphysical Christian churches have a distinctive flavor which no other movement within Christianity duplicates.[20]

A sense of history helps a religious community define itself and understand what its people are doing when they gather on the first day of each week as a community of faith. The *ekklesia* becomes *koinonia* when the people become aware of shared history and the direction they are traveling together.

The Church is People.

Most of all, the Church is people. It is the "gathered community" (*ekklesia*) which joins in fellowship and love (koinonia) under the lordship of Jesus Christ. Most people know the Christian faith through association with other people. We have been have taught by their words and, more importantly, by their lives what it means to be a follower of Jesus.

From its earliest days, the Christian Church was characterized as a body of committed, caring people. "See how these Christians love one another," a Roman pagan wrote in the opening years of church history. If that had remained true, perhaps humankind would not have suffered so much through the subsequent centuries. Certainly, the atrocities visited upon humanity by churchmen in the name of God would not have occurred if we had kept our covenant to be the ekklesia and koinonia, the gathered community of loving fellowship. But for all our faults, the Church is still the people. About that original fellowship Wayne A. Meeks writes:

> One cannot read far in the letters of Paul and his disciples without discovering that it was concern about the internal life of the Christian groups in each city that prompted most of the correspondence. The letters also reveal that those groups enjoyed an unusual degree of intimacy, high levels of interaction among members, and a very strong sense of internal cohesion and of distinction from both outsiders and from "the world."[21]

If the metaphysical churches do anything well it must certainly be to reflect, on our better occasions, some of this original spirit. A strong sense of group identity vibrates in and among Metaphysical Christian churches, an almost Richter-scale-measurable level of excitement tingling in an atmosphere of dynamic, loving fellowship seldom found elsewhere.

While there are dangers in maintaining one's distinction from members of   other groups and from the world at large--especially when arrogance replaces charity in dealing with communicants of other Christian fellowships--most people join a Metaphysical Christian Church because of the excellent caliber of her people as much as anything in the theological flavor of our congregations. As one wag said, "We joined here because of the people, and we stay in spite of them."

Theology of Ministry

No discussion of the Church would be complete without a look at ministry, the other major category under the general heading of Ecclesiology. We briefly discussed the "priesthood of all believers" taught by Protestants in general and Martin Luther in particular. Instead of a special status conferred by supernatural authority of the Church, Protestants tend to look at ministry in terms of function.

When anyone fulfills a task of ministry—i.e., preaches a sermon, visits the sick, teaches new insights—he/she exercises a function of ministry, therefore is a "minister" of Jesus Christ. Since anyone can perform acts of kindness or convey the truth to another, anyone can minister. Luther called it the "priesthood of all believers." Biblically, the concept harks back to these words from the New Testament:

> But you are a chosen race, a royal priesthood, a holy nation, God's own people, in order that you may proclaim the mighty acts of him who called you out of darkness into his marvelous light... As servants of God, live as free people, yet do not use your freedom as a pretext for evil. Honor everyone. Love the family of believers. Fear God. Honor the emperor.[22]

The emphasis is not upon election but *service*. There can be no trace of superiority in the true Christian, who is are called to serve others in utter humility. When Jesus walked among his disciples, he set the highest example—touching, feeding, healing, washing, and loving everyone who would avail themselves of his ministry. Christians are called to do likewise. However, according to the unknown author of Ephesians, some persons are called for special service:

> The gifts he gave were that some would be apostles, some prophets, some evangelists, some pastors and teachers, to equip the saints for the work of ministry, for building up the body of Christ, until all of us come to the unity of the faith and of the knowledge of the Son of God, to maturity, to the measure of the full stature of

Christ.[23]

A "pastor and teacher" was an ordinary Christian with special gifts in speaking, administration, teaching, and other necessary functions to keep the Church in business. The same is still true. Some pastors are talented in a multitude of ways; others (myself included) squeak by with a nimble tongue and a friendly smile. Some are candidates for sainthood; some are villains who should be driven from office. Most of us are somewhere betwixt the two extremes, just like most of our parishioners. Jim Glasse made an important point in his book *Profession: Minister*:

> Leading others in worship does not make the minister religious any more than healing people makes the doctor healthy. In fact, the doctor may lose his own health in the service of others, but this does not necessarily diminish his dedication to the medical profession...It is characteristic of the professional that he continues to function when others falter. He does not practice his profession only when he feels like it, but as the situation demands.[24]

Glasse said as a professional the minister must continue to function even when his/her faith has been shaken by life. All clergy, when we are being honest, must admit that any number of people in the congregation will be more "spiritual" than the minister. The minister is not hired to be the holiest person in church any more than a professional coach is hired to be the best player on the team. But all the players—substandard to super-star—will improve their game under the leadership of a good coach. Professional ministry is good coaching. A pastor is called because of skills and not necessarily because he/she is the most spiritual person in the congregation. "Professional ministry" is just that: a profession requiring skills and education. If the minister is also a highly developed person spiritually, that is an added benefit.

Certainly, the professional pastor should not be a knave whose morality and character is highly suspect, but holding the religious professional to saintly standards is a recipe for disillusionment. The tendency to put clergy on pedestals, the role Sinclair Lewis called the "professional good man," can only result in disappointment for the parishioners. Ministers who cultivate this exalted status without taking reasonable corrective measures are trifling with a fate worthy of Humpty-Dumpty.

If the clergyperson is seen as someone who has already achieved Christ-consciousness, or even as someone who is well on the way, his/her opportunities for growth will be severely limited. One clergyperson told me wanted to attend a workshop on biblical studies that I was conducting at his church but couldn't come, because he didn't want the church members to know he had much to learn about the Bible. I asked, "Who *doesn't?*" Even authentic scholars with PhD's in Bible— and I'm not one of them—shuffle off the seminars held by their peers. But worrying about what congregational members will think if we appear human is not endemic to Metaphysical churches. I know ministers of many denominations who dart into liquor stores to grab a bottle of spirits, even though their churches allow them to drink alcohol.

Divinity students are often offered part-time preaching jobs to earn a little much-needed cash. During my tenure as a graduate student at Lancaster Theological Seminary, I served briefly as student-assistant to a young United Church of Christ minister, whose rural parish stretched along the backbone of the Allegheny Mountains in central Pennsylvania. The UCC is arguably one of the most liberal Protestant denominations in the USA, and Pennsylvania UCC churches are full of ethnic Germans with a long tradition for what Lancaster Seminary President James Glasse called the "beer and baloney" diet. One evening, the young minister told me, he and his wife were eating dinner on their anniversary, drinking wine, when a member of his congregation approached them and scolded, "I caught you!"

Although said with a twinkle in her eye, this church member thought it was a trifle naughty for her minister to be drinking in public regardless of whether their church allowed its people to drink. The ultimate absurdity was that the woman facetiously scolding her minister *owned the restaurant.*

Double standards are unhealthy for everyone, and since the clergy talks about subjects toward which we are all striving, necessarily the professional minister will always fail to practice everything he/she preaches. If we allow our professional clergy to be real people as well as spiritual leaders, Christian love and a sense of ekklesia/koinonia will prevail. But, like ordinary mortals, most of us in the clergy have an occasional lapse into temporary insanity. When Moses came down from the Mountain and found the people sinning, he flew into a rage and smashed the first draft of the Ten Commandments. Even high-level spiritual leaders blow it sometimes. Patience and prayer will always help clergy-laity relationships.

The Church & Ministry

We have seen that the Church is *ideas, heritage* and *people*. Furthermore, ministry is a task which everyone can carry out, although some persons have been set aside as specially trained, professional leaders to help us all do ministry. The Church and her ministry go hand-in-hand, for neither could exist without the other. The word *ministry* refers to the widest possible definition of those tasks which Christians of all vocations perform in service to humanity after the example of Jesus the Christ. Service to humanity occurs in a concrete setting often complicated by competing values. Deciding what to do, or to avoid doing, in the gray area between clearly right and clearly wrong choices requires tools that can be sharpened through the study of theological ethics. This is our next topic.

If there is a natural course of life flowing toward Christ-consciousness, a goal which will be achieved eventually, what does this confidence mean in relationship with the world and other sentient beings? Ignore the pain of others; rest assured in their ultimate victory in Jesus Christ? Or rush about, saving the world? Of theological topics most frequently underrepresented in metaphysical theology, Social Ethics probably qualifies as the loneliest category of all. Into this vital, relatively unexplored region our survey of Christian thought must now venture.

CHECK YOUR KNOWLEDGE

1. Identify/explain: *Ekklesia, Koinonia, Basilica, Diocese, Bishop, Deacon, Presbyter, Pastor, Laity/Layperson, Clergy, Ministry.*

2. What are the two worlds in which some religious people live?

3. Explain Luther's "priesthood of all believers."

4. What three elements does the text say constitutes "the Church"?

5. Is the Church a building? Give a historic example.

6. "Protestants tend to look at ministry in terms of function." Explain.

QUESTIONS FOR DISCUSSION

1. If ultra-conservative Christianity reflects neither the heritage nor current posture of legitimate theology, why do so many people think of *fundamentalism* as "the" Church? Can progressives change this misconception?

2. How could a local church provide more opportunities for members to do ministry? List and discuss possibilities/problems with increased lay involvement in ministry.

3. Why are we here? What is the purpose for the Church?

4. If the pastor is a *professional*, what does that mean?

5. Have you ever considered studying for the ministry?

6. Is the Church a special community? What makes it so?

THEOLOGICAL ETHICS

Decision-making in a Morally Ambiguous World

I fairly sizzle with zeal and enthusiasm as I spring forth
with a mighty faith to do the things that ought to be done
by me.

Charles Fillmore (written in his 94th year)

There is probably no issue more neglected and needful of study by
Metaphysical Christianity than Christian social ethics. But before
exploring the thorny garden paths of today's issues, we need to back off
and take a long look at what is meant by *ethics* in general and *theological*
ethics in particular.

The Word for Today is | Ethics

Ethics is a much misunderstood word. Like other technical terms, it
has acquired a popular meaning which makes the subject difficult to
discuss without confusion. Commonly, people speak of someone person
behaving "ethically," or "unethically," which loosely means "properly"
or "improperly." But when a theologian or philosopher launches into a
discussion of ethics, no such neat dichotomy between good and evil
presents itself.

Philosophically, ethics is the attempt to examine critically those
questions which deal with what is *right, good and proper* in human
values. Plato reported that Socrates said during his trial, "The
unexamined life is not worth living." For Socrates, a good life must
contain periods of reflection about its values and actions.

Another term for ethics is *moral philosophy* , or for religionists, *moral theology*. Moral questions tend to have a stronger "religious" component, although both philosophers and theologians often discuss the same issue with similar language. Recalling a distinction made earlier in this study, philosophers differ from theologians by virtue of their starting points. Theology comes from the context of a supportive community; philosophy does not. When trying to separate moral concerns from ethical issues, a quick scan of online definitions finds pandemonium rather than clarity. One source says ethics is systemic, morality is personal; another authority reverses these. For our purposes, we'll use a sliding scale between both pairs—spiritual and secular, communal and personal.

Some authors limit *ethics* to discussions of appropriate professional conduct, recommending what individuals must do or avoid doing to stay out of trouble. Such discussions are helpful but far too limited for the purposes of this chapter. Theological ethics is not so much a code of conduct as a way to make value decisions. Some people would never tell a lie, run a red light, or steal food might do all of these actions under extraordinary circumstances: If a madman appears at the door, waving a loaded pistol and demanding to know if a certain person is having tea in the parlor, few people would feel compelled to answer truthfully. When driving a critically ill friend to the hospital at four o'clock in the morning, most people would (carefully) run every red light encountered on the deserted city streets. For soldiers are trapped behind enemy lines, stealing food could be interpreted as obeying the in fulfillment of their sworn duty to evade capture and return home safely. The U.S. Army *Code of Conduct* reads in part:

> I will never surrender of my own free will. If in command, I will never surrender the members of my command while they still have the means to resist. If I am captured I will continue to resist by all means available. I will make every effort to escape and to aid others to escape.[1]

What makes some behavior acceptable in one series of events and morally reprehensible in another? What alters the rules, standards and mores? How do people behave in those many, many instances when no clear-cut answer emerges, nothing but gray areas where any choice may prove right or wrong? One learns quickly that where issues of right-and-wrong are concerned, there are as many possibilities as there are participants. Some choices are unspeakably outrageous, some elegant beyond words.

Most lie in that vague hinterland where distinguishing *good, right* and *proper* is like picking a white thread from a gray in the dim light before sunrise. When we move beyond individual ethical considerations and look at the value system of a group, society or nation we are entering the domain of social ethics. Here the problem becomes far more complex because we are now dealing with systems of values that may be in conflict. The Mormon Church of the nineteenth century practiced polygyny, i.e., allowed men to marry more than one wife. That custom ran afoul of the community standards of the nation as a whole and precipitated a near-war between the United States and the Utah territory. In many Islamic societies, a man's right to have multiple wives is unquestioned, although the first wife must accept subsequent spouses or the new arrangement is rejected. In Europe and North America another standard prevails. The Mormons changed their rules in the face of violent opposition by the rest of their country rather than risk further military confrontation with an overwhelmingly superior non-Mormon society.

What makes polygyny acceptable today in the predominantly Christian nation of Uganda but illegal in predominantly Christian Utah? Unless exploitation of minors or forcible unions among adults is involved, what causative factors prompt governments to dictate the way a family must organize itself to be legitimate? The complex interaction of culture, human choice and nature makes groups what they are. Individual ethics looks at moral standards and values by which the person lives his/her life; social ethics asks critical questions about group morality and standards of conduct. As the world grows smaller through technological advance, few topics will be as important for the wellbeing of the human family as an intelligent approach to social ethics in the emerging global village.[2]

Axiology: The Study of Valuing

Life is about choices. When those decisions involve personal or social values; moral standards and appropriate conduct; right and proper attitudes and behavior among people; public policy, social justice, or any other category which impinges on human life in this world, important questions inevitably must be asked. The study of that which people value is called *axiology*.

However, some things which are valued have a moral dimension, others do not. For example, *retirement* is valued by many people, but it is ordinarily considered a lifestyle choice rather than a moral decision. Many axiological questions have no moral or ethical dimension.

> ❖ What do you value in life?
> ❖ What is great art, music, drama?
> ❖ What is beautiful, good, inspirational?

These questions may have great meaning, but they are usually not considered *moral* or *ethical* issues. Wearing a raincoat or carrying an umbrella is a question about which is valued more—hands free or head dry? This is an axiological question without an ethical component. However, because of its controversial labor policies, shopping at Walmart for raincoats or umbrellas might become a values question with moral implications.

One of the ongoing axiological discussions through history—which may or may not have a moral component, depending how it is framed—has been to ask what constitutes the *good life*? An important distinction to make when sifting through historic examples is between lives to *admire* and lives to *envy*.

Some lives people *admire* because they elevate humanity, even if someone might not want to live that way. Mohandas K. Gandhi immediately comes to mind. He chose a life of profound asceticism, corroborated by his bone-thin body and austere living quarters. In the great 1982 movie about the life of the mahatma ("great soul") starring Sir Ben Kingsley, Gandhi remarked: "I have friends who are always telling me how much it costs to keep me in poverty."[3]

Other lives may not be as admirable, but people *envy* their resources and opportunities. Rather than the self-sacrificial Gandhi, names of rock stars, professional athletes, stars of the motion picture industry, high-level politicians, mega-million lottery winners, and other wealthy and powerful figures come to mind. Despite the glitzy aura surrounding the small tribe of celebs who are pursued daily by the paparazzi, most people wouldn't actually want to *be* them, either. But people living "ordinary" lives can fantasize about the seemingly limitless wealth and power which the rich and famous enjoy.

Decision-Making

The ethicist steps forward when questions arise with moral, political or social implications. Sometimes, little discussion of values is required. For instance:

❖ Should humans own other humans?
❖ May a woman have two husbands?
❖ Shall public dueling be legalized to settle private grievances?

While questions about slavery, polygamy, or public dueling *could* be subjects of ethical inquiry, most people already have such firm values on these subjects that critical reflection is unnecessary. Lots of issues remain unresolved in many societies, including: pro-choice/pro-life issues, marriage equality and LGBT rights, status of women and children, criminal justice issues and the death penalty, economic justice, immigration and citizenship, civil rights, inequalities of wealth distribution, war and peace, sexism, racism, urban violence, inequalities in education, health care and biomedical ethics, global climate change and environmental issues, the list goes on and on. Controversy is the arena where theological ethics functions best.

Deontology vs. Teleology

An important distinction to make in the study of theological ethics is whether an person's ethical system is *deontological* or *teleological*. Understanding the difference can open a new level of awareness about the way people approach problem-solving. The basic question is this: When confronted with a problem which has ethical/moral dimensions, do you ask yourself, *"What is the right choice?"* or *"What choice will produce the best outcome?"*

Ethical systems are classified as either deontological *or teleological,* depending on whether the ethicist bases his or her system on *rules* or *goals*. Deontologists start with rules and apply them to life's circumstances. They ask, "What's the *right* thing to do here?" Teleologists envision a goal and base their ethical decisions on how effectively that goal may be achieved. They ask, "What will lead to the *best outcome*?" Teleologists are frustrated when rigidly following the rules hampers an outcome they consider to be right, good, and proper. Deontologists want good results too, but they take refuge in being on the side of the angels. Let the chips fall where they may, deontologists will do the "right" thing, regardless of the outcome.

By now you might be asking why you can't be both? *Because you can't.* Logical though each system may be, they are mutually incompatible. To be a teleologist doesn't mean you won't support reasonable rules; it means when you have a problem to solve, your default mechanism goes to getting the best outcome for the most people, even if the rules may have to bend a little. Deontologists don't necessarily love regulations, but when a problem must be solved they invariably look to governing principles and feel okay with the outcome as long as they can see themselves operating with integrity inside those guidelines.

A person's ethical orientation emerges at the decision-points of life. The way you actually approach an ethical dilemma may surprise you. When teaching this model in seminary, my students will often announce they are definitely one way, and when they're given an ethical scenario to work with they find they really go to the opposite methodology. People who declare themselves goal oriented sometimes discover the first question they ask is, *"What's the right thing to do here?"* A classically deontological response.

Can you see how having both deontologists and teleologists on a church board will definitely cause anxiety from time to time? The two perspectives are fairly well distributed, so you can count on it. Let's take a look at a historic example of deontology vs. teleology, an extraordinary conflict by today's standards. But let me assure you, I did not make this up.

Historic Example: The "Lying Baptists"

In 1804, the congregation of Long Run Baptist Church in Kentucky got into a heated argument about a hypothetical situation involving telling the truth and lying. Suppose a settler had been captured by hostile

Indians while his family was hiding nearby. Was he justified in lying to protect his wife and children?

> The moral question was raised whether a man, when captured by the Indians, was justified in lying to protect his family concealed nearby. Some believed the man had a duty to lie in those circumstances, while others maintained he should tell the truth even if it meant the sacrifice of his family. The argument was so vehement that the church split into two congregations.[4]

If this quasi-racist, anti-Native American scenario disturbs you, substitute runaway slaves and the Fugitive Slave Law, or Jews fleeing the Nazis. The question is the same: Are there conditions under which lying is justified? Some people (rigid deontologists) insisted that obeying God's commandments demanded he should tell the truth, even if it meant sacrificing wife and children. Other people (teleologists) said the man had a duty to his family which superseded the requirement to always be truthful.

The combatants appealed to the Baptist equivalent of a hierarchy, which came down firmly on the side of the "never tell a lie" faction! The two halves of the church never rejoined, and the group which said it was okay to deceive the Indian war party became known as the "Lying Baptists." Their opponents were, of course, the "Truthful Baptists".

Even though the scenario was hypothetical, the radically deontological pronouncement of the church hierarchy shocks the postmodern conscience. People living after the Nazi holocaust to understand have a hard time understanding how anyone could turn Anne Frank over to the Gestapo and call it a righteous act. But rigid deontology is not the only route to ethical disaster. Pushing teleology to the extreme creates an even more disturbing scenario. Do the ends always justify the means? What if the perceived "good" is a perceived "evil" to others? Some readers will recall the notorious comment attributed to a Vietnam era military official.

"It became necessary to destroy the town to save it", a

United States major said today. He was talking about the decision by allied commanders to bomb and shell the town regardless of civilian casualties, to rout the Vietcong.[5]

The jihadist blows himself up to strike at what he considers a crowd of infidels and Zionists and to satisfy his hate-contaminated passion to defend Islam. The problem is not limited to non-Western nations. In the USA, white hooded KKK have a well-documented history of racial violence. Yet, incredibly, the Klan proclaims itself the last bastion of true Christians by burning crosses on the lawns of their enemies! "This ritual has also been called 'cross lighting', a term used by David Duke and other Klansmen in the 1970s to illustrate that 'Christ is the light of the world.'"[6] Have these people even *read* the New Testament? Every murderous fanatic is a radical teleologist, willing to break the law to get his own way.

What separates the teleology of a Klansman or jihadist from the civil disobedience of a human rights activist? Gandhi's magnificent statement about nonviolent resistance aptly describes the radical opposite of terrorism: "I am prepared to die, but there is no cause for which I am prepared to kill."[7] Gandhi staked out a nonviolent path to admire, and his visionary, judicious life has inspired people around the world. But you will recall from the opening of this study that Dietrich Bonhoeffer chose a different ethical path. He plotted the violent overthrow of Adolf Hitler, an ill-fated attempt which many people have also come to admire. Whose choice is *right, good, proper*—Mohandas Gandhi or Dietrich Bonhoeffer?

Methodological sidebar: While adjudicating the ethical case for *Gandhi v. Bonhoeffer*, examine your thoughts. You will be rewarded with a glimpse at your default mechanism in decision making. Did you find yourself wondering what principles might allow Gandhi's non-violence and Bonhoeffer's ethical use of force to coexist? (That's deontology.) Or did you ask, "What difference does it make, as long as justice and freedom are served by their actions?" (That's teleology.) Welcome to the exciting, maddening world of theological ethics.

The first commandment in this course of study has been, *Thou shalt describe before you prescribe.* Ethical decision-making offers at least four general approaches which might be called schools of ethics (Fig.15-1). Actually, these are less content-topical than methodological classifications. Perhaps this brief look at the four approaches will inspire aspiring ethicists among us to begin their work by considering *how* people think rather than going straight to a discussion of *what* they think.

Ranking people on a rigidity-flexibility scale will most likely uncover rigid and flexible people everywhere—liberals, conservatives, or centrists. Name the issue, and you will find rigid and flexible people scattered among the supporters and opponents. Methodologically rigid gun lovers and methodologically rigid gun control advocates; flexible Pro-lifers and flexible Pro-choicers. So, it makes little sense to discuss the content of a person's value system without recognizing the way he or she processes information about the subject.

Methods always trump content. Senior longshoremen are less interested in *what* their people load on outgoing ships (content) than in how carefully they perform the loading process (methods). For our purposes, we are going to play ethics foreman and look at four ways theologians and laypeople load their cargo of values about what is Right, Good and Proper. Much of the following is based on Joseph Fletcher's game-changing book, written half a century ago, *Situation Ethics.*

Four Approaches to Ethical Decision-Making

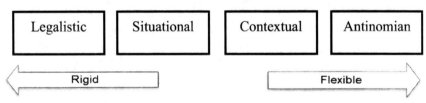

Fig.15-1

LEGALISTIC (PRINCIPLED) ETHICS

Joseph Fletcher used the word *principled* differently in than in popular conversation. "Principled" usually refers to someone whose actions are "based on or manifesting objectively defined standards of rightness or morality," a man or woman who operates in a praiseworthy way based on high values. Someone who is *unprincipled* is considered "lacking principles or moral scruples." [8]

The word *principled* here refers to someone who functions from a rigid set of guidelines, legalistically applying them to all cases with little exception. Earlier we suggested there are some conditions under which a normally honest person might lie or break the law. People who function from unbending principles might argue, like the "Truthful Baptists," that violating a moral principle is never justified. Because nonstandard applications of language pose a problem, Fletcher often called principled ethics *legalism*.

Someone who proceeds from stone-carved principles has several good things going for him. First, eternal principles are quite reassuring in a rapidly changing world, so the principled ethicist has a high degree of Certainty. He has built his house on a rock, and the winds of change will not shake its foundations.

Second, principled ethics relieves people repeated decision-making. Since all questions are referred to unchanging principles which answer any circumstance, they are not creators of ethical systems but only interpreters of Divine decrees.

Third, the viewpoints of the principled ethicist posit infallibility, because they are really not his views but God's. During my Army years, a senior chaplain from another denomination said to me, tongue in cheek, "You may continue to worship God in your own way; I shall continue to worship God in His." It was a humorous moment, but an unspoken assumption hides beneath the joviality. By definition religionists committed to a specific faith believe theirs is the best path to God. If not, why follow it? Applying that stipulation to ethics creates problems, because believers in other systems may not share the norms I take for granted.

To cite a current issue, supporters of equal rights for the LGBT community have difficulty convincing members of conservative religions that pro-gay principles are neither unethical nor immoral. A conservative Christian website writes:

> God loves homosexuals. God does not, however, love homosexuality... God views homosexuality as "detestable" or, as in the King James Version of the Bible, "an abomination." ...If someone is not a

Christian, and is involved in homosexual activity, chances are that no amount of preaching is going to change their mind. Their position is fostered by the sinful nature which dwells within, and from which, without Christ, they have no escape. ...For this reason, the primary goal should be to reach these people with the gospel of Christ. Until and unless they receive the Lord, they will have no reason to seek to change. So proclaiming the gospel to these people is the most loving thing we can do for them. [9]

Contrast the above pronouncement with the following moral position, just as legalistic (inflexible) in its own way, from the copious writings of retired Episcopal Bishop John Shelby Spong.

I have made a decision. I will no longer debate the issue of homosexuality in the church with anyone. I will no longer engage the biblical ignorance that emanates from so many right-wing Christians about how the Bible condemns homosexuality, as if that point of view still has any credibility. I will no longer discuss with them or listen to them tell me how homosexuality is "an abomination to God," about how homosexuality is a "chosen lifestyle," or about how through prayer and "spiritual counseling" homosexual persons can be "cured."... The world has moved on, leaving these elements of the Christian Church that cannot adjust to new knowledge or a new consciousness lost in a sea of their own irrelevance. They no longer talk to anyone but themselves. [10]

Common ground between the above is clearly unreachable. Bishop Spong speaks with the hopeful voice of tomorrow; the other passage reflects abandoned values of yesteryear. Although the *content* of these remarks is important, the key point for our discussion of ethical types is that *methodologically they both exhibit characteristics of unbending principles*. In a way, this impasse describes the cultural stalemate in American society. If my position is good and true and all others false and evil, I cannot ethically compromise. Principled ethics may appear commendable at first glance, but rigidly followed rules paradoxically lead to chaos.

Finally, principle-based ethics relieve people of responsibility for their actions. The rules were made by God, and who can argue with God? In 1970 while attending US Army Rotary Wing Fight School, I had a disquieting discussion with an otherwise rational and likable young Mormon friend on the subject of race. It is an established fact that from the 19th century to the 1970s, the LDS church taught that darker races are spiritually inferior to whites. An article in the New York Times summarized the reason: "The pre-existent spirits of black people had sinned in heaven by supporting Lucifer in his rebellion against God." For this reason, all people of color were excluded from priesthood (ordinary male membership) in the Mormon Church.

When I asked my friend how he could accept such a doctrine, he said if it were up to him, he'd treat everybody as equals. But it was God's law, not his. A few years later, in 1978, the LDS Church received a new revelation from God, which reversed its historic policies of racial discrimination, but the Mormon hierarchy has steadfastly refused to discuss the subject. [11] But before we are too quick to single out one instance of religious bigotry, it might do well to reflect on something Martin Luther King, Jr., said about religion and race relations during a 1963 speech at Western Michigan University: "11 a.m. Sunday is the most segregated hour in America."[12]

The danger of coupling absolute faith with absolute intolerance cannot be overstated. We need only recall some of the terrible experiences of the human family when unbending people of "principle" came to power and sought to make the world in their image. The Spanish Inquisition is one of the most infamous applications of into intolerant righteousness in history, but burnings and beatings were not only handed down by Catholics to "heretics." The great church reformer, John Calvin, had the Unitarian author Michael Servetus burned at the stake in Geneva. Protestant colonists killed witches in British America. Outside the Christian family of religions, Hindus and Muslims continue battle extremists within their faith groups to this day. And the problem is not just confined to organized religion. Fear driven, anti-Communist hunting parties drove countless people from their careers during the McCarthy era.

Are terrorists who die to make a religio-political statement evil people, or are they persons of unbending principle, passionate believers of who will neither compromise nor negotiate? Perhaps the greatest danger of legalistic ethics is its inability to adapt to circumstances without forfeiting its basic premise, i.e., rules must be obeyed. My book, *The Many Faces of Prayer,* opens with a quote from conservative commentator George F. Will. His remarks are insightful enough to repeat here.

> The greatest threat to civility—and ultimately to civilization—is an excess of certitude. The world is much menaced just now by people who think that the world and their duties in it are clear and simple... It has been well said that the spirit of liberty is the spirit of not being too sure that you are right. One way to immunize ourselves against misplaced certitude is to contemplate—even to savor—the unfathomable strangeness of everything, including ourselves.[13]

Not all principled ethic lead to tyranny. Some simply represent deeply held beliefs which lack the flexibility to bend with unforeseen consequences. I knew a parent who decreed his daughter could not go to dances until she was in high school. Then she was picked to be junior high Homecoming Queen, and her father reacted predictably. The result was a fourteen-year-old girl sitting at home, crying inconsolably, never to forget the greatest disappointment of her young life. He hated himself for doing it, but he would not compromise on principles. He was a man of his word, and the principle trumped mere sentiment.

On a much grander scale, something similar has happening in American politics. In the 1970s, televangelist Rev. Jerry Falwell founded the Moral Majority and used it to propel the religious right into political action. "If you're not a born-again Christian," he said, "you're a failure as a human being." Falwell also said, "The idea that religion and politics don't mix was invented by the Devil to keep Christians from running their own country."[14]

When reading these highly conservative, God-and-country remarks by Jerry Falwell, it is important to recalibrate for the difference between *method* and *content*. Falwell was an uncompromising principled ethicist. Arguably, so was Gandhi, who operated from a far different worldview. Some circumstances may call for leaders who will tightly cling to "eternal" principles in a world gone temporarily insane. Students of ethics should be prepared to ask what kind of boundary-pushing circumstances might drive them toward unbending firmness, and if they must respond legalistically under extreme conditions, how rigid is rigid enough?

ANTINOMIAN ETHICS

At the opposite end of the spectrum from principled ethics is a non-system of valuing called *antinomianism*. This term comes from two Greek root words, *anti* (against) and *nómos* (law).[15] Antinomianism was aptly summarized by the slogan of the hippie counter-culture of the 1960s, *"If it feels good, do it."* Sarah Beach writes in Salon.com about growing up during the season of *make love, not war*:

> If it feels good, do it: a rallying cry of the '60s and the root of a lot of really awful parenting…there was a dark side to this intoxicating rejection of rules and boundaries. With everyone embracing spontaneity and the mandates of the id, there was no one left to assume the adult role. People like my parents may have had the best of intentions, but in a wide-eyed quest for social change, they became children. And their actual children suffered as a result.[16]

Raised to its most conventional level, antinomian ethics holds that "ordinary moral laws are not applicable to Christians, whose lives, it is said, are governed solely by divine grace."[17] The idea has a biblical basis. To reach the vast, non-Jewish population outside Judea, the Apostle Paul had preached that Christians were under *grace* and therefore not subject to the Jewish Law. Apparently, Paul wanted to remove two major obstacles to conversion by releasing gentile Christians from the obligation to keep kosher and undergo the painful rite of circumcision. The latter ritual might explain why female converts to Judaism had traditionally surpassed males.

Some of Paul's gentile converts heard Paul's version of the gospel as *really, really good news*. No kosher, no knife, the old rules are history! And they made a natural assumption: If believers are immunized against the law, then anything goes—*so, let's party!* When Paul learned about the salacious behavior at the Church of Corinth, already considered the Las Vegas of the Roman world, he hastily dispatched a disciple with an urgent dispatch in hand. In this First Letter to the Corinthians, Paul sounds like he wanted to float along with the theory of Christian antinomianism, but he recognized the shipwreck awaiting if believers sailed the freedom boat too far from safe harbor in their divine natures.

> "All things are lawful for me," but not all things are beneficial. "All things are lawful for me," but I will not be dominated by anything... Or do you not know that your body is a temple of the Holy Spirit within you, which you have from God, and that you are not your own?[18]

Much of the letter was devoted to settling disputes and quelling the antinomianism rampant in the Church at Corinth. Not only fleshly excesses, but spiritual practices had gotten out of hand. Read chapters 12-13-14 in a modern translation at one sitting and you will understand the battle Paul was fighting with the religious zealots at Corinth.

Antinomianism's great virtue is that it is flexible to circumstances. If there are no standards whatsoever, people are free to adapt behavior to match life experiences. So the madman with a pistol demanding to know if your friend is having tea in your house can be told a technical lie, because there is no such thing as absolute truth anyway. Running red lights is acceptable behavior for antinomian ethicists, as long as no accident results. In fact, one often hears a kind of untutored antinomian ethos when talking to people of the drug culture, or people who drink too much. As long as no one gets hurt, it's okay.

But an antinomian ethicist might not be concerned with another person's pain or discomfort. If there are no standards and no responsibilities, people should just do what seems right at any given minute. Virtually any kind of behavior is ethically permitted under antinomianism. Hitler stands beside Gandhi, Stalin walks hand in hand with Mother Theresa, since they all did what they thought was right.

Metaphysical Churches are especially susceptible to charges of spiritual antinomianism. If God is within everyone, should not each person follow his/her own inner guide and do whatever it says, regardless of the values of society? James Dillet Freeman answered these arguments brilliantly:

> The most important question to ask of any religion is, 'Are you a life-affirming or life-denying religion?' A religion should have beliefs that you can accept without denying your intelligence; it should motivate you to create beauty and revere joy; it should inspire you to be energetic and creative, enable you to find peace of mind and to live well; it should teach you to be kind and tolerant toward all your fellow human beings, even those who do not like you.[19]

Bonhoeffer said Christian faith should call people to discipleship in the footsteps of Jesus Christ, who is the ongoing standard of what is right, good and proper. Antinomianism says there are no external standards whatsoever. A Christian antinomianism is only possible if the free-form valuation process involves shaping the message and person of Jesus Christ to whatever values appeal at the moment. Some skeptics, myself included, have suggested Christology has changed so often through history that an antinomian element in its formulation cannot be denied. Metaphysical Christianity, like Western mysticism through the ages, has lived with the tension between free agency, implicit in direct access to the divine-within, and the need to adapt one's life and thought to the paradigm of Jesus Christ available through Church tradition and biblical sources. Such tension is creative, empowering mindful decision-making when confront with ethical choices, which then can be tested in the free market of Christian theology.

All this presupposes some king of guiding principles. Even clinging to Jesus Christ requires a way of processing the raw information about him, from Bible and tradition, into a value system which helps us make ethical choices. Again, we look to method instead of content. Christians may agree on Jesus; few agree on what it means to follow him. Fewer still agree on how to live by the light of his presence. One way to solve the problem is to boil all the verbiage down to one basic principle which serves as the staple for our whole ethical system.

SITUATION ETHICS

Much maligned and misunderstood, Joseph Fletcher's *Situation Ethics* has weathered a hurricane of anathemas from religious leaders and social conservatives. Part of the controversy is Fletcher's fault. He decided that one of the primary examples of Situation Ethics would be an argument for the liberalization of sexual standards. Matching a new technique for doing ethics with a red-flag issue like the 1960s sexual revolution was an unfortunate alignment, but paradoxically the book attracted a larger readership because of the sexuality issues it raised. The fallout from Fletcher's deployment of the sex-bomb is that the term *situation ethics* has become synonymous with promiscuity and is incorrectly used as a synonym for antinomianism. Joseph Fletcher clearly did *not* advocate doing whatever feels good in any given situation, as some antinomians do. Fletcher's work sketched the categories we have explored so far: principled ethics, which he called *legalism*, and its polar opposite, antinomianism. Fletcher adds his own middle way, which he calls *Situation Ethics*.

> A third approach, in between legalism and antinomian unprincipledness, is Situation Ethics. The situationist enters into every decision-making situation fully armed with the ethical maxims of his community and its heritage, and he treats them with respect as illuminators of his problems. Just the same he is prepared in any situation to compromise them or set them aside in the situation if love seems better served by doing so.[20]

Fletcher wants to establish a true polar star to guide all circumstances, one universal standard against which all other values can be measured. For Fletcher, that criterion is *love*. He would have us ask, in every circumstance requiring moral judgment, "What is the loving thing to do?" He calls upon an impressive array of witnesses to support his ideas, including reports in the gospels about incidents from the life of Jesus.

Fletcher sees the man of Nazareth as the supreme example of Situation Ethics in action. Didn't Jesus heal people on the Sabbath, eat with sinners and converse with foreigners, all acts forbidden by the Jewish Law? And when questioned about his practices did Jesus not say that the Law was made for humanity, not humanity for the Law? What motivation other than love do we need? What better governing principle than the law of love?

Fletcher's argument is tempting, but it begs the question by assuming everyone will agree on what is a loving act in any given situation. The anti-abortionist expresses loving concern for the unborn baby; the pro-choice counselor understands the terrible choice a mother must make and expresses loving concern for the adult female with an unwanted pregnancy that will result in an unwanted child. Which side does the Christian ethicist endorse? Every time *Roe v. Wade* reaches an anniversary, committed believers hold placards on both sides of the street.

Love is the guiding principle for Fletcher, but any suitable reference point could serve as the theological lodestar of an ethical system. Imagine, for example, situation ethics built around pivotal values like *justice, freedom, reciprocity, creativity, courage, detachment,* or even *ecstasy.* Fletcher offers no solution to the subjectivity of Situation Ethics, which perhaps is both his greatest weakness and greatest strength. Although many have tried, no system of ethics can provide prefabricated answers to every life situation. Most ethicists today believe dialogue and discussion of difficult issues is the best way to arrive at answers to tough problems. Even the best answer must be held open to continual review and reconsideration because, paraphrasing Charles Fillmore, what we face today may not be the ethical dilemma of tomorrow.

We still need to consider a fourth way to do ethics, a modus operandi which blends some of the best features of the above three. It is not a perfect system, in every circumstance, but perhaps by now you are aware that perfect systems rarely find their way into the hands of human beings. Let's take a look at this final way of doing ethics next.

Sidebar on Casuistry: Case-Based Ethics

One method of doing ethics, which requires the application of principles based on the circumstances in which people actually find themselves, has been called *casuistry* or *case ethics*. Casuistry actually emerged from the Roman Catholic sacrament of penance. Church members confessed their sins to a priest and were required to do certain acts to make amends for their misdeeds. The problem was some priests were grading confessions harder, assigning more stringent remedies for sinful behavior. To mitigate this drift in propitiatory tasking, they developed a case book for penances. It resolved ethical problems by bundling examples of similar cases and synching new penances with the established precedents. American and British jurisprudence are based on this case study model.

However, for the past three centuries casuistry has fallen in to disrepute among philosophers and theologians alike, who consider case studies far too flexible to provide the kind of definitive answers required in ethical dilemmas. Theological ethicists prefer to search for help among biblical scholars and classical and contemporary theologians. Moral philosophers however prefer to reason from universal principles based on presumptions, often expressed in symbolic logic. For example, if *a* is like *c* and *b* is like *c*, therefore *a* must be like *b*.

$$(a = c) \wedge (b = c) \therefore (a = b)$$

The equation works on paper, but humans don't always do the math. Existence is far more nuanced. Factors in a given moral context are seldom reducible to symbolic logic without pitting principle against principle. For example, if the equation above represents the difficult decision of whether to have an elective abortion, trouble is bound to occur no matter what choice the pregnant woman makes. Let's expand the logic symbols to include more information.

A (Anna) is C (Catholic) who became pregnant by a rapist.

C (Catholics) must carry all B (babies) to term. Therefore,

A (Anna) must carry the B (baby) to term, even if impregnated by a rapist.

Except Anna neither accepts her Church's unbending Pro-Life doctrine nor desires to leave the Catholic faith. In her case, she makes an ethical exception for pregnancies due to rape. Some Catholic ethicists would add incest, severe birth defects, or to save the life of the mother. All of these choices violate Roman Catholic moral principles, yet many people who hold these views are not willing to surrender their Catholic identity. The complexities in a case like this are not due to perfidious church members refusing to obey rules; the rules simply do not apply in certain contexts.[21]

CONTEXTUAL ETHICS

Some ethicists believe no single principle applies in every situation, even the principle of love. To punish a criminal with lengthy imprisonment for misdeeds may result in society's protection; it may even be good for the criminal, who is no longer able to harm himself spiritually by acts of violence. But ethicists must reconfigure the word "love" to interpret an act of imprisonment as a "loving" deed. In this circumstance perhaps a better pivotal principle is *justice*. Jesus showed a loving person can also adjudicate the fairness of a given situation. Witness his stern rebuke of the religious hierarchy and uncompromising, drive-'em-out-with-a-whip response to avaricious moneychangers. However, Jesus tempered justice with reasonableness, so the punishment would fit the crime: No death sentences for selfishness or life imprisonment for petty fraud. To be truly an act of justice, the ethical/social practice must not violate the principles of love, either. It must adapt to the broader context.

Both Pro-Choice and Pro-Life can argue their positions represent a faithful reading of the Apostle Paul's letter to Corinth: "'All things are lawful for me,' but not all things are beneficial." Whenever people start adjusting rules, it must be done with the utmost caution because of the human tendency to rationalize harmful behavior under the banner of free choice. However, societies built on inflexible rules quickly land people in the Lying Baptist dilemma when life presents problems unforeseen by architects of the moral code.

Contextual ethics often looks at case studies but differs from casuistry because it uses a matrix of interactive values which must be understood in relationship to each other. Instead of a series of *unalterable laws* or *binding precedents*, Contextual ethics speaks of *guiding principles* which support each other and give people ways to look at a problem from many vantage points. Instead of one overwhelming principle that takes precedence, contextual ethics offers a chorus of ideas singing in harmony and able to change pitch depending on the music that life places in our hands.

A contextual ethicist has principles, but considers the real-world situation and lets the whole value system mull over the problem instead of doggedly trying to solve every problem by splashing love all over it. The contextual ethicist—having lived and loved, and perhaps after experiencing the failure of love when it is one-sided—knows better. Sometimes, love will be more important than justice, as with our mini-tragedy of the Junior High Homecoming Queen. Other times, justice (or Order) will take precedence, as with criminals facing prison for their misdeeds. The context presents the problem; the value system lets its hierarchy of principles dialogue about possible solutions. Because it is a methodology based on a subset of values, one of the most important questions to ask a Contextual Ethicist is what is the source of that matrix of values which will process the ethical decision?

In 1945 the United States dropped two atomic bombs on Japan, which forced the Japanese to surrender unconditionally, ending the war without a massive invasion of the Japanese main islands. The destruction which those two blasts caused has rightly been called horrific and inhumane by ethical theorists. Other ethicists point to the million-plus deaths among civilians and military forces which would surely have occurred if the Allies had stormed ashore in Japan. The decision was made by President Harry S. Truman, whose home in Independence, Missouri, is a twenty-minute car ride from the Silent Unity Tower at Lee's Summit on the Unity Village campus, where prayer for peace goes up 24 hours a day.

The old argument of the lesser of two evils applies, but does the fact that Truman saved at least a million lives does make his decision to launch nuclear attacks on Hiroshima and Nagasaki *good*? In this instance, where both choices are undesirable, it may be impossible to argue that either option is good. Once an action is taken—lives destroyed, more lives spared—does the ethicist have a moral obligation to declare how wrong it was to drop atomic bombs on human beings? This is a complex, emotional issue. After read Pulitzer Prize-winning author John Hersey's book, *Hiroshima,* I came away with a terrible sense of injustice done to the victims of nuclear violence. How could anyone feel otherwise? However, I was born in 1946, along with many other post-war babies. My father was in the Army when Truman dropped the bombs. May I not selfishly wonder, what if he had been killed while invading the Japanese home islands to end the war? Or what if millions of Japanese fathers, mother, and children had died in what surely would have been horrific, house-to-house fighting, perhaps until the last defender was killed? It had happened on Pacific Islands, and the Samurai fervor to defend the sacred soil of the home islands entangled with myth, history, religion, and the code of Bushido. Truman faced a terrible decision; he made one of the two wrong choices available.

War and peace continue to be some of the most difficult ethical issues for humanity, as Dietrich Bonhoeffer learned firsthand in Nazi Germany. Jesus, the ultimate ethicist, told people to love their enemies. He probably realized we would continue to have enemies despite our best efforts at peacemaking. As long as people divide into opposing groups, the advocates of peace must find new ways to shape a better world. Until then, we'll need Bonhoeffers and Gandhis to walk among us.

Contextual Theory of Ethics for Metaphysical Christians

A promising basis for Contextual Ethics could be Charles Fillmore's *Twelve Powers*, which has applications beyond mere meditative introspection. Value decisions could be considered from the vantage point of those twelve cardinal elements in the makeup of the human-divine paradox. Crowning the whole system is the Christ, the Incarnation of the *I Am* (the image of divinity within) which informs us of the dignity and worth of each sentient being.

Rules such as the Ten Commandments, legal codes of the nation or community, folkways and personal beliefs fall under scrutiny in this value matrix and are held against the standard of the Christ-within each person. No one will ever be written off as utterly lost because the pattern of divinity dwells just below the mask human rebellion. Tough problems still exist. There are no clean, easy answers to ethical issues. But now we have a starting point for discussing individual and social ethics from a mystical perspective. Contextual Ethics offers Metaphysical Christians the kind of freedom we need while firmly grounding us in the Judeo-Christian heritage.

Whether a local church launches a complete social awareness program or just a discussion group to consider world problems from the Christian perspective, the mandate for followers of Jesus to care for his sheep remains in force. How we choose to follow that command is entirely a personal matter and must be left to individual conscience.

The intent of this chapter was to spur discussion about ethical topics and suggest a basis for doing Christian theological ethics that begins and ends with the model of Jesus Christ. Whatever tools we add to our studies--Buddha's meditation on suffering or Fillmore's Twelve Powers--must ultimately come before the only standard of Christian faith for the final test: What would Jesus do? If our ethical systems can answer that question, we are well on the path to a better world.

There is something of a feisty, controversial spirit to theological ethics which may require new religious behavior for Metaphysical Christians. We tend to want peace at any price, without realizing that the founding fathers and mothers of modern Metaphysical Christianity were far from milquetoasts when they gathered to discuss the faith. Charles Fillmore was known for his kindly spirit, but he was also unafraid of disagreement. James Dillet Freeman writes:

> Often in his classes, a student would be answering a question and Mr. Fillmore would ask, "Where did you get that idea?"
>
> The student would reply, "I read that in such-and-such a Unity book, Mr. Fillmore."
>
> "Are you sure?"
>
> "Certainly, Mr. Fillmore, that is right out of page so and so."
>
> "You know," he would say, "that is not exactly right," and then he would go on to explain the point in a way that clarified it.

> Often in his classes, he would interrupt his students, *when they were quoting him*, with the question, "But what do YOU think about it?" The main aim of his teaching was to get his students to think Truth through for themselves. [22]

It is in this kind of free exchange that Truth emerges. Christian community works best when it is not a factory but a marketplace, where varieties of belief and practice lend color and vigor to our spiritual growth. Fillmore knew he must not bottle up a formula and issue it wholesale to his students. One of his favorite affirmations was, "I reserve the right to change my mind."[23] He wrote:

> Beware of the circumscribed idea of God! Always provide for an increase in your concept. Don't write down any laws governing your conduct or your religious ideas. Be free to grow and expand. What you think today may not be the measure for your thought tomorrow.[24]

Pros and Cons of Sacred Social Action

As with any controversial topic, attempts to forge a pattern for social ethics from a mystical basis sometimes generates resistance within the community of faith. In all fairness, it must be admitted that some arguments against exploring this subject are well founded. However, no theology can be complete without addressing the problems of moral theology. Choosing not to speak to questions of social ethics is to make a statement which too often sinks us deep into apathy. Could a responsible Christian live through the slave era and not be an Abolitionist? Could a Christian watch the Civil Rights movement develop in the United States and not be moved to take a stand in favor of integration?

Certainly. Millions did just that.

Slave-owning or slavery-condoning Christians fought the emancipation of blacks before and during the Civil War. Millions of God-fearing Americans prayed they would not have to integrate their schools, prayed African-Americans would keep in their "place", and prayed those "outside agitators" would stop stirring up the local black community with all this marching and civil disobedience. Millions more said not a word when the US government rounded up Japanese Americans and interred them in virtual concentration camps during World War II.

How is that possible? The indignation you likely feel about the way members of racial minorities have been treated—like—is because your society has decided the standards of morality in these situations from recent history. Examine the questions, discover what motivated people to take moral positions which are now seen as clearly repugnant, and you are doing *social ethics.*

It is not enough just to feel that your cause is right; every fanatic claims certitude. People need to understand the process of valuation, to ask critical, empirical questions. To make good choices, the followers of Jesus must be able to handle prickly issues and apply techniques of valuing that flow from the Christian heritage while remaining free from prejudice as possible. That is no easy proposition. As we noted and discussed in Chapter 4, every culture is to some degree ethnocentric.[25] Ethnocentrism creeps into our religious thinking and affects the way we look at ethical/moral problems. Because of this tendency, theological ethics must always be in dialogue--within the community of faith as Christian thinkers discuss problems and cross verbal swords over solutions, and between Christian ethicists and non-Christians who explore moral questions. Only by listening to those who stand outside our house will we ever know what it looks like in its wholeness.

Through critical discussion of ethical issues, opportunities for change naturally arise. We learn quickly which ideas work and which ideas are fantasy when we bring them to market. However, some legitimate arguments against an active involvement in what some people are calling **Sacred Social Action** must be considered. In keeping with this study's ongoing aspiration to promote healthy discussion let's briefly but fairly explore five arguments against social ethics and answer those concerns with the response a Metaphysical Christian ethicist might offer. You are certainly invited to disagree and encouraged to "reserve the right to change" your mind.

OBJECTION #1: Christianity is about spiritual growth.

Mysticism's highest goal is union with God. Those who object to discussing issues raised by theological ethics often contend that involvement with the problems of this world might blunt our drive toward mystical Oneness with God by draining energies on concerns of this world. Too much passion for the problems of this world could bog us down and make us forget spiritual growth as the primary goal of life. Thus, our spirituality might suffer from confrontations with a world that does not yet understand Metaphysical Christian teachings.

RESPONSE: It has always been a challenge for the religious person to live in the world without becoming "worldly" in the pejorative sense of the word. There are countless biblical injunctions to warn believers about the danger of becoming too closely associated with popular causes and fashions; in the mind of some New Testament authors, "the world" is always a term of derision which is contrasted to the Kingdom of God. Yet, even the author of John's Gospel, who rails against "the world" at every opportunity, could not help formulating the central mission of Jesus Christ in these words:

> "For God so loved *the world* that he gave his only Son,
> so that everyone who believes in him may not perish but
> may have eternal life."[26]

It was to help *the world* (meaning the Roman Empire and all its people) that Jesus taught a message of healing love. Several places in the gospels Jesus explicitly commands his disciples to get involved in social action: clothe the naked, feed the hungry, visit the sick and imprisoned, bless the children, heal those facing health challenges, comfort those who mourn, teach all nations, love your neighbor, do the will of the Father, be a neighbor in deed as well as in belief. New Testament support for social ethics runs deep and wide. Parables of Jesus overflow with good deeds and people who took action in the real world: the Good Samaritan, the Father of the Prodigal Son, the Good Shepherd. His teaching was reinforced by a life of compassion and involvement with others: cleansing lepers, healing paralytics, giving sight to the blind, feeding the multitudes, Zacchaeus, healing on the Sabbath, warning of the dangers of violent solutions, and many other instances of proactive compassion by Jesus.

In fact, the only people against whom Jesus went off like Vesuvius were the leaders of the religious community, who had become so concerned about nit-picking at points of the Law they forgot why the Law was given in the first place, i.e., to help people find fellowship with their God and *koinonia* with their neighbor. Perhaps the most powerful statement in the New Testament on the responsibility of Christians others is a passage which the author of Matthew attributes to Jesus. It occurs within the sequence often referred to as the "Little Apocalypse," a series of dire predictions about the imminent end of the world, which can be found in Matthew 24-25:

> "Depart from me, you cursed, into the eternal fire prepared for the devil and his angels; for I was hungry and you gave me no food, I was thirsty and you gave me no drink. I was a stranger and you did not welcome me, naked and you did not clothe me, sick and in prison and you did not visit me." Then they also will answer, "Lord, when did we see thee hungry or thirsty or a stranger or naked or sick or in prison, and did not minister to thee?" Then he will answer them, "Truly, I say to you, as you did it not to one of the least of these, you did it not to me."[27]

Even after de-mythologizing this passage of its fiery eschatology, a frightening admonition remains: Failure to help people in need is tantamount to turning one's back on the Christ. It will lock people into a pattern of no-growth until they learn this lesson. The author of the First Epistle of John continues Matthew's harsh tone:

> Those who say, "I love God," and hate their brothers or sisters, are liars; for those who do not love a brother or sister whom they have seen, cannot love God whom they have not seen. [28]

Can anyone say they love their neighbor and then duck all responsibility to make this a better world? Based on the nearly unanimous testimony of Scripture, reinforced by longstanding tradition of proactive ministry, accelerated by life experience and personal reflection, the Christian Social Ethicist must answer, "No!"

However, there are other arguments against doing social ethics. Some are harder to dismiss.

OBJECTION #2: Others are available to do social action.

Sometimes stated: "Our task is to preach salvation (or teach spiritual enlightenment) to the world. That is the greater need." This is a subtle variation on the first argument, but very popular in some religious circles and among the laypeople of many churches. The Metaphysical Christian equivalent to the argument about the primacy of soul-saving is that the function of a spiritual community is to *promote individual growth*, not become enmeshed in socio-political causes. If we teach people to turn within and find the Christ, they will grow enlightened enough to change the world on their own.

RESPONSE: As mentioned, this objection contains two sub-points.

1) Social activism is not the business of churches because our job is to teach spirituality (or save souls, depending on the religious tradition).

2) If we get about our business and teach people about God, they will accomplish by themselves the good that should be done in the world.

Sub-Point #1. Should churches stick to religion?

Although many clergy took an active part in the Civil Rights era and Anti-War Protests, countless others refused to get involved because they felt it was their duty to save souls, not challenge the status quo. Theodore Parker, nineteenth century Unitarian minister and uncompromising Abolitionist, decried the complacency of even the liberal churches in his day, and the debate continued long after slavery ended. In the book and motion picture *The Hiding Place*, Corrie Ten Boom tells of her Dutch clergyman who refused to get involved in the secret program of sheltering Jewish families from the Nazi's because he felt his first obligation was to care for the souls of his people. Troubled by the inconsistency of a Christian minister without a biblical sense of justice, young Corrie turned to her father, who wisely noted, "Just because a mouse is in the cookie jar doesn't make it a cookie."[29]

Jesus demolished the excuse for non-action based on salvation-centered spirituality when he scolded the religious leaders for superficial piety that took them away from justice and mercy.

> "Woe to you, scribes and Pharisees, hypocrites! For you tithe mint, dill, and cumin, and have neglected the weightier matters of the law: justice and mercy and faith. It is these you ought to have practiced without neglecting the others."[30]

His scalding words impeached leaders of any religion who exempt followers from obligations to real people in the real world. Such practices are not heartfelt religion but an escape mechanism, a fantasy. How could anyone follow God and refuse to feed the helpless hungry?

Buddhists tell the story of Gautama Siddhartha, the first Buddha, whose father attempted to prevent him from seeing the pain of the world. Gautama's father was told by a soothsayer his son will become either a homeless monk or the emperor of all India. Knowing that exposure to suffering often turns people to religion, his father decided to blot out all traces of misery from Gautama's world. Only healthy, young people attended him. Whenever the young prince went riding, his father cleared the highways of old, sick and hungry people. His life contained no hint of suffering.

Then the gods intervened. Young Gautama saw an old man and learned about aging; he met a sick man and discovered disease; he watched a funeral procession and knew there was death. Overwhelmed by grief and anxiety about his own fate, Gautama finally encountered a mystic in a yellow robe whose calm, peaceful demeanor showed that it was possible to live in the real world and yet be a spiritual person. Thus began the quest which ended when he discovered the Noble Eightfold Path and attaining Enlightenment. He became the Buddha, walking a path of moderation in all things.[31]

Buddhists today are as widely varied in lifestyle and politics as the followers of Jesus or the Prophet Muhammad. Some are active in social justice, some follow a singularly ascetic life. Certainly, religious movements must teach spiritual values and stand for personal growth before God. But all the great prophets of humankind have reiterated the necessity for involvement with the problems of society. It was only after Gautama broke free of his isolated, perfect world and faced the sufferings around him that the young prince started down the path to enlightenment as the Buddha.

Call any Divine Messenger to the stand and take testimony: read the writings of prophets and teachers from all the faiths of humanity and see if you can find one which tells us to run away from the world, ignore the cries of the hungry and the oppressed, and seek our own salvation exclusively? Jesus told followers

> Therefore do not worry, saying, 'What will we eat?' or 'What will we drink?' or 'What will we wear?' For it is the Gentiles who strive for all these things; and indeed your heavenly Father knows that you need all these things. But strive first for the kingdom of God and his righteousness, and all these things will be given to you as well. "So do not worry about tomorrow, for tomorrow will bring worries of its own. Today's trouble is enough for today.[32]

He never said, "Strive for righteousness and ignore your responsibilities to neighbor." Right the contrary. Christianity requires engagement with others in concerted effort to make the world a better place. The verse about striving for the kingdom comes immediately after Matthew's Jesus reminded his disciples not to worry about the outcome, because God is with them every step of the way. We need to worry is more than a call to higher consciousness--it is a summons to action, to commitment, to discipleship.

Sub-Point #2. Shouldn't the goal be to *inspire* others?

Christians can inspire people and not get involved themselves. If we teach about God, won't people transform themselves and change the world? In fact, is there any other way lasting change can occur?

Yes and no. One could argue that after everyone becomes

enlightened—fully aware of the divine within—the world will be a much happier place. The only question involves setting the agenda: Work for universal enlightenment, or help people live a better life here and now, during their struggle to achieve Christ-consciousness? Take a look at how this argument works when placed in the context of human evolution. If the DNA-based studies are correct, the species Homo sapiens arose among primates of primordial Africa. Consider what sense it would make if our prehistoric ancestors had decided, "It's nice here on the forest floor, but we can't migrate to better feeding grounds until the last monkey comes down from the trees."

Save the world by universal enlightenment, or work to make a small corner of it a better place—how would Jesus answer? Those who say churches should teach religion and let the people go forth to live an enlightened life are following the "Leaven in the Loaf" model of social ethics. Sprinkle a little yeast into the batter and the whole mass rises to become light, fluffy bread. Sprinkle enlightened souls through the population and human consciousness will rise to higher levels without any apparent effort at reform.

The only problem with this theory is that it doesn't work. History shows that some kind of organized effort is necessary to meet and overcome social evils. Were segregationists "bad" people who needed the example of "good" citizens who favored integration? Were those of us who served in the long, painful conflict in Southeast Asia *wrong* and those who fled to Canada or marched in the streets against that war *right*?

Right and wrong usually get sorted out later by historians. People like us live in the anxiety of a gray world where ethical decisions can usually go either way. It takes more than an enlightened person to raise consciousness; it takes dialogue among people who are struggling to learn God's will. The "Leaven in the Loaf" theory assumes the modernist paradigm, i.e., there is one correct way of living, and if we find the right path and live it effectively, we can influence society in the right way. But what happens when we don't know the right way? What if the post-modernists are correct and there is no airtight *right* way of doing things, not even a single *best* way? What happens in those messy, sticky areas where even enlightened people are confused? This study will suggest that dealing with ethical problems by dialogue and intelligent analysis stands a better chance at reaching some kind of societal consensus than exhortations to enlightenment by word or deed.

OBJECTION #3: There are too many hungry and poor people. How can the Church possibly cope?

A quick look at the monumental problems of underdeveloped nations (hunger, disease, poverty, oppressive regimes, ignorance, overpopulation), or Western society's blind spots (hungry people amid plenty; sexism, homophobia, lingering racism, poverty, drugs, violent crime, apathy, general intolerance) could paralyze an aspiring humanitarian by the enormity of the world's challenges. Even Jesus acknowledged that poor are always with us. What can one person, or one church, do?

RESPONSE: A simple reply to this objection? *Do something!* What might happen if every follower of Jesus Christ decided to improve the world, even in some small way? We may not be able to save planet single-handedly, but we can certainly affect the spaces surrounding our lives. The best illustration for this principle is the well-known starfish story from *Chicken Soup for the Soul.* Tossing one beached starfish back into the water after a storm at sea may not save all of them, but it makes a difference to each animal rescued.[33] What if a church established a program of "adopting" needy children through Child Fund International? CFI, formerly known as the Christian Children's Fund, is a non-denominational, inter-faith foundation through which individuals and groups sponsor children who live under some of the world's most desperate circumstances. Like many other helping agencies, CFI brings food, clothing and education to boys and girls so they may rise from poverty to some degree of adult prosperity.[34]

What if a church decides it will help to fund a new health clinic through an international service agency? Surely we can't save all the hungry and clothe all the naked ourselves, but we can feed some, clothe some. Laziness can masquerade as despair when confronted by problems of this magnitude. We don't have to solve all the problems of the world to get involved with social action. We must simply decide to act, now.

Choosing a plan of attack may be the greatest obstacle facing a church that resolves itself to get started. That's the final objection to be considered.

OBJECTION #4:   Social action is too divisive. Too many people disagree on the issues.

One of the unchallenged bromides in American culture is, "Never discuss religion or politics." And what is Christian social ethics? Religious discussion of political topics. Just about every agenda item for consideration as an ethical concern has socio-political overtones to it. *Hunger* requires economics; *sexism* becomes a discussion about equal pay for equal work and other forms of gender discrimination; *Pro-choice vs. pro-Life* pits social liberals against social conservatives. Why should any church wallow into this quagmire to upset, divide and drive away major blocks of contributing members? The return is not worth the effort.

RESPONSE: Implicit in this argument is the idea that churches should strive for uncritical harmony. Good luck. Christendom has never been a peace garden. When two or more people are involved, conflict is natural. Ask any happily married couple. Whether or not a church formally decides to discuss theological ethics and possible avenues for social action, every church will experience natural, healthy conflict over these issues anyway.

Projects to consider under the category of social ethics could as innocuous as obtaining new street lights in a high-crime area, collecting used clothing for the needy, or offering Alcoholics' Anonymous a place to meet on the church's property. If the church begins with discussions, progresses toward easy-to-achieve projects that have a solid base of support, finally graduates to open consideration of the more controversial topics, spiritual leadership will generate a minimum of unnecessary resistance and discord.

I am not suggesting a church should kick off its social ethics program with a march on city hall, but the choice should never be between inner spirituality and action in the outer world. Spirituality should embolden us to "spring forth with a mighty faith to do the things that ought to be done." Faith without works is an unemployed faith.

CHECK YOUR KNOWLEDGE

1. Explain/identify: ethics, moral philosophy, Christian social ethics.

2. What is the philosophical definition of ethics given in the text?

3. What are the four kinds of ethics? Explain each

4.. What is *casuistry*, and why is it controversial?

5. What major ethical decision did President Harry Truman make which ended World War II? List the reasons for and against this decision.

6. Summarize a few of the objections to discussing/doing Christian social ethics listed in the text.

QUESTIONS FOR DISCUSSION

1. Should local churches discuss or become involved in ethical issues? What about those areas which border on politics, e.g., Women's Rights, racism, Pro-Life/Pro-Choice, LGBT Liberation (i.e., marriage equality), the environment, gun control, war and peace issues?

2. What is the proper function of Christian social ethics for the Church at large? For the local church? For the individual Christian?

3. Each person list his/her ethical issues, prioritized in order of importance. Discuss the lists. Any surprises?

4. Which of the four ethical systems appeals most to you?

5. What would happen at your church if the minister announced she/he is going to take part in a "demonstration" about some ethical issue?

6. What low-threat social action projects could you initiate at your church? Or should the church concern itself with spiritual pursuits and leave social action to others?

- 16 -

PRAYER

Communion with God

Prayer is essential, not to the salvation of the soul, for the Soul is never lost; but to the conscious well-being of the soul that does not understand itself. There is a vitality in our communion with the Infinite, which productive of the highest good. As fire warms the body, as food strengthens us, as sunshine raises our spirits, so there is a subtle transfusion of some invisible force in such communion, weaving itself into the very warp and woof of our own mentalities. This conscious commingling of our thought with Spirit is essential to the well-being of every part of us.[1]

Ernest Holmes

In the multi-cultural family of religions known as Christianity, the more-or-less shared central reason for prayer is communion with God. Everything else said about prayer—from the educated agnostic who considers it mental house-cleaning to the frightened old woman in a nursing home who has been told God will burn her in hell for all eternity if she does not frequently remind him how much she loves him—is pure fancy. As James Dillet Freeman wrote in *Prayer the Master Key*:

> The whole purpose of prayer—whether I pray for myself
> or someone else—is to unify myself with God, the
> Creative Spirit.[2]

Prayer often comes wrapped in a package with meditation, and the most common distinction between them is usually described as active vs. passive involvement. In prayer, people *speak* to God; in meditation, they *listen,* or clear their minds to disengage the thinking mechanism in favor of spiritual *experience.* Popular religious philosopher Deepak Chopra reflects a universalist Hindu heritage when he distinguishes the two approaches:

> Prayer is a mental phenomenon where you actually speak mentally to a deity. Although prayer has many beneficial effects and more and more are scientifically getting validated. Prayer is not meditation because meditation is going beyond the mind, whereas prayer is a mental phenomenon, it's still mental activity. The mental activity is directed to a deity. Whether you believe in a deity or you imagine the deity, or you actually have experience of the deity, the inevitable mystery that we call "God"...[3]

And there are less clinical explanations. Sometimes prayer is a longing, a cry to the Universe for sense amid senselessness. Thomas Merton captured the heart of *I-Thou* communication, by which God-hungry souls have issued their wailing, lonely songs to the One Presence/One Power, like spiritual birds in the night, calling for life to make sense and have meaning. Merton's natural vulnerability speaks with a depth that transcends theology:

> My Lord God, I have no idea where I am going. I do not see the road ahead of me. I cannot know for certain where it will end. Nor do I really know myself, and the fact that I think that I am following your will does not mean that I am actually doing so. But I believe that the desire to please you does in fact please you. And I hope I have that desire in all that I am doing. I hope that I will never do anything apart from that desire. And I know that if I do this you will lead me by the right road though I may know nothing about it. Therefore will I trust you always though I may seem to be lost and in the shadow of death. I will not fear, for you are ever with me, and you will never leave me to face my perils alone.[4]

Six Misconceptions

However the Divine may be understood, both Freeman and Chopra find prayer a gateway to God. Prophets and poets have identified prayer as a source of people mountain-moving strength. However, some skeptics have placed prayer somewhere between *wishing* and *magic*. It is neither. Too many modern people consider prayer a duty or a fantasy. It is not. Too many ministers believe in a God who miraculously intervenes in the world to break the laws of science, which makes prayer *unnatural*, or disbelieve in any kind of divine involvement with the real world, which makes prayer *unnecessary*. These misconceptions represent six common misunderstandings, which must be addressed before refreshing the definition of prayer. The six are listed in couplets forming three pairs of opposites.

If *sin* is, as Ed Rabel said, the willful attempt to negate divine ideas (Ch. 9), then each negation represents a sinful attitude about prayer. Instead of releasing the power of God into everyday existence, sin (error-belief) blocks the flow of divine goodness and leaves people lonely, broken and helpless before an apparently uncaring Universe. Prayer can change all that if properly understood. But first we must examine the easy path away from effective communion with God typified by these popular but mistaken notions about prayer.

1. WISHING – MAGIC. Properly understood, prayer is neither wishing nor magic, and the difference between these two error-beliefs is significant to a discussion of prayer in general. Wishing assumes the person is utterly powerless, a pawn of the cosmos, who can only hope things will work out favorably. Wishing prayer is not unlike the chant of young lovers under the evening sky:

> Starlight, star bright
> First star I see tonight
> I wish I may, I wish I might,
> Have the wish I wish tonight.

To wish is to dream, and there is nothing wrong with dreaming. Walt Disney told generations of young lovers:

A dream is a wish your heart makes
When you're fast asleep
In dreams you lose your heartaches
Whatever you wish for, you keep
Have faith in your dreams and someday
Your rainbow will come smiling thru
No matter how your heart is grieving
If you keep on believing
The dream that you wish will come true.[5]

It is almost impossible to hear the lyrics to Disney songs like "A Dream is a Wish Your Heart Makes," and "When You Wish Upon a Star" without admiring the sentiments of optimism and hope. The line *"No matter how your heart is grieving / If you keep on believing…"* especially resonates with Metaphysical Christianity. Affirming the good regardless of appearances to the contrary is bottom-line metaphysics in the New Thought churches.

But even good dreams are not prayer. Wishing freely admits the unlikelihood of the desired outcome; no one wishes when properly prepared to deal with a situation from available resources. Students who have studied hard for a test seldom wish for a good grade, although they might pray for clarity of thought and memory. Wishing for good grades is the desperate act of a lazy student. When I wish for ideals that seem far-fetched—world peace, happiness for all people, or my boyhood favorite: the Philadelphia Phillies winning the World Series—I am expressing heartfelt desire for good to be established in my life.

However, wishing in the place of prayer is a wasted opportunity. Wishing denies the reality of prayer, opting instead for some kind of miraculous intervention: "If I want something strongly enough, something will happen." Metaphysical Christians generally believe in the natural flow of good throughout the cosmos, whenever we open ourselves to receive that good, but wishing has no real power to affect the world; "first star" hopes are understandable, but prayer to the evening star is ineffectual.

Wishing also brings false hopes. Who hasn't seen long lines at convenience stores where lottery tickets are sold? State governments which sponsor lotteries feed the wish-frenzy by slick advertisements showing average citizens with mansions, yachts, and endless tropical vacations. Yet, the odds against winning are astronomical. If the big prize is $10 million, the State-supported Lottery must sell $20 million in tickets to raise money, which is the whole purpose for having a lottery in the first place. Assuming one ticket wins, the odds would be one in twenty million. It's easier to attract a thunderbolt on a cloudless day.

Instead of wishing to win the lottery, I could use the money to start saving for school, get better skills, and make more over a lifetime than is likely to fall into my lap by gambling. For many people, playing the lottery is just an innocent fantasy; players know they're unlikely to win, no matter ads what the State Lottery Commission might run. But a few tickets purchased in fun is worlds away from whole paychecks poured down the drain by gambling addicts. Most people can decide where to set limits without being wasteful of resources that could be spent in self-improvement or the betterment of others. The error-belief in wishing is that it tries to receive miraculous benefits without increasing awareness of the principles behind prosperity.

Magical thinking is another problem for those who pray. In traditions which practice self-consciously the arts of witchcraft, like Neo-Paganism or Wicca, practitioners of magic believe in unseen powers which can be summoned to do the bidding of the spell-casting witch. Wiccans attempt to align themselves with the supernatural powers of the cosmos and summon these entities to do their will. There is nothing frightening about witchcraft. Witches are *not* in league with Satan; in fact, most of the Neo-Pagans I have met actually deny the existence of a personal Devil. Belief in the magical power of certain spoken words is an ancient spiritual practice, arguably the oldest of all religions. When performed by a Wiccan as an act of ritual, it is part of that pagan heritage which lingers into the twenty-first century and hauntingly provides a glimpse into our collective, pre-Christian past.

Let me be very clear: I have no problem with *magick* or ritual *witchcraft* practiced by people who are celebrating Earth-based spirituality or reawakening the ancient paganisms with ceremonies that approximate the older religions. These practices are culturally grounded in pre-Christian European, traditional Asian or African tribal societies, or linked to other indigenous religions around the globe, from which all humans emerged in the distant past. Earth-based spirituality and seeks to harmonize spiritual energies. *Magick* is generally not about getting your own way.

However, a twenty-first century New Age practitioner, who simply modifies traditional prayer by sprinkling it with the pixie dust of magical thinking, achieves nothing like the Wiccan concept of *magick*. Metaphysical Christians who go that route may find themselves wandering into the danger zone of self-centeredness. Is prayer really about getting my way, or is it better understood as getting myself out of the way? To believe that spoken words have inherent, value-neutral power, which can be invoked for good or ill at the whim of the practitioner, flies in the face of God as One Presence/One Power.

To complicate the question further, *curses* and *blessings* are theoretically indistinguishable in occultism, because magical thinking attempts to bend some plastic power of supernaturalism to the will of the practitioner. This may in part explain the reason Charles Fillmore, universally regarded as a kindly soul, went full Jeremiah on the magical thinkers of his day:

> Certain persons who call themselves "masters" claim that they have forged ahead of the race in their understanding and use of some of the powers of mind and have in personal egotism set up kingdoms and put themselves on thrones. These so-called "masters" and members of occult brotherhoods are attracting susceptible minds away from the straight and narrow path and leading them to believe that there is a short cut into the kingdom. ...The belief that secret and mysterious powers can control the visible world. This procedure is not the way of the Christ Mind.[6]

This, of course, is diametrically opposed to Metaphysical Christian prayer. Its task is to align the individual with God's Presence/Power and let good things break through walls of human resistance to greater supply, vibrant health, and wholeness of life. Instead of seeking to find God's Will and grow in harmony with him, practitioners of magic believe they can assert their will over the hidden, supernatural powers of the cosmos.

Magical thinking represents the ultimate ego-trip. People caught up in its web of nonsense try to make themselves greater than God by forcing Divine Power to obey them. This is a misuse of the Divine-human power of Will and represents the very definition of Sin under which we have been operating. The error-belief in the case of magical thinking is that prayer can manipulate God.[7]

2. DUTY – FANTASY. These are two error-beliefs, held on the one hand by fearful people who cling to authoritarian, judgmental religion, and on the other hand by cynics who consider any belief a weakness or, at best, a cheap tranquilizer for the anxieties of modern life. Young Martin Luther fits the first category, Karl Marx the second.

Luther grew up in a world of dark forests populated by evil spirits. God was a terrible Judge whose holiness was so transcendent that no person dared approach him. When his desperate search for some way to please this frowning, disapproving deity led him to embrace the monk's cowl, even the excesses of asceticism were not enough to quench Luther's thirst for God's approval. For Martin Luther prayer was an unpleasant duty. He almost killed himself "with vigils, prayers, reading and other works."[8] Luther's terrible burden was lifted when he realized that God loves us whether we deserve it or not, and the sacrificial death of Jesus Christ testifies to the certainty of that ceaseless love. With this new consciousness, Luther moved from duty to love, and prayer became an act of joyful communion for him.

Karl Marx never overcame his hostility to religion. He observed how the state-supported churches of nineteenth century Europe helped to keep the people under control by threatening eternal punishment and promising eternal rewards. "Endure the inequities of this life like a good soldier, appointed by God to your lowly post, and you shall receive a kingly crown in the world to come," the religious establishment of his day told the people. Small wonder the brilliant, cynical Marx called that kind of religion the "opium of the masses." For him, prayer was fantasy.

Less hostile but more pervasive and more damaging to the cause of authentic Christian faith, is the patronizing attitude of modern skeptics who see prayer as a kind of benign fantasy, daydreaming, or mental house-cleaning. This position is represented by a cliché which was floating around in religious circles a few years ago:

Q: Does prayer change anything?
A: Prayer changes people, and people change things.

At first glance this seems healthy enough. Prayer certainly does change people and people go forth to change the world. But implicit in this exchange is a denial that praying affects anything but the attitude of the person who prays. Psychological energies are acknowledged-- spiritual energies ignored--in the interests of empiricism. One could just as easily substitute any kind of activity, mental or physical, in the above formula and obtain the same results:

Q: Does football change anything?
A: Football changes people, people change things

Q: Does eating fiber-rich foods change anything?
A: Eating fiber-rich foods changes people, people change things.

Q: Does getting a black belt in Kangaroo Karate change anything?
A: Kangaroo Karate changes people, people change things.

Presumably, something more substantial happens when Prayer is offered than this formula allows. To see prayer as happy fantasy substitutes psychological goals for actual power to affect the world through the prayer itself.

3. MIRACULOUS – UNNECESSARY

The final couplet originates with two schools of religious thought. Those who see prayer as invoking some kind of miraculous power believe God intervenes supernaturally in time and space to work spectacular deeds contrary to the "laws" of science, which the same God presumably set up in the first case. Although *deus ex machina* comforts some believers, Dietrich Bonhoeffer rejected an interventionist theology because it contradicts the New Testament image of God's power released through defenselessness. Bonhoeffer's letter is worth quoting again:

> Man's religiosity makes him look in his distress to the
> power of God in the world: God is the *deus ex machina.*

The Bible directs man to God's powerlessness and suffering; only the suffering God can help.[9]

The metaphysics of this passage are counter-intuitive, especially in a Western tradition which considers armed might the sole vindicator of justice and truth. However, the New Testament shows a strange aversion to applying physical force to solve problems. The cross of Jesus, by its radical vulnerability, injects divine truth into the world like a God-vaccine to heal broken hearts, transform lives and move humanity closer to Christ-consciousness. Miracles are not necessary if the system contains self-correcting, self-healing mechanisms.

On the other extreme we have people who take Bonhoeffer literally and insist God does nothing whatsoever in the real world. God is not involved with life but stands beyond it, waiting in the wings for the final curtain. Therefore, prayer is unnecessary. Instead of a *deus ex machina* we are left with a different solution: *Deism*.

As we have already noted, the Deists' God does not intervene in time and space, so God must be beyond this realm of mechanical law. The favorite analogy of Deist authors, appropriately drawn from eighteenth century technology in the period of Deism's heyday, was a clockwork Universe. God created the cosmos, wound everything up, and left it running. God does not return to tinker with the mechanism but trusts creation to operate independent of its Creator. Deism is out of favor in theology today, but many more people actually believe in a deistic God than postmodern theology likes to admit.

The error-belief of those who believe in a miraculous function of prayer stands at the stark opposite of those who hold deistic inclinations and see prayer as unnecessary because God leaves us entirely alone. Both, however, reject the God of the New Testament, revealed in Jesus Christ, whose power is released through living with spiritual integrity and glimpsing his Oneness with the Divine. It is this model to which we shall return for our definition of Christian Prayer.

Working Definition of Prayer

There are so many clichés about prayer that one is tempted to rehash the best of them rather than seek a new formulation. Anthropologist Anthony Wallace defined prayer simply as "addressing the supernatural."[10] The seventeenth century mystic popularly known as

Brother Lawrence said prayer is "the practice of the presence of God."[11] According to the *Westminster Short Catechism*: "Prayer is the offering up of our desires unto God for things agreeable to His will."[12] Macquarrie called prayer "the ways in which the worshipper expresses himself verbally."[13] All of these have value. However, Charles Fillmore gave a simple formula that seems to encompass all facets of prayer life: "Prayer is communion between God and man."[14]

Note the two-way motion implied in the definition. This bipolarity gets lost in all the other descriptions of prayer quoted above, except perhaps in the mystical insight of Brother Lawrence. Not only is prayer speaking and communicating with God, according to Mr. Fillmore it is also God's reply. Yet, prayer is more than a reply. Prayer as "communion between God and man" suggests continual exchange, first humanity turns to God, initiating the contact, then God responds—or perhaps more accurately, people become aware of God's ceaseless response to all situations in life. Language is not required. Adoration of God stretches beyond words to a place mystics describe as *the Silence*. Eventually the shadowy barriers separating God and man begin to crumble, polarities merge into unity, and we see the world with God's eyes, aware of our Oneness with the Divine.

Is Prayer Real?

If someone has been diagnosed with a terminal illness, can words heal the body? Does prayer overcome addictions, heal marriages, swing wide prison doors? Will prayer restore childlike innocence for world-weary individuals who have made too many harmful choices in their lives? Can prayer conquer poverty, find a job, and provide adequate housing? Is it reasonable to think prayer might end wars, overcome centuries of hostility, and establish world peace?

The answer to these questions—which are basically asking, "Can prayer really accomplish anything in the real world?"—is a resounding *yes and no*. If "accomplish anything" means manipulating the cosmos to get a desired outcome, Metaphysical Christianity must reply, *"No. Prayer is not magic."* But what if the question refers to affecting outcomes by centering in the Presence and Power of God? That kind of prayer might actually reverse downward trends in health or prosperity, clicking good choices into place which give the right response at the right time. If prayer operates by letting Divine Order work in and through every circumstance, then the answer is a triumphant, *"Yes!"*

And one more possibility must be considered. As mentioned previously in this study, any systematic theology built on One Presence/One Power would be "unscientific" to allow no space for miracles. Who has not experienced little twists of fate, coincidences that bring glimpses of Truth, hints of deeper programming in the fabric of the Universe, and events which mystify logic and cannot be rationally called anything but the miraculous acts of gracious, infinite Spirit? The older I get, the more comfortable I am with something Professor Gordon Kaufman of Harvard Divinity School said a generation ago: God is greater than anything we can domesticate in our theologies.[15]

Tillich Taken Seriously

During the investigation of Spirit (Ch. 6), this study suggested all reality is an outpicturing of the power of God. Furthermore, Metaphysical Christianity has long affirmed that only One Presence/One Power exists in the cosmos—God's power. This means reality is an interrelated whole, not a series of separate systems operating in accidental proximity to each other but otherwise independent. Philosophically, these ideas represent a school of thought known as Absolute Idealism, which was the dominant philosophy of the English-speaking world at the beginning of the twentieth century. Theologically, Metaphysical Christianity takes Paul Tillich seriously when he called God the Ground of our being, the very Power to be. Not a plurality of powers, God among them, but only One Presence/Power, God revealed in Jesus Christ as Goodness Omnipotent. This makes any movement of energies within the cosmos a movement of God-power.

Power is useless without intelligence, and intelligence is helpless to prevent self-defeating actions (sin) without goodness, which comes from the harmony with Divine Ideas. When we use God's power to attempt to negate Divine Ideas, we hurt ourselves. If we try to harm others we do more damage to our own soul-growth. Any misuse of the divine-human faculties will result in brokenness and estrangement from our true Divine-human nature. Following this line of reasoning, Metaphysical Christianity finds itself aligned with Tillich when he declared that *sin is separation*. Because there is no actual separation from God in a One

Presence/One Power metaphysical system, perhaps a better way to express this idea is to say choosing maladaptive behavior (i.e., attempting to negate a Divine Idea) ensnares the individual in illusions of separation from God and estrangement from other people.

Instead of a God who reaches into time and space to rescue us, Jesus and other prophets and teachers of humanity have shown humanity a better way of living. In Christianity, the divinity revealed in Jesus Christ represents a Father-Mother God who walks the corridors of time with us and expresses the power to heal, to bring forth prosperity, to mend relationships, to overcome prejudice, to let those coincidences click into place. It is a fundamental premise of Christian theology that God acts in the world, but until we understand that God-power represents all energy, consciousness, intelligence, life and strength, we have no tools to explain how God acts without violating the natural order.

God works through us. We have Divine-human powers of which most people never dream. When we bring the Divine-within into phase with the Divine power at large in the world, seemingly miraculous things are possible. Not repetitious movements from beyond space and time by an interventionist Supreme Being, but welling up from within every situation, circumstance, person, or event. Good planning mitigates the need for intervention by God's Hand into the cosmos, and we must assume that God plans well. There is nothing more "natural" than God's downpour of gracious energy and creative power. When we align ourselves with this ever-flowing power, things happen which seem like miracles but which are in fact natural occurrences springing from God's Presence/Power undergirding all reality.

Just as electricity seems like a miracle to primitive peoples, the natural Divine-human powers seem miraculous to people unaware of their heritage as children of God.

Prayer triggers spiritual energies so vast that our limited minds cannot comprehend the pervasive, far-reaching effects of communion with God. Mystics have called prayer is the most powerful force in the Universe and claimed every atom of the cosmos as Holy Ground. When people understand how to pray effectively, all that mystical hyperbole might not seem so farfetched.

Now we have a theological rationale for prayer which reflects solid biblical principles and is spiritually and intellectually sound. Let's turn to application, which this study has continually said is the true test of theological ideas.

Thirty-Six Prayer Ideas

Prayer is such a vast subject that some kind of limitation must be placed on our investigations, so I have devised a chart (Figure 17-1) to serve as a handy reference in this study.

Goal ⇨⇩ Method	A Healing	B Prosperity	C Relationships	D Wholeness	E Guidance	F Illumination
1 Imagery						
2 Affirmation & Denial						
3 Blessing & Releasing						
4 Centering Prayer						
5 Thanksgiving						
6 Adoration						

Fig. 17-1
Thirty-Six Prayer Goals and Methods

The vertical column presents six frequent prayer goals subjects. Horizontally across the top I have listed six methods of spiritual well-known to students of Metaphysical Christianity (See Fig. 17-1) The vertical and horizontal interfaces to form a grid, combining goals with methods in thirty-six ways. Rather than run down the list of all thirty-six, let's briefly examine six goals and six methods, offering touch-and-go examples of how to combine goal with method to meet different prayer needs. We shall be looking at

1-A   Imagery to meet Healing needs.
2-B   Affirmations and Denials for Prosperity.
3-C   Blessing and Releasing to deepen Relationships.
4-D   Centering Prayer to achieve Wholeness.
5-E   Thanksgiving for Guidance received or anticipated.
6-F   Adoration for greater Illumination.

The column of the left represents six common themes in Metaphysical Christian prayer. Horizontally across the top are listed six spiritual practices. Combine the two, and the result is a grid of thirty-six prayer and meditation opportunities which represent most of the New Thought attitudes about prayer. For example, type E-4 would be *Centering Prayer for Guidance*; type C-2 would be a series of Affirmations and Denials about Relationships.

Of course, this chart is an artificial structure meant to guide your ongoing prayer journeys. Other methods and prayer subject might fill a different chart. Feel free to construct a grid that reflects your actual prayer needs.

The discussion which follows could have combined any goal with any method, but I chose to limit the illustrations for the sake of brevity. Once you grasp the simplicity of this idea, you will be able to fill in the remaining squares and access the prayer form as needed. This also meets the goal of introducing new concepts which Metaphysical Christian students can apply to concrete situations in their lives. (Consider the blanks your homework for this chapter!)

1-A: Imagery — Healing

Significant evidence from the empirical sciences indicates that *healing* can be powerfully affected by prayer, especially *imagery*. Several recent scientific works have been devoted to healing through imagery, and nonscientific works about mental/spiritual healing have never been more popular. We can read about a variety of individual triumphs--from Myrtle Fillmore's victory over tuberculosis back in the late nineteenth century to the story of Norman Cousin's successful assault on a fatal disease through bathing his consciousness in laughter in the mid-twentieth.[16] We can examine the testimony of people who were healed of such dread maladies as terminal cancer like Harry DeCamp, who wrote a book about his use of imagery, *One Man's Healing from Cancer.*[17]

As scientific research and popular literature begin to point to holistic healing through imagery, Metaphysical Christian students fold their arms and say, "It's about time." These techniques have been known and practiced in one form or another for over a century.

Imagery is a powerful medical/spiritual tool which functions at the boundary between conscious control of one's thoughts and the unconscious bodily processes much the same way hypnosis does, except hypnotherapy tends to work faster and have less permanent results than Imagery. Theories abound which describe why mental/spiritual healings happen but none has captured the field. We are faced with an area where science and religion must cooperate because neither can by itself adequately explain the phenomenon, yet science and religion still consider each other skeptically.

Although neither metaphysics nor science is certain exactly why it works, we are beginning to understand what works and how to reproduce results with a fair degree of consistency. Myrtle Fillmore's testimony gives the key elements in her own words:

> I was fearfully sick; I had all the ills of mind and body that I could bear. Medicine and doctors ceased to give me relief, and I was in despair...This is how I made what I call my discovery. I was thinking about life. Life is everywhere--in the worm and in man. "Then why does not the life in the worm make a body like man's?" I asked. Then I thought, "The worm has not as much sense as man." Ah! intelligence, as well as life, is needed to

make a body, Here is the key to my discovery. Life has to be guided by intelligence. How do we communicate intelligence? By thinking and talking, of course. Then it flashed upon me that I might talk to the life in every part of my body and have it do just what I wanted. I began to teach my body and got marvelous results.[18]

If this is your introduction to holistic healing, a likely response at this juncture is healthy skepticism. Talk to parts of her body? Images of a kindergarten class pop into mind: *"Good morning, Mr. Throat! Good morning, Mrs. Kneecap!"* Of course, that ludicrous picture is not what Myrtle Fillmore meant by talking to her body. She intuitively grasped the fact that we talk to our bodies all the time--usually programming negative attitudes into them. Doubtful? Check your memory banks and see if you've said any of the following:

I'm too fat, too skinny, too young, too old, too weak, too slow, too nearsighted, clumsy, ugly, tall, short, stupid. I catch cold easily; I have allergies; I don't sleep well; don't have any energy; I have sensitive skin, an ulcer, bursitis; I can't eat spicy food—I just can't do this!

There is a remarkable correlation between what people think about themselves and what they outpicture. More frightening are new studies which show that, among licensed psychotherapists, sixty-nine percent report feeling so personally inadequate they imagine themselves to be impostors posing as therapists. This woeful sense of inferiority which permeates our whole society has been awarded an official label by the helping professions, the Impostor Phenomenon. Dr. Joan C. Harvey, who created the Harvey IP Scale to test for this condition, explains:

The term "Impostor Phenomenon" was coined by two psychologists at George State University, Dr. Pauline Clance and Dr. Suzanne Imes. They had been observing this phenomenon for several years, studying 150 highly successful female students and career women. Despite good grades, honors, awards, advanced degrees, or promotions, these women persisted in believing they were less qualified than their peers. They suffered from a terrible fear of being "found out" as impostors.[19]

Nor is this bad feeling endemic to females. Dr. Gail Matthews of Dominican College did a study of 41 men and women in a variety of occupations: entertains, judges, attorneys, scientists, etc. In this mixed group seventy per cent confessed to feelings of inadequacy and fears about being caught as an impostor.[20] Coupling this disturbing data with what we know about the power of the mind to create conditions it dwells upon, one cannot help but wonder if modern society consists of a vast parade of "pretenders" hiding their terrors behind masks of gaiety and competence while inside them churn self-generated sicknesses, neuroses, emptiness. This Mardi Gras of self-doubt is marching off toward early coronaries, cancers and broken relationships. It cannot be attacked from outside. Essentially a spiritual problem, it must be solved spiritually. The "discovery" of Myrtle Fillmore becomes one of the most important events in modern times. Listen to her gentle way of countermanding the bad programming she had fed into her bio-computer all those years:

> I told the life in my liver that it was not torpid or inert, but full of vigor and energy. I told the life in my stomach that it was not weak or inefficient, but energetic, strong, and intelligent. I told the life in my abdomen that it was no longer infested with ignorant thoughts or disease, put there by myself and by doctors, but that it was all athrill with the sweet, pure, wholesome energy of God. I told my limbs that they were active and strong. I told my eyes that they did not see themselves but that they expressed the sight of Spirit, and that they were drawing on an unlimited source. I told them they were young eyes, clear, bright eyes, because the light of God shone right through them. I told my heart that the pure love of Jesus Christ flowed in and out through its beatings and that all the world felt its joyous pulsation.[21]

Nor did she give up easily. It took two years before Myrtle Fillmore was completely healed. But she was healed, and recovery from tuberculosis in those days was nothing short of a miracle. Word spread. Soon others came, hungry for health and desperate to try anything which offered hope. They got better, too. In a little while the healing work expanded to general prayer, prayer meetings, Sunday afternoon services, and finally a full ministry. What began for Myrtle Fillmore in moments of quiet prayer, during her search to release Divine-human powers to quiet her fears and cure a sickly body, today has brought healing strength to millions. And it all started as main idea—to meet a *healing* need with *imagery*.

Imagery is a simple process which can be done by anyone, anywhere. Simply see yourself as God sees you—whole, healthy, strong and radiant. Your true nature is spiritual, and spirit doesn't get sick. When you realize that you are not sick—the real, Divine-human spiritual being that you are—you release the image of sickness and bathe yourself in healing energy.

There is clinical and anecdotal evidence this works, but the best data comes from personal experience. Work your imagery continually, seeing yourself whole and well. Read good books on holistic healing; many are available these days. But don't substitute intellectualizations for practice. Healing is no spectator sport; to get better you must work your imagery. Best of all is to let God's power work through you by nonresistance to God's will for you, which is perfect health, happiness, prosperity. John W. Adams writes, "Non-resistance is letting go of personal limiting beliefs and accepting the abundant good God has for you."[22] If everyone believed that, we would most likely need very few hospitals.

2-B: Affirmations and Denials – Prosperity

One of the most popular books available on this subject is Catherine Ponder's signature work, *Open Your Mind to Prosperity*. Her 1971 volume remains one of the most readable books about prosperity consciousness in the English language. Written from a how-to-do-it point of view, Ponder mixes prescriptions with anecdotes to make her book lively. Before readers are through the opening chapter, they have met a dozen people who grew prosperous by following the Ponder principles, including a pair of secretaries whom she hired to type the manuscript. The prosperity of her secretaries increased so much that they quit the job before finishing typing the first draft! Browsing the works of Catherine Ponder, one begins to wonder if anyone need be poor. What about the idea of holy poverty? Ponder will hear none of it:

> How in the world can poverty be a Christian virtue, when poverty causes most of the world's problems?...You can open your mind to prosperity by giving up the ridiculous idea that poverty is a Christian virtue, when it is nothing but a common vice.[23]

Surely this is an exaggeration. Or is it? Ed Rabel's definition of sin was any attempt to negate a Divine Idea. If prosperity is the divine intention for all sentient beings is prosperity, health and happiness, then poverty and the consciousness which brings poverty upon humanity is, in fact, *sin*. This does not mean people locked into hunger, disease, and misery by conditions beyond their control are *sinners* in the classical sense of the word; it means the conditions which prevent the natural flow of prosperity to all God's creatures are sin.

Too many people are caught in the poverty trap today, from the crowded cities of the underdeveloped to the dirt-floor cabins of Appalachia, suffering from sin's burdens. Oppression, prejudice, war, and geo-political conflicts beyond their understanding have created lifestyles of lack, holding people in the grip of ignorance, hunger, and disease. Can anyone seriously doubt poverty is ugly, maladaptive, *sinful*? If everyone understood the natural flow of good from God, would there be crushing poverty at large today? Would nations feed the hungry or continue buying weapons to defend themselves against their neighbors? Can we look into the glazed eyes of a dying child and justify the sins of waste, political expediency, or regional ethnocentrisms? Catherine Ponder believes prosperity is possible for every human:

> In the beginning, God created a lavish Universe, and then created spiritual man and placed him in this world of abundance, giving him dominion over it. You are only trying to open your mind to receive your heritage of abundance bequeathed you from the beginning.[24]

425

Prosperity contains within it much more than wealth. Peace of mind, health of the body and wholeness in human relationships must accompany any increase in material wealth or the person is not truly free to enjoy his prosperity. Two questions immediately step forward to bar the way to Christian prayer for prosperity and must be answered before we can proceed.

1) Can prayer put money in the bank and feed a hungry world?
2) Is it a sin to pray for wealth?

Can Prayer Produce Prosperity?

If God (however understood) wants us to be healthy, happy and prosperous (what kind of God would want anyone sick, miserable or poor?), we have two choices when *not* experiencing wholeness and prosperity. Either God is unable to deliver these blessings, or we are unable to accept them. If the Divine Spirit is unable, we are not encountering the God of Jesus. This leaves the second alternative: we are somehow unable to accept the good that God showers upon humanity. Since prayer for the Metaphysical Christian means harmony with the Divine, prayer can align people with God's good intentions for humanity. By prayer we unclog spiritual arteries blocked by negative thinking and let the circulation of Divine blessings resume. The objective of this kind of prayer is not vast wealth (although that is certainly possible if necessary in the course of life's highest good); the goal is harmony with God and enjoyment of divine blessings. Quality, not quantity, makes a person prosperous.

Is It Sinful to Pray for Wealth?

Easy answer: Certainly, praying for riches is "sinful" if motivated by love of money to the exclusion of human values and spiritual virtues. The rich young man in the biblical story went away sad after Jesus challenged the youthful tycoon to toss away wealth and follow him. That wealthy youngster exemplified people who love things and use people instead of the healthy opposite. However, if Spirit is trustworthy, there is no harm in affirming, in the words of the Lord's Prayer, "Thy will be done." And we have already established that God's "will" for all sentient beings is health, happiness and prosperity. Since prosperity is a divine goal, we might well be slipping into sin by accepting less!

How, then, to pray for prosperity? Perhaps the most effective method is a combination of *Affirmation/Denial*. It is an ancient prayer form found repeatedly in the Bible, especially the book of Psalms where prosperity prayers abound. Normally, prayer means talking to God "out there," in some spiritually distant locale. God presumably hears every prayer because, like Superman, the Super-Being has long-range senses. Our prayers fall into the "up" and "down" language of the biblical cosmology with its three-story Universe: earth sandwiched between heaven in the clouds above our heads and hell underground beneath our feet.

The very language we speak still reflects a prescientific worldview; why else is *highest* better than *lowest*? There is nothing particularly virtuous in greater altitude, but people speak of *lofty* purposes, high morals, *mountaintop* experiences and prayer *ascending to heaven* (a.k.a., into the sky). Humans have subscribed so completely to the God-up-there thinking that this up-down language moved from physical to spiritual terms when the ancient cosmology fell apart during the Copernican revolution. Half a century ago, Bishop John A.T. Robinson wrote in his disturbing, delightful little book *Honest To God*:

> In fact, we do not realize how crudely spatial much of the Biblical terminology is, for we have ceased to perceive it that way...For in place of a God who is literally 'up there' we have accepted, as part of our mental furniture, a God who is spiritually or metaphysically 'out there.'[25]

When praying to the God of the ceiling, how many people realize the idolatry implicit in locating God in space above their heads? Metaphysical Christianity begins with God-within, which renders much of the up-down language of conventional piety meaningless. Not that God is absent from the skies or the top of the church building—the direction toward which much prayer is offered. God is "up there" because Omnipotent Good is everywhere, including outer space. However, God's Presence is best discovered by the individual believer at the center of consciousness, deep within. Prayer turns a different direction, if this inner movement is the premise.

Outward-looking prayer usually tells the Ceiling God what any competent deity presumably already knows. In community gatherings, outward-looking prayer can be covert announcements or exhortations addressed to the congregation by the clergy. Inward-looking prayer begins by telling ourselves what God already knows. Here are some examples of outward-looking, conventional prayer (cp) followed by the same need expressed through inward-looking, affirmative prayer (ap).

> cp) O God, give me strength to do my best in the history test. Let my mind be clear and my memory not fail me.

> ap) God's strength flows through me, clearing my mind of stray thoughts and empowering my memory. I will do well on this history test, because God never fails.

> cp) Lord, if it is Thy Will, let my mother be healed.

> ap) The healing presence of God's spirit surrounds my mother, bringing perfect health, wholeness and divine strength. I see my mother as God sees her—radiant spirit, perfect, whole, and eternally young.

Conventional prayer is a cry for help, a subject-object transaction between creature and Creator. As such it is understandable and healthy, perhaps the most universal form of prayer. I discovered that fact in a highly personal way. When the North Vietnamese shot down my UH-1H Medical Evacuation helicopter on March 21, 1971, I was praying to God, Jesus, Moses, Buddha, Krishna, the Mother Goddess—you never know Who's duty office in Heaven at that moment! If I took time to reflect on the matter theologically, I would have realized how irrational my, "Help, Lord!" was in that context. (I have since decided the most naturally recurring prayer in exigent circumstances is a cry aloud to the Great God of Elimination.) Did God hear and rescue me from the burning wreck, and protect me for several hours in hostile country, until I could be picked up by another helicopter, also under fire? I have no idea. But it was a classic application of Paschal' s wager, and outward-looking prayer seemed wholly appropriate, nay, absolutely necessary.

Having said that, I am willing to concede the need to move theologically beyond elementary notions of a Supreme Being Who can be enticed to do good deeds by petitionary prayer. That does not mean praying to God *out there* is misplaced attention. Who has not stood under the night sky and marveled at the vastness of the Universe, whispering a quiet, "Thank you, God" for life and beauty and the inexpressible joy of existence?

Metaphysical Christianity has long recognized is God's glorious inflexibility. In the words of the late Jim Morrison of the 60s rock group *The Doors*:

> When I was back there in seminary school
> There was a person there
> Who put forth the proposition
> That you can petition the Lord with prayer.
> Petition the lord with prayer.
> Petition the lord with prayer.
> *You cannot petition the lord with prayer!*[26]

The Divine Presence/Power cannot do otherwise than shower creation with good. The problem comes from human inability to receive the good, and it is these blocks to divine grace which affirmation/denial seek to remove.

Affirmation ("The Lord is my shepherd") tells us what is true; Denial ("I shall not want") points to untruth, draining these false notions of their potency. They are used in tandem in the most effective prayer sequences. Some Metaphysical Christian teachers insist Denial must come first, cleaning house before bringing in the new thoughts, but many people find virtually any combination of Affirmation/Denial works as long as the essential elements are covered.

Those essential elements include 1) identifying the goal, 2) identifying and denying the power of obstacles to that goal, 3) identifying oneself with the Power of God in this situation, and 4) remaining open and receptive to divine surprises.

Prosperity, of course, is only one spiritual objective

Affirmation/Denial can address. Figure 17-1 shows five more, but the number of applications for this prayer form is endless, limited only by your imagination and circumstances. Nor must prosperity work be limited to this prayer-form, as the chart shows. Imagery, for example, works quite well in bringing greater success, material wealth and well-being.

One popular way to employ imagery for prosperity work is the Picture Prayer or Treasure Map. A handy guide to this technique, is the little book *What Treasure Mapping Can Do for You* by Mary Katherine MacDougall.[27]

3-C: Blessing and Releasing - Relationships

Perhaps more prayer is offered for hurting relationships than any other topic. Primary *relationships* of our society (parent-child, husband-wife, life partners) have never before received such wide attention and never been so deeply troubled as today. Self-help books for parents and lovers line the paperback shelves, most offering excellent advice. Countless counselors earn their daily bread working with parent-child and husband-wife problems as more and more people take responsibility for their lives and seek competent professional help.

Spiritual counselors and teachers who recognize this need can offer their special assistance. Although psychiatrists and other counseling professionals (psychologists, social workers, licensed marriage and family counselors) get most of the publicity and publish most of the best-selling books in the field, the fact is more marriage and family counseling is done by religious professionals than all the secular agencies together. A priest listens as a troubled teenager spills bitter tears while recalling the fight he just had with his alcoholic father. A Protestant minister works with a young married couple in her office at the church, gentling exploring ways they can open up communication and stop yelling at each other. A rabbi talks with troubled parents whose son expresses real doubts about the Jewish faith and wants to marry a gentile girl.

In countless carpeted little rooms, clergy of every faith are doing Pastoral Care for their people, helping them with Parent-Child, Husband-Wife issues. We'll explore this more deeply in the next chapter, when we look at Pastoral Theology: God's Love with Skin On.[28]

Relationship problems usually arise from different ways of looking at religion, life, love, sex, money, child-raising, and role models. Conflicts are often exacerbated by differences in temperament, personalities, and backgrounds. Outside influences can be powerful levers or wedges in the relationship; peer pressure, social expectations, family, church and school can stress a relationship. Whether we are talking about Parent-Child or Husband-Wife/Life Partners, these conditions apply. There is not enough space in our survey to deal comprehensively with problems of this magnitude. So, this study will focus on single prayer technique applicable to most situations, even if other participants in the problem refuse to cooperate.

Read carefully this caveat: This is not a panacea which will cure all marriage and family problems. No such elixir of truth exists because we are all individuals with highly individual needs and complex life-circumstances. What we offer here is a simple way to start employing God-power in resolving problems through *blessing and releasing* all persons, situations and conditions involved. At the risk of criticism for gross oversimplification, we propose an all-purpose formula which allows someone enmeshed in person-problems to avail herself of the power of this kind of prayer. The formula is not new; many Metaphysical Christian teachers use something like this nearly every day when working with relationships.

When you have identified the person/situation/condition which is causing grief, get quiet and center on the Christ-within. Next, follow this guide:

I bless and forgive [Name] for [specific action].

I see [Name] as God sees him/her, whole and perfect, a child of God.

I release [Name] to god's care, sending loving thoughts as he/she goes forward to meet his/her good.

I now release all persons, situations and conditions involved in these circumstances, placing the problem in God's hands.

(Repeat each element three times before going to the next.)

431

Thomas W. Shepherd

The next step is crucial. Take the above sequence and repeat the whole process, this time reversing subject/object roles.

> [Name] blesses and forgives me for anything I may have done to offend him/her.

> [NAME] sees me as god sees me, whole and perfect, a child of god.

> [Name] releases me to God's care, sending loving thoughts to me as I go forward to meet my good.

> [Name] now releases all persons, situations and conditions involved in these circumstances, placing the problem in God's hands.

> (Also repeats, as above.)

This theology of prayer began by analyzing how the prayer affects the world. We have considered prayer as effective because every person is in fact an incarnation of the Divine-human paradox, representing a bit of condensed God-power. Prayer, then, becomes an effective way to unblock the flow of Divine Goodness through persons, places and circumstances by centering on the Christ-within. This is not simply pretty imaginings, but represent real power to make connections, cause changes, and 'click' those coincidences into place. Such power does not come as intervention from the *deus ex machina*. We need to center ourselves on the God-power already available within us and let its healing, prospering, wholeness-making energy burst forth into our lives and affairs. This is the essential metaphysical theology behind prayer in its many forms. Next, *centering prayer,* applied to the search for *wholeness.*

4-D: Centering Prayer – Wholeness

In a sense, if prayer links individual consciousness with the indwelling divine spirit found in every sentient being, all effective prayer is a variation of *Centering Prayer*. This section considers Centering Prayer to achieve *wholeness*, which may include dealing with guilt, achieving forgiveness, and establishing peace with God and neighbor. Of course, people can approach guilt-forgiveness-peace issues through other prayer paths: Imagery (seeing oneself at the foot of the cross), affirmation/denial, and blessing/releasing immediately spring into mind. We are checking off techniques/goals as we travel through the chart (Fig. 17-1), so pairing wholeness with Centering serves the dual purposes of explaining the categories and offering some practical solutions to real situations.

Centering Prayer wasn't invented by Metaphysical Christianity. Centering was practiced in the early Church and revived by medieval mystics like Meister Eckhart. A Roman Catholic pamphlet laments that more people today are not aware of its advantages:

> One way of entering this "secret place" is being rediscovered in our own day. It is called Centering Prayer. The name is new, but the method itself is the Church's oldest, classical form of private prayer. For at least the last four centuries this treasure of Catholic spirituality has been available only to a handful of monks and nuns in a few enclosed, contemplative communities. Numerous books on prayer (many still on our shelves) warned that this ancient prayer form was not for ordinary Christians, but only for a small number of spiritually advanced souls. The resulting spiritual loss was great...[29]

Despite archaic rules, Catholic theology retains a never-ending ability to discover "new" ideas which in fact represent "the Church's oldest" teachings. Thankfully, the "spiritual loss" was rediscovered and Centering Prayer. However, few Protestants have ever heard of the concept. Centering requires three phases.

1) Preparation
2) Repetition of Prayer Word
3) Re-directing.

1) Preparation. We prepare for Centering Prayer by getting quiet, finding a comfortable body position in a secluded location, and then saying a few simple prayers or affirmations to attune thoughts to God's presence. Perhaps the Lord's Prayer, the Prayer for Protection, or some other meaningful selection could be used. When quiet and ready, move to phase two.

2) Repetition of Prayer Word. Since we are praying for wholeness, our word might be "oneness", or "joy", or just "wholeness" itself. If we are targeting guilt and desiring forgiveness, the word might be "forgiveness" or "peace". Find the word which speaks to you. The word is quietly repeated in your mind, always reaching beyond words for the Silence in which we know our Oneness with God through Christ-within. If we have difficulty maintaining concentration, move to phase three.

3) Re-directing. Whenever we become aware of outside evens, disturbances or stray thoughts, just return gently to the prayer word. After completing our prayer time, re-direct thought to the outside world by returning through spoken or mental prayers again. Also, a period of quiet is best before leaving the prayer place.

I have presented a simple version of Centering Prayer, knowing this example can rightly be critiqued as wading into the shallows of a deep subject. Fortunately, deeper study from masters of the technique is available through retreats and courses dedicated to variations on the basic theme. But even the simple practice introduced above will not be easy at first. Stray thoughts will lead your mind far from the prayer word until you have established the mental discipline necessary. Charles Fillmore believed in regular prayer at the same time of day for a prescribed length of time, whether it went well or not. There is something to be gained from regularity, if nothing more than stretching one's ability to sit quietly for longer and longer intervals.

Other possibilities for Centering Prayer have been suggested by other teachers: Twelve Powers meditations, wordless chanting, and use of music are among these techniques. Whatever releases your mind from captivity to linear thinking and allows you to "go to headquarters" will be best for you.

Two more goals and methods remain. We'll review them together, because they're similar enough to be confusing if handled separately.[30]

5-E: Thanksgiving – Guidance
6-F: Adoration – Illumination

Guidance and *illumination* are complimentary but not the same. Seeking *guidance* means remaining open and receptive to unforeseen possibilities, especially when deciding what action to take. Looking for *illumination* means searching for understanding regardless of what may happen.

Prayer for guidance: What shall I *do* in this circumstance?
Prayer for illumination: How shall I *understand* this circumstance?"

Thanksgiving means to give thanks for some blessing, either received on the way. Adoration is love expressed toward God, the Source of all good, however understood. Adoration differs from thanksgiving in that no specific blessings need be involved; it means to love God because God is love-worthy. People of all faiths celebrate God's goodness by adoration and express appreciation through thanksgiving.

Actually, if someone needs guidance, perhaps to take a new job or go back to school, any prayer form in Figure 17-1 can help. Since the goal of this subsection is to demonstrate each type of prayer through examples, let's match prayers of thanksgiving with our desire for guidance. We'll combine a desire for Illumination with prayer of Adoration to complete our packet of spiritual samples.

Thanksgiving—Guidance prayer might raise a few eyebrows as an odd couple. But to understand Metaphysical Christianity as operating according to principles (strong probabilities and tendencies which function the same for everyone) means giving thanks for guidance not yet received can be one of the best ways of opening the mind to inspiration. In fact, if we truly believe God desires all goodness, health, prosperity and happiness for everyone, then prayers of thanks should accompany every other form of prayer, whether mentioned in this chapter or not. Jesus said confident prayer has a life of its own. "So I tell you, whatever you ask for in prayer, believe that you have received it, and it will be yours.[31]

Forgive the anthropomorphic metaphor, but giving thanks for desired good is like accelerating the blessings-chute leading from God's hands to our lives.

Adoration—Illumination expresses love to God for blessings provided and expected in the future. When struggling with a spiritual concept, it is often possible to break the mental gridlock by giving praise and love to God for the blessing of understanding. Contemplate God as the Source of all knowledge, light, inspiration. Let that knowledge, light and inspiration surround and uplift the quest for illumination, so that a dialogue begins: praise to God comes back as the divine approval in all circumstances. Problems fade in a loving sense of Oneness. Beyond words is the Silence, and beyond the Silence is love eternal.

Remember, no formula applies in all instances. These prayer techniques reveal only a fraction of the possibilities for communion with God-within. You will need to try each for yourself, editing and re-organizing the ideas into a network of applicable prayer principles which will put you in touch with your indwelling Lord.

Love in Action: Pastoral Ministry

Our survey of Metaphysical Christian Theology takes us next to love in action. We have already looked at the Church and her ministries in Chapter 13. Now the focus shifts to the most important ministry of all, ministering to people as they struggle for wholeness in their inner lives and outer relationships. We turn to the study of Pastoral Theology.

CHECK YOUR KNOWLEDGE

1. What is the difference between prayer and wishing?

2. Explain the most effective use of affirmation and denial in prayer.

3. What happens when we bless, release and forgive someone else?

4. Describe Centering Prayer; tell how it can be used in daily devotions.

5. What does Catherine Ponder say about the idea that poverty is a virtue?

6. Explain the difference between *guidance* and *illumination*.

QUESTIONS FOR DISCUSSION

1. Bonhoeffer said that "only a suffering God" can help. This is not a typical idea you'd find in most Metaphysical literature. What do you think it means, and do you agree?

2. How could you improve the quality of your prayer life? Does your church afford opportunities to pray outside the Sunday worship hour? What can a local ministry do to promote prayer as a way of life?

3. The author is highly skeptical about the efficacy of magic. What's your view?

4. Myrtle Fillmore talked to her body and was healed. Discuss this method of healing, as well as other healing techniques. What place should medicine play in healing? How is healing prayer different from a chanting witch doctor?

5. Can prayer change God's mind? If not, why bother? [Or: If God knows what your prayer will be before you say it, and knows if you'll receive your healing or prosperity demonstration or not, why go through the motions?]

6. Have conservative Christian friends or family members ever said they were "praying for you," and it felt like thinly a veiled disapproval of your personal beliefs? Can prayer be a bad thing?

- 17 -

PASTORAL THEOLOGY

God's Love with Skin On

If there is any posture that disturbs a suffering man or woman, it is aloofness. The tragedy of Christian ministry is that many who are in great need, many who seek an attentive ear, a word of support, a forgiving embrace, a firm hand, a tender smile, or even a stuttering confession of inability to do more, often find their ministers distant men, who do not want to burn their fingers. They are unwilling to express their feelings of affection, anger, hostility or sympathy. The paradox indeed is that those who want to be for "everyone" find themselves often unable to be close to anyone.[1]

Henri J.M. Nouwen, *The Wounded Healer*

Earlier in this study, the chapter on Ecclesiology (Ch.14) suggested that ministry belongs to the whole Church, not just the professional clergy. There are some functions of ministry which can be done by either professional staff or trained laypeople, such as visiting hospitalized members; other tasks are best done by laity alone, like ushering and greeting newcomers on Sundays. However, a few jobs are significantly specialized as to require the attention of clergy or lay ministers. Marriage counseling is an example of a task which needs the kind of skill a trained religious professional should bring to the job.

All these person-centered ministries of the Church can be loosely characterized as *Pastoral Care*, although it is important to reiterate that in a healthy religious community not all the care is given by the Pastor. Indeed, most scholars in the field of pastoral theology today contend that the more widely a community of faith participates in the caring ministries, the more effective a local church will be in meeting the needs of the people. If this is the case, an effective program of Pastoral Care seems absolutely essential for a healthy community of faith. The key word is "if".

Other Folks Disagree

Not everyone agrees Pastoral Care is important. Some traditional churches see their ministry as primarily evangelical, a maximum of outreach and a minimum attention to the needs of members. Other congregations emphasize the sacraments, or an intellectualized religion, or emotional experience at worship, or lifestyle issues such as dress codes and abstinence from prohibited substances (usually alcohol, tobacco and recreational drugs). These churches often offer a bare minimum amount of Pastoral Care, so their people go elsewhere or receive none.

This lack of services is only a problem if we conclude that Pastoral Care is a vital part of the ministry to the Christian community, and we have not yet made the case for such an assumption. Indeed, some Metaphysical Christian leaders fail to see the need for an organized, ongoing program of Pastoral Care. Some New Thought ministers believe in scheduling no more than a few appointments with troubled parishioners, then passing the problem along to other professionals for extended psychological work or couples' counseling. I have heard the arguments during my years in the field as a minister:

> ➢ *We don't do therapy.*
> ➢ *Our business is teaching Truth, not extensive counseling.*
> ➢ *When people learn spiritual principles they will overcome any obstacle.*
> ➢ *More than 3-4 sessions creates a dependency in counselees.*
> ➢ *Long-term counseling is a job for psychologists, life coaches, and certified marriage & family counselors.*

These are good points, which need to be addressed before proceeding. It is especially important to affirm the first statement above: *pastoral counseling is not therapy.* An understanding of this distinction is a good place to start a study in the theology of Pastoral Care.

Defining Terms - Accepting the Challenge

Let's begin with a comprehensive definition to provide a baseline for discussion:

> Pastoral Care refers to those functions of ministry which help people grow in their inter-personal skills, foster emotional spiritual health, and improve relationships through individual or group counseling; to support people in times of crises and difficulty such as hospitalization, health challenge, bereavement or personal loss; and to be accessible to people through the "ministry of presence" during church activities, home visitation and regular office hours.

This comprehensive, straight-forward definition requires little explanation. If we accept such a broad concept as our baseline for Pastoral Care, we incur an obligation to show how this much pro-active ministry is needed in a healthy program. As we go along, we will need to present honest objections to Pastoral Care as an integral function of ministry and meet these with arguments drawn from Scripture/Tradition/Experience/Reason. If we succeed in establishing the necessity for Pastoral Care, we must then propose an outline showing the essential elements of this ministry for Metaphysical Christian churches.

We are deliberately excluding group-oriented forms of Pastoral Theology in action, such as preaching or teaching, in order to focus on person-centered ministries that generally involve some kind of one-to-one interaction, like counseling, visitation and the "ministry of presence."

Here, then is the challenge we face in our study of Pastoral Theology. The irony of this endeavor is that Pastoral Care is so deeply entrenched in mainline Protestant churches that readers from this background will wonder what else a minister does; nevertheless, comprehensive Pastoral Care is fairly rare in Metaphysical Christian circles, so readers from those churches might wonder why a ministry should offer these services. Since the author already betrayed a bias in favor of Pastoral Care, we accept the task ahead with eagerness to demonstrate his bias is well founded.

Biblical Basis for Pastoral Care

Both Old and New Testaments offer supportive images for a theology of Pastoral Care. God continually appoints leaders who help bring Israel out of one self-imposed bondage after another. Finally, Jesus appears, and his ministry is a mixture of healing, teaching and empowering people. His charge to those who follow him frequently involves caring/restorative functions of ministry:

> "For I was hungry and you gave me food, I was thirsty and you gave me something to drink, I was a stranger and you welcomed me, I was naked and you gave me clothing, I was sick and you took care of me, I was in prison and you visited me…just as you did it to one of the least of these who are members of my family, you did it to me."[2]

> "Whoever wishes to become great among you must be your servant, and whoever wishes to be first among you must be slave of all. For the Son of Man came not to be served but to serve, and to give his life a ransom for many."[3]

> "Which one of you, having a hundred sheep and losing one of them, does not leave the ninety-nine in the wilderness and go after the one that is lost until he finds it?"[4]

> "I give you a new commandment, that you love one another. Just as I have loved you, you also should love one another. By this everyone will know that you are my disciples, if you have love for one another."[5]

Rarely do all four gospel authors agree on specifics, but there is no doubt their written accounts harmonized in the keynote principles of *servanthood, self-sacrifice, selfless love* (*agape*), and the *beloved community* (*koinonia*). This is the biblical basis for Pastoral Care. But perhaps the most powerful argument for the caring/restorative functions of ministry is the person-centeredness which Jesus demonstrated in his day-to-day activities.

Jesus of Nazareth was more than an itinerant teacher with a gift for healing; he met the needs of hurting people at the point of their suffering. Challenging those who needed to be shaken from complacency, comforting the bereaved and liberating the self-oppressed, Jesus shows us Pastoral Care in action. He may not have had a carpeted office with soft chairs and boxes of tissues, but Jesus Christ was a pastor.

When we move into other parts of the New Testament—some older than the gospels—Pastoral Care becomes a routine category for the authors. In fact, the non-Pauline NT pseudo-correspondence is usually called the *Pastoral Letters*, although that is pushing the meaning a bit too far. Still, there can be no doubt that pastoral concerns motivated Paul's writing and the work of other NT authors. How could anyone read Paul's "Hymn to Love" (I Corinthians 13:1-13) and think otherwise?

Tradition and Pastoring

Early Church Fathers saw their roles as *Fidei Defensor*, Defender of the Faith. Men like Clement, Origen and Augustine expended years of grueling labor combating heresies and schismatics on all sides, only to have their own works suspected in later ages. What motivated their efforts, if not an earnest passion for the people of God? St. Augustine's *Confessions*, his spiritual autobiography addressed to God but aimed at the general public, operated from a pastoral premise. Augustine wanted everyone to learn from his mistakes and lead a whole, happy life instead of thrashing about like he did during his wild youth.

> For the space of nine years (from my nineteenth year to my eight-and-twentieth) we lived seduced and seducing, deceived and deceiving, in divers lusts; openly, by sciences which they call liberal; secretly, with a false-named religion; here proud, there superstitious, every here vain. Here, hunting after the emptiness of popular praise, down even to theatrical applauses and poetic prizes, and strifes for grassy garlands, and the

follies of shows, and the intemperance of desire...[6]

One might criticize Augustine's methods and conclusions, but he longed to spare young people the pain he suffered, something which cannot be faulted by anyone who has raised teenagers. His failure to understand human dynamics gave him the illusory hope that exhortation might work with the young. Augustine was a practicing pastor, if not always a successful one. Caring for one another in Jesus' name became a hallmark of the Christian faith. Sometimes this required food for widows and orphans; more often it meant grieving with survivors of the Plague or nursing the bedridden back to health.

In recent times social agencies have assumed some of the functions of the early church, however social services workers tend to be overworked and impersonal, dealing exclusively with people from the lowest income brackets. The government may be provide care, but it is certainly not pastoral. What agency can people call when feeling lonely and depressed, or when they need marriage counseling, or when their mother is hospitalized?

Fortunately, many churches understand the need for someone to listen and offer support; that is why counseling techniques are taught to young men and women studying to become professional clergy in most denominations. This extension of the caring/restorative function of ministry is an important resources today, especially since more people are seek opportunities for personal growth, better relationships, and psychological-spiritual wholeness. As the tempo of modern life increases, so does the need for Pastoral Care.

For example, when divorce was uncommon because sociopolitical factors prevented breakups, there were probably as many bad marriages as in today's easy-divorce age. When Great-great-grandmother realized she was trapped in a loveless, dead-end relationship, she had few alternatives beyond suffering quietly. If she had gone to her minister back in the nineteenth century, he probably would have told her to try harder, submit herself completely to her husband, who was thought to be biblically ordained as her lord and master, and pray for the grace to endure.

Hopefully, few clergy today are offering similar advice. Most pastors are trained in marriage and family counseling techniques, which begin with a premise of equality. The presumption that persons have alternatives to loveless, dead-end marriages is itself something of a victory for Pastoral Care. This means more people will seek healthy alternatives to suffering in silence, and the Christian clergyperson is high on the list of those sought out for guidance and comfort in times of marital strife. The option to change partners or live as a single person has created a need for more helping persons to walk with us as we make those life-shaking decisions. This need is overloading the support-systems of society. Where can people turn, if not to the clergy?

Experience Factor: The Need for Pastoral Care

Self-help books on pop-psychology have never been more in demand. Authors who mix pop-psychology with quasi-religion sell millions of copies to people hungry for improvement in their lives. The phenomenal success of possibility thinkers like Norman Vincent Peale and Robert Schuller indicates how deeply people hunger to feel good about themselves, to get emotionally healthy and have long-lasting relationships. Go to a bookstore and find the nonfiction bestseller list. Odds are, a book on self-improvement, self-motivation or self-respect is among the top ten.

Reading about personal growth, though helpful, is not enough. Real growth takes practice. Most people find that they can make greater progress if they engage in a systematic of in-depth counseling with a professional counselor. If the problems involve a relationship, both parties must be involved and willing to put forth the necessary effort. If the difficulties are within a system, such as a family unit, many counselors believe every member must be enlisted in the solution.

Options available today—divorce and remarriage, abortion or carrying to term, marriage or single parenthood, gay marriage or life partnering without legal commitments—create enormous difficulties for modern people. These problems are complex, fraught with emotional baggage, freighted by moral values which no longer seem to apply, compounded by society's inability to agree on what questions may be discussed, let alone which solutions are correct. When a pregnant fifteen year old appears in the doorway of her minister's study, she is probably not interested in social justice, the prosperity gospel, biblical studies, or Christian metaphysics. She needs a pastor. Someone who'll listen rather than judge, who cares rather than cures.

Objections Still Unanswered

We have clearly established biblically, historically and existentially the need for Pastoral Care, backing those points with reasonable arguments. Yet, the question remains open for debate on a specific type of support usually offered by today's clergy, Pastoral Care with an unlimited number of sessions. As we have seen, counseling causes specific problems for Metaphysical Christian ministers, who are often impatient with problems requiring long-term management. The trouble centers around three objections:

1) Metaphysical Christian ministers are primarily teachers and should not pretend to be clinical psychologists.

2) Practical Christianity seeks to empower of the individual, allowing the Christ-within to emerge; all we need to do is point the person in the right direction and the Divine-human power within will take over.

3) Long-term counseling creates dependencies in counselees.

All three are worthy concerns which deserve separate responses, during which the goals and limitations of Pastoral Care will become apparent.

First Objection: You're a Pastor, Not a Psychologist

That's absolutely correct. The distinction between ministers as preacher-teachers and their additional role as pastoral counselors often confuses laity and incoming seminary students. Part of the misconception originates in general ignorance about what a clergyperson does during the week. Parishioners have literally expected to find their minister kneeling in ceaseless prayer, engaged in continuous Bible study or practicing sermons to an empty auditorium when they wander into the church building on Thursday afternoon. Instead, they find her perched at the computer, looking for clip-art cartoons to paste in the Sunday bulletin, or e-mailing letters to members whom she'd like to serve on the

Religious Education Committee. Under close scrutiny, illusions about the full-time holiness of professional ministry is sometimes shaken.

Even for a clergyperson who puts long, hard hours into preparation for sermons and classes, the preaching/teaching aspects of ministry take up only a small fraction of the religious professional's workweek. A diligent pastor, studying the biblical backgrounds behind his text and rehearsing his sermon Saturday night, might take ten to fifteen hours preparing a well-constructed Sunday sermon. Most preachers feel like they've done their homework if they put in half that much time. If we add the usual course load of teaching carried by clergy in Metaphysical churches--one class per week--that might add another five-seven total hours of preparation/teaching. So, in the case of Superpastor who maxes out sermon and class preparation time, we could foresee over twenty hours per week alone on the preach/teach aspects of the job.

That's half-time, folks.

No minister worth a full-time paycheck works twenty hours a week. There are endless meetings, administrative details, notes to significant church members, hospital and home visits, financial and planning sessions, composition and publication of bulletins and newsletters, supervision of church volunteers and paid staff, religious education planning and coordination, ordering supplies, recruiting workers, long-range planning, retreats, workshops, prayer meetings, clergy meetings, denominational requirements, choir/music ministries to organize and fund, offerings to supervise and bank books to balance, checks to sign, schedules to coordinate, youth activities to sponsor, telephones to answer, appointments to make...If the pastor survives this workload, he/she gets to go home and help with the kids' homework, o the laundry or wash the car, drive the family to the Mall...All this is on top of sermon and class preparations. The minister is not just a preacher/teacher. These other functions must be carried out or, more appropriately, supervised by the professional clergyperson.

However, it is entirely possible that a pastor may see himself/herself primarily as a preacher, or as a teacher or administrator or any other major function of the ministry. If we're talking self-concept, there is no harm in someone leading with his strengths--as long as all the other vital functions of ministry are being accomplished under his guidance.

Setting oneself up as preacher-teacher and then ignoring church administration, finances and people-management is a short-cut to a short pastorate. A large number of good-hearted but inexperienced first-year ministers learn the hard way that a local church is also a business and must be run effectively or the whole organization suffers. This does not imply cutthroat business practices or laissez-faire capitalism should become our polar star; prosperity teachings have shown us a better way. It suggests that the authentic needs of the organization must be met by the pastor, so a measure of reality must seep into his/her consciousness early in the program or disaster is a distinct possibility. A fair number of fine preachers/teachers botch their first pastorates because of unwillingness or inability to grapple with the realities of managing a local church.

Yet, the basic objection makes a strong case; the pastor is not a psychologist but a religious professional. If we infer from this critique that a psychologist "counsels" and a minister does not, we misunderstand the term. According to Rollo May, counseling is "any deep understanding between two persons which results the changing of personality."[7] However, Samuel Laycock suggests that Pastoral Care involves many activities which constitute "counseling" by ministers:

> The counselor must be aware that the techniques of counseling will necessarily vary with each situation, such as, (1) a pastoral call in a home where the chief object may be to establish good human relationships with parishioners and to express the church's interest in their welfare; (2) a call on a sick parishioner where comfort and support may be the chief objectives; (3) the comforting of the bereaved; (4) the giving of information as to where a parishioner may get the help he needs; (5) referring a parishioner to other professional people— psychiatrist, doctor, lawyer, psychologist, social worker, teacher, or nurse; (6) helping people work through their problems in an interview or series of interview.[8]

Note that "changing of personality" is not necessarily involved in each instance because there is a different emphasis here than in strictly psychological counseling. Pastoring calls for a wider, more holistic approach than clinical psychologists usually permit. It is entirely possible that "Pastoral Counseling" may consist of a chat over coffee after the Sunday sermon or a brief discussion in a supermarket parking lot with a worried father whose teenage daughter has announced she has a steady boyfriend and they want to plan marriage.

The common factor in psychological counseling is change must take place for growth; dealing with an unhealthy situation, the psychologist wants to help the counselee overcome his difficulties and make internal adjustments so he can live more effectively in the future. Psychologists try to cure.

However, the common factor in pastoral counseling is not the necessity for change, although change is both possible and desirable in all living, growing things. Some people need a hand to hold while they are hurting, and if the minister holds a hurting hand she is doing Pastoral Counseling without a word being exchanged. The pastor wants to walk with the counselee/parishioner as he treads the valley of the shadow or stumbles about in the darkness looking for light. Pastors try to care. At least one authority on pastoral counseling, Seward Hiltner, believes the role of the minister engaged in such caring/counseling can best be characterized as a kind of teaching ministry:

> The best word to characterize the attitude and approach of the pastor in counseling and precounseling pastoral work is "eductive." The pastor does not coerce, moralize, push, divert, or direct. Instead he attempts to lead out or draw out resources and strengths which can become operative only as they are helped to well up within the parishioner. The eductive approach implies an acceptance and understanding of what the parishioner is prepared to communicate, not in the sense of agreement but in receiving this as the material which must be examined if clarification is to be achieved. This approach is not passive. It does involve much mirroring of feelings expressed. But it also includes frequent definition and redefinition of the counseling situation. The counselor is a person, not a mere bit of machinery.[9]

Of course, there are similarities between psychological and pastoral counseling, especially if done in a sit-down, one-hour, appointment-at-the-office formula. Although their techniques may be the same, the added dimension which religious counselor bring is the presence of the holy, representing the heritage of the Church that drifts backward through time to the primordial faith stories of our Bible. People seldom come to a pastor to discuss specifically religious problems. Not surprisingly, very few counselees walk into the church office and say, "I have some questions about the Bible." They come when they are hurting and need a friend, a shoulder to cry on, a person to help them put the pieces of shattered lives back together. But although religion is not the object of their quest, people know that behind the pastor stands an unseen Presence and Power. Whether clergy feel worthy or not, the minister represents God to them, and this link is not to be dismissed lightly. God may not be not the main topic, but personal faith is inescapably the backdrop against which pastoral counseling is done.

One further point on this first objection: Since people persist in seeking out religious professionals when they face problems, the question really isn't whether or not ministers will do pastoral counseling, it's whether they will be effective pastoral counselors when the role falls upon them. Good pastoral counselors get training in those techniques which help them do their job. Courses in basic counseling skills are available everywhere. Although a course or two hardly gives anyone the right to hang a shingle and bill clients by the hour for psychological treatment, most theological seminaries require counseling courses for all students completing their first professional degree.

Pastors need to know their limitations, too. One of the functions of good pastoring, listed by Laycock, is to make referrals when the presenting problem exceeds your professional abilities. I have done this frequently in four decades of ministry, and never regretted the decision to refer.

Second Objection: Your Goal is to Let Christ-Within Emerge

At first glance this appears a powerful counter-argument, especially against long-term counseling. Perhaps chatting about problems over the hood of a car in the parking lot or even sitting down for a session or two in organized counseling could be conducive to spiritual growth. But if we engage in weeks or even months of in-depth counseling aren't we losing sight of the primary goal of Metaphysical Christian teaching, which is empowerment of the individual by helping him release his inner divinity?

To demonstrate the validity of this complaint about long-term counseling one would have to argue that fewer sessions are better at promoting spiritual maturity. There have been no studies which indicate that abandoning counselees after two or three sessions does anything except lighten the case load of the counselor. Lyle Schaller's research indicates long-term involvement tends to increase the effectiveness of the leader in reaching/teaching the people.[10]

Accepting the premise that a primary teaching goal of Metaphysical Christian ministry is to identify the divinity in humanity, the likelihood exists that some persons will need only brief encounters with the teacher/pastor while others may require more one-to-one soul-coaching. Actually, the analogy of a coach working with a team is wholly appropriate to understand pastor-parishioner relationships. Coaches may not have the level of talent their players display—they are hired to help others play the game, not to score touchdowns or hit home runs. Any honest pastor will admit that there are members of the "team" (congregation) who have more spiritual savvy than the coach does, but the minister is their leader because of special skills and vocational calling, not for being the most spiritually advanced member on the rolls. The coach teaches the whole team, meets with groups of players who have special skills/needs, and offers personal guidance to athletes struggling with their performance. Sometimes a single session will improve a player's techniques so radically that nothing more is needed; the coach has demonstrated how to release hidden potential and the player catches the new insight like a wide receiver racing for the end zone.

Other players need more help, not because they lack talent but because their technique is flawed due to bad habits or just plain ignorance. The coach will need to work with them regularly for a while, offering expertise as they struggle to develop their potential. Of course, athletic coaches have an option which no pastor could exercise; they can dismiss players who refuse to work or are display an inability to improve themselves. Clergy heed the rules laid down by the greatest player-coach of all, Jesus Christ, and drop no one from the squad regardless of how frustrating the task of coaching them becomes. In the gospels, his team left the field during the final quarter and he went to the cross alone.

The key difference between counseling and coaching is that the coach is free to give advice whereas the counselor who wants to be effective strictly adheres to the eductive game plan. Counseling is not telling people what they ought to think or do. In the military, a social system to which I have had some degree of exposure as a twenty-year career soldier, there is an unfortunate misuse of the word *counseling* which gives it a rather abrasive connotation. (For example, when a drill sergeant takes a new recruit aside and snarls, "Come here, boy; I'm gonna *counsel* you!") It also can mean the military member has been officially advised of what his proper conduct should be—"The soldier has been counseled about his duty requirements in this situation."

Person-centered counseling operates from principles which oblige the counselor to function as a non-judgmental listener, someone who reflects with the counselee about the matters they are discussing. Another good model for understanding non-directive techniques, especially marriage counseling, is also drawn from sports: the counselor as referee. In this capacity she functions as rules keeper of the game, ready to blow the whistle if either side refuses to play fair, either during the face-to-face sessions or outside the pastor's office. And a good referee is inconspicuous, letting the team members play the game, only interceding when absolutely necessary to keep them within agreed boundaries. A good pastoral counselor provides a safe arena for people to solve their own problems, which interfaces with the clergyperson's heartfelt desire to care for all parties involved while letting the Divine-within provide each with healing energy for growth and change. Sometimes, that takes more than one or two sessions.

Third Objection: You Are Creating Dependencies

If more sessions are required, what about the last complaint, that long-term counseling creates dependencies and this flies in the face of our goals to educe divinity from humanity? The most honest response to this is, "Right." Some people need to establish a trusting relationship so desperately that counselors do serve as a crutch for a period of time.

There is nothing wrong with a crutch if a person has suffered a broken leg; there is nothing wrong with an emotional leaning-post if some part of our inner life is broken. Who has not gone to a friend in time of trouble or grief? Did we expect our friend would solve our problems? No. All we wanted was a friend to listen and to care.

Humans are dependent on each other from conception to death. Even Jesus Christ needed parents to get started. Our dependencies begin on a network of supporters as soon as we suck our first breath of air and cry for nourishment and do not end until a handful of survivors carry our bodies to the grave. There is nothing wrong with this fact of human existence: who would want to live in a world where each person was a self-subsisting island? It may be more blessed to give, but it is blessed to receive, too.

What people should avoid is unhealthy dependencies, utilitarian relationships based on loveless symbiosis instead of loving cooperation and care. There is a sense in which counseling can degenerate into such an unwholesome reliance, especially if money changes hands for the counselor's efforts. This is not a plea for volunteerism in counseling ministries. Although well-trained, volunteer counselors can be a vital asset to the local church, there is no substitute for professionalism in counseling ministries. However, clergy who receive payment for their counseling services need to be aware of the trap of commercialization. If people feel they are buying mental-spiritual health services and the only effort required is writing a check it defeats the whole purpose of pastoral counseling.

The opposite danger occurs when the parishioner does not contribute anything for counseling. In our commercialized world, people equate price with quality. When the cost is, nothing is expected. Most churches have some kind of written policy explaining fees and love offering standards, or statements of what is expected of the counselee in exchange for no-fee services. These stipulations may sound crudely businesslike, but the lack of clearly defined guidelines communicates disorderliness and an unprofessionalism which does little to comfort the person seeking help. Also, many people simply do not know if they should pay the minister, give a love offering, or just plop some extra cash into the collection plate next Sunday. Even if no fee is expected, pre-established guidelines will answer those questions with a minimum of embarrassment to the parishioner. Church boards and ministers usually negotiate these matters when drawing up clergy contracts. Of course, any official guidelines for love-offerings should contain a clause allowing the minister to waive the requirement in the case of financial challenges.

Short-term dependencies which occur during longer-term counseling, then, are not necessarily bad. At least one well-known psychiatrist, Dr. William Glasser (1925-2013), believed it was absolutely imperative that all people develop and maintain a trusting relationship with at least one significant other. In *Reality Therapy*, the name Glasser assigned to the method he founded, counselors encourage their counselees to form just this kind of trust-bond. Aloofness and cool detachment are not considered helpful. Warmth, understanding, and concern are the cornerstones of effective treatment.[11]

If wholeness and mental-spiritual health are the goal, certainly long-term counseling must be considered an appropriate response to problems which are not easily dismissed. Ministers today are faced with parishioners who are more likely to seek help for deeper, more entrenched psychological/spiritual dilemmas than were brought to the attention to earlier generations of clergy.

In the first year of his/her ministry, it will not be unusual a clergyperson to hear problems which defy the imagination of daytime television scriptwriters. During my first years in full-time ministry as a U.S. Army chaplain (mid-1970s), here are some of the actual problems brought by walk-in counselees: pregnant girlfriends (note the plural), lingering sense of guilt about abortion as a fait accompli, history of shop-lifting, compulsive drinking/overeating, drug abuse, wife and child abuse, incest (both victim and perpetrator), adultery (publicly, caught in the act by military authorities), homosexuality (which the military then considered a crime), compulsive bad-check writing, habitual lying, raging self-hatred, nightmares, impotence, inability to trust men/women, terror of going to hell, incessant fighting between married couples, looming divorce, premarital worries, rape, and suicidal gestures.

Counselors who try to address problems like these with a three-session schedule of pep-talks about the person's Divine-human qualities, ought to turn in their ordinations and open a lemonade stand at the airport, because that is the degree of involvement they are seeking. Short-term counselors won't be able to do their job as pastor of a congregation of struggling human beings. Perfection is a little way down the track for most of us, and people tend to get themselves tangled in the most incredible webs along the way. A fundamental premise of Pastoral Care is that the pastor must care. Not cure; not bless and send packing. *Care*. And caring requires involvement, which often requires long-term pastoral counseling for those who need it.

Which brings up an important asterisk to the above. Not every parishioner seeking long-term help will *need* it, but some will. Providing a multi-faceted counseling program is absolutely essential if a church wants to meet its obligation to follow Jesus Christ in the modern age. There is no other effective way to minister to the real needs of people today.

Who Does the Counseling, and What Kind is Best?

Having said all that, let's soften this rather Draconian pronouncement about non-counseling pastors by clarifying the role of the minister as one who provides pastoral care in ministry without necessarily doing it all himself/herself. Frankly, some pastors would be better off doing little or no counseling, because they have little or no talent for it. There is nothing wrong with a person entering the pastoral ministry who has no aptitude for or interest in counseling, if someone with the talent and energy to counsel is available to the members of the congregation.

There are special skills involved in ministry, and wise pastors know they can hardly meet everyone's needs. So how can those ministers who have little talent for writing still provide a decent online newsletter? By finding an aspiring journalist in the flock and turning him/her loose to create an internet masterpiece. (People will read the newsletter and say, "Isn't our minister good with words!")

How does the pastor who hates to make home visits get the job done? Empowering a cohort of energetic folk who love to chit-chat over coffee and will be happy to call on every member in the calendar year as the official representative of the church. Some jobs the professional minister must perform, like it or not. If she leans toward "not," she should locate someone to help while working through the church financial statements, making hospital visits, or doing whatever it is she must do but doesn't enjoy doing.

Some of the more effective counseling ministries are operated by trained lay ministers or other helping professionals who work out of the local church. In this model the minister serves as senior professional advisor who coordinates a staff of counselors. Large Protestant congregations employ a staff of full-time professional counselors who may be psychologists, pastoral counselors, or even psychiatrists. Most mega-church ministers gave up one-on-one counseling years ago when their congregations grew so large they could no longer perform all the functions of ministry personally. However, they still provide Pastoral Care for the flock by supervising a staff of assistant pastors and other professionals.

Not every style of counseling will work in every church community, but at least two popular methods of doing Pastoral Care seem to interface nicely with the theology and worldview of Metaphysical Christianity: Reality Therapy and Transactional Analysis (called "T.A."). Although we do not have adequate space to provide an in-depth description of these two counseling approaches, a plethora of books is available on each.[12] More importantly, they are simple enough to be employed by clergy or trained lay counselors without requiring that the helping person return to school for a Ph.D. and several thousand hours of supervised practice, which is the requirement for psycho-therapists in most states.

Shepherd's Rule: When in doubt—*refer, refer, refer!*

But let's get one fact very clear: Pastoral Care is not psycho-therapy. It is care by a pastor or a representative of the Christian community. Be a referee if the problems are manageable, but don't take chances. If a counselee exhibits symptoms of extreme emotional disorder, the only responsible action for the religious professional or paraprofessional to take is to refer that person to a qualified psychiatrist or mental health clinic, immediately.

These folks are not hard to spot; your gut instincts will tell you the person sitting in the chair next to you is out of touch with reality or experiencing extreme mental duress. If the counselee reports hearing voices, seeing visions, or any other obviously delusional tendencies, this is a sign the pastor is out of his league with this case.

This is especially true if a pastoral counselor has even the faintest suspicion that the counselee is suicidal. That person should be referred to a crisis intervention center or suicide hotline. If there is even a whiff of suicidal tendencies in the air, don't be afraid to ask: *How badly are you hurting? Have you been thinking about hurting yourself?* It is a question that saves lives. Immediately refer if there is even a hesitation.

I suggest that all Pastors follow Shepherd's Rule: When in doubt, *refer—refer—refer!* Send anybody in whom you have the slightest hint of deep distress to the next level of professional care, to competent psychological treatment or medical facilities When the clinic calls and says the person really didn't need hospitalization, the pastor can breathe a sigh of relief for being overly cautious on this one.

Essential Ingredients for Pastoral Care

So far our discussion has concentrated on pastoral counseling. However, the comprehensive definition we gave for Pastoral Care calls for much more. Education is a major part of any program aimed at helping people "grow in their inter-personal skills" and "emotional/spiritual health." Most Metaphysical Christian churches do an excellent job in this, offering a bevy of classes and workshops to foster growth and a sense of community.

We must briefly mention Home Visitation, touched on above. It is probably the single biggest headache for the pastor, yet the greatest method for getting to know her congregation and enlisting their support. Here, again, the wise clergyperson knows better than to try to visit personally every member on the books during the first few months of the new pastorate. With all the energetic folks nipping at our heels, the minister has a powerful tool to multiply ourselves a dozen times and make many more home visits than we could alone.

Some churches hold training sessions before launching a comprehensive program during which every member is regularly visited at home. Those home sessions are most effective when two-way communication happens. The pastor or church representative listens to the suggestions, complaints and hopes of the visited member. It is also a chance to explain, on behalf of the congregation and pastor, what services and activities are available at the church. Sometimes the visitor hands the member a short form to complete which asks for creative suggestions, provides space to request help for special needs (marriage counseling, etc.), and allows the parishioner to volunteer for a laundry-list of church activities and opportunities for ministry. When the pastor and the church board sift through these records they will get a powerful indication of how they are doing and what needs are not being met. Of course, plans must include follow-up to meet those needs or the whole process will generate mistrust. ("They asked me what I wanted; I told them, but nothing happened!")

Another aspect of Pastoral Care as defined in this study is "to support people in times of crisis and difficulty such as hospitalization, health challenge, or personal loss." A military chaplain whom I know personally was assigned to the 101st Division when the awful crash of that airliner at Gander, Newfoundland, took the lives of hundreds of soldiers from that famous unit. The men on that plane were a large chunk of the community of Fort Campbell, Kentucky. Not only the families of the soldiers, but literally thousands of people at the Fort went through the grief process. Store keepers, neighbors, teachers at the on-post dependent schools, commissary workers, postmen, military police, fire fighters, clerks at the headquarters—the loss affected them all. Even the surrounding civilian communities went through an equally tough time of trial. Just imagine what it would be like if you lived in a coal mining town and several hundred husbands and fathers died in a mining disaster. That is what happened at Fort Campbell.

The chaplains were, by all accounts, magnificent. They counseled literally thousands of people, some in formal sit-down session in the chaplains' offices, many more informally as the clergy in uniform moved about the stunned, grieving community. A force of less than twenty Army chaplains performed over one hundred and eighty military funerals at locations from Europe to Puerto Rico to as far away as Japan. It was a giant, complex, mind-boggling task in pastoral ministry. For weeks the ministers saw little of their own families as they went about holding hands and helping people cry through their anguish, anger and grief. Their ministries drew strength from their individual understanding of faith, because the chaplains represented many faiths with vast differences among them. Pastoral Care is the great equalizer. No one sitting with a mother after the awful experience of crib death, as I have done, is representing a denomination. They are the face of God in the midst of horrific pain, even while feeling wholly inadequate to assume that role.

It is my profound hope that no minister will ever have to deal with grief on the magnitude which the chaplains faced after the Gander crash, but the world is what it is. Sometimes the words Paul heard from God will have to do: "My grace is sufficient for you, for power is made perfect in weakness."[13] We can see from the aftermath of the Gander crash that pastoral ministry is not optional for the clergy in times of acute distress for his/her parishioners. It is at once an absolute necessity and a high calling, a terrible experience which no one wishes to face but which no pastor would ever shirk from meeting with faith in the God who walks with us through the valley of the shadows as well as the spring sunshine.

Tonight when you say your prayers, include a prayer of thanksgiving for men and women of the clergy who have walked such a lonesome valley with hurting souls in their charge. They are everywhere.

Equally important and sometimes overlooked are those day-by-day instances whereby the clergyperson makes herself "accessible to people through the ministering person's presence in church activities" as well as more conspicuous availability at the church during "regular office hours."

The "Ministry of Presence" ranks second only to Preaching in showing   parishioners what their minister does for them. In the armed forces, chaplains leave their offices and venture into the work areas of their soldiers to greet them in the Name of the Lord. The chaplain might stroll through the motor pool during maintenance time, walking from truck to truck, chatting with soldiers about upcoming field duty, inspections, new policies, trouble spots at work and home, personal and religious problems. Civilian clergy, who might only see their parishioners once a week, do not enjoy the daily contact which military chaplains share with their congregations. However, the pastor of a local church can maximize his visibility by a pro-active "Ministry of Presence." Here are a few miscellaneous ideas:

1. BE A DROP IN. When the ladies' group holds its Thursday morning prayer meeting, the minister drops in for prayer as a participant, not as the leader. If he does this once every other month--or more if time permits--he has established a "presence."

2. OVERBOOK THE FACILITY. If the choir practices on a week night, the crafty pastor schedules important, ongoing committee meetings at the same time. This will frustrate some members, because they won't be able to participate in two simultaneous events, which is exactly what the pastor wants. Conflicting activities say, *"Wow. We're really busy!"* to members, establishing an energy-consciousness which translates into zeal. Those members who cannot be at both activities are invited to help find someone to fulfill the other role, multiplying involvement in the life of the church.

It also doesn't hurt church members to see the pastor at work in the evening. This kind of informal contact increases opportunities to approach the minister with personal problems without calling for an appointment. Many people just need a word or two of support and will not want to "bother" their minister with something so trivial by making a full-fledge office-hours appointment.

3. THE PASTOR IS IN. However, the more opportunities pastors provide for the people to speak with them, the heavier the counseling load will be. This means they must be willing to set up regular office hours and make appointments or recruit/ train qualified lay counselors to handle referrals from these informal encounters. Not all the counseling has to be done by the senior minister, we have said, but the ranking religious professional must supervise the staff to insure the job gets done. That means an office schedule people can depend upon.

4. GROWTH GROUPS offer an exciting alternative which blend the best features of teaching and counseling. The Growth Group meets to talk about problems, challenges and questions members might face on a common subject such as parenting, alcoholism, keeping love alive (couples), health challenges, spirituality issues, or virtually any other topics which combine a need for learning with a need for group sharing to affect growth.

If the pastor initiates a Growth Group every six months, walking with each group for about a year and then turning it over to group members to sponsor and facilitate, soon there will strong little knots of people meeting at the church and sustaining each other in Christian fellowship, the very heart of ekklesia-koinonia. The pastor need only drop by occasionally to renew acquaintances and see if he can meet any needs which are beyond the ken of the group. Again, many good books on this kind of ministry are available from Protestant and Catholic publishers as well as secular works on group counseling.

5. SOCIAL EVENTS are another maximum-exposure time for the clergy. A potluck dinner with light programming could be the local church's most effective outreach tool. This also applies to the minister's own in-house program for outreach (in-reach?). Whether sitting down for apple pie a la mode with Mrs. Zuchovitch or a plate of chili mac with Mr. Dohner, the pastor is the pastor.

6. SHOOT THAT BULL. Newcomers to the parish ministry often complain about how their daily routine is interrupted by people who drop in unannounced at the office or who phone for no particular reason but to "shoot the bull." Veterans know that wise pastors never let a bull go un-shot.

In those casual encounters the parishioner tests his minister to see if his particular bull catches the eye of the matador. Sensitive clergy know to listen carefully for off-hand remarks, jesting and other signals that the person is in trouble. Sometimes a parishioner will laugh and say, "Yeah, Reverend, I ought to come see you myself one of these days! Maybe you could tell me how to keep my wife from complaining." Red flags ought to wave when that kind of remark is made, even light-heartedly.

Something about our society makes it difficult for some people—especially men—to ask for help, but allows them to accept unsolicited assistance. This kind of person will drop all sorts of hints, often cloaked in self-critical humor: "With my luck, I'll probably find a job but get fired for running home to nurse the baby," or "My husband is a real dream—a nightmare!" or "I don't drink any more since I bought a funnel," or "Hey, Reverend, how do you file for divorce in this state?" Gallows humor is often a tip-off that something else is likely going on.

There are jokers in every crowd, but some people use humor to surface their anxieties in a way that signals for help but gives them room to retreat if someone presses too hard. "What, divorce my wife? I was only kidding! I'd never consider divorce. Murder, perhaps." If a clergyperson cultivates a good ear and a notebook-memory, jotting down who said what at the Christmas party, she can follow up on those seemingly stray remarks later in private conversation with the persons. One minister known to the author refers to church socials as "hinting parties," an apt description.

7. CARING PERSONS REPRESENT GOD FOR OTHERS. A story was circulating when the author attended seminary which describes Pastoral Care. A little boy was afraid of the dark, but his mother wanted to break him of the nightlight habit. After a few nights of relative success, a thunderstorm broke across the skies. Terrible flashes and crashes scared the little guy so much he ran to his parents' bedroom where he was comforted until the brief storm passed. Then Momma took him back to his dark room. When he implored her to turn on the nightlight she gently refused, saying, "Don't worry about being alone in the dark, honey. God loves you; He is here with you." The little boy replied, "I know, but I want somebody with skin on." That is the objective of Pastoral Care.

Limited Goals

Pastoral Care has limited goals. Although similar methods may be employed, counseling ministry is not psychotherapy. Home and hospital visitation is not deep involvement but an attempt to get to know as many parishioners as possible. Deeper commerce between ministers and individual members will happen only as these peripheral, touch-and-go encounters bring people a taste of church life and fellowship. The final choice always rests with the parishioner, but if we clergy offer a cup of cold water in Christ's Name to those who thirst we have done our part, fulfilled our calling. Just as Jesus is the Wayshower to God, the Christian clergyperson must be a Wayshower to Jesus Christ. It is a humbling, staggering, exhilarating task.

Henri Nouwen, a Catholic priest much beloved by Protestant clergy for his writing and teaching, became the unofficial spokesperson for Pastoral Care. Father Nouwen offered some closing words on this crucial aspect of ministry:

> A Christian leader is not a leader because he announces
> a new idea and tries to convince others of its worth; he is

a leader because he faces the world with eyes full of expectation, with the expertise to take away the veil that covers its hidden potential. Christian leadership is called ministry precisely to express that in the service of others new life can be brought about. It is this service which gives eyes to see the flower breaking through the cracks in the street, ears to hear a word of forgiveness muted by hatred and hostility, and hands to feel the new life under the cover of death and destruction.[14]

CHECK YOUR KNOWLEDGE

1. Explain/Identify: Pastoral Care, pastoral counseling, growth groups, home visitation, office hours, ministry of presence.

2. According to the text, what are some essential ingredients in a comprehensive program of Pastoral Care?

3. What biblical justification exists, if any, for Pastoral Care? Give examples.

4. How does pastoral counseling differ from psychological counseling?

5. List the main three objections to Pastoral Care; briefly summarize the author's response to each.

6. TRUE/FALSE: The pastor must personally counsel his/her people for an effective program of Pastoral Care? Explain.

QUESTIONS FOR DISCUSSION

1. Discuss the definition of Pastoral Care given in the text. Are all the elements necessary? What other forms of Pastoral Care can you list?

2. How involved in counseling should the laity become? What can be done by trained lay volunteers?

3. Discuss the objections to Pastoral Care. Where do you stand?

4. Is long-term counseling appropriate for Metaphysical Christians? Explain.

5. What is the difference between caring and curing? Which should be the goal of a ministering person?

6. How effective is the Pastoral Care at your church? What could be done to improve it? What can you do?

OPEN UNIVERSE

Where Teilhard Went off the Rails[1]

> The palpable influence on our world of an other and
> supreme Someone...Is not the Christian
> phenomenon, which rises upward at the heart of the
> social phenomenon, precisely that? In the presence of
> such perfection in coincidence, even if I were not a
> Christian but only a man of science, I think I would
> ask myself this question.[2]

Pierre Teilhard de Chardin is a difficult man to criticize. An immensely likeable figure, intellectually brilliant and rather saintly by most accounts, Teilhard performed legionary service by moving a positive treatment of the science of evolution out of the classroom and into the pulpit. Even when his ideas were summarily rejected by ecclesiastical superiors, his writings banned, his ability to teach severely curtailed, Teilhard never repudiated the Catholic Church but prayed instead to die without bitterness, a goal he seems to have achieved. By setting an example of fidelity to science and Church, Teilhard made it easier for generations of Christian leaders who followed him to discuss the origins of life on this planet without fear of ecclesiastical reprisal.[3] Finally, because his thought is so closely related to the science of evolution, some progressive religionists are uncomfortable leveling their guns at Teilhard's system without appearing to attack the established facts of contemporary science.

Besides sharing a hesitancy to assail a stalwart figure of such academic brilliance and virtuous life, I am also in the unenviable position of advocating a perspective which differs markedly from earlier endorsements of Teilhard's system in *Friends in High Places* (1985). This requires me to spend a little time refuting myself, an unhappy task for any theologian.[4]

Marie-Joseph-Pierre Teilhard de Chardin was born on May Day, 1881 at the Chateau of Sarcenat near Clermont-en-Auvergne. The family was of the nobility, so young Pierre received a fine education from his learned father and a Christian upbringing from a deeply pious mother. His sister became a nun, so he quite naturally entered the Jesuit Order at age eighteen.

From early childhood, Teilhard was fascinated with rocks and the earth. He followed this interest as a man and became a world renowned scholar in the discipline of paleontology. But his work as a scientist, as important as it was, would be overshadowed by his meditations on the ultimate nature of reality. He was a passionate, gentle soul who was ill-equipped to weather the storms of controversy which his theological adventuring would generate. His superiors ruled that none of Teilhard's religious writings could be published during his life, and he obeyed without rebellion.

Fr. Teilhard wanted to show how intimately human consciousness is bound up with the physical Universe and to point down the corridors of time at the ultimate goal of evolution, union with God. He called this process *orthogenesis*. It was a profound yet disturbing theory. Scientists accused him of abandoning empiricism; theologians said he reduced God to a scientific formula. Teilhard saw it as simply following truth wherever it led. He could not construct a comprehensive theory of consciousness—of life itself—without a spiritual dimension. He believed a program was running in the Universe, nudging, beckoning, urging sentient beings to grow and mature. Teilhard's God stands at both ends of time, Source and Destination, Alpha and Omega, functioning beneath, in and through history as its propelling energy.

> The entire problem, all my attention, the total attraction of my spiritual life, have been focused on this point and continue to be focused there: how to connect within my person the forces of both these centers—God and the world—or, more exactly, how to make them coincide.[5]

Teilhard believed all reality is moving toward Christ-consciousness, which he called it the *Omega Point*. The whole process of cosmic evolution is under God's guidance, but God allows freedom of choice. Everyone shall all reach Omega, but the course of instruction is self-paced. This is not Calvinist predestination but the unfailing movement through history of a Divine Plan.

Did Teilhard Miss the Mark?

Christianity has just begun to discover the importance of his work. However, in the years since the first edition of *Glimpses* appeared, I've lost my enthusiasm for Teilhardian orthogenesis and would be remiss not to mention those misgivings in a Second Edition. I am not alone in this disquiet with Teilhard. In his systematic theology, *Principles of Christian Faith,* John Macquarrie leveled a powerful critique at any attempt to "construct a metaphysic of history..."

> Our knowledge of history is far too fragmentary to permit anything of the sort. About most of man's long sojourn on earth (so-called prehistory) we know practically nothing, and even about the very recent period of the past five thousand years or so that have emerged into the light of recorded history, we know only a fraction. On this basis it would be impossible to pretend to trace some grand scheme in history. The "sacred" history recorded in the Bible is itself only a tiny fragment, and cannot be used to construct a metaphysic of history, although it may be illuminative and interpretative in other ways. Moreover, the fragments that we do see are as ambiguous as the events of nature, and he would be indeed a bold optimist who would claim that he could see in them the workings out of a providential scheme.

Let me briefly suggest three ways in which Teilhard may have missed the mark. First, *evolution is non-directional*. Organisms are not trying to become anything. Plants and animals adjust over time to

466

environmental and social factors to increase their survivability. The process occurs through random mutations, not a programmed flight from primordial soup to beings of light.

Second, evolution isn't about linear change, it's about *stability*. The prairie isn't trying to become a rain forest. Ecosystems seek stabilizing factors like the symbiotic reciprocity of predator –vs.-prey. Predators feed on the prey, which culls weaker members of the herd and prevents sickness and overpopulation. When the predator kills too many or reproduces too often, the supply of prey shrinks and the stalker starves. If an environment offers long term stability, nothing major will change for a very long while. Think dinosaurs. They lasted 135 million years. Absent a meteor hit 65 million years ago which probably drove them to extinction, they still might be grazing the meadows and forests of an ongoing Jurassic Era. Evolution is response-based; it is going nowhere.

Third, *spiritual life requires neither increased intelligence nor growth higher consciousness*. Some say the trees, raising leafy hands skyward, commune with the Universe as purely as the Buddha under his Bodhi. Pragmatically, there is no ecological pressure to rise to "higher levels," which may be a mythic memory of reverence to sky-gods in bygone ages. A koala doesn't need a graduate degree in philosophy to be all it can be. It already is. Although the cosmos is changing due to entropy, stability is the apparent goal of sentient life. With this preliminary critique in mind, let's look at the deeper implications of Teilhard's work.

Orthogenesis and Omega

Fundamental to an understanding of Teilhard's spiritual-scientific matrix is his concept of *orthogenesis*, the inexorable movement of the evolutionary process toward a specific goal. "Without orthogenesis," he writes, "life would only have spread; with it there is an ascent of life that is invincible."[6] Because everything turns on this focal point, comprehending Teilhard requires the ability to grasp his heavy reliance on *teleology*. In fact, Teilhard's system could be seen as the marriage of teleology and eschatology; he offers not just a goal-driven metaphysical system, but also its ineluctable consummation in the *Omega Point*. Without that distant beacon, Teilhard says, evolution

becomes aimless natural selection, i.e., "life would only have spread..."
To make sense of the Universe, Teilhard finds intelligent design
written into the long-running program of life, an onward-and-upward
movement from pre-biological *geosphere*, through animate *biosphere*,
to consciousness-based *noosphere*.

At the culmination of the evolutionary process, all sentient beings
are taken up into transcendent oneness of the *Omega Point*, which he
identified with the Christ. Upon this foundation Teilhard has
effectively built a scientific version of the biblical model of linear
development, creation through exaltation, Genesis to Revelation.

Working the Borderlands

As with many thinkers who wander along the boundaries between
disciplines, Teilhard has been fired upon by partisans from both
countries—theologians and scientists have taken issue with his
conclusions. Given Teilhard's attempt to synthesize two disciplines
which frequently have long been at odds with each other, it could
hardly be otherwise. There are historic reasons for vigilance whenever
theology attempts to verify itself scientifically. So-called "Creation
Science" researchers of today are seldom more than advocates of an
anti-evolutionist biblicism.

However, even progressives can succumb to the temptation to
validate their ideas by invoking scientific authority. Unity co-founder
Charles Fillmore attempted to build a metaphysical-scientific alliance
between what he believed about the underlying nature of Reality and
what the science of his day was saying about the cosmos. As with any
effort to link eternal spiritual beliefs with contemporary worldviews,
the union cannot last. Human knowledge of the physical world shifts;
today's science becomes yesterday's superstition. Ethers and
ganglionic centers go the way of flat earth theory, and a theology built
on the pillars of current science will likely find its temple cracking in
the earthquake of new discoveries. Earlier, this study referred to a
comment by Harry Emerson Fosdick, which bears repeating:

> The fact that astronomies change while the stars abide is a
> true analogy of every realm of human life and thought,
> religion not least of all. No existent theology can be a final

formulation of spiritual truth.[7]

Although theologians need to be wary about the dangers of a mixed-marriage between science and religion, the task of theology in general requires constant correlation with other fields of knowledge, not the least of which is scientific research. Religious perspectives may never be definitively proven by empirical studies, but the very least theologians should do is strive to keep abreast of new developments to avoid advocating ideas based on fallacious concepts.

Teilhard's observations and conclusions have gained such momentum in spiritual communities that a critical response from metaphysical Christianity is long overdue. As suggested above, I will base my critique on Teilhard's fundamental assumption that biological evolution is a program heading for an inescapable culmination in the Omega Point. Furthermore, I will ask whether evolution has any goals *whatsoever*, suggesting alternative views from traditional Hindu metaphysics, early New Thought Christianity, and current scientific theory. I will contend that the Universe has no specific goals, because existence is a workshop with limitless possibilities.

Evolution is Non-Directional

In his essay "The Idea of Biological and Social progress in the System of Teilhard de Chardin," F.A.Turn says the concept of orthogenesis has little place in current evolutionary thought.

> There has always been some difficulty for biologists in defining, from the evidence, wherein biological progress resides; by what precise criteria we shall recognize it in the pattern of evolutionary sequence. The old-fashioned evolutionary trees of animals and plants are, as everyone knows, always shown upright! Yet, to the biologist, the 'lower' are as perfectly adapted to their special habitats as the 'higher'— sometimes, maybe, better and more perfectly so.[8]

Evolution is non-directional. Nothing in nature suggests that evolutionary forces are shuffling individual species and whole ecosystems along some developmental assembly line. Rather than an orthogenetic, onward-and-upward, progressive march from the primordial soup to Homo sapiens, the process of biological evolution is better understood today as a *response mechanism* by which living organisms attempt to cope with their world. Successes and failures are measured by mutated improvements which, in the environment where the organism lives, add survival traits that can be passed to successive generations.

> The survival and reproductive success of an individual is directly related to the ways its inherited traits function in the context of its local environment. Whether or not an individual survives and reproduces depends on whether it has genes that produce traits that are well adapted to its environment.[9]

Instead of journeying along an evolutionary line, or up a spiral path, organisms seek *balance,* a niche they can successfully occupy within their respective ecosystems. They have little incentive to go anywhere or make changes unless required by environmental pressures. Arguably, some degree of counter-pressure against rapid change must be part of any successful strategy for survival. The hunter species which adapts too quickly can overproduce offspring and literally eat itself to extinction.

Consider, for example, the ecology of a prairie environment, called a *grassland biome.* Factors like latitude, soil composition, and climate will determine what kind of organisms flourish. Annual precipitation amount is crucial, because too little water means the grasses cannot survive, and too much rain and snow melt will allow for the growth of trees, changing the ecosystem from prairie to forestlands. The lighter participation of a prairie ecosystem allows range fires, which also retard the spread of large trees. Grasses survive because they quickly revive from subterranean roots after a fire has swept through.[10]

The point of this biological sketch is to observe that a prairie is not attempting to become a forest. There is no destination toward which the creatures and plants are evolving. They will go on happily maintaining the prairie ecosystem, given a stable climate, a balance among competitive species, geological stability, and other favorable factors. If the annual temperature dips and the climate slides into an ice age, or rises and dries up the sources of moisture creating a desert, the plants and animals will begin to evolve as a direct response to this external pressure. Nature will not send a Toucan to the Yukon, or a penguin to do a parrot's job. The long-term evolutionary objective, if nature can be said to have any objective at all, is neither progress nor growth of consciousness but *long-term stability*. Evolution is less about upward mobility in consciousness than it is about how organisms answer the question, "What's for dinner?"

Monotheistic Metaphysics: Time as Linear

The Judeo-Christian concept of time as linear is partly to blame for the confusion about directional evolution. In Jewish, Christian and Muslim thought, God's cosmos begins with a mighty act of Creation and will end in a Judgment Day. Movement through time is unidirectional, from a primordial act by a monotheistic Creator to an ultimate triumph at the end of time. Many Muslims and Christians believe in various forms of predestination, where the choices people make were known to the Creator before God created them. Therefore nothing like free will actually exists, only its appearance. Monotheists who proclaim free will have contradictorily held the result will be God's inexorable victory and the establishment of the Kingdom of Heaven; only the time required until its arrival remains in doubt.[11] This embedded theology plays in the background of statements of faith and traditional hymns. For example:

> Stand up, stand up for Jesus, ye soldiers of the cross;
> Lift high his royal banner, it must not suffer loss.
> From victory unto victory his army shall he lead,
> Til every foe is vanquished, and Christ is Lord indeed.[12]

An embedded theology of teleological triumph comes from the official website of the Southern Baptist Convention:

> God, in His own time and in His own way, will bring

the world to its appropriate end. According to His promise, Jesus Christ will return personally and visibly in glory to the earth; the dead will be raised; and Christ will judge all men in righteousness. The unrighteous will be consigned to Hell, the place of everlasting punishment. The righteous in their resurrected and glorified bodies will receive their reward and will dwell forever in Heaven with the Lord.[13]

While the above texts are light-years away from the elegant theology of Teilhard, his metaphysical foundation is essentially the same. He holds that life is progressing in a linear or, more charitably, an upwardly spiraling direction from Creation to Omega Point. In other words, Teilhard's prairie is trying to be a forest when it grows up. There is an ultimate destination, and the task of human consciousness is to move toward it. The model Teilhard proposes, while differing in content, is structurally similar to fall-and-redemption schemes advocated cross-culturally since the time of Plato.

Footnotes to Plato

Is philosophy wholly dependent upon a Greek who died in 347 B.C.E.? Alfred North Whitehead famously described modern western thought: "The safest general characterization of the European philosophical tradition is that it consists of a series of footnotes to Plato."[14] Scholars have debated the influence of this ancient sage since his long-ago death, and for our purposes in evaluating Teilhard we must briefly enter the fray. Among his many achievements, Plato is also considered one of the major sources of the unfortunate myth of the fallen nature of humanity. In another context, we have already looked at *Timaeus*, where Plato describes a pre-existent soul which lived among the stars until crash-landing on earth where it was united with a body.

However, according to Plato, not all souls can achieve the "perfect order" of reunion with the divine. Plato says in *Timaeus*:

When a man is always occupied with the cravings of desire and ambition, and is eagerly striving to satisfy them, all his thoughts must be mortal, and, as far as it is possible altogether to become such, he must be mortal every whit, because he has cherished his mortal part. But he who has been earnest in the love of knowledge and of true wisdom, and has exercised his intellect more than any other part of him, must have thoughts immortal and divine, if he attain truth, and in so far as human nature is capable of sharing in immortality, he must altogether be immortal; and since he is ever cherishing the divine power, and has the divinity within him in perfect order, he will be perfectly happy.[15]

Classical Christian theology picked up the central themes of Plato's metaphysics, re-baptizing the pagan elements by dragging Plato's soul through the Garden of Eden and insisting that humanity "fell" at that moment in time and space. The end game of judgment at the Last Day adds an eschatological twist to Plato's mythology, which became the fall-and-redemption system of the dominant form of Roman Christianity.

Teilhard probably cannot be accused of advocating most fall-and-redemption theologies, but his methodology casts a hard shadow into Plato's cave. He compares orthogenesis to a pulse originating at the South Pole, so humanity comes from God, moves to maximum differentiation and distance at the equator, and continues "upward" through time and space existence toward reunion with the Divine at the North Pole, This predetermined goal must be achieved in the fullness of time, after which human consciousness leaps out of the world to the Omega Point, union with the Christ. It is a once-and-forever, spiral-linear experience. The destination is set; only the time required to complete the journey is optional. Teilhardian orthogenesis suggests an Augustinian-Calvinist race to the finish line without a stopwatch. In Teilhard's modification, the goal alone is predestined; take all the time you need.[16] While the image of reconvening in divine consciousness is a comforting idea, there are better models than Omega and orthogenesis to understand the purpose of life.

Hindu Metaphysics: Time as Cyclical

Rather than a grand sweep of evolutionary consciousness moving toward ultimate union with the divine, Hindu thought assumes a continually creating, exploring, destroying, and re-creating cosmos.

> Hindu concepts of time revolve around the periodic and infinite repetition of the creation (srti) and dissolution (pralaya) of the Universe. This aspect of repetition distinguishes the Hindu cosmogony from that of the monotheistic/Semitic religions (Judaism, Christianity, and Islam), wherein the creation and the destruction of the world is strictly linear (i.e., from Genesis to Last Judgment.)[17]

The three chief gods of the Hindu pantheon personify this universal pattern: Brahma the Creator, Vishnu the Preserver, and Shiva the Destroyer. The countervailing elements of preservation and destruction are not enemies but complimentary forces, like the Ying-and-Yang of Taoism. A well-known image from Hindu lore is the Dance of Shiva, which symbolizes the cosmic cycles of creation and destruction, which themselves mirror the daily experience of birth, life, death, and re-birth.[18] Preservation and Destruction dance until the need arises for universal renewal, at which time the Creator acts again.

> During a day of Brahma, he wakes up creates the Universe and when he sleeps at night, the Universe is dissolved. Therefore a day of Brahma equals the age of the Universe. As calculated earlier, the current age of the day of Brahma is around 2 billion years. This is also off from popular science, which dates the start of the Universe as 15 billion years ago.[19]

In classical Hindu cosmology, the creator god Brahma remakes the cosmos continually. There is no linear progression throughout eternity, rather the cycle restarts by absorbing that which came before.

Even if enlightenment is the ultimate goal, the task is less like a student progressing toward graduation than Sisyphus rolling his boulder up the hill only to find it at the bottom once more. Nor is the idea of cyclical time limited to the Indian subcontinent. "Belief in a cyclical conception of time was a common feature of Mayan, Babylonian, Hellenistic, and Hindu worldviews, and this was gradually supplanted by the linear Christian view."[20]

Cyclical Cosmos

There are scientific theories which hold that the physical Universe, which is currently expanding in the aftermath of the Big Bang over 14 billion years ago, will eventually collapse into a "Big Crunch" and recreate itself by subsequent new explosion. This process, if it exists, could be an eternal series of creations, expansions, collapses and re-creations, much like the Hindu model.

> In the new paradigm, each cycle proceeds through a period of radiation and matter domination consistent with standard cosmology, producing the observed primordial abundance of elements, the cosmic microwave background, the expansion of galaxies, etc. For the next trillion years or more, the Universe undergoes a period of slow cosmic acceleration (as detected in recent observations), which ultimately empties the Universe of all of the entropy and black holes produced in the preceding cycle and triggers the events that lead to contraction and a big crunch. Note that dark energy is not simply added on — it plays an essential role. The transition from big crunch to big bang automatically replenishes the Universe by creating new matter and radiation.[21]

At the risk of elevating the obvious to the level of cosmic revelation, any divine *purpose* in a Universe which continually recreates and resets itself cannot rest upon attaining a goal at the *end* of the process, since it never ends. Regardless how lofty the achievement, the mills of God grind past the conclusion of time and space into the next cycle as certainly as seasons turn upon the earth. If there is any objective for life, it must be related to the events which occur along the way to each culmination. To offer a temporal analogy, the purpose of an around-the-world cruise is not to return to Los Angeles; the journey itself is the destination.

Purpose without Particulars

If the objective does not wait for us at the end of time, are we relegated to a feckless existence devoid of meaning? When life's purpose must be sought in everyday encounters, humanity will be free to live for creative expression. The focus of life will move from some distant reunion in God to existential chances to love and be loved, to learn and expand one's consciousness; to fill our sails with to the winds of life and voyage to new lands of creative adaptation; to bring forth colors and beauty and music and art; to chase the dream of harmonious balance and find meaning in daily existence. Ice cream and good wine fit the scheme somehow, too. In other words, *the process is the goal.* Like a vast video game, the program re-boots and consciousness re-spawns to play the adventure of life, not to satisfy the demands of a distant deity but for the sheer joy of living.

This paradigm finds parity in the mythologies of nirvana or heaven; salvation or apotheosis; *moksha, satori, parosia, Valhalla* or beatific vision—all final goals are human inventions because people live and die in a linear flow of time. Hindu metaphysics with its circular concept of time frees the individual from the limitations of finite existence. Cycles repeat. There is an opportunity to try it again. An alluring possibility implicit in a recreated cosmos is the ability to grasp a finalized sense of eternity as *now.* This tracks with certain ideas found in early new Thought writers and continued in the works of Eric Butterworth. We need not wait for all the power and love, which will descend upon humanity as it achieves the Omega Point, because the complete package of God-consciousness is available at every stage. Enlightenment is less a journey than a glimpse, more *"Ah-ha!"* than *"Are we there yet?"*

The Hindu model of a recreating cosmos is also appealing because it offers a reason for existence other than to provide a school corridor to march from Creation to Omega. Life is not a passing phase;

life is the goal so precious that the Universe keeps recreating to afford life an opportunity to grow again. In this paradigm infinite possibilities present themselves; life has purpose without particulars, because the goal is not a specific product but an opportunity to try new thoughts.

Carrying Teilhard across the Thresholds

Teilhard frequently speaks of *thresholds* in evolution. One could just as easily argue thresholds in the Teilhardian system are not inevitable but exist solely as human labels; a threshold is recognized not because it is inevitable but because it has been attained. As such they are descriptive, not prescriptive. If humanity were to suffer some terrible, species-wide cataclysm and revert to fatalism or wild-eyed otherworldliness, would that be a threshold? If Hitler's program for racial purity through genocide and eugenics had succeeded, would that have been a threshold? As we gathered for Lyceum 2011, where I presented most of these ideas in a paper, the United States was marking the 150th anniversary of its Civil War (or as we called it when I lived in Georgia, the *War of Northern Aggression*). What if humanity had decided to solve its issues of diversity by holding certain racial groups in perpetual servitude? Would that constitute a threshold? Are thresholds in human consciousness only recognizable when we like them?

The fact that these very real possibilities from the recent past seem impossible today is mute testimony to the triumph of reason over passion, but the game was not easily won, and it is not over. To see the purpose of life in some distant attainment of higher consciousness runs the risk of disengagement with the world, an ethical antinomianism like the Apostle Paul appears to advocate because he felt the end of the world would happen shortly.[22] An emphasis on attaining spiritual goals in the future can deemphasize the importance of this life, making ethical considerations secondary to enlightenment. Teilhard has the good sense not to go there, as his frank confession of faith in the world testifies.

Mystic, Skeptic, Jesuit

Teilhard, as a mystic, is characteristically original. Rather than deny the world for the love of God, he would deny God for love of the world. The startling description of the bottom line in his Credo is more compelling than any argument from the science of his day:

> If, as a result of some interior revolution, I were to lose in succession my faith in Christ, my faith in a personal God, and my faith in Spirit, I would feel that I should continue to believe invincibly in the world. The world (its value, its infallibility and goodness)—that, when all is said and done, is the first, the last, and the only thing in which I believe. It is by this faith that I live. And it is to this faith, I feel, that at the moment of death, rising above all doubts, I shall surrender myself.[23]

If the cosmos eternally re-creates itself, not the destination but the journey is paramount. In fact, in an endless, cyclical Universe, even the concept of life as a *journey* no longer serves and must yield to something more creative. I have suggested the metaphor of existence as a *workshop*, but I suspect there are many other possibilities which imaginative thinkers can discover.

Some images which come to mind as replacements for life as a journey include an artist exploring her craft, improving technique and producing finer works; lovers maturing as passion yields to comfortable presence; spiritual creatives working with all *Twelve Powers* for a life-art expression; the Ying and Yang as free choice interplaying throughout the cosmos; seekers of enlightenment—to use a Teilhardian term—*groping* for new ideas, new forms of thought, new ways to improve on perfection.[24] Nor do we have to relinquish the belief in divine guidance. However, *guidance* is not the same as structure, and inspiration by its nature is flexible and creative. Take take this passage from *Daily Word:*

> Clearing my mind of any uncertainty about what I can do, I open myself to what God's Presence can do through me. In quiet times of prayer, I receive divinely inspired direction. Free of any doubt or fear, I let divine possibilities flow into my conscious awareness.[25]

"Divine possibilities" is plural, because there are always more than one choice available. Metaphysical Christian thinkers, like Charles Fillmore and Ernest Holmes, have consistently held that every situation offers multiple opportunities for love, growth and creative expression. The important point is to free the mind from any compulsion to follow a prefabricated life plan, however benign. As Ralph Waldo Emerson said in his "Divinity School Address" in 1838:

> Let me admonish you, first of all, to go alone; to refuse the good models, even those which are sacred in the imagination of men, and dare to love God without mediator or veil ... Yourself a newborn bard of the Holy Ghost, -- cast behind you all conformity, and acquaint men at first hand with Deity. [26]

With Emerson's new edition of the Great Commission ringing in the independent minds of humanity, perhaps the time has come to release the need for a pre-set destination, trust your gifts, and sail into the unknown with confidence. As sentient beings with free will, we rise or fall to the dreams we create, not in reply to the tidal pull of some distant objective. Nothing is written. The adventure is in your hands.

CHECK YOUR KNOWLEDGE

1. Why did the author say it's hard to critique Teilhard's thought?

2. What did Teilhard's superiors say about publishing his works?

3. Describe Teilhard's *Omega Point*.

4. What does the author mean when he says, "Evolution is non-directional"? How does that relate to his critique of Teilhard's views?

5. Compare and contrast orthogenesis to the Hindu cyclical model.

6. Describe Teilhard's concept of *thresholds* and summarize the author's counterpoints.

QUESTIONS FOR DISCUSSION

1. Do you accept Teilhard's doctrines of orthogenesis and the Omega Point? Is life going somewhere, or is it an open-ended process of response?

2. How has this chapter affected your views on human consciousness?

3. Is the Universe cyclical or linear? How do the two paradigms—linear and cyclical—affect your God concept?

4. Are there learning experiences which everyone must undergo?

5. Without a directional beacon, onward and upward, what's left?

6. The chapter ends with the words below. Your response?

> "As sentient beings with free will, we rise or fall to the dreams we create, not in reply to the tidal pull of some distant objective. Nothing is written. The adventure is in your hands."

THEOLOGY FROM A GALACTIC PERSPECTIVE

What Changes if We Are Not Alone?

With a third or a half a trillion stars in our Milky Way Galaxy alone, could ours be the only one accompanied by an inhabited planet? How much more likely it is that technical civilizations are a cosmic commonplace, that the Galaxy is pulsing and humming with advanced societies, and, therefore, that the nearest culture is not so very far away...Perhaps when we look up at the sky at night, near one of those faint pin-points of light is a world on which someone quite different from us is then glancing idly at a star we call the Sun and entertaining, for just a moment, an outrageous speculation.[1]

Scientific Assumptions and the "Circle of Faith"

While presenting a new look at the cosmos via his book and PBS TV series, astronomer Carl Sagan was well aware that the existence of life on other worlds would be "an outrageous speculation" even for aliens. When John Wesley (1704-1791) was drawn into the ongoing quarrel over extraterrestrials—about which he was skeptical—the founder of Methodism advised the disputants, "Be not so positive."[2] It was a frank acknowledgement that, at any given point in human history, some things simply cannot be confirmed or discounted.

Taking this inability to know for certain as a starting point, this paper will make no attempt to demonstrate—scientifically, philosophically or theologically—that intelligent life exists on other worlds. Countless papers and books have explored that question from a variety of perspectives, like the (2005) article by Julian Chela-Flores in Science and Belief, "Fitness of the Universe for a Second Genesis: Is It Compatible with Science and Christianity?"[3] Nor will I attempt to explain how humans will learn to travel at faster-than-light speeds, explore unknown star systems, or make first contact with sentient life forms which have evolved under those alien suns. With the advance of human knowledge and the proper technology to investigate observable phenomena, questions about the above can be settled empirically by science in the fullness of time. However, because these ideas exist in human consciousness as possibilities that have been neither validated nor invalidated, one could argue they are not subjective opinions but unverifiable theories based on untested facts, which legitimately remain open to scientific conjecture and theological speculation. As interconnected ideas, beliefs about human destiny and the cosmos constitute an embedded, ersatz eschatology by which some twenty-first century people find themselves inside a circle of faith that includes life on other worlds. Although this starting point has not been reached by careful analysis as much as from a science-fiction derived theology of hope, further theological explorations may nevertheless be mounted from this outpost of unsubstantiated faith. Consequently, this study begins with the following speculative assumptions:

❖ Life exists on a multitude of worlds in billions of galaxies, to include our galaxy.

❖ Some of those life forms are intelligent.

❖ Someday humans will learn how to travel the vast distances between Earth and other biologically friendly planets in a reasonably short span of time.

I proceed with full knowledge that, like Wesley observed, all of the above may be disproved at some future point. As our ancestors sailed toward an unknown horizon where destruction might have awaited over the edge of the world, the journey of human thought must continue. For me, this is not a result of some self-conscious leap of faith; it is simply there, an integral part of my embedded theology as a member of the baby-boomer/Star Trek generation.

Doing the Numbers Leads to Ethical Considerations

Although the existence of extraterrestrial life is yet to be determined, there is an impressive stream of information steadily flowing from the scientific community to comfort true believers like me. Sagan said that even a conservative estimate of the number of advanced civilizations in our Milky Way Galaxy alone could run into the millions. Furthermore, our half-trillion (500 billion) stars represent but one of the billions and billions of galaxies in the cosmos, each with hundreds of billions of stars. Even given conservative estimates, the likelihood that earth is the only inhabited spec in that vast ocean of energy and matter appears to be incomprehensibly slight. The famous Drake Equation, which was developed in 1961 for the first SETI (Search for Extraterrestrial Intelligence) Conference, Frank Drake estimated that the Milky Way galaxy alone harbors from 10 million to 1 billion advanced civilizations. With 50-100 billion galaxies estimated in the Universe, even one advanced civilization per galaxy would mean billions of locations in the cosmos where intelligent life has flourished.[4]

While it was Sagan who introduced this new cosmos to a wide span of people, other baby-boomers, like myself, have harbored a life-long faith in life on other worlds. This optimistic view of a biologically friendly universe was cultivated by a youthful interest in the works of science fiction authors like Arthur C. Clarke, Andre Norton and Isaac Asimov. Science historian Steven Dick says that sci-fi literature has broken new trails of speculative thought but seldom receives the credit due for such innovative thinking.

> Although science fiction is often dismissed by serious scholars (and much of it should be), the best of it is a source of original thought that should not be ignored. And of course the alien has been one of the perennial themes of science fiction.[5]

Long before Sagan or Sputnik, these visionaries of futuristic myth gave us faster-than-light travel to distant worlds populated with exotic, intelligent beings. However, the ethical implications of encountering such life never occurred to me until the greatest icon of pop sci-fi boldly sailed where no man had gone before. Previously, alien contacts in film and TV had never kept pace with the rather sophisticated alienology available in authentic SF literature; movies of the genre were horrific caricatures of the creature-feature variety. Then Gene Roddenberry (1921-1991) introduced the boomer generation to his new vision of life in the universe. Although the inane, wildly humanized, pointy-ear extra-terrestrials of Star Trek probably bear no resemblance to any creature other than homo sapiens—they were not even up to the caliber of exotic species described in hard science fiction works of the time—Roddenberry's Vulcans, Klingons and Romulans were nevertheless intelligent aliens sharing the cosmos with us. Sometimes they confronted humans in warlike conflict, but they never appeared as slimy creatures from space bent on devouring or ravishing our species.6 They were not monsters; they were intelligent alien life forms, or at least an anthropomorphic version of the concept.

One legitimate question which has been raised by scientists and laypeople is called the Fermi Paradox. Enrico Fermi (1901-1954) was an Italian physicist who worked with Robert Oppenheimer on America's nuclear bomb. During a casual conversation while lunching with other eminent scientists in 1950, Fermi asked his colleagues, "Where are they?" Everyone understood, although the remark was spontaneous, that Fermi was talking about extraterrestrials. Fermi later made a series of calculations, which suggested the age of our sun vs. the much greater age of other stars in the galaxy meant there had to be civilizations millions of years older than us, if any existed at all.

He further calculated that any civilization could have completely mapped, visited, and colonized any planets it chose by now. But they aren't here, and there is no evidence they have ever visited us. So, where are they? Maybe nowhere, because we are alone in the cosmos. Sagan remarked that somebody had to be first—why not us? This is a hard question for Trekkies and fans of the actual space program. SETI—then Search for Extra-Terrestrial Intelligence—has heard no verifiable signals from technological civilizations after decades of listening.

There are several possible answers to this cosmological question with vast metaphysical implications. First, the density of stars in our galaxy alone is so great that Sagan said a civilization only two hundred light-years away could find itself sorting through two hundred thousand star systems in the neighborhood which extends from them to us. Even allowing them the luxury of Faster-than-Light travel--which is by no means an assured technology of the future--such a "local" civilization would require hundreds of centuries to weed through the closest stars. During that time, who knows what winds of cultural change will blow through any spacefaring species?

Our Galaxy is so vast that it is entirely possible a world with starflight capability could exist for tens of thousands of years and never encounter another technologically advanced culture, even given the probability that millions exist in the Milky Way alone. Finding our world in its spiral arm of the Galaxy would be like finding a needle in a haystack somewhere on the earth's surface from a vantage point beyond our solar system.

If the civilization has in fact endured millions of years, and has the itch to explore, there is another reason why we have not met them face-to-mandible, a thought experiment known as the "Postage Stamp Theory." There may be billions of star systems in the Galaxy far older than our own. Granting that intelligent life with starflight capability may have existed somewhere in the cosmos for as long as our earth has orbited the sun. If we were visited at all, it might have been millions or perhaps even billions of years ago. To illustrate the problem in relation to extra-terrestrial visitors, let the Empire State Building represent the geological history of the earth. On top of the radio tower poking above the great building let's place a one-foot ruler to represent the million-odd years of human life on this world. Next, put dime flat on the top edge of the ruler; this stands for recorded history, approximately the last seven thousand years. Finally, lick a postage stamp and stick it atop the dime; it will represent modern times, Renaissance to the present.

That thin slice of paper compared to the great Empire State Building must be our period of visitation by alien cultures. In fact, we are really only talking seriously about visits after the dawn of the Twentieth Century, when people might realize what was happening and recognize a starship full of aliens for what it was. If Earth were visited sometime in its geological history by more advanced races, the great likelihood is that any fly-by occurred on the sixty-eighth floor, or some other point in the dim, unrecorded past. Perhaps the vessel took images of our dinosaur-ruled surface and decided this was a nice place to visit but they wouldn't want to live here. Perhaps they never came back.

If the incredible volume of UFO sightings in recent years contain even a grain of truth, this planet must straddle the trade routes and be considered quality entertainment for the amusement of starflight civilizations. Two visits every hundred years would make this corner of space as busy as Chicago's O'Hare International Airport at Christmas.

Theology and Exobiology

Interesting as it may be to speculate about UFO's and alien intelligences, we are engaged in a study of Christian Theology, therefore you may have rightly suspected some ulterior motive for trotting out all this data on the possibility of extra-terrestrial life. Alien life forms are the province of the infant science known as Exobiology, and if we are to take seriously what the exobiologists and speculative astronomers like Sagan have said, we are not alone in the cosmos. So far, few Christian thinkers have lifted up their eyes to the heavens and taken a look at how Christian theology must be affected when viewed from this new. Galactic perspective.

We propose to discuss the rough outlines of how Christian theology must change as we look to the stars, predicated by the firm belief that Divine Mind is active wherever there is life, energy, and love. We propose to view theology from that Galactic perspective. Rather than try to establish the existence of alien life forms through further argument, we shall take their existence as a given. We shall also assume that definitive contact between humanity and other sentient
beings remains for the future, despite all the sightings of UFO's and the hosts of cultists who believe contact has been made. Perhaps it has; there is no way to refute or substantiate the claims of true believers.

However, we shall proceed on the assumption that Definitive Contact, open discourse between our species and races from other worlds, will occur sometime in the future but shall not speculate on the journalistic questions--who, what, when, where and why. Let science fiction play with timetables and scenarios. Our task will be to ask Christian theology to reevaluate itself in the light of humanity's quite probable loss of status as an only child.

Is This Approach Valid?

One might justifiably ask if a paradigm shift from an anthropocentric theology to a multi-species, Galactic perspective is intellectually tenable. We know nothing of civilizations among the stars; why not concentrate on the known and deal with the human condition as it is today? The answer to this objection is that one often gains a better view of subjects by bringing them up against a higher perspective. Life becomes more precious when taken to its limit by considering finitude and death. Our inter-faith dialogues disclose hidden ethnocentrisms which become apparent only when we meet others who think differently, benefiting both parties. The same could be said of any effective cross-cultural interaction, like the Christian-Jewish dialogue underway today in Europe after the historic declarations of Pope John Paul II about the Church's sin and culpability in the persecution of European Jewry throughout the centuries.

Someone Stole My Idea—2.5 Millennia Ago!

Early in my career as a theologian, when I began reflecting on the theological and ethical implications of contact with alien intelligences, my first thoughts were rather self-congratulatory as I mused about how very original my brand-new, postmodern ideas must be. I remember feeling like a time-traveler who had discovered an empty temple of the future, its vaulted ceiling incomplete and open to the moonlight. When researching research the topic now, even a cursory reading of available resources indicates that theologically there is very little new under the moon or sun, no matter which solar system one ponders. To my great chagrin as an erstwhile innovative thinker, there even is a name for this field of study, which I did not get to create—competing names, in fact: Steven Dick's panentheistic term cosmotheology vs. Thomas Hoffman's exotheology and its classical theism.[7] There is also substantial body of literature on the subject, and the discussion has been going on for twenty-five centuries! While there is not sufficient space in a single paper to do justice to the antecedents of these issues, a representative sampling seems obligatory before proceeding to the central questions to be considered.

Warp-Speed Through History

In the fifth century B.C.E. the Greek philosopher Leucippus advocated life elsewhere in the cosmos. He was not alone in this speculation. In the fourth century B.C.E., Epicurus would flavor the discussion with these words: "There are infinite worlds both like and unlike this world of ours. For the atoms being infinite in number are borne far out into space."[8] Michael Crowe cautioned against assuming these ancient atomists had glimpsed twenty-first century astronomy with its myriad suns and orbiting planets. Lacking the tools to comprehend Carl Sagan's universe, some Greeks and Romans were nevertheless convinced that a geo-centric cosmology—earth in the middle, starry kosmos rotating across the dome of sky—was a pattern which the divine powers could have repeated innumerably in alternative realities.[9]

At first, Christian authorities supported the idea of alien life. Pope John XXI sent a bull to the University of Paris in 1277 C.E. which warned scholars against teaching that God could not create new worlds.[10] Ironically, the medieval Church was dragging academia toward a wider view of the cosmos, probably to curtail the drift toward unchecked Aristotelianism. Some of the great minds of the time disagreed. Thomas Aquinas, the "angelic doctor" and staunch Aristotelian who died three years prior, had weighed into the controversy on the side of geo-centrism.[11] The discussion continued for centuries and the Church kept producing advocates of life on other worlds. William of Occam (1290-1350) argued for a plurality of worlds and suggested the extra-terrestrials could be superior to humans. Nicolas of Cusa (1401-1464), a devout Catholic priest who would become a Cardinal, advocated not only a plurality of worlds but speculated about life on the moon and even the sun.[12]

The discovery of the New World seemed to confirm that God had other places where Creation continued under different lineages.13 However, the rise of Nicholas Copernicus (1473–1543) split the intellectual and spiritual world between two camps which Alexandre Vigne has labeled Copernicophiles and Copernicophobes. By publication of his 1547 book advocating a heliocentric (sun-centered) cosmos, Copernicus literally changed the shape and context of everything; one Polish astronomer transformed Earth into a planet instead of the footstool of God.14 Although Copernicus never indicated his views on the existence of other life on other worlds, subsequent Copernicophiles and Copernicophobes frequently did, and they reacted with wild enthusiasm or furious indignation. Martin Luther's co-reformer, Phillip Melanchthon (1497-1560), denounced the Copernican cosmology because he held that postulating life on another planet threatened the unique redemptive act of Jesus Christ in this world.

Jesus Christ was born, died, and resurrected in this

world. Nor does he manifest Himself elsewhere, nor elsewhere has He died or resurrected. Therefore it must not be imagined that Christ died and was resurrected more often, nor must it be thought that in any other world without the knowledge of the Son of God, that men would be restored to eternal life.[15]

Giordano Bruno (1548-1600) strongly advocated the Copernican system and saw its clear implications for life elsewhere in the Universe. He was burned at the stake in 1600, however the death sentence was apparently more related to his denial of the divinity of Jesus Christ and an alleged friendly relationship between Bruno and Satan. After Bruno's blazing exit, other Copernican thinkers—such as Galileo Galilei (1564-1642), René Descartes (1596-1650), and Johannes Kepler (1571-1630)— were far more circumspect about advocating the existence of extraterrestrial life.[16]

One of the key figures of the extraterrestrial life debate is Thomas Paine (1737-1809), eighteenth century political revolutionary who penned pamphlets and essays that nudged the American colonies toward independence from Great Britain. Paine hotly contended other planets orbiting other suns would deal a death-blow to Christian theology:

...to believe that God created a plurality of worlds at least as numerous as what we call stars, renders the Christian system of faith at once little and ridiculous and scatters it in the mind like feathers in the air. The two beliefs cannot be held together in the same mind; and he who thinks that he believes in both has thought but little of either."[17]

Paine was called a Unitarian and an atheist, when living in the late eighteenth century meant the two terms were not synonymous. Paine was certainly an anti-traditionalist on Christian doctrine; he took comfort in raising the discussion to the level of extrasolar worlds to make the physical universe incompatible with established doctrines about the Christian Trinity. With countess worlds to supervise, Paine speculated, can anyone seriously believe the Creator picked Earth as his solitary birthplace? Implicit in this critique is the clash between a human-divine Jesus as Second Person in an eternal Triune God, over and against the very likely reality of millions or billions of worlds with their innumerable creatures. Among all those alien life forms, the news from Earth about a human-divine hypostatic union in Jesus of Nazareth would be a minority report, indeed.[18]

Paine's The Age of Reason was a bestseller in England and America, provoking at least fifty published responses. Paine's skepticism, although not wholly indorsed by even the most progressive thinkers, influenced nineteenth century thought through the works of Ralph Waldo Emerson and Henry David Thoreau. Emerson, who began his professional life as a Unitarian clergyman, told his congregation in 1832 that modern astronomy has nullified certain ancient myths about the life and death of Jesus Christ. He envisioned a Christianity purged of these misunderstandings, an ethical faith which required no atoning blood sacrifice to set right the balance of human and divine economy. Thus purified, Christianity could be shared with intelligent beings from other planets as a religion of moral insights and selfless love, without any need to convince aliens of their unworthiness or to promulgate the barbaric concept of Jesus' blood atonement as necessary for their eternal happiness.[19] Crowe writes, "In short, Emerson, as Paine had earlier, decreed that belief in extraterrestrial life entails rejection of some central Christian doctrines."[20]

Two Camps

The discussion would continue along these lines until the present time. Today, the debate among those Christian thinkers who assume the existence of alien intelligent life forms has generally fallen into two camps, i.e., those who follow along the lines of thought sketched by Paine and Emerson and tend to see Christian doctrine, especially the Trinity, as fatally incompatible with extraterrestrial intelligences, and those who want to maintain the central features of traditional Christianity, to include the sovereignty of a Triune God over this multi-species cosmos. Ironically, conservative churchmen often agree with the skeptics, that Christianity and extraterrestrial life are incompatible, but they balance the equation by subtracting the alien life forms, not by amending Christian doctrine. Catholic author Marie T. George writes:

Paine is not wrong to see the tensions between Christian belief and belief in ETIs existence. The more one looks at how carefully all the details of the central story of the universe, Christ's story, is fitted to its human beneficiaries, the more the introduction of any other kind of material rational being appears as something that would be superfluous and out of place.[21]

George even contends that the logic of redemption precludes alien life forms. "If it is the case that Christ is the savior of all the fallen, and if he came only to save humans, and if God would not leave fallen material rational species unredeemed, it follows that there are no other fallen material rational species in the universe."[22]

Putting aside the need to see any creatures as "fallen" from some primordial state of grace, one response to this kind of Neo-Platonic thinking would be to invoke the Aristotelian requirement for observation rather than relying on abstract speculation from assume universals. If humanity encounters intelligent extraterrestrials in the future, which this chapter assumes will occur, George's sine qua non formula may spell the doom of the fall-and-redemption model, if not all of traditional Christian thought as Thomas Paine envisioned. In any case, Paine's two-centuries-old, withering theological critique—that any model for Christian thought based in a Triune God and uniquely revealed in the human-divine persona of Jesus Christ will crumple at first contact with alien intelligences—remains hard to refute.

Rescuing the Trinity

The intent of this study, however, is not to establish the likelihood of alien life forms but to assume their existence and, from inside that circle of assumptions, ask how a progressive Christian theology which takes the multi-species cosmos seriously could inform and assist human thought. One possible response to the Trinitarian problem is to follow Paine and abandon it. However, for some the idea of God-in-three-pieces is so ingrained in Christian language that one may as well try to dismiss Christmas while retaining the Nativity. One possible solution is multiple incarnations. Catholic scholar Thomas F. O'Meara says this might be possible, but it would not involve Jesus.

> "Incarnation" means a divine force or person becoming an individual of a particular race for the benefit of that species ... If Jesus Christ visited another planet, it would be a celestial miracle and disclosure, but it would not be a further incarnation.[23]

O'Meara is eager to preserve the uniqueness of the Incarnation of God on Earth in Jesus Christ while keeping God's options open for other intelligent beings elsewhere in the cosmos. Yet, his cosmology freely allows for separate covenants between God and extraterrestrials:

> However, the divine generosity that led once to the Incarnation on earth suggests that there might be other incarnations—many incarnations and in various species, many creatures touched in one or another special, metaphysical way by a person of the Trinity.[24]

O'Meara's language sounds precisely chosen to maintain the Triune nature of God in a multi-species cosmos without surrendering the uniqueness of the historical Jesus or maintaining his necessity for alien salvation. He clearly leans in the direction of a Cosmic Christ, which the hypostatic union in Jesus represents but which may be repeatable in other incarnations, although he allows that Jesus may be the only Incarnation and therefore of singular importance to the cosmos, not necessarily as an agent of universal salvation but as a testimony to God's value of Creation. "Further, if there are other intelligent creatures but not incarnations among them, then the union of the Logos and a terrestrial human would be a positive affirmation of the dignity of corporal intelligent life wherever it is found.[25]

O'Meara attempts to cover all the options, because to his thinking other incarnations also work within the Christian framework as further indications of God's infinite goodness.

> Finally, if there are other incarnations, each of them and all of them affirm God's intense love in this or that form,

for incarnation for corporeal intelligences is the highest form of divine love; therein the Incarnation on earth finds a wider incarnational context.[26]

Sojerd L. Bonting, an Episcopal priest and biochemist from the Netherlands, says that all life shares kinship in its descent from energies released in the Big Bang. Eventually, matter condensed from this colossal energy-release and formed galaxies from the stardust, which eventually cooled to star systems with worlds where life could arise.

In this way, we humans have part in are united with the entire cosmos, are made of stardust. Jesus, being fully human, also shares in this cosmic union, and thus through the incarnation he becomes the cosmic Christ. [27]

With his scientific look at the true Genesis event, from Big Bang to life on Earth, Bonting clearly sees the human-divine Jesus having the same common origin in stardust, which makes the man of Nazareth a brother creature to any physical or energetic form which may exist on any world in the cosmos. The Incarnation is literally for all times and places.

Another way to deal with the problem of the uniqueness of Jesus as Second Person of the Trinity is to unapologetically affirm it wherever humans may roam. For example, Thomas Hoffman has called for an "exomissiology" to raise the Christian mission field to a vast new level and teach all nations throughout the universe. When considering a possible Christian mission to other intelligent species, Hoffman attempts to chart a careful course between outright evangelization and liberation theology, although one might legitimately ask what kind of missiology would not be either invasive or imperialistic when presented to tribes of extraterrestrials who doubtless have their own cultural set of theologies and religious traditions.[28]

Monistic Panentheism

Another way to mitigate the damage to Trinitarian theology when it is raised to a galactic standard might be to re-work Steve Dick's cosmotheology through the lens of monistic panentheism. This model, advocated by New Thought Christianity, separates the Christ from the historical Jesus. The Christ becomes the divinity in all sentient beings, not just in the man of Nazareth, even though Jesus is seen as a supreme example of the Christ presence and divine potential of everyone. For a representative example, Charles Fillmore described the inner Christ:

> The Son of God or spiritual nucleus within each person. All our thoughts must harmonize with this spiritual center before we can bring into expression the divine consciousness. Each man has within himself the Christ idea, just as Jesus had. Man must look to the indwelling Christ in order to recognize his sonship, his divine origin and birth, even as did the Saviour.[29]

This universalization of both imago Dei and incarnational theology shows great promise as a basis for a Christian theology which could interact easily with other sentient life in the cosmos. If the Incarnation present in Jesus is the same Divine Mind which permeates the Cosmos, then all sentient beings might be plugged into this network, albeit unconsciously at first. If God-Mind is available to all intelligences, sooner or later all sentient beings must realize their link to the Divine-within, become fully one with God like Jesus of Nazareth, and thus become the Christ, regardless what terms we use for this culmination. "Alien" or "human" is irrelevant; the package makes no difference.[30]

Revolting Development

Christian theology has undergone frequent revolutions in its long history, although most are now taken for granted. We mentioned previously that the up/down language of the ancient world--which the biblical authors took as actual spatial references, since God lived "up there" in the clouds and the land of the dead was "down there" below the flat earth--has been spiritualized by most Christians ever since the earth lost its place as the center of the Universe after Copernicus. God is no longer physically "up there" but has moved to another   dimension, spiritually "up there." Beyond the shrinking fundamentalist fringe, no reputable theologian takes Genesis literally. It, too, has been spiritualized to mean "God created everything" without the crude mechanics of mud-scooping and rib-snatching to bring about man and woman.

Revolutions in Christian thought are barely beginning to seep down from the walls of the ivory towers to the people in the pew. Reading twentieth century theology, students discover pioneers like Rudolf Bultmann, who insisted on "demythologizing" the biblical message of its pre-scientific worldview; Paul Tillich, who said God does not "exist" but is the very Power of existence itself; and Pierre Teilhard de Chardin, who held that sentient life evolves because God has programmed the very atoms of the Universe to yearn for union with the Divine.

With "revolting developments" like these just beginning to draw the attention of the laity, perhaps there is hope for Christian theology after all. Provided, of course, that all the folks turned off by fundamentalism and literalism have not already abandoned Christianity for secular philosophies or Pop-Fad Spirituality by the time these "new" ideas reach the people at First Downtown Church. Fortunately for Metaphysical Christianity, new ideas are not generally a threat to the kind of seeking person who wanders into a Metaphysical Christian Church.

However, before descending into theological elitism, let's hasten to add that there are vast numbers of people in Protestant, Roman Catholic and Orthodox churches equally eager to hear the old, old story told in the language and of today. Courageous scholars, teachers, authors and clergy of every denomination are doing just that, even while exposing themselves to criticism and risking job security by chipping away the comfortable crust of centuries. With pro-active Pastoral Care and a well-balanced theology, priests and ministers are struggling to bring the truth of Jesus Christ to people who live in a space age world.

If we take the modern world seriously, we must ask our spiritual insights to operate in the light of a radically different cosmos than faced our ancestors a few generations ago. Is it not, therefore, an acceptable risk to look forward and outward to find still another method of comparison which might give us pause to reconsider our deepest beliefs?

If we take the postmodern world seriously, we must accept the strong likelihood humanity is not the only intelligent species in the cosmos. Sober reflection from this vantage point will call for profound changes in Christian thought. We quoted Professor John Macquarrie on this subject in another context, but his point is worth repeating because it tolls like a bell at midnight: "The overwhelming probability is that countless billions of 'histories' have been enacted in the cosmos, and a space-age cosmology calls for a vastly enlarged understanding of divine grace and revelation."[31]

We shall look boldly forward and outward, accepting Macquarrie's challenge to enlarge "our understanding of divine grace and revelation." Although one could re-write an entire systematic theology from the Galactic Perspective, we shall limit our discussion to three areas: Christology, soteriology, and social ethics.

First Problem: Christology

The assumption that the cosmos is teeming with sentient life calls for a radical reorientation in the orthodox position on the nature and person of Jesus Christ. Given the probability of intelligent life on other worlds, the claim that the Jesus-event represents God's definitive self-disclosure for all time and space makes little sense. Without raising the issue of non-human intelligences,   theologians today are already asking hard questions about his uniqueness. John Macquarrie believes God works through other faiths to bring the same kind of Good News that Jesus Christ represents to us. It is only a slight extrapolation to conclude God is also at work in all locations where sentient beings yearn for truth.

Classical Trinitarian Christology will not bend this far. A uniquely divine, pre-existent Son of God does not translate easily into a reproducible paradigm for alien worlds. If the man of Nazareth was the Second Person in the Trinity, he and he alone partaking of full divinity with the Father and the Holy Spirit, then extra-terrestrial religions could be nothing but philosophical constructs offering neither grace nor revelation. "Discovery," at best, could be found in their religious views, provided they stumbled on some of the principles revealed by Jesus in his onetime appearance on earth. Authentic commerce with God would be ruled out because non-terrestrials have no access to the sole point of contact between sentient beings and Omniscient, Triune Divinity.

With Classical Christology, we are locked into an elitist view which says, in effect: The only Son of God was born in a small town on the eastern shore of a small sea of a small planet lost somewhere in a spiral arm of an average-sized galaxy. One incarnation of God for millions of potentially inhabited worlds in our galaxy alone, in a cosmos of perhaps 100 billion galaxies? When we raise Christology to a Galactic perspective, the unique divinity of Jesus becomes not just impossible to defend rationally. It becomes ridiculous.

However, if the divinity of Jesus were taken as typical rather than unique, which is the position virtually all Metaphysical Christian teachers have advocated, then it does not matter whether the person is a human being or an alien life form, he/she/it will possess the Christ-within. If the true nature of all   sentient life is spirit, the outer form is almost irrelevant, an outpicturing of organic evolution tempered by climate, chance and chemistry.

Would the music of Handel, Brahms and Beethoven be less breath-taking if created by gifted marsupials on a ringed world with ten moons? Would the sublime concepts of mathematics or the majesty of the Psalms diminish if non-human hands scratched the ideas in an unknown script under a double-sun? Some types of knowledge would be affected, notably social sciences. But intelligent beings in any form will need psychologists and counselors to help them with their problems, philosophers and theologians to wrestle with the hard questions of life, artists and musicians to bring beauty to their world. Where there is life, love and intelligence, God is. Fillmore wrote in *Keep a true Lent*:

> God-mind is located and appears wherever it is recognized by the mind of man. It thus follows that whoever gives his attention to Spirit and seals his identification with it by his word (the Son) starts a flow of Spirit life and all the attributes of Spirit in and through his consciousness. To the extent that he practices identifying himself with the one and only source of existence, he becomes Spirit in expression, until finally the union attains a perfection in which he can say with Jesus, "I and the Father are one."[32]

Rather than creating a problem, raising Christology to a Galactic Perspective validates the deepest theological insights of Metaphysical Christianity into the nature of the Divine-human paradox. We would need only to modify our terms and begin speaking of the "Divine-sentient being paradox."

Second Problem: Soteriology

Once again, classical theology crash-lands in difficulties when its ethnocentrisms are raised to the Galactic Perspective. Let us state the problem fairly without puffing up straw men: Universalism (the belief in salvation for everyone) contradicts the necessity for Christian commitment, yet both are necessary for Christianity in the modern age. The problem breaks down into two sub-points.

First, except for the evangelical wing of American Protestantism, modern theology does not believe in a literal, burning hell. It is somewhat wearisome to reiterate this point continually to groups of Metaphysical Christians and other religious progressives who, frustrated by the vociferous proclamation of an archaic "turn or burn" theology by the Christian Right, simply refuse to believe heaven-or-hellfire is not the viewpoint of Christianity in general. Pervious chapters have repeatedly identified universalism as the dominant, default theological position of mainline Protestant and liberal Catholic thinking today. Recently, even Pope Francis has leaned in the direction of universalism. Making this point one more time, I am certain some people holding this book are shaking their heads in disbelief.

The second sub-point in soteriology raises a more difficult issue— one-way or no way? Even with theology's almost unanimous universalism there remains a hidden problem implicit in any Christocentric system: If Jesus Christ is the way to knowledge of God, how can a person find God without Jesus? And if there are other paths to God, why follow Jesus instead of another Wayshower, or take no guide at all? We discussed this problem earlier, but the complaint rings like a farm bell when the barnyard of human thought expands to a galactic perspective. How can an alien come to a "saving knowledge" of God without Jesus Christ? Opening the barn door and saddling up the old nag of Gnosticism (i.e., knowledge is required, not faith) merely changes horses without changing the difficult terrain ahead.

The difficulty for the progressive Christian confronted by a non-Christian culture, whether terrestrial or ET, centers on the question of exceptionalism, which links this or that group to the divine plan by special covenants enacted through history. Exceptionalism has become a political term of some consequence in the early decades of the twenty-first century. To avoid charges of being unpatriotic, politicians in the

USA are required to affirm their belief in American exceptionalism, i.e., the United States is uniquely blessed with democratic virtues and a history of righting the wrongs of the world, so that the USA is a beacon light for humanity. Flagrant ethnocentrism aside, other nations on this planet have held the exceptionalism perspective, and their names are not as pristine today.

Moving the exceptionalism argument to religion, Christianity so special that everyone—even extraterrestrials—need to hear its teachings? Softening the consequences of non-belief fails to solve square the circle of faith and universalism. If we say there is no hell, we must at least allow that belief in Jesus Christ provides some kind of benefit, or what right do we have to call it "saving" anything? Perhaps the benefits are a better life, warmer relationships, peace of mind, or some sort of empowerment. The goal is almost irrelevant. The question is whether salvation, however defined, comes exclusively through the agency of Jesus, is essentially the same question one might ask about the well-read Hindu who rejects Christian faith because it won't work for him in his milieu. Classical theology would have snorted at him, "I hope you like warm climates!" But today's liberal Christians are caught in a bind; they know there is no hell, but they feel that faith in Jesus is nevertheless the best way for everyone.

If saving knowledge/faith comes only through God's self-disclosure in Jesus Christ, as Karl Barth and others insisted, there is no possible way an alien being could be held accountable for lack of faith. Yet, what alternatives are left? Should a follower of Jesus say, "Faith in Jesus is not required for any kind of spiritual benefit," (invalidating the need to follow Jesus), or say, "Faith in Jesus is required for salvation!" (binding God's truth to a geographical accident of birth).

Even a benign One-Way theology, based on universalism, is still a One-Way theology. But a limp heterodoxy which calls for commitment to Jesus makes no sense. This is a profoundly difficult question and the ambivalence of mainline liberal clergy on this issue can be felt in their sermons, prayers, and programs. Is there any way out of this predicament? Once again, we return to theology's favorite battle-cry when riding the horns of a dilemma: Yes and No.

If we maintain the unique divinity of Jesus Christ as the gateway to salvation (enlightenment, better life, whatever), the answer is no, for all the reasons discussed above. If Jesus is the one Key which unlocks the door to eternal life, love and happiness, we are forever trapped in the logical inconsistency of Christian universalism as an avenue to spiritual benefits not obtainable elsewhere. With neither penalties nor rewards for ejecting/embracing Christianity, doesn't the faith become a moot point?

Is there any value in embracing a religion which fails to distinguish itself from other worldviews by its mindless open-mindedness? However, if we distinguish between faith in Jesus and faith in the Christ, we hear theology's "Yes!" to the question, "Is there any way out of this predicament?"

Students of Metaphysical Christianity will immediately grasp the difference. The classical viewpoint requires every sentient being to see the Christ in Jesus. Only when we eliminate the exclusive divinity of Jesus of Nazareth does Christianity survive the galactic test. Christian theology has rightly insisted that Jesus represents a hypostasis, a union in which his divine and human natures are fully integrated to form one unitary being. Metaphysical Christianity calls that union Christ-consciousness and sees it as ultimately normative for all thinking/feeling entities, human or extra-terrestrial. Christ-consciousness, as the basic nature of all sentient life forms, validates both historic Christianity, in its grasp of the Divine-human paradox represented by Jesus of Nazareth, and postmodern Christian theology with its profound insights about the universality of God's love.

Only Christian panentheism, grounded in Christ-consciousness, allows humanity to look upward and outward to unknown races without the smug superiority of bygone eras when rival factions within the Christian camp pronounced anathemas upon each other with self-righteous confidence that their piece of the cosmic puzzle constituted the whole. Hopefully, Metaphysical Christianity will welcome the chance to discover truth which the Christ-within has spoken to nonhuman religions, even while fully committed to the Wayshower of Christ-consciousness, Jesus of Nazareth.

Third Problem: Social Ethics

War and peace issues dominated social ethics during the twentieth century, which indicated theology was attempting to grapple with the real problems of life. May 3, 1983 the National Conference of Roman Catholic Bishops of the United States approved their now-famous pastoral letter on war/peace issues entitled The Challenge of Peace: God's Promise and our Response. This letter is built on the 1963 encyclical of Pope John XXIII known as "Pacem in Terris" (Peace on Earth). Both called upon Christians and non-Christians alike to make all reasonable efforts to reduce the risk of nuclear war by multilateral disarmament. John XXIII wrote:

> Justice, right reason and harmony...urgently demand that the arms race should cease; that the stockpiles which exist in various countries should be reduced equally and simultaneously by the parties concerned; that nuclear weapons should be banned; and that a general agreement should eventually be reached about progressive disarmament and an effective method of control.[33]

The bishops went beyond this to recognize no peace is possible unless the "effective method of control" included more than promises of on-site inspections. Their letter hints that peace must be accompanied by some sort of political union:

> We support, in an increasingly interdependent world, political and economic policies designed to promote the human rights of every person, especially the least among us. In this regard, we call for the establishment of some form of global authority adequate to the needs of the international common good.[34]

Social ethics includes all areas of human interaction where moral values come into play. Certainly, the greatest issue humanity faces today is the threat of regional conflicts in a world where too many nations have nuclear weaponry. That it is a moral issue cannot be denied. Ethical choices made by world political leaders can create a climate of stability where peace flourishes or mistrust and instability leading potentially to the end of the human species. All other ethical concerns, important as they are, pale in comparison to the lingering vision of nuclear Armageddon. Even if a general thermonuclear exchange is less possible today, the threat of a single act of nuclear terrorism could trigger political repression by frightened masses who will gladly trade their civil liberties for increased security. That scenario is every ethicist's nightmare.

Classical theology places barriers between peoples: If our religion is faithful adherence to God's unique revelation in Jesus Christ and all other forms merely towers of Babel, no meaningful dialogue can transpire between Christians and non-Christians. Social ethics becomes social evangelism. Efforts for World Peace become dreams of a Christendom coextensive with human civilization or, at best, peaceful coexistence with those unenlightened souls who have it all wrong. If the Christian faith represents God's exclusive revelation to this Universe, then the Crusaders were more logically consistent than the Peace Corps, and we should not rest until everyone embraces our form of religiosity. Then, after we have a Christian world, we could eliminate all the heretics within the Church and bring about a Christian Utopia. The nasty images creeping into your mind right now should indicate how awful this argument is. But, based on the exclusivist premise, it is perfectly logical.

Christian social ethics raised to the Galactic Perspective must reflect the kind of tolerant confidence which characterized our discussion of Christology. If the spirit of God resides in every sentient being, there is no need of unanimity. Rather, we can see in the clash of ideas a healthy contrast, an opportunity for creative insights. If I find God-within through Jesus of Nazareth and someone else discovers his/her divine nature through other prophets, teachers or messiahs--human or not--why should my piece of the puzzle invalidate the other pieces? Granting that we might not see how two dissimilar ideas about Reality could be reconciled, could we not learn from the contrast and agree to disagree without destroying the other? Would not both be stronger, wiser for the exposure to alien doctrine? And how shall we present ourselves to other races in the cosmos? As Americans? Russians? Japanese? Arabs? Shall we not begin to see ourselves as one species, inhabiting one world?

The only possible long-term preventative for national conflicts is, in the words of the American Bishops' letter, "...the establishment of some form of global authority adequate to the needs of the international common good." That means one human government, world unity. It is an idea fraught with peril. It is an idea whose time has not yet arrived. It will be the most important sociopolitical issue facing humanity for the next few centuries.

The dangers implicit in world unity are second only to the dangers of continued national anarchy in a world with nuclear technology. Because humans hate each other so viciously, many years will pass before the urge toward pan-humanism becomes the driving force of world political opinion. Our squabbling—Arab against Jew, Irish Catholic against Irish Protestant, tribe against tribe, West against East— will likely continue to dominate the politics of this world for generations to come.

To put this fratricide in proper perspective, let's allow ourselves a flight of science fiction/fantasy and ask, "How would an intelligent alien look upon a car bomb exploding in the Middle East, killing women and children in the name of God?" Perhaps the theory of a Lex Galactica, placing this world off limits, is less for our protection against contamination of new technologies before we are ready and more for the protection of Galactic civilization against the violent Homo sapiens species.

Theological Ethics and First Contact Scenarios

However important the theological questions about first contact with alien life may be, the ethical considerations of inter-species interaction are even more urgent. To begin considering the interaction of humans and non-humans, it is important to realize how truly alien the life which evolved elsewhere might be. Alien life forms may be based on radically different biologies from the carbon cycle web of life which evolved on water rich planet Earth. Sagan famously described himself as a "carbon chauvinist" who could not conceive of life based on any other chemistry.35 However, an article in *Scientific American* magazine by astrobiologist Paul Davies highlighted alternatives to carbon as a basis for life. Davies lists such exotic possibilities as mirror life, in which the typical left-handed DNA double helix is reversed, right-handed; or life based on exotic amino acids which are known to exist in meteorites; or even arsenic life or silicon based life, since these can form long, complex chains which could be the basis for non-carbon life cycles.[36]

While it is impossible anticipate what kind of higher values might motivate a creature whose cycle of life is based on silicon or arsenic, certain basics must apply to any higher intelligence. Surely, any self-aware alien must share with humanity the common values of survival, i.e., life over non-being), the need for safety and resources, and the drive to search for knowledge. Moreover, if a species has progressed to the point of space travel, some sort of cooperative community must exist to support that effort. Regardless of their biologies, one could reasonably argue, as Star Trek creator Gene Roddenberry did, that contact with any such culture should be on the basis of mutual respect and non-intervention into the affairs of alien worlds. An interventionist alternative, he believed, would have disastrous results for both alien and human civilizations.

The impact of this fantastic idea alerted people like me to the real potential for problems which could arise after contact with other civilizations among the stars. A true visionary, Roddenberry anticipated this problem and created one of the most original and potentially important ethical concepts in modern times, the Prime Directive. Binding legislation kept the member worlds of the United Federation of Planets from interfering with the evolutionary cycle of pre-star flight civilization. By this device Roddenberry cogently observed that the real danger is not that alien monsters would try to eat us, but that one culture could easily assimilate or mutate in contact with another, producing monstrous effects. John Hood writes in recent issue of *National Review*:

> By the time of The Next Generation, the Prime Directive was restated to apply most clearly to pre-warp cultures —that is, to cultures lacking the antimatter-based technology to travel at many times the speed of light, and thus limited to their own planets or solar systems. This made a lot more sense. Once a civilization reached warp status, it was capable of wreaking great havoc on the outside world. Non-interference was no longer a practical option, and the Federation developed First Contact protocols to seek to introduce the new space-faring civilization to its neighbors and to basic rules of galactic civil society. (In today's world, the appropriate analogy would be when a Third World state goes nuclear.)[37]

Regrettably, after Hood recalls that fictional captains of Federation starships have overstepped their authority and interfered in alien cultures upon occasion, his discussion begins to sound like a thinly veiled attempt to invoke the First Contact/Prime Directive principles to justify contemporary interventionism in the Middle East.

> The proper conclusion is not that such rules (as the Prime Directive) are useless and their enforcers hypocrites, but instead that it may well be valuable to have a clear rule even though it is understood that well-trained and ethical leaders, acting on their own authority, may on rare occasions find it necessary to break the rule for a greater good. I'm a writer, not a justice department lawyer, but even I can see how this insight may apply to current controversies.[38]

The real danger, which Roddenberry anticipated in several Star Trek episodes but Hood appears unwilling to acknowledge, is not that some rogue civilization will become Klingons and blast their way across the galaxy, but rather that contact between cultures with disparate technological levels will invariably lead to ruin of the "lower" civilization. This has already happened, repeatedly, on the only world which has been discovered where intelligent life actually flourishes. Complex, densely populated Native American and Polynesian societies virtually ceased to exist after contact with technologically advanced European explorers.

As humans expand into the galaxy and encounter intelligent species, who may be far more advanced, the tables could turn. This time we might be the Aztec, running in terror from the roar of Cortez's cannons. Perhaps alien life forms themselves will appear supernatural to humans. Arthur C. Clarke said that, to a pre-scientific culture, any advanced technology is indistinguishable from magic,[39] to which skeptic Michael Shermer added this variation: Any sufficiently advanced extra-terrestrial intelligence is indistinguishable from God."[40]

When, for example, the long U.S. combat involvement in Iraq is viewed through Roddenberry's ethical lens, one could easily argue that the United States and its token allies, in fact, violated the Prime Directive with results more ruinous than even a sci-fi author could have envisioned. History does not speak kindly of its conquistadores. Yet, how much better the fate of natives and European immigrants might have been if, before the discovery of the New World, the social ethicists, philosophers, theologians, and scientists in Europe, Africa and Asia had deliberated on the implications of contact with new human civilizations in unknown regions of the Earth?

Roddenberry's "Prime Directive" has profound implications for human exploration of the universe. Any species which has not achieved basic interstellar transportation via faster-than-light propulsion was quarantined from corrupting influences of advanced technologies until such time as their social consciousness and scientific achievements earned them a place at the inter-species table. Not all extrasolar planets would be off limits under a functioning Prime Directive. The Star Trek creator clearly believed humans had the right to explore, settle and exploit the resources of class M planets (Earth-like worlds) as long as the new world had no intelligent, self-aware species.[41] However, some ethicists have argued for an absolute hands-off policy for any planets with operating biospheres, or even presently sterile worlds where conditions exist which may allow biospheres to evolve in the geological future of the planet. The ethics of exploration and settlement may determine whether humanity can graduate from its terrestrial cradle and colonize on other earth-like worlds.

Non-Intervention Spectrum

In considering the ethical implication of human civilization spreading out through the stars, Dan McArthur and Idil Boran have proposed what they call "agent-centered restrictions" on the interaction of humanity and extraterrestrial life of any kind. Their argument stakes out the extreme anti-interventionist end of a debate which has just begun and which, in the generations to come, will likely crescendo like Ravel's Bolero.[42]

Taking the conquistador view of space exploration—i.e., all "new" worlds are undiscovered lands for humans to exploit without regard to the indigenous life forms, a position which no one as of yet seems to be advocating—as the other extreme end of the debate, there is much room for debate about this question and much work to be done far in advance of the first human starship actually sailing out there to explore the galaxy. In fact, if first contact with any form of extraterrestrial life is considered, humanity may not have until the twenty-third century to decide these issues:

> The discoveries in the past few years of a (possibly)liquid-water ocean under the ice on Europa (one of Jupiter's moons) and the news that Mars might have (or might only recently lost) liquid water below its surface raises the possibility that there might just be some life forms close to home after all. If this is so, humanity might be interacting with its first extraterrestrial ecosystem within the life span of some that are alive today.[43]

Not exactly ET with his globular star craft, but perhaps an alien microbe in the dirt of Mars, or some exotic plankton-like creature under Europa's ice may be the first extraterrestrial life form humanity will encounter. Even this requires well-thought planning based on a shared human vision of our interaction with the cosmos. It is not possible to establish a policy about contact with extraterrestrial life unless all nations with space-faring capability sign onto the agreement. Part of the human race cannot speak for all, because the non-subscribers will simply subvert the goals and make their own arrangements for accommodations on other worlds. The question will eventually be urgent, and it is not too early to raise red flags now.

> Humans have had a deplorable record in their dealings with each other and with their fellow species here on Earth, and some have argued that speculation about our moral obligations to extraterrestrials serve as a call to improve our ethical record on Earth. It is clear that we should seek some ethical guidelines in advance lest we repeat our sorry history elsewhere.[44]

McArthur and Boran argue cogently for a radical hands-off policy based on principles of environmental ethics. They call for an "agent-centered" approach which concerns itself with the responsibilities of the researchers and explorers "rather than being primarily concerned with the objects of human action and identifying obligations as being derivative." In other words, the authors are trying to establish an ethical basis for human interaction with extraterrestrial life separate from any obligations derived from the rights of alien species and their biospheres.[45] They argue that an agent-centered approach places certain moral restraints on human interaction with alien domains, even when exercising the right to perform those acts might benefit individual humans or the human race collectively.

> We are not entitled to harm other planets and potential ecosystems when pursuing our own interests, plans, and projects. We cannot view it as permissible to spoil other environments, for example, that are home to other life forms, great or small. The underlying rational is that we do not have the entitlement to harm other environments, even if disregarding this constraint produces the best available overall outcome for us.[46]

McArthur and Boran are so adamant about their non-interventionist extreme that they would limit human interaction with potential biospheres to "spectrographs taken from orbit or very limited, noninvasive study by carefully sterilized probes."[47] However, they stop short of calling for non-interaction with Earth-type worlds lacking an active biosphere, even if teleologically one could argue that life might arise there sometime in the distant future.

An Ethical Proposal: Prudent Expansion on Native American Model
The arguments presented flow from a sentimentalist view of "M-class planets" as a series of self-contained wildlife preserves where evolution is working itself out to the betterment of the biosphere. Certainly, responsible interaction is absolutely required for all human contact with alien ecosystems, to include the need for much more research about how to adapt the human immune systems to alien environments, which could phase into a true science of exobiology. So, I counter with the proposal that humanity has a moral right, perhaps an obligation, to the self-fulfillment and flourishing of its civilization among the stars. While humanity has certainly made a mess of the only nest we have known, it is possible to argue that past mistakes are not a

disqualifier against settling alien biospheres. McArthur and Boran have not paid sufficient attention to the elements of self-consciousness and intelligence in formulating their policies.

All life is not equal. While few ethicists would argue that it is permissible to kill a child in order to save the life of an adult—even a group of adults—certainly the death of millions of bacteria are a morally acceptable trade-off which we make whenever administering antibiotics to sick infants. The question becomes where to draw the line, and one possible answer refers to the degree of self-awareness and intelligence which an organism or creature may possess.

Instead of the polar extremes—either a drastically non-interventionist ethos for any Earth-type world, or conquistador-style conquest of any life-form whose technology we can take down with human weaponry—one could imagine a balanced, humane and non-exploitative program of exploration and colonization based a more benign model from Earth's prehistory, i.e., the emigration of Native Americans from Asia to the unsettled lands of North and South America. Any self-conscious, intelligent species which humans encountered would be treated with utmost respect, based on the universal principles of the Golden Rule and supplemental "Prime Directive" application of non-intercourse with simpler societies. If a world had an intelligent species, or a species showing great potential for the near future, colonizing that world would be avoided.

After exhaustive scientific studies of the new world are complete, settlements and agriculture would be permissible. Farming would involve either planting adapted terrestrial crops or discovering ingestible native species to develop as food stocks. Taking a cue from Native American cultures, all life forms would be considered sacred, but there would be no moral infringement, for example, if humans killed and ate game on alien worlds, assuming our bodies were able to consume the creature, and providing it was not an intelligent life-form. Humans would need to understand what constitutes intelligence far better than we do today, as studies with non-human animal species on Earth seem to be suggesting. Whether the settlement stayed small or grew into complex cities would depend on the interaction of local population and ecology, as was the case in Mesoamerica before the coming of the European.

Species Time and Call of the Stars

One could argue that humans have no right to worlds where they did not evolve, especially if the planet had the potential to develop an intelligent species sometime in the geological future. However, specific life forms like humans are not living in geological time but in species time, a limited window of existence from the rise of the species to its eventual demise or evolutionary mutation into some other creature. A civilization has even less time to express itself in the cosmos, and when viewed in this perspective all the worlds begin to look less like self-made nests than parking slots which must be surrendered at close of business. In this regard, all life has an eschatological dimension, and teleology beats the drum toward which all sentient beings must march.

For ages in the species time of humanity we have looked up at the night sky and wonders about life, eternity, and the Divine. Many of our poets, prophets and priests / poetesses, prophetesses and priestesses have acknowledged something out there seems to beckon us. The deep mythologies of human culture have often look upward. YHWH of Sinai was a sky God. A roaming star and choir of celestial beings heralded the birth of Jesus. Like Jesus, Muhammad ascended into the heavens, although the Muslim Prophet returned to speak of his journey for the edification of the faithful.

Very likely in centuries to come religious thought will pay serious attention to the questions of Cosmotheology and the ethics of first contact. Carl Sagan taught our pre-starflight civilization that we are literally star stuff; the elements in our bodies formed in the furnace of ancient supernovas. Humanity looks up, into the cosmic ocean, knowing it's where we belong. Like Roddenberry, I have no doubt we will boldly go there one day. Certainly, enormous technological and biological problems await solutions by generations yet unborn, but walk with me under the night sky. Look up and feel the call, the deep, ancient yearning. We did not climb down from the trees to remain earthbound forever. At some level we desperately want to answer the beckoning stars. The question of how the amazing history of humanity will move into the cosmos needs much more discussion by greater minds than mine. We have much to learn from the physical universe and from creatures whose histories and theologies are too amazing to contemplate in absentia.

I conclude this brief discussion with the poem "Christ in the

Universe," quoted in part during the discussion about Eschatology in Chapter 10. In this mystical vision of the future, English author Alice Meynell (1847-1922) presented some of the finest words ever penned on the vision of theological discourse extending across the cosmos, when our grandchildren's grandchildren encounter and embrace sentient beings, more unique expressions of God, yet unknown.

Thomas W. Shepherd

Christic in the Universe

by Alice Meynell

With this ambiguous earth
His dealings have been told us. These abide:
The signal to a maid, the human birth,
The lesson, and the young Man crucified.

But not a star of all
The innumerable host of stars has heard
How He administered this terrestrial ball.
Our race have kept their Lord's entrusted Word.

Of His earth-visiting feet
None knows the secret, cherished, perilous,
The terrible, shamefast, frightened, whispered, sweet,
Heart-shattering secret of His way with us.

No planet knows that this
Our wayside planet, carrying land and wave,
Love and life multiplied, and pain and bliss,
Bears, as chief treasure, one forsaken grave.

Nor, in our little day,
May His devices with the heavens be guessed,
His pilgrimage to thread the Milky Way
Or His bestowals there be manifest.

But in the eternities,
Doubtless we shall compare together, hear
A million alien Gospels, in what guise
He trod the Pleiades, the Lyre, the Bear.

O, be prepared, my soul!
To read the inconceivable, to scan
The myriad forms of God those stars unroll
When, in our turn, we show to them a Man.[48]

FINAL THOUGHTS

The title of this chapter is a misnomer. The tasks of theology never end. Every generation must re-interpret the ancient faith for its children, who will of course reject their parents' conclusions and struggle to come up with a cleaner shadow of the Divine, only to be rejected as hopelessly out-of-date by the next generation. This work has attempted to lay down a baseline for future thinkers, not in any false hope that this represents the final word, but that it will provide ample opportunities for future theologians to spend long summer evenings wrestling with the Divine in the playing fields staked out in this first systematic theology of our Metaphysical Christian tradition.

I am convinced that God loves us, even those of us who are cursed with the interminable need to understand the interplay of life, death, humanity, morality, and the cosmos with the One Presence/One Power undergirding and causing all existence. The lighthouse belief of this effort has always been that God would not have given us an intellect if we were not supposed to use it, which Jesus Christ emphatically declared as a worthy pursuit when he told his disciples to "love the Lord your God with all your heart, and with all your soul, and with all your mind, and with all your strength."[1]

This book aims at franchising the struggle to know God with our minds, not to the exclusion intuitive-meditative searching, but as a supplemental and balancing process. Mind and heart, thinking and feeling--these are the two wings by which the human soul can learn to fly.

When I presented some of these ideas at a small church in the Florida Keys, a young woman came up to me with tears in her eyes. She took my hand and said, "I have always felt guilty because I've wanted to understand more." She thanked me for saying aloud from the pulpit that it was okay to use the head as well as the heart in our spiritual quest.

It is an endless task, because it is utterly impossible. We simply cannot understand God with our minds; the Divine is too vast, too immeasurably wondrous for mortal consciousness to comprehend. However much we learn, more will be unknown. In this respect, the vastness of the Universe itself is an allegory for the knowledge of God. The process of stretching toward the Unreachable must in some way provoke and promote growth.

Certainly, we can never love God enough, yet we leap forward in spiritual growth as we attempt the impossible. In ages to come, as humans sail into the Cosmic ocean, our descendants will learn more and more about God's handiwork without exhausting its delights and diversity. Doubtless, their starships will have computer libraries, and in those memory banks humans will transport the collected wisdom of Earth, to include the words of the Son of Man, Who said as he looked into the skies on the last day of his mortal existence. "Then Jesus, crying with a loud voice, said, 'Father, into your hands I commend my spirit.' Having said this, he breathed his last." [2]

If we step away from earth and look back at our home planet from the Galactic Perspective, the pettiness of these conflicts snaps into focus. There are no lines drawn on the face of this world to separate one segment of humanity from another. The spectrum of human races moves gracefully from the darkest Australian Bushman to the palest Swedish blonde, so that no one can say where one race ends and another begins. We are one species, one race, one family. But we are a family embroiled in seemingly endless feuds, brother against brother, cousin against cousin, ideologue against ideologue, true believer against true believer. Humans are the only form of life on earth that kills for love. Could any attempt to negate Divine Ideas—which is our definition of sin—be more perverse?

No sober person believes heaven on earth will be achieved through sociopolitical union, but at least the hellfire of nuclear holocaust or political repression could be avoided. Yet, as we have noted, there are great dangers to face along the road to world unity. There is the danger that human consciousness will not grow rapidly enough, that we shall destroy ourselves before a vision of the Oneness of humanity captures the imagination of the peoples of the world. There is also the danger that force might be used to compel some nations to join the world federation, defeating the very goal of union, which is to preserve the peace.

The greatest danger of all, the one to hold constantly before our eyes, is the potential tyranny of world-wide dictatorship, an Orwellian nightmare in which some power-hungry demagogue seizes power and rules by force rather than through international law. For this reason there must be no compromise on the basic principles of representative democracy. Fundamental rights to freedom of religion, speech, the press, and other individual liberties of all the peoples of the world must be protected by a full charter of political freedom, like the Bill of Rights to the US Constitution. Economic rights, too, must be addressed, but from a framework which encourages individuals to profit from their own inventiveness and fosters free trade for personal prosperity. This will require a delicate balance between the needs of centralization for stability and order vis-à-vis the rights of the individual world citizen to private enterprise and civil liberties.

Establishing a world federal government based on representative democracy will take centuries. It is the unique opportunity of Metaphysical Christianity to stand in the forefront of this long-term struggle for lasting peace and prosperity through world unity, by emphasizing the dignity of the individual while stressing prosperity, freedom, and corporate oneness through God-consciousness. Biblical Christianity looks backward and forward: backward to the primordial revelation of God in the history of Israel and in the person of Jesus Christ, forward to the establishment of the Kingdom of God. Even though all the images of these goals are tainted by cultural and historical biases, there is an integrated whole obtainable through dialogue with Christian and non-Christian thinkers representing many perspectives, to grapple collectively with morality, survival and quality of life issues facing humanity.

Not a perfect set of doctrines distilled into a creed but an ongoing conversation which continuously reviews and re-works religious and spiritual ideas in the light of new knowledge from the social and physical sciences and new insights from Scripture, Tradition, Experience and Reflection, mediated for the Christian through the model of God-consciousness available in Jesus of Nazareth. Problems facing humanity are great, but not insurmountable.

We began this study with quotes from two hymns of faith. It is entirely proper that we end our discussions with these words from another great old hymn which, if you grew up in a Protestant community of faith, you will doubtless recognize:

O Jesus, you have promised
To all who follow you
That where you are in glory
Your servant shall be too;
And, Jesus, I have promised
To serve you to the end;
O give me grace to follow,
My master and my friend![3]

Notes and Comments

Preface and Foreword

[1] *Wings of Song,* (Unity Village, MO: Unity Books, 1986), 72.
[2] WrongPlanet.net, https://www.wrongplanet.net/forums-posting-quote-p-4705126.html (accessed 09-29-12).
[3] Mohandas K. Gandhi, *The Quote Investigator, Dec 27, 2010,* http://quoteinvestigator.com /2010/12/27/eye-for-eye-blind/ (accessed 09-29-12).
[4] Gandhi, *The Quotations Page,* http://www.quotationspage.com/quotes/Mahatma_ Gandhi (accessed 09-29-12).
[5] Ralph Waldo Emerson, "The Oversoul," in *Ralph Waldo Emerson: Essays and Journals* (Garden City, NY: International Collectors Library, 1968), 211.
[6] Thomas W. Shepherd, unpublished address given upon receipt of the *Charles Fillmore Award* at Unity Worldwide Ministries People's Convention, June 2011.

Chapter 1 - Theology and Life: Christmas Faith In An Easter World

[1] This real-life assassination plot was fictionalized in the motion picture *Valkyrie* starring Tom Cruise. Bonhoeffer did not appear in the story. One blogger called Bonhoeffer the "forgotten man" in the narrative. http://defsi.typepad.com/deafening_silence/2009/02/valkyries-forgotten-man-dietrich-bonhoeffer.html (Accessed 06-14-13).
[2] Paul Johnson, *A History of Christianity* (NY: Atheneum, 1980), 494.
[3] Ibid., 484.
[4] Ibid., 485.
[5] Ibid., 485-486.
[6] Ibid., 487.
[7] Ibid., 484.
[8] "The Oxford Oath," at Oxford Union website, source: http://www.oxford-union.org/about_us (accessed 09-21-13).
[9] "World War I Casualty and Death Tables," PBS website: http://www.pbs.org/greatwar/resources/casdeath_pop.html (accessed 09-21-13).
[10] T.A. Kantonen, *Christian Faith Today: Studies in Contemporary Theology* (Lima, OH: C.S.S. Publishing Co., 1974), 65-66.

[11] Deafening Silence blog, (02-04-09), "Valkyrie's Forgotten Man: Dietrich Bonhoeffer" http://defsi.typepad.com/deafening_silence/2009/02/valkyries-forgotten-man-dietrich-bonhoeffer.html (accessed 06-14-13)

[12] Dietrich Bonhoeffer, *Letters and Papers from Prison* (NY: MacMillan, 1972), 371.

[13] Bonhoeffer in Kantonen, 72.

[14] Bonhoeffer in John Macquarrie, *Twentieth Century Religious Thought* (London: SCM Press, 1971), 331.

[15] Bonhoeffer, *The Cost of Discipleship* (NY: MacMillan, 1963), 47.

[16] Merrill McLoughlin, et al, "The Pope Gets Tough," *U.S. News and World Report*, November 1986, 64-71.

[17] Melissa Eddy, "German Catholic Church Links Tax to the Sacraments," *NY Times* online, October 5, 2012.

[18] Aimée Upjohn Light, unpublished Q&A comments during Lyceum 2011, Unity Institute.

[19] The Pew Forum on Religion and Public Life, "'Nones' on the Rise: One-in-Five Adults Have No Religious Affiliation," Poll, October 9, 2012. http://www.pewforum.org/Unaffiliated/nones-on-the-rise-religion.aspx#profile (accessed 06-17-13).

[20] Ibid.

[21] Pew Forum on Religion and Public Life / U.S. Religious Landscape Survey; online source: http://religions.pewforum.org/pdf/report-religious-landscape-study-chapter-2.pdf (06-17-13).

[22] Ibid., http://religions.pewforum.org/comparisons# (accessed 06-17-13).

23 Jahnabi Barooah, "46% Americans Believe In Creationism According To Latest Gallup Poll," *The Huffington Post* -06/05/2012. Source: http://www.huffingtonpost.com/2012/06/05/americans-believe-in-creationism_n_1571127.html (accessed 06-17-13).

[24] Dean M. Kelley, *Why Conservative Churches Are Growing* (NY: Harper & Row, 1972), viii.

[25] Ibid., 86.

[26] Ibid., 43.

[27] Jonathan Edwards,"Sinners in the Hand of an Angry God," preached at Enfield, CT, July 8, 1741. http://www.ccel.org/ccel/edwards/sermons.sinners.html (accessed 06-22-13).

[28] A descriptive term, coined by Presbyterian author Rev. Dr. James Glasse, referring to the sprawling, independent churches which spring up

in rural locations.

[29] Charles Fillmore, *Dynamics for Living* (Unity Village: 1967), 288.

[30] John Macquarrie, *Twentieth Century Religious Thought* , 20.

[31] Kantonen, 49-50.

[32] John Wallace Suter, *The Book of Common Prayer* (NY: Harper & Brothers, 1952), 6.

[33] Hendrik Hertzberg, "'Father, Even the Atheists?' Even the Atheists," *The New Yorker* online: http://www.newyorker.com/online/blogs/hendrikhertzberg/2013/06/-father-the-atheists-even-the-atheists.html (accessed 06-17-13).

[34] Macquarrie, *Twentieth Century,* 44.

[35] Matthew Fox, *Breakthrough: Meister Eckhart's Creation Spirituality in New Translation* (NY: Doubleday, 1980), 24-25.

[36] Thomas Shepherd, *Friends in High Places* (Unity Village: Unity Books, 1985), 40-48. See 3rd Edition, iUniverse Press for expanded discussion.

[37] Matthew Fox website, http://www.matthewfox.org/press/book-reviews-new/original-blessing-reviews/ (accessed 07-16-13).

Chapter 2 - Tools of Theology: Describe before You Prescribe

[1] Paul Tillich, *A History of Christian Thought* (NY: Touchstone, 1968), xxxviii.

[2] Based on an anecdote repeated by many speakers, origin unknown. Here's a link to one version by atheist author Richard Dawkins http://www.spiked-online.com/index.php/site/article/2503/ (accessed 06-18-13).

[3] Luke 6:27-29.

[4] Trudy Govier, *Forgiveness and Revenge* (New York: Routledge, 2002), 161.

[5] Reference to the iconic 1983 feature film, *A Christmas Story,* based on the writings of Jean Shepherd (sadly, not a relative.).

[6] There are many other options, to be discussed in subsequent chapters.

[7] Hans Kueng, *On Being a Christian* (NY: Simon & Schuster, 1978), 125.

[8] "America Becoming Increasingly 'Post-Christian,' Research Shows," Jeff Schapiro, *Christian Post* (online), http://www.christianpost.com/news/america-becoming-increasingly-post-christian-research-shows-93967/ (accessed 10-10-13).

[9] Ibid.

[10] Thomas Shepherd, *Good Questions: Answering Letters from the Edge of Doubt* (Unity Village, MO: Unity House, 2009), 31.

[11] http://voyager.jpl.nasa.gov/where/ (October 9, 2013).

[12] Rick Gore, "The Riddle of the Rings," *National Geographic*, July 1981, 3-31.

[13] An upgradable religious worldview is the central theme of my book *Jesus 2.1*.

[14] Johnny Mercer and Harold Arlen, "Accentuate the Positive," *The American Bicentennial Songbook* (NY: Charles Hansen Music & Books, Inc., 1978), 160-163.

[15] Eric Gill in Walter J. Burghardt, "Contemplation: A Loving Look at What's Real," Vol. 35, March-April '90 of *Praying* magazine (Kansas City, MO: National Catholic Reporter Publishing Company, Inc., 1990), 11.

[16] Fillmore, Dynamics of Living, 13-14.

[17] James Dillet Freeman, *The Story of Unity* (Unity Village: Unity Books, 1978), 165.

[18] Tillich, *Systematic Theology Vol. I* (Chicago: University of Chicago Press, 1973), 8-11.

[19] John Naisbitt, *Megatrends* (NY: Warner Books, 1984), xxxi-xxxii.

[20] Myrtle Fillmore, *Myrtle Fillmore's Healing Letters,* Francis W. Foulkes, ed. (Unity Village, MO: Unity Books, 1954), 117.

[21] Not in the language of metaphysical churches. Some argument can be made for OP[2] as another form of pantheism or panentheism, which will be discussed later.

[22] Luke 2:10-11; Matthew 2:2.

[23] United Methodist Church, *Book of Discipline* (Nashville, TN: Abingdon, undated), 79.

[24] Pew Research Center, "Changing Attitudes on Gay Marriage," online source: http://features.pewforum.org/same-sex-marriage-attitudes/ (accessed 06-25-13).

[25] Charles Fillmore, *The Twelve Powers of Man* (Kansas City, MO: Unity Books, 1930), 15-18.

[26] Jerome Kagan and Ernest Havemann, *Psychology: An Introduction* (NY: Harcourt, Brace & World, 1963), 259.

Chapter 3   - Epistemology: How Do I Know What's True?

[1] Howard W. Stone & James O. Duke, *How to Think Theologically* (Minneapolis, MN: Fortress Press, 2006), 2.

[2] Eric Butterworth, *Discover the Power Within You* (NY: Harper & Row,

1969), 14.

[3] Freeman, "Is Unity a Cult?" pamphlet, Unity School of Christianity.

[4] Paul B. Horton and Chester L. Hunt, *Sociology* (NY: McGraw-Hill. 1964), 5.

[5] Marvin Harris, *Culture, Man, and Nature: An Introduction to General Anthropology* (NY: Thomas Y. Crowell Company, 1972), 565.

[6] Ibid., 566.

[7] Ibid., 567-568.

[8] William S. Sahakian and Mabel Lewis Sahakian, *Ideas of the Great Philosophers* (NY: Barnes & Noble, 1966), 6.

[9] Ibid., 7.

[10] LeoNora M. Cohen, "Philosophical Perspectives in Education," Oregon State University website, http://oregonstate.edu/instruct/ed416/PP2.html (accessed 10-5-12).

[11] Oregon State University website for Foundational Perspectives in Education course; http://oregonstate.edu/instruct/ed416/PP2.html (accessed 06-20-2013) Happy Birthday, Jim.

[12] William James in *Treasury of World Philosophy*, Dagobert D. Runes, ed. (Patterson, NJ: Littlefield, Adams & Co., 1959), 605.

[13] Charles Fillmore in Freeman, *Story of Unity*, 165.

[14] Fillmore, untitled excerpt from *Unity Magazine*, February 1985, 55.

[15] Macquarrie, 21.

Chapter 4 – No Tiger Gods without Tigers

[1] Harry Emerson Fosdick, *The Living of These Days* (NY: Harper & Brothers, 1956), 230.

[2] Unpublished notes from lecture by Professor Richard Lane of the University of Idaho, Winter Semester 1972, which I attended as an undergraduate.

[3] Esther Inglis-Arkell, io9.com website, http://io9.com/5925324/polyandry- or-the-practice-of-taking-multiple-husbands (accessed 06-20-13).

[4] Harris, 146.

[5] It actually *might* reside in Ethiopia. See: Paul Raffaele, "Keepers of the Lost Ark?" in Smithsonian.com, http://www.smithsonianmag.com/people-places/ark-covenant-200712.html (accessed 10-08-12).

[6] Psalm 137:1-9.

7 Robert R. Carroll, When Prophecy Failed: Cognitive Dissonance in the Prophetic Traditions of the Old Testament (New York: Seabury, 1979).

[8] John S. Spong, "Women: Crux of Ecumenism," *Christianity and Crisis Magazine*, December 9, 1986, 431.

[9] Horton & Hunt, 50.

[10] Ibid., 51.

[11] Ibid., 51.

[12] Ibid., 52.

[13] Ibid., 56.

[14] Ibid.

[15] Ibid., 56-57.

[16] Ibid., 74.

[17] Wade Davis, "Other Cultures" poster, Northern Sun Products, http://www.northernsun.com/ Other-Cultures- Wade-Davis-Poster- (4450) (accessed 07-11-12).

[18] Horton & Hunt, 75.

[19] Peter Stone and Sherman Edwards, *1776: A Musical Play*, excerpt from Imdb/com, http://www.imdb.com/character/ch0029372/quotes (accessed 02-15-14).

[20] Unitarian-Universalist http://www.religioustolerance.org/u-u.htm (accessed 07-19-13).

[21] More full disclosure trivia: I was ordained UUA 1976; all my years of service as a US Army Chaplain was as a UU. My primary fellowship is with Unity, but any given day I'm about 38-42% Unitarian-Universalist.

[22] Connie Fillmore, quoted by Ellen Debenport in *The Five Principles: A Guide to Practical Spirituality* (Unity Village, MO: Unity Books, 2009), http://content.unity.org/HOMEPAGE ARCHIVE/ FEATURES/ THEFIVEPRINCIPLES.HTML (accessed 07-19-13).

[23] Alan Bullock and Oliver Stallybrass, ed., *The Harper Dictionary of Modern Thought* (NY: Harper & Row, 1977), 535.

[24] Horton & Hunt, 80-81.

[25] Ibid., 81.

[26] I Corinthians 6:12.

[27] Catherine Driscoll, "The Problem of Adaptive Individual Choice in Cultural Evolution," pre-published paper, Department of Philosophy North Carolina State University, Source: http://www4.ncsu.edu/~ cmdrisco/publications/The%20Problem%20of%20Adaptive%20Individu al%20Choice%20in%20Cultural%20Evolution.pdf (accessed 02-22-14).

Chapter 5 – Biblical Theology

[1] Isaiah 30:8.

[2] Jackson Ice, *Albert Schweitzer: Sketches for a Portrait* (Lanham, MD:

University Press of America, Inc., 1994), 9.

[3] Miriam-Webster Online Student Dictionary, http://www.wordcentral.com/cgi-bin/student?book=Student&va=allegory (accessed 05-15-13).

[4] Nicholas of Lyra, quoted in G.R. Schmeling, "The Typographical Interpretation of the Old testament," source: http://www.bible-researcher.com/schmeling.html (accessed 05-07-13). The type of *allegory* described here refers to allusions about future events, which is a narrow understanding of the word.

[5] St. John Cassian, *Conferences,* Ben Johnson's Western Orthodox Blogspot, source: http://westernorthodox.blogspot.com/2006/01/ancient-eastern-basis-for-four-fold.html (accessed 05-01-13).

[6] Isaiah 9:2, 6.

[7] ISAIAH 9:5-6[6-7]– IS IT MESSIANIC OR HISTORICAL? Unsigned essay on Jewish website: http://thejewishhome.org/counter/Isa9_56.pdf (accessed 05-07-13).

[8] Kantonen, 24-25.

[9] Martin Luther, *Luther's Small Catechism* (St. Louis, MO: Concordia, 1971), 41.

[10] James 2:14-17.

[11] Paul Alan Laughlin's descriptive term for sweet-sounding but vacuous words.

[12] Fess up. Who hasn't used the Bible like a fortune cookie? Open the book, poke a finger blindly at the page, and see if God has sent you a message.

[13] Robert Frost, "Stopping by Woods on a Snowy Evening," in *Robert Frost's Poems* (NY: Washington Square Press, 1968), 194.

[14] Robert Frost, http://poemshape.wordpress.com/2009/05/24/interpreting-robert-frosts-stopping-by-woods/ (accessed 05-15-13).

[15] Thomas Shepherd, *The Many Faces of Prayer: How the Human Family Meets Its Spiritual Needs* (Unity Village, MO: Unity Books, 2013).

Chapter 6 - Holy Spirit: God as Dynamic Expression

[1] Emmett Fox in *Emmett Fox's Golden Keys to Successful Living* by Herman Wolhorn (NY: Harper & Row, 1977), 51.

[2] Acts 19:1-2.

[3] Macquarrie, *Twentieth Century*, 75.

[4] If you're a Star Trek fan, think *holodeck* and you'll have little trouble envisioning this. Non-Trekkies, bear with me a little longer.

[5] Immanuel Kant in Runes, *Treasury of World Philosophy*, 645.

[6] Archaeology AS website, https://sites.google.com/site/archeologyas/terminology/animism-animatism-and-totemism (accessed 05-17-13).

[7] John B. Noss, *Man's Religions* (NY: Macmillan, 1974), 98.

[8] Paul L. Achtemeier, ed., *Harper's Bible Dictionary* (NY: Harper & Row, 1985), 401

[9] Maltbie D. Babcock (1858-1901), lyricist, "This is My Father's World." from *The Book of Worship for United States Forces* (Washington: US Government Printing Office, 1974), 76.

[10] Harper's Bible Dictionary, 401.

[11] Galatians 4:6-7.

[12] *Harper's Bible Dictionary*, 401

[13] Charles Fillmore, *The Revealing Word* (Unity Village: Unity Books, 1979), 97.

[14] Nels M. Bailkey, ed., *Readings in Ancient History* (Lexington, MA: D.C. Heath and Company, 1969), 54-55.

[15] If you don't know what that means, ask your grandparents. Here's what the NY Times said about the famous Procter & Gamble label: http://www.nytimes.com/1994/05/22/magazine/sunday-may-22-1994-99.44-percent-pure-what.html (accessed 05-17-13).

[16] John 1:29.

[17] We shall explore this in depth later as we first look at Christology (Ch. 8), followed by a study of sin and atonement, Soteriology (Ch. 9).

[18] I Corinthians 6:19.

[19] The "Let It Out/Let It" controversy receives a deeper examination in my book *The Many Faces of Prayer: How the Human family Meets Its Spiritual Needs* (Unity Books, 2013).

[20] Van A. Harvey, *A Handbook of Theological Terms* (NY: Harper & Row, 1978d), 112.

[21] Meister Eckhart in *Silent Fire: An Invitation to Western Mysticism*, Walter Holden Capps & Wendy M. Wright, ed. (NY: Harper & Row, 1978), 114.

[22] For a more extensive discussion of the "Let It In / Let It Out" controversy, see my book *The Many Faces of Prayer* (Unity Books, 2013).

[23] *HBD*, 401.

[24] Fillmore, *Metaphysical Dictionary of the Bible*, 629.

[25] Fillmore, *Revealing Word*, 98.

[26] This is called *panentheism*. More to follow in Chapter 6.

[27] Psalm 23:1-4a

[28] Unsigned article, "Pope Benedict absolves the Jews: A 'major step forward'?"*The Week* online version, March 3, 2011; source: http://theweek.com/article/index/212757/pope-benedict-absolves-the-jews-a-major-step-forward (accessed 06-15-13).

[29] Arthur C. Clarke, "Third Law," in *Lost Worlds of 2001* (Signet New American Library, 1972), quoted at http://www.jessesword.com/sf/view/460 (accessed 05-27-13).

[30] http://www.corita.org/collection/index.php?skip=17&cat=0&search=betti&&fav=358&max=25 (accessed 06-25-13).

[31] I Corinthians 13:4-8.

[32] Galatians 5:19-23.

[33] *HBD*, 990. For more of Paul's lists see Romans 12:6, I Corinthians 12:8-10, 12:28, 12:29-30.

[34] "Is Pentecostalism and Charismatic Christianity growing in South America and Asia?", online Q&A article at http://in.answers.yahoo.com/question/index?qid=20100112032746AAIkjc7 (accessed 05-27-13).

[35] Marcus Bach, *Questions on the Quest* (San Francisco: Harper & Row, 1978), 138.

[36] Ruth Furbee, "Worship," in *Masterpieces of Religious Verse*. James Dalton Morrison, ed. (NY: Harper & Brothers, 1948). 117-118.

Chapter 7 - Divine Mind: God as Father-Mother-Creator

[1] Ralph Waldo Emerson in *Gospel of Emerson*, Newton Dillaway, ed. (Unity Village: Unity Books, 1980), 114.

[2] Sr. Sandra Schneiders, IHM, prolific author and internationally acclaimed innovative thinker, professor emerita of scripture spirituality at the Jesuit School of Theology, Berkeley, CA. Sr, Sandra holds a doctorate in sacred theology from the Pontifical Gregorian University in Rome. Above quote can be found at CatholicCulture.org website: www.catholicculture.org/culture/library/view.cfm?recnum=1267

[3] Pièrre Simon Laplace in T. Parsons and J. Mackay, History of Ideas blog, August 1, 1980. http://www.answersingenesis.org/articles/cm/v3/n3/history-of-ideas (accessed 03-23-14).

[4] Pew Research Forum, "Religion in Public Life," www.pewforum.org/2009/11/05/scientists-and-belief/ (accessed 03-23-14).

[5] Charles Hartshorne, *The Divine Relativity* (New Haven: Yale

University Press, 1974).

[6] Fillmore, *Revealing Word*, 142.

[7] Robert Evans, "Atheists Face Death penalty in 13 Countries," Reuters news service, republished online in the *Huffington Post*, 12-10-13 (accessed 03-01-14).

[8] Hartshorne, 34.

[9] John B. Noss, class lecture notes taken at Franklin & Marshall College, 1976.

[10] Emerson, 58.

[11] Today's gender-consciousness might render the term *Father-Mother*.

[12] HBD, 305.

[13] *IOVC*, 689.

[14] The name *YHWH*, given to Moses at Sinai according to the legend of Israelite origins, is so holy that many Jews will not pronounce it aloud, substituting *Adonai* (Lord) when God's Name appears in the Hebrew text. Some Orthodox publications will not even represent the common English word for the Divine, preferring to write *G_d*.

[15] Macquarrie, *Twentieth Century Religious Thought*, 386.

[16] Max Ehrmann, "Desiderata," written c.1927, has become one of the best known inspirational readings. Online source: http://www.cs.columbia.edu/~gongsu/desiderata_textonly.html

[17] Sahakian, 88.

[18] Ibid., 91-92.

[19] Macquarrie, *Twentieth Century*, 273-274.

[20] Hartshorne, 134.

[21] Macquarrie, in Vernon L. Purdy, American University Studies series, *The Christology of John Macquarrie* (NY: Peter Lang Publishing, Inc., 2009), 233.

[22] William G.T. Shedd (1820-1894); theologian, teacher, pastor; quoted by Values.com – The Foundation for a Better Life; online source: http://www.values.com/inspirational-quotes/4073- A-Ship-In-Harbor-Is-Safe-B- (accessed 07-03-13).

[23] Macquarrie, *Twentieth Century,* 273-274.

[24] The following sections draw upon my book *Good Questions* (Unity Books, 2009).

[25] Acts 17:28, Luke-Acts quotes Paul quoting Epimenides the Cretan, sixth century B.C.E. philosopher.

[26] T.A. Kantonen, *The Christian Faith Today* (Lima, Ohio: C.S.S. Publishing Company, 1974), 98.

[27] Epicurus, quoted at: http://atheistempire.com/greatminds/greatest.php (accessed 07-06-13).

[28] Eckhart in Holden & Capps, 116. Amazingly, Eckhart wrote this Metaphysical Christian passage in the thirteenth century.

[29] Fillmore, *Revealing Word,* 124-125.

[30] II Corinthians 1:20.

Chapter 8   - God the Son-Daughter

[1] Eckhart in Holden & Capps, 116.

[2] Anthony F. C. Wallace, *Religion: An Anthropological View* (NY: Random House, 1966), 72-73.

[3] Rudolf Bultmann, *Kerygma and Myth*, Hans Werner Bartsch, ed. (NY: Harper Torchbooks, 1961), 10.

[4] Ephraim Emerton, *Unitarian Thought* (London: The Lindsey Press, 1913), 164.

[5] Frank B. Whitney, lyrics to "I Behold the Christ in You," *Wings of Song* (Unity Village, Mo: Unity Books, 1989), 65.

[6] Fillmore, *Dynamics*, 43-44.

[7] Ibid., 285.

[8] Humorous story, author anonymous, various forms of the joke available online; first told to the author by a Jewish friend long ago.

[9] The Nicene Creed, in *Book of Worship for US Forces*, 718.

[10] Martin Luther, *Luther's Small Catechism* . Excerpts from 103-105..

[11] Matthew 13:55-57.

[12] Philippians 2:4-11.

[13] Meister Eckhart in Runes, *Treasury of World Philosophy, 348.*

14 See Henri Nouwen's *The Way of the Heart: Desert Spirituality and Contemporary Ministry.*

[15] Fillmore, *Revealing Word*, 179.

[16] Eckhart in *Treasury*, 343.

[17] Ibid.

[18] George Arthur Buttrick, series ed., *The Interpreter's Dictionary of the Bible*, Vol. 3 (NY: Abingdon, 1962), 7.

[19] *Abraham Lincoln: Vampire Hunter* (2012). http://www.imdb.com/title/tt1611224/ Based on the novel by **Seth Jared Greenberg**. "Abraham Lincoln, the 16th President of the United States, discovers vampires are planning to take over the United States. He makes it his mission to eliminate them." (I dabble at writing science fiction novels, but this plot falls off my credibility horizon.)

[20] Luke 1:1-4: "Since many have undertaken to set down an orderly

account of the events that have been fulfilled among us, just as they were handed on to us by those who from the beginning were eyewitnesses and servants of the word, I too decided, after investigating everything carefully from the very first, to write an orderly account for you, most excellent Theophilus, so that you may know the truth concerning the things about which you have been instructed."

[21] Eric Butterworth, quoted at http://www.brainyquote.com/quotes/authors/e/eric_butterworth.html (accessed 10-17-13).

[22] "Up Where We Belong" from the Paramount Motion Picture *An Officer and a Gentleman*, lyrics by Will Jennings, 1981.

[23] Emerson, 100.

Chapter 9 - Soteriology

[1] Plato's "Euthyphro," Benjamin Jowett, trans., *Dialogues of Plato* in *Great Books of the Western World, Vol. 7* (Chicago: University of Chicago Press: 1952), 195.

[2] William Shakespeare, *The Merchant of Venice, Act I, Scene 2*. The works of Shakespeare are readily available online; http://shakespeare.mit.edu/merchant/merchant.3.2.html (accessed 07-01-13).

[3] Romans 7:15-21.

[4] Luke 4:12.

[5] Micah 6:6-8.

[6] Bonhoeffer, *Letters & Paper*, 361.

[7] Al Capone, quoted in Dale Carnegie, *How To Win Friends and Influence People* (NY: Simon and Schuster, 1936), 20.

[8] Romans 6:23.

[9] Luke 9:60.

[10] Connie Fillmore, quoted by Ellen Debenport, *The Five Principles: A Guide To Practical Spirituality*, (Unity Books, 2009), excerpt online at Unity website: http://content.unity.org/ HOMEPAGEARCHIVE/FEATURES/THEFIVEPRINCIPLES.HTML (accessed 07-05-13).

[11] Charles and Myrtle Fillmore, *Dedication and Covenant*, 1892; Unity Archives http://content.unity.org/publications/archives/Homepage/fillmoreCovenant.html (accessed 07-05-13).

[12] Ibid.

[13] Romans 5:6-8.

[14] John 1:29.

[15] Macquarrie, *Principles of Christian Theology* (New York: Charles Scribner's Sons, 1966), 314.

[16] Georgia Harkness, *Understanding the Christian Faith* (Nashville, TN:

Abingdon, 1981), 78.

[17] Macquarrie, *Principles*, 314.

[18] I Corinthians 6:19-20.

[19] Gustaf Aulen, *Christus Victor* (NY: Macmillan, 1969), 11.

[20] Ibid., 4-5n.

[21] Macquarrie, *Principles*, 318-321.

[22] Harkness, 81.

[23] Eric Butterworth, *Discover the Power Within You*, 151-152.

[24] Harry Emerson Fosdick, *Dear Mr. Brown* (NY: Harper & Brothers, 1961), 134.

[25] Kantonen, 32.

[26] Thomas Shepherd, *Jesus 2.1: An Upgrade for the twenty-first Century* (Unity Village, MO: Unity Books, 2010); http://shop.unityonline.org/products/B0022 (accessed 07-05-13).

[27] II Corinthians 5:19.

[28] Fillmore, *Revealing Word*, 112.

Chapter 10 - Eschatology: Where Do We Go from Here?

[1] Richard McBrien, *Catholicism* (Oak Grove, MN: Winston Press, 1981), 1101.

[2] I Samuel 28:3-25.

[3] Luke 16:22-24, 27-31.

[4] Mark Twain, quoted at http://atheistempire.com/greatminds/greatest.php (accessed 07-06-13).

[5] II Peter 3:3-4, 1-10.

[6] John Mark Hicks, "The Lord's Supper as Eschatological Table," monograph available online: http://johnmarkhicks.files.wordpress.com/2008/03/lords-supper-as-eschatological-table.doc (accessed 07-08-13).

[7] Macquarrie, *Christian Hope*, Preface.

[8] Hans Kueng, *Eternal Life?* (NY: Doubleday, 1984), xiii.

[9] Ibid.

[10] Ecclesiastes 3:19-21

[11] 2 Thessalonians 1:6-9.

[12] Romans 9:22.

[13] Job 1. "In the Old Testament the Hebrew word *satan* means to accuse, harass, or hold a grudge. When it is used as a noun it means the accuser, the adversary, or one who tests humans." *HarperCollins Catholic Gift Bible* (NY: HarperOne, 2007), xxviii.

[14] Mark Twain, *Letters from the Earth* (NY: Harper & Row, 1962), 12.

[15] Ibid., 11.

[16] Amazon.com book description of *Heaven is for Real* by Todd Burpo and Lynn Vincent (Thomas Nelson, 2010). http://www.amazon.com/Heaven-Real-Little-Astounding-Story/dp/0849946158 (accessed 07-12-13).

[17] Ibid.

[18] Robert Browning, http://www.brainyquote.com/quotes/quotes/r/robertbrow108884.html (accessed 07-12-13).

[19] Laura Gibbs, "Jesus's (sic) Harrowing of Hell in the Christian Apocryphal Tradition," *Journey to the Sea* blog, posted July 1, 2009 (accessed 07-12-13).

[20] Macquarrie, *Principles,* 367.

[21] T.A. Kantonen, *Life After Death* (Philadelphia: Muhlenberg Press, 1962), 75.

[22] Ibid. Parenthesis added.

[23] *Encyclopedia Britannica,* http://www.britannica.com/EBchecked/topic/496541/reincarnation (accessed 07-15-13).

[24] Mark 8:27-28.

[25] 2 Kings 2:11-12.

[26] John 3:3 (RSV).

[27] Ibid, NRSV.

[28] Hebrews 9:27.

[29] Ibid., 9:24-28.

[30] Mark 8:28.

[31] Richard Rubenstein *When Jesus Became God* (San Diego: Harcourt, Inc.), 1999), 5.

[32] Oracle ThinkQuest Education Foundation website, unattributed essay on "Buddhism and Karma," http://library.thinkquest.org/06aug/00394/karmarein.html (accessed 07-15-13).

[33] "The Bliss of Hinduism" website; http://blissofhinduismwordpress.com/tag/karma-fatalism/ (accessed 07-16-13).

[34] 10:25 PM GMT, July 15, 2013; US Census Department, World Population Clock, http://www.census.gov/popclock/ (accessed 07-15-13).

[35] Macquarrie, *Principles*, 357.

[36] Macquarrie, *Principles,* 172.

[37] Revelation 21:1-4

[38] John 14:12. "Very truly, I tell you, the one who believes in me will also do the works that I do and, in fact, will do greater works than these, because I am going to the Father." (NRSV) Note the connection with God-power: his disciples will be able to work wonders because he is "going to the

Father." The power apparently does not dwell within them but requires a boost from On High. This is inconvenient for Metaphysical Christianity, since it seems to invalidate a key proposition held by Unity and other New Thought groups, i.e., that because we are the Christ our only need is to let that indwelling divinity emerge. No external power source required.

[39] John 10:34-35. Actually, John's Jesus is taking the key quote (Psalms 82:6) out of context. "You are gods" did not refer to all humanity but to the Assembly of Gods, sometimes called the Heavenly Council, over which Yahweh, the god of Israel, presided. YHWH was reading the riot act to His subordinate gods, threatening their very existence because they failed to "Give justice to the weak and the orphan; maintain the right of the lowly and the destitute." (Ps 82:3).

[40] Thomas W. Shepherd, "A Worthy Sacrifice," unpublished poem, 1977.

Chapter 11 - Sacramental Theology: A New Look

[1] 1 Corinthians 11:23-25.

[2] Roland H. Bainton, *The Reformation of the Sixteenth Century* (Boston, Beacon Press, 1956), 92.

[3] Harvey, 88. Sacramental theology is a complex maze of ideas. The description of transubstantiation offered in this chapter does not pretend to be a comprehensive treatment of the subject. Scholars can rightly accuse me of oversimplifying the issues and thereby distorting the meaning.

[4] Ulrich Zwingli in *The Protestant Reformation*, Lewis W. Spitz, ed. (Englewood Cliffs, NJ: Prentice-Hall. 1966), 84.

[5] Tillich, *History*, 261.

[6] Macquarrie, *Principles*, 7.

[7] Ibid., 8.

[8] Ibid., 9.

[9] Ibid.

[10] Karl Barth in Kantonen, *Christian Faith Today*, 32.

[11] Kantonen, 31.

[12] Charles Fillmore in Freeman's *Story of Unity*, 52.

[13] Hartshorne, 4-5.

[14] Luke 10:36.

[15] Madeleine L'Engle, quoted at http://www.homosexuals-anonymous.com/devotional-step-2-ii (accessed 07-20-13).

[16] Hans Kueng, "The World Religions in God's Plan of Salvation," in *Christian Revelation and World Religions*, ed. Josef Neuner (London: Burns & Oates, 1965), pp. 51-53.

[17] HBD, 890.

[18] Ibid.

[19] Harvey, 211.

[20] Ibid., 213.

[21] *HBD*, 577.

[22] Ibid., 890-891.

[23] Andrew M. Greenwell, "Hugo of St. Victor: Sacraments of the Natural Law," *Lex Christianorum* website; http://lexchristianorum.blogspot.com/2010/04/hugh-of-st-victor-sacraments-of-natural.html (accessed 07=-21-13).

[24] Will Durant, *The Story of Civilization, Vol. IV, The Age of Faith* (NY: Simon & Schuster, 1950), 755-56.

[25] Ibid., 755.

[26] Regarding the current work of systematic theology you hold in hand, the author pleads guilty as charged.

Chapter 12 - Twelve Sacraments of Life

[1] Thomas Merton, Catholic mystic, Trappist monk and bestselling author who died tragically in Thailand in 1968 by accidental electrocution. https://www.goodreads.com/author/quotes/1711.Thomas_Merton (accessed 03-23-14).

[2] Psalm 8:3-5.

[3] Because this is by far the most important mysterion/sacramentum in the history of Christian thought, the Eucharist will require more elaboration than the other eleven sacraments. Even so, this slice of a chapter cannot achieve a comprehensive treatment of a subject, which has filled libraries.

[4] Luke 24:30-31; 35 (parenthesis added).

[5] J. Brent Bill, *Holy Silence: The Gift of Quaker Spirituality* (Brewster, MA: Paraclete Press, 2006), 8.

[6] William L. Fischer, *Alternatives* (Unity Village: Unity Books, 1980), 56.

[7] Official Website of the Church of Jesus Christ of Latter-Day Saints, unsigned article, "What Are Mormon Church Services Like?" http://mormon.org/faq/church-welcome-visitors (accessed 07-25-13).

[8] Karen Drucker and Rev. Karyl Huntley, "You Are the Face of God,"

[9] See my book *Jesus 2.1: An Upgrade for the 21st Century* (Unity Books, 2010).

[10] See my book, *Jesus 2.1* (Unity Books, 2010), Chapter 14. *Jesus Christ and Relationships: The Four Kinds of Love.* For another perspective, try C.S. Lewis's classic, *The Four Loves* (NY: Harcourt Brace, 1988).

[11] About.com, *Glossary of Buddhist Terms,*
http://buddhism.about.com/od/buddhismglossaryk/
Glossary_of_Buddhist_Terms_K.htm (accessed 07-29-13).

[12] I Thessalonians 1:1-3.

[13] Emerson, 55-56.

[14] "Repentance and Confession—Introduction," website of the Greek Orthodox Archdiocese of North America,
http://www.goarch.org/ourfaith/ourfaith8493 (accessed 07-29-13)

[15] Macquarrie, *Principles,* 484.

[16] Charles Fillmore, *The Twelve Powers of Man* (Unity Village: Unity Books, 1930), 142-143.

[17] Alfred North Whitehead's importance for theology is discussed with reasonable clarity in Kantonen, *Christian Faith Today,* 94-107. Tackling Whitehead undiluted is for none but the hardy.

[18] *Dialogues of Alfred North Whitehead: As Recorded by Lucien Price,* Boston: Little, Brown, and Company, 1954), 370-371.

[19] Ibid.

[20] Personal recollection of comments by CH (MG) Kermit Johnson, during public event I attended while serving in the US Army chaplaincy.

[21] . Horton & Hunt, 93

[22] Henri J. M. Nouwen, *The Way of the Heart: Desert Spirituality and Contemporary Ministry* (NY: Seabury Press, 1981), 30-31.

[23] Psalm 19:1-4.

[24] Paramahansa Yogananda, *Autobiography of a Yogi* (Los Angeles: Self-Realization Fellowship, 1979), 168.

[25] Ibid., 169.

[26] Ibid.

[27] Charles Fillmore, *Atom-Smashing Power of Mind* (Kansas City, MO: Unity Books, 1949), 89.

[28] Myrtle Page, letter to Charles Fillmore, dated September 1, 1878 (Source: Unity Archives).

[29] Mark 12:30.

[30] Fillmore, *Twelve Powers,* 46.

[31] Cora Dedrick Fillmore, *Christ Enthroned in Man* (Unity Village: Unity Books, 1981), 70.

[32] Fillmore, *TP,* 105.

[33] Francis of Assisi, "Prayer of St. Francis," http://www.catholic-forum.com/ saints/pray0027.htm (accessed 08-01-13).

Chapter 13 - Providence: How Does God Interact with the Universe?

---

[1] St. Francis de Sales, in William R. Parker and Elaine St. John, *Prayer Can Change Your Life* (Englewood Cliffs, NJ: Prentice-Hall, Inc., 1957), 246.

[2] Capps & Wright, 13.

[3] Bart Ehrman's term for the group, among many small groups, whose theology would eventually become the universal (catholic) church. http://www.biblesabbath.org/tss/512/earlychristians.html (accessed 09-21-13).

[4] Tertullian, *De Praescriptione Haereticorum* (*On the Prescription of Heretics*), online source: http://www.tertullian.org/works/de_praescriptione_haereticorum.htm (accessed 08-09-13). Parenthesis added.

[5] Archimandrite George, *Theosis: The True Purpose of Human Life* (Mt. Athos, Greece: Melissa Editions, 2006), 20, 22.

[6] Paige P. Parvin, *Emory Magazine*, "The Revolutionary," Autumn 2006, online source: http://www.emory.edu/EMORY_MAGAZINE/autumn2006/feature-god.htm (accessed 09-06-13).

[7] Ibid.

[8] Charles Fillmore, *Jesus Christ Heals,* (Kansas City, MO: Unity Books, 1939), 118.

[9] Fr. Jean-Pierre de Caussade, SJ (1675-1751), *Abandonment To Divine Providence,* online source: http://www.catholictreasury.info/books/abandon/ab44.php (accessed 09-10-13).

[10] David J. Stewart, "God's Divine Order," online source: http://www.jesus-is-savior.com/Believer's%20Corner/gods_divine_order.htm (accessed 09-10-13).

[11] Fillmore, *Keep a True Lent*, 168-169.

[12] Merriam-Webster online dictionary, http://www.merriam-webster.com/dictionary/grace (accessed 09--5-13).

[13] Oxford online dictionary, http://oxforddictionaries.com/us/definition/american_english/grace, (accessed 09--5-13).

[14] Urban Dictionary online, http://www.urbandictionary.com/define.php?term=grace (accessed 09--5-13).

[15] Fillmore, *JCH*, 121.

[16] Arthur C. Clarke, "Third Law," in *Lost Worlds of 2001* (Signet New

American Library, 1972), quoted at
http://www.jessesword.com/sf/view/460 (accessed 05-27-13).

[17] Fillmore, *Revealing Word*, 56-57.

[18] H. Emilie Cady, *Lessons in Truth* (Kansas City, MO: Unity Books, 1896), 44-45.

[19] Viktor E. Frankl, *Man's Search for Meaning* (Boston: Beacon Press, 1963), 31.

[20] Ibid., 86.

[21] Emerson, *Gospel of Emerson*, 61-62.

[22] Daniel J. Boorstin, *The Discoverers* (NY: Random House, 1983), 401-402.

[23] Ibid.

[24] Bullock and Stallybrass, *Harper Dictionary of Modern Thought*, 517.

[25] Horton & Hunt, 33.

[26] Job 1:6-8.

[27] Job 1:9-10.

[28] II Corinthians 12:7-9a.

[29] II Corinthians 12:9b-10.

[30] Jess Stein, ed., *The Random House College Dictionary* (NY: Random House, 1980), 1053b.

[31] Fillmore, *Revealing Word*, 156.

[32] Job 40:8

[33] Boorstin, 407.

[34] Fillmore, *Dynamics*, 22.

Chapter 14 - Ecclesiology: Church and Ministry

[1] Marcus Bach, *The Unity Way of Life* (Unity Village: Unity Books, 1972), 174.

[2] John Fea, "Understanding the Changing Facade of Twentieth-Century American Protestant fundamentalism: Toward a Historical Definition," *Trinity Journal,* 15:2, Fall 1994, online source: http://www.galaxie.com/article/trinj15-2-04 (accessed 08-01-13).

[3] "Holier Than Thou" website, http://www.holierthanthou.info/denominations/fundamentalists.html (accessed 08-01-13).

[4] Philip S. Gorski, "'Conservative Protestantism' in the United States? Towards a Comprehensive
and Historical Perspective," paper delivered at Christian Conservative Movement and American Democracy Conference, April, 2007;

http://rsfconference.ucr.edu/papers/Gorski2007.pdf (accessed 07-19-13).
[5] Kantonen, 24.
[6] Ibid., 24-25.
[7] Ibid.
[8] Paul Brandeis Raushenbush, "Pope Francis On Gays: Who Am I To Judge Them?" Huffington Post, 07/29/2013; online source: http://www.huffingtonpost.com/2013/07/29/pope-francis-gays_n_3669635.html (accessed 08-02-13).
[9] Laurie Goodstein, "Evangelical Leaders Join Global Warming Initiative," *New York Times*, (02-08-02), http://www.nytimes.com/2006/02/08/national/08warm.html?pagewanted=all&_r=0 (accessed 08-02-13).
[10] Harvey, 142.
[11] Patrick Symmes, "History in the Remaking," http://www.the dailybeast.com/ newsweek/2010/02/18/history-in-the-remaking.html (accessed 03-18-12).
[12] "What Makes a Church a Basilica?" Website of Sts. Peter and Paul Basilica, Chattanooga, TN; http://www.stspeterandpaulbasilica.com/what-makes-a-basilica (accessed 08-02-13).
[13] For a deeper discussion of the early church see Wayne A. Meeks, *The First Urban Christians* (Yale, 1983), especially Chapter 3, "The Formation of the Ekklesia."
[14] Anne Freemantle, *The Great Ages of Man: The Age of Faith* (Alexandria, VA: Time-Life Books, Inc., 1979), 12.
[15] Ibid., 31-32.
[16] Unsigned article, http://www.history.com/this-day-in-history/quakers-executed-for-religious-beliefs (accessed 08-03-13).
[17] Peter S. Field, *The Crisis of the Standing Order: Clerical Intellectuals and Cultural Authority in Massachusetts1780-1833* (Amherst, MA: University of Massachusetts, 1998), 208-210.

[18] Horton & Hunt, 94.
[19] Website of the *Scientific Committed to Evaluate PseudoSkeptical Criticism of the Paranormal*; http://www.debunkingskeptics.com/DebunkingChristians/Page16.htm (accessed 08-06-13).
[20] Sy Miller and Jill Jackson, "Let There Be Peace On Earth" in *Wings of Song*, (Unity Village, MO: Unity Books, 1989), 3. While not found in

every single order of worship, ending the service with "The Peace Song" remains the ubiquitous closing hymn in Unity Churches.

[21] Wayne A. Meeks, *The First Urban Christians* (New Haven: Yale, 1983), 74.

[22] I Peter 2:9, 16-17.

[23] Ephesians 4:11-13.

[24] James D. Glasse, *Profession: Minister* (Nashville, TN: Abingdon, 1968), 65.

Chapter 15 - Theological Ethics

[1] Code of Conduct, quoted from *Army Study Guide* website, (site not affiliated with the US Government) http://www.armystudyguide.com/content/army_board_study_guide_topics/code_of_conduct/the-code-of-conduct.shtml (accessed 03-02-14).

[2] Sulaiman Kakaire, "Uganda: Is Polygamy Misunderstood?" *The Observer*, Kampala, Uganda, 03-20-12. Online source: http://allafrica.com/stories/201203221126.html (accessed 02-09-14).

[3] Vincent Canb, "Ben Kingsley in Panoramic 'Gandhi'", *New York Times*, December 8, 1982, online source: http://www.nytimes.com/packages/html/movies/bestpictures/gandhi-re.html (accessed 08-16-13).

[4] Joe E. Trull, "Making Moral decisions: An Artful Ability," *Christian Ethics Today,* Issue: 74, Page No: 6; http://christianethicstoday.com/cetart/index.cfm?fuseaction=Articles.main&ArtID=1035 (accessed 08-17-13).

[5] *New York Times*, February 8, 1968. The accuracy of this quote has been disputed, but the verbal faux pas is instructive even as fiction.

[6] Michael Fisher, "The Ku Klux Klan," http://home.wlu.edu/~lubint/touchstone/KKK-Fisher.htm (accessed 08-17-13).

[7] Quotations of Mahatma Gandhi, http://mindprod.com/ethics/gandhi.html (accessed 08-17-13).

[8] *The Free Dictionary,* http://www.thefreedictionary.com/principled (accessed 08-18-13).

[9] The Bible Page, http://www.thebiblepage.org/biblesays/homosexuality.shtml (accessed 08-21-13).

[10] John Shelby Spong, "A Manifesto from our friend Bishop John Shelby Spong," http://walkingwithintegrity.blogspot.com/2009/10/manifesto-from-our-friend-bishop-john.html (accessed 08-21-13).

[11] John G. Turner, "Why Race is Still a Problem for Mormons," *NY Times*, 08-18-12, online source: http://www.nytimes.com/2012/08/19/opinion/sunday/racism-and-the-mormon-church.html?_r=0 (accessed 08-21-13).

[12] "Singer Finds Faith Through Gospel Music," Charisma magazine, online edition, http://www.charismamag.com/component/content/article/570-j15/news/featured-news/3538- (accessed 08-23-13).

[13] George F. Will, "Address to University of Miami class of 2005," excerpted by Steven Shapiro's 24/7 Innovation website; online source: http://www.steveshapiro.com/2005/06/19/george-will-certitude-2/ (accessed 08-02-12).

[14] Rev. Dr. Jerry Falwell, online source: http://www.brainyquote.com/quotes/authors/j/jerry_falwell_2. html#k4Stx WHuSQX3joUu.99 (accessed 08-26-13).

[15] Dictionary.com, online source: http://dictionary.reference.com/browse/antinomian (accessed 08-23-13).

[16] Sarah Beach, The Curse of Hippie Parents," Salon.com. Beach writes: "If it feels good, do it: a rallying cry of the '60s and the root of a lot of really awful parenting..." online source: http://www.salon.com/2001/08/22/hippie_parents/ (accessed 08-23-13)

[17] Anthony Flew, *A Dictionary of Philosophy* (NY: St. Martin's Press, 1979), 14.

[18] I Corinthians 6:12, 19.

[19] Freeman, "Is Unity a Cult?"

[20] Joseph Fletcher, *Situation Ethics* (Philadelphia: Westminster Press, 1966), 26.

[21] The application symbolic logic above is vulnerable to attack by professions in the field, which I am not. It is given only to illustrate the complexities of reducing human behavior to mathematical terms. The same can be said of word-equations in systematic theology. We are so much more than our systems contain or describe.

[22] Freeman, *Story of Unity,* 170-171. Italics added.

[23] Ibid., 169.

[24] Ibid., 170.

[25] Horton & Hunt, 74-75.

[26] John 3:16; italics added.

[27] Matthew 25: 41-45.

[28] I John 4:20.

[29] For a discussion of this problem, see http://www.sermoncentral.com/sermons/the-real-mccoy-roger-thomas-sermon-on-christian-values-93166.asp

[30] Matthew 23:23.

[31] Noss, *Man's Religions*, 121.

[32] Matthew 6:31-34.

[33] Jack Canfield and Mark Victor Hansen, *Chicken Soup for the Soul* (Deerfield Beach, FL: Health Communications, Inc., 1993). Cited online; http://www.angelfire.com/ok/bobbiesues/pg2write.html (accessed 08-16-13).

[34] See the ChildFund International; http://www.childfund.org/about_us/ (accessed 08-16-13). Carol-Jean and I have sponsored children through this trustworthy agency since the early 1980s.

Chapter 16 - Prayer: Communion with God

[1] Ernest Holmes, *The Science of Mind* (NY: Dodd, Mead and Company, 1938), 152.

[2] James Dillet Freeman, *Prayer, the Master Key* (Unity Village: Unity Books), 126.

[3] Deepak Chopra, "Take Your Meditation Practice to the Next Level" at *Deepak Chopra's Secrets of Meditation* website; http://secretsofmeditationlaunch.com/FreeVideos/script-7/ (accessed 09-29-13)

[4] Thomas Merton, excerpt from *Thoughts in Solitude,* online source: http://www.goodreads.com/work/quotes/1220202-thoughts-in-solitude (accessed 03-23-14).

[5] "A Dream is a Wish Your Heart Makes," written by Jerry Livingston, Mack David, Al Hoffman, for the animated motion picture *Cinderella,* Walt Disney Productions, 1950.

[6] Fillmore, *Revealing Word*, 130, 141.

[7] For a more extensive discussion, see my book *The Many Faces of Prayer* (Unity Books, 2013).

[8] Martin Luther in Edith Simon, *The Great Ages of Man: The Reformation* (Alexandria, VA: Time-Life Books, Inc., 1966), 15.

[9] Bonhoeffer, *Letters & Paper*, 361.

[10] Wallace, 53.

[11] Brother Lawrence, *The Practice of the Presence of God*, E.M. Blaiklock, trans. (Nashville, TN: Thomas Nelson Publishers, 1982), 35.

[12] Harkness, 122.

[13] Macquarrie, *Principles*, 493.

[14] Fillmore, *Dynamics for Living, 92.*

[15] Gordon Kaufman, *Systematic Theology: A Historicist Perspective* (NY: Charles Scribner's Sons, 1968), Introduction.

[16] Although there is no scientific evidence humor cures cancer, the American Cancer Society acknowledges Norman Cousins' experience as "the most famous story of humor therapy" while pointing out that the disease he reported cured by laughter was never specified. For more info, see http://www.cancer.org/search/index? Query Text= norman+ cousins (accessed 09-26-13).

[17] Harry DeCamp, *One Man's Healing from Cancer* (NY: F.H. Revell, 1983.)

[18] Myrtle Fillmore in Freeman, *Story of Unity*, 47-48.

[19] Joan C. Harvey, *If I'm So Successful, Why Do I Feel Like A Fake?: The Imposter Phenomenon* (NY: St. Martin's Press, 1985), 5-6

[20] Ibid., 6-7.

[21] Myrtle Fillmore in *Story of Unity*, 47-48.

[22] John W. Adams, "The Healing Power of Forgiveness!" Golden Key Ministries website, August 31, 2009; source: http://goldenkeyministry.com/the-healing-power-of-forgiveness/ (accessed 09-27-13).

[23] Catherine Ponder, *Open Your Mind to Prosperity* (Unity Village: Unity Books, 1971), 10-11.

[24] Ibid., 11-12.

[25] John A.T. Robinson, *Honest to God* (Philadelphia: Westminster Press, 1963), 13.

[26] Jim Morrison, "Petition the Lord with Prayer," https://thedoors.com/discography/songs/petition-lord-prayer-721 (accessed 09-27-13). Italics added.

[27] Mary Katherine Macdougall, *What Treasure Mapping Can Do for You* (Unity Village, MO: Unity Publications, 1999); available through http://shop.unityonline.org/products/B0213 (accessed 09-27-13).

[28] Anne Robertson, *God with Skin On: Finding God's Love in Human Relationships* (Morehouse Publishing, 2009). http://www.godwithskinon. com/God_With_Skin_On/The_Book.html (accessed 09-27-13)

[29] John Jay Hughes, "Centering Prayer," pamphlet (Liguori, MO: Liguori Publications, 1981), 7

[30] For a more extensive discussion of Centering Prayer, see my book *The Many Faces of Prayer* (Unity Books, 2013).

[31] Mark 11:24.

Chapter 17 - Pastoral Theology: God's Love with Skin On

[1] Henri J. M. Nouwen, *The Wounded Healer* (Garden City, NY: Doubleday/Image Books, 1979), 71-72.

[2] Matthew 26:35-36, 40.

[3] Mark 10:43-45.

[4] Luke 15:4.

[5] John 13:34-35.

[6] Edward B. Pusey, trans., *The Confessions of Saint Augustine* (NY: Pocket Books, Inc., 1952), 45.

[7] Rollo May, *The Art of Counseling* (Nashville, TN: Abingdon, 1939), 120.

[8] Samuel R. Laycock, *Pastoral Counseling for Mental Health* (Nashville, TN: Abingdon, 1961), 16.

[9] Seward Hiltner, *The Counselor in Counseling* (Nashville, TN: Abingdon, 1952), 10-11.

[10] Schaller, *Mirror*, 142.

[11] William Glasser; website http://www.wglasser.com/ (accessed 10-04-13). Glasser's work spanned half a century. He died while *Glimpses* Second Edition was in progress, but his ideas have influenced the work of many counselors and pastors.

[12] Raymond J. Corsini, *Current Psychotheraphies* (Itasca, IL: F.E. Peacock Publishers, Inc., 1979), 316. This is an old reference, but every major bookstore offers shelves of books on self-help, current psychology, and counseling techniques. Online publishers broaden the choices to a staggering number of choices.

[13] II Corinthians 12:9.

[14] Nouwen, *Wounded Healer*, 75.

Chapter 18 - Open Universe: Where Teilhard Went off the Rails

[1] This chapter demonstrates the theological method by offering a critique of the spiritual evolution paradigm of Pierre Teilhard. The critical analysis is based on classical Hindu metaphysics, early New Thought Christianity, and current evolutionary theory. I presented most of these ideas in a paper delivered at Unity Institute's Lyceum 2011.

[2] Pierre Teilhard de Chardin, *The Phenomenon of Man* (NY: Harper & Row, 1975), 298-299.

[3] T.A. Kantonen, *Christian Faith Today: Studies in Contemporary Theology* (Lima, Ohio: C.S.S. Publishing Company, 1974), 79-80.

[4] Thomas Shepherd, *Friends in High Places* (Unity Village, MO: Unity Books, 1985), 226.

[5] Ibid., 21.

[6] Teilhard, *Phenomenon of Man*, 109.

[7] Harry Emerson Fosdick, http://www.great-quotes.com/quote/1374010

(accessed 04-08-2011).

[8] F.A.Turn, "The Idea of Biological and Social progress in the System of Teilhard de Chardin," in *Teilhard Reassessed: A Symposium of Critical Studies in the Thought of Pierre Teilhard de Chardin,* Anthony Hanson, ed. (London, UK: Darton, Longman & Todd, 1970), 11.

[9] PBS Library Online. "Frequently Asked Questions about Evolution," www.pbs.org/wgbh/evolution/ library/faq/cat01.html (accessed 04-08-2011).

[10] "Grasslands," Blue Planet Biomes, www.blueplanetbiomes.org/ grasslands.htm (accessed 04-08-2011).

[11] http://www.religionfacts.com/islam/comparison_charts/islam _judaism_christianity.htm (accessed 04-08-2011).

[12] "Stand Up, Stand Up for Jesus," lyrics by George Duffield, Jr., music by George J. Webb, http://www.hymnsite.com (accessed 04-08-2011)

[13] "The Baptist Faith and Message, Articled X," SBC Net, the "Official Website of the Southern Baptist Convention," www.sbc.net/bfm/bfm 2000 .asp (accessed 04-08-2011).

[14] Alfred North Whitehead, *Process and reality* (1929), online source: http://plato-dialogues.org/plato.htm (accessed 04-13-2011).

[15] Plato, *Timaeus*, online source: http://classics.mit.edu/Plato/ timaeus.html (accessed 04-13-2011).

[16] Kantonen, 83.

[17] Satish Reddy, "Hindu Concepts of Time," in *The Experience of Time,* Jorge Canestri and Henri F. (FRW) Smith, ed., (London, UK: Karnac Books, 2009), 178.

[18] Subhamoy Das, "Nataraj: The Dancing Shiva," http://hinduism.about. com/od/lordshiva/p/nataraj.htm (accessed 04-12-2011).

[19] Achal Oza, "Cyclical Time and Astronomy in Hinduism," www.achaloza.com/ docs/AchalOza_CyclicalTime.pdf (accessed 04-10-2011).

[20] David Jhirad, "The Concept of Time," book review of *What is Time* by G.J. Whitrow (1972), in *Journal for the History of Astronomy,* http://articles.adsabs.harvard.edu (accessed 04-10-2011).

[21] Paul J. Steinhardt, "The Endless Universe: Introduction to the Cyclic Universe," source: http://wwwphy.princeton.edu/~steinh/cyclintro/ (accessed 04-13-2011).

[22] I Corinthians 8; see also deutero -Pauline Letter to the Ephesians, 6:5.

[23] Pierre Teilhard de Chardin, *Christianity and Evolution* (NY: Harcourt Brace Jovanovich, 1971), 99.

[24] Teilhard, *Phenomenon of Man,* 110.

[25] Unsigned devotional for 13 April 2011, *Daily Word* magazine (Unity Village, MO: Silent Unity, 2011).
[26] Ralph Waldo Emerson, "Divinity School Address," www.vcu.edu/ engweb/transcendentalism/authors/ emerson/essays/dsa.html (accessed 04-13-2011).

Chapter 19 - Theology from a Galactic Perspective

[1] Carl Sagan, Cosmos (NY: Random House, 1980), p. 298.
[2] John Wesley in Michael J. Crowe, "A History of the Extraterrestrial Life Debate," *Zygon* 32, no. 2 (June 1997): 160.
[3] Julian Chela-Flores, "Fitness of the Universe for a Second Genesis: Is It Compatible with Science and Christianity?" *Science and Belief* 17, No. 2 (2005): 187-197.
[4] Milan M. Cirkovic´, "The Temporal Aspect of the Drake Equation and SETI," Astronomical Observatory Belgrade, online article. Source: http://arxiv.org/PS_cache/astro-ph/pdf/0306/0306186v1.pdf (Accessed 11-27-07). The *Drake Equation* reads: $N = R_* f_s f_p n_e f_l f_i f_c L$
[5] Steven Dick, *Many Worlds: The New Universe, Extraterrestrial Life & the Theological Implications* (Phila.: Templeton Foundation Press, 2000), 199. Parenthesis original.
[6] http://www.museum.tv/archives/etv/R/htmlR/roddenberry/roddenberry. htm (accessed 11-09-07).
[7] Thomas Hoffman, "Exomissiology: The Launching of Exotheology," *Dialog: A Journal of Theology*, 43, no. 4 (Winter 2004): 326-327.
[8]Crowe, 148.
[9] Ibid.
[10] Alexandre Vigne, "Extraterrestrials of the New World," *Diogenes* 48: 189 (January 2000): 48.
[11] Ibid., 49.
[12] Crowe, 149.
[13] Vigne, 51.
[14] Crowe, 150.
[15] Phillip Melanchthon quoted in Crowe, 150.
[16] Crowe, 150-151.
[17] Thomas Paine, in Steven J. Dick, *The Biological Universe* (Cambridge, UK: Cambridge University Press, 1996), 22-23.
[18] Ibid., 23.
[19] Crowe, 153-154.
[20] Ibid., 154.
[21] Marie T. George, "ET Meets Jesus Christ: A Hostile Encounter

between Science and Religion?" *Logos* 10: 2 (Spring 2007): 76-77.

[22] Ibid., 77.

[23] Thomas F. O'Meara, O.P., "Christian Theology and Extraterrestrial Intelligent Life," *Theological Studies* 60 (1999): 27-28.

[24] Ibid., 28.

[25] Ibid.

[26] Ibid.

[27] Sojerd L. Bonting, "Theological Implications of Possible Extraterrestrial Life," *Zygon* 38, no. 32 (September 2003): 76-77.

[28] Hoffman,

[29] Charles Fillmore, *The Revealing Word* (Unity Village, MO: Unity Books, 1959), 35.

[30] Thomas W. Shepherd, "Christology After Carl Sagan: Can the Faith of Jesus Survive the Jump to Hyperspace?" *Journal of the Society for the Study of Metaphysical Religion,* 7, no. 1 (Fall 2001): 158.

[31] Macquarrie, *Principles*, 172.

[32] Charles Fillmore, *Keep A True Lent* (Unity Village: Unity Books, 1953), 17-18.

[33] Dean C. Curry, *Evangelicals and the Bishop's Pastoral Letter* (Grand Rapids, MI: Eerdmans, 1984), 3.

[34] Ibid.

[35] Unsigned article at website "Does God Exist?" October 8, 2007 update. Online source: http://www.doesgodexist.org/SepOct07/TheWonderofCarbon.html (accessed 11-26-07).

[36] Paul Davies, "Are Aliens among Us?" *Scientific American* 297, no. 6 (December 2007): 64-65.

[37] John Hood, "Prime Lesson," *National Review Online,* (09-28-07) Parenthesis original. http://www.nationalreview.com/articles/222319/prime-lesson/john-hood (Accessed 09-17-13).

[38] *Ibid.*

[39] Arthur C. Clarke, "Brainy Quotes" website, http://www.brainyquote.com/quotes/quotes/a/arthurccl101182.html (accessed 11-19-07)

[40] Michael Shermer, "Shermer's Last Law," *Scientific American,* (January 2002): 33. See also http://www.skeptic.com/eskeptic/06-03-09.html (accessed 11-19-07)

[41] Unsigned website subdirectory: "Are Class M Planets Common?" Online source: http://www.astrobiology.net/archives/2006/09/are_class_m_pla.html

(Accessed 1-26-07). The fiction-derived term has found its way into popular descriptions of extrasolar worlds by legitimate astronomers.
[42] Dan McArthur and Idil Boran, "Agent-Centered Restrictions and the Ethics of Space Exploration," *Journal of Social Philosophy*, 35, no. 1 (Spring 2004): 148-163.
[43] Ibid., 149. Parenthesis original.
[44] Ibid.
[45] Ibid., 154.
[46] Ibid., 155.
[47] Ibid., 156.
[48] Alice Meynell, "Christ in the Universe." Online source http://www.poetry-archive.com/m/christ_in_the_universe.html (Accessed 11-01-13)

Chapter 20 – Final Thoughts

[1] Mark 12:30
[2] Luke 23:46.
[3] "O Jesus, I have Promised," words by John E. Bode, *Book of Worship for US Forces*, 410.

ABOUT THE AUTHOR

After a long process of re-writing and updating new material, *Glimpses of Truth, 2nd edition*, springs full-grown from the laptop of the Rev. Dr. Thomas W. Shepherd. An ordained minister and retired US Army Chaplain, "Dr. Tom" (as students call him) teaches Historical and Theological Studies at Unity Institute and Seminary. He is best known for his longstanding Q&A column "Good Questions" in *Unity Magazine*. Shepherd is the author several books, including *Glimpses of Truth* (2000), *Friends in High Places* (2006), *Good Questions (2008), Jesus 2.1—Upgrade for the 21st Century (2009)*, and *The Many Faces of Prayer: How the Human Family Meets Its Spiritual Needs* (2013). He hosts *Let's Talk About* It on Unity Online Radio, http://www.unity.fm/program/talkaboutit.

Shepherd's first career path took him soldiering with the US Army, including a tour in Vietnam as a medical evacuation helicopter pilot, where he was awarded two Distinguished Flying Crosses, the Air Medal, the Purple Heart, and the Vietnamese Cross of Gallantry. He left the Army after Vietnam service, graduated college and seminary, and returned to active duty as a military chaplain. Shepherd earned a B.S. Ed. from the University of Idaho, Master of Divinity. from Lancaster Theological Seminary, and Doctor of Ministry from St. Paul School of Theology. Although his primary fellowship is with Unity, Dr. Tom holds ministerial credentials with the Unitarian Universalist Association and the National Association of Congregational Christian Churches. He was Assistant Executive Director and Theologian-in-Residence for the Universal Foundation for Better Living, 2000-2001. The Rev. Dr. Shepherd has served Unity Churches in Georgia, South Carolina, and California. In 2011 he received the Charles Fillmore Award from Unity Worldwide Ministries.

Thomas Shepherd lives in Lee's Summit, Missouri, with his lovely wife, Carol-Jean, a generationally diverse assortment of offspring, and a timid pit bull named Riley. His daughter-in-law, the Rev. Rachel Simpson, was ordained by Unity in 2013.

CPSIA information can be obtained at www.ICGtesting.com
Printed in the USA
LVOW10s1554021015

456698LV00017B/762/P

9 780615 969923